Using SPSS® to Solve Statistical Problems: A Self-Instruction Guide

David M. Shannon
Auburn University

with

Mark A. Davenport
ACT, Inc.

Merrill
Prentice Hall

Upper Saddle River, New Jersey   Columbus, Ohio

This book is dedicated to our wives, Jamie and Liane, and our children, Ian, Phillip, and Kate.

Library of Congress Cataloging-in-Publication Data

Shannon, David M.
    Using SPSS to solve statistical problems : a self-instruction guide/David M. Shannon
  with Mark A. Davenport.
        p. cm.
    Includes index.
    ISBN 0-13-267576-5
      1. SPSS (Computer file) 2. Social sciences—Statistical methods—Computer programs.
  I. Davenport, Mark A. II. Title.

HA32 .S13 2001
519.5'0285'5369—dc21   99-087917

Vice President and Publisher: Jeffery W. Johnston
Executive Editor: Kevin M. Davis
Editorial Assistant: Christina Kalisch
Production Editor: Julie Peters
Design Coordinator: Diane C. Lorenzo
Text Designer: Carlisle Publishers Services
Cover Art: SuperStock
Cover Designer: Jason Moore
Production Manager: Laura Messerly
Electronic Text Management: Marilyn Wilson Phelps, Karen L. Bretz, Melanie Ortega
Director of Marketing: Kevin Flanagan
Marketing Manager: Amy June
Marketing Services Manager: Krista Groshong

This book was set in Garamond Classical BT by Carlisle Communications, Inc.,
and was printed and bound by Victor Graphics. The cover was printed by Phoenix Color Corp.

SPSS is a registered trademark of SPSS Inc. Copyright 2000 SPSS Inc.

Screen Shots 1.1, 1.2, 1.3, and 1.4 reprinted by permission from Microsoft Corporation.

All other screen shots reprinted by permission from SPSS Inc.

Merrill
Prentice Hall

10 9 8 7
ISBN 0-13-267576-5

Preface

The motivation for writing this text comes from ten years of experience with students enrolled in beginning statistics classes. Students in these classes have had to deal with the challenges of learning not only statistical concepts, but also how to use the computer software (SPSS) that will guide them through their statistical analyses. Whether you are a student learning about statistics for the first time or an experienced researcher who has used statistics throughout your career, you are likely to have many encounters with software such as SPSS® for Windows.

Such programs have become more "user friendly" over the years with the introduction of graphical menus and windows. The modern graphical user interface is a far cry from the "old days" of writing code and punching cards. Nevertheless, learning to use a new software program is still difficult, especially when you don't use the program on a regular basis. Learning to use the software package, however, is just the first step. You also need to be able to make sense of the output generated by the software program so you can incorporate it accurately in your research reports. We have written this book to assist you with two tasks: 1) using SPSS to solve statistical problems and 2) making sense of the output.

We believe this book will serve as a valuable supplement in a beginning or intermediate statistics course. Becoming proficient with SPSS for Windows will make the process of statistical analysis less time consuming and painstaking, allowing you more time to think about research design and analysis, and strengthening the overall quality of your work. An overview of the text organization and key features follows.

SPECIAL FEATURES AND TEXT ORGANIZATION

Step-by-Step Illustration of Statistical Procedures. For each statistical procedure addressed in this book, we provide a brief rationale for its use as well as a few examples. In most cases, these examples are drawn from real data gathered from graduate students enrolled in a beginning statistics course. Each statistical procedure is presented in a step-by-step manner using SPSS for Windows. Each menu and screen encountered in these steps has been captured and used to further illustrate the process. Following the illustration of each procedure, we thoroughly discuss and interpret the output generated by SPSS.

Data disk. A data disk is included with this text. It contains all the data files you will need to follow along with each chapter's illustrations. These files are carefully named to correspond with the chapters in which they are used. For example, the data used in Chapter 4 is identified as "chap 4 data." These data files have been created from a larger data set pertaining to graduate students enrolled in a beginning statistics course. To make things easier for you, we have included only the variables you will need for the chapter's illustrations.

Practice Exercises. Practice Exercises are included at the end of each chapter so you can apply and expand upon what you have learned. These exercises are brief and focus on the specific procedures illustrated in that chapter. The answers to these exercises are provided in Appendix D so you can check your work.

Organization of the text. This text is divided into seven sections. The first section (Chapters 1 through 4) provides an overview of SPSS, how to retrieve and save SPSS files, how to define variables and create a data set, and how to import and merge data files. In

Section 2 (Chapters 5 through 7), we explore various data analysis procedures that are used to summarize and describe data. These procedures include frequency analysis and descriptive statistics. The third section includes three chapters (8 through 10), which illustrate how to transform variables, create new variables, and estimate the reliability of variables. The variables created in this section are used throughout the remainder of the text.

The fourth section consists of just one chapter that focuses on the process of hypothesis testing. This chapter serves as a transition into the statistical procedures used to address hypotheses and research questions in the remaining sections of the text.

Section 5 (Chapters 12 through 14) explores a few procedures used to measure relationships among variables. These correlational procedures, which include chi-square, Pearson, and Spearman correlation, are examined as they pertain to different types of variables. We also include a chapter on displaying relationships using scatterplots.

We begin making comparisons between groups in Section 6 (Chapters 15 through 17). Statistical procedures used to make these comparisons include t-tests, one-way ANOVA, and factorial ANOVA. Within-subjects designs are discussed in Section 7 (Chapters 18 through 20). These three chapters focus on paired t-tests, within-subjects ANOVA, and mixed ANOVA designs. We conclude with Section 7 (Chapters 21 through 23), which provides an overview of regression analysis. These chapters illustrate bivariate and multiple regression analysis as well as the use of categorical predictors in regression.

STATISTICS WEBSITE

Merrill has a statistics website that includes, among other things, web links to statistics tools and additional data sets. To link to this site, go to **www.prenhall.com/shannon**.

ACKNOWLEDGMENTS

First of all, we would like to acknowledge the students from our statistics classes over the past ten years who have requested that such a book be written. We have observed these students struggle and succeed while learning statistics and SPSS. These students have been extremely helpful throughout the creation and development of this text. They have used drafts to guide their learning of SPSS and have provided very thoughtful feedback as to how these drafts could be improved.

We would also like to express our gratitude to the reviewers who have carefully and thoughtfully read several drafts and offered constructive feedback regarding our progress. Their expertise and experience in teaching statistics and using statistical software contributed greatly to the organization and content of this text. These reviewers are: Tom Coombs, Duke University; Joe Cornett, Texas Tech University; Beverly J. Dretzke, University of Wisconsin–Eau Claire; Jimmie C. Fortune, Virginia Tech; Thomas T. Frantz, SUNY–Buffalo; Gretchen Guiton, University of Southern California; Wayne I. Gordon, Western Illinois University; Robert Hale, Pennsylvania State University; Basil Hamilton, Texas Woman's University; and Bill Roweton, Chadron State College.

We further acknowledge Kevin Davis, Executive Editor from Prentice Hall, for working with us throughout this project. His critical analysis of our work and recommendations improved the content and organization of this book. In addition, we thank Holly Jennings for her assistance in the coordination of feedback and editorial assistance with the manuscript. Furthermore, we would like to thank Amy Gehl and the staff from Carlisle Communications for their careful editing throughout the production phase. They were instrumental in transforming the original manuscript pages into this book.

Finally, we thank you for using this book and hope it allows you to use SPSS for Windows more proficiently and make sense of all the output you generate. As you follow along with the illustrations in this book, we encourage you to jot down comments. Your feedback will help us to better understand how the next edition can be refined and improved. Please feel free to contact us at:

David M. Shannon
Auburn University
email: shanndm@auburn.edu

Mark A. Davenport
ACT, Inc.
email: davenpor@act.org

Contents

22　MULTIPLE REGRESSION   307

23　REGRESSION WITH CATEGORICAL PREDICTORS   328

SECTION I

Introduction
to SPSS

1 | Orientation to SPSS

We have written this book with two primary goals in mind. Our first goal is to provide you with opportunities to learn and use SPSS (Statistical Package for the Social Sciences), which is one of the most popular statistical analysis software packages available. We believe that the best way to learn how to analyze data is to *do* it, and so you will be using SPSS to perform a variety of statistical procedures throughout this book. Our second goal is to provide an introduction to a variety of statistical analysis procedures that are commonly used by graduate students, researchers, and other professionals.

In our work with graduate students, we have come to realize that many students are very self-conscious about their computer skills. Although personal computers have been around for many years, the technology changes so rapidly that it is often difficult to keep up. The power and complexity of computer software has grown to meet the capabilities of larger, more powerful computers. It seems that as you finally get comfortable with one software system, new technology makes it obsolete and you are forced to acquire and learn a new system. Such is the case with DOS, and Windows operating systems. The authors began working with the original mainframe versions of SPSS produced in the 1980s. Before we knew it, there was a DOS version, which required us to learn slightly different syntax commands. The DOS version was followed by a Windows 3.1 version, which began to use a graphical interface allowing the user to select options from menus. With the recent releases of SPSS for Windows 95, 98, and 2000 environments, we have had to go through the whole process all over again.

We empathize with those of you who are learning how to use a statistical computer package for the first time. It is often difficult to put your faith in a machine that you don't fully understand or trust. For those of you who are familiar and comfortable with computers, you might find your statistics classes to be largely one-dimensional and you can concentrate on learning statistics. However, many students of statistics spend as much time learning how to use a computer as they do learning statistics and have to work twice as hard to keep up with their classmates. We have written this book for individuals who are trying to learn how to use SPSS to solve their statistical problems. We have tried to be particularly sensitive to those individuals who have limited experience with computers. It is important to realize that, no matter which version of SPSS you use, you will actually be using a programming language. The wonderful thing about the current versions of SPSS is that through the use of menus and option buttons, the computer actually writes the syntax for you.

Regardless of your previous computer experience, we have incorporated tips and suggestions to make data entry and analysis easier so you can spend more time answering research questions and less time debugging computer programs. You will inevitably develop ideas and shortcuts that will help you become better computer users and researchers. We strongly encourage you to keep a record of the products of these moments of inspiration. You, and others, will appreciate the time you take now to record these insights. If you are in the situation of learning SPSS in a classroom environment, we suggest that you work together and share ideas outside of class. In most cases, working collaboratively with others is beneficial.

As we mentioned, we will be using SPSS to illustrate many types of statistical procedures that you will encounter as you do research. By using SPSS to perform statistical procedures, you will also become more familiar with your computer. These are skills that will be very useful, if not essential, for most technical, academic and professional careers. We are not suggesting that these are the only statistical analysis skills you will need because it is still essential that you understand the concepts that support the use of each statistical procedure.

For each procedure addressed in this book, we will provide a brief rationale for its use as well as an example. In most cases, these examples will be drawn from real data gathered from graduate students enrolled in a beginning statistics course. Following the illustration of each technique, we will provide an interpretation of the output generated by SPSS. We recommend that you read more about each of these statistical procedures from a statistics textbook with which you are comfortable.

USING COMPUTERS TO ASSIST WITH STATISTICAL ANALYSIS

Computers have become a required tool for anyone engaging in statistical analysis. Without computers, many statistical operations would take days, weeks, even months to complete. The days of calculating everything by hand (or with the assistance of a calculator) are gone even though it hasn't really been that long since computers were developed and first used to assist with statistical analysis.

Electronic computers were not introduced until the early 1960s, about the time we (the authors) were born. How many of your classmates were born during or before this time? These computers were very large, expensive, and frequently needed repair. They were able to perform a variety of mathematical procedures using what were referred to as machine languages, which were associated with specific types of computers. They were also able to complete statistical procedures within hours and greatly assisted those engaged in statistical analysis. With the development of computer programming languages such as *FORTRAN* (short for *Formula Translation*), programs could be written by researchers and used on different computers. These early computer programs, however, were often stored on punch cards. It wasn't uncommon for these punch cards to get mixed up and this often resulted in either a failed program or inaccurate results.

Statistical analysis became much easier in the 1970s with the development of packaged programs. These programs were designed to perform a wide variety of statistical procedures. Perhaps the greatest feature of these packages was that they could be used by individuals who were not computer programmers. One of the earliest statistical packages developed for use by novice programmers was SPSS. This package and others of its kind were available only on large mainframe computers until the mid-1980s, when the use of personal computers began to increase. SPSS introduced its first personal computer product in 1984 when it offered SPSS/PC+ for the DOS environment. It introduced its first Windows-based product in 1992 and since has released products designed for Windows 95 and Windows 98, Windows 2000 environments. For individuals with Internet access, on-line support and information are available via the Internet through SPSS's web site located at http://www.spss.com.

As you can see, SPSS is available in several different versions for mainframe and personal computers. SPSS versions designed for DOS and Windows 3.1 environments are no longer being developed. Therefore, we will concentrate our efforts on SPSS software designed for use with the Windows 95 and later version environments. Throughout the remainder of this chapter, we will explore the basic features of SPSS.

ORIENTATION TO SPSS

Beginning with Version 7.0, SPSS has been designed for use in a Windows 95 environment. More recently, SPSS has released SPSS 9.X and SPSS 10.X, designed for use with a Windows 98 and Windows 2000 environment. In an attempt to become more user-friendly, SPSS for Windows was developed around a graphical user interface (GUI) in which the user selects statistical options from menus using a mouse as opposed to typing specific commands. It is much easier to use and learn as well as being much more fun. Let's get started by activating SPSS.

ACTIVATING SPSS FOR WINDOWS 95/98

Installing any software package for Windows 95 is usually a seamless process. Each software package will create a directory within the Program Files directory on your hard drive. Simply called SPSS, this directory contains the files needed by SPSS and will become the default directory in which all of your data and program files will be located unless you specify otherwise.

Using the Start Key or Start Menu

The installation program will also create a set of icons within the programs directory. You can launch SPSS in Windows 95/98 by pressing the <Start> key (if you are using a Windows 95 dedicated keyboard) or by clicking on the **Start** button on the screen, scrolling up to the **Programs** icon, and clicking with your mouse on the **SPSS** icon, which will appear toward the end of the list of installed programs. You may see another SPSS icon labeled SPSS Production Facility; we will not be using this function. For more information, please consult your SPSS documentation. Selections made from the **Start** menu are illustrated in Figure 1.1. The number and types of installed software programs may be different on the computer you are using.

FIGURE 1.1
Start – Programs –
SPSS for Windows 98
menus

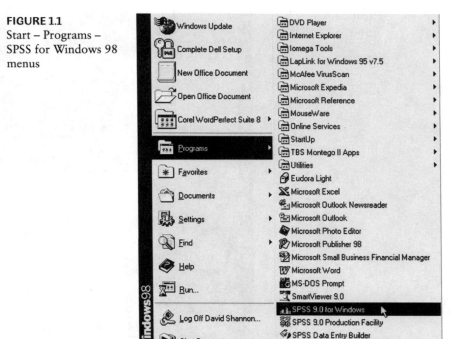

To activate SPSS from the Start menu:

1. Click the **Start** button.
2. Click **P**rograms.
3. Click **SPSS**.

Creating and Using Shortcuts

You can also activate software programs in Windows 95/98 using a **S**hortcut icon. Shortcuts allow you to activate programs directly from your desktop, bypassing the Start menu. You can create one yourself by moving your mouse cursor to an area of your main screen not already taken up by an icon and clicking once with the *right* mouse button. This will open up a small main Window editor, displayed in Figure 1.2. From this desktop menu, highlight **N**ew, which will open up another small window from which you will choose **Shortcut.**

Single clicking with the left mouse button brings up the Create Shortcut dialog box, displayed in Figure 1.3.

Within the dialog box (the white box directly beneath the words **C**ommand Line:) you type the command line that activates the software program. In most cases for SPSS users, this line will be: **"C:\Program Files\SPSS\spsswin.exe"**. (Do not type the period at the end of the filename.) This command line indicates that SPSS is located in the Program Files directory, in a subdirectory called SPSS. The execution file used to activate SPSS is spsswin.

If you are unsure as to the exact location (directory and subdirectory) of SPSS, you can use the **B**rowse... feature. This will allow you to search your directories and subdirectories until you find the exact location of the execution file.

Once you have identified the exact location and file, click on the **N**ext > button. The editor then asks you to name your shortcut icon (see Figure 1.4). By default, the name spsswin is used, but you can name it anything you choose. When finished, left click on

FIGURE 1.2
Windows 98 Desktop
menu–Create
Shortcuts

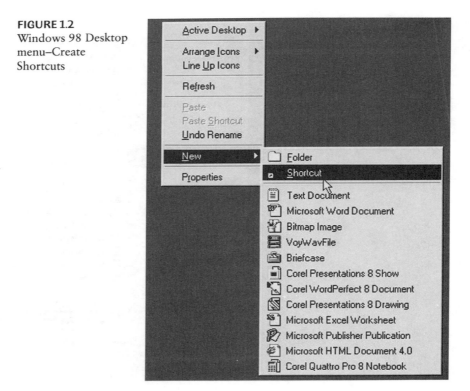

the **Finish** button and the icon will appear on the main desktop anytime you start Windows in the future. From now on, simply double-click on the **Shortcut** icon using your mouse to launch SPSS.

To Create a Shortcut for SPSS:

1. Click the right mouse key.
2. Click on **New.**
3. Click on **Shortcut.**
4. Type the command line which will activate the program in the Command Line box (i.e., "**C:\Program Files\SPSS\spsswin.exe**") or use the **Browse...** feature to search for the execution file (i.e., **spsswin.exe**).
5. Name the **Shortcut** icon.
6. Click **Finish.**

FIGURE 1.3
Create Shortcut dialog box

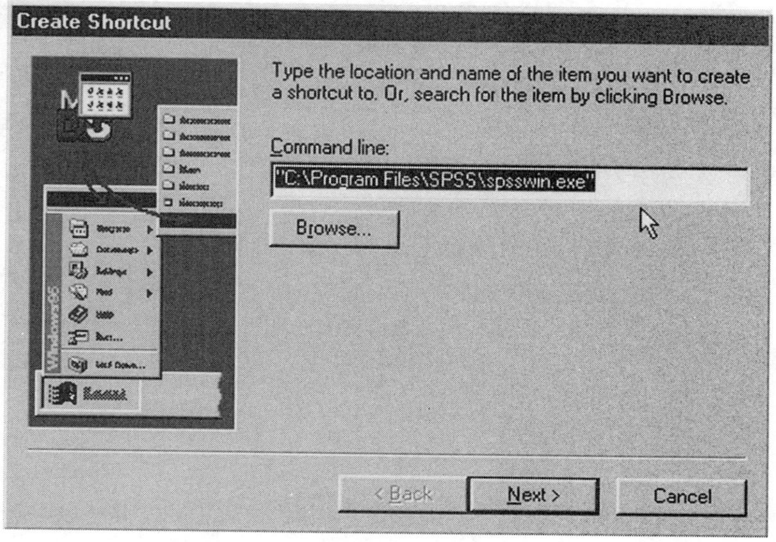

FIGURE 1.4
Select a Title for the Program dialog box

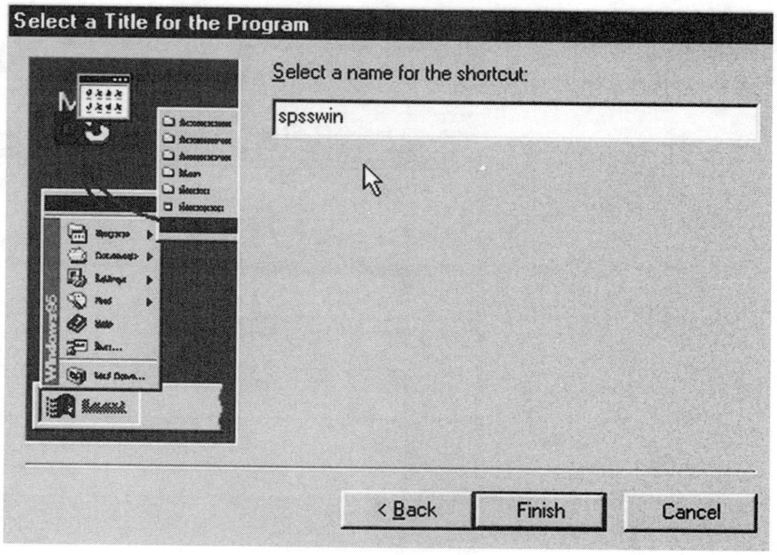

SPSS OPERATING WINDOWS

When you click on the **SPSS** icon from the Start menu or use the shortcut icon from the desktop, the main SPSS logo appears and is followed by the Data Editor screen. However, if you are opening SPSS for the very first time, you will be prompted with the window displayed in Figure 1.5. The window allows you to select which opening window you prefer when you activate SPSS. The default window is the data editor.

Data Editor Window

The data editor is displayed in Figure 1.6. When you activate SPSS, the data editor is automatically opened, awaiting your input. From this editor, we will create new data files and open existing data files so that we can perform a variety of statistical analyses. This editor is a spreadsheet (much like Excel; Lotus 123, Quattro Pro, etc.) that you will use to record your raw data.

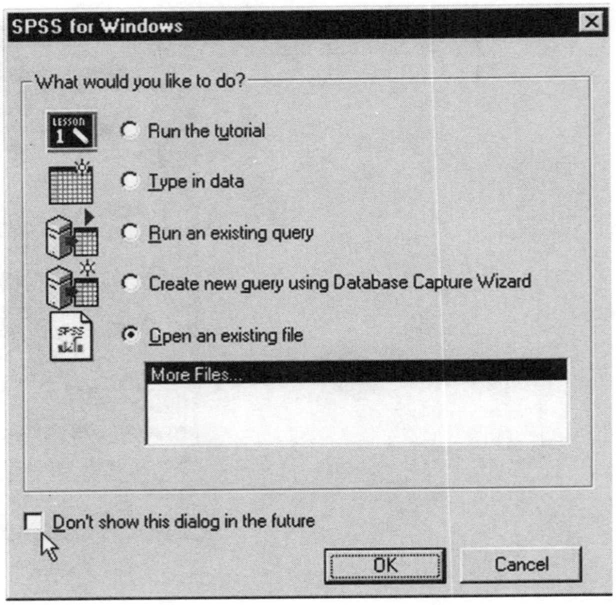

FIGURE 1.5
Opening window for
first session using SPSS

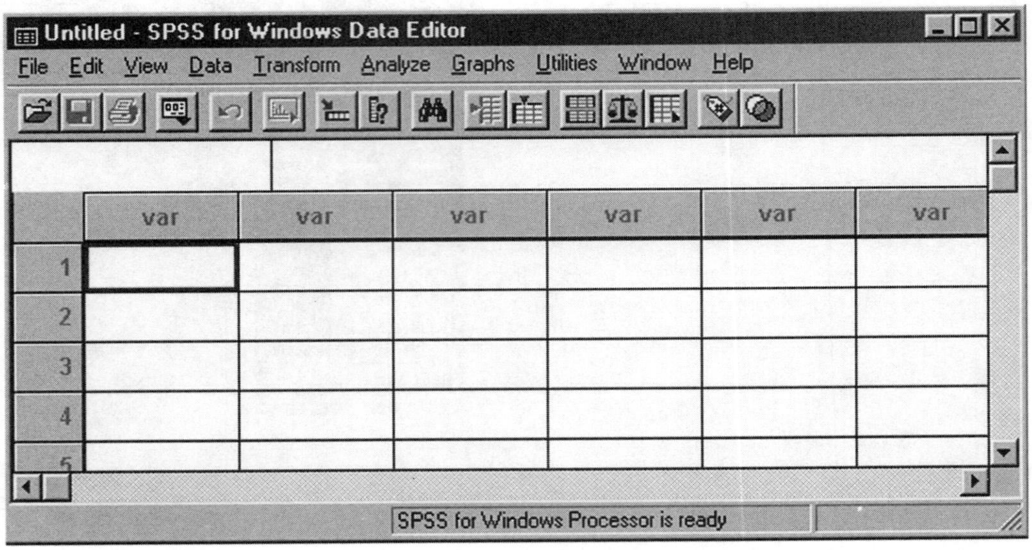

FIGURE 1.6
SPSS Data Editor

Notice that the spreadsheet has an upper margin with column headers labeled **var** and a left margin with row headers numbered sequentially beginning with 1. The columns will represent individual variables, the rows will represent individual cases. If you have not clicked on any functions, buttons, menus, or struck any of the cursor keys on your keyboard, you will notice that the leftmost box or *cell* in row one, column one is bordered with a thick, black outline. If this cell is not highlighted with this outline, move your mouse cursor to this first cell and click with your left mouse button. This should highlight the first data cell. You can move around the data editor using the cursor keys or other function keys, which we will explore later.

You will notice that the name of the window you are presently in appears in the upper left-hand margin of the screen, preceded by the word "Untitled." As soon as you begin to save your work and give your file a name, the word "Untitled" will be changed to the name you give the file.

As with earlier versions of SPSS, there are two critical components used to perform statistical operations. These are the *menu bar* and the *toolbar*. These components are very similar to those used in earlier versions. There are, however, a few improvements which we will now discuss.

Menu Bar.   The menu bar still appears at the top of the screen and will remain there no matter which window you are working in. The menu bar consists of a family of specific functions summarized in a single word (such as File or Analyze). Clicking on one of these words opens up what we will call a *drop-down menu*. From these drop-down menus you will be able to open and close different types of files, print files, perform cut, copy, and paste functions, change the look of the interface (fonts, etc.), perform various data manipulations, perform statistical functions, produce graphs, and access the Help and tutorial programs. This main menu bar appears in Figure 1.7.

There are several options in this menu bar. These options are used to perform different functions in SPSS. We will examine these menu options in more detail as we explore SPSS operations throughout the remainder of this book.

Toolbar.   Below the menu bar is the button bar, or *toolbar*. The toolbar in SPSS for Windows 95/98 has been changed so that only the buttons relevant to the window being used are shown. In this case, the toolbar that contains the data editor buttons is displayed. These buttons can be used to perform certain common functions needed to create and manage the data set. This toolbar is displayed in Figure 1.8.

The buttons in the button bar are illustrated such that the icon on the button is indicative of that button's function. For instance, the **Open File** button is marked by an open manila folder, the **Save** button is marked with a computer disk, and the **Print File** button is marked with the image of a printer. If you have just opened the data editor and have not input any information into the window, the **Save** and **Print** buttons should be muted. Only buttons that you may currently use will be shown in color.

Because only buttons that are specific to a certain window (data editor, output, syntax and graphics) are displayed, fewer buttons appear on the screen at once. This makes learning the functions of the button bar much easier. Many other buttons exist, but are not useful when viewing the data editor. The other buttons, which are not displayed, are relevant to output or graphing functions. We will examine these functions as we explore SPSS further.

FIGURE 1.7
SPSS Data Editor main menu

FIGURE 1.8
SPSS Data Editor toolbar

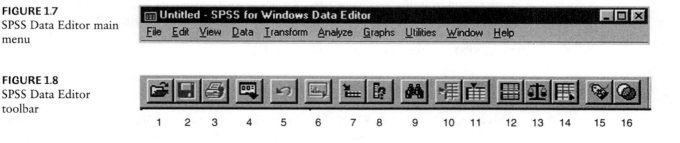

FIGURE 1.9
SPSS Output Viewer

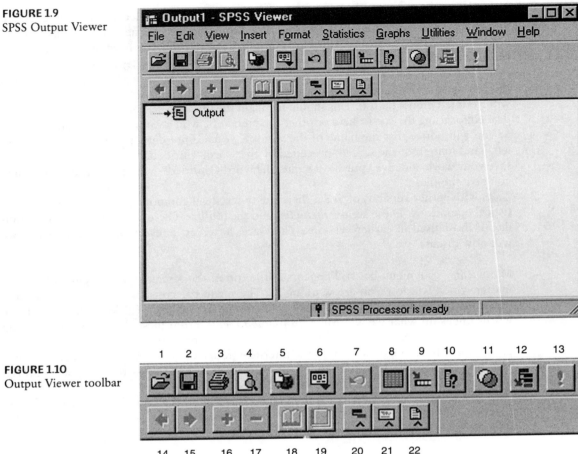

FIGURE 1.10
Output Viewer toolbar

SPSS Output Viewer

There is another window that records all the results of your statistical operations. This window is called the Output Viewer. The SPSS output viewer is displayed in Figure 1.9.

Right now, this window does not display any information because you have not instructed SPSS to do anything yet. As you explore the many statistical operations available using SPSS, you will fill this output viewer with results. As you examine these results, you will also learn how to use the output viewer to sift through all the information, and organize, format, and print it. You will use the output viewer functions as you produce statistical results in the chapters that follow.

Just like the data editor window, this window comes with its own menu and toolbar. The menu options are very similar to those from the data editor; whereas the toolbar buttons are tailored more to those functions that are related to the output navigator (see Figure 1.10). For example, the fifth button on the top of the toolbar is used to export data from the output navigator as an .htm or .txt file. This allows you to post results on the Internet or use them in another software program (e.g., word processor). The last three buttons (20, 21, 22) are used to edit the output generated by SPSS. These options allow you to insert headings, titles, and text. We will explore these, and other features, as we generate results using SPSS throughout the remainder of this book.

EXITING SPSS

This completes your introduction to the SPSS software system. We encourage you to continue exploring the many features of this software. We will be using most of these features in later chapters as we perform statistical analyses. If you want to exit SPSS for now, select the **Exit** option from the **File** menu on the main menu bar.

DATA USED IN THIS BOOK

We will be using several sources of data in this book to illustrate statistical analysis procedures using SPSS. One set of data is small, containing only twenty (20) subjects. These twenty subjects are applicants to a doctoral program. These data were specifically designed to help illustrate a variety of SPSS procedures. We created these data just for you to explore. We will say that it is not a common practice to make up your own data; nor is this practice generally acceptable in the profession.

We have included a second data set, which is real. These data were gathered from graduate students enrolled in statistics classes who were asked questions about their attitudes toward computers and statistics. These data will be used to illustrate most of the statistical procedures addressed in this book. As we encounter statistical procedures that are not appropriate for these data, we will ask you to use other data from the enclosed disk.

Doctoral Applicants Data

In this fictional data set, we have included some common information about twenty applicants to a doctoral program. This information includes the following variables: gender, socio-economic status (SES), ethnicity, Graduate Record Examination—Quantitative (GREQ), Graduate Record Examination—Verbal (GREV), a pretest score in the doctoral speciality area, and two ratings from interviews with faculty members.

If these data were real, a variety of data collection methods may have been used. First, the demographic information (i.e., gender, SES, ethnicity) may have been supplied by the candidate. The test scores from the GRE would have been supplied by Educational Testing Service and included in the applicant's file. The pretest would have been administered by the program area and the results would be kept in the applicant's file. Finally, the faculty rating would have been a result of the applicant's interview. These data can be found in Appendix A. In the following chapters, you will work closely with these data, preparing them for analysis and using a variety of statistical procedures.

Computer and Statistics Attitudes Data

This data set is much larger (and real). Each individual (subject) in this data set was enrolled in a graduate statistics course when this information was collected. Information was gathered from each subject on the first day of class. The survey instrument is reproduced in Appendix B.

Data gathered using this survey instrument included variables regarding each student's background, coursework, degree, and attitudes toward computers and statistics. Because this is a much larger dataset, we have also included these data on the enclosed diskette. This will save you the time it would take to prepare and enter all the data. The information from this data set will be used to help illustrate the many statistical procedures explored in the remainder of this book

We have selected subsets of variables from this data set to illustrate specific statistical procedures in each chapter. These smaller data sets are also stored on the enclosed disk. For example, the data used in Chapter 2 is labeled **chap2 data**. This will make the process more manageable with fewer variables to sift through. The entire data set is also stored on the disk so you can explore it using SPSS. The name of the complete data set regarding computer and statistics attitudes is **compstat total data**.

2 | Retrieving and Saving SPSS Files

In the previous chapter, you explored the basic features of SPSS. During this orientation, you examined the data editor and the output navigator. You also learned about the many functions that can be performed by SPSS using the menus or the toolbar. In this chapter, you will begin to use SPSS to perform some basic, but essential, file management tasks. Specifically, you will be retrieving an existing data file from the enclosed disk, working in the data editor to explore this file, and saving the file. In chapter 3, you will learn how to create a data file by inputting the data yourself. For the current chapter, we have created a small data file for you.

RETRIEVING SPSS FILES

Before you retrieve a file, you must activate the program. Upon opening SPSS, the data editor will be displayed on your screen. Normally, you would begin to define variables and enter data in this data editor. However, we have done this for you in order to save time. The name of the file we will use in this chapter is **chap2 data.sav** and it can be found on the enclosed disk. All you need to do is retrieve this file into the data editor and we can get started. There are two ways in which files can be retrieved; you can use the menu or the toolbar.

Using the Menu to Retrieve SPSS Data Files

Many procedures are executed from the main menu bar. We will be using the options in the **File** menu to open and save files in this chapter. These options are displayed in Figure 2.1.

The options in the **File** menu allow you to create new files, open existing files, capture a file from another database (e.g., Excel), read data that is stored in ASCII format, save files, print files, and exit SPSS. In this SPSS session, we will retrieve an SPSS file and save it. In later chapters, you will read data files from other databases and ASCII files.

To begin, we need to retrieve a data file. From the main menu bar, select **File.** From the file menu, select the second option, **Open...,** by highlighting it and clicking the left button on your mouse. This is illustrated in Figure 2.2. Because the data editor was automatically activated when you began, you do not have to identify the type of file you want to open. An SPSS data file will be opened by default. You will open other types of files (e.g., syntax files, output files) in later SPSS sessions.

Selecting the **Open...** option will open the Open Data File dialog box, which appears in Figure 2.3.

FIGURE 2.1
SPSS File menu
options

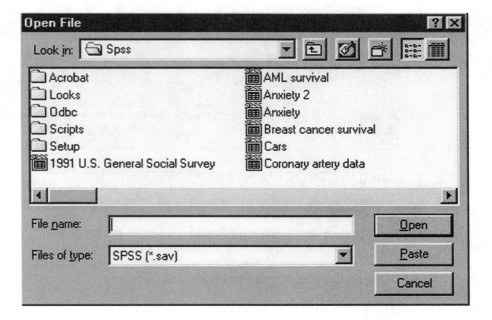

| File | Edit | View | Data | Transform | Analyze | Graphs | Utilities | Window | Help |

New ▶
Open...   Ctrl+O
Database Capture ▶
Read Text Data

Save   Ctrl+S
Save As...

Display Data Info...
Apply Data Dictionary...

Print...   Ctrl+P

Stop Processor   Ctrl+.

Exit

FIGURE 2.2
File–Open menu
selections

| File | Edit | View | Data | Transform | Analyze | Graphs | Utilities | Window | Help |

New ▶
Open...   Ctrl+O
Database Capture ▶
Read Text Data

Save   Ctrl+S
Save As...

Display Data Info...
Apply Data Dictionary...

Print...   Ctrl+P

Stop Processor   Ctrl+.

Exit

FIGURE 2.3
Open Data File dialog
box

Open File

Look in: 🗁 Spss

📁 Acrobat   ▦ AML survival
📁 Looks   ▦ Anxiety 2
📁 Odbc   ▦ Anxiety
📁 Scripts   ▦ Breast cancer survival
📁 Setup   ▦ Cars
▦ 1991 U.S. General Social Survey   ▦ Coronary artery data

File name: [   ]   **Open**

Files of type: SPSS (*.sav)   **Paste**

      Cancel

FIGURE 2.4
List of Directories
(with 3½ Floppy
highlighted)

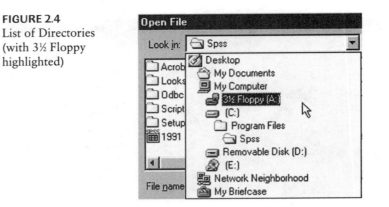

A long text box appears along the top portion of this window, labeled **Look in:**. In this box is a file folder icon labeled SPSS. By default, SPSS begins searching in this directory for files to be opened because this is the directory that contains the SPSS files. If you loaded your SPSS program in a directory with a different name, that one will be displayed by default.

Our data are not located in the main SPSS directory. We stored these data on a 3½-inch computer disk. Use the down arrow at the right of the directory textbar to reveal other directories, as in Figure 2.4. Select the option for **3½ Floppy (A:)**.

We are looking for a file named **chap2 data.sav,** stored on a 3½-inch disk. Find the file folder icon labeled **3½ Floppy(A:)**. The contents of a directory are viewed by double-clicking your mouse on the file folder icon. All files with a .sav suffix found on the 3½-inch floppy disk will be displayed, as in Figure 2.5.

The .sav suffix is attached to SPSS data files. Notice the box at the bottom of this window labeled **Files of type:**. Within this box, the message SPSS(*.sav) appears. This simply means that only SPSS data files are being displayed for your convenience. If you wished to examine other types of files, as you will in later chapters, you would select from a list of file type options by clicking on the arrow button to the right of the box. We need the data file, **chap2 data.sav,** and we double-click on the file icon to retrieve the file into the data editor, as in Figure 2.6. The data are now ready to be analyzed.

The steps we used to retrieve the data from our disk are summarized in the following box.

To Retrieve an SPSS data file:

Step 1   From the menu bar, click on the **File** menu.
Step 2   Select **Open**....
Step 3   Select the drive that contains your file.
Step 4   Identify the type of file you wish to retrieve. The setting is *.sav for SPSS data files.
Step 5   Highlight the file and click twice with your mouse to retrieve it into the data editor.

Using the Toolbar to Retrieve SPSS Data Files

You can also retrieve files using the toolbar, which appears under the menubar. As you explored in the previous chapter, this toolbar contains a series of icons that can be used to perform such operations as opening files, saving, printing, changing windows, and running a syntax file. The active toolbar displays only those buttons that can be used to perform operations that are appropriate when working in the data editor. The first icon at the very left of the toolbar displays an open file, pictured below.

FIGURE 2.5
Directory of SPSS data files (.sav) on 3½ Floppy

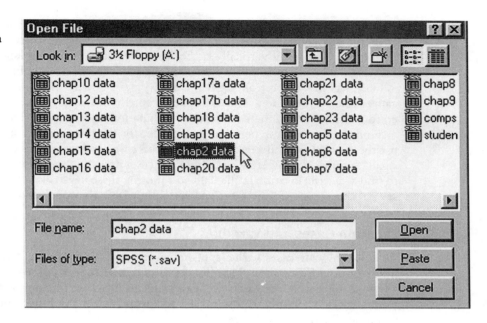

FIGURE 2.6
Data Editor (chap2 data.sav)

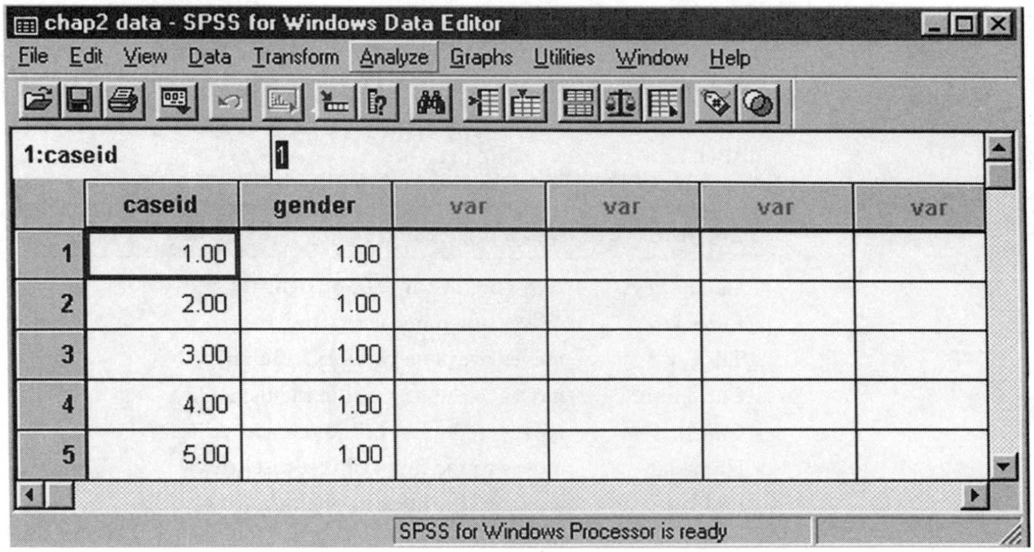

By double-clicking on this open file icon, you will be lead directly to the window containing the names of files found on specific disks. This bypasses the first two steps that we illustrated above. All you need to do to complete the process is select the directory and the desired file to retrieve the data into the data editor.

EXPLORING THE DATA EDITOR

This data file contains several different subjects, found in each row, and variables, found in each column. When a file is opened, the cursor rests in the upper left-hand corner. This area, called the home cell, should be outlined. Using the <Cntl> and <Home> keys together will automatically move your cursor to this cell. The combination of the <Cntl> and <End> keys will move the cursor to the last cell in the data editor. You can also move within the spreadsheet by moving the mouse cursor (within the spreadsheet, this cursor takes the form of a cross-hair) to the desired cell and clicking once.

You can also scroll vertically or horizontally using the arrow keys on your keyboard. Pressing the <Tab> key will move you along a row from left to right, whereas the <Shift> <Tab> will move you from right to left. To move down a column in the data editor, you can use the <Enter> key. The cursor keys can also be used to move around within the data editor. A summary of these keystroke combinations is found in Table 2.1.

Find the information pertaining to gender for the third subject in the data file. You can use the cursor keys and keystrokes to find this case quickly. It helps that this data set is very small. Suppose there were several hundred cases and variables. It would require more time to find a specific location in the data editor using these keystrokes. Fortunately, SPSS offers several shortcuts to locate cases and variables within the data editor.

Locating Cases and Variables

To quickly locate cases with a specific value on a given variable, you use the **Find...** option from the **Edit** menu. Begin by positioning the cursor in the column of the variable you wish to search. For example, if we want to find case number 3, we move our cursor to the 'caseid' column. To use the Find feature, select the **Find...** option from the **Edit** menu, as illustrated in Figure 2.7.

This will open the Search for Data dialog box displayed in Figure 2.8. We want to find case number 3, therefore type a "3" in the box labeled Search for and select the **Search Forward** button. The cursor will now be located in the cell that contains the value 3. We realize that finding the third case would not have taken that long if you simply used the cursor keys. However, there will be times when you are working with much

TABLE 2.1
Summary of Data Editor Keystroke Commands

Keystroke	Function
Cursor keys	move up, down, left, or right
Enter key	moves down one case (row)
Tab key	moves over one variable (column)
Cntl Home	moves to the first cell in the data editor
Cntl End	moves to the last cell in the data editor
Home key	moves to the first cell of a case (row)
End key	moves to the last cell of a case (row)
Cntl ↑	moves to the first case of a variable (column)
Cntl ↓	moves to the last case of a variable (column)

FIGURE 2.7
Edit–Find menu selections

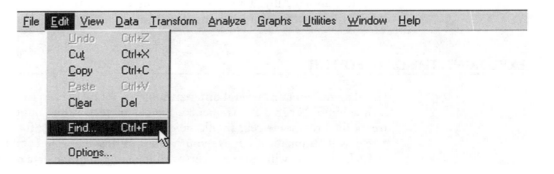

larger data files and the **Find...** option will be a valuable shortcut. This procedure can be used to find any value within any existing variable.

You can also use the toolbar to search for specific values in a row or column. The icon that looks like a pair of binoculars will open the search window. This is the ninth icon from the left. Using this icon, pictured below, will bypass the menu selections.

Another easy way to locate a specific case begins from the **Data** menu. From this menu, select the option for **Go to Case...**, as illustrated in Figure 2.9. Using this procedure, you can locate a specific case simply by typing the desired case number in the box labeled Case Number in the Go to Case dialog box (see Figure 2.10). To locate the third case, type in "3" and click on the **OK** button. Again, this procedure is most helpful when dealing with larger data files.

FIGURE 2.8
Search for Data dialog box

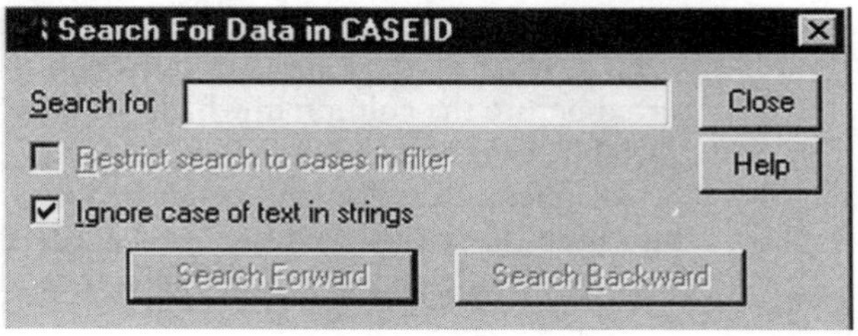

FIGURE 2.9
Data–Go to Case...
menu selections

FIGURE 2.10
Go to Case dialog box

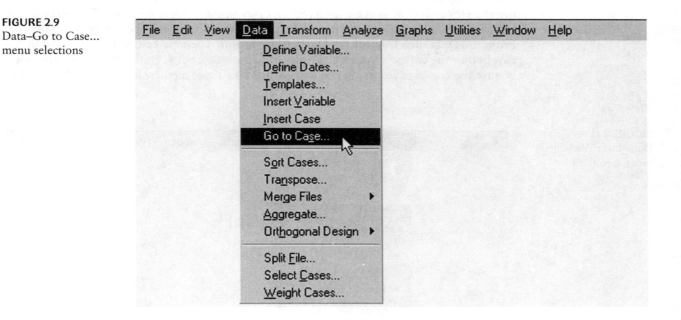

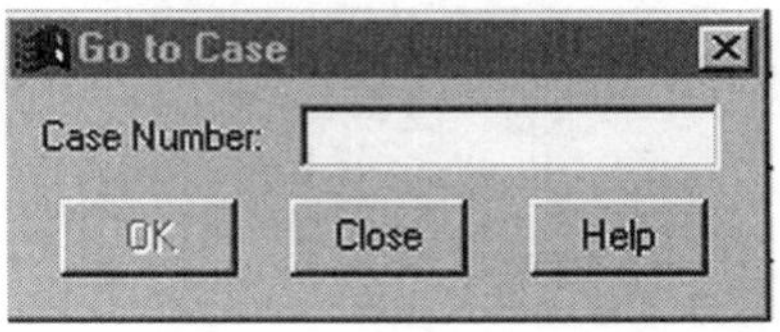

As with the find function, you can bypass the menu by using the toolbar. The seventh icon on the toolbar (shown below) will open the Go to Case dialog box.

Inserting Cases and Variables

Suppose you wanted to add to these data. Adding more cases and/or more variables to a data file is very simple using SPSS.

Inserting Variables.　If you would like to add a variable to the data file, you have two options. First, you can simply add it in the next available column. In this case, we have two existing variables so we would simply add the new variable in the third column. The second option is to add a new variable at some position within the data file. For example, we might want to add a new variable in a column between our case number and gender variables. Should this be the case, we would need to make some selections from the **Data** menu.
　First, be sure to locate your cursor in the gender column. The new variable will be inserted before the column in which the cursor is located. From the **Data** menu, select **Insert Variable,** as illustrated in Figure 2.11.
　This menu selection will result in a new variable being inserted between the two existing variables, as displayed in Figure 2.12. All you need to do now is enter the data for each case. By default, this new variable will be identified as **var00002**.

Inserting Cases.　There are also two ways to insert cases. First, you can simply add to the current cases by using the next available row for the new case. In this case, we would use the eleventh row, as we only have ten cases in the current data file. The second way to insert a case is used when you wish to place the new case at a specific point in the file. From the **Data** menu, select the **Insert Case** option. The new case will be inserted in the row before the cursor's location. To place this new case between the fifth and sixth cases, be sure the cursor is resting in the sixth row. Make these menu selections (as displayed in

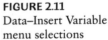

FIGURE 2.11
Data–Insert Variable
menu selections

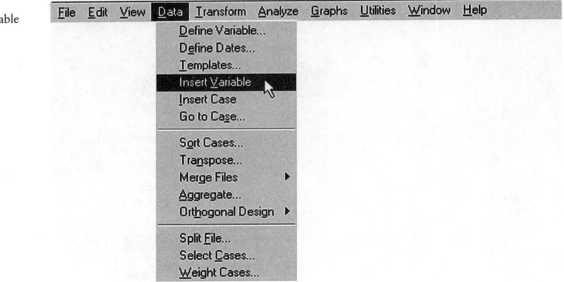

Figure 2.13) and notice that a new case is inserted (see Figure 2.14). Now you are ready to enter the data for this new case.

There are toolbar buttons that will allow you to insert cases or variables without using the menu. To insert a new variable, use the icon displaying a spreadsheet with an arrow pointing to an inserted column. To insert a variable, use the icon with an arrow pointing to an inserted row. These icons are shown below.

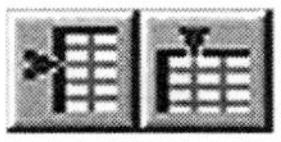

FIGURE 2.12
New variable inserted
in chap2 data.sav

	caseid	var00002	gender
1	1.00	.	1.00
2	2.00	.	1.00
3	3.00	.	1.00
4	4.00	.	1.00
5	5.00	.	1.00
6	6.00	.	2.00
7	7.00	.	2.00
8	8.00	.	2.00
9	9.00	.	2.00
10	10.00	.	2.00

FIGURE 2.13
Data–Insert Case
menu selections

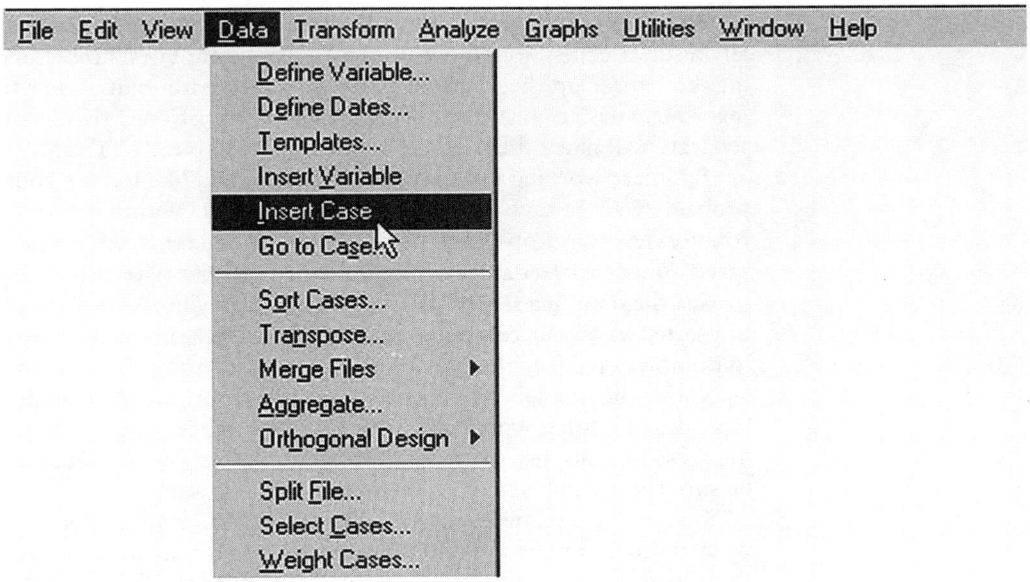

File Edit View **Data** Transform Analyze Graphs Utilities Window Help

Define Variable...
Define Dates...
Templates...
Insert Variable
Insert Case
Go to Case...

Sort Cases...
Transpose...
Merge Files ▶
Aggregate...
Orthogonal Design ▶

Split File...
Select Cases...
Weight Cases...

FIGURE 2.14
New case inserted in
chap2 data.sav

	caseid	gender
1	1.00	1.00
2	2.00	1.00
3	3.00	1.00
4	4.00	1.00
5	5.00	1.00
6	.	.
7	6.00	2.00
8	7.00	2.00
9	8.00	2.00
10	9.00	2.00
11	10.00	2.00

SAVING YOUR DATA IN SPSS

It is always a good idea to save files regularly. In SPSS, files can be saved from the main menu or the toolbar. Using the menu, select the **File** menu and choose the **Save** option, as illustrated in Figure 2.15. SPSS recognizes that a data file will be saved because you are working from the data editor and that this file has been previously saved. Therefore, it will automatically save the changes and retain the same name for the file.

If you want to save this file under a different name, or in a different location, select the **Save As...** option from the **File** menu (see Figure 2.16). These selections will open the Save Data As dialog box, which appears in Figure 2.17.

SPSS files will be saved in the SPSS directory unless you specify otherwise. This is usually a subdirectory found within the **"C:\Program Files\"** directory. It is not usually a good idea to clutter up the main program directory with many other files. We recommend saving your work to a separate working directory of your own creation. Keeping these files separate will make it easier to find them when you need them.

If you are working in a computer lab or would like to take your work with you, you will probably want to save your work on a floppy disk. Within the **Save in:** box, use the down arrow to view the drop-down menu. Using this menu, specify where you want the file to be saved. You can select any existing directory on your hard drive (C:) or floppy disk. We want to save the data to a floppy disk so you can take your work with you. Be sure that your disk is inserted into your computer disk drive and click on the 3½ **Floppy (A:)** icon. All you need to do now is identify the type of file being saved and give it a name.

Notice the box labeled **Save as type:** at the bottom of the dialog box. SPSS data files are typically identified with a .sav suffix. Several types of files can be saved in SPSS. To examine these options, use the pull-down menu. When you are finished exploring these options, be sure the setting is back to the default SPSS (*.sav).

You specify a name in the **File name:** box. Click your mouse in the **File name:** box. We want to give this file a name that tells us something about what the file contains. One of the added benefits of using Windows 95/98 over the Windows 3.1 environment is that file names are not limited to eight characters. Since these data were previously saved, a file-name already exists. The name **"chap2 data.sav"** should appear in the **File name:** box. We could accept this name or we could change it. In order to explore the process of renaming

FIGURE 2.15
File–Save menu
selections

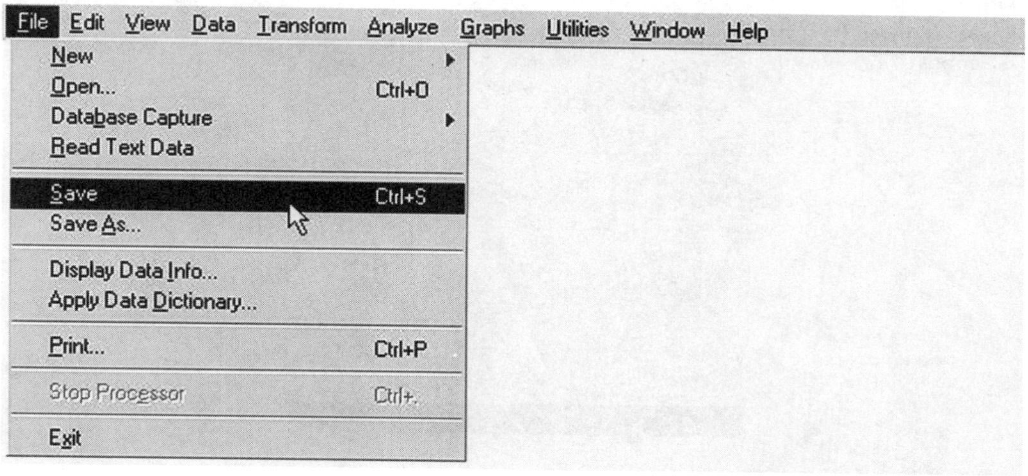

FIGURE 2.16
File–Save As menu
selections

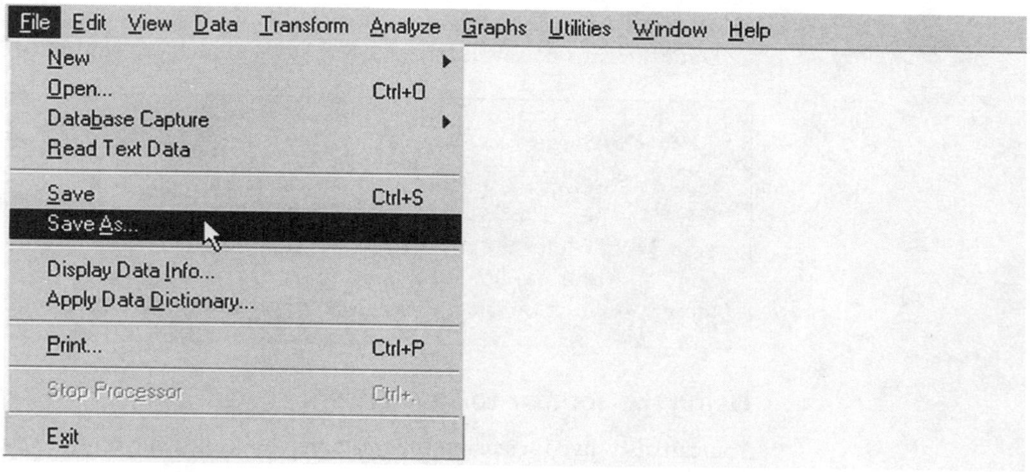

FIGURE 2.17
Save Data As dialog
box

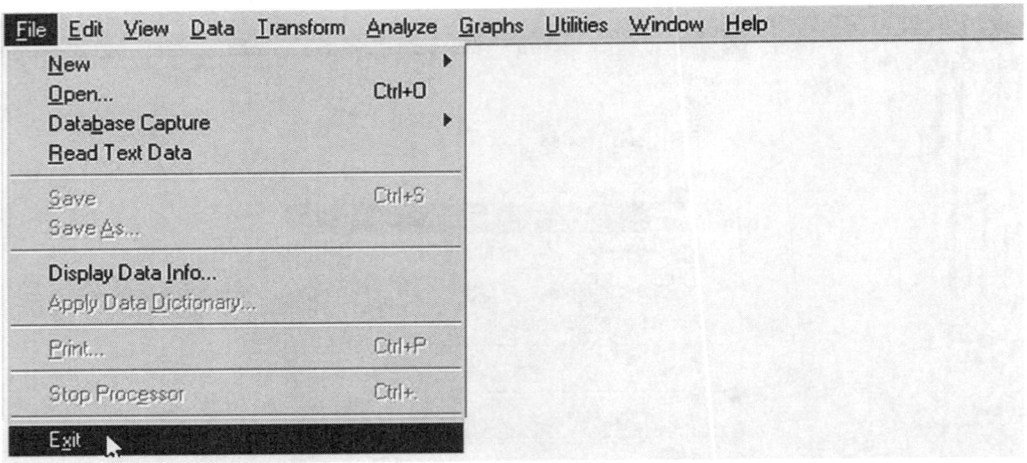

FIGURE 2.18
File–Exit menu
selections

File	Edit	View	Data	Transform	Analyze	Graphs	Utilities	Window	Help

New	▶
Open...	Ctrl+O
Database Capture	▶
Read Text Data	
Save	Ctrl+S
Save As...	
Display Data Info...	
Apply Data Dictionary...	
Print...	Ctrl+P
Stop Processor	Ctrl+.
Exit	

files, change the name of the file to **new chap2 data.** Type "**new chap2 data**" in the **File** name box. You do not have to type the .sav suffix because SPSS will do that automatically. To save this file, use the **Save** button.

Data files can be saved in just a few steps, which are summarized below.

To Save SPSS files:

Step 1   Select the **File** menu from the main menu bar.
Step 2   Select the **Save** option.
Step 3   Specify the drive to which the file will be saved in the **Save in:** box.
Step 4   Indicate name for file in the File name: box.
Step 5   Click on the **Save** command button to save the file.

Using the Toolbar to Save Files

You can also save files using the toolbar. This will save you time if you frequently save your files. The save icon looks like a disk, as shown below.

This shortcut appears on the toolbar, which allows you to update (save) a file you are presently working on without opening up a separate window. Simply click once on the **Save** button on the button bar and your file will be updated to reflect the work you have just completed in addition to any work previously saved. If you wish to save a copy of your file under a separate name, simply choose the **Save As...** option from the **File** menu and follow the procedure outlined above, using a different name.

Exiting SPSS

If you wish to exit SPSS, use the main menu bar. Select the **File** menu and choose the **Exit** option. These selections are illustrated in Figure 2.18.

CHAPTER SUMMARY

In this chapter, you learned how to retrieve SPSS data files, work with the features of the data editor, and save files. We encourage you to continue to explore this data file using the many features of the data editor. In the next chapter, you will create your own data file using SPSS.

3 | **Data Entry and Definition**

Like all computer programs, SPSS will perform only the procedures that you tell it to, using the variables you specify. However, before you are able to perform any statistical procedures, you need to define the variables you will be using. These variables will be stored in an SPSS data file. You retrieved and explored a data file in the previous chapter. In this chapter, you will be using SPSS to define variables and create a new data file. Specifically, you will create the data file pertaining to applicants to a doctoral program, which we described in the first chapter. First we will discuss some ways to stay organized while doing research and data analysis.

ORGANIZING YOUR RESEARCH AND YOUR DATA

Many people's stereotypic impression of the pre-computer age scientist would include a weathered, well thumbed, hardbound laboratory notebook or field book, bound with a rubber band or ribbon and filled with sketches, equations, and roughly copied notes. Although most research is now conducted in and around the computer, it is still necessary for a researcher to keep notes and ideas organized. Although the computer has made it easier for us to process numbers and information, we now find ourselves with desktops and drawers filled with floppy disks with labels that read proj1a.txt or exp1datab.dat or the like. Anyone who has misplaced a disk, only to find it six months later under the desk, knows the frustration that surrounds the examination of a disk full of files with names that one can no longer place. The proper organization of one's research resources has not lost its importance with the coming of the computer age. Years of experience with lost data sets and misplaced files allow us to share with you some suggestions for making your introduction to social and educational research in the computer age a less exasperating affair.

As alluded to previously, the research notebook did not become obsolete with the advent of the computer. Researchers, as students of science, must still keep notes about their daily activities. You will find that as you go through your statistics courses, you will be involved with the creation and manipulation of many data sets, each of which will contain several different variables. For some of these variables, you will likely define value labels (for instance, a marital status variable might include special values that represent the classification "married," "single," "widowed," "divorced," etc.). In the process of analyzing your data, you will likely create new variables and files with names that seem perfectly reasonable now but who's meaning may be lost in the coming weeks or months. This is complicated by the fact that pre-Windows 95 PC software does not allow file names of more than eight characters and none of the current SPSS packages will allow variable names of more than eight characters. With these constraints, it is often difficult to develop variable names that allow for easy recognition. Keeping a research notebook, a place to jot down names, equations, ideas, and results, is an excellent way to keep track of your progress, especially if you are forced to leave the data for a period of time.

We recommend that you begin the process of organizing your data before you start inputting it into the computer using SPSS. One way to keep your data organized is to create a coding guide. A coding guide is a written record of the variable names and descriptions that allow both you and SPSS to keep track of all variables that are a part of your data set. This coding guide will serve as a valuable reference later in the research project when you may have forgotten many of the details about some of the variables. Coding guides for the mainframe and DOS versions would include the exact columns in which the data are located. Using SPSS in Window-based environments, data are organized in a spreadsheet format, therefore the exact column locations are not necessary.

A second thing you can do to organize your data is to code your data on data sheets. FORTRAN coding sheets and graph paper work well for these purposes. This may seem like an extra step in the process and many people prefer to enter data directly into the computer. At a minimum, print a hard copy of your data once you've created a finished data file. If you were ever to lose (or misplace) the disk on which you entered the data or something were to happen to your computer and the data were destroyed, you would have a record from which to re-create the data set.

A third recommendation is to record an identification number for each case. This number should be coded and stored with all the other variables in your data set. In addition, you should record this number on the raw data instrument (e.g. survey, test, observation form, interview guide, etc.). By doing this you will have quick access to the raw data. If you should make a mistake while entering the data into an SPSS file, you can refer to the original raw data and make the corrections. It is also a good practice to verify your data set against the original data to be sure that the data are accurate before performing any analyses.

Once your data are coded and recorded onto a computer disk, store the raw data in a safe, dry place until you are absolutely sure you will never need it again. Unfortunately, it is far too common to lose electronic files due to mechanical or human failure. Always make back-up copies when working with important files (e.g. dissertation data) in SPSS or any other software program, just in case the original files are lost or destroyed. We also suggest that you store your back-up disks and working disks at separate locations. The authors have heard the stories of doctoral students storing a hard copy of their dissertation in the freezer just in case of a fire. Keeping copies of disks and documents at home and at the office would be more than sufficient.

CODING YOUR DATA

We will use the fictitious data about applicants to a doctoral program to illustrate how to code data. These data, found in Appendix A, are reproduced in Table 3.1. There are twenty cases (applicants) found in this data set. Each applicant's record has been assigned an identification number and contains information on eight variables. These variables will be used to determine who will be admitted to the doctoral program. As you can see, some of these data are recorded in numerical form while others are identified by words. For example, the first applicant is a white male coming from a family of middle socioeconomic status. He scored a 667 on the GREQ and a 449 on the GREV, while obtaining an 87 on the pretest and receiving ratings of 9 and 8 from interviews with two faculty members.

These data could be coded just as they are in Table 3.1 and entered into an SPSS file. However, many of the statistical procedures you will be performing require that numbers be used to represent each variable. Therefore, it is necessary that we assign codes to these variables now, before we begin using SPSS. The values (codes) attached to each variable are important and must make sense so that we can use them in later analyses. The numerical values attached to variables in our data set also help to define the level of measurement on

TABLE 3.1
Doctoral Program Applicants

ID	Gender	SES	Ethnicity	GREQ	GREV	Pretest	Rating1	Rating2
01	male	middle	white	667	449	87	9	8
02	female	low	African American	356	480	55	7	5
03	female	middle	African American	445	666	75	8	7
04	male	upper	white	750	679	94	10	9
05	male	middle	African American	589	550	80	8	9
06	female	middle	white	490	450	74	8	6
07	female	middle	Asian	705	405	97	7	7
08	male	low	African American	380	360	55	5	4
09	male	low	Hispanic	450	385	69	7	6
10	female	upper	African American	666	765	85	10	9
11	male	middle	Asian	675	499	88	8	6
12	male	low	white	422	435	72	6	6
13	male	middle	white	555	666	81	8	7
14	female	upper	white	600	755	74	6	5
15	male	middle	Hispanic	533	485	68	7	8
16	female	middle	white	500	535	79	8	7
17	male	low	white	375	490	65	6	6
18	female	upper	white	725	750	95	8	10
19	female	middle	African American	575	650	78	10	9
20	male	middle	white	475	550	63	7	6

Variables:

ID – identification number
Gender – gender of applicant
SES – socioeconomic status of applicant
Ethnicity – ethnicity of applicant
GREQ – score on Graduate Record Examination – Quantitative Section
GREV – score on Graduate Record Examination – Verbal Section
Pretest – score on pretest in area of speciality
Rating1 – rating from an interview with a faculty member
Rating2 – rating from another faculty member

which each variable is measured. These levels of measurement will be important later as we determine the most appropriate analysis for our data.

Levels of Measurement

Researchers in the social sciences must often take into account a subject's membership in a particular group. Numbers are frequently assigned to represent different groups within a variable. For example, males may be assigned a value of "1" and females a value of "2." The same categorical system may be used for ethnicity. In this case, a "1" may be assigned to represent white, "2" for African-American, "3" for Asian, and "4" for Hispanic. For both variables, gender and ethnicity, numbers are simply used to classify people into different groups. There is no order or importance implied by these numbers. Such variables are referred to as nominal level measures.

However, for a variable such as socioeconomic status (SES), the numbers we assign have more meaning. We can assign a "1" for lower SES, a "2" for middle SES, and a "3" for upper

SES. In this case, a higher number represents higher socioeconomic status. There is an order implied by these numerical values. Variables such as this are said to be measured at the *ordinal* level of measurement. Although ordinal variables do maintain such order, the intervals between each point along the scale are not equal. For example, the interval of income that distinguishes between two applicants of low and middle SES may not be the same as for two other individuals of middle and high SES.

The remaining variables, GREQ, GREV, pretest, and ratings are already in numerical form and require no special coding. They will be coded as they appear in Table 3.1. From a measurement perspective, the rating variables are similar to the SES variable. A higher number represents a higher rating, but the intervals between each point on this rating scale may not be equal for all individuals. These intervals may vary depending upon the faculty person doing the rating. Therefore, the rating variables would also be classified as ordinal.

The other three numerical variables (GREQ, GREV, and pretest) would be classified as *interval* variables. Interval variables maintain the order that is the primary characteristic of ordinal variables, but also have equal intervals between points along the scale. In the case of these three variables, a higher score is associated with better performance. In addition, the difference between two people scoring 490 and 500 on the GREQ and two people scoring 690 and 700 on the GREQ is 10 points in either case. The same holds true for the GREV and the pretest. Interval variables, such as these test scores, are very common in behavioral research.

There is one remaining level of measurement that maintains all the properties of interval measurement and has the added property of a lower bound of zero. This level is referred to as ratio-level measurement. Ratio variables have an absolute zero. In other words, a "0" represents the absence of whatever is being measured. These variables are more common in the physical sciences as they include variables such as length, width, and weight. We will encounter some ratio variables in the larger data set on attitudes toward computers and statistics. These variables include age and years of teaching experience. Before we begin working with this larger data set, we will finish organizing our data in the smaller data set.

Constructing a Coding Guide

It is a good idea to construct a coding guide for each data set you encounter. As we noted previously, a coding guide provides you with a record of variable names and descriptions, allowing you to keep track of all variables that are part of your data set. The more variables you have in your data set, the more valuable your coding guide becomes. At a minimum, a coding guide will include names and descriptions of variables. These variable descriptions should include a reference to your original data source and definitions for all levels of each variable. This coding guide is usually kept in a notebook, along with other valuable information about your research procedures and data analysis. Let's examine an example with which most of you will be familiar.

Suppose you were gathering data for your thesis or dissertation. These data were being gathered by administering a survey instrument to a sample of undergraduate students. Like most survey instruments, there was a section for demographic information. One question in this section pertained to the program area in which the student was currently enrolled. You might choose "PROG" to label this variable in your SPSS files. Although this variable name may be perfectly clear to you now, it may not be clear a year from now when you are working with the same data set. We are not suggesting that it will take you a year to complete the data analysis for your thesis. We simply want to emphasize that a coding guide becomes even more valuable if you haven't worked with the data in quite some time.

In order to complete the coding guide entry for this variable, you should include the question from the survey and a list of the response categories. The list of response categories should include each corresponding code number that you used. Suppose that the question included the following response categories: 1 = Business, 2 = Education, 3 = Engineering, 4 = Liberal Arts, 5 = Science and Math, and 6 = Other. This coding information will be necessary if you want to describe students who are enrolled in specific programs.

DEFINING DATA USING SPSS

In this section, we will be using SPSS to organize the data on doctoral applicants (see Table 3.1). Within SPSS, data are organized in spreadsheet format. If you have entered data into a spreadsheet (e.g., Excel, Lotus 123, Quattro Pro), you will find using SPSS's data editor to be quite familiar.

Since data are organized in a spreadsheet format, there is no need to identify starting and ending columns as you may have done with the earlier DOS or mainframe versions. Variables are stored in columns in the spreadsheet while cases (subjects) are stored in rows. The spreadsheet format allows you to keep your data organized. If you have ever used the DOS or mainframe versions of SPSS, you will appreciate the spreadsheet format used in the current SPSS versions.

Although the spreadsheet format displays your data in such a way that it is easy to identify where each variable is located, we still recommend keeping a coding guide as part of your research notebook. The nature of this coding guide is very simple. Keeping a record of the variables in your data set will help keep you organized. Therefore, only a few pieces of information about each variable are necessary. This information might include the variable name, description, coding information, and a reference to the original data (where the variable came from). A sample coding guide for our data on doctoral applicants is displayed in Figure 3.1.

As we illustrate the data definition process, you will see that SPSS has a built-in utility that stores information about each variable. It is still a good idea to keep at least one written

FIGURE 3.1
Coding Guide for
Doctoral Applicants
data

Coding Guide for Doctoral Applicants		
Variable Name	Variable Description	Coding Information
ID	identification number	1 = male
GENDER	gender of applicant	2 = female
SES	Socioeconomic status of applicant	1 = lower 2 = middle 3 = upper
ETHNIC	ethnicity of applicant	1 = white 2 = African-American 3 = Asian 4 = Hispanic
GREQ	GRE quantitative section	200–800
GREV	GRE verbal section	200–800
PRETEST	subject area pretest	0–100
RATING1	rating from faculty interview #1	1–10
RATING2	rating from faculty interview #2	1–10

record and multiple electronic copies of your data in case the working SPSS file cannot be retrieved for some reason.

Defining Data

You define your data by selecting options from a series of menus using your mouse. Before you begin to define data, you'll need to activate the software. Once activated, the data editor is displayed as in Figure 3.2.

Notice that the first cell in the upper left-hand corner of the spreadsheet is highlighted. The heading in the grey box above this cell is labeled "**var.**" At this point, SPSS can do very little without data. You will be entering data directly into this spreadsheet using the information on applicants to a doctoral program presented in Table 3.1. Before you begin entering these data, you must define the variables.

We begin from the **Data** menu. Select the **Data** pull-down menu as shown in Figure 3.3 and select the first option labeled **Define Variable....** This menu selection will open the

FIGURE 3.2
SPSS Data Editor

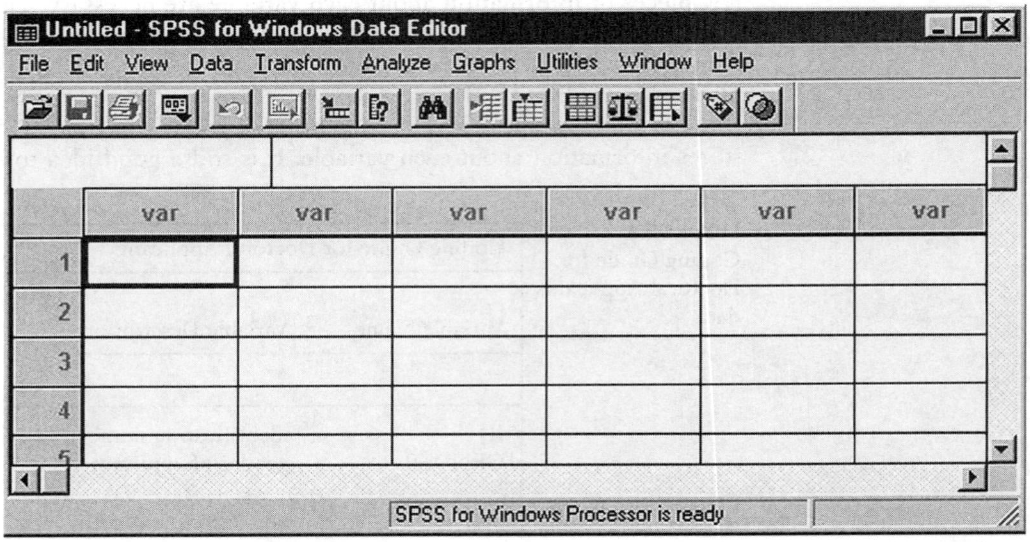

FIGURE 3.3
Data–Define Variable
menu selections

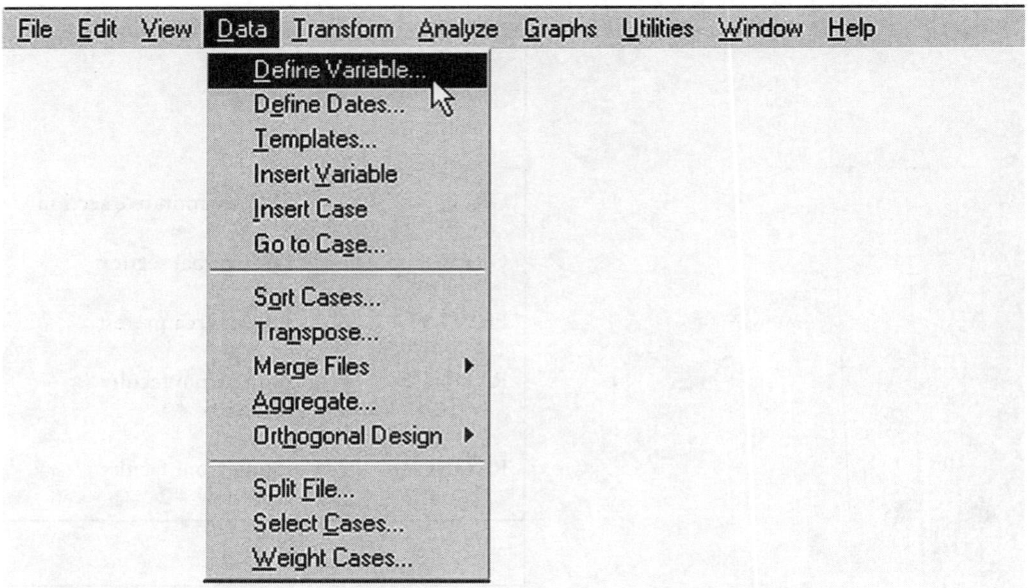

FIGURE 3.4
Define Variable dialog
box

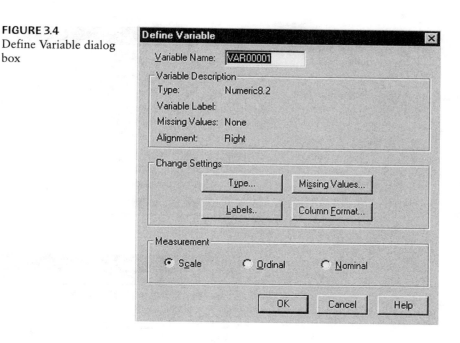

Define Variable dialog box, where we will begin defining our variables. Figure 3.4 displays this dialog box.

Notice your cursor blinking in the box at the top of the window. This box is labeled Variable name: and the variable name that appears highlighted in this box is VAR00001. By default, SPSS will identify variables in numerical order. Since it would be difficult to remember our variables this way, we will create our own variable names. The first variable is the applicant's identification number. We will label this variable ID. First, erase the "VAR00001" by using the <Backspace> key. If the word "VAR00001" is highlighted, you can simply type "ID." If the default variable name is not highlighted, you will need to remove it manually using the <Backspace> key. Once you have removed the default name, type "ID" in its place. Do not press the <Enter> key yet. Look toward the middle of the Define Variable box. Notice that there are four option buttons under the Change Settings heading. These options allow you to: a) define the type of variable you are entering (a dollar amount or a date, for instance), b) provide labels for variables and the codes used for them (for example, a "1" representing males, a "2" representing females), c) decide how to treat missing data, and d) choose the size of the columns in your data file. There is really no need to use any of these options for ID, but we will use them for the next variable. To complete the variable definition process for ID, click your mouse on the **OK** button (or just press <Enter>). Notice that the heading for the first column is now ID, which replaced the old heading of VAR00001.

The next variable to be defined from Table 3.1 is GENDER. From the main menu bar, select the **Data** pull-down menu and the first option labeled **Define Variable....** Erase the "VAR00001" in the variable name box and type "GENDER." The first option button labeled **Type...** is used to identify the type of variable. This screen is displayed in Figure 3.5. The default setting is Numeric. This means the data for this variable are in numeric format, which is the form that most data take. The second most common format for data is alphabetic. Data in the form of letters or words are called string formatted data. Notice the last option is labeled String. If we were to enter our data as "M" for male and "F" for female, we would need to change the data type to String. All of our data are in numeric format, so we will leave this setting alone.

You will notice three command buttons at the right of the screen. The first button, labeled **Continue,** is used to accept the options you have chosen. The **Cancel** button can be used when you wish to cancel the options you have selected and return to the previous windows. Finally, the **Help** button is used if you want more information about what you

FIGURE 3.5
Define Variable Type
dialog box

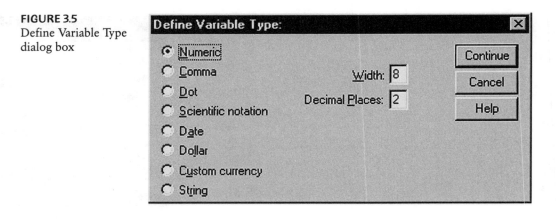

FIGURE 3.6
Define Labels dialog
box (Gender)

are doing, or trying to do. We accept the current settings for type of variable, so click your mouse on the **Continue** button and we will continue defining the GENDER variable.

The button below **Type...** is labeled **Labels....** This option is used to enter a more descriptive label for the variable and labels for the values used in coding the variable. For the GENDER variable, we want to provide a more descriptive label such as "gender of applicant." So, click on **Labels...** and the next screen should appear, as displayed in Figure 3.6.

The cursor is blinking in the Variable Label: box. In this box, type "gender of applicant" and hit the <Tab> key. The next part of the screen is the Value Labels box. The cursor is blinking in the Value: box, waiting for the first value you used to code the data. We already coded these data with a "1" representing males and a "2" representing females. Please note that we add the quotation marks in the text for emphasis; you don't need to add them when you input material in the dialog box. If SPSS needs them, it will add them for you. Enter a "1" and hit the <Tab> key. The cursor is now waiting for your input in the Value Label: box. In this box, enter "male" as a label for the value "1." Click your mouse on the **Add** button. The bottom box now indicates that 1.00 = "male."

Notice that there are two other buttons to the left of the Value Label box. You use the **Change** button if you wish to change an existing value or value label. For example, you may have spelled "male" incorrectly. If so, you would use the **Change** option. The bottom button is labeled **Remove.** If you specified a value and value label that wasn't appropriate for the variable, this option would be used.

The cursor is waiting in the Value: box for the next value. Try to define and label the female applicants by yourself. Remember that we used a value of "2" to represent females. Remember to hit the **Add** button after you finish identifying the female applicants. If you press <Enter> and see a warning box that reads "Any pending Add or Change operations will be lost," it is most likely because you neglected to click the **Add** button after typing your value label. Click on the **Cancel** button to return to the Define Labels: box and click on the **Add** button to complete your additions to the label definition box.

The cursor is now waiting for the next value. Since there are only two values used to identify gender categories, we are finished with the labels for GENDER and are ready to continue this process with the remaining variables. Click on the **Continue** button at the right of the screen. Before you define the remaining variables, let's explore the other two buttons at the bottom of the Define Variable screen. These are the **Missing Values...** and **Column Format...** buttons.

Click your mouse on the **Missing Values...** button. Figure 3.7 shows this window. The options presented to us on this screen allow us to define missing values for a specific variable in our data set. We don't have any missing values for gender, or any other variable in our data set. However, our data set is small and composed of fictitious cases. In a real research data set, you often have missing data. People may fail to answer all the questions on your written instrument or their information may be missing from your records. When there are missing data on a given variable, you have two choices. You can just leave that information blank and SPSS will treat it as missing, or you can indicate a specific value or range of values to identify missing data. Notice that the option labeled No missing values is selected for GENDER. This is the default setting and will be in effect unless you change it. In our case, all data are complete, so we will just leave it blank. Click your mouse on the **Continue** button and move on to the next option.

The last button under the Change Settings heading is **Column Format....** Click on this button and the screen displayed in Figure 3.8 will appear. There are just a few options here. The first is column width. The default is eight characters. If you have a variable that contains more than eight characters, such as a social security number, you should change this setting. The other option allows you to change the alignment of the data within the column. The default setting is alignment of all values to the right side of the cell in the column. Your choice of alignment is a matter of personal preference and will not affect your analyses. If you want values aligned to the left or in the center, change it. However, keep in mind that if you are working with a variable for which values may range between one and one hundred (or even

FIGURE 3.7
Define Missing Values
dialog box (Gender)

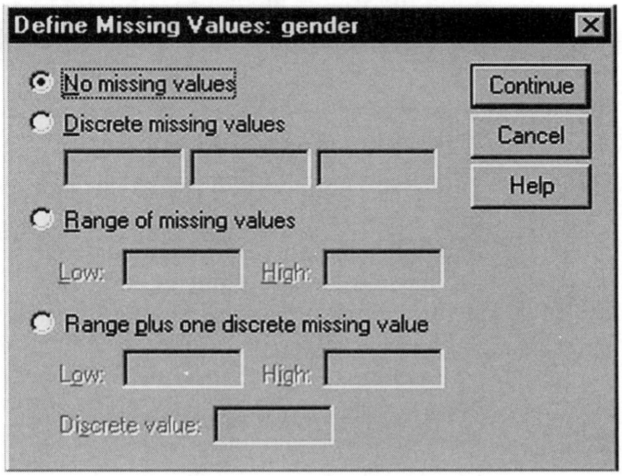

FIGURE 3.8
Define Column Format
dialog box (Gender)

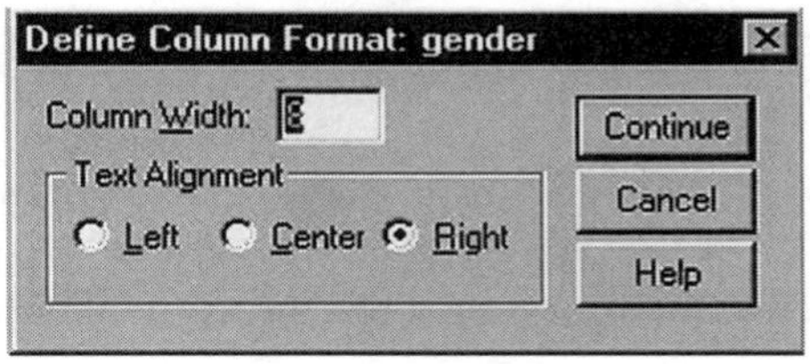

one thousand) and you align values to the center or to the left, your data will not retain decimal alignment. This will not affect your statistics, but it may make the spreadsheet harder to read and may actually lead to typing errors if you are typing in your data. For the sake of consistency and accuracy, we would recommend that you leave your text alignment at the default position (text alignment to the right).

Click on **Continue** to move back to the Define Variable screen. To execute all the options you selected for the variable of GENDER, click you mouse on the **OK** button at the right of the screen. The label GENDER should now be placed above the second column. You are now ready to continue with the definition of the variables in the data set.

To Define a Variable, Use the Following steps:

*Step 1   Click your mouse above the column where the variable information will be stored.

*Step 2   Select the **Data** menu from the main menu bar.

*Step 3   Select the **Define Variable...** option.
          *These three steps can be performed using a shortcut by double-clicking your mouse on the grey heading box above the appropriate variable in your data set.

Step 4   Specify a name for the variable in the box labeled Variable name.

Step 5   Make any necessary changes regarding the **Type** of variable.

Step 6   Select the **Labels...** button and identify variable and value labels.

Step 7   Make any necessary changes to the **Missing Values** setting.

Step 8   Be sure the **Column Format** is to your satisfaction.

Be sure to use the **Continue** button to move from screen to screen and the **OK** button when you have finished defining the variable.

Continue this process for the remaining variables in the data set. Use the information from the coding guide in Figure 3.2 as you define each variable. Also, try the shortcut in place of the first three steps. Hint: All variables are in numeric format and there are no missing data.

Entering Data Using SPSS

Now that you have defined all the variables, you are ready to enter the data. You will start by entering the first applicant's data, beginning with ID. Before you begin to enter this data, highlight the home cell (in the upper left-hand corner). Remember, you can move to this cell instantly by using the <Cntl> and <Home> keys together. As a reminder, other keystroke combinations can be used to quickly move about the data editor. For a refresher, see Table 2.1.

Examine the first applicant's data in Table 3.1. The first applicant from this data set has been assigned an ID of "01." The applicant is a white male from a middle SES household. He scored 667 and 449 on the GREQ and GREV respectively. His pretest score is 87 and he received ratings of 9 and 8 from the faculty interviewers.

Type a "1" for this applicant's ID and press the <Tab> key. A "1" will now appear in the cell below the ID heading and the cell in the next column under the heading of GENDER is highlighted. Enter a "1" for male in this cell, followed by the <Tab> key. Next, enter a "2" to represent his socioeconomic status. The <Tab> key will move the cursor to the next column and the cell below the ETHNIC heading will be highlighted. Enter a "1" for white and press the <Tab> key. In the next cell, enter "667" for his GREQ score, followed by the <Tab> key. His GREV score is "449". Enter this value, and press the <Tab> key. Enter an "87" for his pretest score, press the <Tab> key, enter a "9" for the first interview rating, press the <Tab> key, and enter an "8" for the second faculty interview rating. The first applicant's data have now been successfully entered. You are ready for the second applicant.

First, you need to get in position for the second case. Remember, you can move around the data editor using cursor keys, the <Tab> key, the <Enter> key, and other keystroke combinations. You need to move to the second cell in the first column. You can do this by using your cursor keys to move down one row and left to the first column. You can also move down one row using the cursor and return to the first column by pressing the <Home> key. You can also get back to the first cell by pressing <Cntl> <Home> and then using the down cursor key to move down one row. Use one of these methods to get to the second cell in the first column.

You are now ready to enter the data for the second applicant. To do this, enter the following data for each variable. Remember to use the <Tab> key to move from one variable to the next.

For Variable:	Enter
ID	2
GENDER	2
SES	1
ETHNIC	2
GREQ	356
GREV	480
PRETEST	55
RATING1	7
RATING2	5

Now, move to the third row and begin entering data for the third applicant. Continue this process until all twenty applicants have been entered. You can speed up the data entry process somewhat by using the number pad at the right side of your keyboard. To use the numbers on the number pad, press the <Num Lock> key. If your keyboard does not have a number pad, you will have to use the numbers located at the top of the keyboard. When you are finished, the last cell in the data editor will be highlighted. Move to the first cell using the <Cntl><Home> keys. Your data editor should look like that displayed in Figure 3.9. You may want to maximize the data window so you can see more of your data set.

FIGURE 3.9
Data Editor with student admission data

	id	gender	ses	ethnic	greq	grev	pretest	rating1	rating2
1	1	1	2	1	667	449	87	9	8
2	2	2	1	2	356	480	55	7	5
3	3	2	2	2	445	666	75	8	7
4	4	1	3	1	750	679	94	10	9
5	5	1	2	2	589	550	80	8	9
6	6	2	2	1	490	450	74	8	6
7	7	2	2	3	705	405	97	7	7
8	8	1	1	2	380	360	55	5	4
9	9	1	1	4	450	385	69	7	6
10	10	2	1	2	666	765	85	10	9

You have successfully entered data to create a small data file in SPSS. You will work with much larger data sets in your coursework and future research projects. In the chapters that follow, you will work with a data set that contains over 200 cases. Remember to save your work before you exit SPSS.

Saving Your Data

Notice that this file is untitled. This means that we have not saved the file yet. You will need these data throughout the remainder of this book, so save it to a file. It is a good idea to save your work often while working with any software program, especially when your work involves dissertation or other important research files. We recommend saving your work as you go. In other words, every time you make significant changes in a file, save it. If you feel a need to review the process of saving files in SPSS, please examine the previous chapter. To refresh your memory, the steps are summarized below:

Step 1	Select the **File** menu from the main menu bar.
Step 2	Select the **Save** option.
Step 3	Specify the drive to which the file will be saved in the **Save In** box.
Step 4	Indicate a name for file in the File Name box.
Step 5	Click on the **Save** command button to save the file.

Remember, the first three steps can also be completed in a single action by using the save file icon from the toolbar. (This icon looks like computer disk.)

We will be using this file in later chapters, so give it a name that is easy to remember. These data pertain to students applying for admission to a doctoral program. Therefore, name this file student admission data. Save these data in a location that is most convenient for you. If you are working at home, you could use your hard drive. But, if you are working in a computer laboratory, you will have to save these data on a floppy disk so you can take it with you.

CHAPTER SUMMARY

Congratulations, you have successfully completed data definition and entry procedures using SPSS. In this chapter, you entered and defined fictitious data pertaining applicants to a doctoral program. These data were limited to twenty cases so that you could complete these operations in a reasonable amount of time. In reality, and throughout the remainder of this book, we will use data from larger samples. The process is the same no matter the size of the sample. We will begin working with larger samples in later chapters.

PRACTICE EXERCISES

A group of college faculty members were asked to provide information about several variables. Some of these variables are presented below.

1.   *College:*
     _____ Agriculture
     _____ Business
     _____ Education
     _____ Engineering
     _____ Liberal Arts
     _____ Science and Math

2. *Tenure Status:*
   _____ Tenure-track
   _____ Tenured

3. *Academic Rank:*
   _____ Instructor
   _____ Assistant Professor
   _____ Associate Professor
   _____ Full Professor

4. *Years of Experience:*_____

For each of these variables, identify the level of measurement and how the variable will be coded for SPSS.

Variable	Level of Measurement	Coding Information
College		
Tenure Status		
Academic Rank		
Years of Experience		

4 | Importing and Merging Data Files

You may have data from a pre-Windows version of SPSS or another spreadsheet program, such as Excel, and want to analyze these data using the current version of SPSS. If this is the case, you can import these files into SPSS and use them in the same manner as regular SPSS data files. There will also be times when you have data stored in more than one file and you wish to merge these two data files. In this chapter, we will illustrate how to import data into SPSS and how to merge data files.

IMPORTING DATA

There are two basic forms of data that we will import in this chapter. First, you may have data stored in another spreadsheet program, such as Excel or Lotus. These data are organized in cells just like they are in SPSS and can be converted to SPSS data files in just a few quick steps. Second, many data files, especially ones that are a few years old, are stored in a mainframe or SPSS/PC+ file or have been created as a result of scanning information from scan sheets. These data are typically stored in specific columns or a specific order, but not cells in a spreadsheet. These data can also be imported into SPSS.

Data from Other Spreadsheet Programs

Let's begin with data from other spreadsheet programs because these data can be converted into SPSS files very quickly. We will be using a file created in Excel for this illustration, but the same procedure works for files created in other spreadsheet programs. You begin from the **File** menu, as you would to open an SPSS file. From the **File** menu, select **Open**.... You can also use the open file icon from the toolbar. Either way, the Open File dialog box will appear on your screen (see Figure 4.1). You have selected SPSS data files from this dialog box in previous chapters. The default setting is to display SPSS data files, which are identified with a .sav suffix.

Other types of files can be opened from this dialog box. Scroll down the menu at the **Files of type:** box to view the options. In this session, we want to open a file created in Excel. Excel files are identified with an .xls suffix (see Figure 4.2). While you're scrolling through this menu, let's examine the other types of files that can be opened using SPSS. These include other types of SPSS files (SPSS/PC+, SPSS portable), Systat files, and other spreadsheet files such as Lotus and dBase; and raw data (text) files in the form of delimited text.

You may want to try opening these other types of files on your own as such data files present themselves. For now, continue with the steps necessary to open an Excel file. Once you've specified the Excel option, all Excel (*.xls) files will be displayed in the Open File

FIGURE 4.1
Open File dialog box

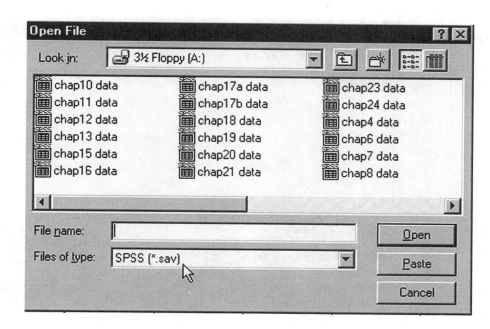

FIGURE 4.2
Open File dialog
box–Files of type menu

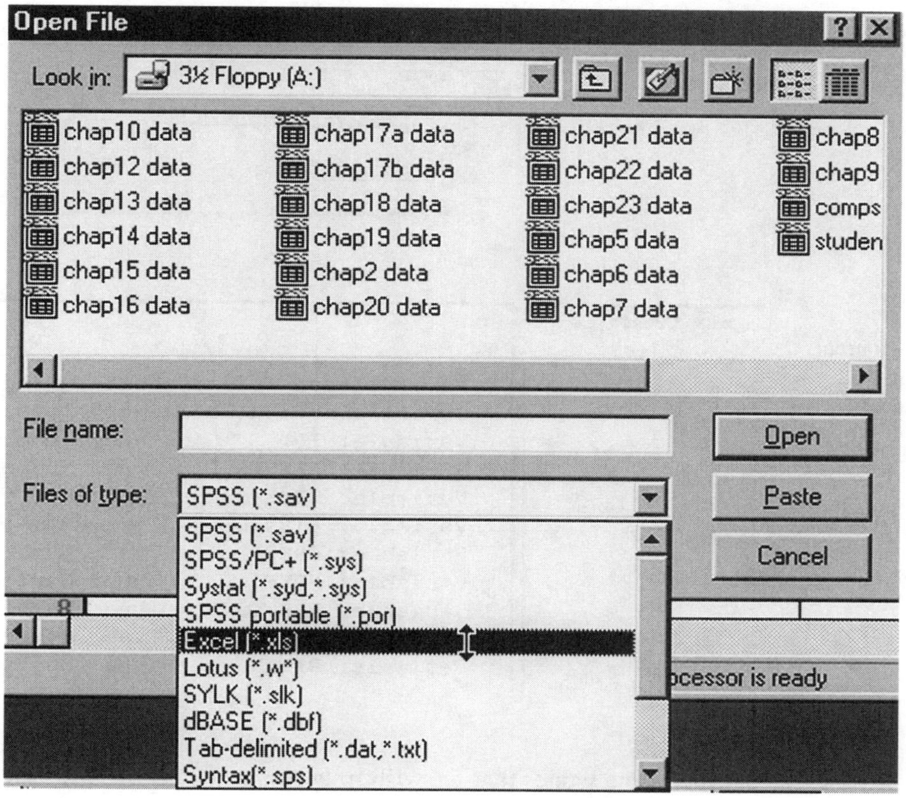

dialog box. It is easy to determine which file we want in this case, as there is only one file listed. The name of the file we want is **student**. This Excel file contains the same student admission data you created in Chapter 3. To open the file, highlight the file and click on the **Open** button (see Figure 4.3).

This will open the Opening File Options dialog box (see Figure 4.4). We've checked the option **Read variable names** because we know that we identified variables in the original

FIGURE 4.3
Excel file (student)
selected

FIGURE 4.4
Opening File Options
dialog box

FIGURE 4.5
SPSS Viewer–contents
and format of
imported Excel file

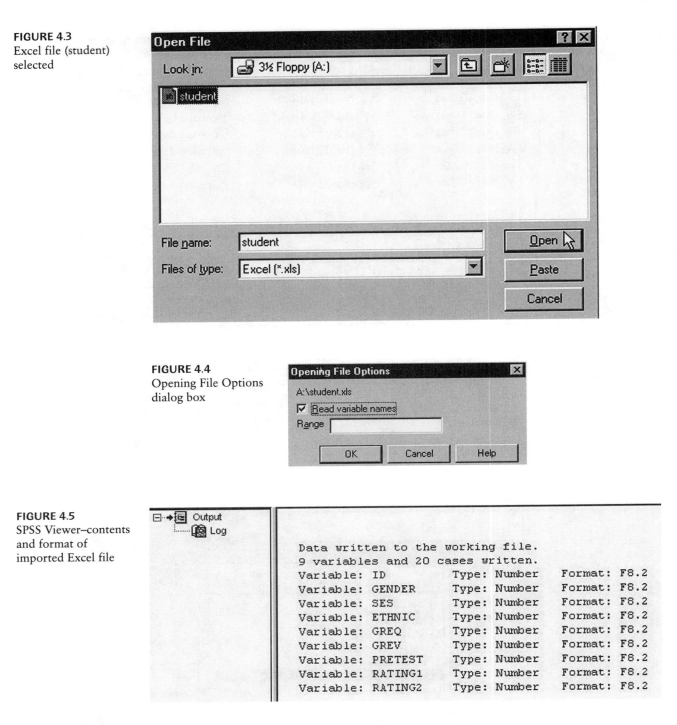

data set using names that we wish to keep in the new SPSS file. You can limit the amount of information that SPSS reads from the old data set by specifying a range of cells. We want the entire file, so we'll leave this option blank.

Click on the **OK** button to open this Excel file. After this file is successfully retrieved, the SPSS viewer will display the contents and format of the SPSS file. This information is displayed in Figure 4.5.

This information lets us know that nine variables and twenty cases were written to the working file. The working file is active in the data editor. The nine variables are listed; each variable is identified as a numeric variable. The format is reported as "F8.2" for each variable. This simply means that the data are stored in columns that are eight characters wide, including two decimal places.

The data are now stored in the data editor. You can view these data and save them as part of an SPSS data file as you would any other SPSS data file. Move to the data editor to view these data. Unless you want another copy of these data, there is really no need to save them.

Reading Text Files

Reading text files requires a few more steps than reading other spreadsheet files. First of all, you need to be sure that the file you are attempting to read has been saved in ASCII format. If you entered the data using a word processing program, there is an option to save files in ASCII format. In most word processing programs, you use the Save As option from the File menu and select ASCII DOS Text as the type of file to be saved. If the file is saved in the word processing format, it will not be read by SPSS.

An ASCII data file basically looks like a bunch of numbers (or letters). Subjects are organized in rows and variables in columns. Each variable is found either in a specific starting and ending column or different variables are separated by commas, spaces, or tabs in the data. When specific starting and ending columns are used to locate variables, the file is stored in a fixed format. On the other hand, when variables are separated by spaces or commas, tabs, or some other character, the file is stored in freefield format. We've created an ASCII file containing the data regarding student admissions. These data appear in Figure 4.6.

As you can see, there are twenty rows of data, one for each subject. The data are just stored columns, not organized in cells. Each variable is located in specific columns. In order to read these data, you need to know what variables are found in what columns. Here is where a coding guide, discussed in Chapter 3, comes in handy. A coding guide for our data is displayed in Table 4.1.

To read ASCII data using SPSS, select the **Read Text Data** option from the **File** menu, as illustrated in Figure 4.7.

These menu selections will display the Open dialog box. You've used this box before to open an SPSS data file. The file we wish to open, asciidat, is found on the 3½-inch floppy. Change the drive to 3½ Floppy (A:) and select this file, as illustrated in Figure 4.8.

FIGURE 4.6
ASCII data file
(student admissions
data)

```
01121667449870908
02212356480550705
03222445666750807
04131750679941009
05122589550800809
06221490450740806
07223705405970707
08112380360550504
09114450385690706
10212666765851009
11123675499880806
12111422435720606
13121555666810807
14211600755740605
15124533485680708
16221500535790807
17111375490650606
18211735750950810
19222575650781009
20121475550630706
```

TABLE 4.1
Coding Guide for ASCII data

Variable	Beginning Column	Ending Column
ID	1	2
Gender	3	3
SES	4	4
ETHNIC	5	5
GREQ	6	8
GREV	9	11
PRETEST	12	13
RATING1	14	15
RATING2	16	17

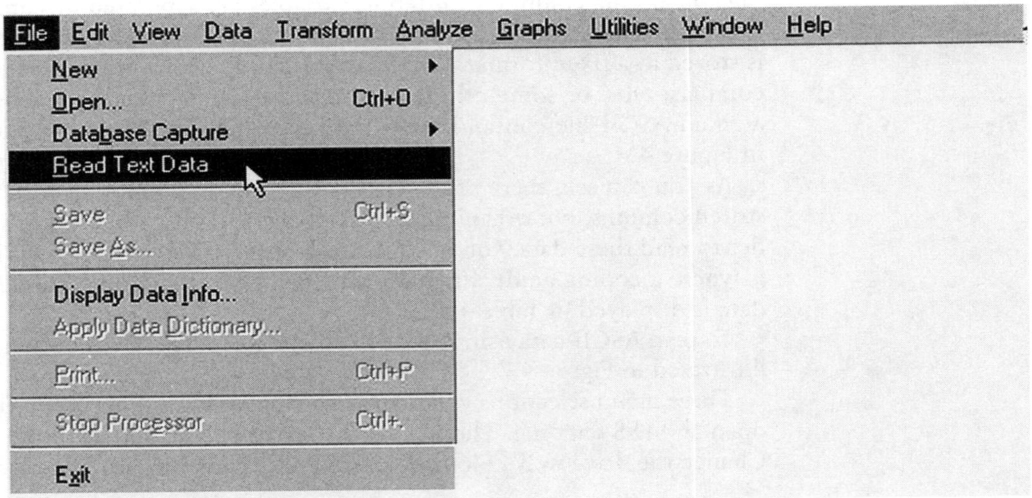

FIGURE 4.7
File–Read Text Data
menu selections

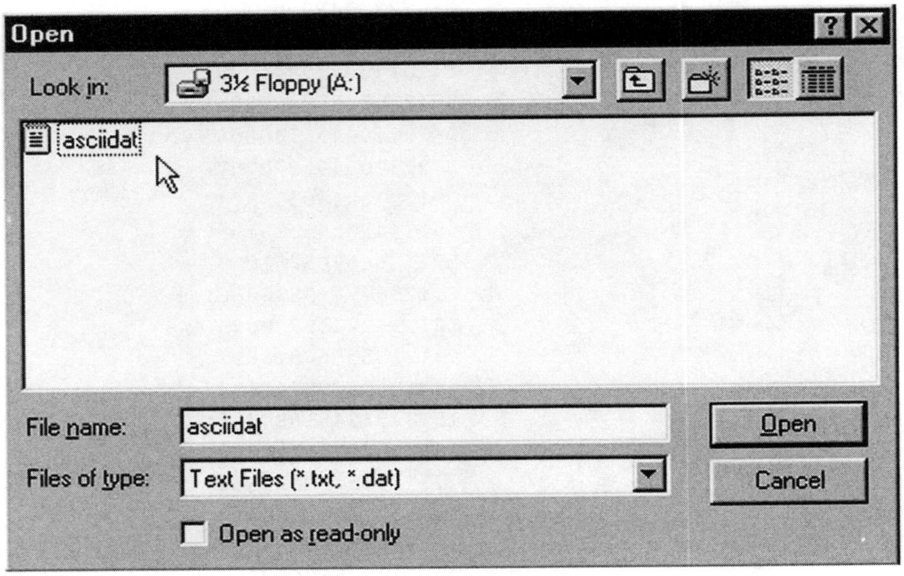

File Edit View Data Transform Analyze Graphs Utilities Window Help

New ▶
Open...   Ctrl+O
Database Capture ▶
Read Text Data
Save   Ctrl+S
Save As...
Display Data Info...
Apply Data Dictionary...
Print...   Ctrl+P
Stop Processor   Ctrl+.
Exit

FIGURE 4.8
Open dialog box
(selection of asciidat
file)

Open   ? ✕

Look in: 3½ Floppy (A:)

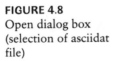
asciidat

File name: asciidat   Open
Files of type: Text Files (*.txt, *.dat)   Cancel

☐ Open as read-only

Once you've selected this file, you can begin working with SPSS's Text Import Wizard to define the variables found in the text file. There are six steps to follow when using the Text Import Wizard. SPSS guides you through these steps, one screen at a time. The first screen appears in Figure 4.9.

Text Import Wizard

Step 1 of 6. Examine the information found in this first Text Import Wizard screen. You are prompted to respond to the following question in the upper right of this screen: "Does your text file match a predefined format?" The default response is No. If our file was predefined using the Text Import Wizard, we would select **Yes**. Since we have not worked previously with this file in the Text Import Wizard, select **No**. Click on the **Next >** button to continue.

Step 2 of 6. In the second step, you are asked to respond to questions about the arrangement of the variables in the text file and whether variable names appear in the file. These questions appear in the upper part of the screen (See Figure 4.10).

There are two options pertaining to the arrangement of variables. Variables can be arranged in a delimited format or a fixed width format. A delimited format uses commas, spaces, or some other characters to separate each variable in the file. Using commas, our first case from Figure 4.6 would look like the following: 01, 1, 2, 1, 667, 449, 87, 09, 08.

Our data, however, are stored in fixed columns as specified in Table 4.1. Therefore, we will select the option for Fixed width format. To respond to the Wizard's second question, select No because the file does not include the variable names. Click on the **Next >** button to continue with the Text Import Wizard.

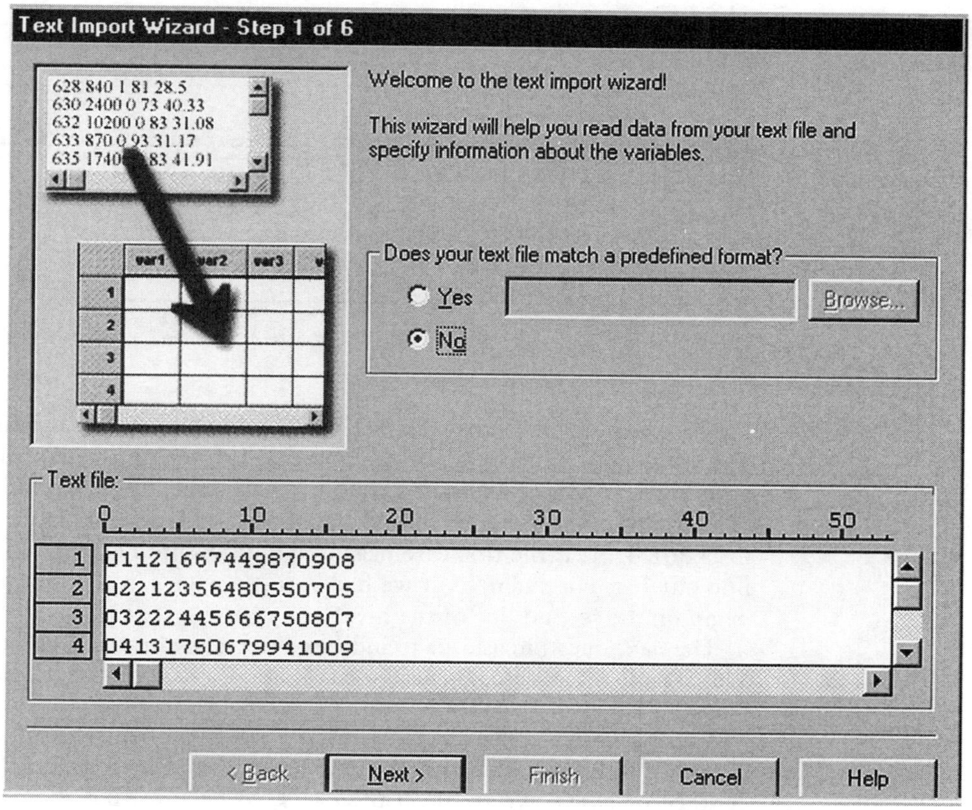

FIGURE 4.9
Text Import Wizard
(Step 1 of 6)

FIGURE 4.10
Text Import Wizard
(Step 2 of 6)

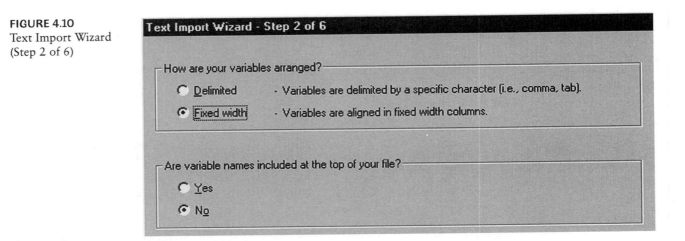

FIGURE 4.11
Text Import Wizard
(Step 3–Fixed Width)

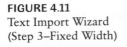

Step 3 of 6. In the third step, we begin to specify the arrangement of cases in the file. Specifically, we indicate where the first case is found, how many lines represent each case, and how many cases we want to import. This screen is displayed in Figure 4.11.

Our first case begins on the first line of the file. This matches the default setting as shown in Figure 4.11. If the first case began on a different line, we would select the appropriate line number. For example, if we had variable names in the first line, our first case would begin on the second line of the file.

The next question asks us to indicate how many lines represent a case. The default is 1. This is true of our data, as each case is stored on a single line. Sometimes, text files contain many variables that cannot be stored in a single line.

Finally, we are asked to specify how many cases from this file we wish to import. The default is to import all cases. You also have the option to select a specific number or percentage of cases. We want all the cases, so be sure that the option All of the cases is selected.

Before you continue to the next step, make sure you have addressed each question as follows:

Question	Setting
The first case of data begins on which line number?	1
How many lines represent a case?	1
How many cases do you want to import?	All of the cases

If these selections are correct, click on the **Next >** button to continue.

Step 4 of 6. The fourth step requires us to specify either the positions (column locations) of each variable (see Figure 14.12A) or the character used to separate variables in the text file (see Figure 14.12B).

Fixed width column format.   We are importing data in a fixed width column format. In order for SPSS to read these data accurately, we must identify the exact location of each variable. We do this by using variable line breaks. The instructions for determining these locations appear at the top of the screen (see Figure 4.12A).

Delimited text format.   In a delimited text file, a character or space is used to separate each variable. Using the Text Import Wizard, all you must do is indicate what is being used. Your options include tab, space, semicolon, comma, or some other character (e.g., period or forward slash). You identify this character in Step 4 of the Text Import Wizard (see Figure 14.12B).

Specify location of variable for fixed column format.   To specify the exact location of variables in your data file, insert variable break lines using the data that appear at the bottom of the screen. A break line appears at the beginning of the line (before the first column). To insert new variable break lines, click your mouse at the top of the file in the area of the ruler bar. The first variable in this file is an identification number (ID). This ID is

FIGURE 4.12A
Text Import Wizard
(Step 4–Fixed Width)

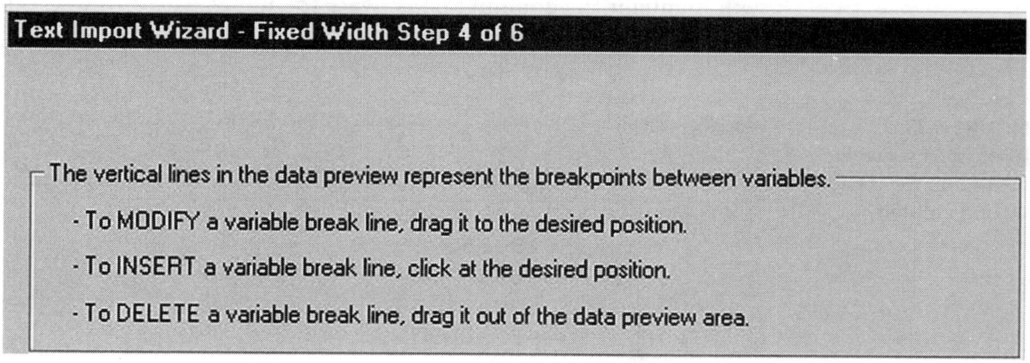

FIGURE 4.12B
Text Import Wizard
(Step 4–Delimited)

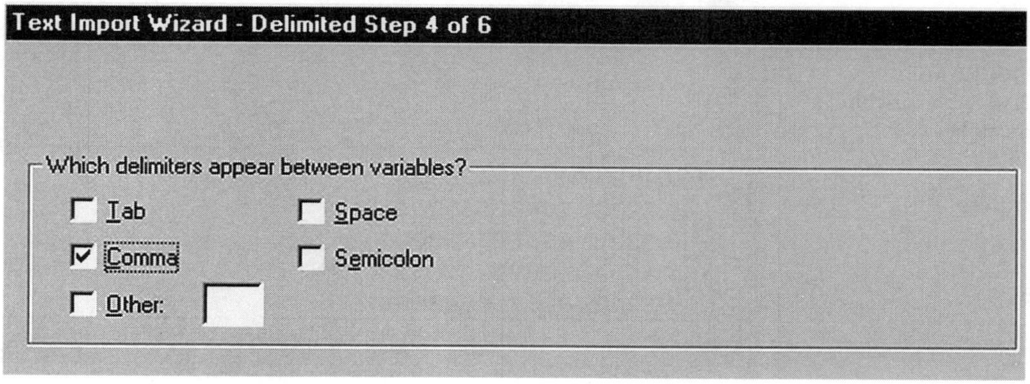

located in the first two columns. Therefore, we need to insert a variable break line between the second and third columns. Click the mouse between the second and third columns to insert this break line. This process is illustrated in Figure 4.13.

To complete the identification of variables, you need to insert the remainder of the break lines. Refer to Table 4.1 for the column locations. No break line is needed after the last variable. To define the variable locations for your file, use the following:

Variable	Columns	Insert Variable Break Line
ID	1–2	after the 2nd column
GENDER	3	after the 3rd column
SES	4	after the 4th column
ETHNIC	5	after the 5th column
GREQ	6–8	after the 8th column
GREV	9–11	after the 11th column
PRETEST	12–13	after the 13th column
RATING1	14–15	after the 15th column
RATING2	16–17	not needed

You inserted a total of eight variable break lines. The data should now look like that displayed in Figure 4.14.

Once you've inserted the variable break lines at the appropriate column locations, click **Next >** to continue.

Step 5 of 6.   In the fifth step, you will indicate names for each of these variables. Before you do so, check the data in the lower part of the screen and make sure there are nine variables, labeled V1 to V9. We want to further define these variables with names that we can better understand, beginning with the first variable. Click on the grey header for V1. This will highlight the column and activate the upper part of the screen so you can further define the variable, as displayed in Figure 4.15.

FIGURE 4.13
Inserting a variable break line for ID at second column

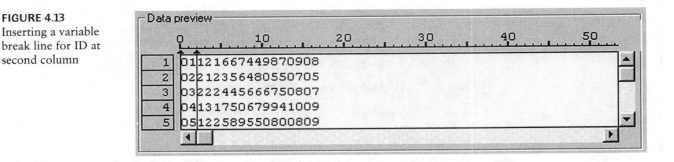

FIGURE 4.14
Data with variable break lines

In the Variable name box, type "ID." In the Data format box, select **Numeric.** The upper part of the screen will look like Figure 4.16.

Continue this process for the remaining eight variables. Each of the variables in this file is stored in a numeric format. We recommend using the following variable names.

V2—GENDER

V3—SES

V4—ETHNIC

V5—GREQ

V6—GREV

V7—PRETEST

V8—RATING1

V9—RATING2

When you have completed defining these variables, click **Next** to continue to the final step.

FIGURE 4.15
Text Import Wizard
(Step 5 of 6)

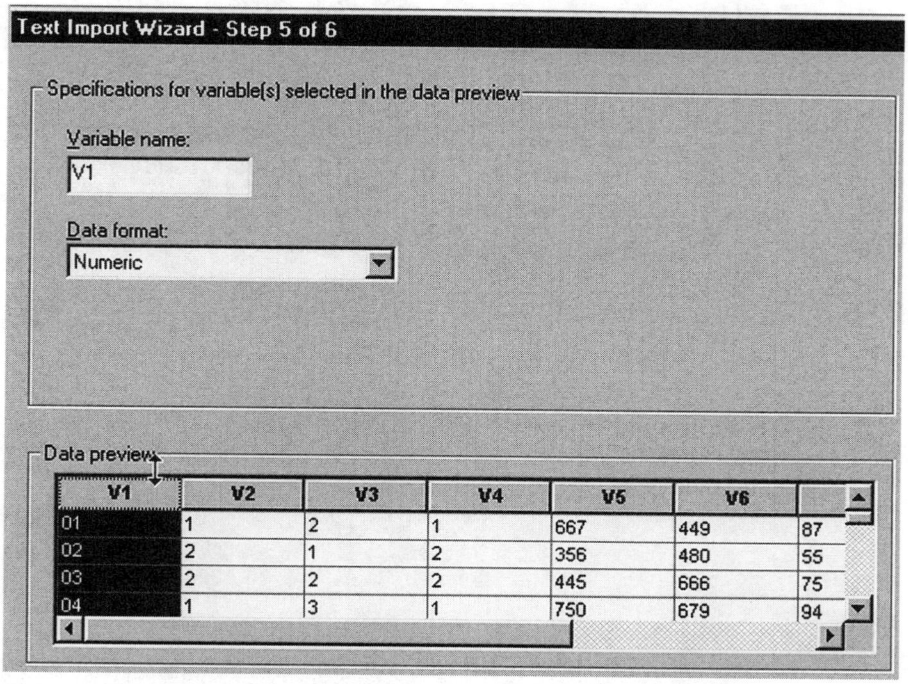

FIGURE 4.16
Text Import Wizard
(Step 5 of 6–defining
variables)

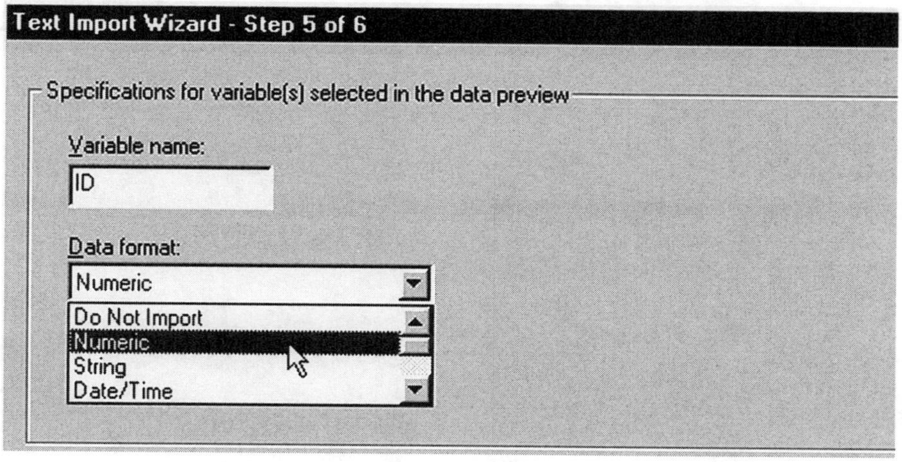

Step 6 of 6. In this final step, you have two options for saving your work. First, you can save the file format that you just created. If you ever have to import similar data later, you'll have a predefined format from which to work. Second, you can copy your work in a syntax file. This will save the SPSS commands you generated in steps 1 through 5. These two options appear in the upper part of the screen (see Figure 4.17).

First, let's examine the option to save the file format for future use. Select Yes and click the **Save As...** button (see Figure 4.18). This will open the Save As dialog box displayed in Figure 4.19. Now give the file a name and click **Save.**

You can also save the syntax commands to a file. SPSS records each selection you make as you work your way through dialog boxes and menus. A record is kept in the form of syntax commands, similar to those used in the PC version of SPSS. If you'd like a record of the syntax commands, select Yes in response to the question: "Would you like to paste the syntax?"

FIGURE 4.17
Text Import Wizard
(Step 6 of 6)

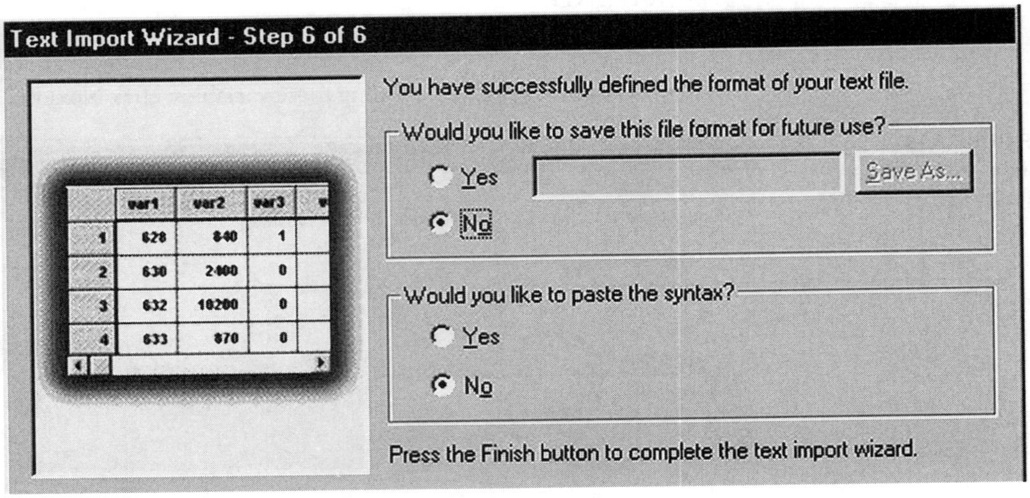

FIGURE 4.18
Saving the file format
for future use

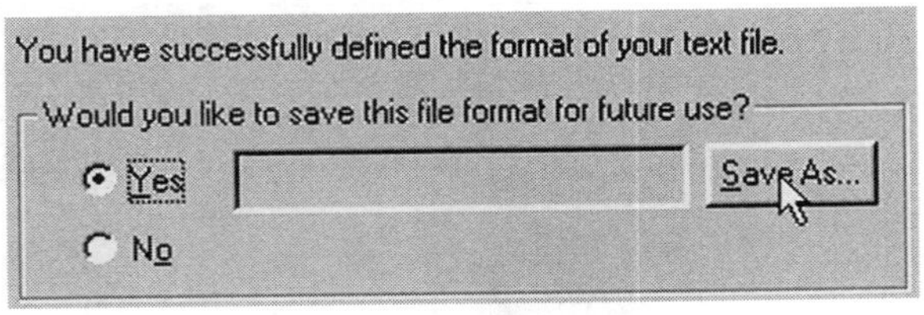

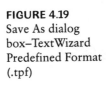

FIGURE 4.19
Save As dialog
box–TextWizard
Predefined Format
(.tpf)

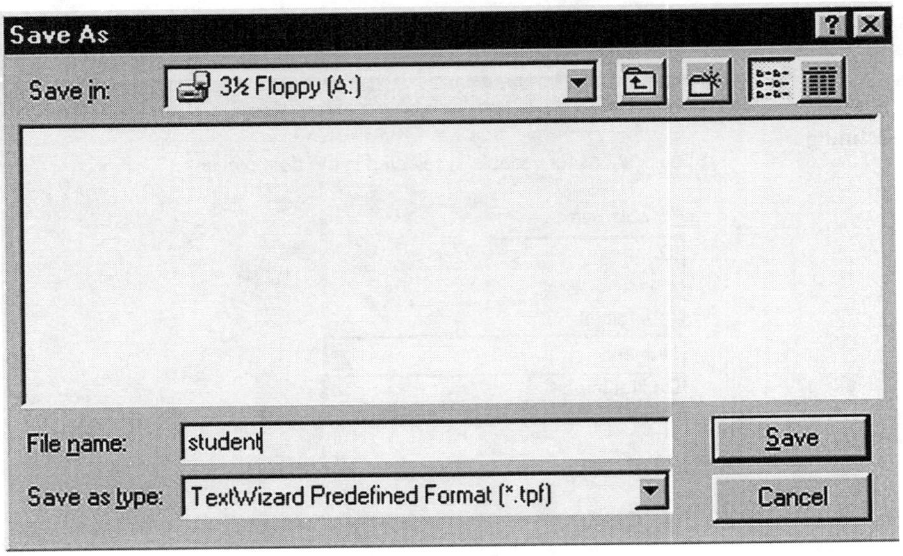

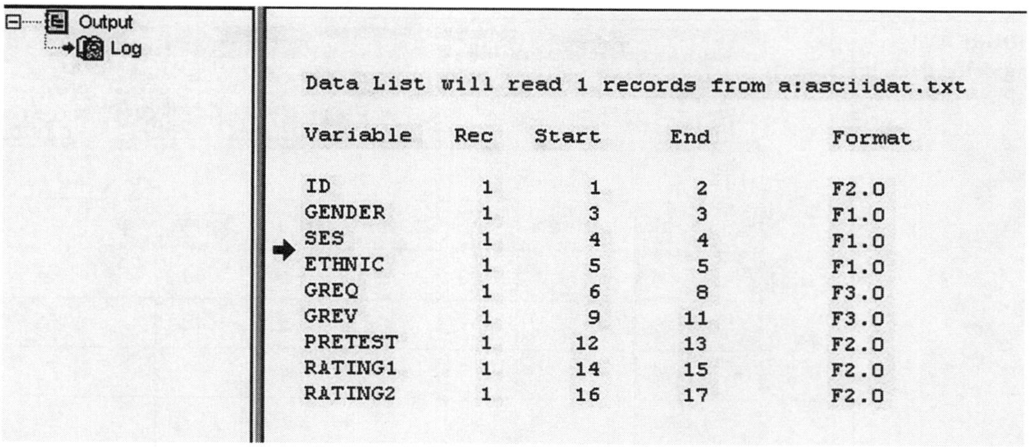

FIGURE 4.20
Output Window Log
of text file
(asciidat.txt)

```
⊟----- 🄴 Output
     ➔ 📷 Log

              Data List will read 1 records from a:asciidat.txt

              Variable    Rec    Start      End       Format

              ID           1       1         2        F2.0
              GENDER       1       3         3        F1.0
           ➔  SES          1       4         4        F1.0
              ETHNIC       1       5         5        F1.0
              GREQ         1       6         8        F3.0
              GREV         1       9        11        F3.0
              PRETEST      1      12        13        F2.0
              RATING1      1      14        15        F2.0
              RATING2      1      16        17        F2.0
```

To complete the process of importing the text file, click on the **Finish** button. The data will now be imported into SPSS. A log of this process will be displayed in the output viewer (see Figure 4.20). This log identifies the variables that were read from the imported file. It is similar to the log you produced when you imported the Excel data set.

The imported data should now appear in the data editor. Move to the data editor by selecting **Untitled—SPSS for Windows Data Editor** from the **Window** menu. You can also use the data editor icon on the toolbar, located just under the **Analyze** menu. These data are displayed in Figure 4.21.

All you need to do is save the file as an SPSS file and you're finished. You already have a data file like this. You created it in Chapter 3. If you'd like to save this data file, please do so. Select **Save** from the **File** menu and give the file a name. You can also use the second icon on the toolbar, the one that looks like a floppy disk.

You have now successfully imported a text file into SPSS. This process involved quite a few steps which we have summarized below:

To Import a text file:

Step 1	Select **Read Text Data** from the **File** menu.
Step 2	Open the text file. This will activate the Text Import Wizard.
Step 3	Text Import Wizard—Step 1
	—If you have a predefined format, select Yes. If not, continue with the Text Import Wizard.
Step 4	Text Import Wizard—Step 2
	—Indicate how the variables are arranged (i.e., fixed columns or delimited format) and whether the file includes variable names.
Step 5	Text Import Wizard—Step 3
	—Identify the location of the first case, how many lines of data per case, and how many cases you wish to import.
Step 6	Text Import Wizard—Step 4
	—For *fixed column* files, insert variable break lines to identify the locations of variables.
	—For *delimited text*, identify the character that separates each variable (e.g., tab, comma, space).
Step 7	Text Import Wizard—Step 5
	—Define variable names and types.
Step 8	Text Import Wizard—Step 6
	—Examine the data, decide if you want to save the file for future use.
	—Click **Finish** to import the data.

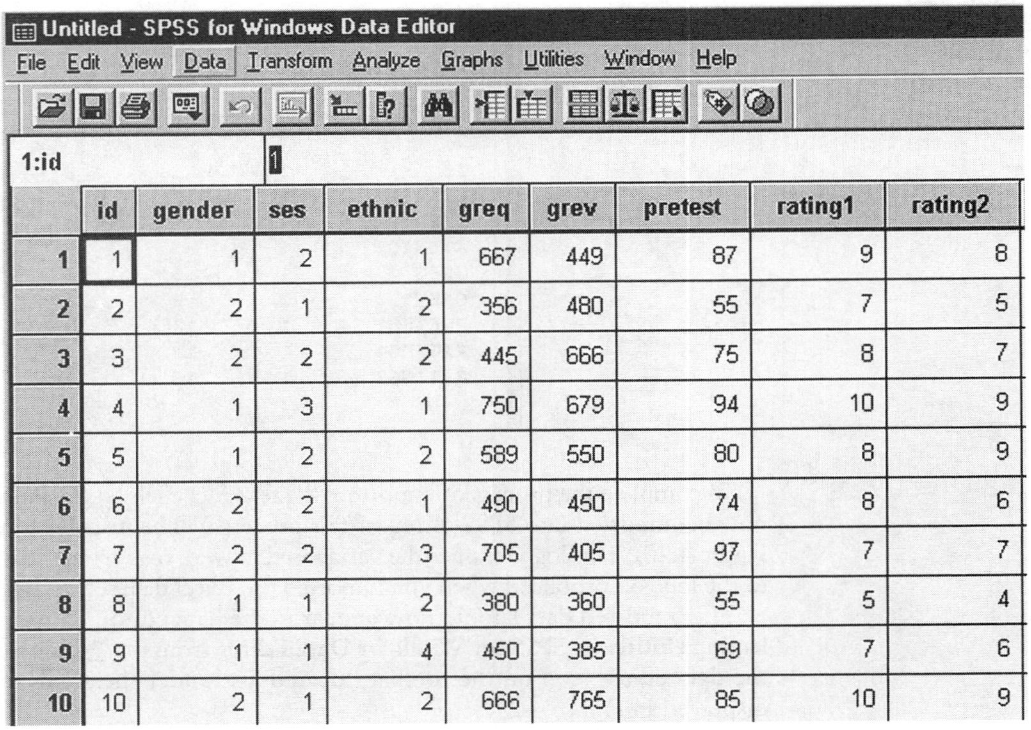

FIGURE 4.21
Imported data in Data
Editor

	id	gender	ses	ethnic	greq	grev	pretest	rating1	rating2
1	1	1	2	1	667	449	87	9	8
2	2	2	1	2	356	480	55	7	5
3	3	2	2	2	445	666	75	8	7
4	4	1	3	1	750	679	94	10	9
5	5	1	2	2	589	550	80	8	9
6	6	2	2	1	490	450	74	8	6
7	7	2	2	3	705	405	97	7	7
8	8	1	1	2	380	360	55	5	4
9	9	1	1	4	450	385	69	7	6
10	10	2	1	2	666	765	85	10	9

MERGING DATA FILES IN SPSS

There will be times when you need to merge different data files. For example, you might have one sample of subjects stored in one file and a different sample in a second file. You also might have additional data (variables) on the same subjects stored in a separate file. In this section, we will illustrate how to merge data files using SPSS. There are two basic ways to merge data. That is, you either want to add more cases to an existing data file or you want to add more variables. The file you wish to add data to is referred to as the working data file in SPSS. We'll use the data you created in the previous chapter as our working data file.

Retrieve this file from the 3½-inch floppy. We named this file **student admission data** so we would remember what it was. (You may have named it something different.)

To merge files, we begin from the **Data** menu. Select **Merge Files** from the **Data** menu, as illustrated in Figure 4.22.

As you can see, there are two options available. These allow us to either add cases or add variables to our working data file.

Adding New Cases

To add cases, select the **Add Cases...** option. This will open the Add Cases: Read File dialog box (see Figure 4.23). This dialog box offers a listing of all the files stored on the floppy disk. From this listing, we need to select the file that contains the additional cases we wish to add. The name of the file we need is **student1.add cases**. Select this file and click the **Open** button. The variables found in this file are the same as those you created for the original working file, student admission data.

This next dialog box illustrates what will be added to the file (see Figure 4.24). This dialog box is labeled **Add Cases from A: \student1.add cases.sav**. This lets us know that the cases are being added from the correct file. The variables found in the new working file appear to the right of the screen under the heading Variables in New Working Data File.

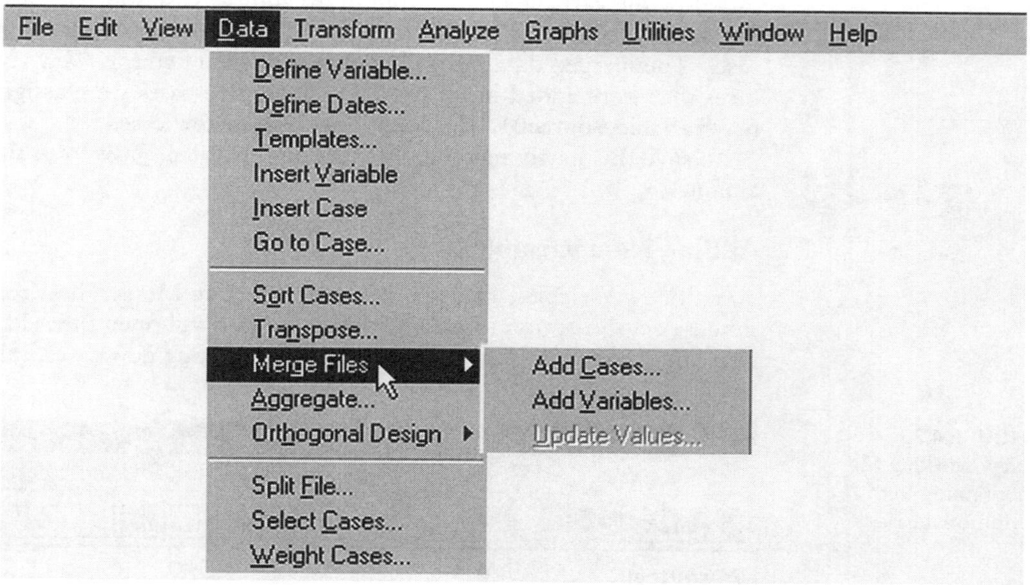

FIGURE 4.22
Data–Merge Files
menu selections

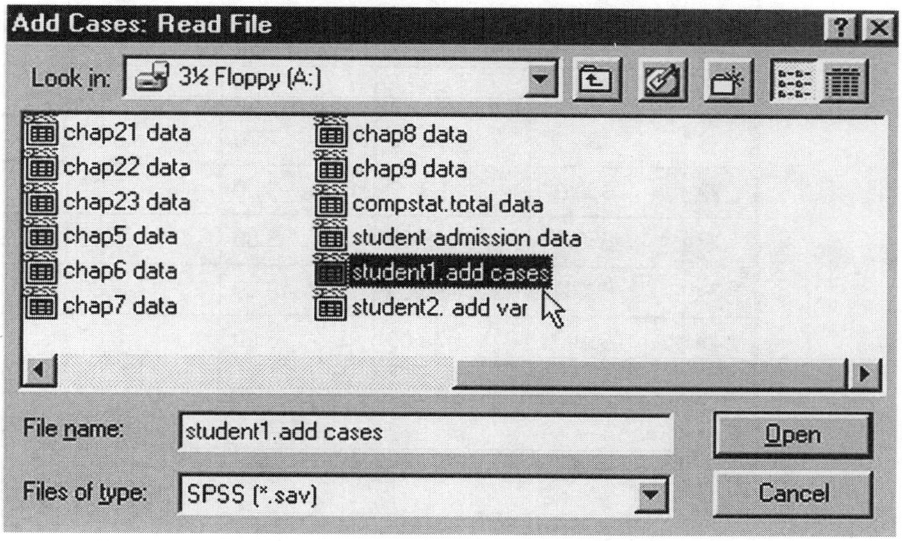

| File | Edit | View | **Data** | Transform | Analyze | Graphs | Utilities | Window | Help |

Define Variable...
Define Dates...
Templates...
Insert Variable
Insert Case
Go to Case...

Sort Cases...
Transpose...
Merge Files   ▶   Add Cases...
Aggregate...   Add Variables...
Orthogonal Design ▶   Update Values...

Split File...
Select Cases...
Weight Cases...

FIGURE 4.23
Add Cases: Read File
dialog box

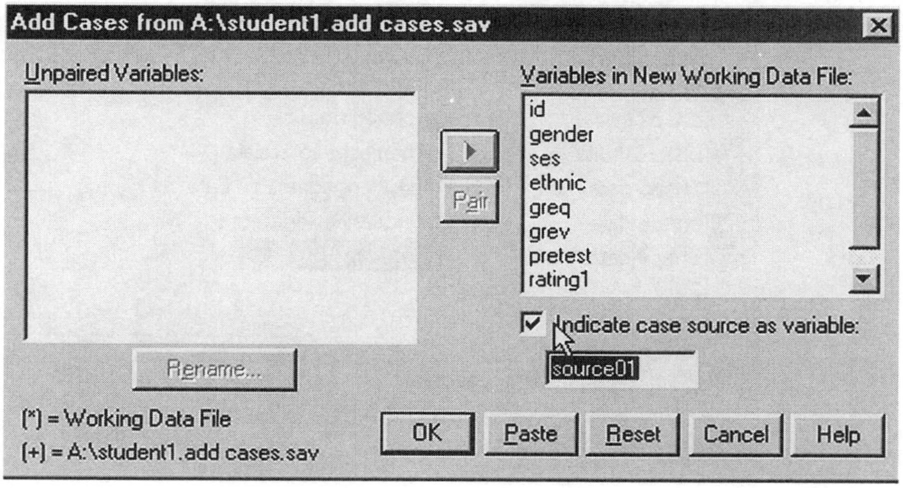

Add Cases: Read File   ? ×

Look in: 3½ Floppy (A:)

chap21 data   chap8 data
chap22 data   chap9 data
chap23 data   compstat.total data
chap5 data   student admission data
chap6 data   student1.add cases
chap7 data   student2. add var

File name: student1.add cases   Open

Files of type: SPSS (*.sav)   Cancel

FIGURE 4.24
Add Cases from
A:\student1.add
cases.sav dialog box

Add Cases from A:\student1.add cases.sav   ×

Unpaired Variables: Variables in New Working Data File:

                                       id
                                       gender
                                       ses
                          ▶   ethnic
                        Pair   greq
                                       grev
                                       pretest
                                       rating1

                        ☑ Indicate case source as variable:
                        source01

Rename...

[*] = Working Data File   OK   Paste   Reset   Cancel   Help
[+] = A:\student1.add cases.sav

Below the variable list is an option to add the case source as a variable in the new data file. Check this box. This will identify which cases were added. Click **OK** to add the new cases. The merged data file will appear in the data editor. We've highlighted the five new cases that were added in Figure 4.25. These five cases were assigned a value of 1 for the new variable, source01. This identifies them as new cases.

To save this newly merged data file, simply select **Save** from the **File** menu and give it a name.

Adding New Variables

To add new variables, you also begin by selecting **Merge Files** from the **Data** menu. This time, select the option to **Add Variables...**. This will open the Add Variables: Read File dialog box (see Figure 4.26). As you did when adding new cases, select the file you wish to

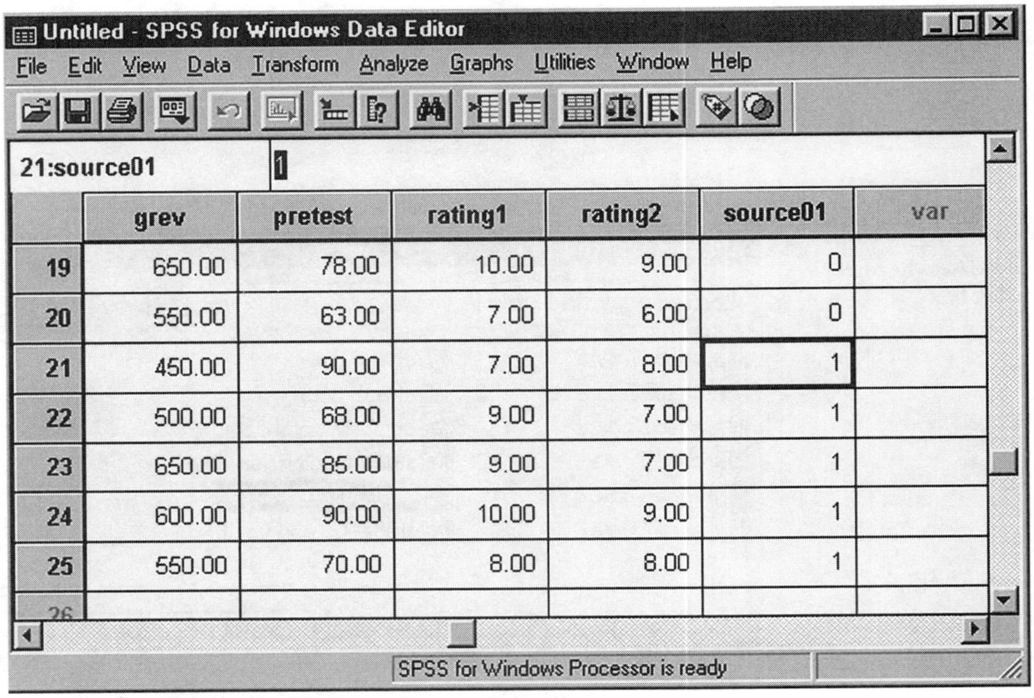

FIGURE 4.25
New working file containing five additional cases

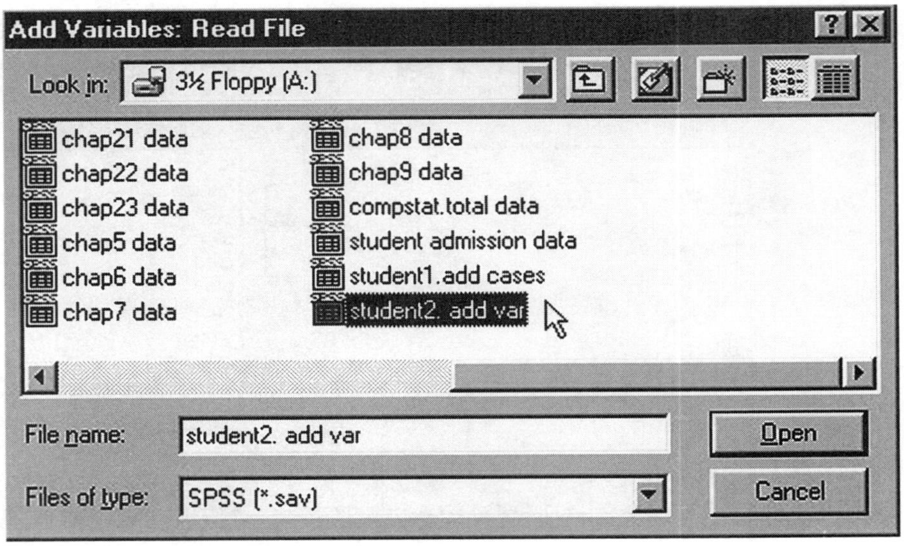

FIGURE 4.26
Add Variables: Read File dialog box

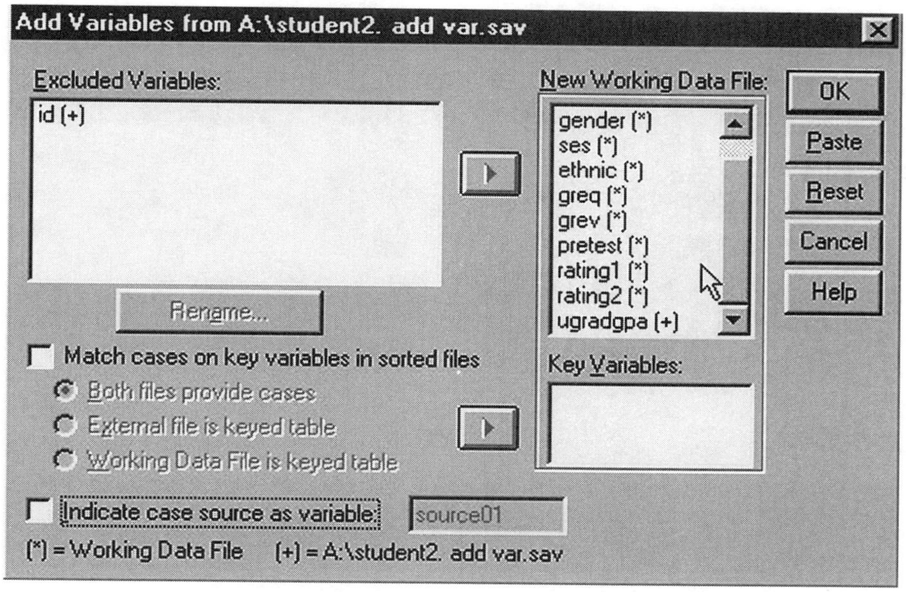

FIGURE 4.27
Add Variables from
A:\student2.add
var.sav dialog box

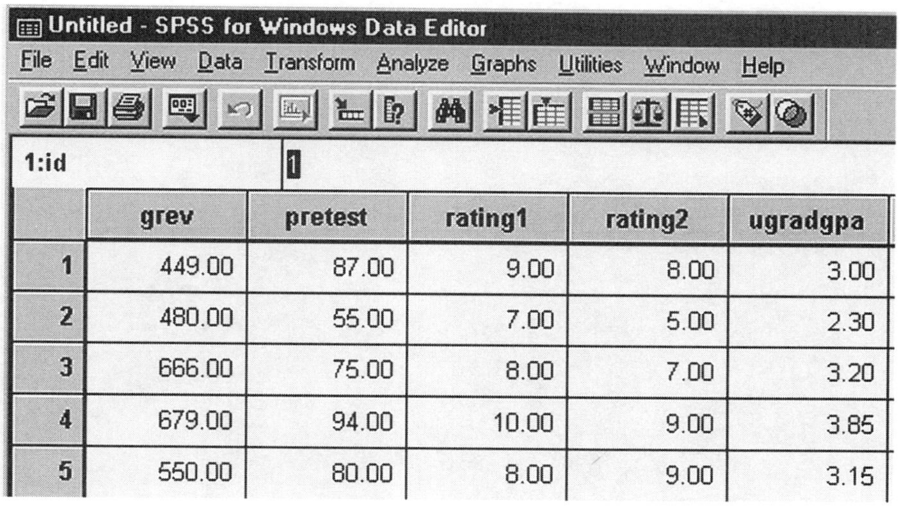

FIGURE 4.28
New working file
containing additional
variable (ugradgpa)

	grev	pretest	rating1	rating2	ugradgpa
1	449.00	87.00	9.00	8.00	3.00
2	480.00	55.00	7.00	5.00	2.30
3	666.00	75.00	8.00	7.00	3.20
4	679.00	94.00	10.00	9.00	3.85
5	550.00	80.00	8.00	9.00	3.15

merge with the working data file. The file we wish to merge is **student2.add var.** This file contains the same twenty cases as the one you created, but includes a different variable. The additional variable is undergraduate GPA. Select this file and click **Open.**

This will open a dialog box which illustrates the variables that will be merged (see Figure 4.27). These variables are listed to the right of the dialog box. Notice that some variables have an asterisk (*) behind them while others have a plus sign (+). If you examine the key at the bottom of the dialog box, you will see that variables with an asterisk were part of the original working file while those with a plus sign are from the new file. Scrolling down the list of variables, you will see that the only variable with a plus sign is UGRADGPA, undergraduate GPA.

Click **OK** to merge the new variable with the existing ones. The new variable will be added to the existing file, as displayed in Figure 4.28.

CHAPTER SUMMARY

In this chapter, you imported data from another spreadsheet format (Excel) and read ASCII data into SPSS. These procedures will be used quite frequently as you analyze data, as data come in many different formats. Being able to convert data to a form that you can work with is essential. Being able to merge data files is also essential as you accumulate multiple data files.

SECTION II

Summarizing Data

5 | Frequency Analysis

Now that you've had a chance to explore some of the features of SPSS and have learned how to enter and define your data, you can begin exploring some statistical procedures. The type of statistical analysis that will be applied to your data is determined by your research questions. However, the calculation of some basic descriptive statistics (with the assistance of the computer) is always a good place to begin your data analysis. Summarizing and describing your data using frequencies, measures of central tendency, and variability will allow you to organize and report the results in a clear, concise manner. In addition, as you encounter other statistical procedures, such as correlations, t-tests, and ANOVA, you will find it necessary to obtain descriptive statistics.

This chapter focuses on the use of frequencies and percentages to summarize your data. These procedures are most useful for determining how many people in your sample have a particular score or belong to each group within a variable. Examining the variables in our data set of applicants to a doctoral program (see Appendix A), you find several categorical variables that are suitable for frequency analysis. These variables include gender (GENDER), ethnicity (ETHNIC), and socioeconomic status (SES). Using frequency analysis, you would be able to address many questions about the individuals who applied for admission to the doctoral program. For example, how many males and how many females applied for admission? What percentage of the applicants was African-American? Was the majority of applicants from lower or higher socioeconomic backgrounds?

As you become more familiar with data entry and data analysis, you will find another reason to run frequencies on your data. As you examine frequency distributions of your data, you can check the accuracy of your data entry efforts. For example, if gender is coded as a "1" or a "2" and you notice a "3" in the distribution, you have found a mistake. Each time you find a value that is out of the possible range for a given variable, you know a mistake was made when the data were entered. Once you find mistakes, you can sort through the raw data (e.g., surveys, coding sheets, etc.) to determine the correct values and correct the mistakes in your SPSS data file.

After you have examined all of the frequency distributions and corrected all of the mistakes, you still can't be sure that all of the data are correct. What if you entered a "1" for a person's gender when it should have been a "2?" A mistake of this type would not be detected from a frequency distribution. As we discussed in the previous chapter, the most thorough way to verify your data is to check the raw data against the data in your data file. This will allow you to catch all types of mistakes and should be done before any analyses are performed.

In the remaining sections of this chapter, we will explore frequency analysis using SPSS. We will illustrate the frequencies procedure by showing you how to work your way through the SPSS menus.

VARIABLES USED IN THIS CHAPTER

The variables we will be using come from the graduate student data set. You will be using these data throughout the remainder of the book as you explore other statistical procedures. In this chapter, we will use four variables from the data set to illustrate the frequencies procedure. Two of these variables, GROUP and GENDER, are measured on the nominal level. The other two variables, COMPEXP and DEGREE, would be classified as ordinal. GROUP is a categorical variable with eight levels. Each level represents one of eight separate sections (or classes) of about 26 students taking a graduate level introductory statistics course. For example, one of these sections is "672f92." The "672" is the numerical code for the beginning statistics course and the "f92" indicates that the course was offered in the fall quarter of 1992. GENDER is dichotomous with values of "1" and "2" representing males and females, respectively. The categories of gender could have also been represented using "M" and "F", as SPSS will read letters as well as numbers.

The variable COMPEXP (computer experience), has five levels that correspond to the following coding scheme: 1 = less than 1 week, 2 = 1 week to 1 month, 3 = between 1 and 6 months, 4 = between 6 months and 1 year, and 5 = more than 1 year. DEGREE corresponds to the degree program in which a student is currently enrolled. This variable has four levels: 1 = Bachelors, 2 = Masters, 3 = Specialist, and 4 = Doctorate. Since all students in our sample are enrolled in a graduate program, the Bachelor's category will be empty.

Using frequency procedures to examine the above variables, we will answer many questions about the nature of our sample of graduate students. For example, which had the largest enrollment? How many students were male and how many were female? How much computer experience do students have when they enroll in a beginning statistics class? What types of degrees are these graduate students pursuing?

We encourage you to follow closely and reproduce our illustrations. You will be given additional opportunities to apply these statistical procedures using other variables found in this data set in later chapters.

USING SPSS TO PERFORM FREQUENCIES

In SPSS, you perform statistical analyses by selecting the appropriate commands and subcommands from a series of menus. The menus and windows that we illustrate are captured from the version 9.X of SPSS software. These menu selections are similar to those found in earlier Windows-based versions of SPSS, as are the statistical procedures themselves. In this section, we will illustrate the procedures used to generate frequencies, pointing out some of the critical differences between the current and earlier versions of SPSS.

The format of the output generated by SPSS does depend somewhat on the version you are using. Whereas SPSS for the Windows 3.1 environment (Version 6.X) output is similar to that of the previous DOS (Version 5.X) and mainframe versions, the output from the latest versions of SPSS is quite different. Although the look of the output may be different, the basic contents of frequencies output is the same no matter which version of SPSS you are using.

Retrieving the Data

Before any analysis can occur, you must activate SPSS and retrieve your data, as you did in previous chapters. If your data had not been entered, you would simply input it into the data editor following the guidelines provided in Chapter 3. However, the data that we will be using have already been entered, saving you a lot of time. These data can be found on the enclosed 3½-inch floppy disk. The name of the data file you will use in this chapter is chap5 data.

As a reminder, you can open a file using the main menubar or the toolbar. From the main menu, select the **Open** and **Data** options from the **File** menu. Or, you can double-click on the **Open File** icon in the toolbar. This will activate the Open Data dialog box. Once you activate the Open Data dialog box, all you need to do is identify the file you wish to retrieve. You may need to change the drive location from the default (c:\spsswin) to either A: or B:, as these data are stored on the enclosed 3½-inch disk. Once you select this file, it will be retrieved into the data editor.

Analyzing Data in SPSS

The data from **chap5 data** should appear in spreadsheet format on your screen. Now that we have data with which to work, we can begin running some frequencies. When analyzing data, you will usually begin with the **Analyze** menu, which appears in the middle of the main menubar. Once you've selected the **Analyze** menu, a series of additional menus will be made available from which you choose the statistical techniques to be applied to selected variables in your data set. The **Analyze** menu is displayed in Figure 5.1.

The options from this menu will allow you to summarize data, compare means, correlate variables, use regression analysis, and perform a variety of other statistical procedures. Notice the option for the general linear model. This option will be used in later chapters to perform analysis of variance (ANOVA). If you are using an earlier version of SPSS for the Windows 3.1 environment (Version 6.X), this option will not be included. Instead, an option for ANOVA models is used.

Running Frequencies Using SPSS

What follows is our first contact with the **Analyze** menu. Most of the statistical procedures we will use in this book can be found within this menu. Follow the steps outlined below to locate the Frequencies menu.

Step 1	We begin at the **Analyze** menu.
Step 2	After selecting the **Analyze** menu, choose the **Descriptive Statistics** option.
Step 3	A drop-down menu will appear, from which you should select the **Frequencies** option.

These three steps are illustrated in Figure 5.2.

FIGURE 5.1
Analyze menu options

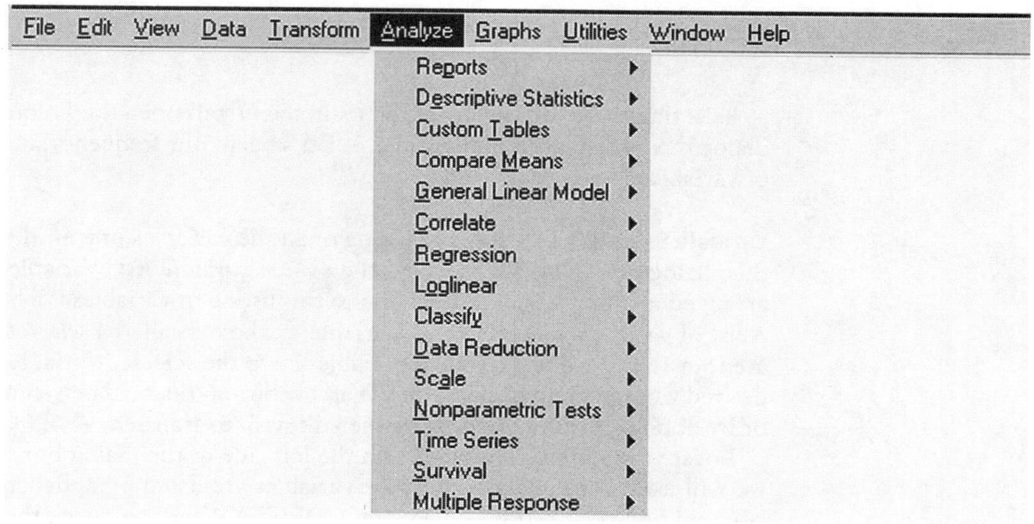

FIGURE 5.2
Analyze–Descriptive
Statistics–Frequencies
menu selections

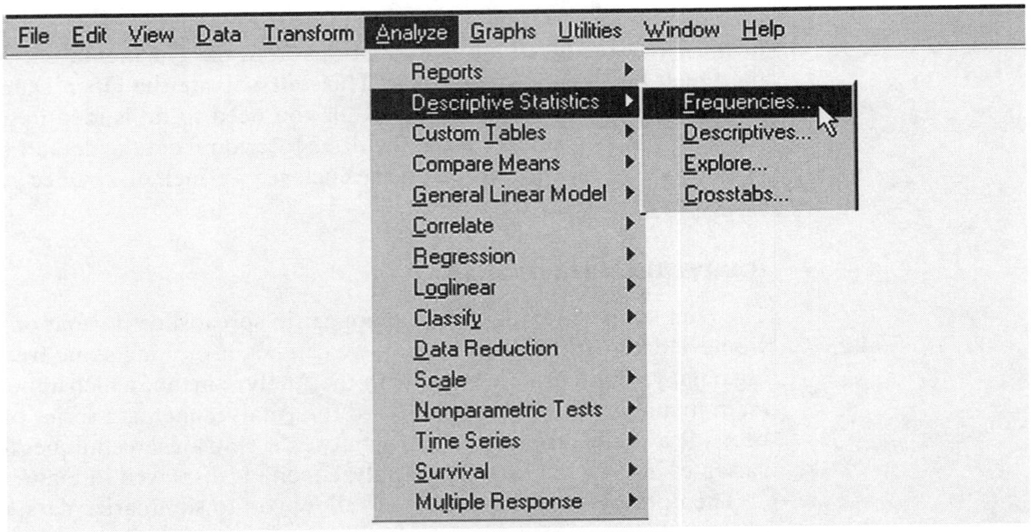

FIGURE 5.3
Frequencies dialog box

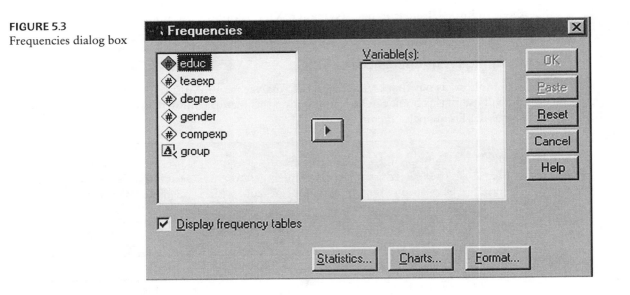

Selecting these options from the main menu will open the Frequencies dialog box. This dialog box is displayed in Figures 5.3. Let's begin our frequency analysis with the selection of variables.

Variable Selection.   There is a listing of all the variables in your data set on the left side of this dialog box. This list is called the *source variable list*. Variables in this source list are arranged in alphabetical order. Next to this listing of variables is a box labeled **Variable(s):**. A list of variables placed in this **Variable(s):**. box is called a *selected variable list*. Variables are transferred from the source variable list to the selected variable list by highlighting the desired variables and clicking on the arrow button (located between the variable list boxes) or by double-clicking on the variable you wish to transfer.

Locate the source variable list on the left side of the dialog box. These are the variables we will use in our analysis. Because variables are listed in alphabetical order, the first one you will find is COMPEXP. Click on COMPEXP and then click the arrow button to transfer it over to the selected variable list. The variable COMPEXP should now appear in the selected variable list (the box to the right of the arrow button). We will repeat this process for the remaining three variables for which we want frequencies.

One at a time, select the variables **DEGREE, GENDER,** and **GROUP** with your mouse and transfer them to the selected variable list using the arrow button. Once all four variables are selected and placed in the selected variable list, the Frequencies dialog box will look like that displayed in Figure 5.4. Note that this process of variable selection will be similar for other statistical procedures.

Now that these variables have been selected, we are ready to proceed with the frequency analysis. We are interested in obtaining frequency tables, descriptive statistics, and visual displays (e.g., bar charts, histograms) for our data.

Frequency Tables.   The basic output generated from frequency analysis is a frequency table. Notice the small box below the source variable list labeled Display frequency tables. By default, this box is checked. If this box is not checked, click your mouse inside the box to select this option. Choosing this option will result in the production of frequency tables for each of the variables you have selected.

We will also obtain additional information about these variables. There are three buttons that we will use to select descriptive statistics, charts, and the format of our output. These buttons are labeled **Statistics…, Charts…,** and **Format….**

Descriptive Statistics.   The options to calculate measures of central tendency and variability are presented to you after you select the **Statistics…** button at the bottom of the dialog box. Click on this button with your mouse. The Frequencies: Statistics dialog box will appear, as displayed in Figure 5.5.

From this window, you can select the statistics that are appropriate for your selected variables by clicking your mouse in the check box (☐) beside each option you desire. SPSS will allow you to select as many check boxes as you like. We will select only those that are appropriate for the variables we are using in this session. The first grouping of options appear under the Percentile Values heading. These options are used to calculate quartiles and percentiles and would be more appropriate for interval-level data. The next option box is labeled Central Tendency. Here you specify mean, median, mode, and sum for your data. Since we are working with nominal and ordinal level variables, it would be appropriate to use the mode to describe the nominal variables and median for the ordinal variables. Click your mouse on the boxes next to the option for **Median** and **Mode.** We'll examine measures of central tendency in more detail in the next chapter.

FIGURE 5.5
Frequencies: Statistics
dialog box

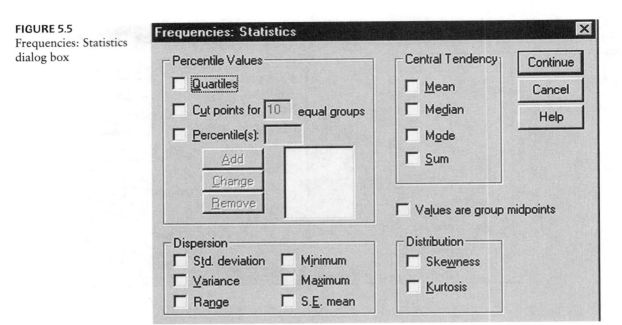

In the lower portion of the screen, notice the box labeled Dispersion. There are several options available here regarding the variability of your data. The only measure of variability that would be meaningful for these nominal and ordinal variables would be the range. We can also select an option to report the minimum and maximum values for the ordinal variables (COMPEXP and DEGREE). However, when you examine continuous variables such as age (AGE) and number of credits earned (AUCRED), you may want to select some of the other options. The final box in the Frequencies: Statistics dialog box is labeled Distribution. The Distribution options provide information about skewness and kurtosis. These options, pertaining to the shape of the distribution of the data, are more applicable to data measured at or above the interval level.

To continue with your current frequency analysis, click on the **Continue** button. You should be seeing the familiar Frequencies main dialog box, in which you have previously selected your variables for this analysis. There are two more buttons at the bottom of the screen. These are the **Charts...** and **Format...** buttons.

Charts.   As you might expect, the **Charts...** button will allow you to create charts to visually display the frequency data. The types of charts available to you with this option are limited to bar charts, pie charts, and histograms. Additional graphs are available using the **Graphs** option on the main menu bar. We will discuss these options later. Click on the **Charts...** button to open the Frequencies: Charts dialog box, displayed in Figure 5.6.

Beside each option is a circle, or an option button (◯). Unlike the check boxes (☐) you encountered earlier, option buttons are mutually exclusive. Therefore, only one option button can be selected at a time. The default option in SPSS is *not* to display the data visually using charts. Notice that the option button next to the **None** option is selected and the word "**None**" has a border around it. Let's visually display these data using a bar chart. To do this, you need to select the option for bar charts under the Chart Type heading. When you click your mouse on the circle next to **Bar Charts**, the default option will be overridden and your data will now be visually displayed in bar chart format. We will see these charts when we examine the output later in the chapter. To continue with this frequency analysis and return to the Frequencies dialog box, click on the **Continue** button.

Format.   The last button at the bottom of this screen is labeled **Format...**. This option allows you to select the format in which you want the data displayed. Click on the **Format...** button. The Frequencies: Format dialog box will appear, as displayed in Figures 5.7.

FIGURE 5.6
Frequencies: Charts
dialog box

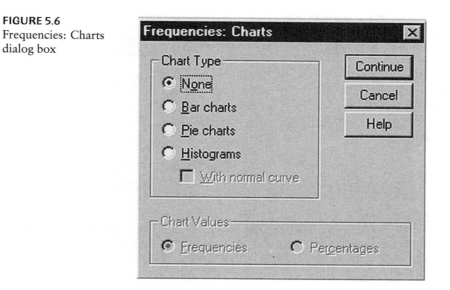

FIGURE 5.7
Frequencies: Format
dialog box

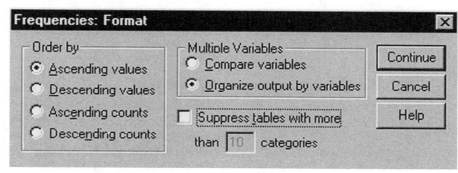

Here, we have a few options regarding the order in which the results will appear in our output and the output page format. Typically, values appear in a frequency table in ascending order. Therefore, because we coded males as a "1" and females as a "2," males will be the first category, followed by females. Under the heading, Order by, you'll notice that Ascending values has been selected. We could just as easily order the results in descending order, in which case females would appear first, followed by males. The other two options are Ascending counts and Descending counts. These options will order the results according to how many cases fall into each category.

The output will be displayed in presentation-quality pivot tables. We will discuss working with these pivot tables and the output navigator in more detail later when we examine the output. Click on the **Continue** button again to return to the Frequencies dialog box.

Command Pushbuttons. There are a few more buttons that appear on the Frequencies main screen (see Figure 5.3). These are called *command pushbuttons* and appear in a column at the far right side of the screen. These command pushbuttons are also displayed in Figure 5.8.

The top button, labeled **OK,** will allow us to run all the options that we just selected. The second button, **Paste,** is used to generate syntax commands. Syntax commands can be used to perform analyses and options that are not available as menu selections. We will generate syntax commands later in this workbook.

The third button, **Reset,** will reset the dialog box to its default settings, erasing all of the selections that you just made. You don't want to click on this button at this time. However, the next time you use the Frequencies procedure, you may find this helpful to clear out the

FIGURE 5.8
Command
Pushbuttons

old variables from the selected variable list and begin with the new ones. The fourth button, **Cancel,** cancels any changes you have made recently and closes the dialog box. If you select this option, you will exit the Frequencies dialog box and cancel what you have done thus far. So, please don't let your mouse near this command pushbutton.

The last button, **Help,** allows you to access further screens which will describe the procedure in more detail. Click on the **Help** button and explore. When you are finished reading about the Frequencies procedure, select the **File** option at the top lefthand side of the Help screen menu bar and choose the **Exit** option. This will return you to the Frequencies dialog box.

Running the Frequencies Procedure

We are ready to run the Frequencies procedure on the variables you have selected. Since you have already defined the variables of interest and selected all the desired options, all you need to do is click your mouse on the **OK** button. It won't take long to run frequencies on just these four variables. There will be messages printed at the bottom lefthand corner of the SPSS for Windows screen. While the procedure is running, the message will read "Running FREQUENCIES." Once the procedure is completed, the message will read "SPSS Processor is ready." Click on the **OK** button and watch for these messages.

SPSS FREQUENCIES OUTPUT

Your output will be displayed in the output navigator. Earlier versions of SPSS (Version 6.X) stored output in the output window and you viewed the bottom, most recent results, of this output when opening the window. Current SPSS versions display the beginning of the output when the output navigator is opened.

Your window is untitled because you haven't saved your output yet. SPSS will remind you to save this file as you exit. It's a good idea to save your files regularly in case your session in interrupted. You save output just like you saved your data file earlier. From the **File** menu, choose the **Save** option. The Save As dialog box will open so that you can specify the name and location of the file to be saved. This process can also be shortcutted by using the toolbar. The second icon on this toolbar is a picture of a disk and is used to save SPSS files. In order to keep your files organized, output viewer files use a **.spo** suffix. Since this output was produced in Chapter 5, we recommend naming this output, **chapter 5.spo.**

Once the output is saved, use your cursor or the scroll bar to move down the output until you locate the first frequency table from this analysis. This first frequency table will summarize information regarding the variable of computer experience (COMPEXP). This, and other selected output, is discussed in the final section of this chapter.

Printing SPSS Output

You may find it more convenient to interpret your output using a printed copy. You can print your output in whole, or in part in much the same manner as you saved it; by using the main menu or the toolbar. First, using the **File** menu, select the **Print...** option. A file can also be printed directly from the toolbar. The third icon on the toolbar is a printer. Clicking on this icon will print the SPSS file you are viewing.

In this session, we requested basic frequency counts for four variables so the output file isn't large. However, in later sessions you will be using many more variables and the output file will become quite large. SPSS will only display a limited amount of information on each page. Printing often wastes a lot of paper and, depending on your computer and printer, might also take some time. We recommend viewing the output on your screen, editing it, and printing only what you need. You can select segments of the output to print using the Output Viewer. We will explore this later.

Finally, you can copy output from SPSS and paste it into a word processing program. This feature is extremely useful when preparing reports or other important documents such as a thesis or dissertation. Once viewed in a word processor, the file can be edited and printed as a word processing document. Using the word processor allows you to make comments, change the margins and fonts, and add page breaks where you want them. We will illustrate this process in a later chapter.

INTERPRETING SPSS FREQUENCIES RESULTS

The first frequency table displays information pertaining to the COMPEXP variable. This is shown in Figure 5.9.

In this frequency table, you'll notice that the name of the variable is reported at the top of the table and its values are listed in the left most column. The values for COMPEXP range from 1 to 5. The next column in the frequency table is labeled Frequency. The numbers reported under this heading simply indicate how many people fall into each category. For example, the largest group is the fifth category, "1 year or more," which was represented by 145 of the 209 students in our sample. The next column, labeled Percent, indicates what percent of the entire sample each group represents. In other words, 69.4% of the entire sample indicated that they had one or more years of computer experience. The following column is labeled Valid Percent. This percentage is based on the number of people who answered the question. In this case, there are no missing cases. Therefore, the Percent and Valid Percent are the same. The final column is labeled Cumulative Percent. This percentage is calculated by adding up the valid percentages as you move down the list of categories. For the last category, the cumulative percentage is 100%. Examine the cumulative percentage for the third category. The value is 18.2%, meaning that 18.2% of our sample had six months or less of computer experience.

We also requested some descriptive statistics, which are displayed in a separate output table (see Figure 5.10). This information includes the median, mode, range, minimum, and

FIGURE 5.9
Frequency results
(COMPEXP)

COMPEXP

		Frequency	Percent	Valid Percent	Cumulative Percent
Valid	1	9	4.3	4.3	4.3
	2	10	4.8	4.8	9.1
	3	19	9.1	9.1	18.2
	4	26	12.4	12.4	30.6
	5	145	69.4	69.4	100.0
	Total	209	100.0	100.0	

FIGURE 5.10
Frequencies results:
Statistics summary for
COMPEXP

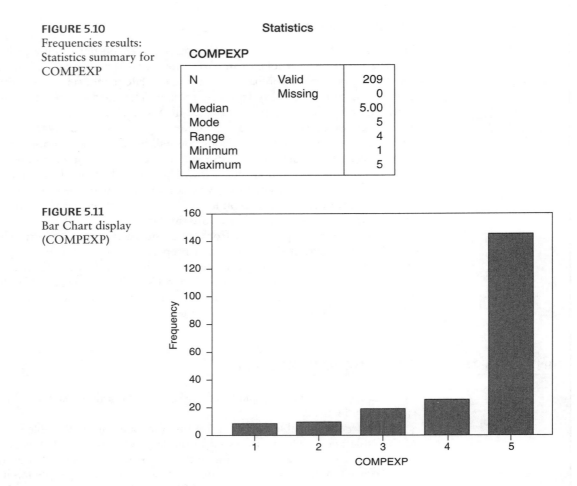

Statistics

COMPEXP

N	Valid	209
	Missing	0
Median		5.00
Mode		5
Range		4
Minimum		1
Maximum		5

FIGURE 5.11
Bar Chart display
(COMPEXP)

maximum values. The median and mode are 5, while the range is 4. This simply means that the fifth category (one year or more) is the midpoint of the distribution and it has the highest frequency. The range of 4 indicates that the responses ranged from a low of 1 to a high of 5, resulting in a range of 4.

Bar Chart Displays

We requested a bar chart in this frequency analysis. This chart appears with the other frequency results (see Figure 5.11). Earlier versions of SPSS (Version 6.X) required you to click on a Chart Carousel icon, which opened a chart editor.

Examining this bar chart, you can see that the majority of our sample has had some computer experience. The bar at the far right represents the fifth level of computer experience (one year or more). This bar is a great deal taller than the other bars on the chart, indicating that this level of experience was reported most frequently by students. This level of experience represents the mode of the distribution. The mode is easily determined by locating the highest point on the chart. The bars to the left of this level are much shorter, indicating that very few students chose these options.

Saving Charts.   When using the current version of SPSS, charts are saved as part of the output file. Earlier versions (Version 6.X) required you to save charts as separate files. As you might have guessed from saving other SPSS files, you can save chart files two ways: using the main menu or the toolbar. We will make some modifications to the output using the output navigator in the next section. After making these changes, we will want to save the output file, and these charts will be saved as part of the output.

Using the Output Viewer in SPSS

One of the most noticeable differences between the current SPSS series and earlier Windows 3.1-based versions is the output interface. Calling this window a "viewer" instead of a window is descriptive of the interface's function. In earlier versions (version 6.X), output was displayed in contiguous pages in what was essentially a very simple text editor. The limitations of this output window/text editor were numerous. It is our impression that the SPSS output window was not designed to be a fully functional word processor. It was designed to give you output, fair and simple. However, if you wanted to see a particular part of your printout, you had to manually scroll down to the portion of interest. If what you were looking for was located toward the end of a thirty-five page printout, you had little choice but to scroll past thirty or so pages of printout to find the results you wanted to examine. Also, if you wanted to transfer a part of the output to a word processor for, say, a homework assignment or for publication, you had to transfer it by cutting and pasting from the SPSS output window into a word processing program and formatting the pasted output manually.

The output viewer was designed to make information within the output easier to find and easier to transfer into other formats, such as a word processing format. This window contains two separate window panes that allow your output to be neatly organized. Figure 5.12 displays the output navigator.

These two window panes are called the *outline pane* and the *output pane*. The larger of these panes, the output pane, contains the output. It is in this pane that frequency tables, descriptive statistics, and charts will be displayed. The other pane, the outline pane, contains a cumulative outline of all of the output, syntax, graphics, and text that you have prepared in your current SPSS session. It is this outline pane that offers you the versatility to expand or collapse various aspects of the output and to quickly find and move to the output of interest. You can also add text, headings, and titles so that you can produce publishable graphics and output right in SPSS, without having to export and reformat output into a word processor.

Using the Outline Pane. The outline pane is controlled using the set of shortcut buttons located just above it. These buttons are displayed in Figure 5.13.

Three of these buttons are usually active. These buttons, labeled "1","2", and "3" in Figure 5.13, are used to insert headings, titles, and text in the output pane. This is a very important feature because, by default, SPSS will give your tables and graphs titles that reflect the variable names of the data being analyzed. These names are likely abbreviations of some kind. In the output pane, you can edit the titles to more accurately reflect the contents of each table or chart.

To give these results a title, select the Insert Title button, labeled "2" in Figure 5.13. A text box will appear at the top of your output window, awaiting a title. The default font is

FIGURE 5.12
Output Viewer

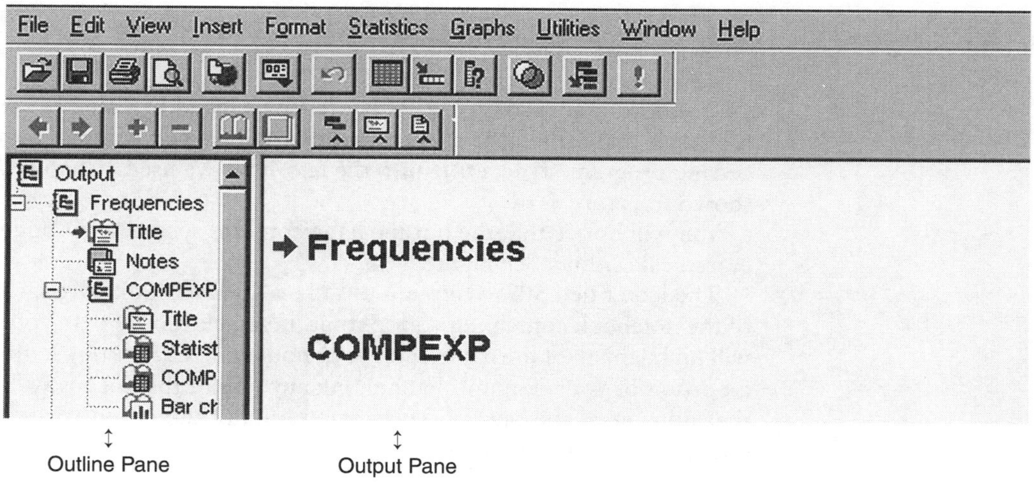

Outline Pane   Output Pane

FIGURE 5.13
Outline Pane shortcut
buttons

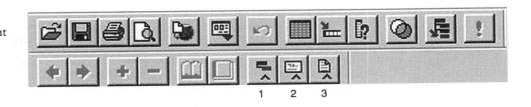

FIGURE 5.14
Inserting a title using
the Output Viewer

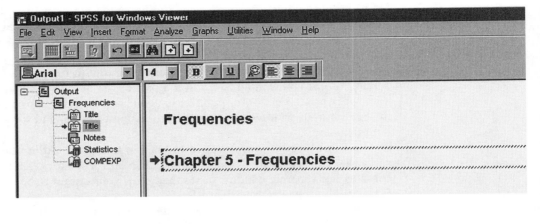

FIGURE 5.15
Outline Pane

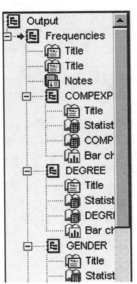

14-point boldface Arial type. This can be changed by using the text format toolbar. This toolbar is quite similar to the formatting toolbars you will find in many popular word processing program. Type a title into the text box. We used "Chapter 5–SPSS Frequencies," as shown in Figure 5.14.

You will notice that the outline pane contains special icons and names presented as a hierarchical outline. See Figure 5.15.

The icon titled SPSS Output looks like a stylized book cover. This, in fact, is the "cover" of the notebook containing your output. If you click once with your mouse on this icon, you will highlight all of the contents of your notebook. Each listing in this outline pane represents a portion of your output. Highlighting any one of these icons will take you immediately to that portion of the output. Try moving around the output to examine the remaining frequency tables and bar charts.

As you can see, it is easy to insert headings, titles, and text using the output viewer. This viewer can also be used to modify the format of your output for presentations and manuscripts. We will explore these capabilities in a later chapter.

CHAPTER SUMMARY

In this chapter, you used the Frequencies procedure to produce frequency tables and bar charts for nominal and ordinal variables in a data set. This information was useful in determining how many students belonged to each category within a variable. We used the mode, or most frequently occurring value, to describe each of the nominal variables and the median, or midpoint, for the ordinal variables. We were also able to identify a range of values for each of the ordinal variables. In the next chapter, we will be working with variables measured at the interval level and using additional descriptive statistics to summarize them in terms of central tendency and variability.

PRACTICE EXERCISES

For Question 1, use the data set you created in Chapter 3 (i.e., student admission data).

1. Perform a frequency analysis for each of the following variables:
   GENDER, SES, ETHNIC, RATING 1, RATING 2
   a. Frequencies and Percentages
      1. How many students in the sample are female?
      2. How many come from low SES backgrounds?
      3. What percentage of the sample is African-American?
      4. What percentage of the applicants received a faculty rating of 8 or lower?
   b. Determine which measure of central tendency and variability is most appropriate and report it for each of the four variables.

For Question 2, use the same computer/statistics attitude dataset that you used in this chapter (i.e., chap5 data).

2. Perform a frequency analysis for each of the following variables:
   EDUC, TEAEXP
   a. Frequencies and Percentages
      1. How many students in the sample have previous teaching experience?
      2. How many students have earned a Bachelor's degree?
      3. What percentage of the sample earned a Master's degree?
   b. Determine which measure of central tendency and variability is most appropriate and report it for each variable.

6 | Measures of Central Tendency and Variability

In the previous chapter, you ran basic frequencies in which data were summarized in a frequency table. You obtained some basic descriptive information such as frequency counts and percentages. Using the Frequencies procedure, information about central tendency and variability was also reported. However, since we were working with nominal and ordinal variables, we limited these descriptive statistics to the mode, median, and range.

In this chapter, you will use other descriptive statistics to describe the central tendency and variability of variables measured at the interval level. The most common measure of central tendency is the mean, while the standard deviation is typically used to describe variability. These measures provide concise summaries of your data without all the detail from the frequency analysis.

MEASURES OF CENTRAL TENDENCY

There are three basic measures of central tendency. These are the *mean, median,* and *mode.* These measures are used to describe the center of a variable's distribution, or the typical performance on a particular variable. Your choice of the most appropriate measure of central tendency will depend primarily on the type of variable and on the shape of the distribution. If a distribution is severely skewed, the mean will be heavily influenced by extreme scores and may not represent typical performance. In the case of a skewed distribution, the median usually serves as a more representative measure of central tendency.

You used the mode and median in the previous chapter when working with the Frequencies procedure. Recall that the mode is most appropriate for variables measured at the nominal level. It simply defines the score (or category) of the variable that occurs most frequently. We used the mode to indicate which statistics section (GROUP) had the most students enrolled. We also use the mode to indicate that there were more females than males in our sample. We used the median for two ordinal variables, computer experience (COMPEXP) and degree program (DEGREE). Using the median, we were able to identify the midpoint of the distribution.

In this chapter, we will begin to use the mean to describe central tendency. The mean is simply the average of a group of values. You have used a mean many times. When you calculate your average grade in a class or your average gas mileage for several tanks of gas, you are using the mean. In order to use the mean, the values that define the variable must make sense when they are added to each other and averaged. A mean makes sense for grades or gas mileage. Examining the variables from our doctoral applicants (see Appendix A), it would also make sense to report a mean for the GRE scores and pretest scores. However, a mean for the ethnicity variable would be meaningless because ethnicity is measured at the nominal level. In the case of a nominal value, the mode is the most appropriate measure of central tendency.

Comparisons are generally made on the basis of a mean. For example, final grades in a course are typically assigned after examining your average (mean) performance. Using a criterion-referenced grading system, your mean performance is compared to predetermined criteria to determine your final grade. If your mean is over 90%, you would earn an "A" in most courses. On the other hand, if grades are determined in a norm-referenced manner, your mean performance would be compared to the performance of other individuals to determine your grade. In either case, means are used to make these comparisons and determine final grades. It would be rare for an instructor to use medians or modes to make these comparisons.

MEASURES OF VARIABILITY

The three primary measures of variability are *range, standard deviation,* and *variance.* These measures are used to describe how spread out the values are in a distribution. A measure of variability is typically reported along with a measure of central tendency to describe a group's performance on a given variable. Generally, the range is reported for ordinal variables, while the standard deviation and variance are used for variables measured at the interval or ratio level.

The range is the simplest measure of variability. It is the difference between the largest and smallest values in the distribution. You used the range to describe the variability in computer experience, measured at the ordinal level, in the previous chapter. A range can also be used for variables measured at the interval or ratio levels, but is not meaningful for variables measured at the nominal level, such as gender or ethnicity. A range is usually reported with the median when describing a variable in terms of central tendency and variability.

The standard deviation and variance are more commonly used measures of variability. These measures describe variability in terms of how individual scores deviate from the mean of a given variable. The variance represents the average squared deviation from the mean, while the standard deviation is the square root of the variance. Therefore, the standard deviation is reported in the same units as the original score and is commonly reported with the mean to describe a variable.

When you calculate your average (i.e., mean) grade or gas mileage, all of the values that define these variables are used. In most cases, values will not be the same. In other words, it would be rare for all of your grades to be exactly the same. The extent to which grades are different is reflected in a measure of variability. If all of your grades were exactly the same, there would be no variability and the value of the standard deviation and variance would be zero.

In general, variances and standard deviations closer to zero represent less variability. For example, if all of the grades in a particular class are between 85 and 90, student performance is very consistent and the standard deviation of grades is very low. However, suppose that grades range from as low as 70 to above 90. In this case, grades are very different and the standard deviation is larger.

As with measures of central tendency, the value obtained for a measure of variability will depend somewhat on the variable being measured. Using the information on our doctoral applicants, we would use a standard deviation to describe the variability in GRE scores and pretest scores. We would expect the standard deviation and variance to be higher for GRE scores as compared to pretest scores because GRE scores use larger units of measurement. This does not necessarily mean that performance on the GRE was more varied than that on the pretest.

To be meaningful, the standard deviation must be interpreted in relationship with the mean. Smaller deviations from the mean will have greater impact when a variable has a very small standard deviation. Suppose the overall mean grade for your class is 80. A final grade average of 90 is far more impressive when the standard deviation is 5, as opposed to 10. In the first instance, your grade is two standard deviations above the mean, while only one standard deviation above the mean in the other.

The interpretation of the standard deviation also depends somewhat on the shape of the distribution. If a variable follows a normal distribution, the standard deviation is used to divide the distribution into different areas, as discussed in the following section.

NORMAL DISTRIBUTION

The normal distribution serves as a model for many of the variables used in behavioral research. A normal distribution is a symmetrical distribution, with the mean, median, and mode being equal to the same value. The normal distribution is often referred to as a bell-shaped distribution with most scores occurring in the center and fewer at the extremes. The normal distribution is displayed in Figure 6.1.

The areas under the normal distribution are well defined in standard deviation units. First, approximately 68% of scores in a normal distribution will fall within one standard deviation on either side of the mean (−1SD to +1SD). Second, approximately 95% of scores will be distributed within two standard deviations of the mean (−2SD to +2SD). Finally, over 99% of all values will fall within three standard deviations of the mean (−3SD to +3SD). Scores will rarely extend beyond three standard deviations from the mean in either direction.

For example, the population mean for intelligence scores (IQ) as measured by the Weschler scales is 100, having a standard deviation of 15. Three standard deviations in each direction would create a range from 55 to 145. How many people do you know who have an IQ score less than 55 or greater than 145? It isn't very likely that a person's IQ score would be so extreme. In other words, the probability that a person obtains an IQ score of 145 or greater is very small. We will find the normal distribution and the probabilities associated with it very helpful as we explore a variety of statistical procedures in later chapters of this book.

For now, let's use the normal distribution to explore the use of standard scores. Standard scores are expressed in standard deviation units, making the comparison between variables measured on different scales much easier.

FIGURE 6.1
Normal Distribution

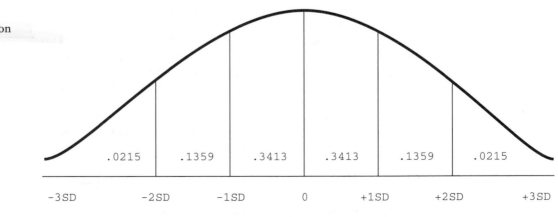

STANDARD SCORES

Suppose we wanted to make comparisons among the applicants to the doctoral program. We have several important variables such as GRE scores, pretest scores, and faculty ratings that might be used in our selection process. We want the best candidates for our doctoral program. Ideally, the students we select would be above average on the important variables such as GRE, pretest, and faculty rating. We might also want students with consistent performance across these important selection variables.

As long as we know the mean of each of these variables, we can determine the extent to which each student's score deviates from the group average on each variable. However, these variables are measured in different units, so comparisons will be difficult. Twenty points above the mean on the GRE is much less impressive than twenty points above the mean on the pretest, and twenty points above the mean on the faculty rating would be impossible because the upper limit for this rating is 10.

When making these comparisons of variables measured on different scales, we must also use the standard deviation of each variable. The standard deviation for GRE scores will be the largest, followed by the pretest and the faculty rating. Therefore, 20 points above the mean on the GRE will be less than one standard deviation. However, 20 points would most likely be more than one standard deviation above the mean on the pretest. Thus, an applicant who scored twenty points above the mean on both the GRE and pretest would be ranked much higher on the pretest than on the GRE.

We need some common scale that can be used to help us make these comparisons easier. Using standard scores, we represent a person's performance in standard deviation units. If a person scores above the mean, his/her standard score will be positive. On the other hand, scores below the mean will be negative. The most common standard score is the *z score*.

Z scores have a mean of 0 and a standard deviation of 1. Therefore, when scores are expressed as z scores, they indicate the distance and direction from the mean in exact standard deviation units. For example, a z score of +1.0 represents a score that is exactly one standard deviation above the mean, regardless of the original scale of the variable. If you want to select applicants who are above average on each selection variable, then you would only consider those with positive z scores.

In the remaining sections of this chapter, we will explore the use of these descriptive statistics with SPSS.

VARIABLES USED IN THIS CHAPTER

The variables we will be using come from the graduate student data set. We have chosen three variables to illustrate the use of descriptive statistics. These variables are AGE, AUCRED, and TEAEXP. The values for AGE represent the actual age of the student when he or she was enrolled in the beginning statistics course. AUCRED represents the number of credits completed at Auburn University by each student beyond his/her most recent degree. The final variable, TEAEXP, is dichotomous. Each student was asked to respond to a yes/no question regarding whether or not they had any teaching experience. For this variable, the values of "0" and "1" were used to code responses of no and yes.

Using descriptive statistics to examine the above variables, we will be able to answer many descriptive questions about the sample of graduate students. Some of these questions include the following: What is the average age of students enrolled in a beginning statistics class? How many credits, on average, have these students completed at Auburn University? What proportion of these students have had teaching experience?

USING SPSS FOR DESCRIPTIVE STATISTICS

The process of obtaining descriptive statistics is similar to the one that you followed in Chapter 5 to perform frequency analysis. You will select the commands and subcommands necessary for descriptive statistics from a series of windows and menus. As you continue to use SPSS to perform statistical procedures, you will find that there are many similarities from procedure to procedure. As we mentioned in the previous chapter, you will usually begin with the **Analyze** menu. In the previous chapter, we performed frequency analysis for a few variables pertaining to graduate students' attitudes toward computers and statistics. In this chapter, we will be using the same data to calculate descriptive statistics. Open the data file **chap6 data** by selecting the **Open** and **Data** options from the **File** menu. Again, you can save some steps by clicking on the **Open File** icon on the toolbar.

Analyzing the Data

The procedure used to run descriptive statistics is **Descriptives....** To run this procedure, we begin with the **Analyze** menu and follow the steps illustrated in Figure 6.2.

Step 1	Begin at the **Analyze** menu.
Step 2	After selecting the **Analyze** menu, choose the **Descriptive Statistics** option.
Step 3	A new menu will appear, from which you select the **Descriptives...** option.

As a result of these three steps, the Descriptives dialog box will open. This dialog box is displayed in Figure 6.3.

Many features of the Descriptives dialog box should look familiar from previous SPSS procedures. The source variable list on the left, the selected variable list, and the arrow button in between were all part of the Frequencies dialog box. The five command pushbuttons that appear at the right of the window were also part of the Frequencies dialog box. You will find that these basic features are part of most of the procedure dialog boxes you encounter when performing statistical analyses using SPSS for Windows.

Using the Descriptives Procedure

We need to select the variables to be used in this analysis. These varialbes are AGE, AUCRED, and TEAEXP. Transfer these variables from the source variable list to the selected variable list using the arrow button, or by double-clicking on the variable.

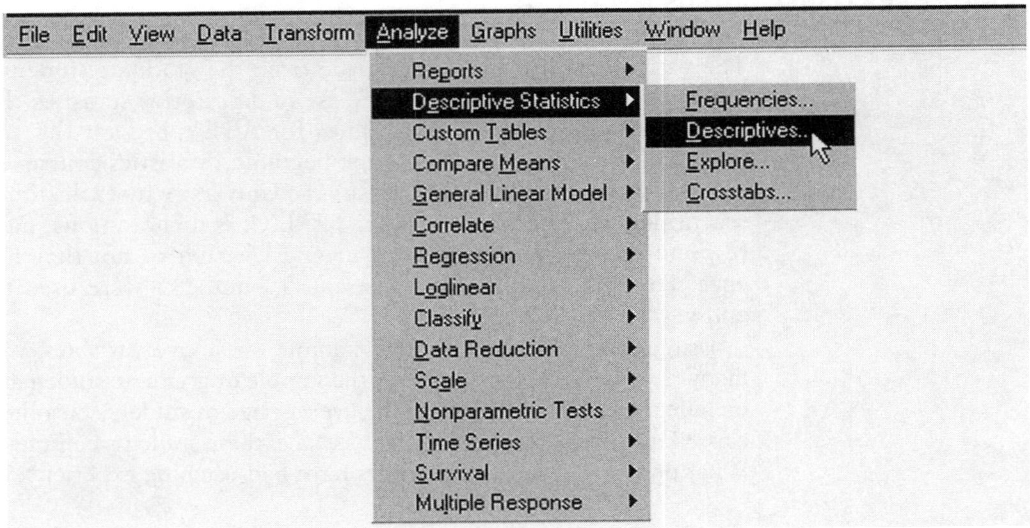

FIGURE 6.2
Analyze–Descriptive Statistics–Descriptives menu selections

Below the listing of variables, there is an option box labeled Save standardized values as variables. Notice that the "z" is underlined. If you would like to transform the variables into z scores, you would select this option. We want to calculate z scores, so select this box with your mouse.

There is one last important feature in this Descriptives dialog box. Notice the **Options...** button at the bottom right-hand corner of the window. You need to click on this button in order to specify the statistics you desire. Click on the **Options...** button to open the Descriptives: Options dialog box. This dialog box is displayed in Figure 6.4.

Default Statistics

You will notice many options in the Descriptives: Options dialog box that were also available using the Frequencies procedure. These options include the mean and sum, measures of variability, and measures of distribution. Notice that some of these options have

FIGURE 6.3
Descriptives dialog box

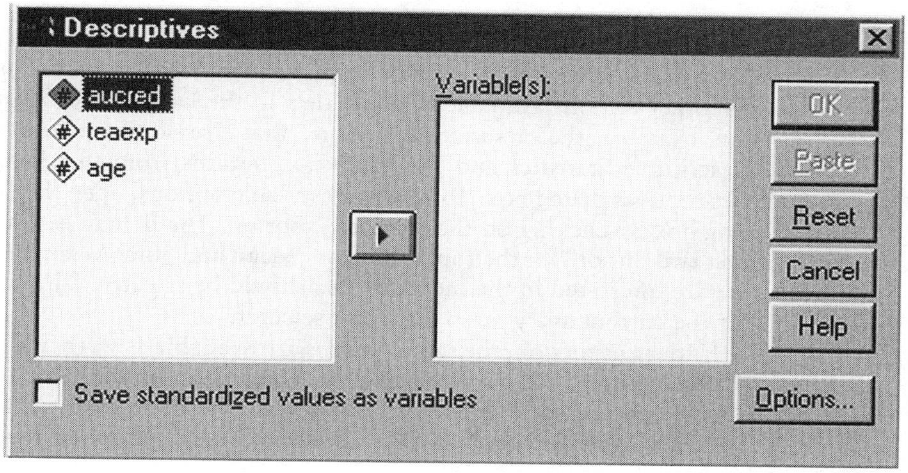

FIGURE 6.4
Descriptives: Options dialog box (with default statistics)

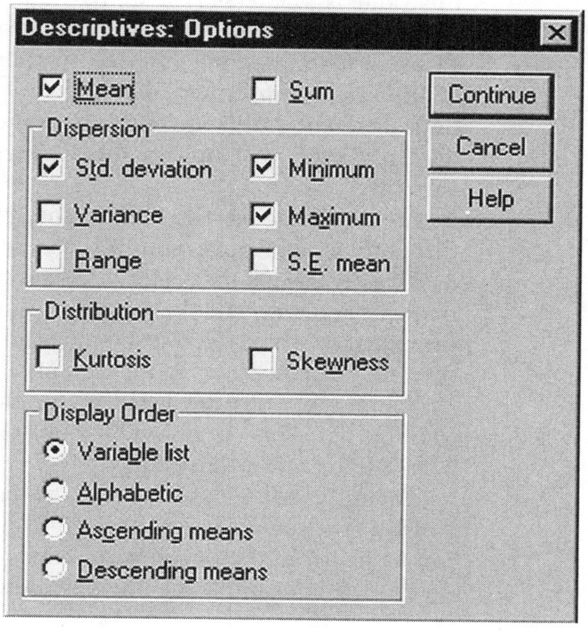

already been selected. These are the default options for the descriptive procedure. For our first descriptive analysis, we'll accept these default options. The options for **Mean**, **Std. deviation**, **Minimum**, and **Maximum** should be selected.

Examine the box labeled Display Order. The default setting is **Variable list**, which will present the variables in the order they were selected for analysis. The other options include **Ascending means**, **Descending means**, and **Alphabetic**. There is no definite advantage to any of these display orders. If you are examining variables that are measured on the same scale, the ascending or descending order of means would be helpful so that you could easily determine which variables had the lowest or highest means. On the other hand, if variables are measured on different scales, this order is not as useful. For this SPSS session, leave the default settings in place.

Click on the **Continue** button to return to the Descriptives dialog box. To perform the analysis, click the **OK** command pushbutton. Your screen should be displaying the output from this analysis. Before we examine these results, let's specify some additional descriptive statistics using SPSS.

Additional Descriptive Statistics

Now that you've completed a descriptive analysis using the default options, let's explore the other options available to us. Return to the Descriptives: Options dialog box so you can examine the descriptive options that are available. As a reminder, select the **Descriptive Statistics** and **Descriptives...** options from the **Analyze** menu to open the Descriptives dialog box. To view the available options, open the Descriptives: Options dialog box by clicking on the **Options...** button. The default settings are still in place. The first two options, at the top of box, are **Mean** and **Sum**. Mean should already be selected. We are interested in the mean, so this should be selected. The sum is not that important for the current analysis, so we won't select it.

Under Dispersion, the same options are available as were in the Frequencies: Statistics dialog box from the previous chapter. The default options for **Std. deviation**, **Minimum**, and **Maximum** have already been selected. The three remaining options are **S.E. Mean**, **Variance**, and **Range**. You should select these options so that you can examine the results.

S.E. Mean identifies the standard error of the mean. This statistic provides us with an indication of how well our sample mean represents the population mean. The smaller this value is, the less error we have in our sample and, therefore, our sample mean provides a better estimate of the population mean. The **Variance** option will calculate the variance for our sample on each variable. The variance represents the amount of variability in our sample just like the standard deviation. However, the variance is measured on a different scale. Squaring the standard deviation results in the variance. The final option, **Range**, will indicate the distance between the smallest and largest value for each variable.

The next heading, Distribution, has two options: **Kurtosis** and **Skewness**. Select both of these options with your mouse. The measure of kurtosis will describe the extent to which the data cluster around the center of the distribution. Distributions can be described as platykurtic (wide and flat), mesokurtic (normal), or leptokurtic (tall and skinny). Skewness describes the extent to which the distribution is not symmetric. If any of these distributions is severely skewed, we should use the median, instead of the mean, to describe the central tendency.

The last options are listed under the heading Display Order. The default option is **Variable list**. This option will list our results in the order they appear in our variable list. This is fine for our illustration.

Having selected these options, the dialog box should look like that in Figure 6.5.

Now that you are finished selecting these options, click your mouse on the **Continue** button to return to the Descriptives dialog box. Everything is ready to go. Click your mouse on the **OK** button to generate these descriptive statistics.

FIGURE 6.5
Descriptives: Options dialog box (with additional statistics selected)

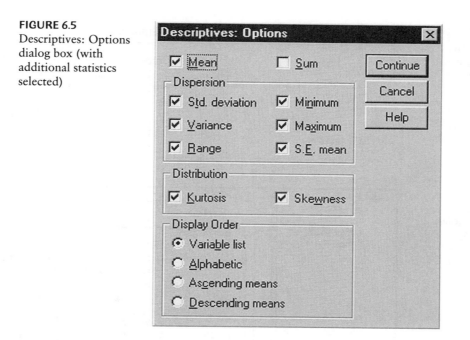

INTERPRETING SPSS DESCRIPTIVES RESULTS

We generated two sets of descriptive results in this SPSS session. In the first descriptive analysis, we accepted the default options. These options included the mean, standard deviation, minimum, and maximum values. In the second analysis, we selected additional statistics such as the standard error of the mean, variance, range, kurtosis, and skewness. We'll examine these results next.

Output with Default Statistics

Before we begin our examination of this output, let's save this output file. SPSS will remind you to save this file as you exit. However, it is a good idea to save your files regularly in case your session is interrupted. This process can be completed from main menu or by using the save icon in the toolbar. Since this output was produced in Chapter 6, we recommend naming this output **chap6.spo**.

Move down the output file until you locate the table of descriptive results. This output is displayed in Figure 6.6.

Examine the output from our analysis. TEAEXP has the lowest mean of .64. Recall that this variable is coded "0" if a student did *not* have teaching experience and "1" if they did have experience. Therefore, the mean indicates the proportion of 1s, or yes responses. In this case, a mean of .64 indicates that 64% of our sample (N = 209) had some type of teaching experience.

The highest mean given was for the AGE variable. The average age in our sample is 32.68, having a standard deviation of 8.9. The youngest student is 21, most likely enrolled in a Master's program fresh out of his or her undergraduate program. On the other hand, the oldest student is 58. Two students did not reveal their age. Therefore, the descriptive statistics computed for age are based on 207 students.

The average number of credits completed toward their current academic degree (AUCRED) is 20.86. However, our sample is quite varied, having a large standard deviation (19.6) and the wide range. Some students were enrolled in their first quarter, having completed 0 credits, while at least one student had already completed 85 credits. This descriptive information is based on 201 students.

FIGURE 6.6
SPSS Descriptives
Output (default
options)

Descriptive Statistics

	N	Minimum	Maximum	Mean	Std. Deviation
AUCRED	201	0	85	20.86	19364
TEAEXP	209	0	1	.64	.48
AGE	207	21	58	32.68	8.90
Valid N (listwise)	199				

FIGURE 6.7
Using Output
Navigator to Reveal
notes in SPSS

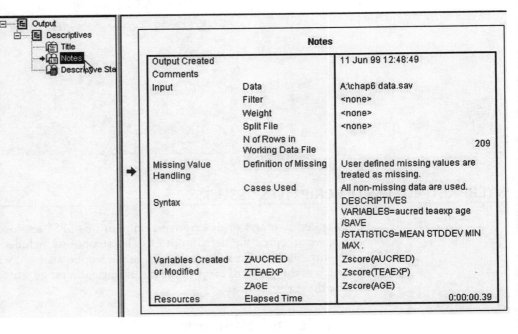

Outline Pane   Output Pane

The final piece of information you requested was a z score for each variable. These z scores have been created and added to your data file. To see confirmation of this, view the **Notes** section in the output viewer. Click on **Notes** in the outline pane to the left of the screen. This will reveal a text box in the output part of the viewer (see Figure 6.7). For each of our variables, a z score has been created. Each of these newly created variables is denoted with a "Z" as the first letter. To confirm the calculation z scores, highlight the icon for **Notes** in the outline pane as illustrated in Figure 6.7. If you examine your data file, these z scores have been added and appear in the last three columns for each subject in our sample.

Output with Additional Options

In the second analysis, you specified several additional descriptive statistics such as the standard error of the mean, variance, range, kurtosis, and skewness. Let's examine a sample of these results. This output appears in Figure 6.8.

Examine the information pertaining to the variable AGE. Many of the statistics reported here are the same as we examined earlier using the default options. Again, you will find information regarding the mean, standard deviation, minimum, and maximum. One new statistic is the standard error of the mean. This value provides an estimate of how well the sample mean estimates the population mean. The standard error of the mean is .62 for AGE. The standard error of the mean is a standard deviation. Specifically, this value repre-

	N	Range	Minimum	Maximum	Mean		Std.	Variance	Skewness		Kurtosis	
	Statistics	Statistics	Statistics	Statistics	Statistics	Std. Error	Statistics	Statistics	Statistics	Std. Error	Statistics	Std.Error
AUCRED	201	85	0	85	20.86	1.38	19.64	385.540	1.064	.172	.573	.341
TEAEXP	209	1	0	1	.64	3.3E-02	.48	.231	−.593	.168	−1.665	.335
AGE	207	37	21	58	32.68	.62	8.90	79.278	.520	.169	−.954	.337
Valid N (listwise)	199											

FIGURE 6.8
Descriptive Statistics Results (with additional statistics)

[handwritten annotations: "look at statistics column", "the higher the value, the less normal", "Neg. = flatter Platykurtic", "Pos. = taller leptokurtic"]

sents the standard deviation of a normal distribution of sample means, with the mean of this distribution being equal to the population mean. We will discuss the sampling distribution of the mean in more detail later when we examine statistical procedures used to compare means (e.g., t-tests, ANOVA).

Using the normal distribution (see Figure 6.1), we can estimate the range in which the population mean for AGE will fall. For example, approximately 68% of the distribution falls within −1 and +1 standard deviations in a normal distribution. Therefore, to determine a range in which the population mean for AGE would fall 68% of the time, you construct a confidence interval using the sample mean (32.68) and the standard error of the mean (.62). If you add and subtract .62 to and from 32.68, you will have constructed a 68% confidence interval. This interval would extend from 32.06 to 33.30.

Several additional measures of variability are reported. We examined the standard deviation in the prior output. Two additional measures of variability are reported in these results. These are the variance and the range. The variance is calculated by squaring the standard deviation. For example, the variance of the AGE variable is reported 79.278, or $(8.90)^2$. The range is simply the difference between the largest and smallest values. The range for AGE is 37, ranging from a minimum of 21 to a maximum of 58.

There are two additional measures reported in this SPSS output that describe the shape of the distribution. These are skewness and kurtosis. The closer these values are to 0, the more likely it is that the variables follow a normal distribution. The skewness for AGE is .520, indicating that there are some extreme scores on the positive, upper end of the distribution. The skewness for AUCRED, however, is larger (1.064). This also indicates more extreme scores at the upper part of the distribution. The kurtosis value is negative (−.954) for AGE and positive (.573) for AUCRED. A negative kurtosis indicates that the distribution is slightly flatter than what you would expect in a normal distribution, while a positive kurtosis identifies a taller distribution.

These two properties are easier to understand through a graph of the distribution. A histogram would be used to display the distribution. This display was an option in the previous chapter when examining the Frequencies procedure. Remember that a normal distribution can also be superimposed on the histogram. There are also a variety of graphs available in SPSS that can be selected from the **Graphs** menu. We will explore some of these in later chapters.

We produced the following histograms using the options available in the Frequencies procedure. To reproduce these from the main menubar:

Step 1	Select **Analyze—Descriptive Statistics—Frequencies**.
Step 2	Select the variables of AGE and AUCRED.
Step 3	Click on the **Charts...** button.
Step 4	Select the **Histograms** option and check the **With normal curve** box.
Step 5	Click **Continue** to return to the Frequencies dialog box and click **OK** to produce the histograms.

The selections made in the Frequencies: Charts dialog box are illustrated in Figure 6.9. The histograms for AGE and AUCRED appear in Figure 6.10A and 6.10B.

We requested that a normal curve be superimposed over these distributions so that you can see the extent to which they deviate from normal. First, let's examine the property of skewness. This value was .520 for AGE and 1.064 for AUCRED. The skewness of AGE is closer to 0, indicating a more symmetrical distribution. Next, examine the property of kurtosis. The distribution of AGE appears to be somewhat flatter than the normal curve, while AUCRED is somewhat taller. The kurtosis value for AGE was reported as −.954, compared to .573 for AUCRED.

We encourage you to examine these descriptive properties for the remaining variables. After you have finished examining these results, try some of the practice exercises at the end of the chapter. Do not forget to save your work before you exit.

FIGURE 6.9
Frequencies: Charts
(histogram and normal
curve)

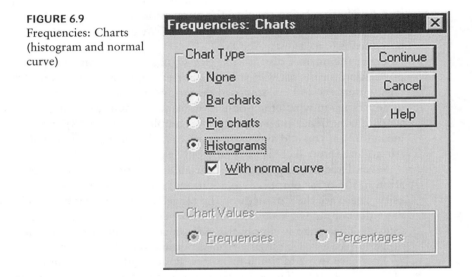

FIGURE 6.10A
Histogram of AGE

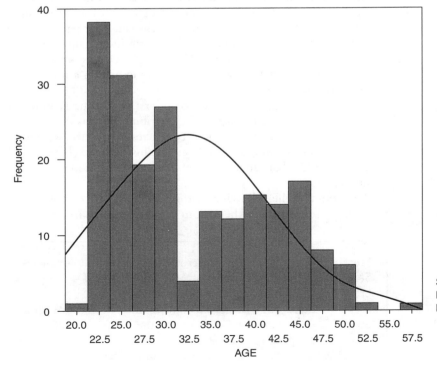

Std. Dev = 8.90
Mean = 32.7
N = 207.00

FIGURE 6.10B
Histogram of
AUCRED

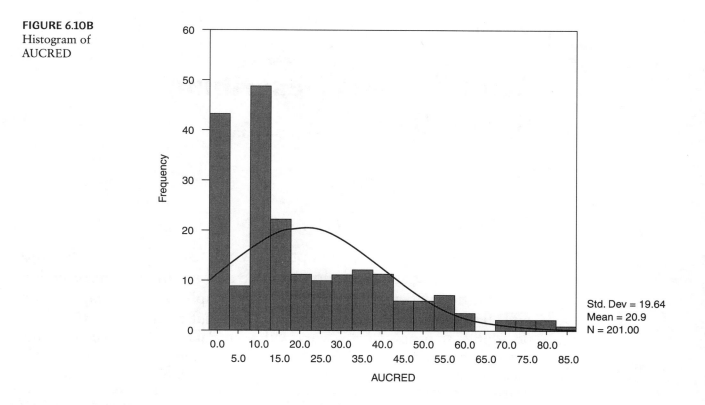

CHAPTER SUMMARY

In this chapter, you used a variety of statistics to describe the central tendency and variability of a sample of graduate students. The mean and standard deviation are the two most common of these descriptive statistics, available as default statistics in SPSS. You used other statistics, such as kurtosis and skewness, to describe the shape of each sample distribution and the standard error of the mean as an index of the extent to which the sample mean represents the population mean. In the next chapter, you will use some of these same descriptive statistics to describe subgroups within the overall sample, such as male and female graduate students.

PRACTICE EXERCISES

Use the data set you created in Chapter 3
(i.e., student admission data).

1. Perform a descriptive analysis for each of the following variables:
   GREQ, GREV, PRETEST, RATING
   a. For each of these variables, report the following descriptive statistics: mean, standard deviation, skewness, kurtosis.
   b. Is our pool of applicants more varied in terms of verbal or quantitative ability? Support this response with the appropriate sample statistics.
   c. Which variable appears to be the most skewed? Report the value that describes this skewness and explain what it means.
   d. Create z scores for each variable and identify which applicant performed better for each of the four variables.
   e. Based on this descriptive information, select three candidates for admission to the doctoral program. Support your decision using information regarding their performance on these four variables.

7

Selecting and Describing Subgroups

In the previous two chapters, you used frequencies and descriptive statistics to help organize and summarize information about different variables for an entire sample. In this chapter, you will first break down the sample into subgroups and then use descriptive statistics. As you work with your data, you will encounter the need to compare two or more subgroups. After you have thoroughly summarized the information for the overall sample, you, or someone else (perhaps a committee member), will wonder what the data might look like if it were broken down into subgroups. For instance, there is a story about a data analysis specialist who was asked by the boss, "How many employees do we have broken down by sex?" To which, the reply was: "None, most of our employees are broken down by alcohol."

If gender were an important variable in your data set, for example, separate descriptive summaries of males and females would be valuable so that you could compare the responses of males with those of females. Furthermore, this breakdown is essential for other statistical procedures such as t-tests and ANOVA, which are used to compare group means.

Using SPSS, the selection of subgroups for analysis can be done in several ways. If you are interested in only a comparison of means and standard deviations across subgroups, the Means procedure is appropriate. However, if you want to obtain frequencies or perform other statistical procedures for each subgroup, you must first select the cases that belong to the subgroup and then perform your analysis, filtering out all other cases. First, let's examine the variables that we will use in this chapter.

VARIABLES USED IN THIS CHAPTER

Subgroups can be formed using any combination of variables. We have already examined several variables from the computer and statistics attitude data set that can be used for subgroup analysis. Simple subgroups can be formed using levels of existing variables, such as gender, course section, and computer experience. For gender, two subgroups would be formed. Also, there are eight different sections of this particular beginning statistics course and five levels of computer experience.

Subgroups, however, are not limited to existing levels for variables in a data set. You can combine variables to create more specific subgroups. For example, you might want to examine males and females separately, broken down by levels of computer experience. There are five different levels of computer experience and two levels of gender. As a result of this breakdown, ten subgroups would be formed. As long as you can specify the conditions that define a subgroup, SPSS will be able to create it.

Throughout the remainder of this chapter, we will use SPSS to describe subgroups in our sample. Specifically, we will use three variables to form subgroups, including gender

(GENDER), computer experience (COMPEXP), and teaching experience (TEAEXP). Once we have formed subgroups, we will use three other variables as dependent variables. These include age (AGE), hours worked each week (EMPHOURS), and hours committed to other activities and organizations (OTHHOURS).

USING SPSS TO DESCRIBE SUBGROUPS

In the previous two chapters, we described several variables regarding graduate students' attitudes toward computers and statistics using the Frequencies and Descriptives procedures. In this chapter, we will first select subgroups from our overall sample and then describe these subgroups.

We will be using the same data, so you should retrieve the data from your disk. As a reminder, you can open a data file from the **File** menu or by using the disk icon from the toolbar. Retrieve the data, **chap7 data,** and we'll get started.

There are several ways to describe subgroups using SPSS. We will illustrate two procedures. First, **Select Cases...** can be used to select a subgroup of cases according to your specifications. Once a subgroup is selected, any SPSS procedure can be applied. The second procedure used to identify and describe subgroups is the Means procedure. The Means procedure can be used to compare the means and standard deviations of subgroups from existing variables in your data set.

SELECT CASES COMMANDS

Subgroups can be selected in SPSS for Windows using the Select Cases command. The Select Cases commands are accessed through the **Data** menu. This is the same menu you used in Chapter 5 to define your variables and values. From the **Data** menu, choose the **Select Cases...** option, as illustrated in Figure 7.1.

The Select Cases dialog box, which is displayed in Figure 7.2, is used to select cases meeting your specifications. Notice that the first option in this box, **All cases,** is selected. This means that the overall sample has been selected for your analysis. Unless you change this option, SPSS will use all available cases. Other options are available for selecting subgroups.

The option labeled **If condition is satisfied** allows you to specify the conditions that define a subgroup. For example, if you wish to select only males, which are coded as "1," you

FIGURE 7.1
Data–Select Cases
menu selections

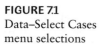

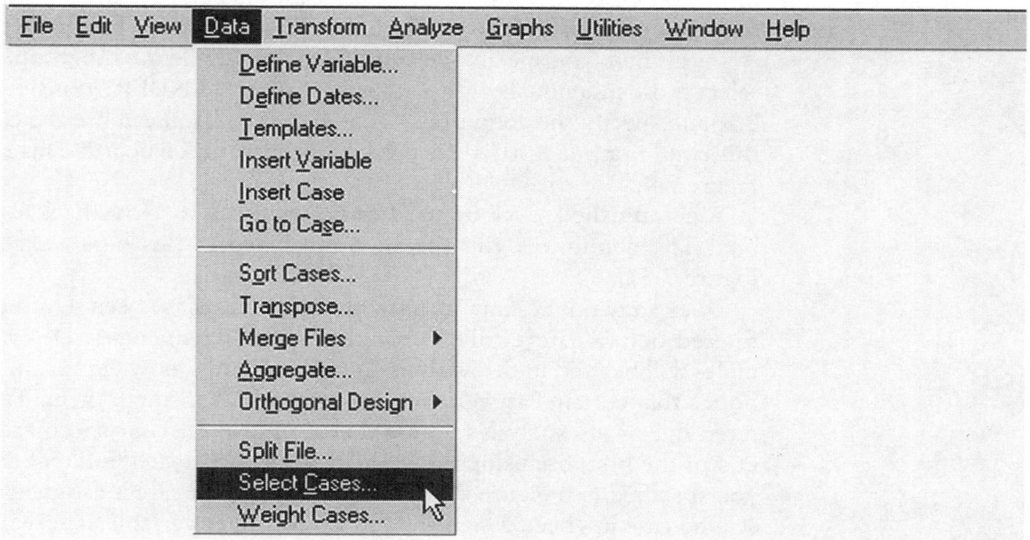

File Edit View **Data** Transform Analyze Graphs Utilities Window Help

- Define Variable...
- Define Dates...
- Templates...
- Insert Variable
- Insert Case
- Go to Case...

- Sort Cases...
- Transpose...
- Merge Files ▶
- Aggregate...
- Orthogonal Design ▶

- Split File...
- Select Cases...
- Weight Cases...

FIGURE 7.2
Select Cases dialog box

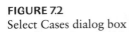

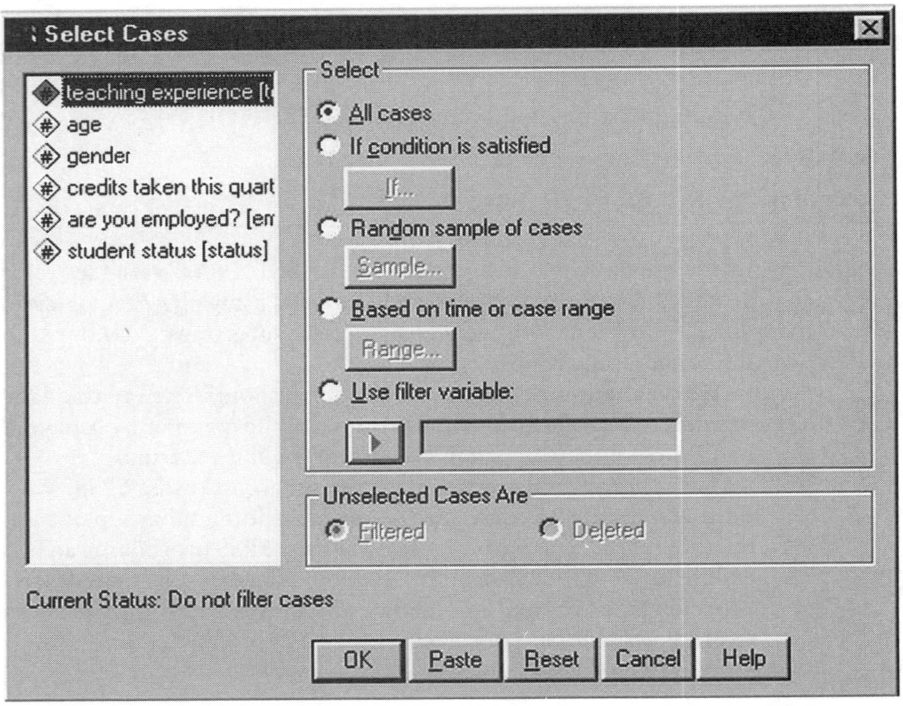

would specify that only those cases with a value of 1 for GENDER be selected for the analysis. The next option, **Random sample of cases,** is used to draw a random sample from your data set. Choosing the option **Based on time or case range** is useful when you want to select a range of cases according to the order in which they appear in the Data Editor. This option is useful when performing time series analysis. The final option is labeled **Use filter variable.** Choosing this option will allow you to filter out cases having a value of "0" on any specified variable.

If Condition Is Satisfied

First, we'll illustrate how to use the option **If condition is satisfied.** For this option, you specify the conditions used to define a subgroup. We'll select males, identified with a value of "1" on GENDER. From the Select Cases dialog box (see Figure 7.2), select this option and click on the **If...** button. The Select Cases: If dialog box in Figure 7.3 will appear.

In this box, you specify the conditions that define the subgroup. In our case, we want to select those individuals with a value of "1" for GENDER. Transfer GENDER to the upper box and specify the condition "GENDER = 1." You can use the calculator pad to express this condition, or just type it directly using your keyboard. This condition is specified in Figure 7.4.

When finished, click on the **Continue** button to arrive back at the Select Cases dialog box. The conditions you specified are listed in this box, next to the **If...** button (see Figure 7.5).

To execute this command, click on **OK.** Males have been selected and females have been filtered out. Whatever SPSS procedures (e.g., Frequencies, Descriptives) you select, only males will be used in the analysis. Your data should now appear on the screen, and you will notice that certain case numbers have a slash (/) through them. These cases have been filtered out of the analysis because they do not meet your specifications. Also, move to the end of the first case using the <End> key. SPSS created a filter variable to select the cases you specified (see Figure 7.6). Notice that the first case is assigned a value of "0" while the second case has been assigned a "1" on this filter variable. Those cases with a value of "0"

FIGURE 7.3
Select Cases: If dialog
box

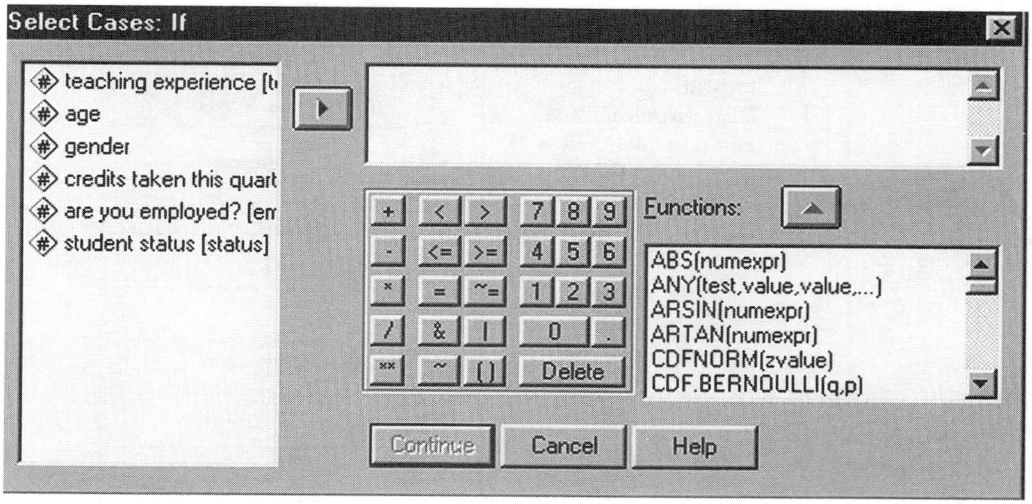

FIGURE 7.4
Select Cases: If dialog
box (GENDER = 1)

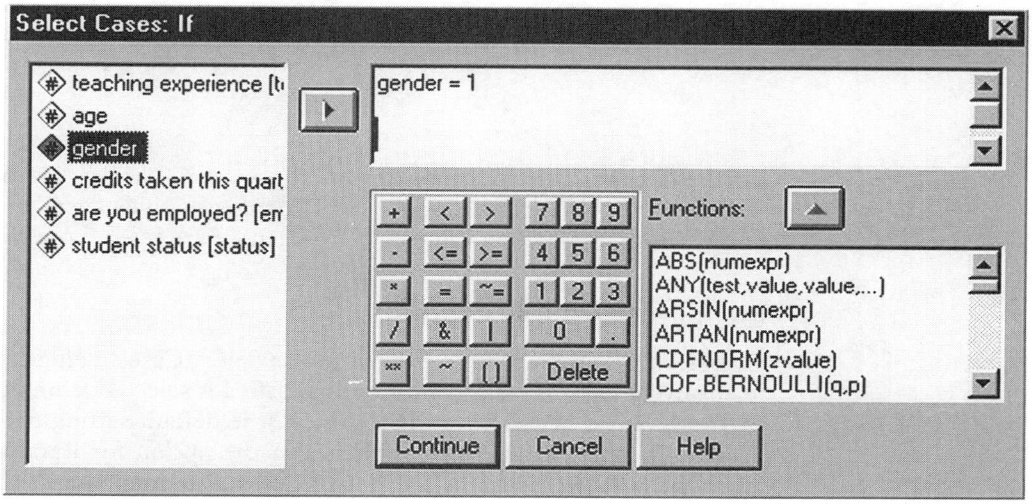

FIGURE 7.5
Select Cases dialog box
(If GENDER = 1)

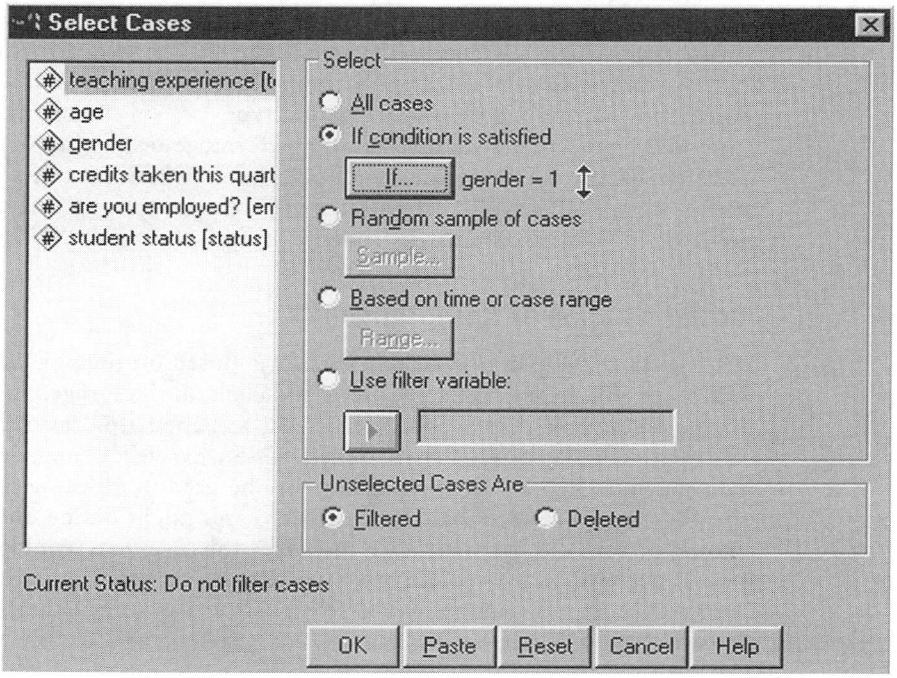

FIGURE 7.6
Filter variable in Data
Editor (If GENDER = 1)

	gender	filter_$
1	2	0
2	1	1
3	2	0
4	2	0
5	2	0
6	2	0
7	2	0
8	1	1
9	2	0
10	2	0

on the filter variable are dropped from the analysis. Notice that those cases with a "1" on the filter variable also have a value of "1" on the variable of gender, which is what you specified. Those cases with a value of "2" on gender are filtered out of the analysis.

Random Sample of Cases

To select a random sample, return to the Select Cases dialog box (located in the **Data** menu). The option for **If condition is satisfied** is selected from our previous illustration. If you had just begun your SPSS session, the default setting for **All cases** would be selected. To select a random sample, select the option for **Random sample of cases** and click the **Sample...** button. The Select Cases: Random Sample dialog box, displayed in Figure 7.7, will appear.

You can specify a random sample in two ways. The first method is by indicating the approximate percentage of cases you wish to sample. If you want to sample 25% from the date set, then type "25" in the box next to the %. The second method requires you to specify the exact number of cases you want in the random sample. If we wanted to sample fifty cases from our sample of 209, we would type "50" in the first box and "209" in the second box. Once you have identified the percentage or number of cases, click on **Continue** to arrive back at the Select Cases dialog box and **OK** to execute the Random Sample command. Again, SPSS will create a filter variable, consisting of 1s and 0s. The cases with a value of "0" will be eliminated from the analysis.

Based on Time or Case Range

The next available option to select cases is **Based on time or case range.** To choose this option, highlight the circle next to it and click on the **Range...** button. The Select Cases: Range dialog box, displayed in Figure 7.8, will appear. In this dialog box, you must identify the first and last case to be sampled. SPSS will select a subgroup which spans the range you specify. This option is more likely to be used in a time series situation where cases can be selected in sections. The first fifty cases might define one section or interval and should be selected for analysis. If this were the case, you would specify a "1" in the first box and a "50" in the second box. The first fifty cases will be selected for your analysis. To execute such a command and select this sample, click on the **Continue** button, followed by the **OK** button.

FIGURE 7.7
Select Cases: Random
Sample dialog box

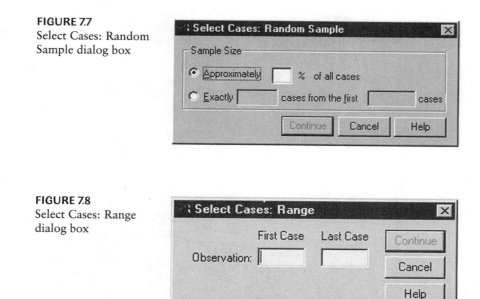

FIGURE 7.8
Select Cases: Range
dialog box

Use Filter Variable

The final option available to select a subgroup is to use a pre-existing variable as a filter variable. If your data set contains a variable which has values of "0," you can specify a filter variable. Choosing the final option, **Use filter variable,** allows you to use an existing variable as a filter variable. In our data set, the variable of teaching experience (TEAEXP) is coded using 1s and 0s. A "1" indicates that the student has some teaching experience, while a "0" indicates that the student has no teaching experience. If we use TEAEXP as a filter variable, those students with no teaching experience will be filtered out.

Select this option by highlighting the circle next to it. To identify TEAEXP as the filter variable, select it from the source variable box and transfer it to the filter variable box using the arrow button, or by double-clicking on the variable name. The Select Cases dialog box should look like that displayed in Figure 7.9.

The filtered sample will be drawn by clicking on the **OK** button. If you examine your data, you will see that all subjects with no teaching experience have been filtered out. Until you change the filter, all subsequent analyses would be performed only on students having teaching experience.

We encourage you to try the practice exercises pertaining to the selection of cases at the end of the chapter. If you are exiting SPSS for Windows, save any SPSS output you may have generated. If you are continuing to follow the illustrations in this chapter, return to the Select Cases dialog box and select the option for **All cases** because we will be using every case with the Means procedure in the next section.

As a reminder, use the **Data** menu and choose the **Select Cases...** option. This will open the Select Cases dialog box in which you select the option for **All cases.** Another way to eliminate the filter variable is to simply delete it from the data editor. To do so, click on the grey column heading above the filter variable to highlight the variable column and hit the <Delete> key.

FIGURE 7.9
Select Cases dialog
box: using teaching
experience (TEAEXP)
as a filter variable

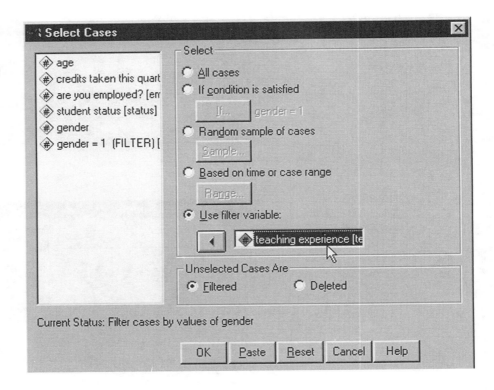

MEANS PROCEDURE

The Means procedure is used to describe levels of existing variables in your data set. As you did with the Frequencies and Descriptives procedures, you begin with the **Analyze** menu. From this menu, select the **Compare Means** and **Means...** options as illustrated in Figure 7.10.

Selecting these options will open the Means dialog box, displayed in Figure 7.11.

In this dialog box, you will recognize many features. The source variable list which contains the names of all the variables in your data set appears at the left. As with previous SPSS procedures, you select variables from this list and place them in one of two boxes to the right. The first box, labeled Dependent List, is where you identify the dependent variable or variables. The dependent variable is the variable you wish to describe.

Before we specify variables for the Means procedure, let's explore the available options. Click on the **Options** button to reveal the Means: Options dialog box as displayed in Figure 7.12.

The default options have already been selected. These include the mean, number of cases (count), and standard deviation. These options appear under the Cell Statistics heading. There are a few other options available. We could also calculate the variance and sum for these data. There are additional options listed in this box labeled Statistics for First Layer. You would use the first option to request an analysis of variance (ANOVA) for the data and the second option for tests of linearity. We will explore these options in greater detail using other SPSS procedures. The default options are fine for our purposes. Be sure that the default options are selected (Mean, Standard Deviation, and Number of Cases) and continue with your analysis by clicking on the **Continue** button to return to the Means dialog box.

Tables with One Independent Variable

These tables display statistics (e.g., means, standard deviations) for a dependent variable for each level of the independent variable. For this illustration, select age (AGE) and credits taken during the current quarter (CREDNOW) as the dependent variables by placing

FIGURE 7.10
Analyze–Compare
Means–Means menu
selections

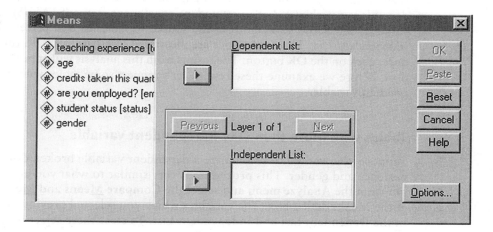

FIGURE 7.11
Means dialog box

FIGURE 7.12
Means: Options dialog
box

FIGURE 7.13
Specifications for one
independent variable
using Means Procedure

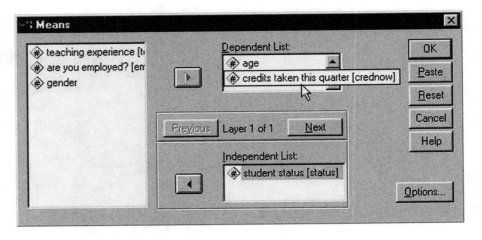

them in the Dependent List box using the arrow button. Next, we need to identify the independent variable(s). Let's use student enrollment status (STATUS) as the independent variable. Select this variable from the source variable list and place it in the box labeled Independent List. These selections are illustrated in Figure 7.13. To run the Means procedure, click on the **OK** button. The results from this analysis will appear in your output window. Before we examine these results, let's request some tables with more than one independent variable.

Tables with More than One Independent Variable

Suppose you wanted to summarize a dependent variable broken down by computer experience and gender. This procedure is very similar to what you just did. Again, you begin from the **Analyze** menu and select the **Compare Means** and **Means** options to arrive at the Means dialog box. The variables which you selected previously should still appear in the Dependent List and Independent List. To clear these selections, click on the **Reset** button.

For this illustration, we will summarize the variables of AGE and CREDNOW, broken down by student enrollment status (STATUS) and employment status (EMPLOYED). The selection of the dependent variable(s) is just as you've previously done for a one-way table. In this case, select the dependent variables AGE and CREDNOW and place them in the Dependent List box.

The selection of the independent variables is different. They will still be placed in the Independent List box. However, you will be creating layers of a two-way table with each independent variable representing a different layer. First, select STATUS and place it in the Independent List box. Notice the two buttons above this box labeled **Previous** and **Next**. These buttons are used to identify layers of your output. Between these buttons, a message reads Layer 1 of 1. This means you have identified one layer of independent variables that includes STATUS. We want to identify a second layer that will include the variable EMPLOYED. To identify the second layer, click on the **Next** button. An empty Independent List box should appear. Select EMPLOYED and place it in this box. You can move between layers using the **Previous** and **Next** buttons. Each layer should have one independent variable, as illustrated below in Figure 7.14.

If these layers are identified correctly, continue with the analysis by clicking on the **Continue** button. To run this procedure, click on the **OK** button. This procedure will produce two tables, one for each dependent variable. If you wanted to add a third independent variable, you could create a third layer by using the **Next** button. In the next section, we will examine the output that was generated earlier in this chapter using the Means procedure.

FIGURE 7.14

Specifications for a
Means Table with two
independent variables

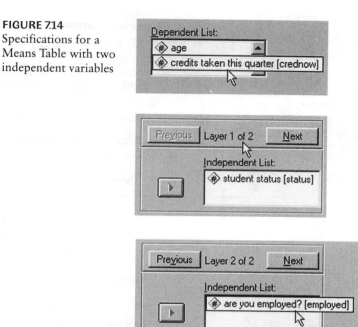

INTERPRETING SPSS MEANS RESULTS

You generated several Means tables in this SPSS session. In this section of the chapter, we will discuss samples from your SPSS output.

Table with One Independent Variable

In the first table, we summarized the variables AGE and AUCRED by different levels of computer experience. This table appears in Figure 7.15.

The results for both dependent variables are presented in one table. Earlier SPSS versions for the Windows 3.1 environment (version 6.X) presented a separate table for each dependent variable. Locate these tables from your output so we can begin to make sense of them. The basic information summarized in these tables includes the mean, standard deviation, and the number of cases in each subgroup. The information for the overall group is reported in the last row of the table. Let's take a closer look at some of the subgroup information.

Examine the subgroup means for credits taken during the quarter (CREDNOW) for part- and full-time students. For the fifty-eight part-time students, the average number of credits taken is reported as 7.03. However, the average number of credits reported for the 149 full-time students is 12.21. Of course, we would expect part-time students to be enrolled in fewer credits for the quarter. Many part-time students have obligated their time to other things such as work and family. Therefore, they aren't able to take as many courses. Take a look at the standard deviations reported for each subgroup. The variability is higher for part-time students (3.07 vs. 2.26). This also makes sense, as part-time students might enroll in one course or four courses in a given quarter, but full-time students would have to consistently enroll in three or four courses per quarter to maintain their full-time status.

Examine the information pertaining to the dependent variable AGE. As you might expect, part-time students are older. The average age is reported as 38.81, compared to 30.29 for full-time students. It appears that more full-time students enter graduate school soon after receiving their undergraduate degree, whereas part-time students return to graduate school several years after finishing their college.

FIGURE 7.15
Means Results
(STATUS)

Case Processing Summary

	Cases					
	Included		Excluded		Total	
	N	Percent	N	Percent	N	Percent
AGE *Student Status	207	99.0%	2	1.0%	209	100.0%
credits taken this quarter *student status	207	99.0%	2	1.0%	209	100.0%

Report

Student Status		AGE	Credits Taken This Quarter
Part-Time	Mean	38.81	7.03
	N	58	58
	Std. Deviation	7.64	3.07
Full-Time	Mean	30.29	12.21
	N	149	149
	Std. Deviation	8.21	2.26
Total	Mean	32.68	10.76
	N	207	207
	Std. Deviation	8.90	3.42

Table with Two Independent Variables

You generated a table summarizing each of the dependent variables by the variables of student status (STATUS) and employment status (EMPLOYED). The information for both dependent variables is summarized in the same table. In this section, however, we'll focus on the information regarding the dependent variable of credits taken during the quarter (CREDNOW). This information is displayed in Figure 7.16.

This table is more complex than the previous one. Once again, the means, standard deviations, and number of cases for the overall group (N = 207) are reported. Instead of having just the two subgroups like the previous table, four different subgroups are reported. The largest of these four subgroups is the employed, full-time students (n = 107), while the smallest is the non-working, part-time students (n = 7).

As with the previous table, the lowest means are reported for the part-time students and the highest means belong to full-time students. However, this table offers us more. We can examine the means for those students who are employed and those who are not employed at each level of student status. Examine the means reported for part-time students.

The mean for part-time students who are not employed is 9.0, compared to 6.76 for those part-time students who are employed. Students who are not working have time to enroll in more classes. This pattern is not as evident for full-time students. Those full-time students who are not working are enrolled in an average of 12.45 credits. This is only slightly higher than those full-time students who are employed, as they averaged 12.11 credits for the quarter.

After examining the tables generated for the dependent variable of age, we encourage you to try the practice exercises with the Means procedure at the end of the chapter. If you are exiting SPSS, save your output. To keep your files organized, name this output file **chap7.spo**. We will use some features from the SPSS viewer to modify the format of this output in the following section of this chapter.

FIGURE 7.16
Means Results
(STATUS by
EMPLOYED)

Report

Student Status	Are You Employed?		AGE	Credits Taken This Quarter
Part-Time	Not Employed	Mean	39.57	9.00
		N	7	7
		Std. Deviation	10.80	3.27
	Employed	Mean	38.71	6.76
		N	51	51
		Std. Deviation	7.24	2.97
	Total	Mean	38.81	7.03
		N	58	58
		Std. Deviation	7.64	3.07
Full-Time	Not Employed	Mean	29.88	12.45
		N	41	42
		Std. Deviation	8.75	1.86
	Employed	Mean	30.44	12.11
		N	108	107
		Std. Deviation	8.03	2.40
	Total	Mean	30.29	12.21
		N	149	149
		Std. Deviation	8.21	2.26
Total	Not Employed	Mean	31.29	11.96
		N	48	49
		Std. Deviation	9.59	2.41
	Employed	Mean	33.09	10.39
		N	159	158
		Std. Deviation	8.67	3.60
	Total	Mean	32.68	10.76
		N	207	207
		Std. Deviation	8.90	3.42

USING THE OUTPUT VIEWER

In this section of the chapter, we will modify the format of our output so that it is more suitable for presentations and manuscripts. Let's use the Means table displayed in Figure 7.15. This table is presented in the default style used by SPSS.

Highlight this in your output pane by double-clicking your mouse anywhere in the table. The table should be outlined in a grey border with a red arrow pointing from the left. Since we are modifying the format in which this table is presented, select the **TableLooks...** option from the **Format** menu, as illustrated in Figure 7.17.

This will open the TableLooks dialog box (see Figure 7.18). A long list of TableLook Files will appear in the box to the left. For this illustration, select the **Academic** setting. Click on the **Save Look** button and **OK** to make this change and return to the output table. The format of the output table has been changed. This academic format is more suitable for presentations and manuscripts.

This new output table is displayed in Figure 7.19.

Return to the TableLooks dialog box and try a few other formats, to see which style you prefer. We'll explore other features in later chapters. Don't forget to save the output before you exit SPSS.

FIGURE 7.17
Format–TableLooks menu selections

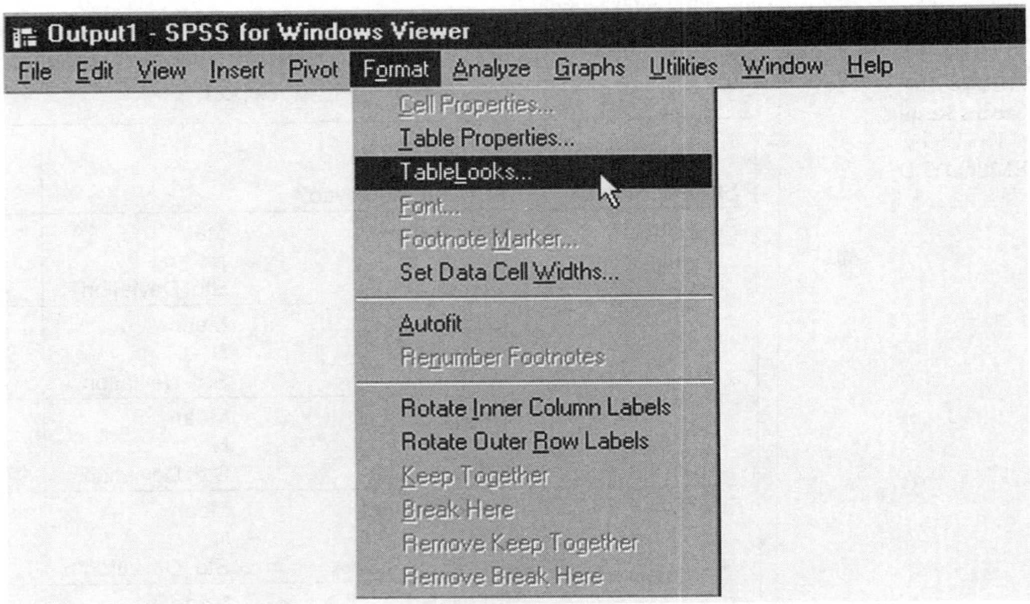

FIGURE 7.18
TableLooks dialog box
(Academic setting)

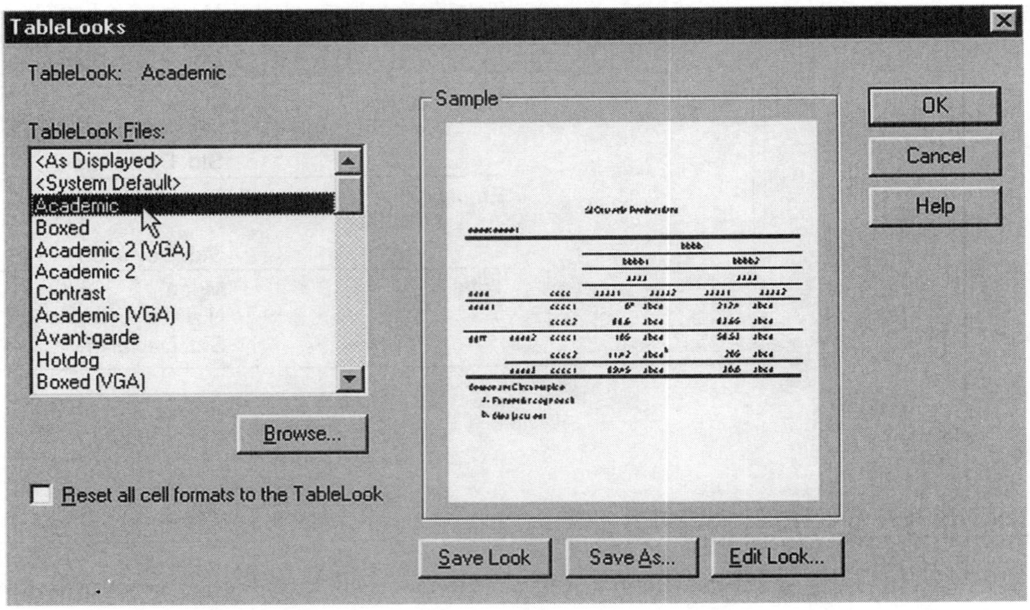

FIGURE 7.19
Means Report Table in
Academic format

Report

Student Status		Age	Credits Taken This Quarter
Part-Time	Mean	38.81	7.03
	N	58	58
	Std. Deviation	7.64	3.07
Full-Time	Mean	30.29	12.21
	N	149	149
	Std. Deviation	8.21	2.26
Total	Mean	32.68	10.76
	N	207	207
	Std. Deviation	8.90	3.42

CHAPTER SUMMARY

In this chapter, you used the Select Cases and Means procedures to select subgroups from your overall sample. Using the output from the Means procedure, you were able to look for possible patterns when comparing means across the various subgroups. In the next chapters, you will be exploring patterns in data using various measures of association.

PRACTICE EXERCISES

Use the data set you created in Chapter 3 (i.e., student admission data).

1. Use the Select Cases procedure to answer the following questions.
   a. What is the average GREQ score of students from a lower SES background?
   b. What is the average rating of female students? For Rating1 & Rating2
   c. What is the average GREV for students who received a rating of 8 or above?

2. Use the Select Cases procedure to select a random sample of five students. Repeat this procedure five times and list the ID numbers of the students in each sample.

	ID numbers
Sample 1	
Sample 2	
Sample 3	
Sample 4	
Sample 5	

   a. How many students were selected in more than one of the five random samples?
   b. Were any students not sampled at all?

3. Use the Means procedure to generate the following summary tables.
   a. Summarize GREV and GREQ scores by GENDER.
   b. Summarize GREV and GREQ scores by SES.
   c. Summarize GREV and GREQ scores by GENDER *and* SES.

SECTION III

Transforming Data and Creating New Variables

8 | Recoding Variables

In Chapters 5 and 6, you used frequencies and descriptive statistics to summarize "raw" data. These data are referred to as raw data because they haven't been changed in any way. Sometimes it is necessary to change the data before you begin your analyses. We are certainly not suggesting that you go about changing your data simply because you don't like the way it looks. However, there will be occasions when you find mistakes in the datafile which you can and should correct. When corrections need to be made for individual cases, it is a simple matter to highlight the incorrect cell and make the necessary changes. However, if you had to change something for all the cases in your data set, highlighting and changing each cell could take a great deal of time and effort.

The techniques that we explore in this chapter will allow you to change existing variables or create new variables using data transformation procedures in SPSS. These procedures will allow you to transform the data for some or all cases on one or more variables much more easily and accurately than doing so on a case-by-case basis. In this chapter, you'll use the Recode procedure to transform existing variables in the data set. In the next chapter, you'll use the Compute procedure. Let's begin with a discussion of data transformation techniques and some reasons why you might want to recode data.

RECODING VARIABLES

Recoding existing variables results in a change in the values that define the original variable. You can either change these values and retain the variable or create a new variable. You may want to recode existing variables or create new ones for various reasons. We will describe a few of these reasons and then illustrate some examples using SPSS.

RECODING EXISTING VARIABLES

It is often necessary to recode data before the appropriate analysis can be performed. Perhaps the most common application of recoding is made when scoring raw data. Using SPSS to score instruments as well as manipulate the resulting scores often requires that you enter individual item responses as variables. Often, the computing of scores as a function of a set of items requires you to make systematic changes to one or more items. One common instance of such systematic manipulation of items is called reverse coding. This applies to items that are worded negatively on a survey instrument and need to have their values reversed before a total score is computed. Another example of recoding involves the combining of categories for a given variable into a broader category, such as the collapsing of the categories "General Motors", "Ford", and "Chrysler", into the broader category "American cars." Let's look at some more explicit examples of situations that require data transformation.

Scoring a Test

Before you score a test, you would have first coded the data from this test and entered each person's responses to each question into an SPSS data file. In this case, each person represents a row within the data editor and each item represents a separate variable and thus a separate column. Suppose you had a test that consisted of ten four-option, multiple-choice questions. The easiest way to code a person's responses to these questions would be to assign a "1" if he or she responded using the first option, a "2" for the second option, "3" for the third option, and "4" for the final option. You could just as easily code these data using "A," "B," "C," and "D" to represent the four options (remembering to identify these variables as string variables when you define them.

Once the data are entered in an SPSS file, you would probably want to know how many people got each question correct so that you can determine the difficulty of your test. You can do this by tallying all the responses to each option using the Frequencies command (see Chapter 5) and examining the percentage of people who responded using the correct option. The correct option, however, will not be the same for every question, so you must keep the scoring key handy when examining the results of the frequency analysis. To make the interpretation of these results easier, you might want to score the test items before running the frequency analysis.

You can score the test by recoding each item as either correct or incorrect. When recoding the data, you typically assign the value of "1" to a correct response and "0" to an incorrect response. For example, suppose everyone in your sample was asked the following question:

Which of the following universities has a mascot that is *NOT* a tiger?

A. Auburn
B. Clemson
C. Louisiana State
D. Penn State

The correct response to this question is D because the mascot for Penn State is a nittany lion, not a tiger. In recoding your data, everyone who selected the correct option "D" would receive a value of "1," while everyone who selected "A," "B," or "C" would receive a value of "0." Repeating this recoding procedure for the remaining questions on the test would complete the scoring process. Once all items are scored, a total score can be easily obtained by summing all items. The resulting score represents the number of questions a person answered correctly.

There are several advantages to scoring the data using SPSS procedures. The greatest advantage is time. Using SPSS procedures, the scoring is applied consistently to each person (case), saving you the time and frustration associated with having to physically change each person's responses in the data file. If you were to score each item on the test before entering the data, it would also take much longer. The second advantage is accuracy. If you change each variable on a case-by-case basis, you are more likely to make some mistakes. Using a global recoding procedure will help prevent these mistakes.

Recoding Negatively Worded Items

A related application to scoring a test is recoding negative items from a survey instrument. One of the most common formats used with surveys is a Likert (pronounced "Lick-ert") scale. Using Likert scales, people respond to a series of statements by indicating the extent to which they agree (or disagree) with a given statement. The number of options presented on a Likert scale usually range from two to seven. A few examples are shown in Figure 8.1.

2-point Likert scale:						
Disagree	Agree					
3-point Likert scale:						
Disagree	Neutral	Agree				
4-point Likert scale:						
Strongly Disagree	Disagree	Agree	Strongly Agree			
5-point Likert scale:						
Strongly Disagree	Disagree	Neutral	Agree	Strongly Agree		
6-point Likert scale:						
Strongly Disagree	Slightly Disagree	Disagree	Agree	Slightly Agree	Strongly Agree	
7-point Likert scale:						
Strongly Disagree	Slightly Disagree	Disagree	Neutral	Agree	Slightly Agree	Strongly Agree

FIGURE 8.1
Likert scale examples

Responses to Likert scales are easily coded in numerical order. For example, if a five-point Likert scale were used, responses would be coded from 1 to 5. This makes the entry of data very easy. However, many survey instruments contain negatively worded items, and agreeing to a negative statement is not the same as agreeing to a positive statement. Therefore, before a total score can be determined on the entire survey, the negative items must be reverse coded so that a higher value represents a more positive attitude for each statement.

Let's use the information from our data set as an illustration. A copy of the survey instrument used to gather these data appears in Appendix B. The information regarding attitudes toward computers and statistics is gathered using a four-point Likert scale format. Consider the first two items on the *Survey of Attitudes Toward Learning About and Working With Computers* (Loyd & Gressard, 1984).

1. Computers do not scare me at all.
2. I'm no good with computers.

A person with a positive attitude would most likely agree with the first item because it is positive, but disagree with the second because it is negative. Initially, all items might be coded consistently (e.g., 1=strongly disagree, 2=disagree, 3=agree, and 4=strongly agree). This coding process would make the entry of data easier. However, before these items are combined to form a score for each person, the second item must be recoded.

If you want a higher score to represent a more positive attitude, then these two items would be coded as follows:

1. Computers do not scare me at all (positive item):
   1=strongly disagree, 2=disagree, 3= agree, and 4=strongly agree.

2. I'm no good with computers (negative item):
   4=strongly disagree, 3=disagree, 2=agree, and 1=strongly agree.

Because item 2 is worded negatively, the values assigned to each response are exactly the opposite of those assigned for item 1. Now, when items are combined to form an overall attitude score, a higher value is always associated with a more positive attitude. This process is called reverse coding. All you must do is recode the negative items so that their values are the reverse of the positive items.

Examine the survey instrument in Appendix B. Look over the items regarding attitudes toward working with computers and try to find the ones which should be reverse coded. You should have identified twenty items which are stated negatively. These items appear in Table 8.1. We will illustrate reverse coding using SPSS later in this chapter.

Combining Existing Categories

Recoding may also be necessary when you need to combine categories of a given variable. For a given question (variable) on your measurement instrument, there may be many possible categories. However, when people respond to questions, some categories may not be selected, or you simply don't have a need to retain all the detail that the existing category structure provides.

We mentioned one example involving American cars. A survey may include a question that requires each respondent to select the type of car he or she drives. Some categories may not be chosen very often, and a recoding procedure can be used to group several categories together. Also, the researcher might simply be interested in comparing people who drive American cars and those who drive foreign cars. Should this be the case, responses like "Ford," "General Motors," and "Chrysler" would be coded as "American cars" while categories such as "Honda," "Toyota," and "Nissan" would be categorized as "foreign cars."

TABLE 8.1
Negatively Worded items on Attitudes Toward Computers

Variable	Item from Survey
COMP2	I'm no good with computers.
COMP5	Working with a computer would make me very nervous.
COMP7	The challenge of solving problems with computers does not appeal to me.
COMP8	Learning about computers is a waste of time.
COMP10	I don't think I would do advanced computer work.
COMP13	I feel aggressive and hostile toward computers.
COMP15	Figuring out computer problems does not appeal to me.
COMP18	I'm not the type to do well with computers.
COMP20	I expect to have little use for computers in my daily life.
COMP21	Computers make me feel uncomfortable.
COMP23	I don't understand how some people can spend so much time working with computers and seem to enjoy it.
COMP24	I can't think of any way that I will use computers in my career.
COMP26	I think using a computer would be very hard for me.
COMP29	I get a sinking feeling when I think of trying to use a computer.
COMP31	I will do as little work with computers as possible.
COMP32	Anything that a computer can be used for, I can do just as well some other way.
COMP34	I do not think I could handle a computer course.
COMP37	Computers make me feel uneasy and confused.
COMP39	I do not enjoy talking with others about computers.
COMP40	Working with computers will not be important to me in my life's work.

Suppose people responded to this question by writing in the type of car they drive. With all the types and models of cars manufactured today, there would most likely be a wide variety of responses to this question. Some people are also likely to indicate specific model and types like "Honda Accord EX", while others will simply indicate the manufacturer like "Honda." After coding all responses, you might use a recoding procedure to group similar responses together in broader categories.

Another example regards the item pertaining to computer experience from the *Survey of Attitudes Toward Learning About and Working With Computers*. This item is listed below.

Experience with learning about or working with computers:

( ) 1 week or less
( ) between 1 week and 1 month
( ) between 1 month and 6 months
( ) between 6 months and 1 year
( ) 1 year or more

It is reasonable to expect attitudes toward computers to depend somewhat on a person's experience with computers. Therefore, you might want to compare the attitudes of persons from each of these five categories of experience and determine if their attitudes are different. However, you may find that when all surveys are coded and prepared for analysis, that very few individuals responded using the first two categories: "1 week or less," and "between 1 week and 1 month." Without a sufficient number of people in each of these first two categories, it may be necessary to combine them before performing any further analysis. This is done by recoding each of the first two category values to the same value.

By combining categories, some detail is lost. For example, if these two categories were combined, you could no longer tell whether a person had less than a week of experience or between one week's and one month's experience. All you know is that all individuals in the combined group have one month or less of experience with computers. This loss of detail, however, is often better than the inappropriate application of statistical procedures to groups of only one or two subjects.

RECODING VARIABLES USING SPSS

Before you begin using SPSS to transform data, you need to activate the software and retrieve data into the data editor, as in previous chapters. The data are stored on the enclosed disk as **chap8 data.** Retrieve the data into the data editor and we'll get started.

The recoding of existing variables in SPSS is accomplished by selecting options from a series of menus and dialog boxes. The options available in these menus for the most current version of SPSS software are similar to those in previous versions. Therefore, those of you upgrading from a previous version will have little difficulty.

To recode variables, begin from the main menu bar and select **Transform**. The pull-down menu, displayed in Figure 8.2, should appear.

From this menu, select the fourth option labeled **Recode**. A second menu appears to the right, containing two options. These options are **Into Same Variables...** and **Into Different Variables....** Selecting Into Same Variables will allow you to simply recode the values of the existing variables, whereas the Into Different Variables option creates a new variable based on the recoding of an existing variable. These menu options appear in Figure 8.3.

In other words, if you want to change the values of an existing variable, select **Into Same Variables....** The recoded values will be physically changed and the new values will appear in your data file. If you want to maintain the existing variable as it was originally coded and create a new variable, then you would select **Into Different Variables....** Selecting this option will create a new variable in your datafile.

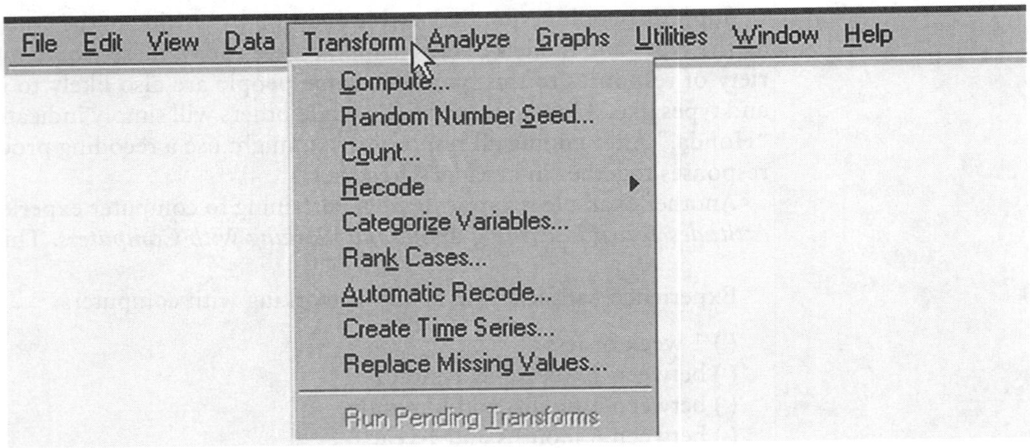

FIGURE 8.2
Transform menu
options

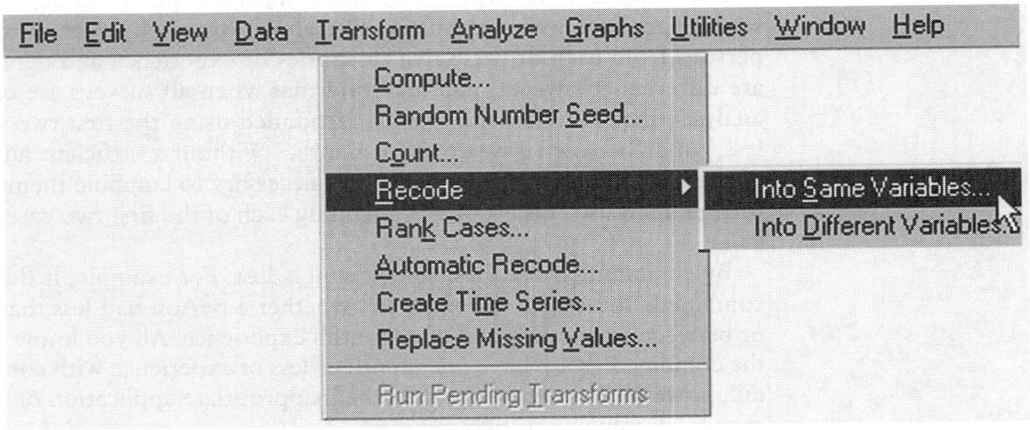

FIGURE 8.3
Transform–Recode–
Into Same Variables
menu selections

We will be recoding the negatively worded items from our survey of graduate students' attitudes toward computers and statistics. Once we recode these items, we will be able to combine them with the positively worded items to form an attitude score for each student. Therefore, we do not need to create different variables, just recode the existing ones. Select the **Into Same Variables...** option, and the dialog box displayed in Figure 8.4 will appear. This screen is called the Recode into Same Variables dialog box.

You've already identified the negatively worded items (see Table 8.1) that we will recode in this session. Locate the source variable list on the left side of the dialog box. Using your mouse, begin by scrolling the list of variables to find the first negatively worded item, COMP2. Single-click your mouse on COMP2 and use the arrow button to transfer it to the selected variable list or double-click on the variable. This variable should now appear in the selected variable list on the right side of the window. Repeat this process for the other variables listed in Table 8.1.

One at a time, select these variables with your mouse and transfer them to the selected variable list using the arrow button. When all of these variables are selected and placed in the selected variable list, you are ready to recode them. There should be twenty variables listed in the selected variable list box, as illustrated in Figure 8.5.

Be sure that the twenty items you have selected are correct. Check them with those in Table 8.1. If any are missing, select them from the source variable list on the left. If any have

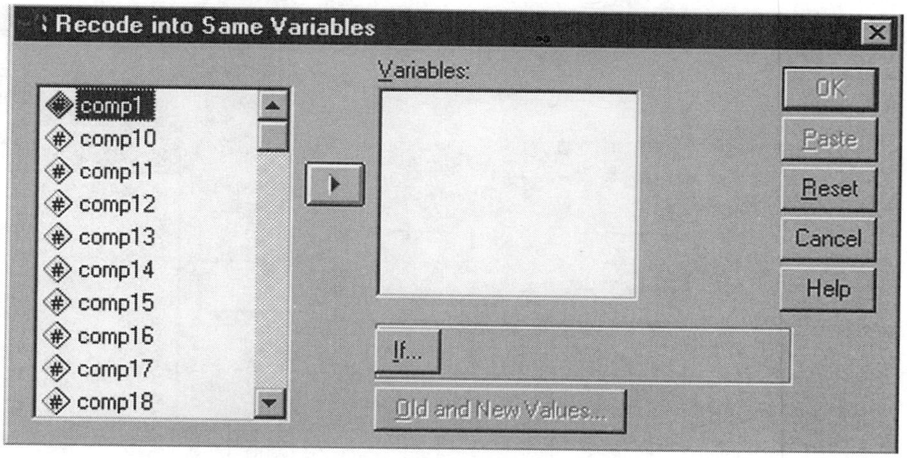

FIGURE 8.4
Recode into Same
Variables dialog box

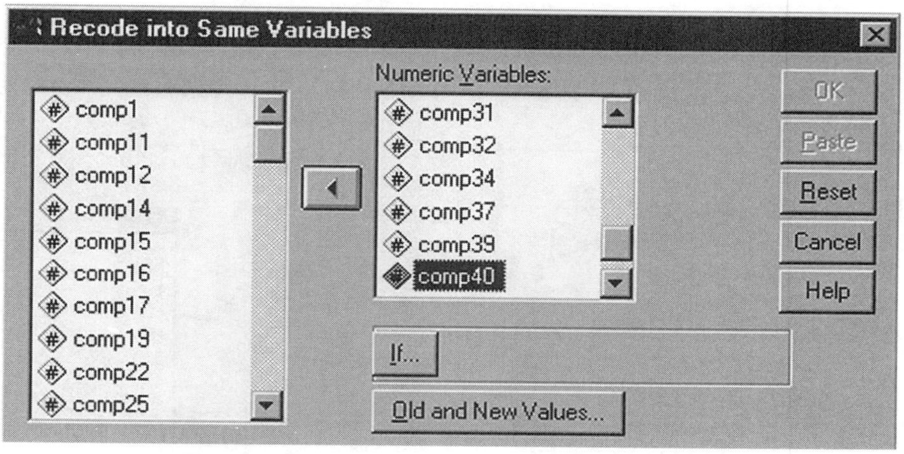

FIGURE 8.5
COMP items selected
to be recoded

been selected by mistake, you can move them back by highlighting the variable and using the arrow button. When everything is correct, continue with the recoding process.

We want to change the values for these selected variables. Click on the **Old and New Values...** button at the bottom of the screen. The Old and New Values dialog box will appear, as in Figure 8.6.

There are two sides to this box for old and new values. You will specify the old values on the left and the new ones on the right. The old values may be specified as specific values, ranges of values, or missing values. As a reminder, all of these items were coded on a four-point Likert scale according to the following guidelines: 1=Strongly Disagree, 2=Disagree, 3=Agree, 4=Strongly Agree.

The cursor is in the Old Value box on the left side of the window waiting for you to specify the first old value. We want to reverse code these items, so the old value of "1" will become a new value of "4." In the Old Value box, type "1." You can use the <Tab> key to move the cursor to the New Value box. Be sure that the cursor is blinking inside the New Value box. You'll have to press the <Tab> key twice. In the New Value box, type "4." Click on the **Add** button and your command will be displayed in the Old -> New box on the right side of the window.

The cursor is waiting for the next value to be recoded in the Old Value box. Type "2" in the Old Value box, hit the <Tab> key twice, and type "3" in the New Value box. Click on the **Add** button and the recode statement is complete. Next, type "3" in the Old Value box

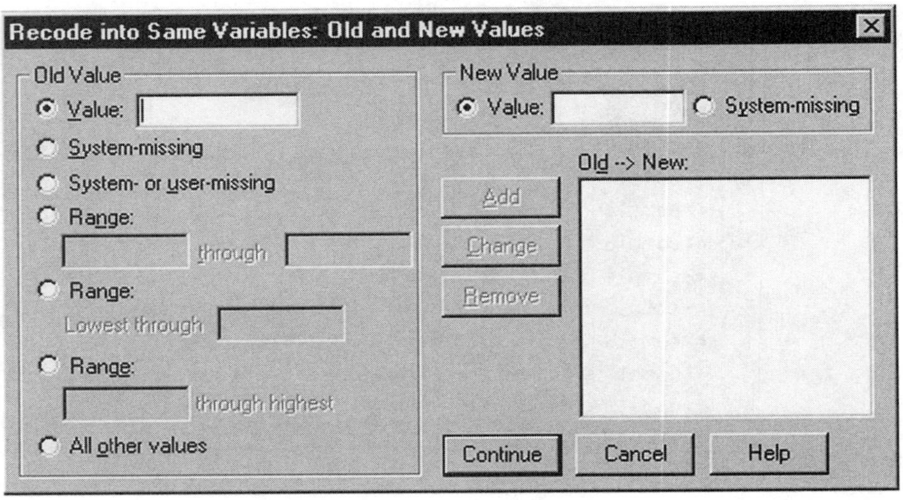

FIGURE 8.6
Recode into Same
Variables: Old and
New Values dialog box

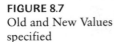

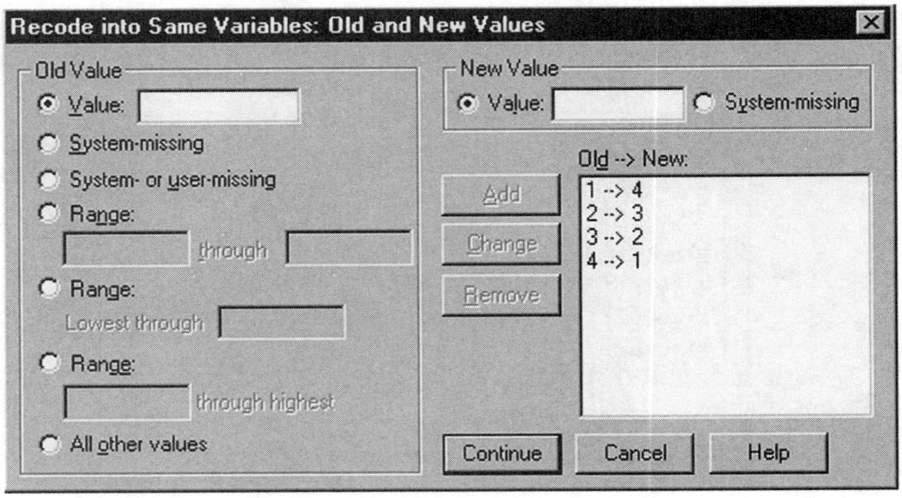

FIGURE 8.7
Old and New Values
specified

and "2" in the New Value box. Finally, "4" should be typed in the Old Value box and "1" in the New Value box. Don't forget to click on the **Add** button after you specify each recode statement. The Old and New Values dialog box now contains all your recoding instructions, as in Figure 8.7.

To continue with the recoding process, click on the **Continue** button at the bottom of the window. You are back to the Recode into Same Variables dialog box, where you first specified the variables to be recoded. To execute your recode commands, click on the **OK** pushbutton at the right of the window. The data editor will appear on your screen and the message "running EXECUTE. . ." will appear at the bottom of the editor in the grey status bar.

The values for the twenty selected variables have now been recoded. For all forty computer attitude items, a higher value now indicates a more positive attitude. Before you sum these items for a total attitude score, you should recode the items relating to attitudes toward statistics. These items were written to parallel the computer items, so the item numbers are exactly the same. Whereas the computer items were identified as COMP1 to COMP40, the statistics items are identified as STAT1 to STAT40. Try to recode the remaining negatively worded items on your own. Use Table 8.1 to be sure that the correct item numbers are identified.

To Recode Variables:

Step 1   From the main menu bar, select **Transform**.
Step 2   Select **Recode**, then select.
               Into Same Variables....
Step 3   Select the variables to be recoded from the source variable list.
Step 4   Select the **Old and New Values...** button.
Step 5   Specify the old and new values.
               Be sure to click on **Add** after each recode statement.
Step 6   When finished with old and new values, click on **Continue**.
Step 7   To execute the recode statements, click on the **OK** button.

You have now recoded all the negatively-worded items from our survey. Before we use these recoded items to create new variables, let's try one more application of recoding existing variables into different variables.

RECODING EXISTING VARIABLES INTO DIFFERENT VARIABLES

You have recoded variables using the Recode procedure and, as a result, your original variables were changed. This is not a problem as long as you no longer need them. In the case of negatively worded items, such as those we recoded, they are more valuable to us since they've been recoded. However, there will be times when you may want to recode an existing variable, but also maintain the original variable. We will explore one such application in this section of the chapter.

Again, you begin from the **Transform** menu and select the **Recode** option. However, because we want to maintain the original variables, select the option for **Into Different Variables...**, as illustrated in Figure 8.8.

This will open the Recode into Different Variables dialog box displayed in Figure 8.9. Many features of this box are identical to the Recode into Same Variables dialog box you used earlier. This dialog box contains the source variable list, **If...**, and **Old and New Values...** option buttons, and the five command pushbuttons. Some of these features appear in different locations than in the earlier dialog box, but they still perform the same functions.

Notice that the heading for the selected variable list box is labeled Input Variable -> Output Variable. The input variable is the original variable from your data set, while the output variable is the new variable that will be created as a result of the recoding process.

FIGURE 8.8
Transform–Recode–
Into Different
Variables menu
selections

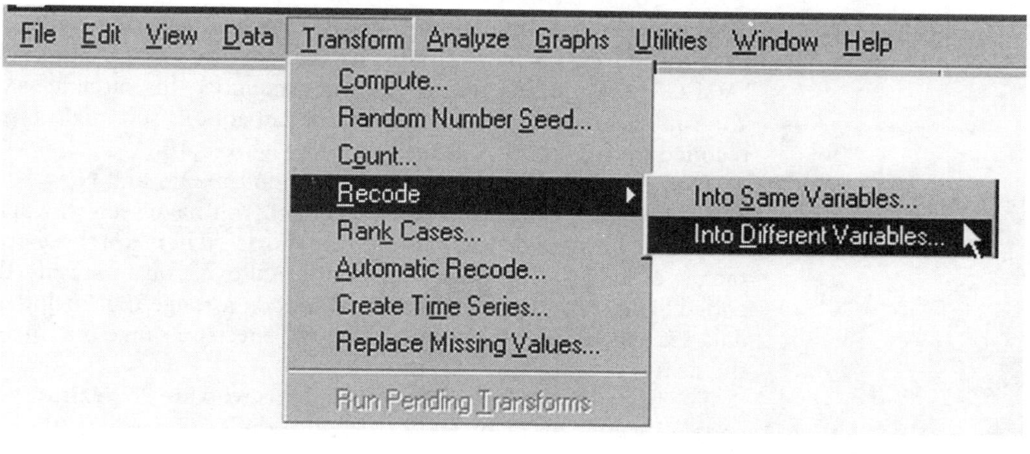

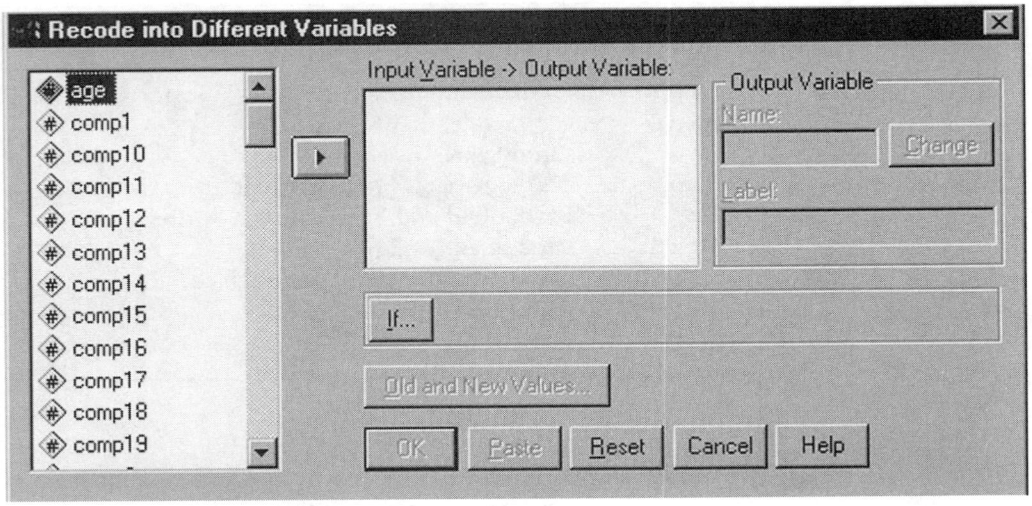

FIGURE 8.9
Recode into Different
Variables dialog box

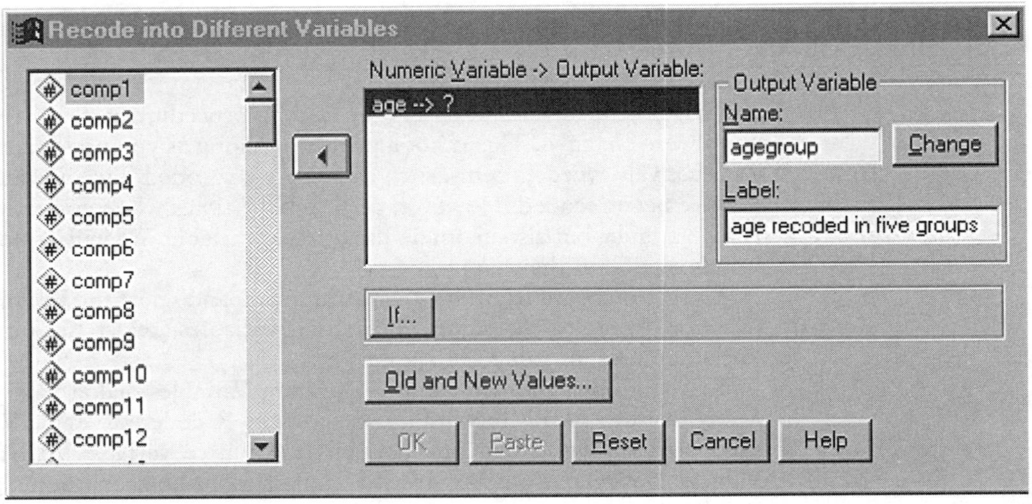

FIGURE 8.10
Output Variable
(AGEGROUP)
identified

To illustrate this process, we will recode age into different categories. The AGE variable exists as a continuous variable in our data set. We want to recode AGE into a categorical variable using the following five categories: 1=25 or under, 2=26–30, 3=31–40, 4=41−50, 5=51 or older.

Transfer AGE to the selected variable list box using the arrow button, as you did in earlier procedures. The new variable name is specified in the Output Variable Name box. Type "AGEGROUP" in this box so you will remember this variable as categories of age groups. You can also type a variable label in the Label box. You might type in something like "age recoded in five groups," as displayed in Figure 8.10.

To specify the old and new values, open the Old and New Values dialog box by clicking on the **Old and New Values...** button. You have seen this dialog box before. We will be recoding ranges of ages into new categories. There are three options available to recode ranges of values. The first **Range** option allows you to specify the exact range to be recoded. The second option is used to specify a range that includes the lowest value in the data set, while the third option is used to specify a range that includes the highest value in the data set.

The first age category identifies students who are 25 years or younger. Therefore, to recode all values of 25 or less as "1", use the option which allows you to specify a range

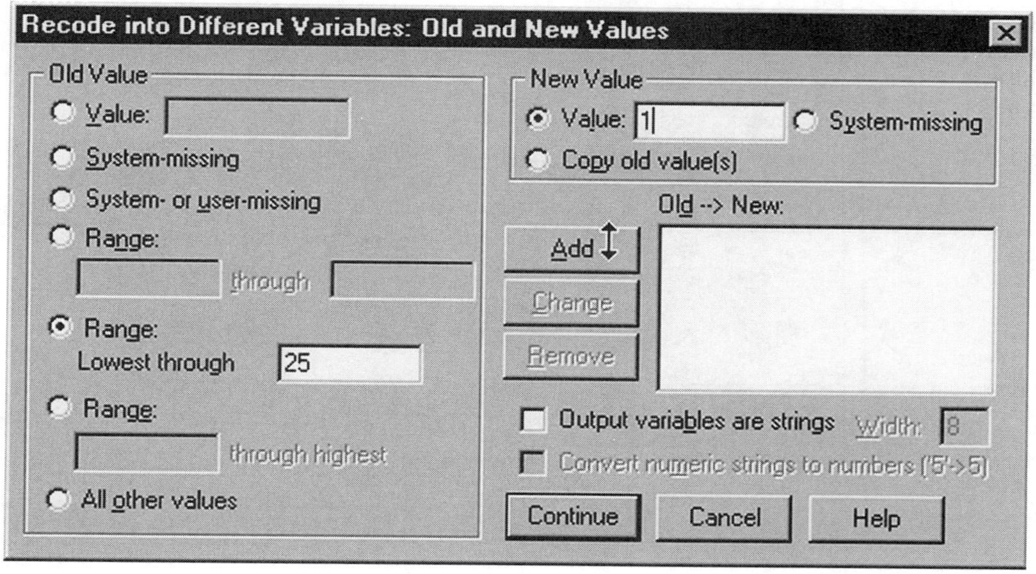

FIGURE 8.11
Recode "Lowest through 25" into new Age category "1"

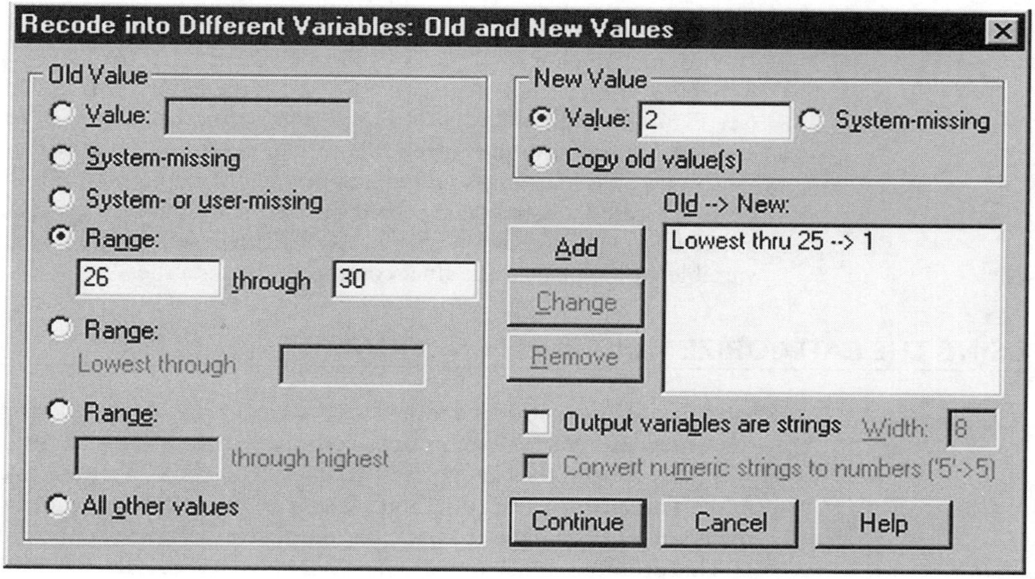

FIGURE 8.12
Recode "26 through 30" into new Age category "2"

from the lowest value in the data set (see Figure 8.11). Specify "25" in Range: Lowest through box and "1" in the New Value box. Click on the **Add** button to implement this change.

The next three age categories will be recoded using the first Range option, which allows you to specify the exact range of values. The second category should include individuals between the ages of 26 and 30. Therefore, select the first Range option (see Figure 8.12) and use the values of "26" and "30" to define this range. In the New Value box, type "2" for the second age category and click on the **Add** button.

Repeat this process for the next two age categories.

Old Value	New Value
Range 5 31 through 40	3
Range 5 41 through 50	4

FIGURE 8.13
Recode "51 through highest" into new Age category "5"

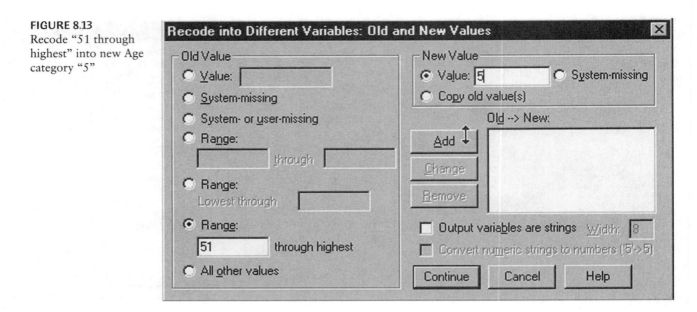

The final category will include all individuals who are 51 years or older. Use the third Range option for this category. Type "51" in the empty box and "5" in the New Value box (see Figure 8.13). Finally, click on the **Add** button to make the change.

Click on the **Continue** button to return to the Recode into Different Variables dialog box.

To make these changes and create the new variable, AGEGROUP, click on the **Change** button, located where you specified the output variable earlier. Click on the **OK** command pushbutton, and the new variable, AGEGROUP, will be created in the data set. This new variable will appear in the final column in the data file.

USING THE CATEGORIZE VARIABLES FUNCTION

SPSS for Windows offers another way to categorize a continuous variable like AGE. Select the **Categorize Variables...** option from the **Transform** menu (see Figure 8.14).

This will open the Categorize Variables dialog box. We want to create five categories for AGE. Therefore, select AGE and place it in the Create Categories box. Next, type "5" in the Number of categories box. The completed dialog box appears in Figure 8.15.

This process is much quicker than having to use the 'Recode into Different Variables' approach, where we had to specify the parameters for each category. The difference is that you decide how you want the variables categorized when you make the specifications. Using the **Categorize Variables...** function will divide the variable into categories using percentiles in the distribution. For example, two categories would be determined by dividing the distribution in half, based on the median, or 50th percentile. To create four categories, the distribution would be divided into quartiles, separated by the 25th, 50th, and 75th percentiles.

We want five categories for AGE. Therefore, the existing variable, AGE, is subdivided into five categories, separated by the 20th, 40th, 60th and 80th percentiles. The first category includes those ages below the 20th percentile. The remaining categories include ages between the 20th to the 40th percentiles, 40th to 60th, 60th to 80th, and 80th and above.

Saving Your Work

Congratulations, you have computed several new variables. We will be using these variables as we explore a variety of statistical procedures in the remaining chapters of this book. Save all your hard work so we can use it later.

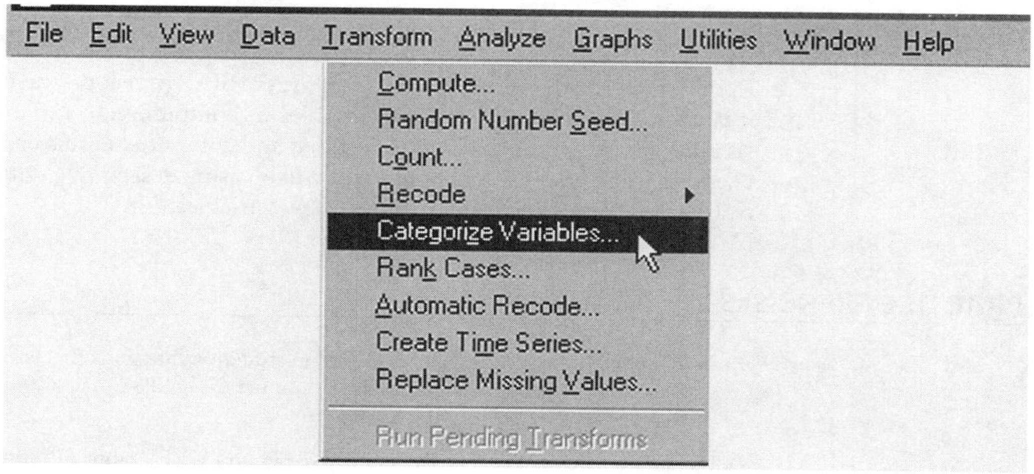

FIGURE 8.14
Transform–Categorize
Variables menu
selections

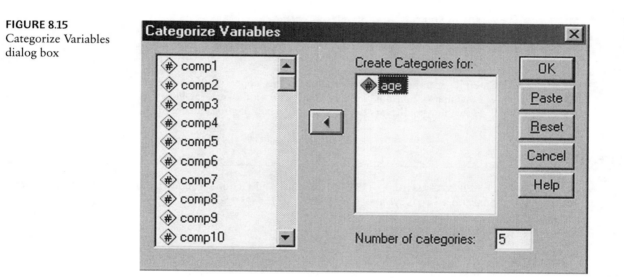

FIGURE 8.15
Categorize Variables
dialog box

These data now contain additional variables that you created from existing variables in the original data set. Since we modified the original data set, it would be a good idea to save the current file as a different name, **new chap8 data.** This name will remind us that the original data file was revised in Chapter 8.

If you need more review on saving SPSS files, see Chapter 2. As a refresher, we have summarized the necessary steps below:

To Save a file:

*Step 1   Select the **File** menu from the main menu bar.
*Step 2   Select the **Save** option.
 Step 3   Specify the drive to which the file will be saved in the Save In box.
 Step 4   Indicate name for file in the File Name box.
 Step 5   Click on the **Save** command pushbutton to save the file.

*The first two steps can also be completed using the save file icon from the toolbar.

CHAPTER SUMMARY

In this chapter, you used several procedures in SPSS to recode and compute variables. Often it is necessary to recode existing variables or compute new variables before further analysis takes place. The variables you recoded and computed in this chapter will be used in later chapters. In the next few chapters, we will be using descriptive statistics to describe the central tendency and variability of these new variables.

PRACTICE EXERCISES

1. In Chapter 3, you created the data file on student admissions (i.e., student admission data.sav).
   a. Describe the process of retrieving a data file using SPSS.
   b. Retrieve this data file using SPSS.

2. Using SPSS, recode each GRE score (GREQ and GREV) into different categorical variables. **BE SURE TO MAINTAIN THE TWO ORIGINAL VARIABLES.**

   1=0 to 400
   2=401 to 500
   3=501 to 600
   4=601 to 700
   5=701 to 800

   Carefully examine these new variables as they appear in the data editor.
   a. How many applicants have a GREQ score in the fifth category (i.e., 701–800)?
   b. How many applicants have a GREV score in the first category (i.e., 0–400)?

REFERENCE

Loyd B & Gressard, C. (1984). Reliability and factional validity of the computer attitude scale. *Educational and Psychological Measurement, 44*(1), 501-505.

9 | Computing New Variables

In the previous chapter, you used the Recode procedure to change the values of existing variables and create new variables. New variables can also be created using the Compute procedure. This is particularly useful when you are combining more than one existing variable to form a new one.

COMPUTING NEW VARIABLES

Often you will want to create a new variable based on some combination of variables which currently exist in your data set. For the majority of survey instruments, existing variables (items) are combined to form a score. Usually, variables are recoded before they are combined to form such a score. This holds true for scoring a test or recoding negative items measured using a Likert scale. Once all variables have been recoded, some type of computing procedure is frequently used to create new variables. New variables are computed using a wide variety of mathematical functions.

One of the most frequently used computing procedures is a sum. Existing variables are added together to get a total score (sum) on a test or survey instrument. An example from our data of applicants to a doctoral program are GRE scores. GRE scores, like SAT scores, are commonly reported as total, or combined scores. In our data, we have GRE-Quantitative (GREQ) and GRE-Verbal (GREV) identified separately. To compute a total GRE score, we would simply sum GREQ and GREV.

From our data regarding graduate students' attitudes toward computers and statistics, we will have several opportunities to create new variables. These attitudes are measured in four areas that include anxiety, confidence, liking, and usefulness. To arrive at a score for each of these four areas, specific items from the survey must be combined. The complete survey appears in Appendix B. The ten items associated with computer anxiety are listed in Table 9.1.

As you examine these items, you'll notice words such as nervous, threatened, bother, uncomfortable, and uneasy. All of these words pertain to anxiety. As we discussed in the previous chapter when describing the recoding process, students responded to each item using a four-point Likert scale. Five of these items are written in a positive manner (i.e., COMP1, COMP9, COMP17, COMP25, COMP33), whereas the other five items are written in a negative manner (i.e., COMP5, COMP13, COMP21, COMP29, COMP37). A person who is not anxious would tend to agree with the positive statements and disagree with those that are negative. To produce a consistent score, you recoded the negative items in the previous chapter.

A total score on these ten items represents how comfortable a person is with computers. The higher a score is, the less anxious the person is in regard to working with computers. Because the negative items have been recoded, a total score can be computed by adding all ten items together.

TABLE 9.1
Items Regarding Computer Anxiety

Variable	Item from Survey
COMP1	Computers do not scare me at all.
COMP5	Working with a computer would make me very nervous.
COMP9	I do not feel threatened when others talk about computers.
COMP13	I feel aggressive and hostile toward computers.
COMP17	It wouldn't bother me at all to take computer classes.
COMP21	Computers make me feel uncomfortable.
COMP25	I would feel at ease in a computer class.
COMP29	I get a sinking feeling when I think of trying to use a computer.
COMP33	I feel comfortable working with a computer.
COMP37	Computers make me feel uneasy and confused.

Computing a sum is only one way to transform existing variables. You can apply a wide variety of mathematical operations when computing a new variable. The basic operations include adding, subtracting, multiplying, and dividing. Also, you can specify operations such as rounding to the nearest integer, calculating a square root, taking the natural log, sine, or cosine, and applying an exponent. These are just a few of the possibilities.

Whatever mathematical operation you wish to apply to existing variables, you need to have a reason for doing so. As we mentioned before, the most common reason to compute a new variable is to arrive at a total score on an instrument, or a subscale score. We will be computing scores for various subscales measuring attitudes toward computers and statistics.

USING SPSS TO COMPUTE NEW VARIABLES

Before you begin to compute new variables using SPSS, you must activate the program and retrieve the data. The data for this chapter are found on the enclosed disk, stored in the file **chap9 data**.

To compute new variables, begin at the main menu bar with the **Transform** menu, then select the first option, **Compute...** (see Figure 9.1). As a result of this menu selection, the Compute Variable dialog box will appear as in Figure 9.2.

The list of variables on the left should look familiar. This is the source variable list. The box at the upper left-hand corner, labeled Target Variable, is where you will identify the new variable. The box to the right, labeled Numeric Expression, is where you will specify how this variable will be created. Notice the equal sign (=) in between these two boxes. Whatever you specify in the Numeric Expression box will be used to define the new variable.

The calculator pad and the **Functions:** menu, both located under the Numeric Expression box, can be used to define your target variable. The basic operations of addition, subtraction, multiplication, division, and raise to power are defined by the +, −, *, /, and ** keys along the left-hand side of the calculator pad. The other keys on this pad are used to specify the operations and logical expressions identified below:

<	less than
>	greater than
<=	less than or equal to

FIGURE 9.1
Transform–Compute
menu selections

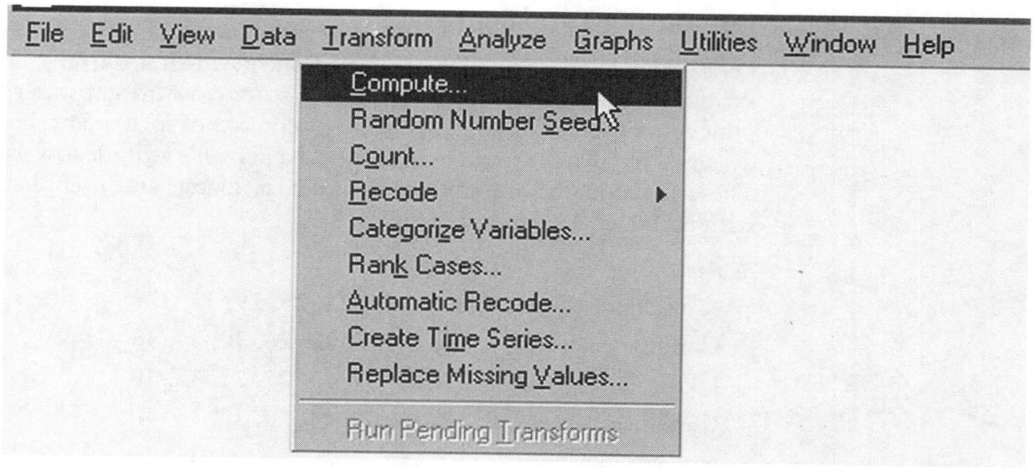

FIGURE 9.2
Compute Variable
dialog box

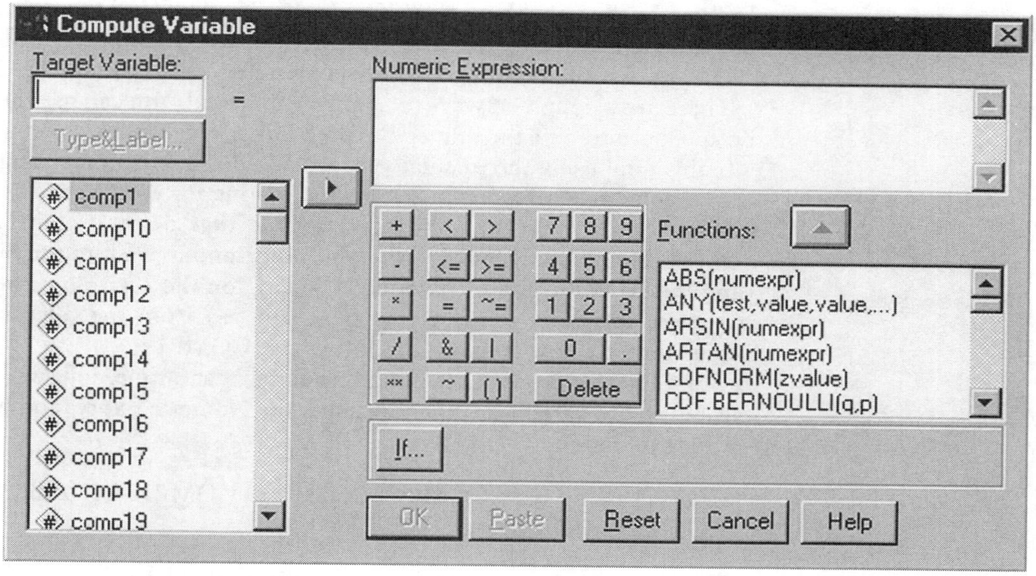

$>=$	greater than or equal to
$=$	equal to
$\sim=$	not equal to
&	and
|	or
$\sim$	not
( )	parentheses used to separate variables and/or operations

The **Functions:** menu; to the right of the calculator pad, is used to specify numerous mathematical functions such as absolute value, sum, mean, square root, cosine, sine, and natural logarithm. You can explore the wide variety of functions by using the scroll bar at the right of the menu box.

Computing Total Scores

Let's compute some total scores, based on specific items from our survey. The items measuring attitudes toward computers and attitudes toward statistics will be used again to compute new variables. Each of the sections consists of forty items. Each set of forty items was designed to measure four components of a person's attitude toward computers or statistics. These components are anxiety, confidence, liking, and usefulness. The items associated with each area are identified below.

Area	Items
Anxiety	1, 5, 9, 13, 17, 21, 25, 29, 33, 37
Confidence	2, 6, 10, 14, 18, 22, 26, 30, 34, 38
Liking	3, 7, 11, 15, 19, 23, 27, 31, 35, 39
Usefulness	4, 8, 12, 16, 20, 24, 28, 32, 36, 40

Recall that the items regarding attitudes toward computers were identified as COMP1 to COMP40, and those associated with statistics were STAT1 to STAT40. Let's begin by computing the total for computer anxiety. We will identify this new variable as COMPANX. Type "COMPANX" in the Target Variable box. Click on the **Type&Label...** button below this box. In the Label box, type "Computer Anxiety" and then click on the **Continue** button. You are now ready to specify the numeric expression used to define this new variable. COMPANX is the sum of the following ten items: 1, 5, 9, 13, 17, 21, 25, 29, 33, 37.

There are a couple of ways to compute this total. You can use the calculator pad, and/or the keyboard to type the numeric expression or you can use the function menu. Let's compute this total using the calculator pad. We'll do the next one using the Function menu.

The numeric expression box is empty, waiting for you to specify the variables and operations. Begin by selecting the first variable that defines COMPANX. This variable is COMP1. Highlight COMP1 with your mouse and move it to the Numeric Expression box using the arrow button or by double-clicking on the variable name. You want to add this and other variables, so select the plus sign (+) from the calculator pad. The Numeric Expression box now contains the following: COMP1+.

Continue this process, selecting one variable at a time, followed by "+" until you have selected all ten variables. When finished, the Numeric Expression box will contain the following expression:

COMP1+COMP5+COMP9+COMP13+COMP17+COMP21+COMP25+ COMP29+COMP33+COMP37

The above numeric expression could also be typed directly, which is often faster when using this many variables. Check to be sure that you have identified the correct variables to be added together. At this point, the dialog box should look like that displayed in Figure 9.3.

When you are ready, click your mouse on the **OK** button at the bottom of your screen to execute the Compute statement. The data editor will now appear, and the message "running EXECUTE..." will appear at the bottom of the editor in the grey status bar.

You have just created a new variable, COMPANX, for each person in the data set. This variable will be stored in the last column of your data spreadsheet. To see the results of your efforts, move to the end column of the first case. You can do this using your right cursor key. To get there more quickly, press the <Cntl> and right cursor keys at the same time.

Use the following steps to get the Compute Variable dialog box.

Step 1	Select **Transform** from the main menu bar.
Step 2	Select the **Compute...** option.

The information you specified for COMPANX has remained on the screen. Clicking on the Reset button will clear your previous selection. The next variable to be computed is computer confidence. Use COMPCON to identify this variable. Change the target variable

FIGURE 9.3
Compute computer
anxiety score
(COMPANX)

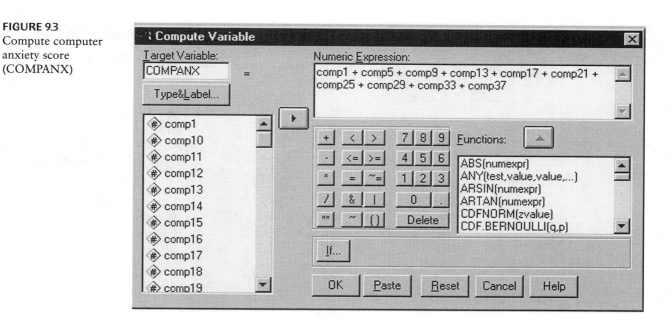

to COMPCON. You can add the label "computer confidence" by clicking on the **Type&Label...** button. We'll use the **Sum** function to compute this variable.

Click your mouse in the Numeric Expression box and delete everything. Now, scroll down the Functions menu until you find the option, **SUM(numexpr,numexpr, . . .)**. Highlight this function and paste it in the Numeric Expression box using the arrow button that points up from the Functions menu. "SUM(? , ?)" now appears in the Numeric Expression box. Position your mouse at the first question mark, between the parentheses. Using the backspace key, erase the "? , ? ." Be sure to leave the parentheses. Each variable used to define the target variable will be placed between the parentheses, separated by commas.

If the variables used to define the target variable are in consecutive order, a shortcut is possible. For example, if you were computing a total score of five consecutive items (e.g., ITEM1, ITEM2, ITEM3, ITEM4, ITEM5), the following **SUM** function would be used.

SUM (ITEM1 to ITEM5)

In the case of computing COMPCON, the variables do not follow this format. Therefore, you must identify each variable between the parentheses, separated by commas. COMPCON is the sum of the following ten items: 2, 6, 10, 14, 18, 22, 26, 30, 34, 38. Select the first variable, COMP2, from the source variable list and move it to the Numeric Expression box using the arrow key. This variable should be between the parentheses. Type a comma (,) and then select the next variable, COMP6. Type a comma and go on the next variable. Continue until all ten variables have been selected. The Numeric Expression box should contain the following expression, as displayed in Figure 9.4.

SUM(COMP2,COMP6,COMP10,COMP14,COMP18,COMP22,COMP26,COMP
30, COMP34,COMP38)

The expression displayed in the Numeric Expression box should read as above. If any variables are missing, select them from the source variable list on the left. If any have been selected by mistake, you can move them back by highlighting the variable and using the arrow button. When everything is correct, continue by clicking on the **OK** button, and the command will be executed. The data editor will now appear and the message "running EXECUTE. . ." will appear at the bottom of the editor in the grey status bar.

Another new variable, COMPCON, has been created. This variable will be stored in the last column of your data spreadsheet, next to the COMPANX variable you created earlier. To see the results of your efforts, move to the end column of the first case. You can do this using your right cursor key or by pressing the <Cntl> and right cursor keys at the same time.

FIGURE 9.4
Compute computer confidence score (COMPCON)

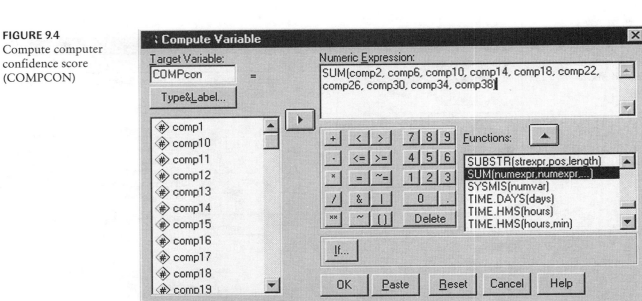

Now you are ready to compute a few more new variables. There are two remaining variables that measure computer attitudes. These are computer liking and computer usefulness. There are also four scores to be computed for statistics attitudes. These are statistics anxiety, statistics confidence, statistics liking, and statistics usefulness. The variables that define each of these scores are presented below. In addition to these subscales, compute a total score for each section.

Score	Sum of the Following Variables:
COMPLIK	3, 7, 11, 15, 19, 23, 27, 31, 35, 39
COMPUSE	3, 7, 11, 15, 19, 23, 27, 31, 35, 39
STATANX	1, 5, 9, 13, 17, 21, 25, 29, 33, 37
STATCON	2, 6, 10, 14, 18, 22, 26, 30, 34, 38
STATLIK	3, 7, 11, 15, 19, 23, 27, 31, 35, 39
STATUSE	4, 8, 12, 16, 20, 24, 28, 32, 36, 40
COMPTOT	COMP1 through COMP40
STATTOT	STAT1 through STAT40

Remember, each of the computer variables is identified using COMP (i.e., COMP1 to COMP40) and the variables measuring attitudes toward statistics are identified using STAT (i.e., STAT1 to STAT40).

To Compute new Variables:

Step 1	From the main menu bar, select **Transform**.
Step 2	Select **Compute**.
Step 3	Identify the new variable as the Target Variable.
Step 4	Click on the **Type&Label...** button to specify a variable label.
Step 5	Specify the numeric expression in the Numeric Expression box. You may use the calculator pad or the Function menu.
Step 6	Check to be sure the numeric expression is correct.
Step 7	To execute the Compute statement, click on the **OK** button.

FIGURE 9.5
Compute COMPTOT
using keyword "to"

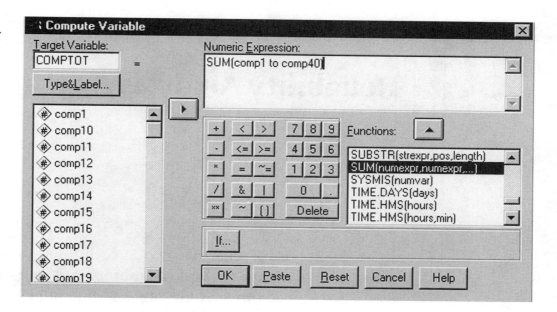

Hint: There are two shortcuts that can be used to compute the total scores. First, you can use the **Sum** function and if all variables are consecutive, you just need to specify the first and last variable between the parentheses, separated by the keyword, "**to**". Second, you can use your newly computed variables to compute the total scores. That is, the variables COMPANX, COMPCON, COMPLIK, and COMPUSE can be combined to create COMPTOT.

Let's illustrate one of these shortcuts for COMPTOT. In Figure 9.5, we use the keyword "to" to compute COMPTOT because COMP1 to COMP40 are arranged consecutively in our data file. Click on the **OK** command button to compute COMPTOT.

CHAPTER SUMMARY

In this chapter, you used the Compute procedure to create new variables. Specifically, you computed four computer attitude scales and four statistics attitude scales. These new scores are useful in determining a student's attitude toward computers and statistics. We will use these new attitude scores as we illustrate other statistical procedures in later chapters.

PRACTICE EXERCISES

In Chapter 3, you created the data file on student admissions (i.e., student admission data.sav).

1. Compute a GRE Total Score by adding GREV and GREQ.
2. Compute an Average GRE by dividing the new GRE Total by 2.

10 | Reliability Analysis

In the previous chapter, you computed several variables measuring attitudes toward computers and statistics. You will be using these new variables throughout this book as you explore a variety of statistical procedures. In most cases, these variables serve as dependent variables. You will examine relationships among these and other variables, and make comparisons between and within groups of subjects regarding their performance on these variables. You will also make many decisions based on the results of the analysis of these variables. Therefore, it is extremely important that these variables, and others, have sound measurement properties.

Two important properties that you have heard about many times are validity and reliability. In this chapter, we will provide only a brief overview of these two measurement properties. We will, instead, focus our efforts on using SPSS to perform an analysis of items that are grouped together, such as those you used to compute the attitude scales in the previous chapter. Using SPSS, you will perform a reliability analysis to determine the extent to which items belong together and are related to the same construct, such as computer anxiety.

VALIDITY

The property of *validity* can be described as the extent to which the measurement scale, or variable, represents what it is supposed to and yields the type of information you need. It is also important that the information you gather be used appropriately. Therefore, the variable you computed pertaining to computer anxiety should actually measure the extent to which people feel anxious about using computers. There are many ways to gather evidence of validity. The manner in which you gather this information will depend on your purpose for using the measure. In other words, you must not just ask yourself, "Is this measure valid?", but, also "Is this measure valid for the purpose it is intended?". There are many purposes for doing research and measuring variables. As you might expect, there are also many different types of validity. You must evaluate the measurement instruments that you use according to the most appropriate type(s) of validity.

Perhaps the most important type of validity is *content validity*. Content validity is the extent to which the content of the measurement instrument reflects what is supposed to be measured. In other words, if you are measuring computer anxiety, the items used to define the computer anxiety variable should pertain to computer anxiety. You examined these items in the previous chapter, when computing the new variable. In addition, the developers of the measurement instrument wrote these items to reflect computer anxiety. In developing your own measurement instrument, you would also write items that reflect the content of what you want to measure. In addition, you could get feedback from other content experts to see if they agree that your items are measuring what you intended them to measure.

Another type of validity, for which it is very simple to gather evidence, is *face validity*. Face validity is evaluated by those who are responding to the measurement instrument. If a measurement instrument appears to be valid in the eyes of those responding, it can be said to have face validity. In other words, this is the extent to which the respondents believe your measurement instrument is valid.

Other types of validity refer to the extent to which your measurement instrument relates to other measures. *Concurrent validity* is evaluated in terms of how consistent the results from your measurement instrument are with the results of other instruments that are designed to measure the same thing. In other words, if the results from the computer anxiety measure you are using related to another existing measure of computer anxiety, then you have evidence of concurrent validity. A second type of criterion-related validity is *predictive validity*. Predictive validity refers to the extent to which the results on your measurement instrument can be used to predict some future performance. In other words, if the scores on the computer anxiety measure relate to students' future performance in a computer class, then we have evidence of predictive validity.

Finally, there is a type of validity known as *construct validity*. Construct validity is perhaps the most difficult type of validity to establish. This is because many constructs are difficult to identify and measure accurately. Constructs are general traits or abilities such as intelligence, personality, anxiety, or self-esteem. These traits are often made up of a variety of skills or abilities. Because of their complex nature, it is difficult to produce a single valid measurement instrument that reflects specific constructs. The validation of an evaluation instrument designed to measure a construct is somewhat more involved than for other types of validity. When evaluating a test for evidence of construct validity, several criteria are often considered.

The criteria used to evaluate construct validity depend upon the construct being measured. For most constructs, there have emerged "theories" that attempt to explain them. For example, some theories of intelligence have indicated that a person's intelligence is demonstrated through such things as verbal skills, problem-solving ability, academic achievement, and conceptual ability. If this theory is true, then a valid intelligence test should be highly related to most, if not all, of these traits. In order to establish construct validity for our measure of computer anxiety, we would have to establish its relationship to other traits which related to anxiety.

RELIABILITY

Reliability may be thought of in terms of consistency. The more consistent the results from a measurement instrument are, the more reliable they are. This consistency may be evaluated in a variety of ways. Some reliability measures require that the measurement instrument be given two different times or in two different forms, while others require only one form to be given one time. The reliability of a measurement instrument is often described as having four related forms: consistency over time, consistency of parallel forms, consistency of items, and consistency across people.

Consistency over time is referred to as *stability,* or alternatively as test-retest reliability. Measuring stability often involves giving the same instrument to the same group of people twice and comparing the results. The correlation coefficient used to estimate the stability of the results over time is called a *coefficient of stability*. If a measurement instrument is reliable, it should yield consistent results over time, resulting in a high, positive coefficient of stability. This means that those individuals who scored high on the test the first time would be expected to score high when the test is given the second time. Also, those individuals who scored low on the test the first time would be expected to score low when the test is given the second time.

A second type of reliability is that of *equivalence,* or parallel forms reliability. Parallel forms reliability is assessed by correlating the scores of two parallel forms of a measure given to a single group. The resulting correlation coefficient is called a *coefficient of equivalence.* The more consistent the results are between the two parallel forms, the greater the evidence of reliability.

A third type of reliability is a combination of the previous two, or *stability and equivalence.* In other words, the consistency of parallel forms is evaluated over a period of time. The results from each of the parallel instruments are correlated with each other to arrive at a *coefficient of stability and equivalence.*

A fourth method used to establish reliability is *inter-rater reliability.* Inter-rater reliability is especially important when information is collected through some observational method. When two people are observing a person's behavior or rating a work project, they will not always agree. It is important, however, that the results of these two observations or ratings be consistent with each other. Greater amounts of consistency, or agreement, indicate higher reliability.

The consistency of two observers, or two raters, can be evaluated in several ways. The easiest way is to simply determine how often the two people agree. This is called a *percent of agreement.* This represents the proportion of times in which the two observers saw the same behavior or assigned the same score to a student's work. When rating behaviors or scoring student projects, only those cases that received exactly the same score from both raters would count as an agreement.

You may not expect the raters to agree frequently on the exact score they assign a project, but the scores that they assign should be very similar. A second way to determine the reliability between raters is to calculate a correlation coefficient between the sets of ratings. Each rater scores every project and the scores assigned by the first rater are correlated with those assigned by the second rater. This process is very similar to those previously discussed in this chapter when evaluation results were correlated between two different times, or different forms, or both. The resulting correlation represents the inter-rater reliability coefficient.

Finally, reliability can be determined by assessing the consistency of items within a measurement instrument. This is called *internal consistency.* Internal consistency estimates reliability in terms of how consistent the actual items are within the instrument. In other words, if an evaluation instrument is designed to measure some content area, then the items that comprise the overall instrument should all be consistent with each other. They should be measuring the same content and therefore be highly correlated with each other. This should be the case for our measures of computer and statistics attitudes.

Internal consistency is typically estimated using a split-half procedure. In other words, if you divide the items of a measurement instrument into two halves, the correlation between the two halves should give you some idea of how consistent, or reliable, the scores from the two halves are. However, this correlation coefficient is basically just an estimate of the equivalence of the two "half" tests. Only one step remains before we can arrive at the overall internal consistency estimate of reliability for the measurement instrument. A correction must be made so that the reliability of the overall instrument may be obtained. A formula that can be used to correct for this is called the Spearman-Brown Prophecy Formula.

A more common measure of internal consistency, especially for attitudinal measures like those used in our data, is called Cronbach's *coefficient alpha.* This coefficient represents the average of all possible split-half estimates. Internal consistency reliability requires a thorough examination of the results from each item on the measurement scale, or what is referred to as item analysis. If items are a consistent measure of the same construct, then the items themselves should be correlated. Using item analysis, you examine the extent to which items perform as consistent measures of a single construct. More consistent items will result in a higher coefficient alpha, representing a higher level of reliability. In the next section of this chapter, you will use SPSS to examine items from several measurement scales and estimate internal consistency reliability.

VARIABLES USED IN THIS CHAPTER

In this chapter, we will use the attitude scales you created and used in previous chapters. There are eight variables; Four of these variables regard attitudes toward computers (i.e., COMPANX, COMPCON, COMPLIK, COMPUSE) and four pertain to attitudes toward statistics (STATANX, STATCON, STATLIK, STATUSE). Each of these eight attitude scales is comprised of ten items.

USING SPSS FOR RELIABILITY ANALYSIS

In this section, you will take a closer look at the reliability of these attitude scales. We will get started with the computer attitude scales and let you examine the statistics attitude scales later on your own. The data you will need are stored in the file identified as chap10 data on the enclosed disk.

To perform reliability analysis, you begin from the **Analyze** menu. From this menu, select the **Scale** and **Reliability Analysis...** options, as illustrated in Figure 10.1.

These menu selections will open the Reliability Analysis dialog box, displayed in Figure 10.2.

FIGURE 10.1
Analyze–Scale–
Reliability Analysis
menu selections

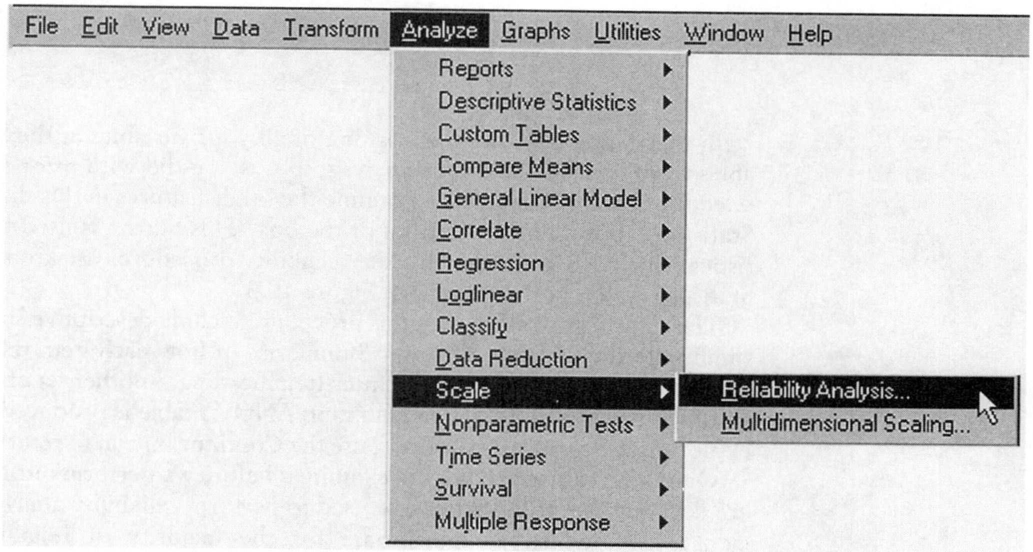

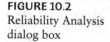

FIGURE 10.2
Reliability Analysis
dialog box

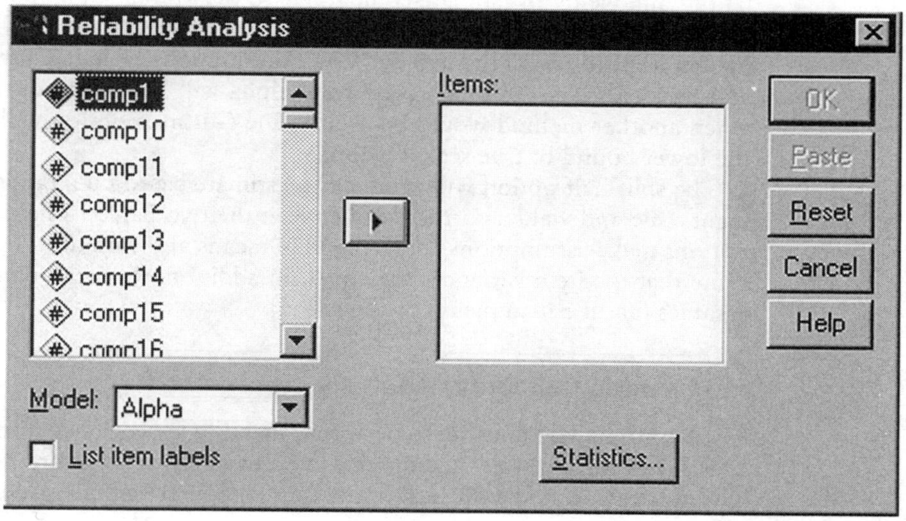

FIGURE 10.3
Reliability Analysis:
Statistics dialog box

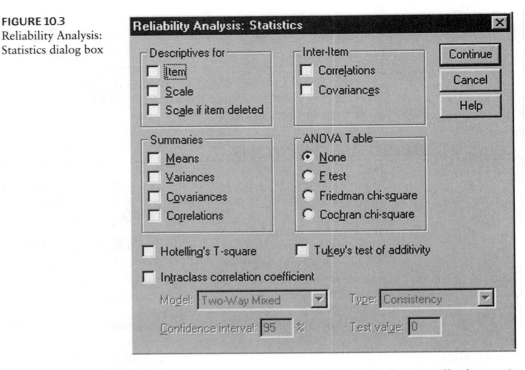

In this dialog box, there is a listing of all your variables at the left. You will select variables from this source list for analysis, just as you did with prior SPSS procedures. Before selecting these variables, let's examine the other features in this dialog box. First, there is a **Statistics...** button at the bottom of the box. This button is used to explore the many statistics which are available with the reliability procedure. Click on this button to open the Statistics dialog box displayed in Figure 10.3.

The statistics available with this procedure include descriptive statistics for each item and summaries for the scale of items. Summaries of how each item relates to the others in the scale are also available under the Inter-Item heading. Another set of options pertain to analysis of variance (ANOVA). By default, no ANOVA table is produced. When you are finished exploring these statistical options, use the **Continue** button to return to the main dialog box.

One final feature needs to be examined before we perform our reliability analysis. There are different methods that can be used to perform reliability analysis. The default is coefficient alpha, which is appropriate for the majority of reliability analysis situations. Remember, coefficient alpha provides an estimate of reliability based on inter-item correlations and yields an estimate comparable to the average of all possible split-haves.

There are, however, additional methods available. Scroll down the **Model** menu (see Figure 10.4) to reveal the choices. The other options include Guttman, Split-half, Parallel, and Strict parallel. Although coefficient alpha will be used frequently, there may be times when another method would be useful. The Guttman option will result in an estimate of the lower bound of true scale reliability.

The split-half option will produce an estimate based on a random split of the measurement scale and yield a correlation between the two halves. The parallel and strict parallel options make assumptions about the item means and variances. Both of these methods assume that the item variances are equal. In addition, the strict parallel model of reliability assumes that the item means are equal.

Performing Reliability Analysis

The first thing you must do to perform reliability analysis is identify the items belonging to each measurement scale. You did this in Chapter 8 when you first computed these variables. The items associated with each of the four computer attitude scales are listed in Table 10.1.

FIGURE 10.4
Model options for
reliability analysis

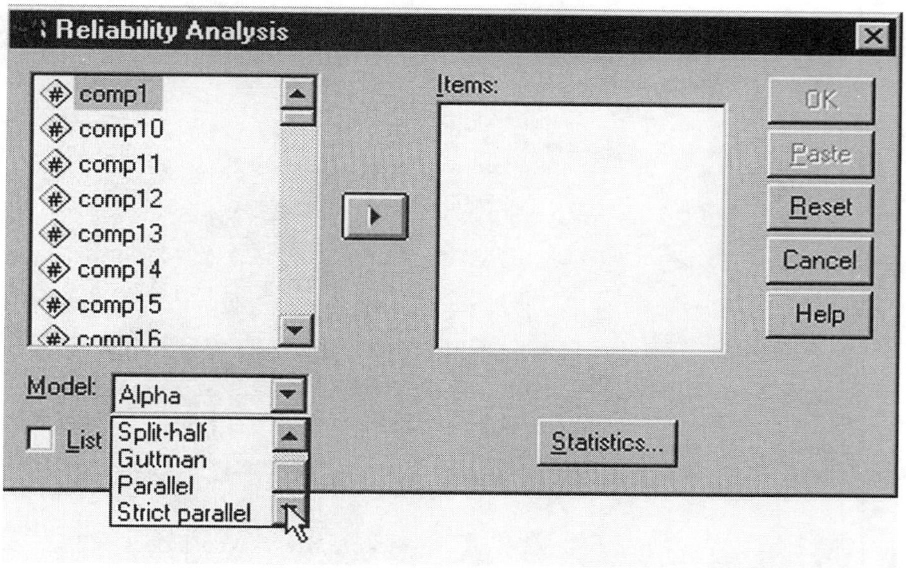

TABLE 10.1
Computer Attitude Scales

Attitude Scale	Items
Computer Anxiety	COMP1, COMP5, COMP9, COMP13, COMP17, COMP21, COMP25, COMP29, COMP33, COMP37
Computer Confidence	COMP2, COMP6, COMP10, COMP14, COMP18, COMP22, COMP26, COMP30, COMP34, COMP38
Computer Liking	COMP3, COMP7, COMP11, COMP15, COMP19, COMP23, COMP27, COMP31, COMP35, COMP39
Computer Usefulness	COMP4, COMP8, COMP12, COMP16, COMP20, COMP24, COMP28, COMP32, COMP36, COMP40

The items that define the four statistics attitudes scales are the same, except they are identified with a "STAT" prefix. We'll let you examine these later. Return to the Reliability Analysis dialog box (see Figure 10.2) and we'll begin with the computer anxiety scale.

From the source variable list, select the ten items that define the computer anxiety scale. Once these ten items are selected, click on the **Statistics...** button so you can select useful statistical options, found in the Statistics dialog box (see Figure 10.3). We'll select a few of these statistics for our reliability analysis.

First, select all three options in the first box. These options will provide us with descriptive information for each of the ten items and the overall scale. We will also be able to see what would happen to the scale if a particular item were not included. Under the Inter-Item heading, select the **Correlations** option. This information will be very helpful as we examine the extent to which these ten items correlate with each other.

Next, there are several options that provide summary information. We will select the options for means, variances, and correlations. This will provide us with an overview of the central tendency and variability of all the items, as well as the relationships among them. The last option we will select will be an **F test** under the ANOVA Table heading. This will summarize the results from an analysis of variance for the ten items and allow us to examine the extent to which the means of these ten items are equal.

The selections you made are summarized in Figure 10.5. Check your selections, then return to the main dialog box by using the **Continue** button.

The last thing to decide before you run the reliability analysis is which method of reliability should be used. The default method is coefficient alpha, identified in the **Model:**

FIGURE 10.5
Statistics selections for
reliability analysis

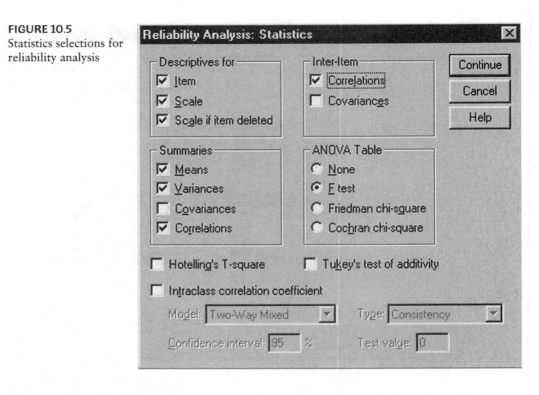

menu. Coefficient alpha is the appropriate choice for our data. Click on the **OK** button to perform the reliability analysis for the computer anxiety scale.

Before we examine the results, let's perform reliability analysis using a different reliability model. For this illustration, use the split-half method. When you return to the main reliability dialog box, all the options you previously selected will still be there, as long as you didn't exit SPSS. Running a second reliability analysis is simple. All you need to do is change the reliability model from the default option, Alpha, to Split-half. After you make this change, select the **OK** button to perform the reliability analysis. We'll discuss the results from this analysis in the final section of this chapter.

Now that you have performed a reliability analysis on the computer anxiety scale, you may wish to try a few on your own. There are three remaining computer attitude scales (confidence, liking, usefulness). As a reminder, the steps to follow are summarized below. Following these steps, specify the conditions for the confidence, liking, and usefulness scales.

Step 1	Select the variables that make up the measurement scale. You might want to consult Table 10.1.
Step 2	Select the statistical options you desire for the analysis. We selected all three descriptive options, inter-item correlations, summaries for means, variances, and correlations, and an F test.
Step 3	Select the method of reliability analysis. The default option for coefficient alpha is appropriate.

INTERPRETING SPSS RELIABILITY RESULTS

In this final section of the chapter, we'll examine the results of the reliability analyses you performed in this chapter. We'll begin with all the output from the reliability analysis of the computer anxiety scale, but highlight selected output from the other three scales.

FIGURE 10.6

Descriptive Summary
of Computer Anxiety
items

Computer Anxiety Scale

****** Method 2 (covariance matrix) will be used for this analysis ******

R E L I A B I L I T Y   A N A L Y S I S   —   S C A L E   (A L P H A)

		Mean	Std Dev	Cases
1.	COMP1	2.9330	.8745	209.0
2.	COMP5	3.0718	.8318	209.0
3.	COMP9	**2.8804**	.8027	209.0
4.	COMP13	**3.3780**	.6473	209.0
5.	COMP17	3.0144	.8055	209.0
6.	COMP21	3.0335	.8049	209.0
7.	COMP25	2.9856	.7626	209.0
8.	COMP29	3.1818	.7439	209.0
9.	COMP33	3.0431	.7552	209.0
10.	COMP37	3.0813	.7833	209.0

FIGURE 10.7

Inter-Item Correlation
Matrix for Computer
Anxiety items

Computer Anxiety

Correlation Matrix

	COMP1	COMP5	COMP9	COMP13	COMP17
COMP1	1.0000				
COMP5	.7469	1.0000			
COMP9	.5159	.4810	1.0000		
COMP13	.4272	.4851	**.3373**	1.0000	
COMP17	.6361	.5940	.4191	.3768	1.0000
COMP21	.7682	.8006	.5569	.5016	.6518
COMP25	.6762	.6989	.5234	.3909	.7361
COMP29	.6396	.7480	.4392	.5655	.6135
COMP33	.7179	.7375	.5400	.4780	.6234
COMP37	.7169	.7879	.5049	.4986	.6687

	COMP21	COMP25	COMP29	COMP33	COMP37
COMP21	1.0000				
COMP25	.7057	1.0000			
COMP29	.7686	.6488	1.0000		
COMP33	.7490	.7024	.6878	1.0000	
COMP37	**.8497**	.7022	.7831	.7662	1.0000

We have broken down the reliability output for the computer anxiety scale into four parts so that we can examine it more closely. The first section of output is summarized in Figure 10.6. This information simply provides a summary of means and standard deviations for each of the ten items. You have generated similar output many times using SPSS. From this output, you can see that most of the item means are close to 3, ranging from 2.88 to 3.37.

The next section of output is a matrix of correlations, displayed in Figure 10.7. These correlations should all be positive because we expect these items to be measuring the same thing, that is, computer anxiety. We also want these correlations to be high. The higher they are, the more our items are related. This is an indication of internal consistency. That is, students' performance is consistent on these items. Most of these inter-item correlations are at least .50. There are a few that are lower and several that are much higher. We've highlighted the lowest (r=.3373) and highest correlation (r=.8497) in the matrix. The lowest correlation exists between COMP9 and COMP13. In fact, several of the correlations that involve COMP9 or COMP13 are lower than .50. The strongest correlation is between COMP21 and COMP37.

The third section of output (see Figure 10.8) provides a summary of item and scale information. This summary includes the central tendency and variability for the overall scale of ten items and summaries for item means, variances, and inter-item correlations. The scale mean is 30.6029 with a standard deviation of 6.3708. You computed these statistics in Chapter 6 and will do so many more times in later chapters. The next two rows summarize item means and variances. The information regarding variances can be very helpful because if items don't vary, resulting correlations will be very small. This is not the case for these ten items, as the item variances range from .4189 to .7647.

Finally, the inter-item correlations are summarized. As you can see, the average inter-item correlation is .6215, with values ranging from .3373 to .8497. The largest correlation is approximately 2½ times larger than the smallest correlation. A smaller ratio indicates greater consistency among the inter-item correlations. The last piece of information reported is a variance of the inter-item correlations. This value appears to be small (.0174). Values closer to zero indicate greater consistency among the inter-item correlations.

The final section of output from the computer anxiety reliability analysis reports information about item-total statistics, ANOVA, and the reliability coefficient. There are several important pieces of information in this section (see Figure 10.9). The item-total statistics table summarizes the relationships between each item and the total score, which is simply a sum of the items. If items are consistent with each other, they will correlate with the total score. Therefore, you would like to see strong, positive item-total correlations. Examine the correlations listed in the third column. All of these values are above .50, with six of them in the .80s. This indicates that items are consistent with the scale. They must have something to do with computer anxiety because they correlate well. What you don't want to see here are negative correlations or values close to 0. A negative correlation would indicate that the item measures something different from the other items, while a zero correlation would indicate the lack of a relationship.

The next column reports a squared multiple correlation. This value describes the amount of variance shared with all of the other items. In other words, if you used regression analysis to correlate the other nine items with COMP1, the R^2 would be .6794. That

Computer Anxiety

Statistics for Scale	Mean	Variance	Std Dev	N of Variables		
	30.6029	40.5867	6.3708	10		
Item Means	Mean	Minimum	Maximum	Range	Max/Min	Variance
	3.0603	2.8804	3.3780	.4976	1.1728	.0193
Item Variances	Mean	Minimum	Maximum	Range	Max/Min	Variance
	.6135	.4189	.7647	.3458	1.8254	.0085
Inter-item Correlations	Mean	Minimum	Maximum	Range	Max/Min	Variance
	.6215	.3373	.8497	.5124	2.5191	.0174

FIGURE 10.8
Summaries for Computer Anxiety scale

is, COMP1 shares approximately 68% of its variance in common with a combination of the remaining nine items. Again, you want the R^2 values to be high, indicating a large amount of consistency among the items.

The other three columns report information about what would happen to the scale if an item were deleted. This provides you with some information about the influence of the item. If the deletion of an item changes the scale statistics substantially, that item is worth a closer look. The first two columns report what would happen to the scale mean and variance. Perhaps a more important column is the last one, which reports what would happen to the reliability coefficient of the scale if an item were deleted. An item that negatively impacts the reliability of the scale should be examined carefully and possibly removed.

If you skip to the information reported below the ANOVA table, you'll find the reliability information. A coefficient alpha of .9432 is reported. Examining the last column

---

Computer Anxiety

Item-total Statistics

	Scale Mean if Item Deleted	Scale Variance if Item Deleted	Corrected Item-Total Correlation	Squared Multiple Correlation	Alpha if Item Deleted
COMP1	27.6699	31.8857	.8036	.6794	.9355
COMP5	27.5311	32.0098	.8377	.7438	.9337
COMP9	27.7225	34.5092	.5761	.3719	.9460
COMP13	27.2249	35.9925	.5376	.3437	.9463
COMP17	27.5885	33.2241	.7230	.6068	.9392
COMP21	27.5694	31.9291	.8805	.8075	.9317
COMP25	27.6172	33.0355	.7951	.6855	.9359
COMP29	27.4211	33.1296	.8062	.7050	.9355
COMP33	27.5598	32.8630	.8262	.6921	.9345
COMP37	27.5215	32.2507	.8680	.7968	.9324

Analysis of Variance

Source of Variation	Sum of Sq.	DF	Mean Square	F	Prob.
Between People	844.2038	208	4.0587		
Within People	468.2000	1881	.2489		
Between Measures	**36.2699**	**9**	**4.0300**	**17.4661**	**.0000**
Residual	431.9301	1872	.2307		
Nonadditivity	6.2511	1	6.2511	27.4756	.0000
Balance	425.6791	1871	.2275		
Total	1312.4038	2089	.6282		

Grand Mean   3.0603

Reliability Coefficients   10 items

Alpha = .9432   Standardized item alpha = .9426

FIGURE 10.9
Item-Total Statistics for Computer Anxiety scale

FIGURE 10.10
SPSS Reliability
Output–Split-half
model

RELIABILITY ANALYSIS — SCALE (SPLIT)

Reliability Coefficients

N of Cases =   209.0   N of Items =   10

Correlation between forms = .9085   Equal-length Spearman-Brown =   .9520

Guttman Split-half =   .9496   Unequal-length Spearman-Brown = .9520

  5 Items in part 1   5 Items in part 2

Alpha for part 1 =   .8376   Alpha for part 2 =   .9334

---

in the item-total table, it appears that the deletion of a few items might result in only a very slight increase in the reliability coefficient. These are COMP9 and COMP13. Let's examine the other information for these items. Both correlate moderately with the total scale (.5761 and .5376). They also share over 30% with the remaining items. They are contributing to the reliability of this scale and, therefore, should be maintained with the remaining items.

There is also an ANOVA table as part of the reliability output. We've highlighted the information pertaining to differences between item means. This is labeled Between Measures in the ANOVA table. Because there are ten items, there are 9 degrees of freedom. The resulting F ratio is 17.4661 with a probability of less than .0001. This indicates that there is a significant amount of variation among the ten items in this scale.

Examine the information reported in Figure 10.10. These are the results from the split-half reliability analysis. These results are also very supportive of the scale's reliability. First, we know that the analysis was based on 209 cases responding to ten items. After this ten-item scale was split into two equal parts, a correlation was computed to be .9085. This indicates a great deal of consistency between the two halves. Applying the equal-length Spearman-Brown formula, to adjust this estimate for the entire scale of ten items, resulted in a reliability estimate of .9520. This value is very high, supporting the internal consistency of the computer anxiety scale. There is also an unequal Spearman-Brown estimate, which would be used if the two parts were not based on the same number of items.

Other information is reported as part of this output. This includes a Guttman split-half estimate, which is similar to the Spearman-Brown estimate. The Guttman method, however, does not assume that the two halves are equally reliable. Some evidence exists that the two parts are not equally reliable when examining the coefficient alpha estimates for each half. The reliability estimate for the first part is .8376, whereas the second half reliability is estimated to be higher at .9334. In this case, the more conservative estimate of scale reliability reported from the Guttman method is valuable. This estimate is .9496, also highly supportive of the scale's internal consistency.

Now that we've examined the output from the reliability of the computer anxiety scale, let's highlight some information from the other three computer attitude scales. This output is highly abbreviated so we can focus on a few specific findings. In Figure 10.11, we present some reliability output that summarizes the item means, variances, and inter-item correlations. This information indicates that attitudes are most positive in regard to computer usefulness because this scale has the highest scale and item means. On average, the variability of the usefulness scale is the smallest of the three scales (.3752 compared to .4964 and .5240). However, the computer usefulness scale also has the lowest average inter-item correlation (.3498). The average inter-item correlations are higher for computer liking

Computer Confidence

Statistics for Scale	Mean 30.6077	Variance 28.0280	Std Dev 5.2941	N of Variables 10		
Item Means	Mean 3.0608	Minimum 2.6124	Maximum 3.3780	Range .7656	Max/Min 1.2930	Variance .0663
Item Variances	Mean .4964	Minimum .2921	Maximum .8191	Range .5269	Max/Min 2.8036	Variance .0256
Inter-item Correlations	Mean .5255	Minimum .3908	Maximum .6736	Range .2827	Max/Min 1.7233	Variance .0047

Computer Liking

Statistics for Scale	Mean 29.6603	Variance 28.2542	Std Dev 5.3155	N of Variables 10		
Item Means	Mean 2.9660	Minimum 2.5550	Maximum 3.2919	Range .7368	Max/Min 1.2884	Variance .0471
Item Variances	Mean .5240	Minimum .4306	Maximum .6616	Range .2310	Max/Min 1.5366	Variance .0069
Inter-item Correlations	Mean .4885	Minimum .3553	Maximum .7951	Range .4398	Max/Min 2.2380	Variance .0077

Computer Usefulness

Statistics for Scale	Mean 34.9187	Variance 15.2097	Std Dev 3.9000	N of Variables 10		
Item Means	Mean 3.4919	Minimum 3.1005	Maximum 3.8086	Range .7081	Max/Min 1.2284	Variance .0425
Item Variances	Mean .3752	Minimum .1940	Maximum .6293	Range .4353	Max/Min 3.2443	Variance .0177
Inter-item Correlations	Mean .3498	Minimum .1590	Maximum .5963	Range .4373	Max/Min 3.7496	Variance .0103

FIGURE 10.11

Reliability Analysis Summary Statistics for Computer Confidence, Liking, and Usefulness scales

(.4885) and confidence (.5255), indicating a greater amount of internal consistency among the items on these scales.

Examine the information summarized in Figure 10.12. This information pertains to the item-total statistics for the three computer attitude scales. The overall estimate of internal consistent (coefficient alpha) is also displayed in this figure. As you might expect, the lowest estimate of reliability is reported for the computer usefulness scale (alpha = .8370). The estimates for computer confidence and liking are .9143 and .9050 respectively. This is consistent with the information we reviewed in Figure 10.11. Computer usefulness had the least amount of variability and lowest inter-item correlations. This

FIGURE 10.12
Item-Total Statistics for Computer Confidence, Liking, and Usefulness scales (continued next page)

Computer Confidence

Item-total Statistics

	Scale Mean if Item Deleted	Scale Variance if Item Deleted	Corrected Item-Total Correlation	Squared Multiple Correlation	Alpha if Item Deleted
COMP2	27.5167	21.7990	.7341	.5696	.9029
COMP6	27.6268	22.7158	.6903	.5179	.9053
Comp10	27.9713	21.6530	.6596	.4527	.9096
COMP14	27.2297	23.5143	.6523	.4462	.9075
COMP18	27.4976	22.4820	.7870	.6378	.8998
COMP22	27.4545	24.1530	.5856	.3813	.9110
COMP26	27.4258	22.5726	.7329	.5785	.9028
COMP30	27.4833	24.2317	.6585	.4645	.9081
COMP34	27.2679	23.9471	.6658	.4962	.9073
COMP38	27.9952	22.1202	.7476	.5907	.9018

Reliability Coefficients   10 items
Alpha = .9143   Standardized item alpha = .9172

Computer Liking

Item-total Statistics

	Scale Mean if Item Deleted	Scale Variance if Item Deleted	Corrected Item-Total Correlation	Squared Multiple Correlation	Alpha if Item Deleted
COMP3	26.4067	23.7232	.6415	.4859	.8969
COMP7	26.6794	22.2862	.7230	.6839	.8915
COMP11	26.5694	23.0637	.7103	.5491	.8927
COMP15	26.8134	22.0179	.7668	.7099	.8885
COMP19	26.7177	23.5497	.6303	.4810	.8975
COMP23	26.6603	22.9369	.6516	.4732	.8963
COMP27	27.1053	22.5177	.6574	.4806	.8962
COMP31	26.3684	23.1953	.7151	.5236	.8926
COMP35	26.7512	23.9282	.5842	.4452	.9002
COMP39	26.8708	24.0553	.5441	.3142	.9026

Reliability Coefficients   10 items
Alpha = .9050   Standardized item alpha = .9052

indicates a lesser degree of internal consistency and, therefore, results in a lower estimate of reliability.

We are not suggesting that the reliability of the usefulness scale is unacceptable. Actually, .8370 offers support for the reliability of these ten items, just not as much as the remaining computer attitude scales. In order to thoroughly evaluate scale reliability, we should also examine the item-total correlations. As you recall, these correlations should be positive and the stronger, the better. All the item-total correlations from the usefulness scale are positive, ranging from a low of .4291 to a high of .6981. In contrast, the item-total correlations

FIGURE 10.12
Continued

Computer Usefulness

Item-total Statistics

	Scale Mean if Item Deleted	Scale Variance if Item Deleted	Corrected Item- Total Correlation	Squared Multiple Correlation	Alpha if Item Deleted
COMP4	31.3876	11.9885	.6709	.4940	.8081
COMP8	31.1100	13.5407	.4551	.3422	.8294
COMP12	31.2632	13.1660	.4757	.3309	.8271
COMP16	31.8182	11.5726	.5573	.4016	.8214
COMP20	31.3397	12.1292	.6981	.5309	.8069
COMP24	31.2679	12.5529	.6128	.4511	.8152
COMP28	31.4545	12.2684	.5138	.3064	.8241
COMP32	31.4163	13.0038	.4291	.2381	.8313
COMP36	31.6459	12.9221	.4993	.2708	.8249
COMP40	31.5646	12.2855	.4644	.2747	.8306

Reliability Coefficients   10 items
Alpha = .8370   Standardized item alpha = .8432

FIGURE 10.13
Summary of Reliability
Estimates for
Computer Attitude
scales

	Reliability Estimate				
	Cronbach's Alpha	Split-half	Guttman's Split-half	Alpha for	
				Part 1	Part 2
Computer Attitude Scale:					
Anxiety	.9432	.9520	.9496	.8376	.9334
Confidence	.9143	.9207	.9120	.8505	.8321
Liking	.9050	.8762	.8752	.8632	.8090
Usefulness	.8370	.8291	.8289	.7612	.6836

for the confidence and liking scales are higher, most of them are above .60, indicating a greater degree of internal consistency.

Finally, examine the contents of Figure 10.13. In this figure, we've summarized the reliability estimates from each of the four computer attitude scales. These scales are presented in order in terms of their reliability from highest to lowest. The order is the same for each type of reliability model (alpha, split-half, Guttman) used. From this comparison of the four attitude scales, you will see that the computer anxiety scale is estimated to have the greatest amount of internal consistency. This was also evidenced in earlier examinations of inter-item correlations and item-total statistics. On the other hand, the least reliable scale is computer usefulness. Again, you examined other information that would lead you to this conclusion.

CHAPTER SUMMARY

In this chapter, you explored the reliability of four computer attitude scales. Specifically, you examined the internal consistency of these attitude scales. In doing so, you explored relationships among individual items and between items and total scale scores. Relationships among items, or inter-item correlations, are used to describe the extent to which people respond to different items on a scale in a similar manner. If these items measure the same construct, such as computer anxiety, individuals' responses should be consistent across the items. In addition, individuals' responses to items should positively relate to their total scale score. High, positive inter-item correlations and item-total correlations offer support for internal consistency. Finally, you estimated reliability using Cronbach's alpha and the split-half models.

PRACTICE EXERCISES

Using the information of attitudes toward statistics (found in chap10 data), perform reliability analysis for each of the four attitude scales. Follow the process illustrated in this chapter. Obtain all the appropriate statistics and address the following questions.

1. Summarize the reliability estimates (alpha) for each of the four statistics attitude scales.
2. Examining the inter-item correlations from each of these four analyses, describe the relationships that indicate the greatest amount of consistency and identify those which lack consistency.
3. What is the average inter-item correlation from each reliability analysis? What does this indicate about the reliability (internal consistency) of each attitude scale?
4. When examining the item-total statistics, are there any items which should be further examined? In other words, did you detect any items which are not contributing strongly to the internal consistency of the scale?
5. Compare the reliability findings from these four attitude scales with those from the four computer attitude scales. As a group, which set of attitude scales are more reliable? Use evidence from your results to support your response.

SECTION IV

Introduction to Hypothesis Testing

11 | Introduction to Hypothesis Testing

In this chapter, we will not illustrate any SPSS procedures, but will introduce some important concepts that you will use in the remaining chapters. Understanding the logic of hypothesis testing is critical in research and statistics. There are many concepts involved in the process of hypothesis testing that apply to many of the statistical tests of significance, that you will explore in the remainder of this book. Specifically, we will discuss the central limit theorem, sampling distribution of the mean, null and alternative hypotheses, alpha and probability levels, Type 1 and Type 2 errors, and power.

CENTRAL LIMIT THEOREM

Perhaps one of the most important concepts in statistics is the central limit theorem. This theorem is the foundation for many of the statistical tests that you will use in this book. You have already used several procedures to describe samples. Frequencies and histograms were useful for describing the distribution of the sample, while other descriptive statistics, such as the mean and standard deviation, were used to describe the sample's central tendency and variability.

Using these descriptive procedures, we are able to describe different types of samples. Some samples are symmetrical while others are skewed. Samples also differ in terms of their central tendency, variability, and size. Given that all samples are not the same, and that the results of your research depend on the information provided by your sample, you want to be sure to base your results on a good sample. That is, you want your sample to be representative of the overall population. While this may be true, and you will make every effort to obtain a representative sample, samples will still vary a great deal.

For example, the population mean of IQ scores is 100. That is, the tests used to measure intelligence yield means of 100. As you know, individuals' scores will vary from the mean. Some individuals will have below average intelligence while others have above average. Depending on which IQ test is used (e.g., Stanford-Binet, Wechsler), individual scores will rarely be below 50 or above 150. In fact, approximately 2/3 of all IQ scores will fall between 68 and 132, as measured by the Stanford-Binet, and between 70 and 130 when measured by the Wechsler scales. Therefore, most samples drawn from the overall population will have means close to 100 and rarely outside of the 68 to 132 range.

This does not mean that every sample of individuals you find will have a mean IQ score close to 100. Some samples may be more extreme because they are comprised of exceptional individuals. Most samples, however, will have means close to 100 if they are representative

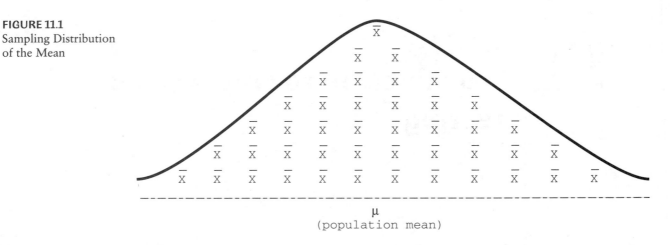

μ
(population mean)

of the general population. More extreme sample means are less likely to occur. How many people, other than yourself, do you know who have an IQ near 130? Imagine a random sample of thirty individuals having a mean IQ of 130. A sample with a mean this extreme would just not occur very often if it were drawn from the general population. In other words, the probability of obtaining a sample with a mean this high by chance would be very low. It would be equally unlikely to obtain a random sample of thirty individuals with a mean IQ as low as 70. Sample means will vary from their population mean just due to chance, or sampling error.

This is an example of the logic of the central limit theorem. Using the central limit theorem, we know that if all samples of a certain size are drawn, these sample means will be distributed symmetrically around the population mean. This distribution is called the *sampling distribution of the mean*. Samples with extremely low or extremely high means are not as likely to occur as those with means closer to the population mean. We also know that as the size of these samples becomes larger (i.e., approximately thirty or more), this distribution will approach a normal distribution, as illustrated in Figure 11.1.

The mean of the sampling distribution of the mean will always be the population mean (μ). Most sample means will be distributed close to the center of this distribution, while fewer will occur toward the extremes, or tails, of the distribution. The variability of this distribution depends largely on the size of the samples. Therefore, sampling distributions based on smaller samples will be more widely distributed around the population mean than those based on larger samples.

Larger samples capture more of the population and, therefore, tend to be more representative. Thus, they will tend to have sample means that are closer to the population mean. We know how sensitive the sample mean is to extreme scores, and this impact is much greater in smaller samples. If the sample consists of only five cases, one extreme score would have a great impact on that sample mean. However, if the sample is larger (e.g., n = 100), the influence of a few extreme scores will not be as great. This is true because there will be many more scores near the center of the distribution to overcome the effect of the extreme scores in larger samples.

HYPOTHESIS TESTING

Using the central limit theorem, we would expect the mean of any given sample to be equal to the mean of the sampling distribution, or the population mean. The farther a sample mean is from the population mean, the more likely it does NOT belong to that population. In other words, an extreme sample mean may in fact belong to a different population, having a different mean. You would think this was the case if you had drawn a sample and computed a mean IQ of 130. It is just not very probable that a sample would have a mean IQ as high as 130 if it had been drawn from the general population having a mean of 100.

To determine whether or not a sample with mean IQ of 130 belongs to the general population, we would use a hypothesis testing process. We begin by stating a hypothesis about the population mean. If our sample did come from the general population, we would expect its population mean to be 100. Therefore, we would hypothesize that the population mean of our sample is equal to 100. This is called the *null hypothesis*. A null hypothesis is used to make an initial statement about our beliefs regarding some population parameter, such as a mean or variance. The null hypothesis is our best guess about the population parameter, and we will assume it is true until we have sufficient evidence to reject it. In this case, we are making a statement about the population mean being equal to 100. The other alternative is that the population mean is NOT equal to 100. This is called the *alternative hypothesis*.

Hypotheses can be stated in a directional or nondirectional manner. The hypotheses stated in the above paragraph are *nondirectional*. A nondirectional hypothesis is also called a *two-tailed hypothesis* because the alternative hypothesis allows for the results of the study to occur in either tail of the sampling distribution. In other words, the null hypothesis could be rejected if the mean IQ of our sample is less than or greater than 100.

A *directional* or *one-tailed hypothesis* is more specific, indicating the direction of the outcome of the study. For example, if theory and/or prior research efforts indicate that your sample of individuals should have a mean IQ higher than 100, you might use a directional hypothesis. Using a directional hypothesis, you would only expect your sample mean to occur in one tail of the sampling distribution. Suppose we had evidence suggesting that graduate students are superior in terms of their IQ scores. This evidence could be drawn from theory or prior research efforts regarding graduate student intelligence. If this were the case, you would expect your sample to have a mean higher than 100 and would state a one-tailed hypothesis. You should be careful when deciding whether to state a one- or two-tailed hypothesis. If there is no solid theoretical basis, or prior research efforts are mixed, a nondirectional hypothesis should be used.

After stating the hypotheses, the next step is to compare the statistics from the sample to the parameter(s) in the hypothesized population, as specified by the null hypothesis. Using the appropriate statistical procedure, we determine the likelihood that the sample results occurred, given the conditions stated in the null hypothesis. In other words, how likely would it be to obtain a sample mean IQ of 130, given the sample was drawn from a population having a mean IQ of 100? This doesn't seem very likely. After all, 30 points is a large difference as far as IQ scores are concerned. But, the question is: How large is large enough to conclude that our sample did not come from a population having a mean IQ of 100?

How many points would it take to convince you that this sample has a different mean IQ than the general population? 5 points? 10 points? 20 points? Are 30 points enough? Although 30 points may seem like a large difference using IQ scores, it would not seem as large if we were using student GRE scores. Therefore, 30 points may be enough to convince you to reject the null hypothesis regarding IQ, but not if GRE scores were being compared. If you had to determine different cut points for rejecting the null hypothesis in every situation, the process would become very subjective. To prevent this process from being too subjective, we will follow a consistent process which can be applied to differences regardless of what is being measured. In previous chapters, when we faced the problem of comparing people on variables measured on different scales, we transformed raw scores into standard scores, or z scores. When variables are converted to the same scale, comparisons can be easily made.

In the hypothesis testing procedure, we do the same thing. We first convert each difference to a standard statistical score (e.g., χ^2, z, t, F), having a known distribution. By doing this, the process of evaluating these differences and making a decision becomes more objective. Second, using the appropriate statistical procedure, we will determine the probability of our sample results occurring under the conditions specified by the null hypothesis. For some situations, the z distribution will be used to determine this probability, while in others, the χ^2, t, or F distribution will be more appropriate. Finally, we make a decision about the null hypothesis. If the probability of our sample results occurring is high, we will retain the null hypothesis. However, if the probability is very low that these results would occur under the conditions of the null hypothesis, we reject the null hypothesis and accept an alternative hypothesis.

This is the process of hypothesis testing that we will follow when using the statistical procedures illustrated in this book. This process can be summarized in a few steps.

Step 1	Specify the null and alternative hypotheses.
Step 2	Gather information from your sample.
Step 3	Compare this sample statistic(s) to the hypothesized population parameter(s) using the appropriate statistical procedure (e.g., χ^2, z, t, F).
Step 4	Determine the probability of your sample results occurring, given the conditions specified in the null hypothesis.
Step 5	Make a decision about whether to retain or reject the null hypothesis.

MAKING A DECISION AND REACHING CONCLUSIONS

Before you make a decision about whether to retain or reject the null hypothesis, there are a few things you must consider. Because you are basing your decision on results from a sample and not the entire population, you can never be sure that you are reaching the correct conclusion. You make your decision about the null hypothesis based on a probability of being wrong. The question is: How much risk are you willing to take in being wrong about your decision? In the hypothesis testing process, you predetermine the amount of risk you are willing to take in being wrong. You determine this risk prior to analysis, this risk, or significance level, is represented using the Greek letter alpha (α) and referred to as the *alpha level*. You have control over the level of risk by establishing an alpha level for each statistical procedure you perform.

Generally, it is acceptable to set your level of risk at 5%. What this means is that you could be wrong up to 5 times in 100 when you reject the null hypothesis. Depending on the consequences of being wrong, you might want to take less risk. For example, if a wrong decision could cost a substantial amount of money, or even worse, illness or loss of life, you would want to lower the risk of being wrong. If lives would be in danger, you might want to limit your risk of being wrong to 1 time in 1,000, or $\alpha = .001$.

Each statistical procedure you perform will yield two important pieces of information that are used to help you make a decision about the null hypothesis. These are the obtained statistical value (e.g., χ^2, z, t, F), and a probability level associated with this value. The *statistical value* is the result of the statistical procedure used to test the null hypothesis. This value represents the position of your sample results in the sampling distribution. The more extreme this value, either in a positive or negative direction, the more extreme your sample results are and the less likely they are to have occurred by chance. This statistical value will be compared to a value in the distribution that defines the maximum amount of risk you are willing to take, determined by your alpha level.

The value in the distribution that is used for comparison is called the *critical value*. You can consult the appropriate statistical distribution table (e.g., χ^2, z, t, F) to determine the precise critical value. These distributions are found in the appendix section of most statistics textbooks. As statistical values become larger, the likelihood of the results occurring by chance becomes smaller. For each statistical value, a *probability level,* or *p value,* is computed to indicate the likelihood of this value occurring by chance, given the conditions stated in the null hypothesis. Let's examine some qualities of the standard normal z distribution as we continue to explore hypothesis testing.

Figure 11.2 displays the standard normal distribution of z scores. We have identified just a few of the infinite number of z scores that make up this distribution. A complete table of z scores associated with the standard normal distribution can be found in almost any statistics textbook. A z score identifies the distance from the mean in terms of standard devi-

FIGURE 11.2
Standard Normal
Distribution

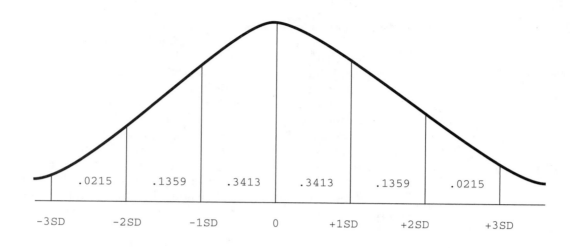

TABLE 11.1
Critical z values

z value	Probability	
	One-tailed (Directional)	Two-tailed (Nondirectional)
1.645	.05	.10
1.96	.025	.05
2.33	.01	.02
2.58	.005	.01

ation units. That is, a z value of $+1.0$ represents the point in the distribution that is one standard deviation above the mean. On the other hand, a z value of -1.0 identifies a point one standard deviation below the mean. For example, the Wechsler scales, used to measure intelligence, follow a distribution with a mean of 100 and a standard deviation of 15. Therefore, if these scores were converted to z scores, a score of 115 would correspond to a z score of $+1.0$, exactly one standard deviation (i.e., 15 points) above the mean. As z scores get farther from the mean (above or below), they become more extreme. Therefore, the likelihood, or probability, of these more extreme values occurring by chance becomes smaller. Let's take a look at some of the properties of the normal distribution in order to further understand probability and chance.

The standard normal distribution exhibits certain basic properties that are particularly helpful when evaluating the results from statistical procedures. First, approximately 2/3 (68.26%) of this distribution is contained within one standard deviation of the mean (-1.0 to $+1.0$). In addition, over 95% (95.44%) is distributed within two standard deviations (-2.0 to $+2.0$). Z scores in excess of two standard deviations from the mean are unlikely to occur. Locate a z score of $+2$ in the standard normal distribution (see Figure 11.2). You will notice that the area above this point represents approximately two percent (2.28%) of the distribution. Z values of 2 or greater are rather unlikely due to chance. This would be equivalent to having an IQ score of 130 or above, measured by the Wechsler scales, which is not very likely in the general population.

Understanding the basic properties of the standard normal distribution will be very helpful when engaging in null hypothesis testing. Because we understand these properties, we can determine, in advance, the critical value needed to reject the null hypothesis. Examine the z values reported in Table 11.1. We have identified these as critical values because they correspond to points along the standard normal distribution typically set as criteria for rejecting the null hypothesis.

Remember that hypotheses can be stated as directional or nondirectional. This will have an impact on your decision. If a nondirectional, hypothesis is being tested, we need to take into account that our sample results could occur in either tail of the sampling distribution. On the other hand, a directional hypothesis would dictate that we examine only the results if they occur in one end of the distribution.

Suppose we set our alpha level at .05, a level widely used in null hypothesis testing. If we were performing a nondirectional test, the critical z value set for the rejection of the null hypothesis would be 1.96. In other words, if we obtain a z value equal to or more extreme than +/− 1.96, we would reject the null hypothesis because our results would have a low probability (equal to or less than .05) of occurring under the conditions specified by the null hypothesis. If, however, the results from our z test yielded a value less extreme than +/− 1.96, we would retain the null hypothesis. In this case, the probability of such a result occurring would exceed 5 times in 100, the criteria set by our alpha level.

Let's examine a directional, or one-tailed, hypothesis. In this case, we expect our results to occur in a specific direction. Using our IQ example, we might expect graduate students to have higher IQ scores. Therefore, we would expect the results of our statistical procedure (i.e. z test) to yield only positive results. Examine the values presented in Table 11.1. Based on an alpha level of .05, the critical z value would be 1.645. If we expected our results to be negative, the critical value would be −1.645. What if we decided to use a more stringent alpha level, like .01? Take another look at Table 11.1 and determine the critical z values for a one- and two-tail test. You should have selected critical z 2.33 for a one-tailed test and 2.58 for a two-tailed test.

Two things should have influenced your selection of an appropriate critical value. First, you needed to determine the alpha level. The alpha level determines the amount of risk you are willing to take when rejecting the null hypothesis. Using an alpha level of .05 assumes more risk than one set at .01. Therefore, you will decide to reject the null hypothesis more often when using an alpha level of .05.

Second, you needed to know whether the test was directional or nondirectional. When using the alpha level of .05, the one-tail critical z value was 1.654, while the two-tail value was +/− 1.96. The critical value is smaller when testing a directional hypothesis because you are examining results in only one tail of the distribution. Using a two-tail test, however, you might expect results to occur in either direction, and therefore, you must assume risk in either direction.

What if your decision about the null hypothesis is wrong? There are two basic types of mistakes, or errors, you could make when making your decision about the null hypothesis. First, you could reject the null hypothesis when it is in fact true. In our previous example using IQ scores, we might have determined that the probability of our sample coming from a population with a mean IQ of 100 is very low and therefore reject the null hypothesis when, in reality, the population mean is equal to 100 and our sample mean differs just because of sampling error, or chance. This type of mistake is called a *Type 1 error.* It is very difficult to tell when you've made a Type 1 error because you never have access to the entire population. You have to make decisions based on your sample.

Fortunately, you have some control over Type 1 error. You define the amount of risk you are willing to take when you set your alpha level. If your alpha level is set at .05, you are taking up to a 5% risk in being wrong when you reject the null hypothesis. Your alpha level will determine your risk in committing a Type 1 error. If you set your alpha level lower (e.g., .01), you will take less of a risk in making a Type 1 error. We recommend using a lower alpha level if you are performing a series of related statistical tests, because Type 1 error will increase with each additional statistical test.

Unfortunately, setting your alpha level lower to decrease the likelihood of making a Type 1 error increases the probability of making a second type of mistake, called a *Type 2 error.* A Type 2 error occurs when you fail to reject the null hypothesis when it is, in fact, false. Using a lower alpha level (e.g., $\alpha = .01$ or .001) makes it more difficult to reject the null hypothesis, because the sample results must be more extreme to meet the more stringent criteria and, therefore, will increase your chances of committing a Type 2 error.

Often, researchers make Type 2 errors due to methodological reasons. For example, if the study is poorly designed or the sample is not representative, your chances of rejecting a false null hypothesis may decrease, increasing the probability of a Type 2 error.

What you want to do is make the correct decision and reject the null hypothesis when it is false. The probability of rejecting the null hypothesis when it is false is called *power*. You want to do everything you can to increase the power of your statistical test so you will make the right decision in rejecting the null hypothesis. There are a few things you can do to increase the power of a statistical procedure. First, be sure that your sample is sufficiently large and representative so that it will provide a good estimate of the population parameter(s). Second, pay close attention to the details in your methodology so that you can maximize your chances of finding a treatment effect. As you develop treatment and measurement procedures, be sure to pilot test them and revise them so that you minimize errors in the process that could prevent you from rejecting the null hypothesis when it is false. The reliable and valid measurement of your dependent variable is essential. Finally, use a very stringent alpha level ($\alpha = .001$) only when the consequences of making a Type 1 error are severe, because this makes it more difficult to reject the null hypothesis and decreases power.

STATISTICAL TESTS OF SIGNIFICANCE

In the chapters that follow, we will illustrate a variety of statistical procedures. Most of these statistical procedures are used with the hypothesis testing process to help you make a decision and reach conclusions about your research study. Some of these statistical procedures are intended to be used for one sample, while others are used when comparing two or more samples. Statistical procedures are used to make comparisons between different groups and within the same group. Other procedures are used to examine relationships between different variables.

In the next section of this book, we will examine relationships among variables. In examining such relationships, we will determine the extent to which they occur by chance under the null hypothesis. We will compare the probability associated with our statistical result with a predetermined alpha level. If the probability is equal to or less than our alpha level, we will reject the null hypothesis and assume that a relationship exists. If the probability of chance is greater than our alpha level, we will retain the null hypothesis. We examine relationships among categorical variables in Chapter 12, while Chapter 14 focuses on relationships between variables measured at the ordinal, interval, and ratio level.

One-sample tests of significance are generally used to compare a sample mean to a hypothesized population mean and determine how likely it is that the sample came from that population. A one-sample test would be used to determine whether our sample with a mean IQ of 150 came from the general population having a mean IQ of 100. Two general statistical procedures are used for one-sample situations. These are the z test and the t test. Because the z test requires information about the population standard deviation and this is generally not available, the t test is more common and will be illustrated in Chapter 15.

Two-sample tests of significance are used to determine whether two samples came from populations having the same mean. For example, we may have two samples of students; one is comprised of undergraduates and the other is a graduate student sample. A two-sample test will allow us to determine whether the population means of these two samples differ. As with one-sample tests, both a z and t test can be used, but a t test is more commonly used because the information required for the z test (i.e., population standard deviation) is often not available. The two-sample, or independent-samples t test will also be illustrated in Chapter 15.

What if you have more than two groups? If you want to compare two or more groups on some dependent variable, such as IQ, a one-way analysis of variance (ANOVA) would be used. This statistical procedure is illustrated in Chapter 16. A one-way ANOVA could be used if you wanted to compare the IQ scores of undergraduates and graduates, but it would certainly be used if you had a third group, such as faculty. You might want to break down each group by gender so that males and females can also be compared. This adds a second independent variable to the study. A situation such as this would call for a factorial analysis of variance, illustrated in Chapter 17. Factorial ANOVA is used to examine the effects of more than one independent variable.

Not all comparisons will be made between different groups or samples. Sometimes, you will want to make comparisons within the same group or related groups. A t test can also be used to compare groups that are related. Suppose you wanted to compare parents and their children by their IQ. In this case, it is very important to keep each parent-child pair together when you apply the statistical procedure. A special t test called a dependent t test would be used in this situation. A dependent t test could also be used if you measured the IQ of the same sample before (pre-test) and after (post-test) you provided them with a treatment to increase their IQ score. This procedure is illustrated in Chapter 18. If you decided to follow-up with these students six months after the posttest, a repeated measures ANOVA would be used to compare IQ scores across all three times. This procedure is illustrated in Chapter 19.

You can also use statistical procedures that allow you to make comparisons between groups *and* within groups. For example, you might want to compare three groups (i.e., undergraduates, graduates, and faculty) over time (i.e., pre-test, post-test, follow-up). These comparisons are referred to as mixed models because they include both between-group and within-group comparisons. Mixed model analysis of variance procedures are illustrated in Chapter 20.

Statistical procedures are also used to help you make predictions about an outcome, or dependent variable. These statistical procedures include correlation and regression analysis. If you wanted to predict the success of graduate students, you would use correlation and regression analysis. These predictions are made using variables called predictor variables. We will illustrate bivariate regression, which uses only one predictor variable, in Chapter 21 and multiple regression in Chapter 22.

CHAPTER SUMMARY

In this chapter, we discussed the importance of the sampling distribution of the mean and the central limit theorem and their role in the process of hypothesis testing. These concepts guide us through statistical procedures and help us to make decisions about what the data tell us. We will apply these important concepts as we explore a variety of statistical procedures in the chapters that follow. We will be using these procedures to test hypotheses concerning differences within one group, between two or more groups, and predictions about the influence of one or more variables on another. The importance of the concepts discussed in this chapter will become more apparent as we explore statistical procedures using SPSS.

PRACTICE EXERCISES

Use the standard normal distribution as a reference (see Figure 11.2) to address the following questions.

1. It has been discovered that when students complete their statistics coursework, they tend to suffer from withdrawal. Often they become so ill that they must spend time in the hospital and receive professional treatment. The distribution of length of stay in the hospital follows a normal distribution with a mean of 5 days and a standard deviation of 1 day.
   a. What percent of students spend seven or more days in the hospital?
   b. What is the length of stay for students found at the 84th percentile in this distribution?
   c. Of a class of fifty students, how many would be expected to spend between four and six days in the hospital?
   d. What percent of students would spend between three and six days in the hospital?

SECTION V

Measures of
Association

12 | Crosstabulation of Variables

Thus far, you have had a chance to explore SPSS and to produce output, such as frequency tables and descriptive statistics for your data. You have also recoded variables, created new ones, and performed a reliability analysis. In this chapter, we will begin to explore some other statistical procedures that will allow you to summarize your data and describe relationships between variables.

This chapter focuses on the use of crosstabulation of variables to help summarize your data. By crosstabulating variables, you will be able to determine how many people in your sample belong to groups formed by a combination of categorical variables. For example, if you examine the variables in our data set on applicants to a doctoral program (see Appendix A), you will find several categorical variables such as: gender (GENDER), ethnicity (ETHNIC), and socioeconomic status (SES). These variables help to describe the applicant pool for the doctoral program. Using frequencies, you are able to determine the percentage of applicants belonging to each category of each variable. Of the overall applicant pool, you are able to determine the percentage who were male, or African-American, or from low socioeconomic background.

Using crosstabulation procedures, you will be able to describe this applicant pool in more specific terms. You will be able to determine the percentage of applicants who were male, African-American, and from a higher SES background, or those who are white, female, and from a lower or middle SES background. This information about your sample could be very valuable. Crosstabulation would be used to summarize information pertaining to gender, ethnicity, and SES in a table with each cell representing a specific subgroup of the applicant pool. In addition, crosstabulation can be used to determine the extent to which two or more categorical variables are related.

There are many statistical procedures used to measure relationships. The statistical procedures used to assess the extent to which variables are related depend largely on the type of variables being used. Before we explore these procedures using SPSS, we'll discuss the measures of association that are appropriate for variables measured at different levels of measurement. We will focus on nominal and ordinal variables in this chapter. In the next chapter, we will examine relationships between variables measured on interval and ratio scales.

MEASURES OF ASSOCIATION

Measures Used for Nominal Variables

There are several procedures that can be used to assess the relationship between two nominal variables. As a group, these procedures are referred to as nonparametric statistics. We encourage you to read more about nonparametric statistics in your introductory statistics textbook. An overview of the statistical procedures explored in this chapter follows.

Among the nonparametric measures of association, the *chi-square* procedure is the most commonly used. This statistical procedure is used to test the null hypothesis that two categorical variables are not related. We discussed null hypothesis testing in the previous chapter.

Specifically, the chi-square procedure is used to compare observed cell frequencies with what you would expect if the two variables were independent (i.e., not related). As the difference between observed and expected frequencies gets larger, so does the chi-square statistic. Because the chi-square statistic follows a known distribution, it is possible to determine the extent to which a specific chi-square value would occur by chance. This is expressed in the form of a probability (*p* value) or significance level. As chi-square values get larger, the probability of chance decreases. Should the probability of a result occurring by chance be equal to or less than your pre-determined criterion (i.e., alpha level), you will reject the null hypothesis and conclude that a relationship exists between the variables.

Another simple measure of association used for nominal variables is the *phi coefficient*. The phi coefficient, which is computed from the chi-square statistic, is used for dichotomous variables. As this value approaches 1, the relationship gets stronger. As this value approaches 0, the relationship is weaker. The phi coefficient would be appropriate for determining the magnitude of the relationship between a variable such as GENDER and a variable that requires a yes or no response.

For assessing the magnitude of the relationship between two variables that are not dichotomous, the *contingency coefficient* should be used. For example, the relationship between socioeconomic status and ethnicity would call for the use of the contingency coefficient. Again, the closer to 1 the stronger the relationship is between the two variables.

Another measure, *lambda,* can also be used for categorical variables. Lambda, however is interpreted somewhat differently. Instead of indicating the magnitude of the relationship between two variables, lambda indicates the extent to which error is reduced in predicting one variable using the other variable. For this reason, lambda is known as a proportionate reduction in error measure. Like other measures, the closer lambda is to 1, the better. To use lambda, you must distinguish between the independent and the dependent variables. The lambda statistic would be useful if you wanted to use ethnicity (ETHNIC) as the independent variable to predict socioeconomic status (SES), the dependent variable.

Measures Used for Ordinal Variables

When you are assessing the relationship between ordinal variables, other measures of association are available. These measures include Spearman's rank-order correlation, gamma, Somers' d, Kendall's tau-b and tau-c. Measures such as chi-square, the contingency coefficient, and lamda can also be used with ordinal variables.

For data that are arranged in the form of ranks, the *Spearman rank-order correlation coefficient* is commonly used. This coefficient will range from -1 to $+1$. The closer the correlation is to -1 or $+1$, the stronger the relationship. A positive relationship indicates that individuals ranked high on the first variable tend to be ranked high on the second variable, while those ranked low on the first variable tend to be ranked low on the second variable. A negative relationship indicates the opposite. Therefore, individuals who are ranked high on the first variable tend to be ranked low on the second variable, while those ranked low on the first tend to be ranked high on the second. We will introduce the use of the Spearman rank-order correlation procedure in this chapter, but explore it in more detail in the following chapter.

Gamma is another measure that can be used to assess the relationship between two ordinal variables. Like the Spearman rank-order coefficient, this statistic ranges from -1 to $+1$, with the sign indicating the type of relationship between the two variables. Specifically, the gamma statistic examines the extent to which the ranks for each variable agree. If the ranks on each variable agree perfectly, a gamma of $+1.0$ will result. If the ranks of each variable are exactly the opposite, a gamma of -1.0 will result. A positive gamma statistic indicates that the ranks agree more often than disagree, while a negative gamma indicates that the opposite is true. A limitation of gamma is that it ignores ranks that are tied. In other words, if more than one subject receives the same ranking on the same variable, these data will be ignored.

There are several other measures that account for ties. One measure, *Somers' d* is an extension of the gamma statistic. Like the lambda statistic, Somers' d makes a distinction between the independent and dependent variables when assessing their relationship. The values of Somers' d will range from -1.0 to $+1.0$. Two other measures, *Kendall's tau-b* and *tau-c,* can also be used for ordinal data. Like Somers' d, these measures of association account for ranks that are tied. However, the values for Kendall's tau-b will range from -1.0 to $+1.0$ only for variables having the same number of levels (ordered categories). Kendall's tau-c will work well with variables having a different number of levels.

Other Measures of Association

One simple measure suitable for both nominal and ordinal data is the *kappa* statistic. Kappa measures the agreement between paired variables. Kappa is useful for determining the extent to which pairs of raters or interviewers agree. If doctoral applicants are interviewed by more than one faculty member, kappa would determine the extent to which the faculty members' ratings of the candidate agreed. Like most previous measures discussed, kappa ranges from -1.0 to $+1.0$, with a $+1.0$ indicating perfect agreement and a -1.0 indicating perfect disagreement.

Eta is another useful statistic. If you were interested in determining the extent to which a nominal variable related to an interval variable, eta would be appropriate. For example, eta would be used to describe the relationship between ethnicity and scores on the Graduate Record Examination. When the eta statistic is squared, it represents the amount of variability in the dependent variable accounted for by the independent variable. Eta and eta^2 will be very useful to us when we explore analysis of variance and regression in later chapters.

Before we begin to work with SPSS, let's examine the variables we will use to illustrate these procedures.

VARIABLES USED IN THIS CHAPTER

The variables we will be using come from our graduate student data set. Several variables will be used throughout this chapter. Some of these variables are measured on a nominal scale, while others are measured on an ordinal scale. We will be using computer experience (COMPEXP), educational level (EDUC), employment status (EMPLOYED), gender (GENDER), enrollment in night course (NIGHT), and student status (STATUS). You have worked with the computer experience and gender variables in previous chapters. COMPEXP has five categories and GENDER has two categories. Educational level (EDUC) is defined as the highest degree earned. There are four possible levels, 1=Bachelor's, 2=Master's, 3=Specialist, and 4=Doctorate.

The remaining three variables, employment status (EMPLOYED), enrollment in night courses (NIGHT), and student status (STATUS) are dichotomous. EMPLOYED is a question pertaining to the student's employment status during the quarter they were enrolled in the course. The next variable, NIGHT, indicates whether or not a student is enrolled in evening courses only. Both of these variables are coded as "0" or "1" to represent "no" and "yes" responses to these questions. The last variable, STATUS, identifies whether a student is enrolled part- or full-time. STATUS is coded as a "1" if the student is part-time and a "2" if he or she is enrolled full-time.

Using crosstabulation procedures, we will be able to summarize these variables and answer a variety of questions about the relationships among them. For example, are more males or females enrolled as full-time students? Also, is there a relationship between gender and computer experience? Finally, is enrollment status dependent upon employment status?

We will use SPSS to perform crosstabulation procedures and answer these questions. Focusing on the information pertaining to the SPSS version that you are using, please follow closely and reproduce our illustrations. You will be given additional opportunities to apply these statistical procedures using other variables found in the data set.

USING SPSS FOR CROSSTABULATION

In the previous few chapters, you summarized and described several variables pertaining to graduate students' attitudes toward computers and statistics using the Frequencies, Descriptives, and Means procedures. In this chapter, you will be crosstabulating variables to summarize them and explore relationships between them. The primary command used to generate crosstabulations of variables is Crosstabs.

Before you specify this command, you need to activate the SPSS for Windows and retrieve the data file named **chap12 data** on your data disk.

CROSSTABS PROCEDURES

As with each of the previous SPSS procedures, you begin with the **Analyze** menu. From this menu, select the **Descriptive Statistics** and **Crosstabs...** options, as illustrated in Figure 12.1. Selecting these options will open the Crosstabs dialog box, displayed in Figure 12.2.

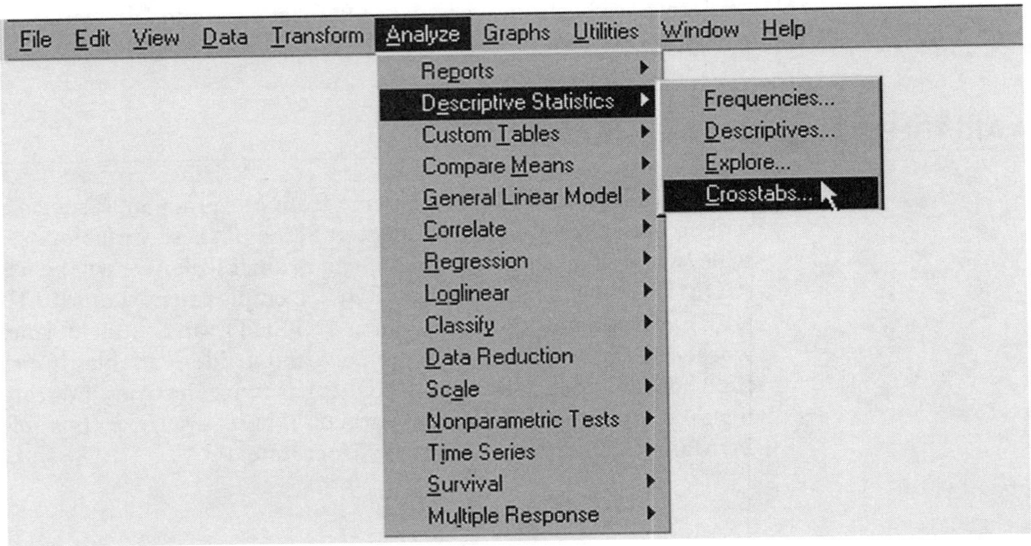

FIGURE 12.1
Analyze–Descriptive Statistics–Crosstabs menu selections

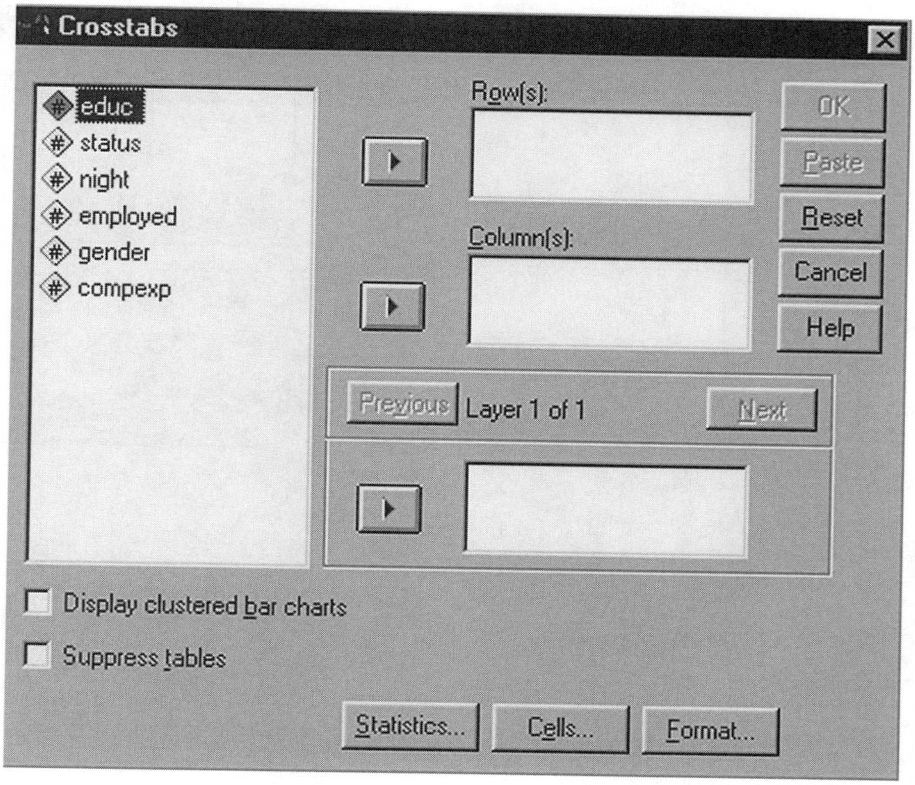

FIGURE 12.2
Crosstabs dialog box

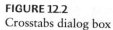

This dialog box offers many of the same features as those you worked with when running the Frequencies, Descriptives, and Means procedures. At the left of the window, the names of all your variables are listed in the source variable list. You identify which variables you want to summarize by selecting them from the source variable list and placing them in the boxes labeled **Row(s):** and **Column(s):**.

Two-Way Tables

To generate a summary of gender (GENDER) and computer experience (COMPEXP), select GENDER from the source variable list and place it in the box labeled **Row(s):** and select COMPEXP and place it in the box labeled **Column(s):**.

The selection you made will create one table, summarizing GENDER and COMPEXP. We want to generate more than one table in this SPSS session. To do this, you select additional variables from the source variable list and add them to the boxes labeled **Row(s):** and **Column(s):**. If you wanted to summarize other variables with GENDER, you would select them and transfer them to the box labeled **Column(s):**. Select the following variables: EDUC, EMPLOYED, NIGHT, STATUS and move to the **Column(s):** box.

You should now have the variable of GENDER in the **Row(s):** box and the remaining five variables in the **Column(s):** box, as illustrated in Figure 12.3. Upon clicking on the **OK** command button, SPSS will produce five tables. By default, each table will include the number of people in each crosstabulated category (cell). For example, the first table (GENDER by COMPEXP) will summarize the number of males and females at each level of computer experience.

However, before you request these tables, let's explore some other options available using the Crosstabs procedure. There are three buttons at the bottom of this dialog box. The first button, **Statistics...**, is used to request statistics along with the summary table. These statistics are used to assess the relationship between the crosstabulated variables. The next button, **Cells...**, is used to request additional information to be summarized in each cell of the table. Finally, the last button, **Format...**, allows you to specify the format in which you want the information summarized.

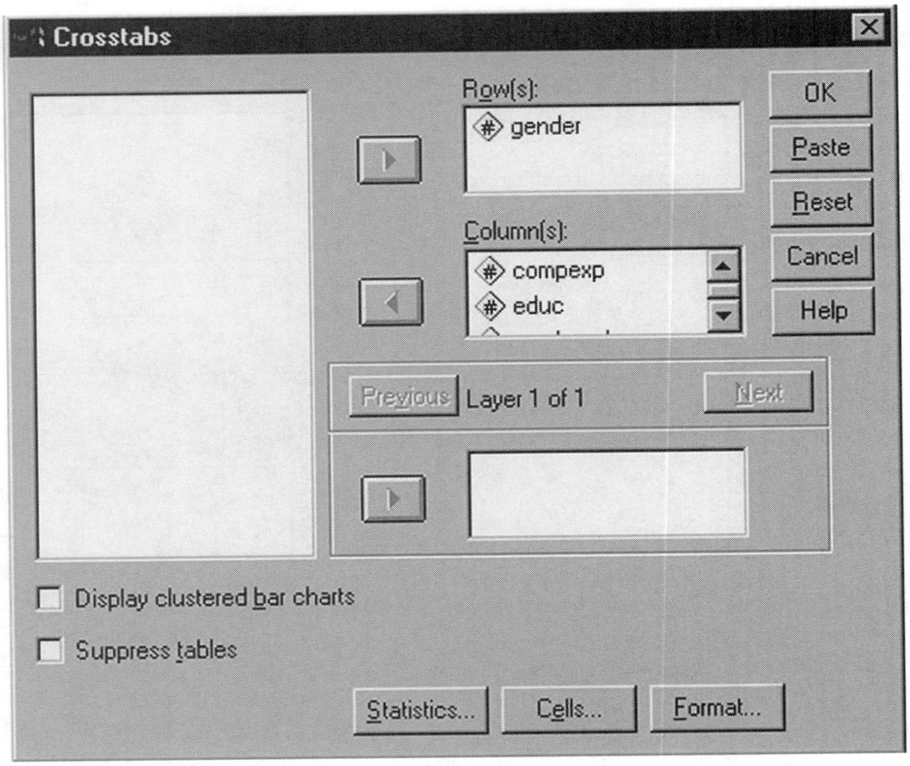

FIGURE 12.3
Specifications for two-way tables

If you do not want SPSS to produce any tables, select the option under the source variable list which allows you to suppress the tables. In choosing this option, only the information requested using the Statistics option will be reported in the SPSS output.

Statistics Option.   Click your mouse on the **Statistics...** button to open the Crosstabs: Statistics dialog box, displayed in Figure 12.4.

You will notice that there are several statistics available. As we discussed in the beginning of this chapter, the choice of which of these statistical procedures to use depends largely on the type of variables being used. Notice that most of the options presented in this Statistics dialog box are organized under headings. There are four options under the Nominal heading and four under Ordinal. One additional option is listed under the Nominal by Interval heading. SPSS helps guide your selection of these statistical procedures by organizing them under the appropriate heading. The remaining options can be used for variables measured on different levels.

The most frequently used statistic is the chi-square. Remember, the chi-square procedure is used to test the null hypothesis, that the two variables are not related. If the two variables are related, there will be a difference between the observed frequencies and those expected by chance, resulting in a large chi-square value. You will usually want to request the chi-square statistic.

Several other statistics can also be used to assess the relationship between the variables summarized by the Crosstabs procedure. Other measures that are suitable for nominal-level variables (i.e., GENDER, EMPLOYED, NIGHT, STATUS) include the phi coefficient, contingency coefficient, lambda, and the uncertainty coefficient. Measures appropriate for ordinal variables, which exist in the form of ranks, include Kendall's tau-b and tau-c, Somers' d and gamma.

We will not request all these statistics because many of them will not be useful for the variables included in this analysis. First, we will request the chi-square statistic, which will be useful in evaluating the difference between observed frequencies and those expected by

FIGURE 12.4
Crosstabs: Statistics
dialog box

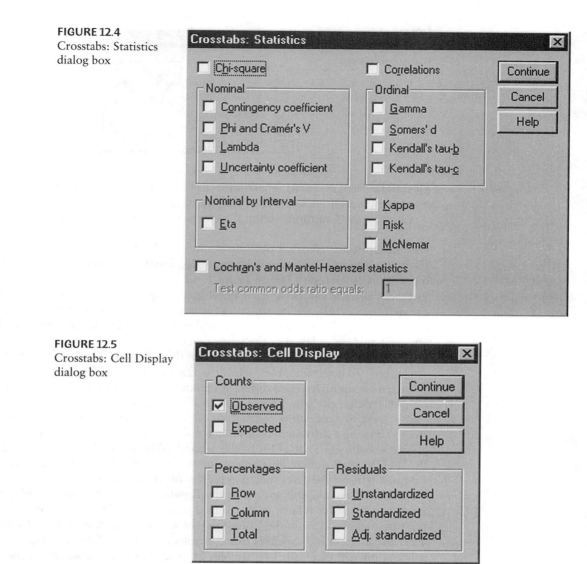

FIGURE 12.5
Crosstabs: Cell Display
dialog box

chance for each table. Second, we will request the contingency coefficient, which provides an index of the magnitude of the relationships between the categorical variables. The third statistic we will request is the phi coefficient, which will be useful in assessing the relationship between the dichotomous variables, GENDER, EMPLOY, NIGHT, and STATUS. Select these three statistics by clicking on each box with your mouse. When they have been selected, the box next to each of these options should be checked. Click on the **Continue** button to return to the Crosstabs dialog box.

Cells Option. Select the **Cells...** button at the bottom of the dialog box. The Crosstabs: Cell Display dialog box, displayed in Figure 12.5, will appear on your screen.

By default, the only information that will appear in the tables will be observed counts, or frequencies. To provide a more detailed summary, we'll select a few additional options. First, under the default **Observed** option is an option for **Expected** counts. Select this option. This will display the frequencies for each cell which would be expected if the two variables were not related. This information, along with the chi-square statistic you selected earlier, will be helpful in determining the extent to which crosstabulated variables are related.

In the box labeled Percentages, there are three options. Select all three. This will result in the calculation of row percentages, column percentages, and total percentages. One additional option under the Residuals heading will be valuable. Select the option for

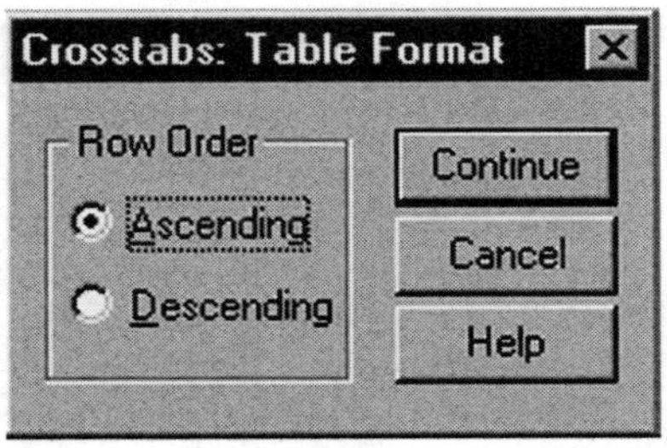

FIGURE 12.6
Crosstabs: Table
Format dialog box

Crosstabs: Table Format

Row Order
- ⦿ Ascending
- ○ Descending

[Continue] [Cancel] [Help]

<u>U</u>nstandardized residuals. This option will display the difference between the observed and expected frequencies for each cell in the table.

Click on the **Continue** button to return to the Crosstabs dialog box.

Format Options.   Format options pertain to the format of the SPSS output. Select the <u>F</u>ormat... button at the bottom of the dialog box to open the Crosstabs: Table Format dialog box, as displayed in Figure 12.6.

By default, the values for each variable are displayed in the output table in ascending order. In other words, the information for males would appear first because males are coded as "1" and females, coded as "2," would follow. The results are displayed in table format and each table is indexed in the output viewer.

Accept the default settings and click on the **Continue** button to return to the Crosstabs dialog box. To generate tables, select the **OK** command pushbutton. Five tables will be generated, each summarizing a different variable with GENDER. Before we examine the SPSS output, let's specify some different tables.

We want to generate two different tables, each summarizing student enrollment status (STATUS) with a different variable. In the first table, we will summarize STATUS with night course enrollment (NIGHT). In the second table, we will summarize employment status (EMPLOY) with student enrollment status (STATUS). Before we can select these variables, we must remove the ones specified for the previous tables.

GENDER should still appear in the **R<u>o</u>w(s):** box. To remove it, highlight it with your mouse and transfer it back to the source variable list using the arrow button. The remaining variables are listed in the **<u>C</u>olumn(s):** box. These variables can be cleared the same way. You can also clear old variables from the selected variable lists using the Reset button. Using this option will clear all the variables at once, but it will also set all the options for the Crosstabs procedure back to the default settings.

To generate our next two tables, select STATUS and place it in the **R<u>o</u>w(s):** box. Next, select the EMPLOY and NIGHT variable and place them in the **<u>C</u>olumn(s):** box. As long as you haven't exited SPSS or selected the Reset option, all your options for **<u>S</u>tatistics...,** **C<u>e</u>lls...,** and **<u>F</u>ormat...** are still in effect. To generate these tables, select the **OK** command pushbutton. Before we examine the output from these two-way tables, let's illustrate how to generate tables with three variables.

Three-Way Tables

SPSS will also produce tables with more than two variables. Additional variables serve as control variables. For example, we might want to summarize enrollment status (STATUS) and night course attendance (NIGHT), but control for differences in employment status (EMPLOYED). In this situation, the variable of EMPLOYED would serve as a control variable.

You generate a three-way table similar to how you generated two-way tables. From the Crosstabs dialog box, select the variables of STATUS and NIGHT and place them in the boxes labeled **R<u>o</u>w(s):** and **<u>C</u>olumn(s):.** To add the third variable, EMPLOYED, select it from the source variable list and place it in the box labeled **Layer 1 of 1.** After selecting these three variables, your Crosstabs Rows, Columns, and Layer boxes should be like those displayed in Figure 12.7.

FIGURE 12.7
Specifications for a
three-way table

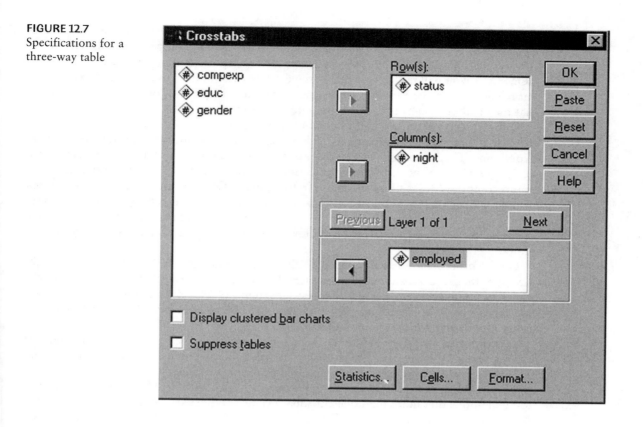

SPSS will produce two subtables. The first subtable will summarize STATUS and NIGHT for students who are not employed, while the second will summarize these two variables for employed students. Browse through the **Statistics...**, **Cells...**, and **Format...** menus. As long as you haven't exited SPSS, all the options you selected earlier are still in effect. Return to the Crosstabs dialog box and select the **OK** command pushbutton to generate the three-way table.

INTERPRETING SPSS CROSSTABS RESULTS

In this SPSS session, you generated several tables using the Crosstabs procedure. In this section, we will examine selected tables from your SPSS output and discuss all the information generated by the Crosstabs procedure. These samples will include two- and three-way tables. Before we begin to examine these results, you might want to save your work. Once again, to keep your files organized, we recommend using **chap12.spo** so you know these results were generated in Chapter 12.

Two-Way Tables

The first table we will examine appears in Figure 12.8. These crosstabulations summarize the gender (GENDER) and computer experience (COMPEXP) variables.

The GENDER variable is summarized in the rows of the table, while COMPEXP is displayed in the columns. The legend for the table is displayed in the table itself. For example, the first piece of information appearing in each cell is the count, or observed frequency. Listed below this count are the expected frequency, row percentage, column percentage, total percentage, and the residual.

Listed in the far right margin/column are the combined frequencies and percentages for GENDER (both males and females). These are called marginal totals. The marginal totals for COMPEXP are listed at the bottom margin/row of the table. From these marginal totals, you can see that there are more females than males (131 compared to 78). Of the entire sample (N = 209), 62.7% of the students are female. Examining the marginal totals for COMPEXP, you will notice that there are very few cases in the lower levels of experience, but many in the highest level of experience. Overall, 145 (69.4%) of our sample indicated that they had one year or more of computer experience.

Our sample is broken down into more specific subgroups in each cell. For example, the first cell (upper left-hand corner), identifies males with one week or less of computer experience. There are only three students from our sample who have these characteristics. Examine the row and column percentages. This information indicates that this subgroup comprises 3.8% of all the males in the sample. Of those students having one week or less of computer experience, 33.3% are male. The total percentage, 1.4%, indicates the percentage of the overall sample (N = 209) that this subgroup constitutes. The group of males with one week or less computer experience is a very small part of the overall sample.

On the other hand, examine the last cell in the second row of the table. This cell indicates that there are 91 students who are female and have one year or more of computer experience. Of all females, this is the largest subgroup (69.5%) and of those students having one year or more of experience, most of them (62.8%) are female. This is the largest subgroup (43.5%) in our sample of 209 students.

In addition to the tables of frequencies and percentages, the Crosstabs procedure reports information pertaining to the relationship between the two tabled variables. You will find this information summarized in a separate table (see Figure 12.8).

The first pieces of information we will examine in this table are the chi-square statistics. You will notice that more than one chi-square value is reported. We will briefly discuss the Pearson chi-square in this chapter. This statistic examines the extent to which the observed cell frequencies differ from those you would expect to find if the two variables are not related. Our reported chi-square is 2.179. Also reported with this chi-square are the degrees of freedom (df) and a significance level. This significance level is the probability that the observed and expected frequencies in the crosstabulation differ by chance.

The value reported for df is 4. This can be determined by a simple formula that accounts for the number of categories in each variable. The formula used is (# of rows − 1)(# of columns − 1). Since there are two rows for GENDER and five columns for COMPEXP, the degrees of freedom can be determined as $(2-1)(5-1)= 4$.

The significance level reported for the Pearson chi-square is .703. This value is listed under the Asymp. Sig (2-sided) heading. The significance level is interpreted as a probability. Because the chi-square procedure examines the extent to which the observed frequencies differ from those expected if there were no relationship, this probability indicates the extent to which the observed and expected frequencies differ by chance. A value of .703 is very high, meaning that we would expect the observed and expected frequencies to differ as much as they do by chance about 70 times out of 100. In other words, it is very likely that these frequencies differ by chance and not because there is a relationship between gender and computer experience. This is referred to as a nonsignificant finding.

Examine the table one more time and compare the observed and expected frequencies. You can also examine the residuals. The differences between our observed frequencies and what we would expect if there were no relationship are very small. For example, we observed three cases in the first cell when we would have expected 3.4, a difference (residual) of only −0.4. In the last cell, which identifies females with one or more years of computer experience, the residual is even smaller. We observed 90 cases in this condition, expecting 90.1, which results is a very small residual of 0.1.

Further evidence that no statistically significant relationship exists between gender and computer experience is found in the remaining statistics at the bottom of the table. The contingency coefficient describes the magnitude of the relationship. This value, .102, is very low (.102). In addition, the probability, .703, listed under the heading Approximate Significance can be interpreted as the likelihood of this relationship occurring by chance.

gender of student * computer experience Crosstabulation

			computer experience					Total
			1 week or less	between 1 week and 1 month	between 1 month and 6 months	between 6 months and 1 year	1 year or more	
gender of student	male	Count	3	2	9	10	54	78
		Expected Count	3.4	3.7	7.1	9.7	54.1	78.0
		% within gender of student	3.8%	2.6%	11.5%	12.8%	69.2%	100.0%
		% within computer experience	33.3%	20.0%	47.4%	38.5%	37.2%	37.3%
		% of Total	1.4%	1.0%	4.3%	4.8%	25.8%	37.3%
		Residual	−.4	−1.7	1.9	.3	−.1	
	female	Count	6	8	10	16	91	131
		Expected Count	5.6	6.3	11.9	16.3	90.9	131.0
		% within gender of student	4.6%	6.1%	7.6%	12.2%	69.5%	100.0%
		% within computer experience	66.7%	80.0%	52.6%	61.5%	62.8%	62.7%
		% of Total	2.9%	3.8%	4.8%	7.7%	43.5%	62.7%
		Residual	.4	1.7	−1.9	−.3	.1	
Total		Count	9	10	19	26	145	209
		Expected Count	9.0	10.0	19.0	26.0	145.0	209.0
		% within gender of student	4.3%	4.8%	9.1%	12.4%	69.4%	100.0%
		% within computer experience	100.0%	100.0%	100.0%	100.0%	100.0%	100.0%
		% of Total	4.3%	4.8%	9.1%	12.4%	69.4%	100.0%

Chi-Square Tests

	Value	df	Asymp. Sig. (2-sided)
Pearson Chi-Square	2.179[a]	4	.703
Likelihood Ratio	2.283	4	.684
Linear-by-Linear Association	.106	1	.745
N of Valid Cases	209		

a. 2 cells (20.0%) have expected count less than 5. The minimum expected count is 3.36.

Symmetric Measures

		Value	Approx. Sig.
Nominal by Nominal	Phi	.102	.703
	Cramer's V	.102	.703
	Contingency Coefficient	.102	.703
N of Valid Cases		209	

a. Not assuming the null hypothesis.
b. Using the asymptotic standard error assuming the null hypothesis.

FIGURE 12.8
SPSS Crosstabs two-way table (GENDER by COMPEXP)

Like the significance for the chi-square statistic, this probability is very high, preventing us from concluding that any systematic relationship exists between the gender and computer experience variable for our sample.

The second table we would like to examine summarizes the student enrollment status (STATUS) and night course enrollment (NIGHT) variables. This table appears in Figure 12.9.

As with the previous table, this table provides a great deal of information about our sample. Examining the marginal totals, we see that the majority of the students are enrolled full-time (71.8%) and are *not* enrolled exclusively in night courses (82.8%). The largest subgroup of students is full-time and not enrolled just in night courses (n = 142, 67.9%). On the other hand, those students who are enrolled full-time and exclusively in night courses are the smallest subgroup (n = 8, 3.8%). This is not surprising in that a student would have to attend classes at least three nights a week to be enrolled as a full-time student.

If you examine the information in this table more closely, you will find that the proportion of students who attend courses exclusively at night is very different for part- and full-time students. Of those students who are part-time, nearly one-half of them (47.5%) attend only night courses, whereas only 5.3% of full-time students attend courses exclusively at night. In other words, night course enrollment depends largely on student status.

Let's examine a few of the other statistics reported for these variables. First, the value for the Pearson chi-square is very large, 52.699. Remember, the larger the chi-square value, the greater the difference between your observed frequencies and those you would expect to see if there were no relationship. The next value reported is also appropriate for this situation. It is called the continuity correction and is used for tables with variables having just two levels. This number is also very large, 49.786. Look at the reported significance level for this statistic. Remember, this is the probability of chance being responsible for differences between observed and expected frequencies. The value reported in the SPSS output is ".00000." This does not mean that the probability is zero. This probability is carried out only five decimal places. If it were worked out farther, you would eventually see a number other than 0.

Be careful how you interpret a probability like this. In most cases, you would report this probability value as being less than 1 in 1,000, or .001. When writing this in a report or manuscript, you would use "p" to represent "probability" and "$<$" to represent "less than." Therefore, you would write "$p < .001$."

If the probability of this finding happening by chance is this low, it usually means that something else is going on. Examine the value for the phi coefficient below. Remember, the phi coefficient is appropriate for dichotomous variables. This value is $-.502$, which indicates a moderate negative relationship. In other words, those students who are enrolled full-time tend to not be exclusively enrolled in night courses. If you compare observed and expected frequencies in the table, you will notice that the residuals are very large compared to what they were in the previous table (GENDER by COMPEXP) where no relationship could be established.

Three-Way Tables

The next output we will examine is the three-way table you generated for the variables student enrollment status (STATUS), night course enrollment (NIGHT), and employment (EMPLOY). Two subtables were produced as a result of your efforts. These tables are displayed in Figures 12.10A and 12.10B.

Each of these subtables summarizes the variables of enrollment status (STATUS) and night course enrollment (NIGHT) at different levels of employment status (EMPLOY). We examined the variables of STATUS and NIGHT in the previous table (see Figure 12.9) and concluded that full-time students were less likely to be enrolled exclusively in night courses. These tables allow us to examine this relationship, while controlling for employment status (EMPLOY). The first table is the summary for students who were not working, while the second displays the summary for employed students. Sometimes the relationship between two variables is dependent upon a third variable. In other words, there could be a relationship at one level of a third variable, but not at another level.

student enrollment status * night course enrollment Crosstabulation

			night course enrollment		
			NOT just enrolled in night courses	just enrolled in night courses	Total
student enrollment status	part time	Count	31	28	59
		Expected Count	48.8	10.2	59.0
		% within student enrollment status	52.5%	47.5%	100.0%
		% within night course enrollment	17.9%	77.8%	28.2%
		% of Total	14.8%	13.4%	28.2%
		Residual	−17.8	17.8	
	full time	Count	142	8	150
		Expected Count	124.2	25.8	150.0
		% within student enrollment status	94.7%	5.3%	100.0%
		% within night course enrollment	82.1%	22.2%	71.8%
		% of Total	67.9%	3.8%	71.8%
		Residual	17.8	−17.8	
Total		Count	173	36	209
		Expected Count	173.0	36.0	209.0
		% within student enrollment status	82.8%	17.2%	100.0%
		% within night course enrollment	100.0%	100.0%	100.0%
		% of Total	82.8%	17.2%	100.0%

Chi-Square Tests

	Value	df	Asymp. Sig. (2-sided)	Exact Sig. (2-sided)	Exact Sig (1-sided)
Pearson Chi-Square	52.699[b]	1	.000		
Continuity Correction[a]	49.786	1	.000		
Likelihood Ratio	47.940	1	.000		
Fisher's Exact Test				.000	.000
Linear-by-Linear Association	52.447	1	.000		
N of Valid Cases	209				

a. Computed only for a 2 X 2 table
b. 0 cells (.0%) have expected count less than 5. The minimum expected count is 0.00.

Symmetric Measures

		Value	Approx. Sig.
Nominal by Nominal	Phi	−.502	.000
	Cramer's V	.502	.000
	Contingency Coefficient	.449	.000
N of Valid Cases		209	

a. Not assuming the null hypothesis.
b. Using the asymptotic standard error assuming the null hypothesis.

FIGURE 12.9
SPSS Crosstabs two-way table (NIGHT by STATUS)

student enrollment status * night course enrollment * employment status Crosstabulation

employment status				night course enrollment		Total
				NOT just enrolled in night courses	just enrolled in night courses	
not employed	student enrollment status	part time	Count	5	2	7
			Expected Count	6.4	.6	7.0
			% within student enrollment status	71.4%	28.6%	100.0%
			% within night course enrollment	11.1%	50.0%	14.3%
			% of Total	10.2%	4.1%	14.3%
			Residual	−1.4	1.4	
		full time	Count	40	2	42
			Expected Count	38.6	3.4	42.0
			% within student enrollment status	95.2%	4.8%	100.0%
			% within night course enrollment	88.9%	50.0%	85.7%
			% of Total	81.6%	4.1%	85.7%
			Residual	1.4	−1.4	
	Total		Count	45	4	49
			Expected Count	45.0	4.0	49.0
			% within student enrollment status	91.8%	8.2%	100.0%
			% within night course enrollment	100.0%	100.0%	100.0%
			% of Total	91.8%	8.2%	100.0%
employed	student enrollment status	part time	Count	26	26	52
			Expected Count	41.6	10.4	52.0
			% within student enrollment status	50.0%	50.0%	100.0%
			% within night course enrollment	20.3%	81.3%	32.5%
			% of Total	16.3%	16.3%	32.5%
			Residual	−15.6	15.6	
		full time	Count	102	6	108
			Expected Count	86.4	21.6	108.0
			% within student enrollment status	94.4%	5.6%	100.0%
			% within night course enrollment	79.7%	18.8%	67.5%
			% of Total	63.8%	3.8%	67.5%
			Residual	15.6	−15.6	
	Total		Count	128	32	160
			Expected Count	128.0	32.0	160.0
			% within student enrollment status	80.0%	20.0%	100.0%
			% within night course enrollment	100.0%	100.0%	100.0%
			% of Total	80.0%	20.0%	100.0%

FIGURE 12.10A
Three-way table (STATUS by NIGHT by EMPLOY)

Chi-Square Tests

EMPLOYED		Value	df	Asymp. Sig. (2-sided)	Exact Sig. (2-sided)	Exact Sig (1-sided)
0	Pearson Chi-Square	4.537[b]	1	.033		
	Continuity Correction[a]	1.917	1	.166		
	Likelihood Ratio	3.251	1	.071		
	Fisher's Exact Test				.092	.092
	Linear-by-Linear Association	4.444	1	.035		
	N of Valid Cases	49				
1	Pearson Chi-Square	43.333[c]	1	.000		
	Continuity Correction[a]	40.600	1	.000		
	Likelihood Ratio	41.697	1	.000		
	Fisher's Exact Test				.000	.000
	Linear-by-Linear Association	43.062	1	.000		
	N of Valid Cases	160				

a. Computed only for a 2x2 table
b. 2 cells (50.0%) have expected count less than 5. The minimum expected count is .57.
c. 0 cells (.0%) have expected count less than 5. The minimum expected count is 10.40.

Symmetric Measures

EMPLOYED			Value	Approx. Sig.
0	Nominal by Nominal	Phi	−.304	.033
		Cramer's V	.304	.033
		Contingency Coefficient	.291	.033
	N of Valid Cases		49	
1	Nominal by Nominal	Phi	−.520	.000
		Cramer's V	.520	.000
		Contingency Coefficient	.462	.000
	N of Valid Cases		160	

a. Not assuming the null hypothesis.
b. Using the asymptotic standard error assuming the null hypothesis.

FIGURE 12.10B
Three-way table (chi-square tests and measures of association)

There are several things to note in these two tables. First, let's examine the marginal totals in each table. A much larger percentage of unemployed students are enrolled as full-time students. Over eighty-five percent (85.7%) of these students are enrolled full-time, compared to only 67.5% of those students who are working. On the other hand, a larger percentage of employed students attend courses exclusively at night (20% vs. 8.2%). These findings are not terribly exciting. After all, if a student has to work, he or she will likely enroll part-time and usually at night, after working hours. In all, there are eight subgroups identified in these two tables. The largest of these subgroups are those students who are employed, enrolled full-time, but not just in night courses (n = 102). The smallest subgroups are those students who are not employed and not taking courses exclusively at night.

To determine the extent to which the relationship between enrollment status (STATUS) and night course enrollment (NIGHT) depends upon employment status (EMPLOY), let's examine the statistics presented below each of these subtables. The first table, which includes unemployed students, reports a Pearson chi-square value of 4.537, with a significance level of .033. If you were to stop here, you would interpret this finding as being statistically significant because the significance level, or p value, is less than .05.

However, in this case, we must first examine the value of chi-square after the continuity correction has been applied. In situations where both variables only have two levels, the resulting chi-square value tends to become inflated and can result in deciding that a relationship is present when it is most likely due to chance. An inflated chi-square value is especially likely when there are expected frequencies below 5. Notice the statement below the chi-square values. It indicates that two of the four cells in this table have an expected frequency of less than 5.

In our situation, the chi-square value reported after the continuity correction is much lower, 1.917, having a significance level of .166. This means that the probability of chance being responsible for this finding may be as high as 16.6 times in 100. Therefore, if we conclude that a relationship exists between STATUS and NIGHT for unemployed students, we are taking a 16.6% risk of being wrong. This risk is too high. In most situations, a predetermined risk level of 5% is acceptable. Therefore, we should conclude that no relationship exists between STATUS and NIGHT for unemployed students.

The situation for employed students on the next table is different. In this case, the corrected chi-square value is very high, 40.600, with a reported significance level of .000. As with a significance level reported earlier, this doesn't mean that the probability of chance being responsible for this finding is zero. It simply means that the probability is very low, less than 1 time in 100,000. When reporting this in a report or manuscript, it is common to report these probabilities as being less than 1 in 1,000, or "$p < .001$." We therefore conclude that a relationship does exist between the variables of STATUS and NIGHT for employed students.

The magnitude of this relationship is shown by the phi coefficient. Remember, the phi coefficient is appropriate for dichotomous variables. This value is $-.520$, which indicates a moderate negative relationship. In other words, those students who are enrolled full-time tend to not be exclusively enrolled in night courses. If you compare observed and expected frequencies in the table, you notice that the residuals are very large compared to those found in the table summarizing the same information for students who are not employed.

CHAPTER SUMMARY

In this chapter, we have explored several applications of the Crosstabs procedure. This procedure was used to crosstabulate variables and describe subgroups within our sample. Subgroups were usually formed by combining two variables. We also examined the same information after including a third variable, or control variable. From this information we were also able to examine relationships between these variables. The chi-square statistic was used to test whether relationships existed between variables from our data, while the phi coefficient and contingency coefficient were used to describe the magnitude of the relationship. In the next chapter, we will explore the use of plots to summarize relationships visually.

PRACTICE EXERCISES

Use the data set you created in Chapter 3 (i.e., student admission data).

1. Use the Crosstabs procedure to generate a two-way table for the variables of GENDER and SES.
   a. Identify the smallest and largest subgroups.
   b. What is the reported Pearson chi-square value and significance?
   c. Is there a relationship between GENDER and SES?
   d. Report the appropriate measure of association for this relationship.

13 | Displaying Relationships

In the previous chapter, you summarized categorical variables and examined relationships between them. In this chapter, you will be examining relationships between variables that exist in rank-order or continuous form. The two most common correlation coefficients used to describe these relationships are the Spearman rank correlation coefficient (r_s) and the Pearson product moment correlation coefficient (r).

Before you compute these correlation coefficients, it is a good idea to plot the data so you can examine the relationship between the two variables visually. If two variables are related, a pattern will be noticeable in the plot. A plot of two continuous or rank-order and is useful in examining different types of relationships. In general, correlation coefficients describe the extent to which a linear relationship exists between two variables. Scatterplots are also useful in detecting relationships which are not truly linear, but follow a curvilinear pattern.

Correlation coefficients range from −1.0, a perfect negative relationship, to +1.0, a perfect positive relationship. The closer the correlation coefficient is to either −1.0 or +1.0, the stronger the relationship. When displayed in a scatterplot, a perfect relationship is illustrated as a straight line that rises at a 45° angle. On the other hand, the closer the coefficient is to zero (0), the weaker the relationship. When a relationship is close to zero, the points on a scatterplot will be widely scattered in a random manner. Examples of a perfect positive (+1.0), perfect negative (−1.0), and no relationship (0) are illustrated in Figure 13.1.

The first scatterplot displays a perfect positive relationship. Notice that all the points in this plot are arranged in a straight line. The points plotted in this scatterplot rise from the lower left-hand corner to upper right-hand corner of the scatterplot. In other words, lower scores on the X variable are associated with lower scores on the Y variable, and higher scores on X are plotted with higher scores on Y. This scatterplot also has a positive slope, that indicates what happens to Y scores as X scores increase. In this scatterplot, as scores increase on X, they also increase on Y, indicating a positive slope and a positive relationship. The second scatterplot displays the opposite. As scores increase on X, they decrease on Y. This straight line falls from the upper left of the scatterplot to the lower right, indicating a negative relationship.

The final scatterplot in Figure 13.1 displays a random arrangement of X and Y scores. Some low scores on X are associated with low scores on Y, but some are also associated with high scores on Y. High scores on X are also plotted with a wide range of Y scores. There is no linear pattern that can be used to help describe the relationship between X and Y in this scatterplot. The points in this plot are extremely scattered with no clear pattern in either direction, indicating a correlation close to zero.

In general, the nature of relationships between variables can be described quickly by examining the pattern of points on a scatterplot. Points grouped in a straight line represent a perfect one-to-one relationship between two variables. In very few instances will the points line up in a perfectly straight line, because very few relationships are perfect. The direction

FIGURE 13.1
Examples of
correlation $(+, -, 0)$

Perfect Positive Relationship

Perfect Negative Relationship

No Relationship

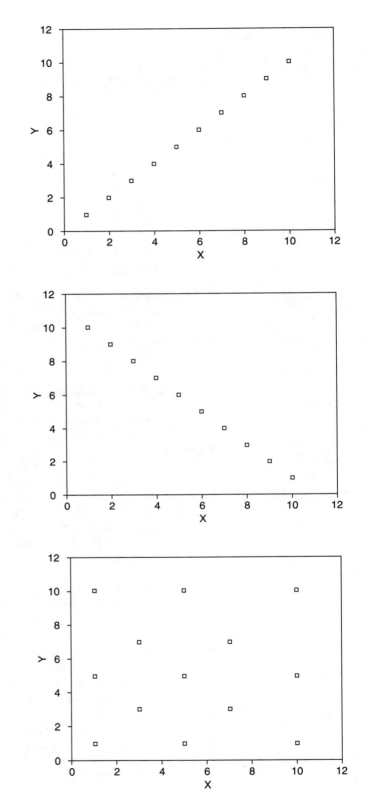

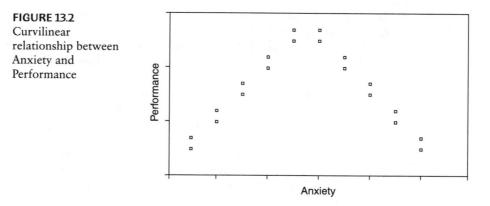

FIGURE 13.2
Curvilinear relationship between Anxiety and Performance

of the line, or slope, will always indicate the type of relationship. For positive relationships, the slope indicates that scores increase on Y as they increase on X. If the slope indicates that scores are decreasing on Y as they increase on X or vice versa, the relationship is negative. If the points in a scatterplot do not fit closely to a line, the relationship is weak. When the scatterplot looks like a random arrangement of points, the linear relationship is at or near zero.

Not all relationships can be described as linear. Some relationships between variables are curvilinear. Perhaps the most widely used example of a curvilinear relationship exists between the measures of anxiety and performance. Becoming anxious about your performance (e.g., academic, athletic, musical) may lead you to study more, practice harder, and/or psych yourself up. This helps performance, as long as you do not become too anxious. If you overstudy for the examination, or practice too much before the big game or recital, your performance may suffer. This type of curvilinear relationship is illustrated in Figure 13.2.

Examining the variables in our data set on applicants to a doctoral program (see Appendix A), we could explore several potential relationships. There are several variables that are continuous and measured at the ordinal and interval levels. These variables include GREQ, GREV, pretest, and interview ratings. Ideally, this information would also be available for those students admitted in the past. If so, we could examine the relationship between each of these four variables with some measure(s) of success in the doctoral program. Knowing how well each of these variables related to future success in the doctoral program would be quite valuable in the selection process.

In the remaining sections of this chapter, we will explore the use of scatterplots with SPSS.

VARIABLES USED IN THIS CHAPTER

The variables we will be using come from our graduate student data set. Some of these variables are measured on an ordinal scale, while others are interval. The ordinal variables include computer experience (COMPEXP) and educational level (EDUC). We will also be examining several interval variables pertaining to attitudes toward working with computers and statistics (i.e., anxiety, confidence, liking, usefulness). Other variables used in the chapter, measured on a ratio scale, include student's age (AGE), hours employed (EMPLOY), years of teaching experience (TEAYEAR), and number of credits taken in the current quarter (CREDNOW).

USING SPSS TO DISPLAY RELATIONSHIPS

In the previous chapter, you used the Crosstabs procedure to summarize variables and explore relationships between them. In this chapter, you will be using graphs (scatterplots) to visually represent the relationship between variables. Before you begin, you need to activate SPSS and retrieve the data. As you might have expected by now, the name for the data in this chapter is **chap13 data.**

With the previous SPSS procedures, you began with the Analyze menu. To produce graphs for your data, you will begin from the **Graphs** menu. From this menu, select the **Scatter...** option, as illustrated in Figure 13.3.

Selecting these options will open the Scatterplot dialog box displayed in Figure 13.4.

In this dialog box, there are four options displayed on four different buttons. The first option (upper left) will produce a simple scatterplot. A simple scatterplot is what you will need in most cases. Simple scatterplots allow you to display the relationship between two variables. The option below the simple scatterplot is labeled Overlay. This option will allow you to examine more than one scatterplot on the same graph. These multiple scatterplots are displayed using different symbols so you can distinguish between them. The option for Matrix is used to summarize several individual scatterplots in different parts of the graph. The final option, 3-D, is used to produce three-dimensional graphs.

Simple Scatterplot

We will begin with a simple scatterplot. Select the Simple option with your mouse. To define the variables for this scatterplot, click on the **Define** button. This will display the Simple Scatterplot dialog box.

As with many dialog boxes you have seen before, the variables from your dataset are displayed at the left in the source variable list. To identify the variables to be plotted, select them

FIGURE 13.3
Graphs–Scatter menu
selections

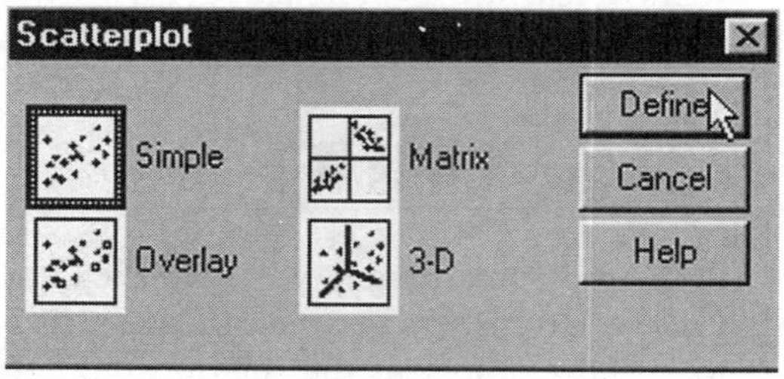

FIGURE 13.4
Scatterplot dialog box

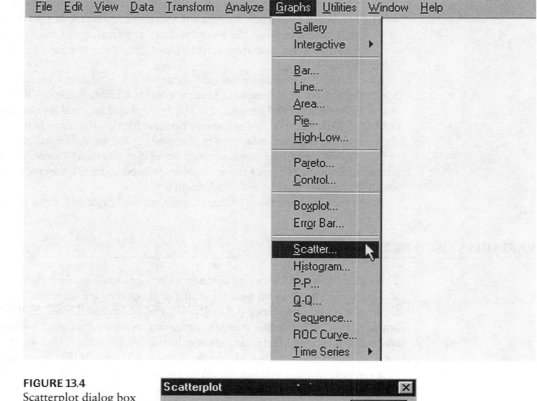

from the variable list and place them in the boxes labeled **Y Axis:** and **X Axis:** (see Figure 13.5). The variable chosen for the Y-axis will be displayed on the vertical axis, while that selected for the X-axis will be shown on the horizontal axis. Select employment hours (EMPHOURS) for the Y-axis and age (AGE) for the X-axis. There are two additional boxes in this dialog box that we will use in a later example. At the bottom of the screen, there are two buttons. The first is Titles and the second is Options. Click on the **Titles...** button to open the Titles dialog box.

Specifying Titles. As you would expect, this box is where you specify titles for the scatterplot. You can specify two title lines and one subtitle line. You can also specify up to two footnote lines for the scatterplot. In the first title line, you might type something like "Plot of Background Variables" so you have a meaningful title for the scatterplot. As a subheading, you might identify the variables displayed in the plot. Our title and subtitle are specified in Figure 13.6. You are welcome to use a more exciting title of your choice. If you want to add a footnote, feel free to do so. When finished, click on the **Continue** button to return to the Simple Scatterplot dialog box.

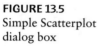

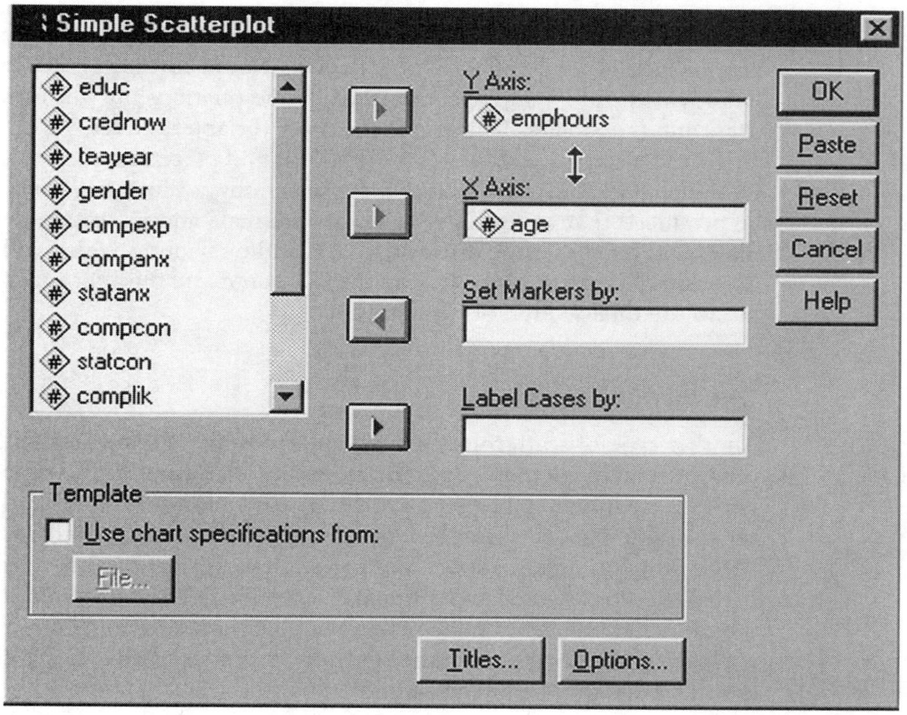

FIGURE 13.5
Simple Scatterplot dialog box

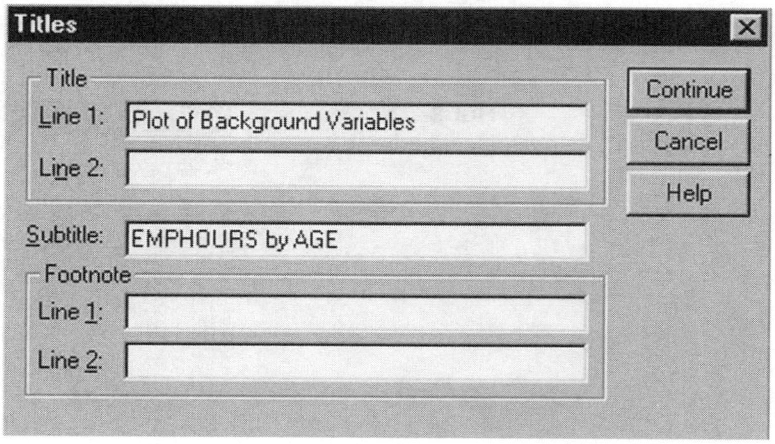

FIGURE 13.6
Titles dialog box (EMPHOURS by AGE)

Options Dialog Box.   The other button at the bottom is labeled **O̲ptions....** Click on this button to open the Options dialog box illustrated in Figure 13.7.

As you can see, there are very few options to choose. The options that appeal pertain to the treatment of missing values. By default, missing cases are excluded on a listwise basis. Therefore, if a person is missing information on any variable, he/she will be excluded. This option is fine for our current scatterplot. If you were producing more than one scatterplot, we might want to exclude cases on a variable-by-variable basis. You also have the option to display the groups that you have defined with missing values in the graph. The default settings are fine for this simple scatterplot. Click on the **Continue** button to return to the Simple Scatterplot dialog box. Click on the **OK** button to produce this simple scatterplot.

Before we examine this plot, let's request other types of plots. To return to the data editor, select **chap13 data** from the **W̲indows** menu, or use the data editor icon from the toolbar. This icon looks like a spreadsheet.

Simple Scatterplot with a Third Variable

Suppose you wanted to examine the relationship between employment hours and age, but also include a third variable, gender. This would further define the relationship between employment hours and age. Specifically, the relationship will now be examined for each subgroup (i.e., males, females) of the third variable, gender.

To add a third variable, select GENDER and place it in the box labeled **S̲et Markers by:** (see Figure 13.5). As a result of these selections, a plot of age and employment hours will be produced that identifies which cases are male and which are female. SPSS will identify males and females using different colors and/or symbols which will be defined in a legend. To create this scatterplot, click on the **OK** command pushbutton. We will examine the output in the final section of this chapter.

Overlay Scatterplots

Another type of scatterplot that is available is an overlay scatterplot. This type of scatterplot is useful in comparing two or more sets of relationships. For example, you could compare the relationship between age (AGE) and employment hours (EMPHOURS) with the relationship between number of credits (CREDNOW) and employment hours (EMPHOURS). You might expect that age and employment hours would be positively related. In general, the older a student is, the more likely he or she would be employed full-time. On the other hand, you might expect number of credits and employment hours to relate in a negative manner since number of hours a person has to work each week limits the number of credits that he or she can take.

To create an overlay scatterplot using these variables, select the **S̲catter...** option from the **G̲raphs** menu. You should arrive at the Scatterplot dialog box as you did earlier. Choose the **Overlay** option and click on the **Define** button to arrive at the Overlay Scatterplot dialog box.

FIGURE 13.7
Options dialog box

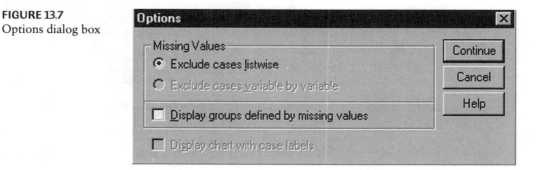

As with previous dialog boxes, the source variable list appears to the left. To the right is a box labeled Y-X Pairs. You select these pairs of variables one at a time. When you select the first variable, it will appear in the box labeled **Current Selections** next to the Variable 1 line. When you select the second variable, it will also appear in this box, next to the line labeled Variable 2. To transfer this pair to the selected variable list under the heading Y-X Pairs, use the upper transfer arrow button, directly to the left of the **Y-X Pairs:** box.

Select the pairs of variables needed for the overlay scatterplot. The first pair is age (AGE) and employment hours (EMPHOURS). The second pair is number of credits in which a student is enrolled (CREDNOW) and employment hours (EMPHOURS). These selections are displayed in Figure 13.8.

Before we continue, notice the arrangement of these variables in the Y-X Pairs box. The first pair lists EMPHOURS first, while in the second pair it is listed last. We want EMPHOURS to be listed as the first variable in each pair so that it will be plotted on the Y-axis. Click on the second pair (**CREDNOW — EMPHOURS**) and use the **Swap Pair** button to reverse this listing. This will display the second pair with EMPHOURS listed first, as in the first pair (see Figure 13.9).

When you are finished, you may wish to specify some titles or subtitles. Click on the **Titles...** button to open the Titles dialog box. Again, you can specify whatever title you feel best describes the plot.

When you are finished with the titles and subtitles, click on the **Continue** button to return to the Overlay Scatterplot dialog box. To produce this overlay scatterplot, click on the **OK** pushbutton. We will discuss this overlay scatterplot in the final section of the chapter.

Scatterplot Matrix

To produce a matrix of scatterplots using several different variables, select the **Scatter...** option from the **Graphs** menu. You should arrive at the Scatterplot dialog box as you did earlier. Choose the **Matrix** option and click on the **Define** button to arrive at the Scatterplot Matrix dialog box.

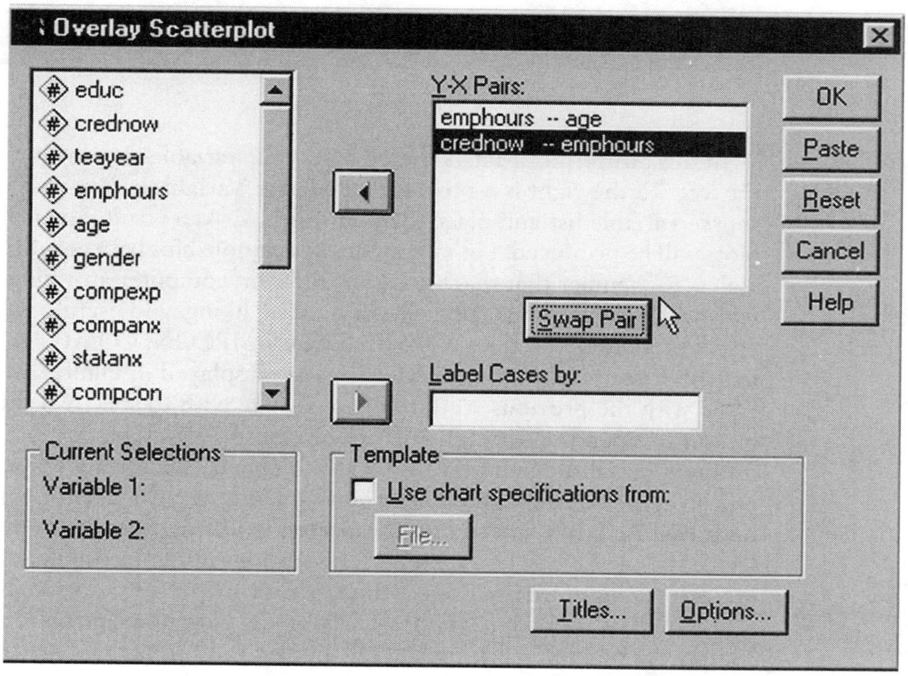

FIGURE 13.8
Overlay Scatterplot dialog box

FIGURE 13.9
Overlay Scatterplot
dialog box–Swap Pair

FIGURE 13.10
Scatterplot Matrix
dialog box

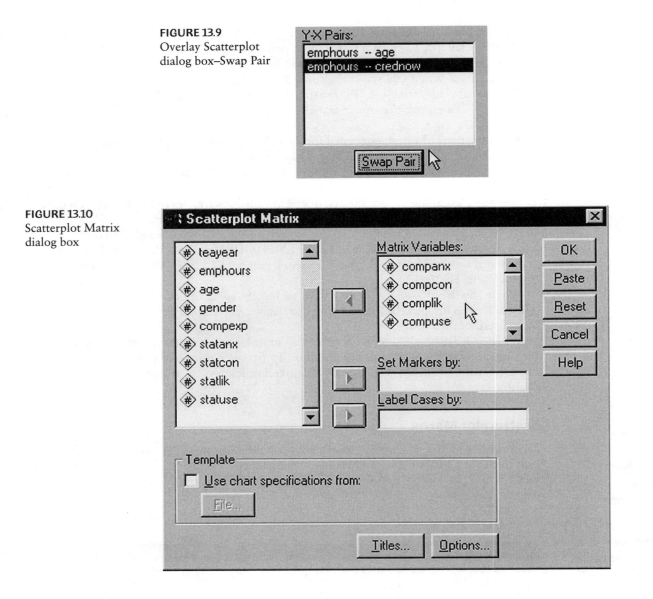

In this Scatterplot Matrix dialog box, your variables appear in the source variable list at the left. To the right is a box labeled **Matrix Variables:**. You will select variables from the source variable list and place them in this box. As a result, a matrix of all possible scatterplots will be produced. Let's examine the relationships between different computer attitude scales. Remember that there are four different computer attitude scales in our data. These scales measure students' anxiety, confidence, liking, and usefulness in regard to computers. Select these four variables (COMPANX, COMPCON, COMPLIK, COMPUSE) to create a matrix of scatterplots. These selections are displayed in Figure 13.10.

As with the previous scatterplots, you may wish to specify a title. Click on the **Titles...** button to open the Titles dialog box. Because several scatterplots will be produced using different variables, you may also want to change the setting for missing values. Select the button at the bottom of the screen labeled **Options....** By default, missing cases are excluded on a listwise basis. Therefore, if a person is missing information on any variable you selected, he or she will be excluded. This option is fine for simple scatterplots. However, we are producing more than one scatterplot, so the option to exclude cases variable by variable would be more appropriate. Click on the **Continue** button to return to the Scatterplot Matrix dialog box. Click on the **OK** button to produce this matrix. We will examine this scatterplot matrix in the final section of this chapter.

FIGURE 13.11
3-D Scatterplot dialog
box

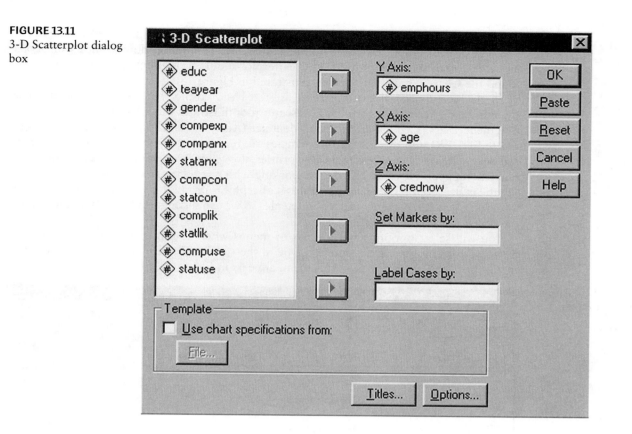

3-D Scatterplots

The final type of scatterplot available is a three-dimensional scatterplot. Using this type of scatterplot, you can display the relationship between three different variables in a single plot. Three-dimensional plots can often be very difficult to interpret. Although you may not use 3-D scatterplots as often as the other types, they are useful in detecting cases that are extreme, called outliers. When a case does not appear to fit in with the rest of the cases, there is usually a good reason.

Let's examine the relationship among three different variables: age (AGE), number of credits in which students are enrolled (CREDNOW), and employment hours (EMPHOURS). To produce a 3-D scatterplot, select the **Scatter...** option from the **Graphs** menu. You should arrive at the Scatterplot dialog box as you did earlier. Choose the **3-D** option and click on the **Define** button to arrive at the 3-D Scatterplot Matrix dialog box.

In the 3-D Scatterplot dialog box, select the three variables from the source variable list and transfer them to the three boxes to the right. Select EMPHOURS for the <u>Y</u>-Axis, AGE for the <u>X</u>-axis, and CREDNOW for the <u>Z</u>-axis (see Figure 13.11).

As with previous scatterplots, you can specify a title. Click on the **Titles...** button to open the Titles dialog box. The default option for missing cases is listwise, so there is no reason to change this setting. In this case ignore the options button. To produce this three-dimensional scatterplot, click on the **Continue** button to return to the 3-D Scatterplot Matrix dialog box and click on the **OK** button. We will examine this plot, along with the others, in the final section of this chapter.

EDITING CHARTS IN THE CHART EDITOR

Like other SPSS output, scatterplots can be edited directly in SPSS. You have used the editing functions in the output viewer to modify the format of frequencies and other descriptive output. We will use it to modify the scatterplots. Let's begin with the second scatterplot we requested. This scatterplot shows the relationship between the variables of age

(AGE) and employment hours (EMPHOURS), controlling for gender (GENDER). Locate this part of your output using the outline pane. Once you find it, double-click your mouse anywhere on the scatterplot itself. The scatterplot should be highlighted with a box around it and the Chart Editor will open, as illustrated in Figure 13.12.

In this section, we'll explore some of the basic editing features available in SPSS. Examine the scatterplot carefully. This scatterplot illustrates the relationship between employment hours (EMPHOURS) and student age (AGE), controlling for the variable of gender (GENDER). On this scatterplot, females are represented by green boxes and males by red boxes. If you have access to a color printer, this scatterplot would look great when displayed on paper. However, if you are working with a regular printer, it will be difficult to tell the males from the females when this scatterplot is printed. Therefore, change the type of marker which represents males and females so we can distinguish between them. We will also explore some other editing features.

You will select options from a series of menus when editing charts. There are several menu options on the main menu bar. One of these is the **Chart** menu. Click on the **Chart** menu to explore your options. This menu appears in Figure 13.13.

FIGURE 13.12
SPSS Chart Editor

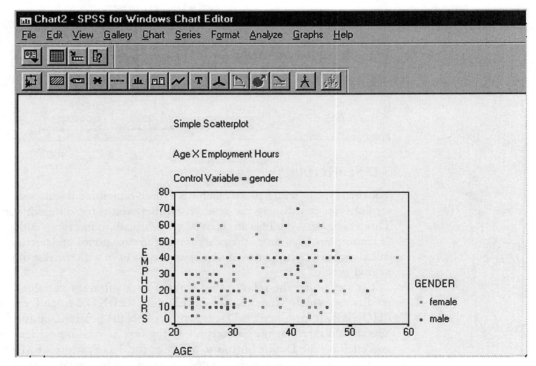

FIGURE 13.13
Chart Editor–Charts
menu selections

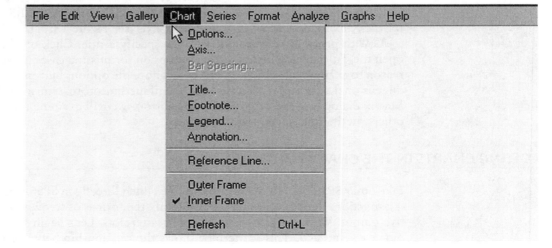

Chart Menu

There are several features on the Chart menu that you might use to edit a chart. We'll explore a few of these with our scatterplot. The only option which has already been marked is Inner Frame. This is a default option which outlines the scatterplot. There is also an option for Outer Frame. Selecting this option will enclose the entire scatterplot, including titles, legend and footnotes in a box. This is a good option to choose when you are using a scatterplot in a report. The outer box helps to separate the scatterplot from your narrative.

At the top of this menu, there are two options. The first is labeled Options and the second is labeled Axis. Select **Options...** to view the Scatterplot Options dialog box, displayed in Figure 13.14. The exact options displayed in this dialog box depend on the type of scatterplot you are editing.

There are many options available in this dialog box, grouped under four categories. The first category is labeled Display Options. The option, **Show subgroups,** is selected. This indicates that the subgroups of females and males are displayed in the scatterplot. The **Case Labels** option is set at the Off setting. You can display the ID number of each case in the scatterplot if you turn this option on. This would be useful if you wanted to identify individual cases in the scatterplot. The next box is labeled Sunflowers and allows you to represent cases in the scatterplot using sunflower symbols. If there is more than one case at a particular location, the sunflower will have more than one pedal. Each pedal of the sunflower will represent a certain number of cases. For our purposes, sunflowers are not necessary.

The upper right box is labeled Fit Line. The options in this category are useful in estimating the type of relationship which exists between the plotted variables. As we discussed in the beginning of the chapter, some relationships are linear while others are curvilinear. These options are especially useful when you are performing regression analysis. We'll discuss this analysis in a later chapter. The last category is labeled Mean of Y Reference Line. Choosing this option will display a line on the scatterplot representing the mean of the Y variable. This line can be used as a reference point to judge how far from the group average each case performed. Reference lines can be displayed for the overall sample and for each subgroup. The distance between each case and the reference line can also be connected by selecting the option Display spikes to lines. When you are finished exploring these options, return to the Chart window by clicking on the **OK** button so we can explore other editing features.

From the **Chart** menu, select the second option, **Axis....** This option allows you to edit the X- and Y-axes. The first window to appear is used to select the axis you wish to edit. In the Axis Selection box, select the X scale and click on the **OK** button (see Figure 13.15).

You are now viewing the X Scale Axis dialog box, displayed in Figure 13.16. Let's explore the available options. The first option, **Display axis line,** is already checked, resulting

FIGURE 13.14
Scatterplot Options
dialog box

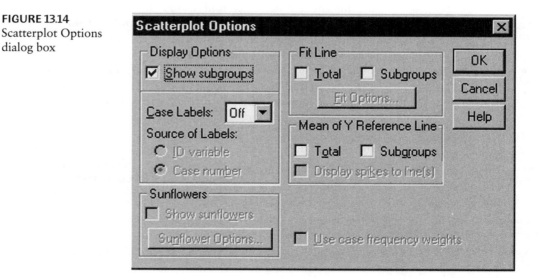

FIGURE 13.15
Axis Selection dialog
box

FIGURE 13.16
X Scale Axis definition
dialog box

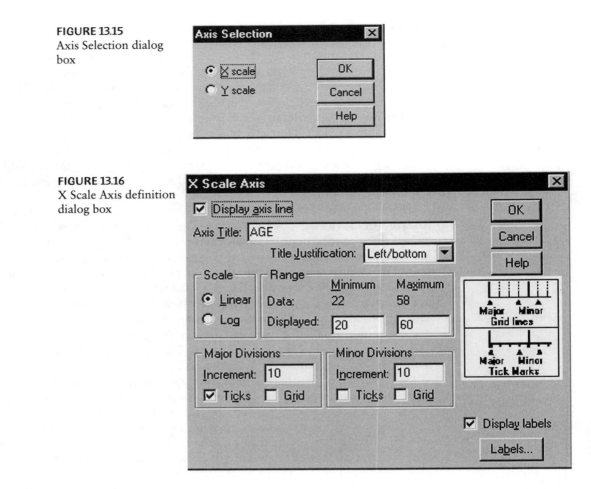

is the display of the X-axis line. The box labeled **Axis Title:** is also completed. This title is the variable name. You can edit this title if you'd like, but the variable name is usually sufficient. The **Title Justification:** box is set to the Left/bottom setting. This is the default setting for the X-axis, but you can change this location if you'd like.

The next two options regard the scale of the axis. The Scale is set to Linear, which is the most common setting. In some cases, the axis might be displayed using a log scale. The Range box identifies the range of values displayed on the scale. Next to the Data label are the minimum and maximum values observed in your data. In the boxes next to the Displayed label are the minimum and maximum values displayed on the axis. These displayed values are determined based on the observed data. If you want to increase or decrease the range of displayed values, just change these values.

There is no need to change these settings for our scatterplot. The next two options regard major and minor divisions along the axis. These divisions can be made using tick marks or complete lines. Tick marks are used by default. Each mark, or line, will be displayed at specified increments along the axis. Our current scatterplot will display a tick mark, as a major division, every 10 units along the X-axis. Finally, the **Labels...** button, at the bottom of the dialog box, can be used to indicate the format of the labels for the axis. Selecting the Labels button will allow you to specify the number of decimal places for each scale label and the arrangement of scale labels along the axis. Again, the default settings are fine for our current scatterplot. Please explore these options. When you are finished, return to the Chart Window.

Let's return to the **Chart** menu to examine the remaining options. The second grouping of four options is used to provide titles, footnotes, legends, and annotations. You may have already specified a title and a footnote when you generated this scatterplot. If so, you

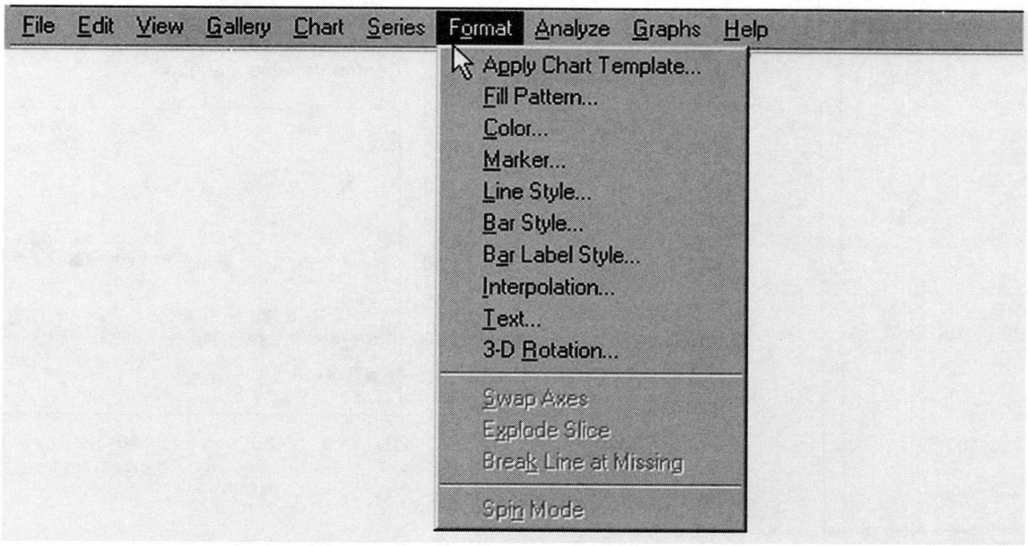

FIGURE 13.17
Chart Editor–Format
menu selections

can edit them using these options. As you might expect, the Title option is used to specify or edit titles, while the Footnote option is used for footnotes. The Legend option is used to define the legend of the scatterplot. By default, the variable label will be used as the title for the legend and value labels to label subgroups. In our scatterplot, "student gender" is used as the legend title with "male" and "female" serving as labels. The last option in this grouping is Annotation. Using this option, you can include explanations at various points on the scatterplot. When you are finished exploring these options, return to the Chart window.

Using the **Chart** menu, locate the option for Reference Line. This option is used if you want to display a reference line on the scatterplot and is similar to the earlier option for Mean of Y Reference Line. Using the current option, you can set the reference line at any value, not just the mean. For example, if you wanted to see how many students worked full-time, you might set the reference line at 40. Try this and return to the Chart window when you are finished.

Format Menu

Next, we want to edit the markers so that we can distinguish between males and females. We will do this by selecting options from the **Format** menu shown in Figure 13.17.

As with the Chart menu, there are many options available. This menu functions somewhat differently from the Chart menu. First, you must highlight a section of the scatterplot and then select an editing option from the menu. We will explore only a few of these options for our current scatterplot. First, we want to change the symbols used to represent males and females so we can tell them apart when this plot is printed in black and white. To do so, click your mouse on a female marker (see Figure 13.18). Next, select the **Marker...** option from the **Format** menu (see Figure 13.19). The Markers dialog box, displayed in Figure 13.20, will appear in the window.

In this dialog box, you can change the size and shape of the symbols used to represent females. The default symbol is a box, and the size setting is Tiny. When many points are represented in a scatterplot, the size of each point cannot be too large or the points will blend together. Let's change this to a solid box and increase the size to Small. When you have finished making these selections, click on the button labeled **Apply.** The symbols representing females should now be solid boxes. If so, click on the **Close** button to return to the Chart window. The symbols used to represent females and males are easier to distinguish now (see Figure 13.21). When this plot is printed in black and white, it will be easier to interpret. If you'd like to change the markers for males, please do so.

FIGURE 13.18
Selected female
markers in scatterplot

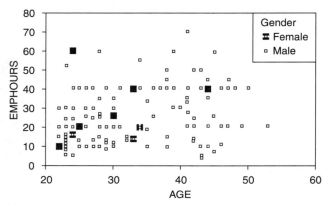

Simple Scatterplot
Age X Employment Hours
Control Variable = gender

FIGURE 13.19
Format–Marker menu
selections

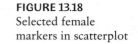

If you are changing the male markers, remember to:

1. Click on a male marker.
2. Select the **Marker...** option from the **Format** menu.
3. Change the marker style and click on the **Apply** button.

The final option we want to explore regards the text used to label this scatterplot. You have already specified titles, subtitles, footnotes, and legends. Each of these is displayed in a slightly different font size. You can edit each label by clicking on it and selecting the Text option from the menu. Highlight the main title and then choose the **Text...** option from the **Format** menu (see Figure 13.22). This will open the Text Styles dialog box, displayed in Figure 13.23.

Your actual title may be different from our title, but it should be displayed in Arial font with font size of 14. This is probably large enough, but you might want to explore the types and sizes of fonts available. To select a different font and size, scroll the menu and select using your mouse. Click on the **Apply** button to apply your selections to the scatterplot. When you are finished exploring, select the **Close** button.

FIGURE 13.20
Markers dialog box

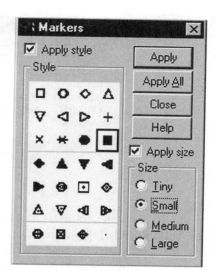

FIGURE 13.21
Scatterplot with new
marker style

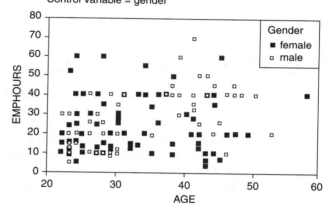

FIGURE 13.22
Format–Text menu
selections

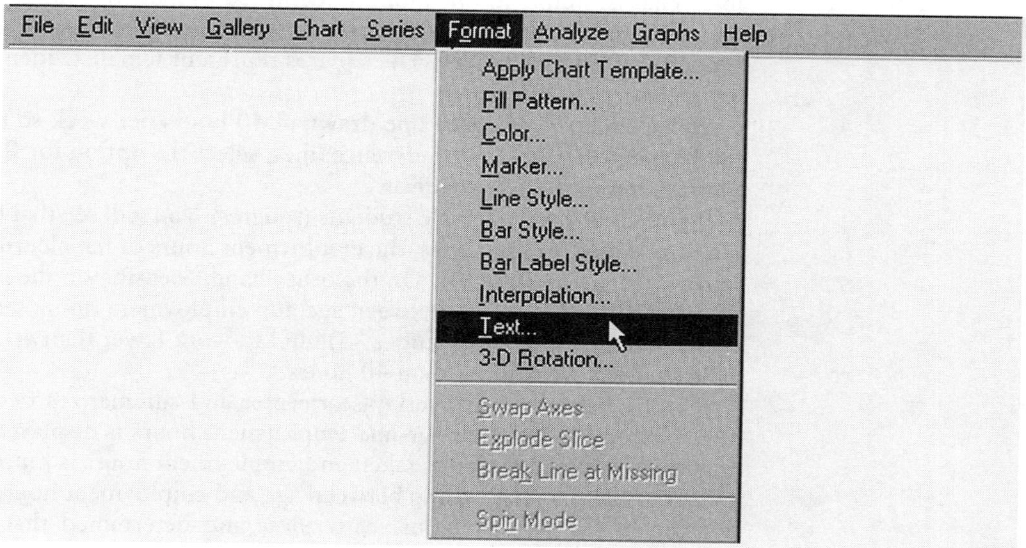

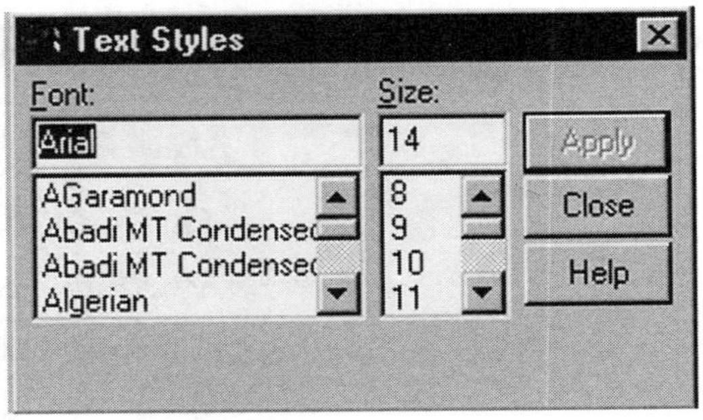

FIGURE 13.23
Text Styles dialog box

There are several other options available in this menu. For example, if you wish to change the background of the scatterplot, use the option for **Fill Pattern....** Our background is clear, which works well for scatterplots. There are many other backgrounds available, such as solid, horizontal lines, vertical lines, diagonal lines, and grids. There are also many different colors available using the **Color...** option.

The option for **Line Style...** is used for line graphs, and the options for **Bar Style...** and **Bar Label Style...** are used for barcharts. **Interpolation...** allows you to connect the points in the graph. When there are many points to connect, this makes the graph difficult to interpret. Finally, there is an option for **3-D Rotation...**, used to rotate the image and examine it from a variety of angles.

INTERPRETING SPSS SCATTERPLOT RESULTS

Now that you've generated a variety of plots, it's time to take a closer look at them.

The first scatterplot (Plot 13.1) displays the relationship between students' age (AGE) and hours employed per week (EMPHOURS). Points in this plot tend to follow a positive relationship, as younger students tend to work fewer hours while older students work more. This relationship is far from perfect because the points do not fall close to a straight line from the lower left to the upper right of the plot. If you were to draw an imaginary line from the lower left corner to the upper right of this plot, many points would be placed far away from that line. Therefore, this plot displays a positive relationship, but not a strong one.

The second plot (Plot 13.2) displays the same relationship but includes a control variable. That is, points in this plot are identified as male or female students. With this plot, we can determine the extent to which the relationship between age and employment hours depends on student gender. The squares represent female students while the circles identify males.

We've added a reference line drawn at 40 hours per week so that further comparisons can be made easily. To add reference lines, select the option for **Reference Line...** from the **Chart** menu in the Chart Editor.

If you focus on the female students (squares), you will see that they are widely scattered across this plot. At most ages, the employment hours of female students range from almost zero to as high as 50 or 60. On the other hand, focusing on the males (circles), this is not the case. The relationship between age and employment hours seems clearer for male students. Younger males (i.e., under 35) tend to work fewer than 40 hours, while many older male students work more than 40 hours.

Plot 13.3 displays an overlay scatterplot and summarizes two different relationships. The relationship between age and employment hours is displayed using circles, while the relationship between credits taken and employment hours is represented by squares. First, let's examine the relationship between age and employment hours. We examined this relationship in the two previous scatterplots and determined that the two variables were

PLOT 13.1
Simple scatterplot (Age by Employment Hours)

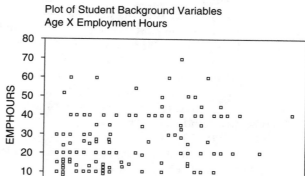

Plot of Student Background Variables
Age X Employment Hours

PLOT 13.2
Simple scatterplot with control variable (GENDER)

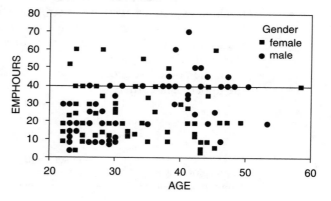

Simple Scatterplot
Age X Employment Hours
Control Variable = gender

PLOT 13.3
Overlay scatterplot

Overlay Scatterplot

Age X Employment Hours
Credits X Employment Hours

CREDNOW EMPHOURS
AGE EMPHOURS

related in a positive direction with older students tending to work more hours per week and younger students working fewer hours.

The second relationship between credits taken and employment hours, represented by squares in Plot 13.3, appears to be stronger than the one between age and employment hours because the points (squares) are grouped more tightly together. This relationship, however is negative with the tendency for those students who are enrolled in more credits to work fewer hours per week. Again, this makes sense as both variables are related to time. The more time you spend taking classes, the less time you have to work and vice versa.

Plot 13.4 displays a matrix of scatterplots that illustrates relationships among four computer attitude scales. The more scatterplots in the matrix, the more difficult it is to view them. There are twelve scatterplots in this matrix and they appear rather small. Nevertheless, patterns can be seen between pairs of computer attitude scales. In each scatterplot, a pattern from the lower left to the upper right is displayed, indicating a positive relationship. This is expected because each of these scales measures related attitudes. For example, a person who feels comfortable with computers is also likely to have confidence in his/her ability to use computers, like working with computers and finding them useful in his/her life.

The final plot is a 3-D scatterplot. This scatterplot allows us to view three different relationships. In order to view each of these relationships more closely, this scatterplot can be rotated. We've already viewed each of these relationships and determined that age and teaching experience were more strongly related than age and employment hours. The relationship between age and employment hours is displayed in the left portion of Plot 13.5. Notice that most of the points tend to be grouped toward the lower right corner (near the center of Plot 13.5), not extending upward in a linear pattern. On the right portion of Plot 13.5, the points are grouped along a line that begins in the lower left and extends toward the upper right corner.

PLOT 13.4
Scatterplot matrix
(computer attitudes)

Scatterplot Matrix
Computer Attitudes

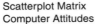

PLOT 13.5
3-D scatterplot

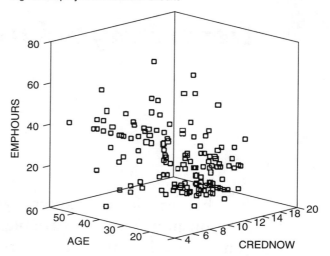

3-D Scatterplot
Age X Employment Hours X Credits

CHAPTER SUMMARY

In this chapter, you generated several types of scatterplots that were useful in displaying relationships. It is a good practice to plot data when examining relationships, so that patterns can be detected. A visual display helps identify patterns in the data quicker than examining numbers. In the next chapter, we will begin to assign numerical values to relationships as we compute correlation coefficients.

PRACTICE EXERCISES

Use the data set you created in Chapter 3 (i.e., student admission data).

1. Produce the following scatterplots.
   a. GREQ and GREV scores
   b. GREQ and GREV, controlling for GENDER
   c. Overlay scatterplot
      GREQ and PRETEST
      GREV and PRETEST

2. Identify the strongest and weakest relationship from these scatterplots.
   What reasons might exist to support these relationships, or lack of relationships?
3. Using the data from this chapter (chap13 data), produce a scatterplot matrix using the four statistics attitude scales.
4. With one of more of the produced graphs, explore some of the editing features illustrated in this chapter (e.g., change marker styles, add reference lines, change text style).

14 Describing Relationships

In the previous chapter, you used SPSS to summarize relationships between variables in scatterplots. In this chapter, you will explore the use of correlation coefficients to describe the magnitude of these relationships. When two variables exist in rank-order form, the most appropriate measure of association is the *Spearman rank correlation coefficient* (r_s). When variables are measured on a continuous interval level, the *Pearson product moment correlation coefficient* (r) should be used.

As with other measures of association, these correlation coefficients indicate the strength of the relationship between two variables. Both the Spearman and the Pearson coefficients range from -1.0 to $+1.0$. A correlation coefficient of -1.0 indicates a perfect negative correlation, while a $+1.0$ describes a perfect positive relationship. The closer the correlation coefficient is to either -1.0 or $+1.0$, the stronger the relationship. On the other hand, the closer the coefficient is to zero (0), the weaker the relationship.

In reality, very few relationships are perfect and very few are so weak as to be equal to zero. For two variables to be perfectly correlated, the relationship between the two variables must be the same for each individual. For example, in a group of students with IQ scores of 100, 110, and 120, and SAT scores of 1000, 1100, and 1200, respectively, the ratio of IQ to SAT score is exactly the same for each student resulting in a perfect correlation. For a perfect negative correlation, the reverse is true. The relationship between variables will still be identical across all cases. However, in this case, high values on one variable will be associated with corresponding low values on the other. If two variables are not related, the correlation coefficient will be zero. When the correlation is zero, the relationship between variables is completely random. That is, for all cases in the data set, a high score on one variable may be paired with a high score, a low score or a moderate score on the other variable. There will be no systematic pattern to the relationship.

Correlation is a measure of covariation. In other words, the more two variables vary together, the stronger the correlation is between them. In fact, another term used to describe the relationship between two variables is *covariance*. A covariance is simply a measure of association which hasn't been standardized. Whereas correlation coefficients range from -1.0 to $+1.0$, the range of a covariance depends on the variability of the variables being correlated and the number of people in the sample. This dependence makes covariances difficult to interpret and compare. The comparison of variables and their relationships becomes easier when the variables have been standardized. Therefore, correlation coefficients are used to describe relationships between variables because they are reported on a common scale and can be more easily interpreted.

A correlation coefficient can also be squared to represent a percentage of variance shared by two variables. A squared correlation coefficient is called the *coefficient of determination*. This coefficient offers you a practical way to determine the magnitude of the relationship between two variables, since you know that variables can only share up to 100% of their variance. Obviously, two variables that share 100% of their variance are perfectly correlated. The coefficient of determination is also useful in determining how well one variable can be predicted from the other. For example, if you examine the variables in our data set on applicants to a doctoral program (see Appendix A), you will see that there are several variables that might be useful for predicting the score of graduate students' final comprehensive written examinations. These potential predictor variables include GRE–Quantitative, GRE–Verbal, pretest in area of specialty, and ratings from an interview with a faculty member. The variable that shares the most in common with scores on final comprehensive written examinations will produce the strongest correlation and the highest coefficient of determination and will, therefore be most useful. We will explore prediction and explanation of variance in greater detail in Chapters 21, 22, and 23, when we discuss regression analysis.

In the remaining sections of this chapter, we will explore the use of correlation coefficients to describe relationships among several variables in our data set using SPSS. Before we begin, let's examine the variables we will use to illustrate these procedures.

VARIABLES USED IN THIS CHAPTER

We will use the same variables that we used in the previous chapter to illustrate scatterplots. Each of these variables comes from our graduate student data set. Some of these variables are measured on an ordinal scale (computer experience, educational level) while others are interval (computer and statistics attitudes) or ratio level variables (age, employment hours, teaching experience, and number of credits taken).

USING SPSS TO PERFORM CORRELATIONS

In the previous chapter, you used scatterplots to visually display relationships between variables. In this chapter, you will be using the Correlations procedure to describe the magnitude of these relationships. Before you specify this command, you need to activate SPSS and retrieve the data file labeled **chap14 data** on the enclosed disk.

Correlations Procedure

As with most statistical procedures, you will start from the **Analyze** menu. From this menu, select the **Correlate** and **Bivariate...** options, as illustrated in Figure 14.1.

FIGURE 14.1
Analyze–Correlate–
Bivariate menu
selections

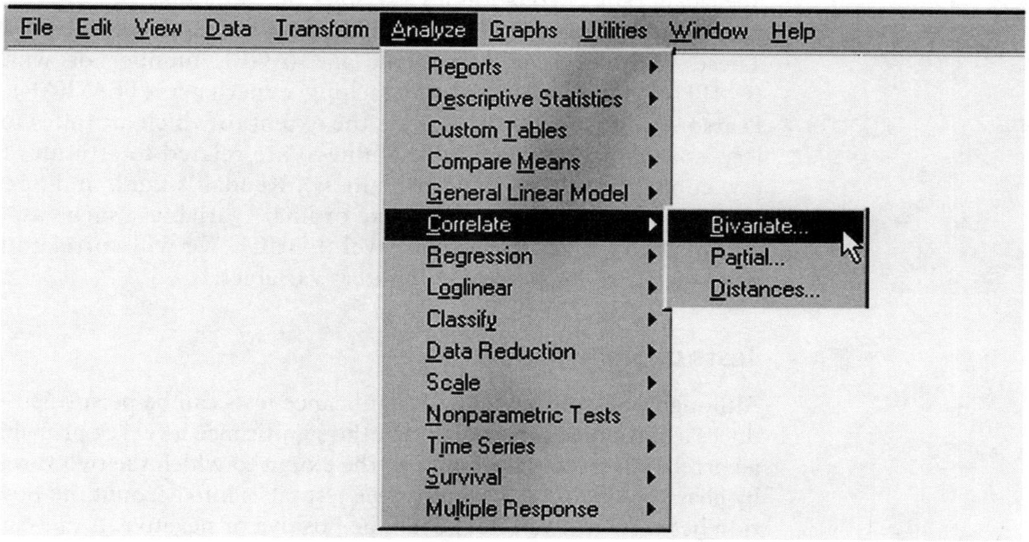

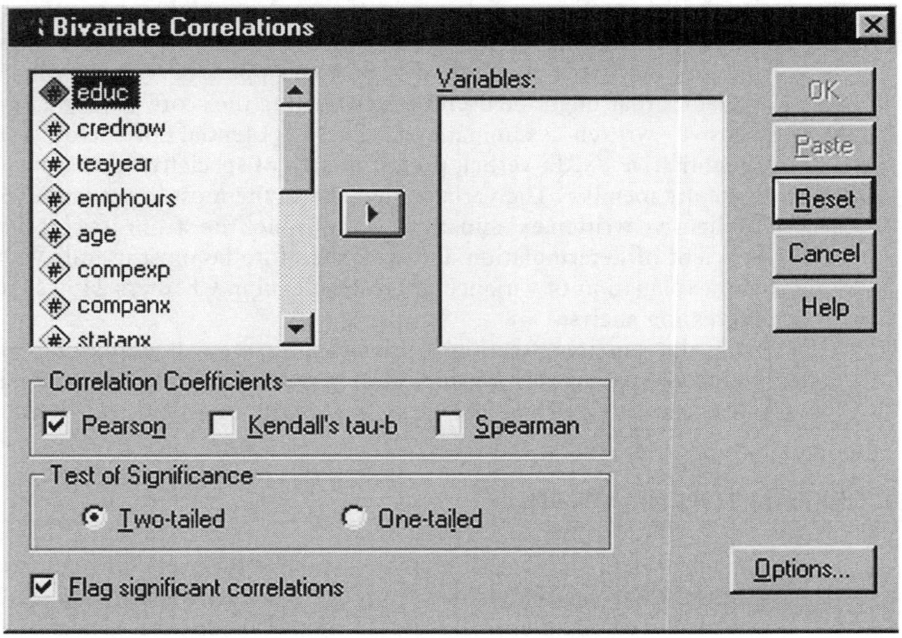

FIGURE 14.2
Bivariate Correlations
dialog box

Selecting these options will open the Bivariate Correlations dialog box, displayed in Figure 14.2. You will recognize several features from previous procedures, such as Frequencies, Descriptives, Means, and Crosstabs. At the left of the window, the names of all your variables are listed in the source variable list. You will select the variables from the source variable list and place them in the **Variables:** box for analysis. Finally, the five command pushbuttons, used in all previous procedures, appear at the far right.

Correlation Coefficients

Below the source variable list is a box labeled Correlation Coefficients. The option for **Pearson** has already been selected as the default option. This option will produce a Pearson product moment correlation, which is most appropriate for variables measured at the interval or ratio level. The second option, **Kendall's tau-b,** can be used to compute a measure of association for ordinal variables. Finally, the **Spearman** option is used to compute the Spearman rank correlation for variables that are ranked.

We will compute Pearson correlations for several interval variables from our data set. These variables include student age (AGE), number of working hours per week (EMPHOURS), and years of teaching experience (TEAYEAR). We will also use the Pearson correlation to determine the extent to which attitudes toward computers (anxiety, confidence, liking, and usefulness) are related to attitudes toward statistics (anxiety, confidence, liking, and usefulness). Kendall's tau-b and Spearman's Rank correlation will be used to correlate ordinal variables such as computer experience (COMPEXP) and educational level (EDUC). We will correlate these ordinal variables with the attitudes toward computers variables.

Tests of Significance

Although one- and two-tailed significance tests can be performed, the default setting produces a two-tailed test. Recall that the significance level is a probability. The significance of a correlation coefficient indicates the extent to which the two variables may be related just by chance. A two-tailed significance test takes into account the possibility that the correlation between two variables could be positive or negative. A one-tailed level of significance

FIGURE 14.3
Bivariate Correlations:
Options dialog box

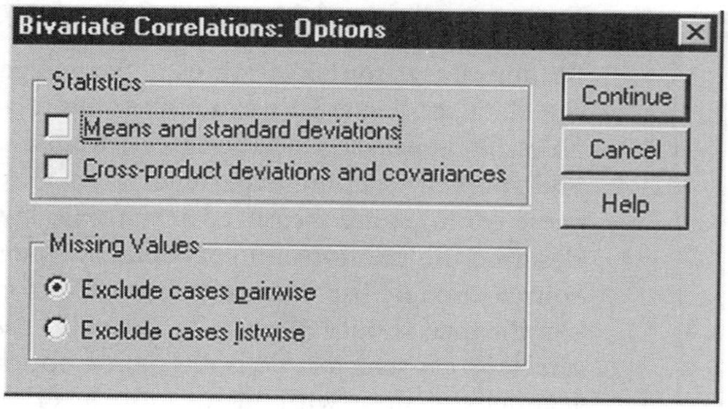

is used less often, and only in situations where you have specific expectations about the direction of the relationship. Your expectations must be supported on sound theory and/or prior research findings in order to warrant the use of one-tailed test of significance.

The actual significance level of each correlation coefficient will be displayed in the SPSS output by default. The displayed significance level will be based on a one- or two-tailed test, whichever option was selected. For our illustrations, the default setting of a two-tailed test of significance will be used. The default option to flag significant ($p < .05$, $p < .01$, $p < .001$) correlations should also be checked.

Options

Click on the **Options...** button to investigate the remaining options. These options are displayed in the Bivariate Correlations: Options dialog box in Figure 14.3.

There are two sets of options available. The first set pertains to descriptive statistics and the second set pertains to missing values. You computed means and standard deviations earlier using the Descriptives and Means procedures. You can also compute these statistics while executing the Correlations procedure. You would want to request this option only for variables measured at the interval level and for which a mean and standard deviation would be meaningful. This option would be useful for the variables age, employment hours, teaching experience, and attitudes toward computers and statistics, but not for computer experience and educational level.

Another set of descriptive statistics you can obtain are cross-product deviations and covariances for each pair of variables. These statistics are necessary when you calculate the Pearson product moment correlation coefficient by hand. As with the correlation coefficient, these statistics can be either positive or negative. Also, the larger the absolute value of these statistics, the stronger the relationship. The values that these statistics, however, depend on the variables being correlated and the number of people in the sample. Therefore, these values are not easily interpreted unless all correlations are performed on similar variables with the same number of people.

The second set of options affect the treatment of missing values. By default, cases missing values for either variable will be excluded on a pairwise basis. In other words, each correlation coefficient will be based on the number of cases that have valid values for the two variables being correlated. If a case has a missing value for either of the two variables, it will be excluded from the analysis.

Another way to treat cases with missing values is listwise deletion. When this option is selected, cases will be excluded if they have a missing value on any of the variables selected for the correlation matrix. This option is useful when you wish to base all correlations on the same number of cases. We will use this option later when we compute correlations as part of a regression analysis. For our current correlation analysis, use the default setting for pairwise deletion.

Return to the Bivariate Correlations dialog box (see Figure 14.2) by clicking on the **Continue** command pushbutton and we'll begin to produce some correlations using SPSS.

Pearson Product Moment Correlation

Student Background Variables.   We will generate several correlations using variables from our data set. First, let's examine some relationships among the student background variables. We have selected the three variables age (AGE), employment hours (EMPHOURS), and years of teaching experience (TEAYEAR) for our first correlation matrix. Since all of these variables are measured at the ratio level, the Pearson correlation will be computed to describe the relationship between each pair. Select each of these three variables from the source variable list. The default settings for the Pearson correlation and Two-tailed test of significance should already be selected. Also by default, the **Flag significant correlations** check box is selected. This is a handy option that will automatically flag statistically significant correlations with one or more asterisks, depending on the significance of the correlation. Be sure these default settings are selected in the Bivariate Correlations dialog box before proceeding with the analysis.

With the default settings in place, let's explore the Options dialog box (see Figure 14.3). Click on the **Options...** button. Select both options in the Statistics box so that means, standard deviations, cross-product deviations, and covariances will be computed for these variables. Leave the default setting for missing values as it is so that missing cases will be excluded on a pairwise basis. Click on the **Continue** button to return to the Bivariate Correlations dialog box. To generate this correlation matrix, select the **OK** command pushbutton. A correlation matrix for these three variables will be generated, as well as descriptive statistics for each variable and variable pair. Before we examine the SPSS output, let's generate a few more correlation matrices.

Return to the Bivariate Correlations dialog box to continue. From the **Analyze** menu, select the **Correlate** and **Bivariate...** options.

Attitudes Toward Computers and Statistics.   The second set of correlations will summarize relationships among students' attitudes toward computers and their attitudes toward statistics. These attitude scales, measuring anxiety, confidence, liking and usefulness were computed in Chapter 7. As with the student background variables, the Pearson correlation will be used to summarize these relationships.

The student background variables should still be selected. To remove these variables, highlight them with your mouse and transfer them back to the source variable list. Select the computer attitude measures from the source variable list. These four scales are COMPANX, COMPCON, COMPLIK, and COMPUSE. Click on the **Options...** button, you will notice that the options you selected for the previous analysis are still highlighted. We will use the same options for these attitude scales. Return to the Bivariate Correlations dialog box using the **Continue** button and run the correlations by selecting the **OK** command pushbutton. You have produced a correlation matrix that summarizes relationships regarding attitudes toward computers.

Next, let's summarize the relationships for attitudes toward statistics. Clear the computer scales from the selected variable list. Select the four statistics attitudes scales: STATANX, STATCON, STATLIK, and STATUSE. Return to the Bivariate Correlations dialog box and run these correlations by selecting the **OK** command pushbutton. Now that you've summarized relationships among the computer attitude scales and among the statistics attitudes scales, let's describe relationships between attitudes toward computers and attitudes toward statistics.

Return to the Bivariate Correlations dialog box and select all eight attitude scales (COMPANX, COMPCON, COMPLIK, COMPUSE, STATANX, STATCON, STATLIK, and STATUSE). You have already summarized relationships among the computer scales and statistics scales, therefore what we want to summarize now is how each computer scale relates to each statistics scale. If you choose to produce these correlations now, you will get a large matrix that contains many correlations you have already performed. To avoid needless duplication, we can modify the procedure using syntax commands and remove unwanted (or unneeded) variables before we run the analysis.

SPSS for Windows keeps a record of each command and subcommand you select as you navigate through each window. After you've selected all the options you desire, you can paste the commands and subcommands you've selected into a syntax file. Once commands are stored in a syntax file, they can be edited so that options that were not available through the windows you viewed can be added. Let's try this using our current example.

First, be sure that all eight variables have been selected. Next, click on the **Options...** button and make sure the options that you selected for the previous analysis are still highlighted. Return to the Bivariate Correlations dialog box using the **Continue** button. Now, use the **Paste** command pushbutton to paste your selected commands and subcommands to a syntax file (see Figure 14.4). The commands and subcommands should now appear in a window labeled Syntax Editor as displayed in Figures 14.5.

This file contains all the commands and subcommands necessary to execute the Correlations procedure. These commands are similar to those used in SPSS/PC+, the old DOS version of SPSS. You can use the Help menu to find out more about these syntax commands. From there, you will be able to examine all the subcommands available through the Correlations procedure. You might want to explore this on your own. For now, let's examine the commands and subcommands in the current syntax file.

The main command line reads "**CORRELATIONS.**" This is followed by a subcommand "**/VARIABLES=**", that lists all the variables you selected. To read the entire line, you will need to scroll to the right. The next subcommand, "**/ = TWOTAIL SIG,**" indicates that a

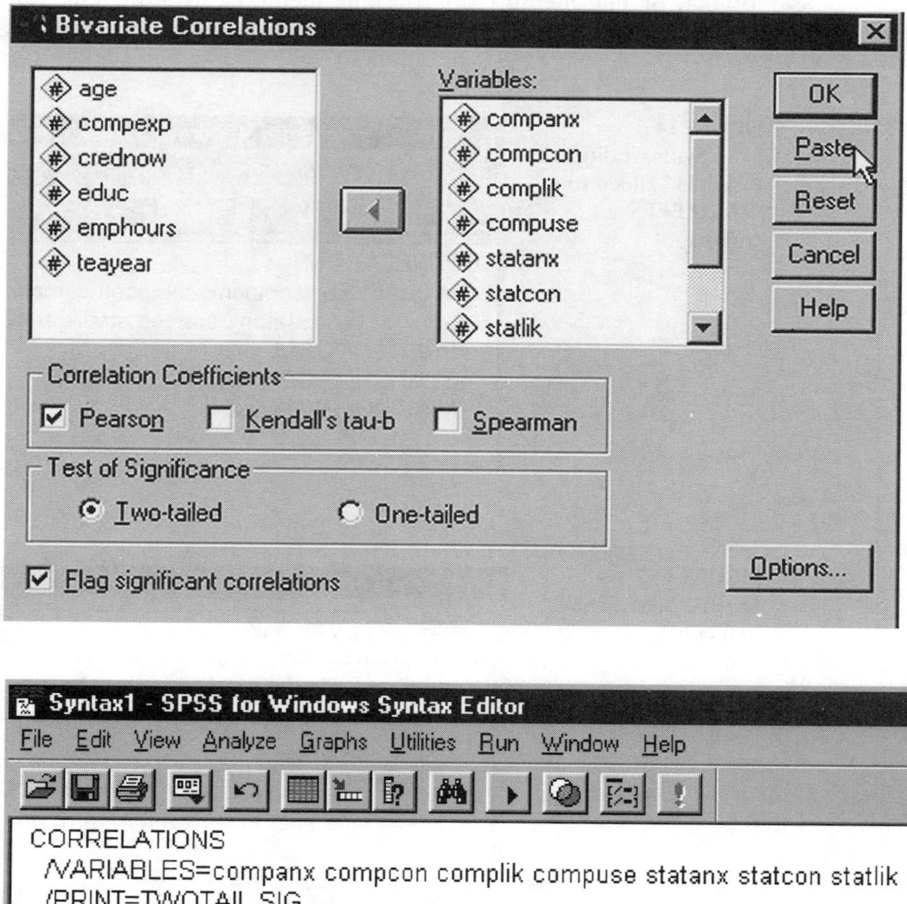

FIGURE 14.4
Using Paste button to paste commands to syntax file

FIGURE 14.5
Syntax Editor with pasted correlation commands

```
CORRELATIONS
  /VARIABLES=companx compcon complik compuse statanx statcon statlik statuse
  /PRINT=TWOTAIL SIG
  /STATISTICS DESCRIPTIVES XPROD
  /MISSING=PAIRWISE .
```

two-tailed test of significance will be performed and the actual significance level of each Pearson correlation will be displayed. The next subcommand, "/STATISTICS DESCRIP- TIVES XPROD," instructs SPSS to calculate the descriptive statistics (i.e., means, standard deviations, cross-products, and covariances) you selected in the Options dialog box. Finally, the "/MISSING = PAIRWISE" subcommand indicates that missing cases will be excluded on a pairwise basis. At the very end of these subcommands is a period (.), which identifies the end of the command.

In order to specify a correlation matrix that just summarizes how each computer scale relates to each statistics scale, we need to make one change. The VARIABLES subcommand is used to identify the variables in the correlation matrix. The keyword WITH is used to separate variables into sets. When the procedure is run, variables in one set (the set of vari- ables prior to the 'WITH' keyword) will be correlated with those variables in the other set (the set following the WITH keyword). Contrast this to the same procedure without the WITH keyword, where in each variable is allowed to correlate with every other variable. A procedure that includes the WITH keyword will produce a much smaller matrix than one without. Position your cursor after the fourth computer scale, COMPUSE. Type the key- word "WITH" between the variables of COMPUSE and STATANX. Use the <Enter> key to move the names of the four statistics attitude scales to the next line. The syntax file should now look like that displayed in Figure 14.6.

Before we execute these commands, let's give this syntax file a name. Syntax files are saved in the same manner as other SPSS files. Begin by using either the save icon from the toolbar, or File menu. Using the **File** menu, choose the **Save** option. The Save As SPSS Syntax dialog box will open, displayed in Figure 14.7. Syntax files are identified within

FIGURE 14.6
SPSS Syntax Editor ("WITH" added to /VARIABLES command)

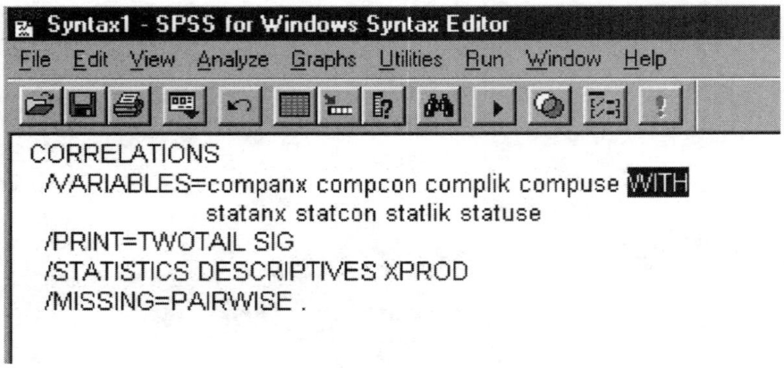

FIGURE 14.7
Save As SPSS Syntax dialog box

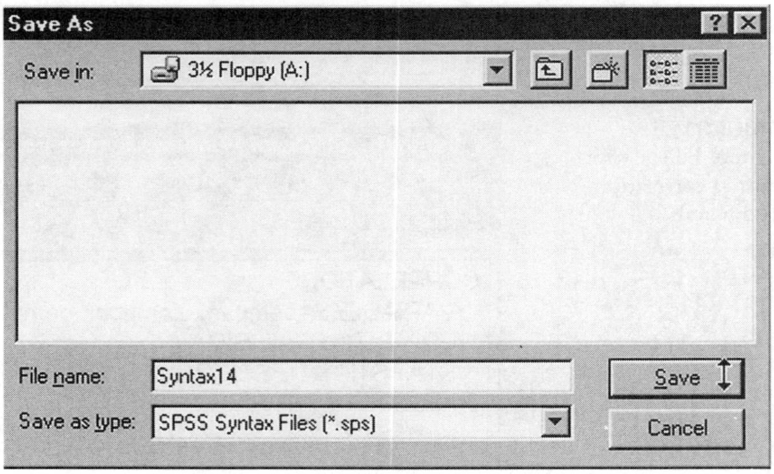

SPSS by a .sps suffix. In order to keep your files organized, we recommend naming this file Syntax14.sps, so that you remember it was created in Chapter 14.

Running SPSS Procedures from Syntax

Now that you've modified and saved the syntax file, it is time to execute the correlations procedure once again. This time, we will be running the procedure from the syntax file instead of the OK command pushbutton. On the toolbar, there is a button with an arrow pointing to the right. This button looks like the PLAY button on the VCR. Figure 14.8 shows the SPSS syntax toolbar. This toolbar contains only the buttons that are appropriate for the syntax editor.

This right arrow button is used to run the commands listed in the syntax file. Click this button with your mouse to run the commands in the syntax file you created. This will generate a reduced correlation matrix that summarizes only the relationships between attitudes toward computers and attitudes toward statistics rather than a full matrix that displays correlations among every variable. We will examine this SPSS output later, so return to the Bivariate Correlations dialog box and we will generate a final set of correlations.

Spearman Rank Correlations

The final set of correlations will summarize the relationship between two ordinal variables: computer experience (COMPEXP) and educational level (EDUC). This matrix will also include correlations between these two variables and attitudes toward computers (i.e., COMPANX, COMPCON, COMPLIK, and COMPUSE). In SPSS, Spearman rank correlations are performed in a manner similar to the Pearson correlations.

Begin by selecting the **Correlate** and **Bivariate...** options from the **Analyze** menu. The Bivariate Correlations dialog box appears, which was displayed in Figure 14.2. Under the Correlation Coefficients heading, the default setting (Pearson) should still be marked. Select the option for **Spearman** and cancel the selection for **Pearson**. Retain the default settings for two-tail tests of significance and the display of the actual significance level. Select the variables for analysis from the source variable list in the same manner as you've done before. For the current analysis, select the following variables: COMPANX, COMPCON, COMPLIK, COMPUSE, COMPEXP, and EDUC, as in Figure 14.9.

Use the **Options...** button to explore the Options dialog box. Because the Spearman correlation is intended for ordinal variables, the options under the Statistics heading are not available (see Figure 14.10). If you try to click on them, nothing will happen. These statistics are not appropriate for ordinal level data. Retain the setting for missing values and use the **Continue** button to recall the Bivariate Correlations dialog box.

The Spearman correlation procedure will first arrange all the data for each variable in rank order. Then, a correlation coefficient will be computed to describe the extent to which these variables are related. To execute the Spearman rank correlations, use the **OK** command pushbutton.

Save Your Results

All of the correlations you generated are stored in the SPSS output viewer. You might want to save this file, using the name **chap14.spo,** so you remember that this file contains the SPSS output from Chapter 14. We will examine some of these results in the final section of this chapter.

FIGURE 14.8
SPSS Syntax Editor
toolbar

↑
Run syntax commands

FIGURE 14.9
Bivariate Correlations
dialog box (with
Spearman selected)

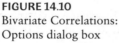

FIGURE 14.10
Bivariate Correlations:
Options dialog box

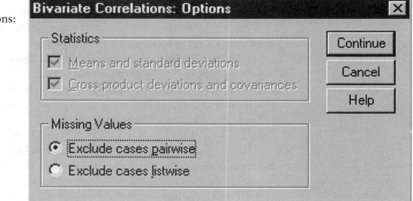

INTERPRETING SPSS CORRELATIONS RESULTS

You have generated correlations for several sets of variables, including student background variables, computer attitudes, and statistics attitudes. Now it is time to interpret this output. SPSS displays correlation output in a series of matrices and tables. Each matrix, or table, is often displayed on a different page of the SPSS output. We will examine selected matrices and tables from your SPSS output and discuss the information generated by the Correlations procedure.

Student Background Information

The first example of your SPSS output appears in Figure 14.11. These results summarize relationships among the student background variables age, employment hours, and years of teaching experience. Three different correlations were produced. As you examine these results, be aware of the danger of inflating Type 1 errors when performing multiple tests of

Descriptive Statistics

	Mean	Std. Deviation	N
AGE	32.68	8.90	207
EMPHOURS	25.30	14.29	151
TEAYEAR	6.81	6.35	128

Correlations

		AGE	EMPHOURS	TEAYEAR
AGE	Pearson Correlation	1.000	.335**	.564**
	Sig. (2-tailed)	.	.000	.000
	Sum of Squares and Cross-products	16331.314	6130.450	3439.429
	Covariance	79.278	40.870	27.515
	N	207	151	126
EMPHOURS	Pearson Correlation	.335**	1.000	.194
	Sig. (2-tailed)	.000	.	.058
	Sum of squares and Cross-products	6130.450	30615.987	1687.937
	Covariance	40.870	204.107	17.768
	N	151	151	96
TEAYEAR	Pearson Correlation	.564**	.194	1.000
	Sig. (2-tailed)	.000	.058	.
	Sum of Squares and Cross-products	3439.429	1687.937	5116.867
	Covariance	27.515	17.768	40.290
	N	126	96	128

**. Correlation is significant at the 0.01 level (2-tailed).

FIGURE 14.11
SPSS Correlations output (student background variables)

significance using the same, or related, variables with the same sample. In this case, we recommend being more conservative when judging statistical significance. One method for controlling type 1 error inflation involves dividing your alpha level of .05 among all of the correlations in the matrix. In your example, you have 3 correlations. You could increase your control over the inflation of type 1 error by using an alpha of .05/3, or .017 to assess the significance of your correlations rather than the more liberal alpha of .05.

SPSS output includes two tables. The first table summarizes descriptive information, including the mean and standard deviation for each variable. The second table summarizes all the information about the relationships between pairs of variables including the correlation coefficient, significance level, sum of cross-product deviations, covariance, and number of cases for each pair of variables. This arrangement is somewhat different from earlier versions of SPSS (Version 6.X), so please follow our interpretations closely.

The information in the descriptive table is nothing new as you have seen this with several earlier procedures. First, look at the number of cases reported in the descriptive information versus that reported in the correlation section. Notice that the number of cases is less when the results pertain to pairs of variables. That is because this number reflects the number of students who have complete information of both variables identified in the pair. For example, there were 151 students who were employed while attending graduate school and 128 students who had some teaching experience. However, only 96 students were employed and had some years of teaching experience.

Next, look at some of the information that describes the relationship between these pairs of variables. Examine the sum of the cross-product deviations and the covariance for each of the three pairs of variables. Remember that these values indicate the strength of the relationship between the two variables, but are dependent upon the variables being compared and the number of people used in the analysis. These values are all positive, which indicates a positive relationship between each pair of variables. The largest coefficient is listed for the relationship between age and employment hours, while the smallest is listed for the relationship between employment hours and years of teaching experience. You will also notice that the relationship between age and employment hours is based on the largest number of students, while the relationship between employment hours and teaching experience is based on the fewest. This information can be misleading. That's why we need to examine the Pearson correlation coefficient.

These coefficients are displayed in the top of each cell. In the diagonal of this matrix (upper left-hand corner to lower right-hand corner) you will see perfect positive correlations ($r = +1.0$) displayed. These values describe the correlation of each variable with itself. On either side of the diagonal, the relationships between the pairs of variables are summarized. If you folded the matrix on the diagonal, the information from each side would be identical. Therefore, we need to examine only the information from one side of the diagonal. We have highlighted the information above the diagonal for clarity.

There are three different correlations in all. Two of these correlations are statistically significant. The strongest correlation exists between age and years of teaching experience, in the upper right-hand cell of the matrix. The reported Pearson correlation coefficient is .564, indicating a moderate positive correlation. Remember that these coefficients have a range from -1.0 to $+1.0$. This relationship makes sense because older students are likely to have more years of teaching experience than the younger students. This coefficient can also be squared to produce the coefficient of determination. In this case, $(.564)^2 = .3181$, or 32%. In other words, approximately 32% of the variance in teaching experience can be attributed to student age, or vice versa.

If you examine the sample size, you will see that this correlation was computed using 126 students. Finally, note the significance level. This is the probability that this relationship would occur just by chance. In this case, $p = .000$. This does not mean that the probability is zero. This probability is carried out only to three decimal places. If the decimal were carried forward, you would eventually see a number other than 0. Be careful how you interpret a probability like this. In most cases, you would describe a probability like this as being less than 1 in 1,000, or .001. When reporting this in a manuscript or thesis, you would use "p" to represent "probability" and "$<$" to represent "less than." Therefore, you would write "$p < .001$." Because this relationship is not very likely to have occurred by chance, you will conclude that a statistically significant relationship does exist between age and teaching experience.

The second highest correlation exists between age of employment hours ($r = .335$). This relationship is not as strong as the one between age and teaching experience. If you square this correlation, you find that these two variables share approximately 11% of common variance, which is only about one-third as much as the relationship between age and teaching experience. Nevertheless, you will also conclude that a statistically significant relationship exists between age and employment hours because the likelihood of this correlation occurring by chance is very low ($p < .001$). In layman's terms, there is a tendency for older students to work more hours per week and for younger students to work fewer hours per week.

The third correlation is that for the variables teaching experience and employment hours. This value is lower than the previous two (r = .194) and is based on only 96 students. Another difference between this relationship and the previous ones is that it is more likely to have occurred by chance (p = .058). This means that approximately 6 times out of a 100, a correlation of this magnitude could occur just by chance. The probability of a chance occurrance is too high for us to conclude that a statistically significant relationship exists between employment hours and teaching experience. Remember that the level of risk is predetermined by your alpha level. In most cases, this alpha level would be set at 5 times in 100 by chance. We decided to be more conservative to guard against Type 1 error inflation and set the alpha level at .0167. Because your finding happens nearly 6 times in 100 by chance, you will conclude that the relationship is most likely due to chance.

Computers and Statistics Attitudes

Attitudes Toward Computers. The second example of your SPSS output appears in Figure 14.12. These results summarize relationships among the computer attitude scales (i.e., anxiety, confidence, liking, usefulness).

Again, descriptive information (means and standard deviations) and information about relationships (i.e., covariances, correlation coefficients) are reported in this SPSS output. You've seen the means and standard deviations before in an earlier chapter. Let's begin by examining the sum of the cross-product deviations and covariances. These values are more meaningful than those presented for the student background variables because all four computer attitude scores are measured in a similar manner and based on the same number of students. However, the four computer attitude scales still have different means and standard deviations, so you should be cautious when interpreting these and making comparisons. All of the covariances are positive, so you can expect positive relationships among these attitude scales.

Let's examine the correlation matrix. Remember that a higher score indicates a more positive attitude. Therefore, students who are more comfortable with computers tend to have more confidence in their ability to work with computers. Again, the coefficients in the diagonal represent correlations of each variable with itself and, therefore, they are reported as 1.0. In figure 14.12 we have highlighted the six correlations that describe the relationship between each pair of computer attitude scales. These correlations are all positive, as expected, and all statistically significant ($p < .001$). The highest correlation exists between the computer anxiety scale and the computer confidence scale (r = .885). This is a very strong correlation. If we square this correlation, we find that these two variables share approximately 78% of their variance. The weakest relationship exists between the computer usefulness scale and the computer anxiety scale. This correlation is moderate (r = .438), indicating that these two variables share approximately 19% of common variance. Students who are more comfortable with computers also tend to find them more useful in their lives.

Attitudes Toward Statistics. Relationships among attitudes toward statistics are summarized in Figure 14.13. This output contains the same types of information as reported in the previous output. As with attitudes toward computers, all covariance values are positive, indicating positive correlations among the attitude scales.

Examining the correlation matrix, you'll notice that the pattern of correlations is similar to those found for attitudes toward computers. The highest correlation exists between statistical anxiety and statistical confidence (r = .872), while the lowest is found between statistical anxiety and statistical usefulness (r = .300). All correlations in this matrix are positive and statistically significant ($p < .001$). Yet, they are consistently lower than those found among the computer attitude scales.

Descriptive Statistics

	Mean	Std. Deviation	N
COMPANX	30.6029	6.3708	209
COMPCON	30.6077	5.2941	209
COMPLIK	29.6603	5.3155	209
COMPUSE	34.9187	3.9000	209

Correlations

		COMPANX	COMPCON	COMPLIK	COMPUSE
COMPANX	Pearson Correlation	1.000	.885**	.772**	.438**
	Sig (2-tailed)	.	.000	.000	.000
	Sum of Squares and Cross-products	8442.038	6208.435	5439.804	2263.249
	Covariance	40.587	29.848	26.153	10.881
	N	209	209	209	209
COMPCON	Pearson Correlation	.885**	1.000	.829**	.555**
	Sig. (2-tailed)	.000	.	.000	.000
	Sum of Squares and Cross-products	6208.435	5829.828	4855.144	2383.330
	Covariance	29.848	28.028	23.342	11.458
	N	209	209	209	209
COMPLIK	Pearson Correlation	.772**	.829**	1.000	.580**
	Sig. (2-tailed)	.000	.000	.	.000
	Sum of Squares and Cross-products	5439.804	4855.144	5876.880	2499.225
	Covariance	26.153	23.342	28.254	12.016
	N	209	209	209	209
COMPUSE	Pearson Correlation	.438**	.555**	.580**	1.000
	Sig. (2-tailed)	.000	.000	.000	.
	Sum of Squares and Cross-products	2263.249	2383.330	2499.225	3163.617
	Covariance	10.881	11.458	12.016	15.210
	N	209	209	209	209

**. Correlation is significant at the 0.01 Level (2-tailed).

FIGURE 14.12
Pearson correlation matrix (attitudes toward computers)

Attitudes Toward Computers and Statistics. Figure 14.14 summarizes the relationships between attitudes toward computers and attitudes toward statistics. We are displaying only the table of correlations because you viewed the descriptive statistics in the previous two figures. As with previous correlation output, sums of cross-product deviations and covariances are displayed. However, the correlation matrix found in Figure 14.14 is somewhat different from the others you have examined.

Descriptive Statistics

	Mean	Std. Deviation	N
STATANX	26.4211	6.8018	209
STATCON	29.0478	5.2089	209
STATLIK	27.0813	4.2684	209
STATUSE	32.9139	4.6886	209

Correlations

		STATANX	STATCON	STATLIK	STATUSE
STATANX	Pearson Correlation	1.000	.872**	.597**	.300**
	Sig. (2-tailed)	.	.000	.000	.000
	Sum of Squares and Cross-products	9622.947	6427.789	3603.842	1989.579
	Covariance	46.264	30.903	17.326	9.565
	N	209	209	209	209
STATCON	Pearson Correlation	.872**	1.000	.712**	.491**
	Sig. (2-tailed)	.000	.	.000	.000
	Sum of Squares and Cross-products	6427.789	5643.522	3291.187	2493.861
	Covariance	30.903	27.132	15.823	11.990
	N	209	209	209	209
STATLIK	Pearson Correlation	.597**	.712**	1.000	.589**
	Sig. (2-tailed)	.000	.000	.	.000
	Sum of Squares and Cross-products	3603.842	3291.187	3789.617	2450.464
	Covariance	17.326	15.823	18.219	11.781
	N	209	209	209	209
STATUSE	Pearson Correlation	.300**	.491**	.589**	1.000
	Sig. (2-tailed)	.000	.000	.000	.
	Sum of Squares and Cross-products	1989.579	2493.861	2450.464	4572.450
	Covariance	9.565	11.990	11.781	21.983
	N	209	209	209	209

**. Correlation is significant at the 0.01 level (2-tailed).

FIGURE 14.13

Pearson correlation matrix (attitudes toward statistics)

In the diagonal of the previous matrices, you found perfect positive correlations. Values below the diagonal were mirror images of the values above the diagonal. In this correlation matrix, the diagonal does not contain correlations of each variable with itself. These correlations describe relationships between the set of computer attitude scales and the set of statistics attitude scales. The correlations summarized on either side of the diagonal describe different relationships among computer attitudes and statistics attitudes. Therefore, they are not mirror images of one another.

Correlations

		STATANX	STATCON	STATLIK	STATUSE
COMPANX	Pearson Correlation	**.502****	.532**	.445**	.255**
	Sig. (2-tailed)	**.000**	.000	.000	.000
	Sum of Squares and Cross-products	**4525.947**	3672.971	2515.751	1584.852
	Covariance	**21.759**	17.659	12.095	7.619
	N	**209**	209	209	209
COMPCON	Pearson Correlation	.529**	**.622****	.566**	.393**
	Sig. (2-tailed)	.000	**.000**	.000	.000
	Sum of Squares and Cross-products	3964.526	**3564.923**	2658.670	2028.938
	Covariance	19.060	**17.139**	12.782	9.755
	N	209	**209**	209	209
COMPLIK	Pearson Correlation	.377**	.519**	**.645****	.438**
	Sig. (2-tailed)	.000	.000	**.000**	.000
	Sum of Squares and Cross-products	2834.895	2987.397	**3041.775**	2271.885
	Covariance	13.629	14.362	**14.624**	10.923
	N	209	209	**209**	209
COMPUSE	Pearson Correlation	.161**	.306**	.425**	**.608****
	Sig. (2-tailed)	.020	.000	.000	**.000**
	Sum of Squares and Cross-products	888.158	1291.813	1472.383	**2312.536**
	Covariance	4.270	6.211	7.079	**11.118**
	N	209	209	209	**209**

**. Correlation is significant at the 0.01 level (2-tailed).
*. Correlation is significant at the 0.05 level (2-tailed).

FIGURE 14.14
Pearson correlation matrix (computer and statistics attitudes)

We've highlighted the correlations in the diagonal because they examine the extent to which similar attitudes are related. In the upper left-hand corner, the correlation between computer anxiety and statistical anxiety is displayed. This correlation (r = .502) is the lowest of the four in the diagonal. The strongest correlation is between the computer liking and statistical liking scales (r = .645). All of these correlations are positive, which indicates that students have similar attitudes toward computers and statistics. Those students who like working with computers, have confidence in their computer ability, find computers useful, and are comfortable with computers also tend to like statistics, have confidence in their statistical ability, find statistics useful, and be comfortable working with statistics.

Spearman Rank Correlations

The final correlations are summarized in Figure 14.15. In this output, there are no descriptive statistics, only a correlation matrix.

Correlations

			COMPANX	COMPCON	COMPLIK	COMPUSE	COMPEXP	EDUC
Spearman's rho	COMPANX	Correlation Coefficient	1.000	.882**	.793**	.508**	.514*	.004
		Sig. (2-tailed)	.	.000	.000	.000	.000	.958
		N	209	209	209	209	209	209
	COMPCON	Correlation Coefficient	.882**	1.000	.833**	.609**	.514*	.034
		Sig. (2-tailed)	.000	.	.000	.000	.000	.624
		N	209	209	209	209	209	209
	COMPLIK	Correlation Coefficient	.793**	.833**	1.000	.603**	.496*	.137*
		Sig. (2-tailed)	.000	.000	.	.000	.000	.047
		N	209	209	209	209	209	209
	COMPUSE	Correlation Coefficient	.508**	.609**	.603**	1.000	.373*	.078
		Sig. (2-tailed)	.000	.000	.000	.	.000	.264
		N	209	209	209	209	209	209
	COMPEXP	Correlation Coefficient	.514**	.514**	.496**	.373**	1.000	.091
		Sig. (2-tailed)	.000	.000	.000	.000	.	.188
		N	209	209	209	209	209	209
	EDUC	Correlation Coefficient	.004	.034	.137*	.078	.091	1.000
		Sig. (2-tailed)	.958	.624	.047	.264	.188	.
		N	209	209	209	209	209	209

**. Correlation is significant at the .01 level (2-tailed).
*. Correlation is significant at the .05 level (2-tailed).

FIGURE 14.15
Spearman correlation matrix

This matrix displays the Spearman rank coefficients for the two ordinal variables computer experience (COMPEXP) and educational level (EDUC), and the four computer attitude scales. Each of these variables was ranked before a correlation coefficient was computed. The Spearman rank correlation coefficient describes the extent to which students' ranking on one variable is similar to their ranking on the other variable.

Examine the last two columns highlighted in your SPSS output (see Figure 14.15). These two columns display the correlations between computer experience and educational level and with each of the computer attitudes scores.

Each of the correlations between computer experience and the four computer attitudes is statistically significant ($p < .001$). These correlations describe the extent to which computer experience relates to each of the four computer attitudes. The strongest relationships exist between computer anxiety and computer confidence. Both of these correlations are reported as .514. This means that students with more experience with computers tend to be more comfortable with computers and have more confidence in their ability. The relationship between experience and computer liking ($r_s = .496$) is nearly as strong. The fourth correlation, between computer experience and computer usefulness ($r_s = .373$), is somewhat weaker. All of these relationships suggest that the more experience a student has, the more positive his/her attitudes are toward computers.

Of the correlations between educational level and the four computer attitudes, only the correlation between educational level and the computer liking scale ($r_s = .137$) is statistically significant. This is also much lower than the correlations you found between computer attitudes and computer experience. Being concerned about the inflation of Type 1 error, you will judge this result using a more stringent alpha level. There are four correlations involving educational level. Therefore, a more appropriate alpha level would be $.05/4 = .0125$. Using this criteria, you will conclude that the relationship between educational level and the computer liking scale is most likely due to chance.

The final correlation highlighted in this matrix is between educational level and computer experience. The reported coefficient is .091, with a probability of .188. This relationship is most likely due to chance. The remaining correlations summarized in this matrix represent the relationships among the various computer attitude scales. You already examined these relationships in Figures 14.12. The correlations in the current matrix indicate the magnitude of these relationships after all the attitude scales have been converted to rank order. The Pearson correlations discussed earlier are more appropriate.

USING THE OUTPUT NAVIGATOR

Now that you have examined the output from the Correlations procedure, let's make a few modifications using the output navigator. We will use the correlations between computer attitudes and statistics attitudes for this illustration (see Figure 14.14). The first thing to do is to activate the pivot table by double-clicking on this table in your output file, as you did when you modified previous SPSS output.

In this application of the output navigator, you will modify this correlation output so that it is more suitable for a presentation or manuscript. When you examine correlation tables in research articles, you rarely see all the information that SPSS includes. Generally, correlation coefficients, number of subjects, and some indication of significance levels are included in most correlation tables found in research articles. Other information, such as sums of cross-product deviations and covariances, is rarely included. The actual significance level is also rarely included. Usually, asterisks (*) are used to identify the statistically significant relationships displayed in tables. If you examine the SPSS output, you will notice that asterisks are already in place. Finally, because all correlations are based on a sample of 209 cases, we can delete the sample size information N as well.

To delete tabled info, first select the rows containing the labels for informatin you wish to delete, as illustrated in Figure 14.16.

Next, from the **Edit** menu, choose the options for **Select** and **Data and Label Cells.** These selections are illustrated in Figure 14.17.

This will highlight the entire row associated with each label you selected as shown in Figure 14.18. Press the Delete key, and all this information will be deleted from the table shown. The only rows remaining should be those containing the correlation coefficients.

Not much of the original table remains (see Figure 14.19). This abbreviated table contains the basic information from a correlation analysis. All variables and coefficients are displayed, and an asterisk system is used to represent probability levels.

Let's delete one more thing. The label Pearson Correlation appears in each row. We don't need that, so highlight the table by double-clicking with your mouse. Now, single-click one of the Pearson Correlation labels. They will all be highlighted. Delete them using the <Delete> key. What is left appears in Figure 14.20.

Before we leave this correlation table, try changing the format to Report as you did earlier when examining descriptive results. As a reminder, you must first select the output table. Then choose the **TableLooks** option from the **Format** menu. Select **Report** and click on **OK.** Your table should now look like that displayed in Figure 14.21.

FIGURE 14.16
Highlighted rows with mouse

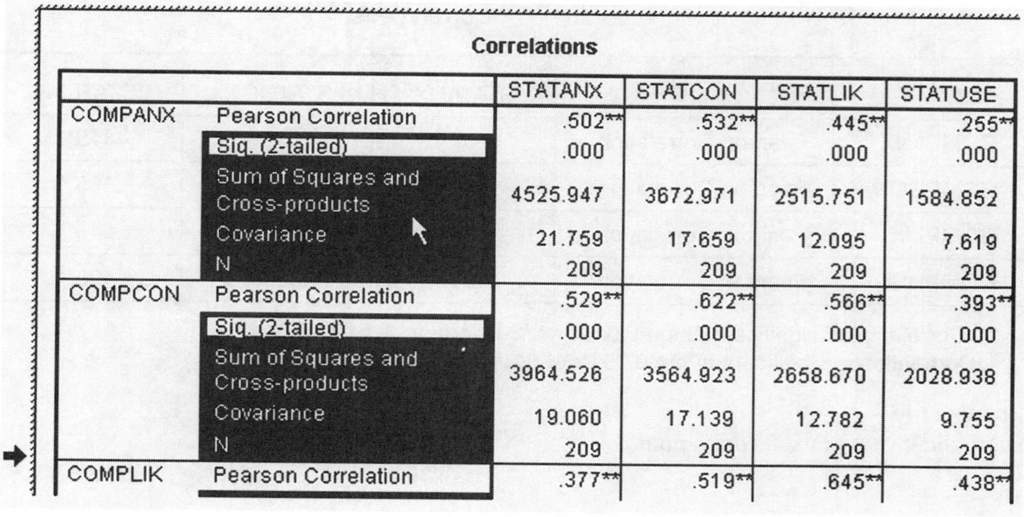

Correlations

		STATANX	STATCON	STATLIK	STATUSE
COMPANX	Pearson Correlation	.502**	.532**	.445**	.255**
	Sig. (2-tailed)	.000	.000	.000	.000
	Sum of Squares and Cross-products	4525.947	3672.971	2515.751	1584.852
	Covariance	21.759	17.659	12.095	7.619
	N	209	209	209	209
COMPCON	Pearson Correlation	.529**	.622**	.566**	.393**
	Sig. (2-tailed)	.000	.000	.000	.000
	Sum of Squares and Cross-products	3964.526	3564.923	2658.670	2028.938
	Covariance	19.060	17.139	12.782	9.755
	N	209	209	209	209
COMPLIK	Pearson Correlation	.377**	.519**	.645**	.438**

FIGURE 14.17
Edit–Select–Data and Label Cells menu selections

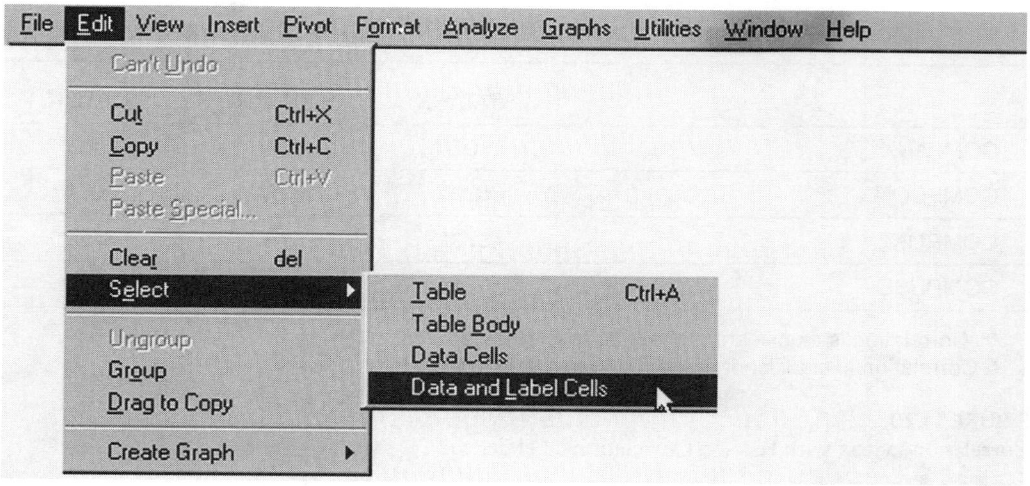

File Edit View Insert Pivot Format Analyze Graphs Utilities Window Help

Can't Undo

Cut   Ctrl+X
Copy   Ctrl+C
Paste   Ctrl+V
Paste Special...

Clear   del
Select   ▶   Table   Ctrl+A
                    Table Body
Ungroup   Data Cells
Group   Data and Label Cells
Drag to Copy

Create Graph ▶

FIGURE 14.18
Rows selected for deletion

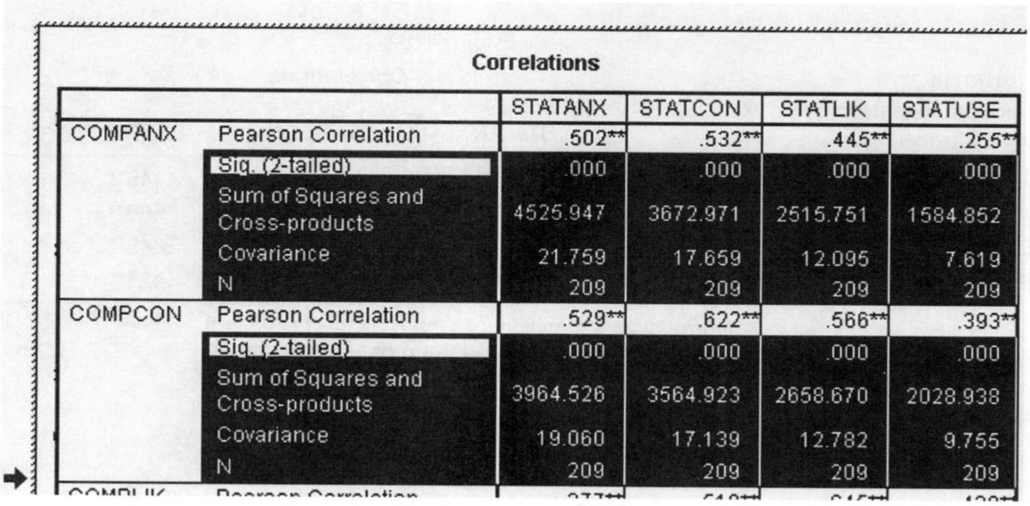

Correlations

		STATANX	STATCON	STATLIK	STATUSE
COMPANX	Pearson Correlation	.502**	.532**	.445**	.255**
	Sig. (2-tailed)	.000	.000	.000	.000
	Sum of Squares and Cross-products	4525.947	3672.971	2515.751	1584.852
	Covariance	21.759	17.659	12.095	7.619
	N	209	209	209	209
COMPCON	Pearson Correlation	.529**	.622**	.566**	.393**
	Sig. (2-tailed)	.000	.000	.000	.000
	Sum of Squares and Cross-products	3964.526	3564.923	2658.670	2028.938
	Covariance	19.060	17.139	12.782	9.755
	N	209	209	209	209
COMPLIK	Pearson Correlation	.377**	.519**	.645**	.438**

Correlations

		STATANX	STATCON	STATLIK	STATUSE
COMPANX	Pearson Correlation	.502**	.532**	.445**	.255**
COMPCON	Pearson Correlation	.529**	.622**	.566**	.393**
COMPLIK	Pearson Correlation	.377**	.519**	.645**	.438**
COMPUSE	Pearson Correlation	.161*	.306**	.425**	.608**

**. Correlation is significant at the 0.01 level (2-tailed).
*. Correlation is significant at the 0.05 level (2-tailed).

FIGURE 14.19
Matrix limited to Pearson correlations

Correlations

	STATANX	STATCON	STATLIK	STATUSE
COMPANX	.502**	.532**	.445**	.255**
COMPCON	.529**	.622**	.566**	.393**
COMPLIK	.377**	.519**	.645**	.438**
COMPUSE	.161*	.306**	.425**	.608**

**. Correlation is significant at the 0.01 level (2-tailed).
*. Correlation is significant at the 0.05 level (2-tailed).

FIGURE 14.20
Correlation matrix with Pearson Correlation label deleted

FIGURE 14.21
Correlation matrix in report format

Correlations

	STATANX	STATCON	STATLIK	STATUSE
COMPANX	.502**	.532**	.445**	.255**
COMPCON	.529**	.622**	.566**	.393**
COMPLIK	.377**	.519**	.645**	.438**
COMPUSE	.161*	.306**	.425**	.608**

**. Correlation is significant at the 0.01 level (2-tailed).
*. Correlation is significant at the 0.05 level (2-tailed).

CHAPTER SUMMARY

In this chapter, we used the Correlations procedure to summarize relationships between variables measured at the ordinal and interval levels. We used the Spearman rank correlation coefficient to describe relationships between ordinal variables and the Pearson product moment correlation to describe relationships between interval variables. In the next few chapters, we will explore procedures used to make comparisons among sample means and make inferences about population means.

PRACTICE EXERCISES

Use the data set you created in Chapter 3 (i.e., student admission data).

1. Which measure of association (i.e., Pearson or Spearman) would be most appropriate for the following pairs of variables.
   a. GREQ and GREV
   b. Pretest and GREQ
   c. Interview Rating1 and SES

2. Use the Correlations procedure in SPSS to investigate the relationships between the following pairs of variables.
   a. GREQ and GREV
   b. Pretest and GREQ
   c. Interview Rating1 and SES

3. Based on the information from your SPSS output, what can be concluded about each of these relationships? Use specific information from your output to support your conclusions.
   a. GREQ and GREV
   b. Pretest and GREQ
   c. Interview Rating1 and SES

SECTION VI

Between-Subjects Designs

15 | T-Tests

In this chapter, we will explore the use of t-test procedures to answer questions about a single sample and pairs of samples. In single-sample situations, the purpose is to determine whether or not a specific sample belongs to a hypothesized population. For example, you may want to know whether a specific class of graduate student is similar to or different from the overall population of graduate students? For two-sample situations, the purpose is to determine the extent to which two groups differ from each other in regard to some population parameter. For instance, you may wish to compare two cohorts of graduate students on their GRE scores.

ONE-SAMPLE T-TEST

A *one-sample t-test* is used to compare a sample mean to a hypothesized population mean. Specifically, a one-sample t-test will help you determine the likelihood that the sample came from a population, given the conditions you specify in the null hypothesis. For example, if a particular sample of graduate students was randomly drawn from the general population, we would expect the sample mean of their GRE scores to be equal to 500. Because of the central limit theorem, discussed in Chapter 11, we understand that sample means will be distributed symmetrically around the mean of the population from which they were drawn. Using this sampling distribution of the mean, we will be able to determine the probability of our sample mean belonging to a population with a mean of 500.

Following the hypothesis testing process discussed in Chapter 11, we will either reject or retain the null hypothesis based on the results of the t-test. If the obtained t value is small, close to 0, it would have a high probability of occurring, given the conditions stated in the null hypothesis. Therefore, we would retain the null hypothesis and conclude that any differences between our sample and population are most likely due to chance. However, if the obtained t value is more extreme, whether positive or negative, the probability of it occurring by chance, under the condition of the null hypothesis, will be smaller. If this probability is lower than our predetermined risk level (i.e., alpha level), we would reject the null hypothesis in favor of an alternative hypothesis.

We make two assumptions when using a one-sample t-test. The first is that our sample was drawn randomly from some population. The second assumption is that this population follows a normal distribution. Before we use SPSS to illustrate a one-sample t-test, let's discuss the two-sample, or independent-samples t-test.

INDEPENDENT-SAMPLES T-TEST

Independent-samples t-tests are used to determine the likelihood that two samples came from populations that have the same mean. If two samples were drawn from the same population, we would expect the difference between these samples to be equal to 0. Therefore, our null hypothesis would indicate that the two population means are equal. Again, using the central limit theorem, we know that even if both samples are drawn from the same population, the sample means could still vary due to sampling error. However, if we sampled all possible samples and calculated differences between each pair of sample means, the distribution of sample mean differences would be symmetrical, and its mean would be equal to the difference between the two population means.

Under the null hypothesis, we would state that the difference between the two population means is 0. As with a one-sample t-test, we reject this null hypothesis if the probability of being wrong is low (e.g., $\leq .05$). On the other hand, if the probability of being wrong is too high, we would retain the null hypothesis and conclude that differences between the two means are most likely due to chance.

There are a few assumptions we need to make when using an independent-samples t-test. The first two are the same as for the one-sample t-test in that these samples were randomly drawn from populations that are normally distributed. Another assumption is that of *independence*. This means that the scores on the dependent variable for subjects in one group are not related to those of subjects in the other group. This also means that the treatment received by individuals in one group was not influenced by the way individuals were treated in the other group.

Finally, there is the assumption of *homogeneity of variance*. This assumption maintains that the variances in the two populations are equal. A violation of this assumption will increase the likelihood of making a Type 1 or Type 2 error. Examine the two populations displayed in Figure 15.1a. Both populations have a mean GRE of 500. However, one population is more varied than the other one. Therefore, the range from which a sample might be drawn is wider in one population than in the other. If a sample is drawn from each population, as illustrated in Figure 15.1a, the difference between these two sample means might be large enough to reject the null hypothesis, when, in reality, the null hypothesis is true because the population means are equal. In this case, lack of homogeneity would lead to a Type 1 error.

In Figure 15.1b, an illustration of how a lack of homogeneity could lead to a Type 2 error appears. In this case, the population means are different, but the population variances are also quite different. If two sample are drawn, with a result as shown in this figure, we would fail to reject the null hypothesis when it should be rejected, committing a Type 2 error.

FIGURE 15.1A
Lack of homogeneity of variance resulting in a Type 1 error

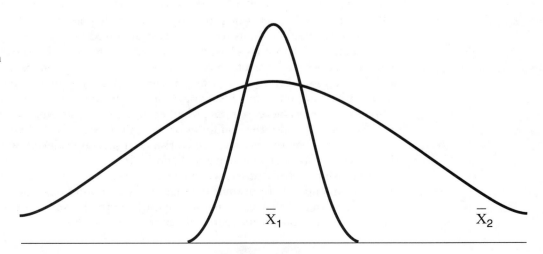

$\overline{X}_1$ $\overline{X}_2$

$\mu_1 = \mu_2$

FIGURE 15.1B
Lack of homogeneity
of variance resulting in
a Type 2 error

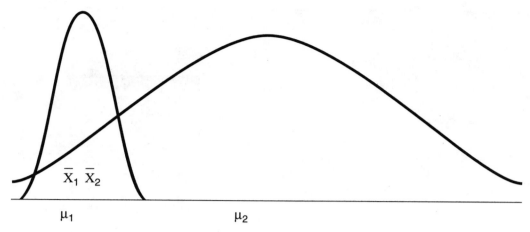

$$\overline{X}_1 \; \overline{X}_2$$

$$\mu_1 \qquad\qquad\qquad \mu_2$$

In the remaining sections of this chapter, we will explore the use of the t-test to test hypotheses about one- and two-sample situations using SPSS. Before we begin, let's examine the variables we will use to illustrate these procedures.

VARIABLES USED IN THIS CHAPTER

Once again, we will use variables from our graduate student data set. In order to illustrate a one-sample t-test, we will compare the number of credits hours taken (CREDNOW) by part-time students in our sample to a hypothesized value for the population. For our two-sample tests, we will use the variables degree program (DEGREE) and student enrollment status (STATUS) as independent variables. Attitudes toward computers and statistics (i.e., COMPANX, COMPCON, COMPLIK, COMPUSE, STATANX, STATCON, STATLIK, STATUSE) and a few demographic variables will serve as dependent variables. The demographic variables include student age (AGE), credits taken (CREDNOW), and employment hours (EMPHOURS).

USING SPSS TO PERFORM T-TESTS

In this session, you will be using the T Test procedure to perform one-sample and independent-samples t-tests. Before you perform these statistical procedures, you need to activate SPSS and retrieve the data. The name of the data you will be using in this chapter is **chap15 data**.

As with previous procedures, you begin with the **Analyze** menu. From this menu, select the **Compare Means** option. You'll notice that there are three options for performing t-tests. These options include the **One-Sample T Test...**, **Independent-Samples T Test...**, and **Paired-Samples T Test....** In this chapter, we will be exploring the one-sample t-test and the independent-samples t-test. We will explore the paired-samples t-test in a later chapter.

One-Sample T-Test

From the **Analyze** menu, select the **Compare Means** and **One-Sample T Test...** options, as illustrated in Figure 15.2.

Selecting these options will open the One-Sample T Test dialog box, displayed in Figure 15.3. You will recognize many features in this dialog box; they are common to many procedures. At the left of the window, the names of all your variables are listed in the source variable list. You will select the variables from the source variable list and place them in the Test Variables box for analysis. The five command pushbuttons, which you've used in all previous procedures appear at the far right.

FIGURE 15.2
Analyze–Compare
Means–One-Sample T
Test menu selections

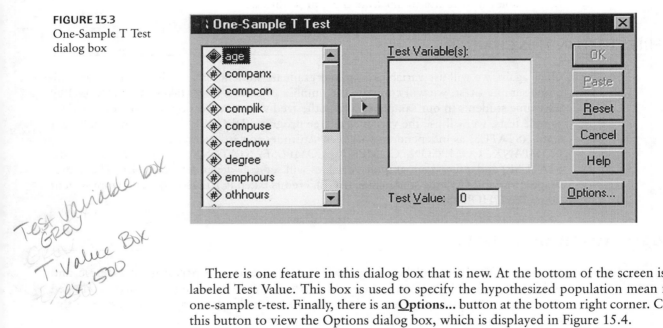

FIGURE 15.3
One-Sample T Test
dialog box

There is one feature in this dialog box that is new. At the bottom of the screen is a box labeled Test Value. This box is used to specify the hypothesized population mean for the one-sample t-test. Finally, there is an **Options...** button at the bottom right corner. Click on this button to view the Options dialog box, which is displayed in Figure 15.4.

In this Options dialog box, you specify a confidence interval, and indicate how missing values should be treated. By default, a 95% confidence interval will be computed, and missing values will be excluded on an analysis-by-analysis basis. These default settings are fine for most t-tests you will run. If you want a smaller or larger confidence interval, type that number in place of the 95. In other words, if you wanted a 99% confidence interval, you would erase the 95 and type 99. If you wish to exclude missing values on a listwise basis, select that option.

Running a One-Sample T-Test

For our illustration of a one-sample t-test, we will use only part-time students and determine whether part-time students are enrolled in just one course during the quarter they are taking statistics. If these students are enrolled in just one course, we would expect the population mean to be 4 credit hours, or one course. Before we perform a t-test to determine whether our sample of part-time students comes from a population having a mean of 4 credit hours, we must select these students.

FIGURE 15.4
One-Sample T Test:
Options dialog box

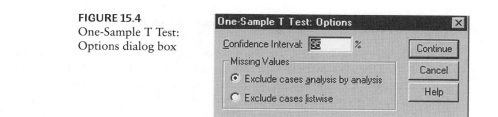

FIGURE 15.5
Select Cases dialog
box: (STATUS = 1)

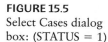

Selecting Part-Time Students.   Subgroups can be selected using the Select Cases command, accessed through the Data menu. You used this procedure in chapter 10 when you selected subgroups for analysis. From the **Data** menu, choose the **Select Cases...** option. The Select Cases dialog box, which will appear on your screen, is used to select cases according to criteria that specify. The option labeled **If condition is satisfied** allows you to specify the conditions that define a subgroup. We want to select part-time students, identified with a value of 1 on the variable of STATUS. From the Select Cases dialog box, select this option and click on the **If...** button. The Select Cases: If dialog box will appear. In this box, you specify the conditions that define the subgroup. In our case, we want to select those individuals with a value of 1 for STATUS. Transfer STATUS to the upper box and specify the condition STATUS = 1. You can use the calculator pad to express this condition, or type it in directly using your keyboard. When you are finished, click on the **Continue** button to arrive back at the Select Cases dialog box. The conditions you specified are listed in this box, next to the If button, as displayed in Figure 15.5.

To execute this command, select **OK.** Part-time students are selected, while full-time students have been filtered out. Examine your data on the screen and you will notice that certain case numbers now have a slash (/) through them. These cases have been filtered out of the analysis because they are full-time students and do not meet your specifications for selection. Be sure that this procedure worked before doing any further analysis.

Specifying Conditions for a One-Sample T-Test.   Now that you have selected part-time students for the analysis, it's time to perform the t-test. Return to the One-Sample T Test dialog box by selecting the **Compare Means** and **One-Sample T Test...** options from the **Analyze** menu.

In this one-sample t-test, we want to determine whether the number of credit hours taken (CREDNOW) by part-time students in our sample differs from our hypothesized population. In this population, we hypothesized that students would be enrolled in only one course, or 4 credit hours. In the One-Sample T Test dialog box, transfer the variable CREDNOW to the **Test Variable(s):** box and type "4" in the **Test Value:** box. This identifies the dependent variable as CREDNOW and the mean of the hypothesized population as 4. What appears in Figure 15.6 should appear on your screen.

Review the Options dialog box by clicking on the **Options...** button. We will use the default settings for this analysis. Therefore, a 95% confidence interval will be computed and missing cases will be excluded on an analysis-by-analysis basis. In this case, there is only one analysis. Return to the One-Sample T Test dialog box by using the **Continue** button. To run this one-sample t-test, click on the **OK** command pushbutton.

Before we examine the results of a one-sample t-test, let's try a few independent-samples t-tests.

Independent-Samples T-Tests

As with a one-sample t-test, you begin with the **Analyze** menu. From this menu, select the **Compare Means** and **Independent-Samples T Test...** options, as illustrated in Figure 15.7.

FIGURE 15.6
One-Sample T Test
dialog box with test
variable and test value

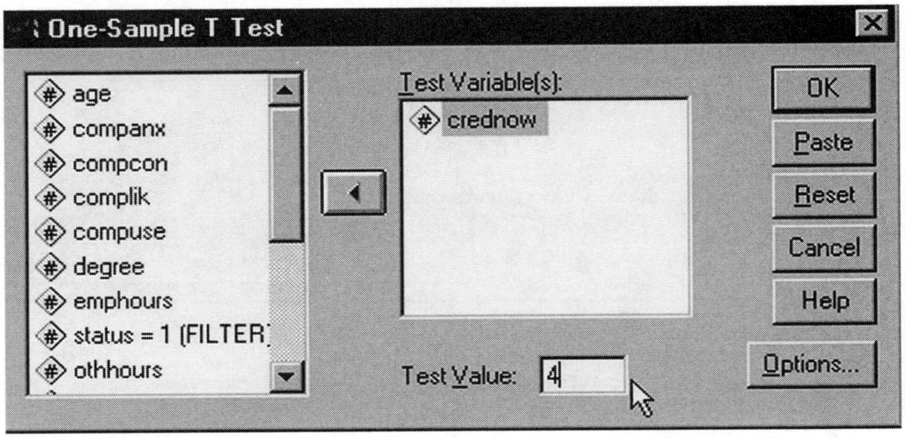

FIGURE 15.7
Analyze–Compare
Means–Independent-
Samples T Test menus

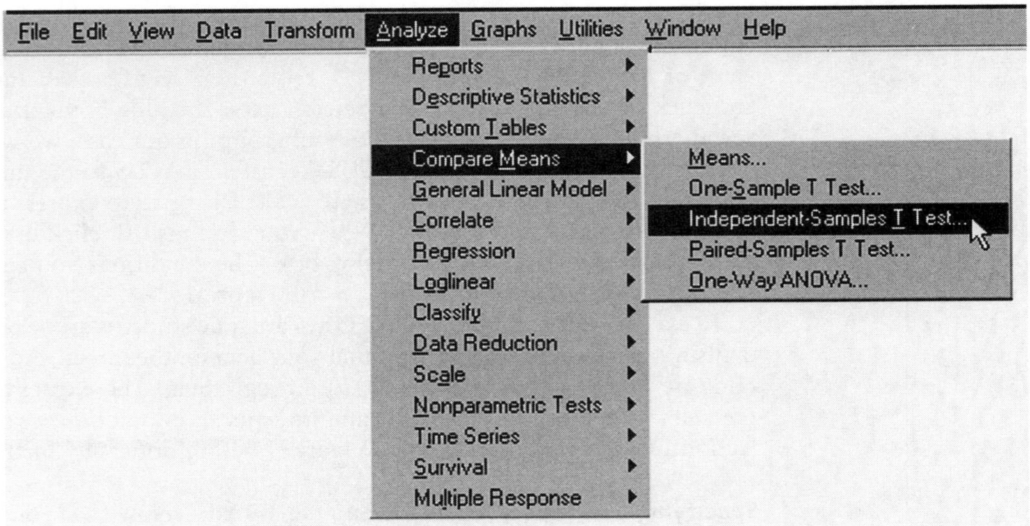

Selecting these options will open the Independent-Samples T Test dialog box, displayed in Figure 15.8. Again, most features in this dialog box should look familiar. At the left of the window, the names of all your variables are listed in the source variable list. You will select the dependent variables from the source variable list and place them in the **Test Variable(s):** box for analysis.

Notice the box labeled **Grouping Variable:**. You specify the independent variable here. This is the variable that you will use to group cases so a comparison can be made. Below this box is a **Define Groups...** button. This option allows you to define the groups that you will be comparing. Finally, there is an **Options...** button at the bottom right corner. Click on this button to view the Options dialog box, which is displayed in Figure 15.9.

These options are the same as they were for one-sample t-tests. In this Options dialog box, you specify a confidence interval, and how missing values should be treated. By default, a 95% confidence interval will be computed and missing values be excluded on an analysis-by-analysis basis. These default settings are fine for t-tests you will run in the next section.

Running Independent-Samples T-Tests

When you performed the one-sample t-test earlier, you selected a subgroup of part-time students for the analysis. We will use all students for these t-tests, not just part-time students. Therefore, be sure that all cases are selected before executing any t-tests in this section. From the **Data** menu, choose the **Select Cases...** option and then select the first option; **All cases....** Select **OK** to execute this command.

Masters vs. Doctoral Students.   Return to the Independent-Samples T Test dialog box by selecting the **Compare Means** and **Independent-Samples T Test...** options from the **Analyze** menu. In this dialog box, we will identify the variables for the first group of t-tests which

FIGURE 15.8
Independent-Samples
T Test dialog box

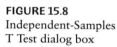

FIGURE 15.9
Independent-Samples
T Test: Options dialog
box

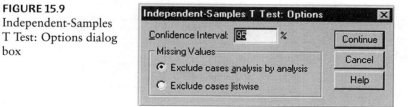

will use student degree program as an independent variable. The variable from our data set that defines a student's degree program is called DEGREE. This variable has four categories: 1=bachelors, 2=masters, 3=specialist, and 4=doctorate. We wish to compare masters students with doctoral students regarding their attitudes toward computers and statistics. These attitude variables will serve as dependent variables. They are identified in our data set as COMPANX, COMPCON, COMPLIK, COMPUSE, STATANX, STATCON, STATLIK, and STATUSE.

Select each of the above dependent variables from the source variable list and transfer them to the Test Variables box. In the **Grouping Variable:** box, place the independent variable DEGREE. These variable selections are illustrated in Figure 15.10.

Next, click on **Define Groups...** to open the Define Groups dialog box, illustrated in Figure 15.11.

This is where you define the groups to be compared in the t-test procedure. This can be done two ways. First, you can specify the values of each group by entering them in the boxes for Group 1 and Group 2. You can use any existing value to define each group for analysis. The second way to define groups is to specify a cut point. When a cut point is specified, cases in your sample will be divided into two groups. The first group will be comprised of cases with a value smaller than the cut point, while the second group will be defined as having a value equal to or larger than the cut point.

We want to compare students enrolled in a masters program, represented by a value of 2, with those enrolled in a doctoral program, represented by a value of 4. Therefore, type "2" in the box for Group 1 and "4" for Group 2. Return to the Independent-Samples T Test dialog box using the **Continue** button. This dialog box should look like that displayed in Figure 15.12.

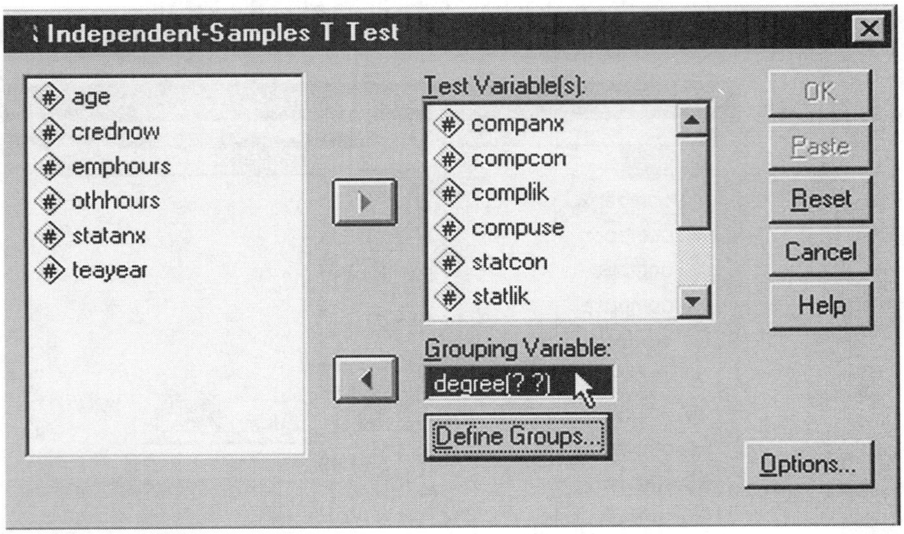

FIGURE 15.10
Variables selected for
Independent-Samples
T Test

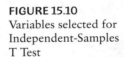

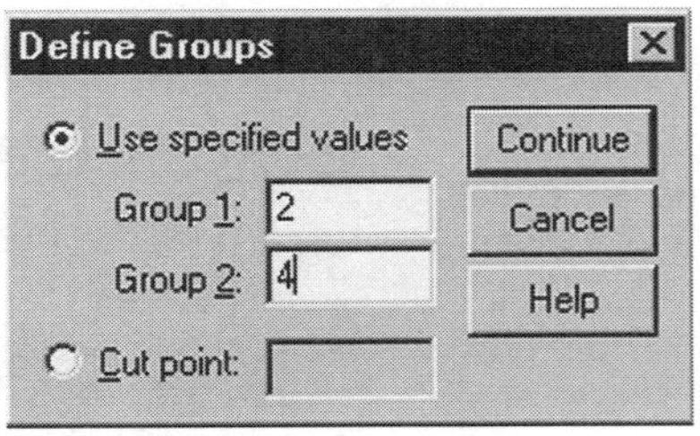

FIGURE 15.11
Define Groups dialog
box (Group 2 vs.
Group 4)

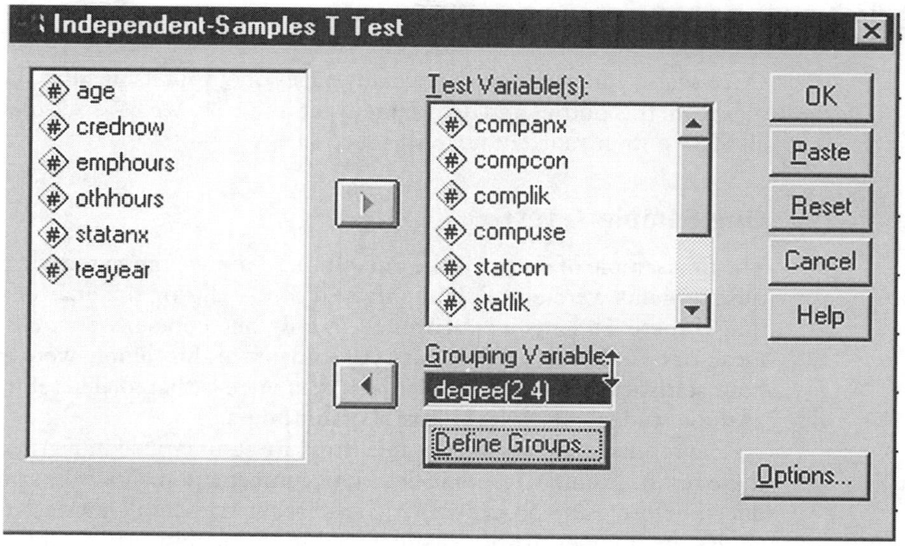

FIGURE 15.12
Variables selected and
groups defined for
Independent-Samples
T Test

FIGURE 15.12
Variables selected and groups defined for Independent-Samples T Test

In Figure 15.12, all eight computer and statistics attitude scales are listed in the Test Variables box as dependent variables. In the Grouping Variable box, the independent variable DEGREE appears with the numbers 2 and 4 specified in parentheses. To run these t-tests, use the **OK** command pushbutton at the top right corner of the dialog box. These choices will produce eight t-tests.

Part-Time vs. Full-Time Students. The second group of t-tests will compare part-time and full-time students on several background variables. To run these t-tests, return to the Independent-Samples T Test dialog box by choosing the **Compare Means** and **Independent-Samples T Test...** options from the **Analyze** menu. The information from the previous t-tests should still be in this dialog box. You can clear this information two ways. First, you can select the variables in the **Test Variable(s):** and **Grouping Variable:** boxes and transfer them back to the source variable list. This method will retain any options you might have selected beyond the default settings. Since we did not change the default settings, a second method can be used. If you use the **Reset** command pushbutton at the right of the dialog box, all information will be reset to the original default setting.

After you have cleared the previous variables from the dialog box, select the ones we will use next. The dependent variables we will be using are background variables. They include student age (AGE), credits taken (CREDNOW), employment hours (EMPHOUR), hours obligated to other activities each week (OTHHRS), and years of teaching experience (TEAYEAR). Select these variables from the source variable list and transfer them, one at a time, to the Test Variables box. Now select the independent variable of STATUS and transfer it to the Grouping Variable box. Using the **Define Groups...** button, define the two groups with the existing values of 1 and 2. Part-time students are represented by a 1, while full-time students are represented by a 2. Return to the Independent-Samples T Test dialog box using the **Continue** button, and use the **OK** command pushbutton to execute these t-tests.

Save Your Work

The results from all the t-tests you produced in this session are stored in the output file. You should save this output file so that you have a record of all your efforts. We recommend using the name **chap15.spo** to identify this file as a listing of the results from Chapter 15. We will examine samples of this output in the final section of this chapter.

INTERPRETING SPSS T-TEST RESULTS

Once again, you have generated many pages of output using SPSS. Let's examine some samples from this output and determine what it means. We have selected samples of your overall SPSS output to examine in this section.

One-Sample T-Test

The first sample of output is the one-sample t-test we ran to see whether our sample of part-time students were enrolled in only one course during the quarter they were taking statistics. If these students were enrolled in only one course, we would expect the population mean to be at least 4 credit hours. All students in this sample were enrolled in a four-credit hour statistics course at the time these data were gathered. Therefore, the population mean of these students must be at least 4 credit hours.

The results from our one-sample t-test are summarized in Figure 15.13. The first part of these results summarizes some descriptive information about the sample, that you have produced before using procedures such as Frequencies and Descriptives. This information includes the number of students included in the analysis, the mean, standard deviation, and standard error of the mean. There are 58 part-time students enrolled in an average of 7.03 credits, with a standard deviation of 3.07. The standard error of the mean is .40. You specified a test value of 4 to represent the mean of our hypothesized population. The test value is displayed in the top row of the second table of the SPSS output (see Figure 15.13).

The next part of the SPSS output summarizes the results of the t-test. First, the reported mean difference of 3.03 is displayed. We will examine this information in two parts. First, let's examine the information pertaining to the mean difference and the 95% confidence interval. The value reported for the mean difference is 3.03. This is the difference between our sample mean (7.03) and the hypothesized population mean (4). The next piece of information is the 95% confidence interval, which ranges from 2.23 to 3.84. This interval provides an estimate of the true difference between our sample mean and the population mean. In other words, if we sampled part-time students over and over again, the differences between our sample mean and our population mean would range from as small as 2.23 to as large as 3.84 in 95 out of every 100 samples. This range includes only positive values. Therefore, we would expect our sample mean to be higher than the hypothesized

One-Sample Statistics

	N	Mean	Std. Deviation	Std. Error Mean
CREDNOW	58	7.03	3.07	.40

One-Sample Test

	Test Value = 4					
					95% Confidence Interval of the Difference	
	t	df	Sig. (2-tailed)	Mean Difference	Lower	Upper
CREDNOW	7.537	57	.000	3.03	2.23	3.84

FIGURE 15.13
One-sample t-test results

population mean. This interval is calculated using the mean difference and the standard error of the mean.

Finally, let's examine the results of the t-test. A t value of 7.537 with 57 degrees of freedom is reported. Degrees of freedom are determined based on the number of cases minus one (n−1). There are 58 students, therefore there are 57 degrees of freedom. The 2-tail significance is reported as .000. As with previous output you've read, this doesn't mean that the probability of this result occurring by chance is equal to zero. It is reported to only three decimal places. Based on these results, the probability that our sample mean differs from our hypothesized population mean by chance is less than 1 in a 1,000 (p < .001). Therefore, we reject the null hypothesis that the population mean of these part-time students is equal to 4 credit hours and that these students are enrolled in just one course. Because our sample mean is higher than 4, we can conclude that this sample of part-time students is enrolled in more than 4 credit hours.

Independent-Samples T-Tests

Next, let's examine some output from independent-sample t-tests. You generated several t-tests in this chapter, two of which were independent-samples t-tests. The first group of these tests was conducted to examine the extent to which masters students and doctoral students differed in terms of their attitudes toward computers and statistics. The second group of t-tests was used to examine differences that might exist between part-time and full-time students in terms of background variables such as age, credits taken, employment hours, hours obligated to other activities, and years of teaching experience.

Attitudes Toward Computers and Statistics. In order to compare masters and doctoral students' attitudes, eight t-tests were required. Because these eight dependent variables are related (you examined these relationships in Chapter 14), you should use these results cautiously. We are aware of the increased risk of Type 1 error involved with multiple tests of significance. Therefore, instead of using the typical alpha (α) level of .05 to evaluate each t-test for statistical significance, we will divide .05 by the number of comparisons we are making. Dividing .05 by 8 results in a more stringent alpha level of .00625. This correction is called a Bonnferoni adjustment. By using a more stringent alpha level to evaluate each t-test for statistical significance, we control for the inflation of Type 1 error across the multiple tests. However, by controlling for Type 1 error, we do increase the risk of making a Type 2 error. In other words, we are more likely to retain the null hypothesis when, in some cases, it may be false in the population.

The results of all eight t-tests are summarized in one table. We have highlighted two of these eight tests for interpretation. Examine the information pertaining to the scales of COMPLIK and STATLIK, which measure the extent to which students like computers and statistics. These results are summarized in Figure 15.14.

Once again, descriptive information for each group (i.e., masters students and doctoral students) is presented. This information includes number of students, mean, standard deviation, and standard error of the mean for each group of students. Let's examine the results of t-test for the dependent variable of COMPLIK. From the descriptive summary, we can see that the mean computer liking score for doctoral students is higher. Additionally, it appears that the group standard deviations are similar. This is good because we want to maintain the homogeneity of variance assumption. The standard error of the mean is smaller for the group of doctoral students, indicating that their sample mean better represents the population mean than does the mean of the masters students. However, the sample of doctoral students is also much larger than the sample of masters students, and larger samples generally represent the population better.

Let's examine the other information summarized in the SPSS output. The remaining information pertains to the test for homogeneity of variance and subsequent t-tests. First, let's check the test for homogeneity of variance for the dependent variable of

FIGURE 15.14
Independent-Samples
T Test results
(computer and
statistics attitudes)

Group Statistics

	DEGREE	N	Mean	Std. Deviation	Std. Error Mean
COMPANX	2	70	30.5286	6.4375	.7694
	4	131	30.3435	6.7707	.5916
COMPCON	2	70	29.9429	5.6051	.6699
	4	131	30.5878	5.7698	.5041
COMPLIK	**2**	**70**	**28.1286**	**5.7153**	**.6831**
	4	**131**	**30.1069**	**5.6149**	**.4906**
COMPUSE	2	70	33.6143	4.3080	.5149
	4	131	35.3435	4.1580	.3633
STANTANX	2	70	26.7714	6.1836	.7391
	4	128	26.0313	7.2394	.6399
STATCON	2	70	28.4714	5.3642	.6411
	4	128	29.1563	5.3953	.4769
STATLIK	**2**	**70**	**25.5143**	**4.5452**	**.5433**
	4	**128**	**27.6719**	**4.1604**	**.3677**
STATUSE	2	70	31.2714	4.9076	.5866
	4	128	33.7109	4.4317	.3917

COMPLIK. We know that unequal variances can impact the results of t-tests, making the probability of committing Type 1 and Type 2 errors more likely (see Figures 15.1A and 15.1B).

To test the assumption of homogeneity of variance, Levene's Test for Equality of Variances a form of F test is used. For the dependent variable of COMPLIK, an F ratio of 1.85 with a probability (p value) of .175 was produced. This indicates that the difference between our two group variances is likely to occur by chance as many as 17.5 times out of 100. You want a high probability of chance being responsible for any difference between the group variances. As long as the probability (p) exceeds our alpha level of .05, we fail to reject the null hypothesis that the variances are different and maintain the assumption of homogeneity.

With this assumption maintained, we examine the results of the t-test for equal variances. This information is found in the first row of the t-test results. The reported t value is −2.931, based on 199 degrees of freedom (df). The df for each group is determined by subtracting 1 from the number of subjects in the group. The overall degrees of freedom can be determined by adding each group's df together, $(n_1 - 1) + (n_2 - 1)$. For this first t-test, there are 70 masters students and 131 doctoral students. The df would be determined as follows: $(70 - 1) + (131 - 1) = 199$.

The 2-tailed significance is the probability of these results occurring by chance, given the null hypothesis is true. In other words, if there wasn't any difference between masters and doctoral students, sample means would still differ just by chance. The probability of this t-test is .004, which means that differences between the two groups this large or larger could occur by chance up to about 4 times in 1,000. This doesn't seem very likely, given the typical level of risk (alpha level) is 5 times in 100.

However, we are being cautious because we are performing eight related t-tests, so our level of risk for each t-test is actually much lower. Earlier, we adjusted our acceptable level of risk for each t-test downward to p = .00625, so that the overall risk is equal to .05. Therefore, a mean difference for a single t-test must happen less than 6.25 times in 1,000 for us to reject the null hypothesis and conclude the group means are truly different. Since

Independent Samples Test

| | | Levene's Test for Equality of Variances | | t-test for Equality of Means | | | | | | |
| | | | | | | | | | 95% Confidence Interval of the Difference | |
		F	Sig.	t	df	Sig. (2-tailed)	Mean Difference	Std. Error Difference	Lower	Upper
COMPANX	Equal variances assumed	.063	.803	−.046	199	.964	−4.395E-02	.9616	−1.9402	1.8524
	Equal variances not assumed			−.046	142.737	.963	−4.395E-02	.9577	−1.9370	1.8491
COMPCON	Equal variances assumed	.034	.853	−1.077	199	.283	−8569	.7955	−2.4256	.7118
	Equal variances not assumed			.−1.060	134.752	.291	−.8569	.8084	−2.4558	.7419
COMPLIK	Equal variances assumed	**1.852**	**.175**	**−2.931**	**199**	**.004**	**−2.2989**	**.7844**	**−3.8457**	**−.7521**
	Equal variances not assumed			**−2.825**	**127.131**	**.005**	**−2.2989**	**.8138**	**−3.9093**	**−.6885**
COMPUSE	Equal variances assumed	2.060	.153	−3.620	199	.000	−2.0346	.5621	−3.1430	−.9261
	Equal variances not assumed			−3.399	118.298	.001	−2.0346	.5986	−3.2200	−.8491
STATANX	Equal variances assumed	2.461	.118	.685	199	.494	.6921	1.0106	−1.3008	2.6850
	Equal variances not assumed			.717	160.145	.475	.6921	.9659	−1.2153	2.5996
STATCON	Equal variances assumed	.014	.907	−1.028	199	.305	−.7987	.7768	−2.3304	.7330
	Equal variances not assumed			−1.023	139.203	.308	−.7987	.7804	−2.3416	.7443
STATLIK	Equal variances assumed	**2.748**	**.099**	**−3.570**	**199**	**.000**	**−2.2092**	**.6189**	**−3.4295**	**−.9888**
	Equal variances not assumed			**−3.446**	**127.652**	**.001**	**−2.2092**	**.6411**	**−3.4778**	**−.9405**
STATUS	Equal variances assumed	.694	.406	−3.572	199	.000	−2.4033	.6728	−3.7300	−1.0765
	Equal variances not assumed			−3.453	128.171	.001	−2.4033	.6960	−3.7804	−1.0261

FIGURE 15.14 *Continued*
Independent-Samples T Test results (computer and statistics attitudes)

.004 is less than our risk level (.00625), we reject the null hypothesis and conclude that masters and doctoral students do differ significantly in terms of their liking for computers.

Finally, let's examine the information regarding the difference between the two group means and its confidence interval. A mean difference of −2.2989 is reported in the SPSS output. This mean difference was computed by subtracting the doctoral sample mean from the masters mean. Therefore, the sample of masters students has a mean which is 2.2989 lower than the group of the doctoral students. A standard error of the mean difference and a 95% confidence interval is also reported. This information can be used to estimate the difference that might exist in the populations. Using the confidence interval reported for the equal-variances t-test, we can state that the difference between the population means of these two groups could range from -3.8457 to $-.7521$ ninety-five percent of the time. As with other confidence intervals, the smaller this interval, the better the estimate. Also, confidence intervals should not contain zero. If so, the true difference in the population could be 0, which would support the null hypothesis. In this case, all points in the interval are negative, which indicates if we repeated sampled students over and over, masters students would be lower than doctoral students 95 times in 100.

The results of the t-test for STATLIK describe if, and to what extent masters and doctoral students differ in their liking of statistics. In the descriptive summary, doctoral students again have the higher mean, indicating their greater liking of statistics. The standard deviations are similar, but not as similar as they were for the previous example using COMPLIK as the dependent variable. Again, the standard error of the mean is smaller for doctoral students.

The results of the Levene's Test for Equality of Variances allow us to maintain the assumption of homogeneity. The F ratio is 2.748, having a probability of .099. Therefore, differences between our two variances could occur by chance as often as 9.9 times in 100, which exceeds 5 times in 100. We fail to reject the null hypothesis and conclude that any difference between group variances is most likely due to chance.

Results of the equal-variances t-test show a t value of -3.570 (df $= 199$). The probability that our group means differ by chance is reported as .000, or less than 1 time in 1,000 but we are willing to risk committing a type 1 error .00625, or 6.25 times in 1,000. Therefore, we reject the null hypothesis and conclude that a difference does exist between masters students and doctoral students in terms of the extent to which they like statistics. Based on this sample's results, we suggest that doctoral students like statistics more than masters students do.

The difference between the two group means is -2.2092, which indicates that masters students averaged 2.2092 points less than doctoral students on the STATLIK scale. The 95% confidence interval ranges from -3.4295 to $-.9888$. As with the 95% CI reported for COMPLIK all of the values in the interval are negative, which indicates if we repeated sampled students over and over, that masters students mean STATLIK score would be lower than doctoral students 95 times in 100.

We have presented the results from only two of our eight attitude t-tests. Take a few minutes to examine the remaining six t-tests in your output. First, examine the results of the Levene's Test for Equality of Variances to be sure that the homogeneity of variance assumption can be met. Then, examine the results of the t-tests, keeping in mind that we are working with a more stringent alpha level ($\alpha = .00625$) when evaluating the statistical significance of each t-test.

You should have maintained the homogeneity assumption for each of the six remaining t-tests because each probability level exceeded .05. There are also two additional t-tests that are statistically significant. These tests include the attitude scales COMPUSE (t $= -3.620$, p $< .001$) and STATUSE (t $= -3.572$, p $< .001$). In both cases, doctoral students had significantly higher means, indicating that they find computers and statistics more useful than masters students.

So, what do we know about masters and doctoral students? Doctoral students like statistics more and find both computers and statistics more useful. This seems reasonable, given that doctoral students have generally had more experience working with computers and statistics. Doctoral students are also required to complete more courses in statistics and will need to be able to use statistics and computers to analyze their dissertation data. Therefore, statistics and computers may be more relevant for doctoral students.

Student Background Variables. The second group of t-tests pertain to student background variables. Five t-tests were necessary to compare part-time and full-time students on the background variables age (AGE), credits taken (CREDNOW), employment hours (EMPHOURS), hours obligated to other activities each week (OTHHOURS), and years of teaching experience (TEAYEAR). As with the multiple t-tests required to examine attitudes toward computers and statistics, these tests are related. In order to control for the inflation of Type 1 error, we will use an alpha (α) level of .05/5, or .01, to evaluate each t-test for statistical significance.

The results for these t-tests are summarized in Figure 15.15.

Group Statistics

	STATUS	N	Mean	Std. Deviation	Std. Error Mean
AGE	1	**58**	**38.81**	**7.64**	**1.00**
	2	**149**	**30.29**	**8.21**	**.67**
CREDNOW	2	**58**	**7.03**	**3.07**	**.40**
	2	**149**	**12.21**	**2.26**	**.19**
EMPHOURS	1	47	35.21	13.77	2.01
	2	104	20.83	12.15	1.19
OTHHOURS	1	28	15.39	11.51	2.18
	2	54	18.50	15.30	2.08
TEAYEAR	1	45	9.62	6.02	.90
	2	83	5.30	6.02	.66

Independent Samples Test

		Levene's Test for Equality of Variances		t-test for Equality of Means					95% Confidence Interval of the Difference	
		F	Sig.	t	df	Sig. (2-tailed)	Mean Difference	Std. Error Difference	Lower	Upper
AGE	Equal variances assumed	**.836**	**.362**	**6.836**	**205**	**.000**	**8.52**	**1.25**	**6.06**	**10.98**
	Equal variances not assumed			**7.059**	**111.185**	**.000**	**8.52**	**1.21**	**6.13**	**10.91**
CREDNOW	Equal variances assumed	**14.212**	**.000**	**−13.313**	**205**	**.000**	**−5.17**	**.39**	**−5.94**	**−4.41**
	Equal variances not assumed			**−11.674**	**82.260**	**.000**	**−5.17**	**.44**	**−6.06**	**−4.29**
EMPHOURS	Equal variances assumed	1.397	.239	6.460	149	.000	14.39	2.23	9.99	18.79
	Equal variances not assumed			6.162	79.675	.000	14.39	2.33	9.74	19.03
OTHHOURS	Equal variances assumed	1.044	.310	−.944	80	.348	−3.11	3.29	−9.66	3.44
	Equal variances not assumed			−1.032	69.455	.306	−3.11	3.01	−9.11	2.90
TEAYEAR	Equal variances assumed	.499	.481	3.875	126	.000	4.32	1.12	2.11	6.53
	Equal variances not assumed			3.875	90.388	.000	4.32	1.12	2.11	6.54

FIGURE 15.15
Independent-Samples T Test results (student background variables)

We have selected two of these t-tests to discuss in this section. These two t-tests pertain to the dependent variables age and number of credit hours taken during the quarter a student was taking beginning statistics. The results of these two t-tests are what you might expect. First, examine the descriptive information regarding age. On average, part-time students are older than full-time students by 8.52 years. The standard deviations are similar for each group, but the standard error of the mean is smaller for full-time students, of which there are almost three times as many as part-time students.

The results of the Levene's test support the assumption of homogeneity of variance as the probability of the two variances differing by chance is .362. Therefore, the equal-variances t-test is used to determine if the two groups of students differ in terms of their age. A t value of 6.836 is reported, based on 205 degrees of freedom. The 2-tailed significance is reported as .000, which means that the probability of these two means differing by chance is less than 1 in 1,000 ($p < .001$). We therefore reject the null hypothesis, which stated that these two groups did not differ in age, and conclude that part-time students are older than full-time students.

The next t-test pertains to the dependent variable credit hours taken in one quarter. This t-test is hardly worth examining, being that one group of students is part-time and therefore will be enrolled in fewer credits. The average number of credits taken by part-time students is 7.03, compared to 12.21 for full-time students. Not only is there a difference in the group means, but the standard deviations also appear to be different. The group of part-time students is more varied than the group of full-time students. The results of the Levene's Test for Equality of Variance revealed a large F ratio of 14.212. The probability level is reported at .000, which should be interpreted as $p < .001$. This means that the group variances would differ as much as they do less than 1 time in 1,000 by chance. If this difference in variances is not likely due to chance, we would reject the null hypothesis and conclude that the population variances differ. Therefore, the assumption of homogeneity can not be maintained, and an unequal-variances t-test must be used.

The unequal-variances t-test resulted in a t value of -11.674 (df = 82.26), with a reported 2-tailed significance of .000. Notice that the degrees of freedom appear to be much lower than you would expect. This is an adjustment for the lack of homogeneity of variance. The more severe the violation of homogeneity, the more the df are adjusted. The formula used to make this adjustment can be found in most beginning statistics textbooks. With a reported 2-tailed significance level of .000 ($p < .001$), we can safely reject the null hypothesis and conclude that full-time students enroll in more credit hours than part-time students.

Take a few minutes to examine the remaining three t-tests. You should find that these two groups differ in terms of employment hours (t = 6.46, $p < .001$) and years of teaching experience (t = 3.87, $p < .001$). Part-time students are employed more hours each week and have more teaching experience. Again, these results are not very exciting. Part-time students have more time to work during the week and are part-time primarily because they work. Part-time students are also older that full-time students and therefore will have accumulated more years of teaching experience than full-time students. Full-time students did commit themselves to slightly more hours for other activities each week, but this difference was not statistically significant (t = $-.94$, p = -9.66 to $+3.44$. This interval contains 0, which would support the null hypothesis.

CHAPTER SUMMARY

In this chapter, we used the T Test procedure to perform one-sample and independent-samples t-tests. The one-sample t-test allowed us to determine whether a sample came from a hypothesized population. Specifically, we were able to compare the mean of our sample with a population mean stated in our null hypothesis. Using an independent-samples t-test, we were able to determine whether two samples came from the same population. If a comparison of the two sample means revealed a difference that was not likely due to chance, we concluded that the two samples came from populations having two different means. In the next chapters, we will explore procedures used to make comparisons between two or more sample means and make inferences about their population means.

PRACTICE EXERCISES

Use the data set you created in Chapter 5 (i.e., student admission data).

1. Using a one-sample t-test, test the following null hypotheses.
   H_o: The doctoral applicants do not differ from the typical student in terms of the GRE-Q and therefore come from a population having a mean of 500.
   H_o: The doctoral applicants do not differ from the typical student in terms of the GRE-V and therefore come from a population having a mean of 500.

   Use SPSS to perform the appropriate t-tests. Summarize the information from your SPSS output below.

	GRE-Q	GRE-V
Sample mean		
Test value		
Mean difference		
95% CI		
t		
df		
2-tail Sig.		
Decision about the null hypothesis (Reject/Fail to Reject)		

   What conclusions can be made based on these t-test results?

2. Using the independent-samples t-test procedure, test the following null hypotheses.
   H_o: Male doctoral applicants do not differ from female doctoral applicants in terms of the GRE-Q.
   H_o: Male doctoral applicants do not differ from female doctoral applicants in terms of the GRE-V.

   From your SPSS output, summarize the following information for each t-test:

	GRE-Q	GRE-V
Means		
Males		
Females		
Standard deviations		
Males		
Females		
Levene's Test for Equality of Variances		
F		
Sig.		
Can homogeneity of variance be assumed?		
t		
df		
2-tail Sig.		
Mean difference		
95% CI		
Decision about the null hypothesis (Reject/Fail to Reject)		

   What conclusions can be made based on these t-test results?

3. Examine the following null hypothesis carefully.
   H_o: The students you selected for admission (see Practice Exercises in Chapter 12) do not differ on the GRE-Q, GRE-V, and pretest.
   Using the Select Cases, Recode, and/or Compute procedures, create a group of five applicants that you would select. Then, using the independent-samples t-test procedure, run the appropriate t-tests.

   Summarize the information from your SPSS output, as you did in question 2.

16 | One-Way ANOVA

In the previous chapter, you used t-tests for both one- and two-sample situations. In one-sample situations, you compared a sample mean to a hypothesized population mean, while in two-sample situations, you compared the means of two groups to determine whether or not they came from the same population. There will be times when you need to compare more than two groups and a t-test will not be useful. You will need to use another statistical procedure, analysis of variance (ANOVA).

ANOVA is a statistical procedure that can be used to address research questions that involve one or more independent variables. Using ANOVA, comparisons can be made between individuals in different groups or within the same group. In this chapter, we will focus on one type of ANOVA procedure used to make comparisons between two or more independent group means. This procedure is called a *one-way ANOVA* because there is only one independent variable, that is used to group individuals for comparison. This procedure is also referred to as a one-factor ANOVA, with factor being another name for independent variable.

One-way ANOVA is an extension of the independent-samples t-test. The same assumptions you made when applying the t-test procedure, normality, independence, and homogeneity of variance also apply to ANOVA. First, each sample must be drawn from a normally distributed population. Second, each person's score must be independent of all other scores, and each treatment level (i.e., group) must be independent of the others. Finally, the variances from each population must be equal.

Using a one-way ANOVA, we also follow a hypothesis testing process. Like the process you followed with the t-test procedure, a null hypothesis is tested. Fron the perspective of the t-test, the null hypothesis is the presumption that both groups come from the same population and therefore have the same population mean. Using a one-way ANOVA, we will make the same assumption under the null hypothesis for as many groups as we are comparing. Suppose we were comparing the IQ scores of undergraduates, graduates, and faculty members. Under the null hypothesis, we would assume that all three groups had the same population mean. We would continue to believe this null hypothesis is true until we gather sufficient evidence from our sample that makes this hypothesis improbable.

If the null hypothesis is rejected, it doesn't mean that all three groups come from different populations, having different population means. A rejection of the null hypothesis simply indicates that not all groups have the same population mean. In other words, you conclude that there is a significant amount of variation among the treatment group means and therefore, a treatment effect exists for the independent variable being examined. To determine which groups differ, you must make more specific comparisons among the different group means. These comparisons are called *multiple comparisons*.

Two types of comparisons can be made. The first type, called *a priori tests,* are carefully planned from the beginning of the study. These comparisons should be based on theory and/or evidence from prior research efforts and never on your sample results because they are built into your research design. The second type of tests are called *post-hoc tests*. These comparisons are made after you have examined the results from your sample. There are many different post-hoc tests that can be used, each offering varying degrees of protection against Type 1 error. Because a priori tests are carefully planned and limited to those comparisons that are supported by theory and/or prior research findings, they generally have more power than post-hoc tests and offer more protection against the inflation of Type 1 error.

In the remaining sections of this chapter, we will explore the use of one-way ANOVA to make comparisons between more than two groups. Before we begin, let's examine the variables we will use to illustrate these procedures.

VARIABLES USED IN THIS CHAPTER

Once again, we will use variables from our graduate student data set. In illustrating the one-way analysis of variance procedure, we will use computer experience (COMPEXP) as the independent variable, and attitudes toward computers (i.e., COMPANX, COMPCON, COMPLIK, COMPUSE) will serve as the dependent variables for each one-way ANOVA procedure. Using one-way ANOVA we will be able to determine the extent to which attitudes toward computers depend on students' experience with computers. In other words, do students with different amounts of computer experience have different attitudes toward computers?

USING SPSS FOR ONE-WAY ANOVA

In this chapter, you will be using the One-Way ANOVA procedure. Specifically, we will use one-way ANOVA to compare students with varying amounts of computer experience on their attitudes toward working with computers. Activate SPSS and retrieve the data file named **chap16 data**.

One-Way Procedure

As with the other statistical procedures you already used, begin with the **Analyze** menu. From this menu, select the **Compare Means** and **One-Way ANOVA...** options, as illustrated in Figure 16.1.

FIGURE 16.1
Analyze–Compare
Means–One-Way
ANOVA menus

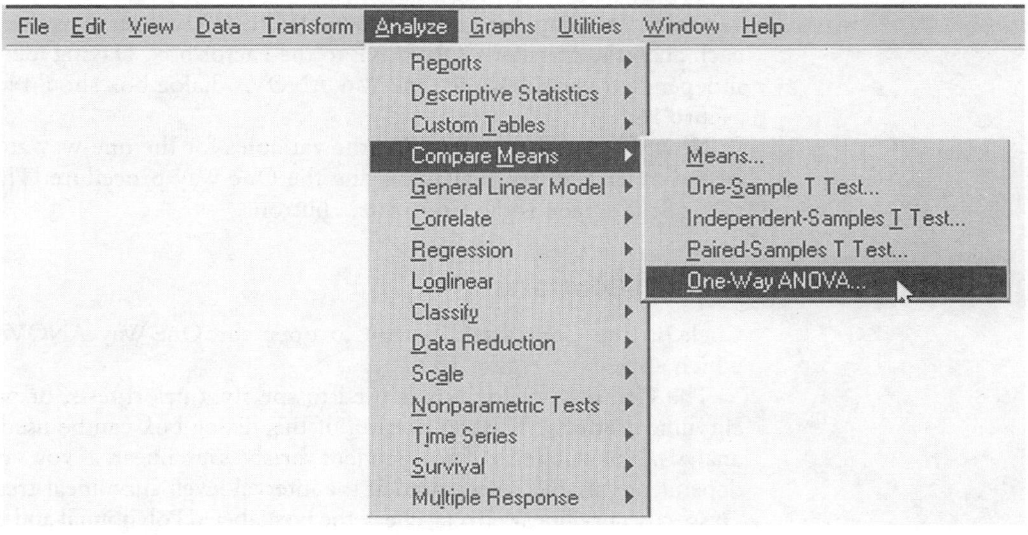

FIGURE 16.2
One-Way ANOVA
dialog box

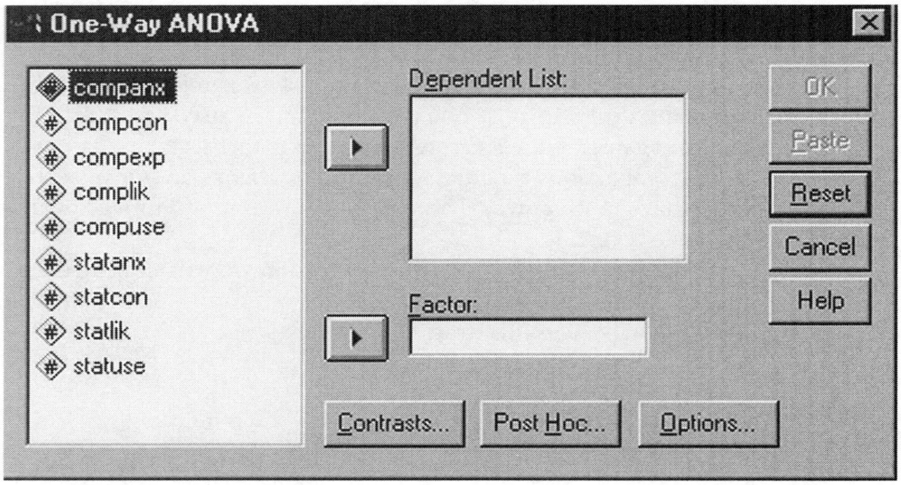

Selecting these options will open the One-Way ANOVA dialog box, displayed in Figure 16.2. As with previous procedures you have used, the names of all your variables are listed in the source variable list at the left. You will select the dependent variables from the source variable list and place them in the **Dependent List:** box for analysis. The independent variable is placed in the **Factor:** box. Remember, ANOVA uses the word *factor* to identify the independent variable. By default, all groups of the independent variable selected for the Factor box will be included in the analysis. Finally, the five command pushbuttons, which you've used in all previous procedures, appear at the far right.

There are three buttons at the bottom of this dialog box. We will use these buttons to specify group contrasts, post-hoc tests, and descriptive statistics for our analysis. First, let's select the dependent and independent variables.

Selecting Dependent and Independent Variables

As you have done with previous procedures, you will select each variable from the source variable list at the left of the dialog box. We will use the four computer attitude scales as dependent variables in this session. Select COMPANX, COMPCON, COMPLIK, and COMPUSE from the source variable list and transfer them to the Dependent List. We wish to compare students with varying amounts of computer experience on each of these four dependent variables, so computer experience (COMPEXP) will serve as the independent variable for each analysis. Transfer COMPEXP to the Factor box. Having identified the dependent and independent variables, the One-Way ANOVA dialog box should look like that displayed in Figure 16.3.

Now that you have identified the variables for the one-way analysis, let's explore some of the other features available using the One-Way procedure. The first button at the bottom of the screen is the **Contrasts...** button.

A Priori Contrasts

Click on the **Contrasts...** button to open the One-Way ANOVA: Contrasts dialog box, which appears in Figure 16.4.

The Contrasts dialog box is used to specify a priori tests, or pre-planned contrasts, and curvilinear effects. The top portion of this dialog box can be used to specify trends for the analysis. Not all effects of independent variables are linear, as you saw in Chapter 14. If the independent variable is measured at the interval level, curvilinear trends might be worthwhile. To specify curvilinear effects, check the box labeled Polynomial and specify effects such as qua-

FIGURE 16.3
One-Way ANOVA with
variables identified

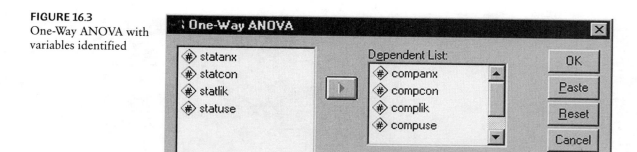

FIGURE 16.4
One-Way ANOVA:
Contrasts dialog box

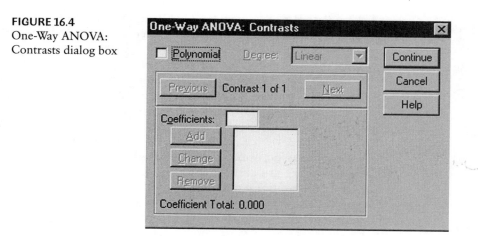

dratic and cubic using the Degree menu. Our independent variable, computer experience, is ordinal, so trend analysis would not be meaningful.

To specify a particular contrast, indicate the coefficients for each group of the independent variable in the **Coefficients:** box. The only condition is that the sum of these coefficients must equal 0, providing a balance of positive and negative weights. You can specify more than one contrast, but should limit these to a minimal number in order to minimize Type 1 error inflation.

Suppose you wanted to compare those students who had one year or more of computer experience with all others, you would balance the value of the coefficients between the first four groups and the fifth group. In other words each of the first four groups of students would receive a −1 coefficient, while the fifth group would receive a coefficient of 4. With four groups receiving a value of −1 and one group a value of 4, the sum of these values is equal to 0.

You specify the coefficient for one group at a time, beginning with the first group. Type "−1" in the Coefficients box and click on the **Add** button. Continue this process for the remaining groups. Remember, the second, third, and fourth groups will receive a coefficient of −1, but the fifth group will receive a 4. The coefficient total should sum to 0, and the Contrasts dialog box should look like that illustrated in Figure 16.5.

To specify additional a priori tests, select the **Next** button. We will specify only one contrast in our example, so click on the **Continue** button to return to the One-Way ANOVA dialog box.

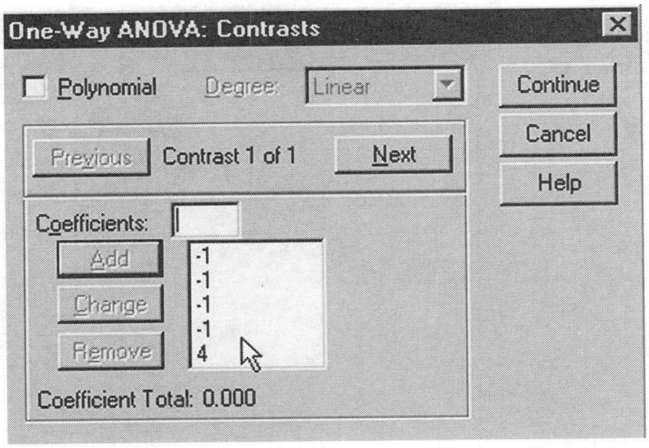

FIGURE 16.5
Contrasts specified for
COMPEXP (-1, -1,
-1, -1, 4)

Post-Hoc Tests

Click on **Post Hoc...** to open the One-Way ANOVA: Post Hoc Multiple Comparisons dialog box. In this dialog box, specify the type(s) of post-hoc tests you want to use to make comparisons among treatment group means. As you can see, there are several post-hoc tests available. Earlier versions of SPSS (Version 6.X) included only seven post-hoc procedures, all of which were designed with the homogeneity of variance assumption maintained. These same post-hoc procedures, as well as several others, are currently available in SPSS under the heading Equal Variances Assumed. In addition, SPSS now offers four procedures that can be used when equal variances are not assumed. SPSS also allows you to determine the significance level (i.e., alpha level) for each of these procedures.

With so many post-hoc procedures available, how do you know which one(s) to use? These tests differ primarily in terms of their protection against the inflation of Type 1 error. The least-significant difference (LSD) test allows for the most inflation of Type 1 error. In our situation, ten t-tests would be required to make all pairwise comparisons. However, using the LSD test would allow Type 1 error to inflate above our established risk level (i.e., alpha level). The most conservative post-hoc test, the Scheffe test, offers the most protection against Type 1 error. The Scheffe test is a popular one, as is Tukey's test. Tukey's test allows you to make all possible pairwise comparisons, while Scheffe allows for pairwise and more complex comparisons between group means. For our one-way ANOVA, let's specify three post-hoc tests, **LSD**, **Tukey**, and **Scheffe**, so you will be able to compare the results from each test (see Figure 16.6).

Earlier versions of SPSS (Version 6.X) required that you indicate sample sizes for your groups in situations where they were not based on the same number of people. This is the case in our example, as each of our five computer experience groups is based on a different sample size. Most post-hoc tests are intended to compare groups of equal size. When groups are of different size, an adjustment needs to be made before applying a post-hoc test. Typically, a harmonic mean is used. A harmonic mean is a weighted average sample size computed for each pair of groups being compared. In the current series of SPSS, the use of the harmonic average of pairs is the default.

Options Available with One-Way ANOVA

After returning to the One-Way ANOVA dialog box, click on the **Options...** button to open the One-Way ANOVA: Options dialog box.

There are only a few options available for the One-Way procedure. The first two options, listed under the Statistics heading, will be useful for our example. As you might expect, **Descriptive** is used to compute descriptive statistics such as the mean, standard deviation, and standard error of the mean for each treatment group. The second option, **Homogeneity-of-variance**, is used to calculate the Levene's tests for equality of variances

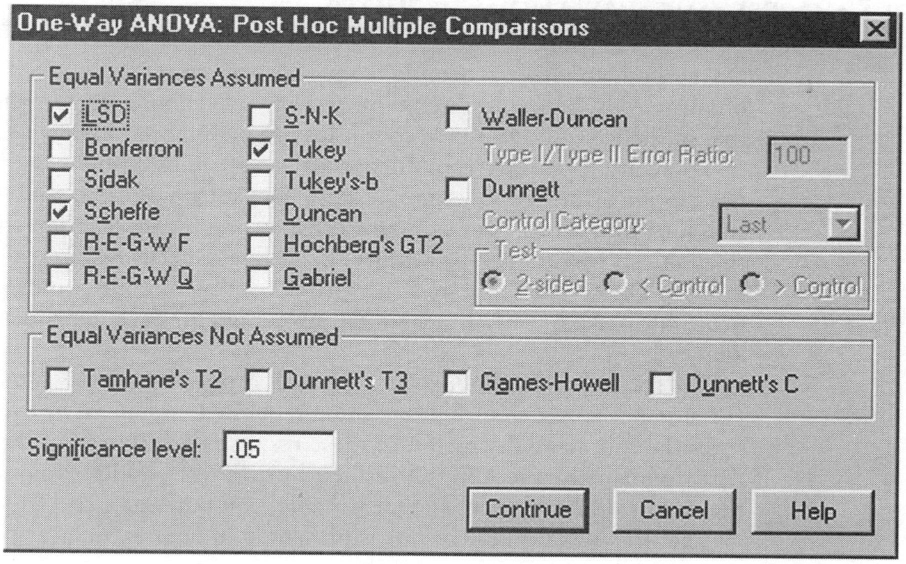

FIGURE 16.6
One-Way ANOVA:
Post Hoc Multiple
Comparisons dialog
box

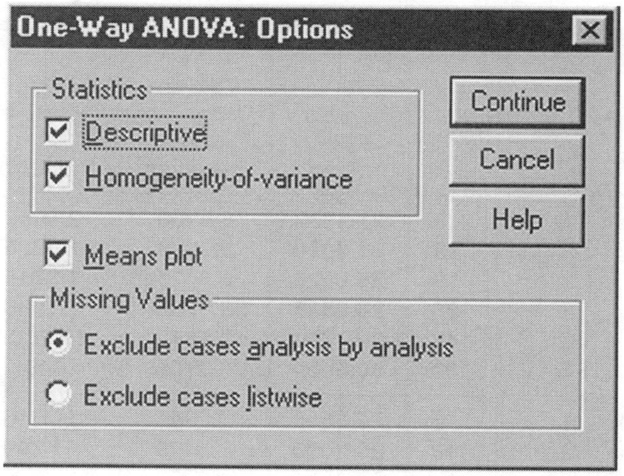

FIGURE 16.7
One-Way ANOVA:
Options dialog box

so that the homogeneity of variance assumption can be tested. Check both of these statistics options. There are also two options available to specify how you want missing data will be treated. We will use the default setting; missing cases will be excluded on an analysis-by-analysis basis.

There is one option for a **Means plot,** which will result in a visual display of group means. This display is a simple line graph, but it is still worthwhile. It is often much easier to determine the nature of effects if you can visualize them. It is also good to include visual displays of data in reports for others to view, so select this option.

After you have made the selections illustrated in Figure 16.7, return to the main dialog box using the **Continue** button.

Running One-Way ANOVA

We are ready to run these four one-way ANOVAs. As with previous SPSS procedures, use the **OK** command pushbutton to execute your commands. The results from your work in this session are once again stored in the output file. You should save this output file so that you have a record of your efforts. We recommend using **chap16.spo** to identify this file as a listing of the results from Chapter 16. We'll examine samples of this output in the final section of this chapter.

INTERPRETING SPSS ONE-WAY ANOVA RESULTS

Once again, you have generated many pages of output using SPSS. We will examine the first one-way ANOVA in our discussion and let you examine the remainder on your own. Recall that in the first ANOVA procedure, we used computer anxiety as a dependent variable.

There are several parts to the output produced by a one-way ANOVA. First, there is the descriptive information you requested. This information includes statistics such as means, standard deviations, and standard error of the mean. Second, there are the results from the analysis of variance procedure, including sums of squares, df, mean squares, and the F ratio. Third, you requested an a priori contrast. Finally, you requested several post-hoc procedures. All of this information is presented for each dependent variable listed for your analysis.

The results are organized by the type of information you requested. Earlier versions of SPSS (Version 6.X) presented all information requested, organized by each dependent variable.

In the following discussion of these results, we will present the descriptive information first, followed by the ANOVA results, a priori tests, and post-hoc results. We will focus on the results of the first dependent variable, computer anxiety (COMPANX).

The first part of these results is presented in Figure 16.8.

Descriptives

		N	Mean	Std. Deviation	Std. Error	95% Confidence Interval for Mean		Minimum	Maximum
						Lower Bound	Upper Bound		
COMPANX	1	9	21.3333	6.0208	2.0069	16.7053	25.9613	13.00	30.00
	2	10	22.8000	5.7889	1.8306	18.6589	26.9411	11.00	34.00
	3	19	26.0526	5.5425	1.2715	23.3812	28.7240	20.00	40.00
	4	26	28.0385	5.8068	1.1388	25.6931	30.3839	16.00	39.00
	5	145	32.7724	5.1542	.4280	31.9264	33.6185	20.00	40.00
	Total	209	30.6029	6.3708	.4407	29.7341	31.4716	11.00	40.00
COMPCON	1	9	22.5556	5.2941	1.7646	18.4861	26.6250	14.00	29.00
	2	10	25.2000	2.1499	.6799	23.6620	26.7380	22.00	29.00
	3	19	27.4211	4.3756	1.0038	25.3121	29.5300	21.00	38.00
	4	26	28.2692	4.4950	.8815	26.4537	30.0848	17.00	36.00
	5	145	32.3172	4.6244	.3840	31.5582	33.0763	22.00	40.00
	Total	209	30.6077	5.2941	.3662	29.8857	31.3296	14.00	40.00
COMPLIK	1	9	21.8889	3.3333	1.1111	19.3267	24.4511	17.00	27.00
	2	10	24.5000	4.6007	1.4549	21.2088	27.7912	13.00	30.00
	3	19	25.4211	4.7178	1.0823	23.1472	27.6949	17.00	37.00
	4	26	28.4615	4.0913	.8024	26.8090	30.1140	19.00	39.00
	5	145	31.2690	4.7247	.3924	30.4934	32.0445	17.00	40.00
	Total	209	29.6603	5.3155	.3677	28.9354	30.3851	13.00	40.00
COMPUSE	1	9	31.6667	5.8310	1.9437	27.1846	36.1487	18.00	38.00
	2	10	32.5000	3.6893	1.1667	29.8608	35.1392	28.00	37.00
	3	19	32.8947	4.0674	.9331	30.9343	34.8552	26.00	40.00
	4	26	32.8846	3.7452	.7345	31.3719	34.3973	25.00	39.00
	5	145	35.9172	3.3717	.2800	35.3638	36.4707	26.00	40.00
	Total	209	34.9187	3.9000	.2698	34.3868	35.4505	18.00	40.00

FIGURE 16.8
SPSS results–Descriptive statistics for One-Way ANOVA

Descriptive Statistics

This information includes descriptive statistics for each of the five treatment groups. This information is similar to what you produced earlier using the Means procedure (see Chapter 7). All the information displayed in Figure 16.8 pertains to the dependent variable of computer anxiety (COMPANX). Information regarding each of the other dependent variables is also summarized. We have highlighted in boldface the information from the SPSS output that pertains to COMPANX.

As with all the attitude scales you computed, a higher score indicates a more positive attitude. Specifically, a higher score on the computer anxiety scales indicates that a student is more comfortable and less anxious around computers. As you would expect, the highest mean is reported for the group having the most computer experience, and the lowest mean belongs to the group with the least experience. The variability (i.e., standard deviation) is very similar for each of the five treatment groups.

The fifth group, which is the largest, does have the lowest standard error, and the first group, which is the smallest, has the largest standard error. This makes sense because larger samples tend to be more representative of the population and will therefore have smaller standard errors. Applying the standard error of each group, the 95% confidence interval is reported. Again, this is smallest for the group having over one year of experience.

The second part of this SPSS output, the ANOVA summary table, is displayed in Figure 16.9.

ANOVA Summary Table

The ANOVA summary table is used to summarize the results from the overall one-way ANOVA procedure. In this table, each source of variation is identified, along with their associated sums of squares (SS), degrees of freedom (df), mean squares (MS), the F ratio, and the probability of the F ratio. The information in this table will allow us to make a decision regarding our null hypothesis. Our null hypothesis assumes that our five groups,

ANOVA

		Sum of Squares	df	Mean Square	F	Sig.
COMPANX	Between Groups	**2629.040**	**4**	**657.260**	**23.066**	**.000**
	Within Groups	**5812.999**	**204**	**28.495**		
	Total	**8442.038**	**208**			
COMPCON	Between Groups	1634.852	4	408.713	19.876	.000
	Within Groups	4194.976	204	20.564		
	Total	5829.828	208			
COMPLIK	Between Groups	1563.888	4	390.972	18.493	.000
	Within Groups	4312.992	204	21.142		
	Total	5876.880	208			
COMPUSE	Between Groups	483.667	4	120.917	9.204	.000
	Within Groups	2679.950	204	13.137		
	Total	3163.617	208			

FIGURE 16.9
One-Way ANOVA results

differing in terms of their computer experience, do not differ on 4 measures computer related attitudes. That is, they have the same population mean. Let's examine this information more closely. We have performed four F-tests, and for each attitude measure, and will evaluate each test using an adjusted alpha level (.05/4 = .01225).

First, two sources of variation are identified: between groups and within groups. The variation between groups is of particular interest to us because this variation represents the degree to which our groups' means differ. Within-group variation represents the degree to which individuals' scores vary in each group. What we hope to do is maximize between-group variation and minimize within-group variation. In other words, we want scores on the dependent variable to vary because of differences among our treatment groups, not because of sampling error within each group.

We calculate the degrees of freedom for ANOVA in much the same manner as for the t-test. There are a total of 209 students in the overall sample, therefore the degrees of freedom is n − 1, or 208. The write out or abbreviate thought for between-groups variation is k − 1, where k equals the number of groups. As there are the five between groups df = 5 − 1 or 4. Finally, the df for within groups is reported as 204, which is the result of adding up the df for each treatment group. The df for each treatment group is determined by subtracting one from the number of people in the group.

The sum of squares (SS) represents the sum of the squared deviations from the mean. The value of the total SS is computed by summing each student's squared deviation from the overall mean, or grand mean. Therefore, the total SS represents the extent to which individuals vary from the overall mean. The total SS is further divided in between- and within-group sources. The SS for between groups represents the variability of the group means from the overall grand mean, and the SS for within groups represents the variability of students' scores from their group mean. Mean squares, estimates of population variance, are computed by dividing SS by df. There is an MS for between and within groups. In our example, the MS value for between groups is much larger, which is good. Remember, we want to maximize the variation between groups.

Finally, the F ratio is reported. The F ratio is computed by dividing the MS (between groups) by the MS (within groups). In our case, the reported F ratio is 23.066, having a probability of .000. With this probability, our chances of being wrong when rejecting the null hypothesis are less than 1 time in 1,000. Recall our adjusted alpha of .01225. As .000 is less than .012, we will reject the null hypothesis and accept the alternative hypothesis that the population means of these five groups are not all the same. Yet, the question remains, which groups are different? The information from the a priori and post-hoc comparisons will be helpful in addressing this question.

A Priori Tests

The information summarized in Figure 16.10 pertains to the a priori test we used in this session. A priori tests are performed no matter what the result of the overall F-test, whereas post-hoc tests can be performed only if the overall F-test is statistically significant. We used an a priori test to compare those students with over one year of computer experience to students with less than one year of experience. The coefficients we used to specify this contrast are reported for each group. Using these coefficients, we formed a two-group comparison, with the students in the first four treatment groups belonging to one group and those in the fifth group in the other. To compare two groups, a t-test is used.

The results of two different t-tests are reported. One is based on a pooled (equal) variance estimate, while the other is based on a separate (unequal) variance estimate. We faced this type of situation when using t-tests in Chapter 15. Remember, if we can assume homogeneity of variance, we use a pooled, or equal-variance, t-test. If not, we need to use a separate, or unequal-variance, t-test.

The Levene's test statistics are reported in the first column, and the probabilities that the variances differ by chance (Sig.) are found in the last column. Each of these tests resulted

Test of Homogeneity of Variances

	Levene Statistic	df1	df2	Sig.
COMPANX	.173	4	204	.952
COMPCON	1.966	4	204	.101
COMPLIK	1.173	4	204	.324
COMPUSE	.748	4	204	.560

Contrast Coefficients

	COMPEXP				
Contrast	1	2	3	4	5
1	−1	−1	−1	−1	4

Contrast Tests

		Contrast	Value of Contrast	Std. Error	t	df	Sig. (2-tailed)
COMPANX	Assume equal variances	1	32.8652	3.4286	9.585	204	.000
	Does not assume equal variances	1	32.8652	3.6365	9.038	49.290	.000
COMPCON	Assume equal variances	1	25.8231	2.9126	8.866	204	.000
	Does not assume equal variances	1	25.8231	2.7787	9.293	43.986	.000
COMPLIK	Assume equal variances	1	24.8044	2.9533	8.399	204	.000
	Does not assume equal variances	1	24.8044	2.7622	8.980	70.708	.000
COMPUSE	Assume equal variances	1	13.7229	2.3280	5.895	204	.000
	Does not assume equal variances	1	13.7229	2.7935	4.913	29.640	.000

FIGURE 16.10
SPSS–A priori contrasts and homogeneity tests

in a probability above .05. Therefore, we maintain the assumption of homogeneity. With this assumption supported, we turn to the pooled (equal) variance t-test to evaluate the results of our contrasts.

The reported t value for COMPANX is 9.585 with a probability of .000, or less than .001. Based on these results, we know that the differences mean computer anxiety scores between the two groups being compared are not likely due to chance (p < .001). Therefore, we conclude that there is a difference in mean scores between the groups being compared. We can refer to our group means (see Figure 16.8) and see that those students having more than one year of computer experience are more comfortable with computers.

Multiple Comparisons

Dependent Variable: COMPANX
LSD

(I) COMPEXP	(J) COMPEXP	Mean Difference (I–J)	Std. Error	Sig.	95% Confidence Interval	
					Lower Bound	Upper Bound
1	2	−1.4667	2.453	.551	−6.3025	3.3692
	3	−4.7193*	2.160	.030	−8.9782	−.4604
	4	−6.7051*	2.064	.001	−10.7756	−2.6347
	5	−11.4391*	1.834	.000	−15.0546	−7.8235
2	1	1.4667	2.453	.551	−3.3692	6.3025
	3	−3.2526	2.085	.120	−7.3645	.8592
	4	−5.2385*	1.986	.009	−9.1548	−1.3221
	5	−9.9724*	1.745	.000	−13.4135	−6.5313
3	1	4.7193*	2.160	.030	.4604	8.9782
	2	3.2526	2.085	.120	−.8592	7.3645
	4	−1.9858	1.611	.219	−5.1624	1.1908
	5	−6.7198*	1.302	.000	−9.2877	−4.1519
4	1	6.7051*	2.064	.001	2.6347	10.7756
	2	5.2385*	1.986	.009	1.3221	9.1548
	3	1.9858	1.611	.219	−1.1908	5.1624
	5	−4.7340*	1.137	.000	−6.9755	−2.4924
5	1	11.4391*	1.834	.000	7.8235	15.0546
	2	9.9724*	1.745	.000	6.5313	13.4135
	3	6.7198*	1.302	.000	4.1519	9.2877
	4	4.7340*	1.137	.000	2.4924	6.9755

*. The mean difference is significant at the .05 level.

FIGURE 16.11A
LSD Multiple Comparisons

Post-Hoc Tests

The final part of our one-way ANOVA shows the results of our post-hoc tests. Remember, we requested several different tests so that we could compare their results. The results of the LSD, Tukey's HSD, and Scheffe post-hoc tests are summarized in Figures 16.11A, B, and C.

We have abbreviated the original SPSS output to include only the comparisons for computer anxiety. In your output, multiple comparisons for all four computer attitude scores will be summarized in the same table. As you can see, this is a very large table that would be difficult to fit on one page. Therefore, we separated the results as they pertain to each type of multiple comparison (i.e., LSD, Tukey, and Scheffe). Figure 16.11A summarizes the results from the LSD tests. The results from the Tukey tests are summarized in Figure 16.11B; while Scheffe results are displayed in Figure 16.11C.

When examining these tables, you will notice that the same information will appear twice, as in previous correlation results. For example, look at Figure 16.11A. In the first row, you see the results comparing group 1 with each of the four remaining groups. Of

Multiple Comparisons

Dependent Variable: COMPANX
Tukey HSD

(I) COMPEXP	(J) COMPEXP	Mean Difference (I–J)	Std. Error	Sig.	95% Confidence Interval	
					Lower Bound	Upper Bound
1	2	−1.4667	2.453	.975	−8.1570	5.2237
	3	−4.7193	2.160	.185	−10.6115	1.1729
	4	−6.7051*	2.064	.010	−12.3366	−1.0737
	5	−11.4391*	1.834	.000	−16.4411	−6.4370
2	1	1.4667	2.453	.975	−5.2237	8.1570
	3	−3.2526	2.085	.523	−8.9414	2.4361
	4	−5.2385	1.986	.064	−10.6567	.1798
	5	−9.9724*	1.745	.000	−14.7332	−5.2117
3	1	4.7193	2.160	.185	−1.1729	10.6115
	2	3.2526	2.085	.523	−2.4361	8.9414
	4	−1.9859	1.611	.732	−6.3806	2.4089
	5	−6.7198*	1.302	.000	−10.2725	−3.1671
4	1	6.7051*	2.064	.010	1.0737	12.3366
	2	5.2385	1.986	.064	−.1798	10.6567
	3	1.9858	1.611	.732	−2.4089	6.3806
	5	−4.7340*	1.137	.000	−7.8351	−1.6328
5	1	11.4391*	1.834	.000	6.4370	16.4411
	2	9.9724*	1.745	.000	5.2117	14.7332
	3	6.7198*	1.302	.000	3.1671	10.2725
	4	4.7340*	1.137	.000	1.6328	7.8351

*. The mean difference is significant at the .05 level.

FIGURE 16.11B
Tukey Multiple Comparisons

these comparisons, those pairing group 1 with groups 3, 4, and 5 are statistically significant. That is, the reported significance (p value) is below .05. Now, examine the second row. This row displays comparisons between group 2 and each of the other groups. Since you already examined the comparison between groups 2 and 1 from the first row of results there are only three additional comparisons in this row. Of these, we see that the two comparisons between group 2 and groups 4 and 5 are statistically significant.

Move on to the third row of comparisons. The only two comparisons you have not examined before are between group 3 and groups 4 and 5. Of these two, only the comparison between group 3 and group 5 is statistically significant. Moving to the fourth row, you will find just one additional comparison. That is between groups 4 and 5, which is also statistically significant. Finally, examine the fifth row. You have already examined these comparisons in the previous four rows.

In all, you should have found seven statistically significant between group differences. To determine the specific nature of these differences, you need to re-examine the group means (reported in Figure 16.8). For each difference, the group with the higher mean has more computer experience. This is what you would expect.

Multiple Comparisons

Dependent Variable: COMPANX
Scheffe

(I) COMPEXP	(J) COMPEXP	Mean Difference (I–J)	Std. Error	Sig.	95% Confidence Interval	
					Lower Bound	Upper Bound
1	2	−1.4667	2.453	.986	−9.0912	6.1578
	3	−4.7193	2.160	.315	−11.4342	1.9956
	4	−6.7051*	2.064	.035	−13.1229	−.2874
	5	−11.4391*	1.834	.000	−17.1395	−5.7386
2	1	1.4667	2.453	.986	−6.1578	9.0912
	3	−3.2526	2.085	.657	−9.7357	3.2304
	4	−5.2385	1.986	.143	−11.4132	.9363
	5	−9.9724*	1.745	.000	−15.3979	−4.5469
3	1	4.7193	2.160	.315	−1.9956	11.4342
	2	3.2526	2.085	.657	−3.2304	9.7357
	4	−1.9859	1.611	.823	−6.9942	3.0226
	5	−6.7198*	1.302	.000	−10.7685	−2.6711
4	1	6.7051*	2.064	.035	.2874	13.1229
	2	5.2385	1.986	.143	−.9363	11.4132
	3	1.9858	1.611	.823	−3.0226	6.9942
	5	−4.7340*	1.137	.002	−8.2681	−1.1998
5	1	11.4391*	1.834	.000	5.7386	17.1395
	2	9.9724*	1.745	.000	4.5469	15.3979
	3	6.7198*	1.302	.000	2.6711	10.7685
	4	4.7340*	1.137	.002	1.1998	8.2681

*. The mean difference is significant at the .05 level.

FIGURE 16.11C
Scheffe Multiple Comparisons

Examine the results reported in Figures 16.11B and 16.11C, showing five statistically significant differences in each figure. The Tukey and Scheffe tests produced similar results, while the LSD test indicated two additional significant differences. You would not expect these post-hoc tests to agree all the time, because they differ in their control for Type 1 error. Remember, the weakest of these tests is the LSD. In other words, the LSD test allows for the most error. Therefore, the LSD test would be more likely to reveal a significant difference between any given pair of treatment group means. However, you cannot tell which of these differences are real and which are due to error. If you want to be sure, then use a more conservative test, such as Tukey or Scheffe. In the current example, Tukey and Scheffe agree that there are five significant group differences. Specifically, the group of students having more than one year of experience differs from each of the other four treatment groups. In addition, the group of students with six months to one year of experience differs from the group of students having less than one week of computer experience.

We have examined the results from only one analysis. You performed three other one-way ANOVAs in this chapter. Take a few minutes to examine the results of these analyses.

You should have found that all three of the remaining one-way ANOVAs were statistically significant (p < .001) and that the group means were highest for the group having the most computer experience and lowest for the group having the least amount of experience. Again, this would be expected; as one gains more experience with computers, one's attitudes usually become more positive.

CHAPTER SUMMARY

In this chapter, we have used the One-Way ANOVA procedure to compare five treatment group means. One-way ANOVA can be used to compare two or more group means on one dependent variable. One-way ANOVA is limited to one independent variable. In the next chapter, we will examine the impact of more than one independent variable using the same analysis.

PRACTICE EXERCISES

Using the data created in Chapter 3 regarding student applicants (i.e., student admission data), perform the following analyses.

1. Using SPSS, perform three one-way ANOVAs (one for each dependent variable).
   a. Independent variable = SES
   b. Dependent variable = GREQ, GREV, RATING average

2. Report the following from each analysis.
   a. Means for each level of SES
   b. F ratio and probability level

3. Select a post-hoc procedure to examine potential pairwise differences.
   a. Which post-hoc test did you choose? Why?
   b. What can be concluded from these post-hoc comparisons for each dependent variable?

4. Using preplanned contrasts, compare high SES to the other two SES categories. What can be concluded from this contrast for each analysis?

17 | Factorial ANOVA

In the previous chapter, you used analysis of variance (ANOVA) to examine the effects of one independent variable. Using one-way ANOVA, you were able to compare two or more treatment group means on a dependent variable. In this chapter, you will be able to examine the effects of more than one independent variable using ANOVA. When two independent variables are included in the analysis, the procedure is called a two-way, or two-factor ANOVA. Generally, when the ANOVA includes two or more independent variables, it is called a factorial ANOVA.

A factorial ANOVA analysis provides much more information about multi-level groups than any number of multiple one-way ANOVAs ever could. Multiple one-way ANOVAs will allow you to examine the effects of each independent variable separately. Factorial ANOVA will also allow you to determine the effects of each independent variable separately as the *main effects*. However, a factorial ANOVA will also allow you to examine any potential *interaction effect* of the independent variables. An interaction effect occurs when the effects of one independent variable are dependent upon levels of another independent variable. For example, a researcher is interested in reducing the risk of heart disease and wants to investigate the effectiveness of three different treatments (drugs, diet, and exercise). There is some reason to believe that these treatments might work differently depending on a variety of other factors, such as gender or weight. In other words, preventive treatment for heart disease might have an interactive effect with gender or weight. If this were found to be true, physicians might change the way they treat heart disease, prescribing different treatments for the patients depending on their gender and their weight.

Independent variables, or factors, are generally considered to be either fixed or random. *Fixed factors* are those in which the levels are determined naturally or set by the researcher. For example, gender naturally has two levels. Another example of a fixed independent variable is computer experience, as we have described it in this book. Recall that levels of computer experience were defined, or fixed, by five different categories. When a fixed factor is used in the design, the researcher has no intentions of generalizing the results to levels other than those represented in the study. In other words, conclusions regarding computer experiences are confined to those levels selected to define the variable.

On the other hand, a *random factor* is one that has levels as a random subset of the population. In this case, the researcher does intend to generalize findings to a larger population. Suppose you were interested in examining the impact of class time. Because of the many different times classes meet, you might randomly sample six classes that meet at six different times. You are interested in generalizing your findings to the overall population of class times, and because the levels of class time were selected randomly, you are able to make these generalizations.

The assumptions for a factorial ANOVA are similar to those of one-way ANOVA. These include normality, independence, and homogeneity of variance. First, each sample is drawn from a normally distributed population. Second, each person's score is independent of all other scores, and each treatment level (i.e., group) is independent of the other levels of groups in the study. Finally, the variances of each population are equal.

An additional requirement for factorial ANOVA design is that cell sample sizes are proportional. This doesn't mean that each cell must contain the *same* number of cases, but equal cell sizes would be beneficial (as we will describe later in the chapter). To illustrate proportional cell size, let's use an example with two independent variables: gender and socio-economic stats (SES). Gender has two levels while SES has three levels. To meet the requirements of proportionality, the same proportion of males and females should be represented in each level of SES. It is important to maintain proportional cell sizes when using factorial ANOVA. We'll examine this in more detail as we examine the results in this chapter.

VARIABLES USED IN THIS CHAPTER

We will illustrate factorial ANOVA using two different examples. Both examples are based on the data with which you have become familiar. The first example examines the influence of computer experience and degree program on computer attitudes. In the previous chapters examining t-tests and one-way ANOVA, both of these variables were found to have some influence on computer attitudes. The computer experience variable has five different categories. However, many of the categories that represent less experience do not contain many students. Therefore, we recoded this variable into just two categories for use in this chapter. The first category represents those students with less than one year of computer experience, while the second category contains those students with one or more years of experience. This variable is identified as COMPEXP2 in the data file. The second variable, MASTDOC, has two levels. The first represents students enrolled in a Masters program, while the second represents those enrolled in a Doctoral program. Because we want to work with an equal number of students in each of the four conditions (cells), we randomly sampled equal numbers of subjects by category for inclusion in this illustration.

The second example examines the potential influence of GENDER and MASTDOC on the number of hours a student works each week. For this second illustration, we used all subjects with complete information for the variables being examined. This resulted in unequal treatment condition cell sizes. However, the cell sizes are proportional.

USING SPSS FOR FACTORIAL ANOVA

We will be illustrating two different factorial ANOVA examples in this chapter. We have provided a separate data file for each example on your data disk. We have named these two data files **chap17a data** and **chap17b data**. To use Factorial ANOVA, you will need to become familiar with the General Linear Model (GLM) procedure.

RUNNING GLM–EXAMPLE #1

In the first example we will examine the impact of computer experience (COMPEXP2) and degree program (MASTDOC) on the degree to which students like working with computers (COMPLIK). These data can be found in the file named **chap17a.data**. Again, we have randomly sampled students from the overall sample in order to create a balanced design. That is, one with equal cell sizes. Retrieve these data and we will begin.

As you have done so many times before, begin with the **Analyze** menu. From this menu, select the **General Linear Model** and **Univariate...** options, as illustrated in Figure 17.1.

Selecting these options will open the Univariate dialog box. The names of all your variables are listed in the source variable list at the left. Also, the command pushbuttons for this procedure appear at the bottom of this dialog box.

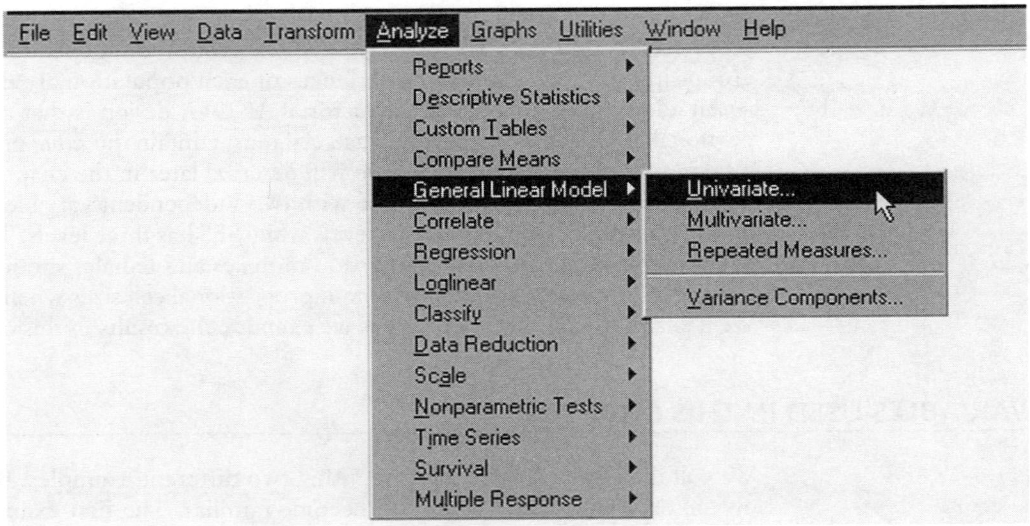

FIGURE 17.1
Analyze–General
Linear Model–
Univariate menus

Selection of Variables

From the source variable list, you will select variables for the analysis. The dependent variable is placed in the **Dependent Variable:** box. Only one dependent variable can be specified in this box. The independent variables are placed in either the **Fixed Factor(s):** or **Random Factor(s):** boxes, depending on the type of factor you are using. If a variable is to be used as a covariate, it is placed in the box labeled **Covariate(s):**. Finally, a weighting variable if needed could be placed in the **WLS Weight:** box.

First, identify the dependent variable. For our first factorial ANOVA, the dependent variable will be the computer liking score, COMPLIK. Select COMPLIK from the source variable list and place it in the **Dependent Variable:** box.

Second, identify the independent variables. There are two independent variables in this illustration. These are computer experience (COMPEXP2) and degree program (MASTDOC). Both of these variables are fixed; that is, we set the levels to ourselves to serve our research needs. We measured computer experience using five predetermined categories and then recoded it as a new variable with only two categories (less than 1 year of computer experience, and 1 year or more). Initially, degree program had four categories. We computed a new variable (MASTDOC) that contained only Masters and Doctoral Students. Select these two independent variables from the source variable list and place them in the **Fixed Factor(s):** box.

There are no random factors, covariates, or weighting variables in this illustration. Therefore you are finished selecting the variables for the analysis. Check to be sure that COMPLIK is identified as the dependent variable and that COMPEXP2 and MASTDOC are identified as fixed factors, as shown in Figure 17.2. If so, you are ready to explore some other features of the GLM-Univariate procedure.

Specifying the Model

The first button is labeled **Model....** You will use this to specify the way you want to model the effects of the variables (factors) included in your design. Click on this button to open the Univariate: Model dialog box, displayed in Figure 17.3.

Initially, the default options are displayed in this dialog box. By default, a full-factorial model is specified. This model will include all main effects, interactions, and covariate effects. For most situations, this option will be appropriate. If you want to specify interaction effects involving a covariate, which would be useful in an analysis of covariance ANCOVA design, or if you just want a partial listing of interaction effects, you would specify a custom model. When

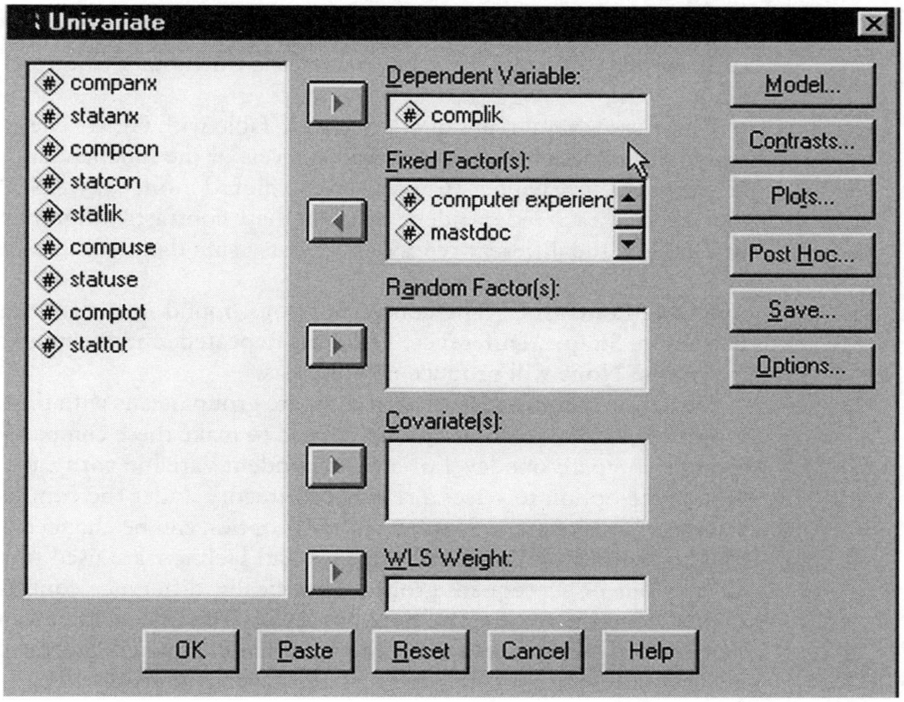

FIGURE 17.2
Univariate dialog box

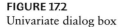

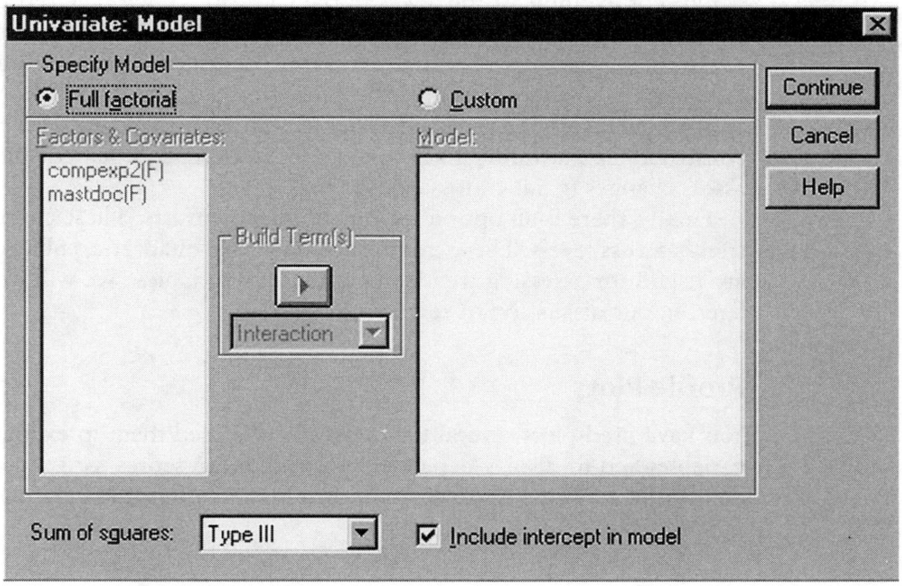

FIGURE 17.3
Univariate: Model
dialog box

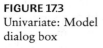

specifying a custom model, you need to select the terms that define the model, including main and interaction effects.

The final piece of information found in this dialog box pertains to specifying the sums of squares used in the analysis. By default, Type III sums of squares are used. Other types of sums of squares can be specified for different situations. For example, you would specify Type I sums of squares to examine the effects in a hierarchical model. Type II sums of squares would be appropriate for a regression model, and Type IV would be used in situations where you have empty cells. For most of the situations you will encounter, Type III sums of squares will be appropriate.

Contrasts

Click on the **Contrasts...** button to open the Univariate: Contrasts dialog box, displayed in Figure 17.4.

There are several types of contrasts available with GLM. These contrasts are used to examine differences between the various levels of the independent variables. You used similar contrasts in Chapter 16 when you explored a one-way ANOVA. Since there are only two levels of each independent variable, these contrasts will not be necessary. However, we will explain the different types of contrasts using them with example 2.

Available Contrasts.   The contrast options, found in the contrasts menu, include None, Deviation, Simple, Difference, Helmert, Repeated, and Polynomial. As you would expect, the option None will produce no contrasts.

Deviation contrasts are used to compare group means with the overall grand mean. Each group, except the reference group, is used to make these comparisons. Simple contrasts are used to compare one level of an independent variable with each of the remaining levels. Notice the option to select a reference category under the contrasts menu. By default, the reference category is the last group. This option can be changed to the first group.

The contrast options for Difference and Helmert are used to compare group means to all previous or subsequent groups. Specifically, difference contrasts compare the mean of each level to the mean of all previous levels. The first group mean is not included because there are no previous levels. On the other hand, Helmert contrasts are used to compare the mean of each group to the mean of all subsequent groups. The last group is not included for the same reasons that the first group was not used for difference contrasts. Difference and Helmert contrasts are useful when there are increasing or decreasing levels to be compared. For example, if the levels in the COMPEXP variable represented increasing or decreasing levels of computer experience, these two types of contrasts would be useful.

Another option is repeated contrasts. Repeated contrasts are used to compare each group mean with the mean of the subsequent group. These contrasts would be useful in contrasting levels of a repeated variable. If our study included several measures of the same construct (e.g., attitude) given over a period of time, repeated contrasts would be useful to assess changes (gains or losses) over time.

Finally, there is an option for polynomial contrasts. These contrasts are used to estimate trends across levels. These trends include linear, quadratic, cubic, etc. Polynomial contrasts are useful for assessing trends in continuous variables. We will explore polynomial trends later, in our discussion of regression analysis.

Profile Plots

You have used plots several times already. We used them to examine relationships between variables and to display dependent variable mean scores for groups defined by an independent variable. Visual displays of interactions and effects are helpful in determining the nature

FIGURE 17.4
Univariate: Contrasts
dialog box

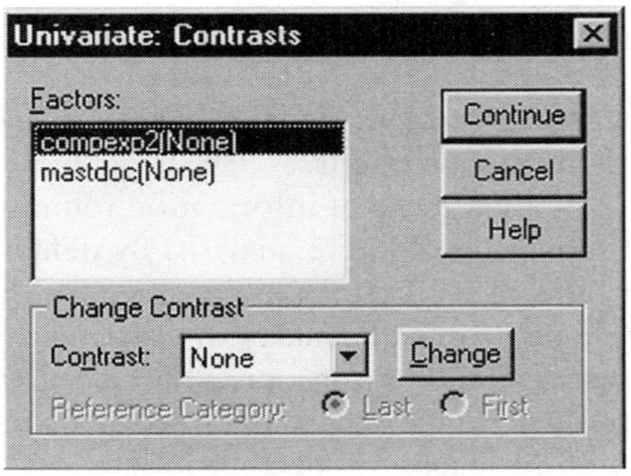

FIGURE 17.5
Univariate: Profile
Plots dialog box

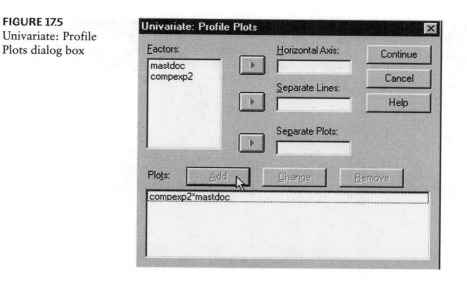

of the effect. Click on the **Plots...** button so we can explore the options that are available. The Univariate: Profile Plots dialog box appears in Figure 17.5.

Profile plots are especially helpful for identifying interaction effects. Our current factorial model includes only two independent variables (COMPEXP2 and MASTDOC). To build a profile plot, you must select one independent variable to plot on the horizontal axis and one to plot as separate lines, representing group membership on that variable.

Select COMPEXP from the source variable list at the left and place it in the **Horizontal Axis:** box. Next, select MASTDOC and place it in the box labeled **Separate Lines:**. Next, click the **Add** button to specify a two-way plot. This will result in a plot of the computer liking scale means for masters and doctoral students at two levels of computer experience. This plot will be identified in the lower section of the box, labeled Plots.

If there were a third independent variable in the design, it would be useful to examine a three-way interaction effect. The box labeled **Separate Plots:** can be used to plot a third grouping variable, if desired. To return to the Univariate dialog box, click on the **Continue** button.

Post-Hoc Multiple Comparisons

Click on the **Post Hoc...** button to open the Univariate: Post Hoc Multiple Comparisons dialog box, displayed in Figure 17.6.

As you can see, there are several different post-hoc multiple comparison tests available. These tests are used to compare the dependent variable means for levels of your independent variables. You explored these options when performing a one-way ANOVA in Chapter 16. These tests are grouped according to their utility when assumptions of the homogeneity of variance have been rejected. We will not be using any of these post-hoc tests in the current example, because both of our independent variables have just two levels. Therefore, should a main effect exist, there is only one difference that can exist between the two means (i.e., one mean can be higher than the other). You could select post-hoc options if at least one of the independent variables had three or more levels. For a review, please examine the section of Chapter 16 pertaining to post-hoc comparisons. Return to the Univariate dialog box and we will examine the remaining options.

Saving New Variables

Using the GLM procedure, predictions can be made for each case regarding his or her performance on the dependent variable. Specifically, predictions are made based on the relationship between the independent variable(s) and the dependent variable. The stronger

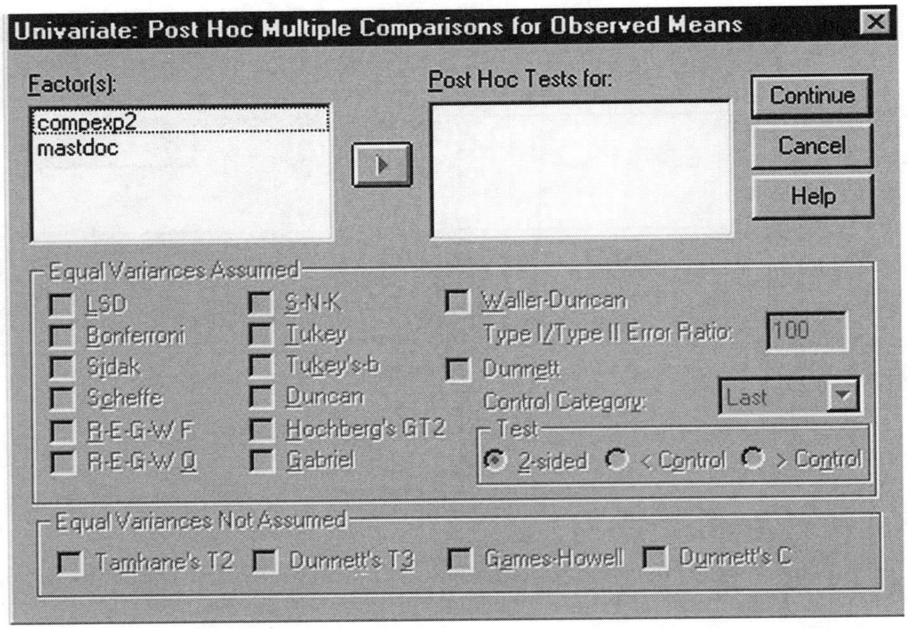

FIGURE 17.6
Univariate: Post Hoc
Multiple Comparisons
dialog box

FIGURE 17.6
Univariate: Post Hoc
Multiple Comparisons
dialog box

the relationship, the better the prediction. These relationships (or effects) are evaluated using the analysis of variance procedure.

Predictions made using the GLM Univariate procedure can be saved for each case. In addition, information about residuals (error) and diagnostics can be saved. To explore these options, click on the **Save...** button (see Figure 17.7). We will not be saving any new variables in the current analysis. However, we will examine these options in more detail when we discuss regression analysis. Return to the Univariate dialog box using the **Continue** button.

Options

To examine the remaining options available for the GLM—Univariate procedure, click on the **Options...** button. This will open the Univariate: Options dialog box displayed in Figure 17.8. There are many options listed in this dialog box. These options pertain to descriptive statistics, comparisons of main effects, effect size, and parameter estimates. You can also adjust the significance level used for post-hoc tests and the width of the confidence interval.

Our current analysis includes two independent variables, COMPEXP2 and MASTDOC. In addition, there may be effects created by the interaction of these two variables. Select the two I. U. and the interaction term from the left box and place them in the box labeled **Display Means for:**. Then select the option **Compare main effects**. This information will be useful in determining the extent to which the different treatment conditions differ.

Under the Display heading, there are many more options. Select the **Descriptive statistics, Estimates of effect size,** and the **Observed power** options. These options will produce means, standard deviations, effect size, and power estimates. We will explore the other options (parameter estimates and matrices) in the following chapters. For our current example, we will not select any additional options. However, we will examine many of these statistical options later when using regression analysis in later chapters. Finally, leave the significance level set at the .05 default.

Return to the Univariate dialog box (see Figure 17.2) using the **Continue** button and you are ready to produce some more statistical output. As with previous SPSS procedures, click the **OK** button and allow SPSS to process your data. Before we examine the output, let's try another GLM example.

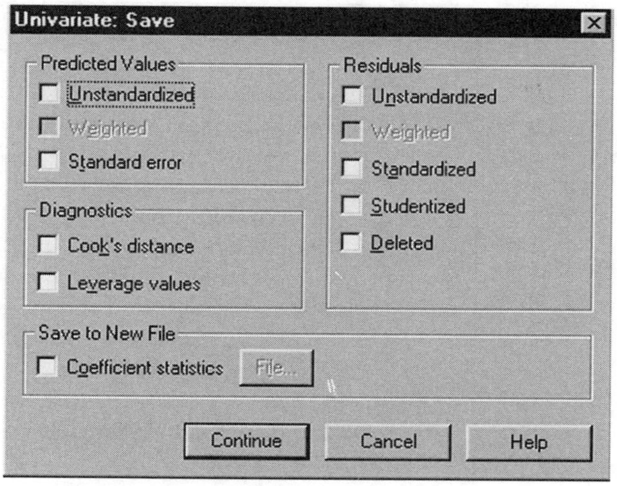

FIGURE 17.7
Univariate: Save dialog
box

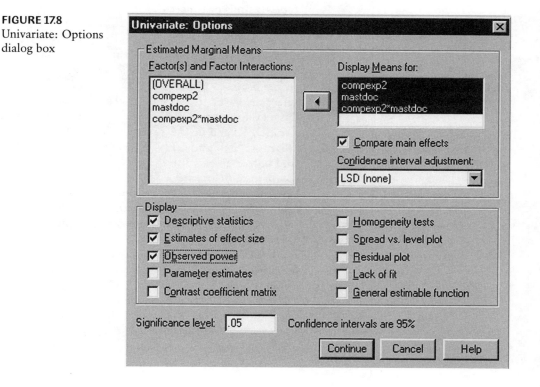

FIGURE 17.8
Univariate: Options
dialog box

GLM–EXAMPLE #2

In the second example we will examine the influence of gender (GENDER) and degree program (MASTDOC) on the number of hours students work per week (EMPHOURS). These data are stored in the file named **chap17b data.** Retrieve these data into the data editor.

The procedure you will follow is similar to the one you just completed. Therefore, we will not display each dialog box, but ask you to refer to those shown in the first example. However, we will summarize the steps involved in using the GLM—Univariate procedure, prompting you to make menu selections throughout.

SPSS steps necessary to perform a factorial ANOVA:

Step 1   *Menu selections*
From the **A**nalyze menu, select **GLM** and **U**nivariate....

Step 2   *Dependent variable*
Select the dependent variable. In this example, the dependent variable is employment hours (EMPHOURS).

Step 3   *Independent variables*
Select the independent variables for the analysis. In doing so, you must also decide whether these variables are fixed or random. In this situation, both variables (GENDER and MASTDOC) are fixed, so place them in the **F**ixed Factor(s): box.

Step 4   *Covariates and weighting variables*
Identify any covariates or weighting variables. There are none in this example.

Step 5   *Model*
In the Model dialog box, retain the default setting of full factorial and Type III sums of squares.

Step 6   *Contrasts*
Specify any desired contrasts in the Contrasts dialog box. As with the prior example, both independent variables have only two levels. Therefore, we will not specify any contrasts.

Step 7   *Profile plots*
Select the variables to be plotted as part of the interaction effect(s). In this example, a potential two-way interaction exists between gender (GENDER) and degree program (MASTDOC). Select MASTDOC for the horizontal axis and GENDER to be plotted using separate lines. Use the **Add** button to confirm these selections.

Step 8   *Post-hoc comparisons*
Select the post-hoc comparisons you wish to apply to the main effects of each independent variable. In this example, there are only two levels for each independent variable, making post-hoc comparisons unnecessary.

Step 9   *Save variables*
If you wish to save any predicted variables from this analysis, select them from the options listed in the Save New Variables dialog box.

Step 10   *Other options*
Display means for each independent variable and combinations of them. Also, check the box labeled **Compare main effects**. Finally, select the **D**escriptives and **E**stimates of effect size options.

Step 11   Check the selections you have made. When these selections meet your satisfaction, use the **OK** command button (or push button) not sure what the convention is to generate output.

Save Your Work

Now that you have produced two factorial ANOVAs, save your work. As with prior results, it is good to give this file a name that you will remember. We recommend identifying these results as **chap17.spo** so you know this file is an output file produced in Chapter 17. You're welcome to use a more creative name, if you'd like.

INTERPRETING SPSS UNIVARIATE FACTORIAL ANOVA RESULTS

In this chapter, you examined two examples of a factorial ANOVA design. The first example was a balanced design in which each of the treatment conditions, or cells, contained

CHAPTER 17 | Factorial ANOVA

the same number of subjects. The second example was not balanced. In this example, each one of the cells contained a different number of subjects. Let's examine the balanced example first.

Example # 1–The Effects of Computer Experience and Degree Program on Computer Liking

In the first example, we examined the influence of two independent variables, computer experience (COMPEXP2) and degree program (MASTDOC) on student attitudes pertaining to their enjoyment of working with computers (COMPLIK). We will examine three types of results from this first example: descriptive results, statistical results, and visual output. Descriptive statistics are presented in Figure 17.9.

As with most other statistical procedures, descriptive statistics are important. Descriptives allow you to compare performance on the outcome variables (dependent variable) across different levels of the independent variables. Examining the data presented in Figure 17.9, we can determine that there are 120 subjects in our sample, equally divided into four different conditions. Recall that we randomly sampled to achieve this balance.

Examine the means and standard deviations for each of the four groups. The lowest mean occurred for masters students with less than one year of computer experience (M = 25.9), whereas doctoral students with more than one year of experience had the highest mean (M = 31.83). What else can we tell from these data? First, examine the rows labeled "Total" associated with the two computer experience categories. Those students with one year of computer experience had higher means than those students with less computer experience (31.38 vs. 26.0). Second, compare the means of all masters students and all doctoral student's found in the bottom row of the descriptives table. For these groups, the means are only slightly higher for doctoral students (28.96 vs. 28.41).

FIGURE 17.9
Factorial ANOVA descriptive results (COMPEXP2 by MASTDOC)

Between-Subjects Factors

		Value Label	N
computer experience	1.00	less than 1 year	60
	2.00	1 year or more	60
MASTDOC	1.00	masters	60
	2.00	doctoral	60

Descriptive Statistics

Dependent Variable: COMPLIK

computer experience	MASTDOC	Mean	Std. Deviation	N
less than 1 year	masters	25.9000	4.5814	30
	doctoral	26.1000	4.8661	30
	Total	26.000	4.6868	60
1 year or more	masters	30.9333	5.8659	30
	doctoral	31.8333	3.5534	30
	Total	31.3833	4.8296	60
Total	masters	28.4167	5.8027	60
	doctoral	28.9667	5.1188	60
	Total	28.6917	5.4554	120

Next, examine the results displayed in Figure 17.10. These results summarize the significance tests used to examine the main effects and the interaction of the two independent variables (i.e., computer experience and degree program).

The reported F value for computer experience (COMPEXP2) is very large, F = 37.92 (df = 1, p < .001). The probability of this result occurring by chance is very low, p < .001. The other two significance tests did not yield statistically significant F ratios. For degree program (MASTDOC), the reported F is .396, (df = 1) with a probability of .530. In other words, the difference between masters and doctoral student means is likely due to chance. Finally, the interaction effect (COMPEXP2 × MASTDOC) is not statistically significant (F = .160, df = 1, p = .690).

To further document the effect of computer experience, examine the information reported under the Eta Squared column. The value reported for COMPEXP2 is .246. This means that the computer experience variable accounts for 24.6% of the variance in the dependent variable, computer liking. The eta squared values reported for degree program (MASTDOC) and the interaction effect are less than 1 percent (i.e., .003, .001). Finally, examine the observed power for each effect. Remember, power indicates the likelihood, or probability, of finding a significant effect when one exists in the population. The power estimate for computer experience is 1.0, whereas the power estimates for degree program and the interaction are much lower.

Next, examine the profile plot in Figure 17.11. This plot shows that doctoral students have a higher mean than masters students for each level of computer experience. The lines for masters and doctoral students are displayed in different colors on your screen. However, these colors are not visible when the plot is black and white (as displayed in Figure 17.11). We will explore some editing features later in the chapter so that we can better distinguish these two groups. The differences are somewhat less noticeable when examining those students with less than one year of experience, but doctoral students still have a higher mean. The relative consistency of mean attitude scores of masters and doctoral students (MASTDOC) at each level of computer experience (COMPEXP2) indicates a lack of an interaction effect.

Example #2–Gender and Degree Program Effects on Employment Hours

As with the first factorial ANOVA example, we will examine descriptive, statistical, and visual output for the second example. In Figure 17.12, we can show group sizes, means, and standard deviations. Overall, there were only 146 subjects in this analysis, because

Tests of Between-Subjects Effects

Dependent Variable: COMPLIK

Source	Type III Sum of Squares	df	Mean Square	F	Sig.	Eta Squared	Noncent. Parameter	Observed Power[a]
Corrected Model	882.158[b]	3	294.053	12.826	.000	.249	38.478	1.000
Intercept	98785.408	1	98785.408	4308.853	.000	.974	4308.853	1.000
COMPEXP2	869.408	1	869.408	37.922	.000	.246	37.922	1.000
MASTDOC	9.075	1	9.075	.396	.530	.003	.396	.096
COMPEXP2 * MASTDOC	3.675	1	3.675	.160	.690	.001	.160	.068
Error	2659.433	116	22.926					
Total	102327.000	120						
Corrected Total	3541.592	119						

[a]. Computed using alpha = .05
[b]. R Squared = .249 (Adjusted R Squared = .230)

FIGURE 17.10
Univariate Factorial ANOVA Between-Subjects Effects (COMPEXP2 by MASTDOC)

only those students that were employed were included. Of these students, most of the them were enrolled in doctoral programs and a majority were females. Let's take a closer look at the specific cell sizes. The first thing to note is that all four conditions do not have equal numbers of subjects. Of the male students, 17 were enrolled in masters programs and 40 were enrolled in doctoral programs. Of the females, 28 were masters students and 61 were doctoral students. However, 30% (17/57) of the male students and 31.5% (28/89)

FIGURE 17.11
Profile Plot
(COMPEXP2 by
MASTDOC)

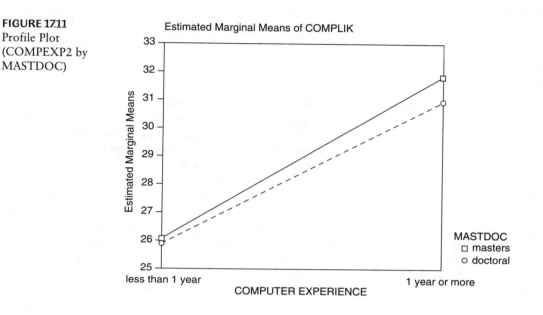

FIGURE 17.12
Descriptive results
(GENDER by
MASTDOC)

Between-Subjects Factors

		Value Label	N
GENDER	1	male	57
	2	female	89
MASTDOC	1.00	masters	45
	2.00	doctoral	101

Descriptive Statistics

Dependent Variable: EMPHOURS

GENDER	MASTDOC	Mean	Std. Deviation	N
male	masters	22.59	12.36	17
	doctoral	31.25	15.14	40
	Total	28.67	14.81	57
female	masters	24.71	14.83	28
	doctoral	22.30	13.29	61
	Total	23.06	13.75	89
Total	masters	23.91	13.85	45
	doctoral	25.84	14.65	101
	Total	25.25	14.39	146

of the female students were enrolled in masters programs, 38% of the masters students and 39.6% (40/101) of the doctoral students were male. As you can see, the cell sizes are not equal, but they are proportional. Therefore, we can, at least assume that the data are proportional.

Let's examine the descriptive statistics for these four conditions. In general, male students work more hours than female students (28.67 > 23.06) and doctoral students work more hours than masters students (25.84 > 23.91). However, take a closer look at the four individual group means and you'll see that male doctoral students work more hours per week than female doctoral students (31.25 > 22.30). However, male masters students work fewer hours per week than female masters students (22.59 < 24.71). So, the amount of hours employed per week depends upon some combination of gender and degree program. Let's take a look at the statistical results.

Figure 17.13 summarizes the tests of between-subjects effects. There are three F-tests, one for each of the main effects and one for the interaction effect. Of these three F-tests, only the interaction effect is statistically significant (F = 4.594, p = .034). The other two effects are more likely due to chance. In addition, the eta squared and power estimates for the interaction effect are larger than those reported for the two main effects.

Examining a profile plot will help us visualize and interpret the interaction effect. This plot is displayed in Figure 17.14.

Although we already examined means from each of the four groups, a visual display is usually easier to understand. As indicated in this plot, female students work more hours than males students when enrolled in masters programs. However, the opposite is true for students in doctoral programs. When the effect of one independent variable (GENDER) is different at various levels of the other independent variable (MASTDOC), an interaction is present. When plotted, lines representing group performance will not be parallel when an interaction effect is present, as in Figure 17.14.

Results Summary

What do we know, having performed these two factorial ANOVAs? First, in regard to computer attitudes, it appears that doctoral students like computers more than masters students, and those students with more computer experience like computers more than those with less experience. This is not surprising. As is true of many activities, you tend to

Tests of Between-Subjects Effects

Dependent Variable: EMPHOURS

Source	Type III Sum of Squares	df	Mean Square	F	Sig.	Eta Squared	Noncent. Parameter	Observed Power[a]
Corrected Model	2101.103[b]	3	700.368	3.562	.016	.070	10.686	.779
Intercept	74818.987	1	74818.987	380.526	.000	.728	380.526	1.000
GENDER	343.066	1	343.066	1.745	.189	.012	1.745	.259
MASTDOC	286.686	1	286.686	1.458	.229	.010	1.458	.224
GENDER * MASTDOC	903.309	1	903.309	4.594	.034	.031	4.594	.567
Error	27920.020	142	196.620					
Total	123080.000	146						
Corrected Total	30021.123	145						

[a.] Computed using alpha = .05
[b.] R Squared = .070 (Adjusted R Squared = .050)

FIGURE 17.13
Between-Subjects effects (GENDER by MASTDOC)

FIGURE 17.14
Profile Plot
(GENDER by
MASTDOC)

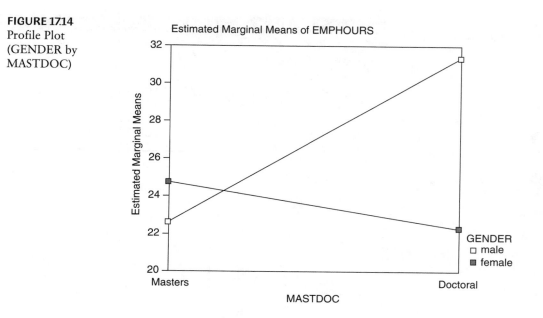

like them more as you gain more experience. Doctoral students also tend to have more computer experience because they are generally required to take more courses that involve the use of computers, like courses in statistics. You also tend to become more skilled and more confident as you gain more experience; this increase in ability and confidence tends to increase your interest and enthusiasm.

Our second example examined the influence of gender and degree program on the number hours a student was employed per week. Generally, we found that doctoral students and males worked more hours than masters students and females. However, these main effects were not statistically significant. What was significant was the finding that the number of hours employed per week was dependent upon a combination of gender and degree program. Whereas female masters students worked more hours than male masters students, male doctoral students worked more hours than female doctoral students. This finding is not easy to explain without more information. Other variables may be influencing these results. For example, age or marital status might be important. Without exploring these influences, we cannot tell. All we can do is interpret the data that we have.

USING THE OUTPUT NAVIGATOR

We have used functions of the output navigator several times in this book to edit SPSS results. In this section, we will use some editing features to change the appearance of a profile plot. Specifically, we will edit the profile plot displayed in Figure 17.14. In this plot, the lines cross and it is difficult to tell which line represents males and which line represents females without looking back at the table of means. If the lines were different, the plot would be more effective.

Locate this plot, then double-click your mouse on it to view it in the chart editor, as displayed in Figure 17.15.

Let's change the female line style so we can distinguish between males and females. Click your mouse on the line representing females. Next, select the **Line Style...** option from the **Format** menu, as illustrated in Figure 17.16.

This will open the Line Style dialog box, displayed in Figure 17.17.

FIGURE 17.15
Profile Plot in Chart
Editor

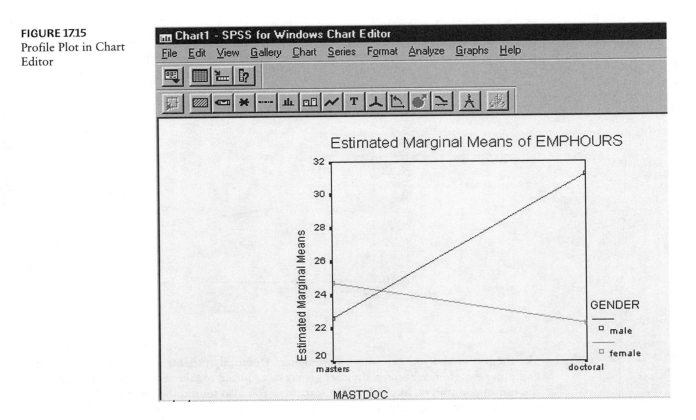

FIGURE 17.16
Chart Editor–
Format–Line Style
menu selections

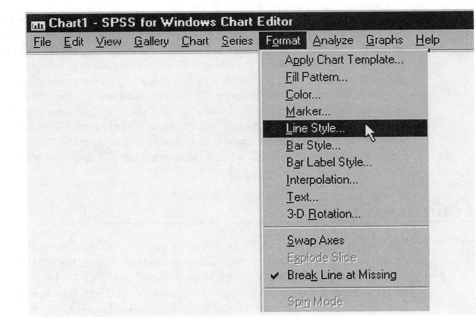

The current style and weight of line is highlighted. By default, it is a thin, solid line for each group. Let's change the female line style to a dotted line; the third option. Let's also make this line thicker by choosing the fourth option. These selections are illustrated in Figure 17.18.

To apply these selections, simply click on the **Apply** button. Finally, click on the **Close** button to view the revised profile plot. The revised profile plot is displayed in Figure 17.19.

FIGURE 17.17
Line Styles dialog box

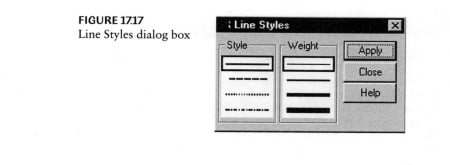

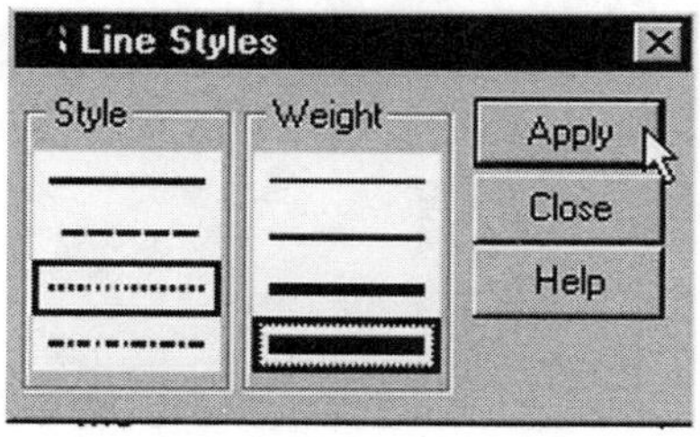

FIGURE 17.18
Selection of new line
style and weight

FIGURE 17.19
Revised profile plot

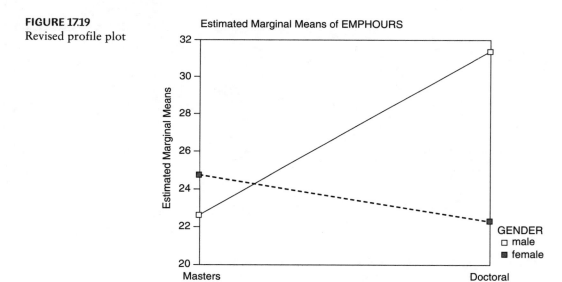

It is now easy to tell which line represents males and which represents females. We encourage you to modify other elements of this plot using features of the chart editor.

CHAPTER SUMMARY

In this chapter, you examined the main effects and interaction of two independent variables. All these effects were between-subjects effects in that comparisons were made between different groups of subjects. In the next section, we will explore within-subjects effects. That is, we will make comparisons within the same group of subjects.

PRACTICE EXERCISES

Using the data from this chapter (chap17a data), perform a factorial ANOVA.

1. Use the statistics liking (STATLIK) score as the dependent variable.
   Use COMPEXP2 and MASTDOC as the independent variables.
2. Obtain a profile plot, identifying MASTDOC with separate lines.
   Does the plot indicate an interaction effect?
3. What can you conclude from this factorial ANOVA based on the main and interaction effects?
   Report and interpret the F ratios (and significance levels) for each main effect and the interaction effect.

SECTION VII

Within-Subjects Designs

18 | Paired-Samples T-Test

In Chapter 15, you used the t-test procedure for one- and two-sample situations. In one-sample situations, the purpose was to determine whether a specific sample mean differed from a hypothesized population mean, whereas in two-sample situations the purpose was to determine the extent to which two independent groups differed from each other in regard to their population mean. In this chapter, we will also be making comparisons between two groups. However, the two groups of scores being compared will not be independent of each other.

The paired-samples t-test, or dependent t-test is used to make two types of comparisons. The first type of comparison is made between two scores that belong to the same group. A common example is a pre-post repeated-measures experiment where individuals are measured on the dependent variable twice, before and after a treatment. For example, if you were asked to evaluate your statistics anxiety at the first week of a statistics class and then again at the end of the quarter/semester, a paired samples t-test would be used because the two evaluations are not independent and this lack of independence must be accounted for during the analysis. A paired-samples t-test would be appropriate for a pre- and post-test design.

Second, comparisons can be made between two related samples on the same dependent variable. This is often referred to as a matched-pairs design. For example, suppose a sample of husbands and wives was asked to respond to a measure of marital satisfaction. When making comparisons between husbands and wives, it is important to keep each husband's response with his wife's response and vice versa. The two groups (husbands and wives) are related and we would want to account for this relatedness during the analysis. Therefore, a paired-samples t-test would be appropriate.

When using a paired-samples t-test, we will follow the traditional null hypothesis testing process. Paired-samples t-tests are used to determine the likelihood that two groups of scores come from populations that have the same mean. If two samples are drawn from populations having the same mean, we will expect the difference between the two sample means to be equal to 0. Therefore, our null hypothesis will indicate that the two population means are equal. Again, using the central limit theorem, we know that even if both samples are drawn from the same population, the sample means could still vary due to sampling error. However, if we sampled all possible samples and calculated differences between each pair of sample means, the distribution of sample mean differences would be symmetrical, and its mean would be equal to the difference between the two population means.

Under the null hypothesis, we state the difference between the two population means is equal to 0. We reject this null hypothesis if the probability of the outcome occurring by chance is low (e.g., $p < .05$). On the other hand, if this probability is too high, we will retain the null hypothesis and conclude that differences between the two means are most likely due to chance. There are a few assumptions we need to make when using a paired-samples t-test.

These assumptions are similar to those made when using the independent-samples t-test in Chapter 15. First, we assume that the population distribution of each variable is normal. Second, within a same group, each person's score is independent of the scores of others in that group. Finally, the population variances for the two sets of scores are equal.

In the remaining sections of this chapter, we will explore the use of the paired-samples t-test to test hypotheses about differences between two related means. Before we begin, let's examine the variables we will use to illustrate these procedures.

VARIABLES USED IN THIS CHAPTER

In order to illustrate the paired-samples t-test, we will compare student attitudes toward computers (i.e., COMPANX, COMPCON, COMPLIK, COMPUSE) with their attitudes toward statistics (i.e., STATANX, STATCON, STATLIK, STATUSE). We know that these attitudes are related because we used the Correlations procedure earlier to describe these relationships. The Pearson correlations between attitudes toward computers and attitudes toward statistics ranged from .5006 to .6445, with a median of .6086. In all, four t-tests will be necessary to compare students' attitudes toward computers with their attitudes toward statistics.

USING SPSS TO PERFORM A PAIRED-SAMPLES T-TEST

In Chapter 15, you used the T Test procedure to perform one-sample and independent-samples t-tests. Much of what you do to perform paired-samples t-tests is the same. Before you get started, activate SPSS and retrieve the data identified as **chap18 data** on your data disk.

Paired-Samples T-Test Procedure

You begin with the **Analyze** menu. From this menu, select the **Compare Means** and **Paired-Samples T Test...** options, as illustrated in Figure 18.1

Selecting these options will open the Paired-Samples T Test dialog box, displayed in Figure 18.2. Many of the features in this dialog box should be familiar by now. At the left of the window, the names of all your variables are listed in the source variable list. You will

FIGURE 18.1
Analyze–Compare
Means–Paired-Samples
T Test menu selections

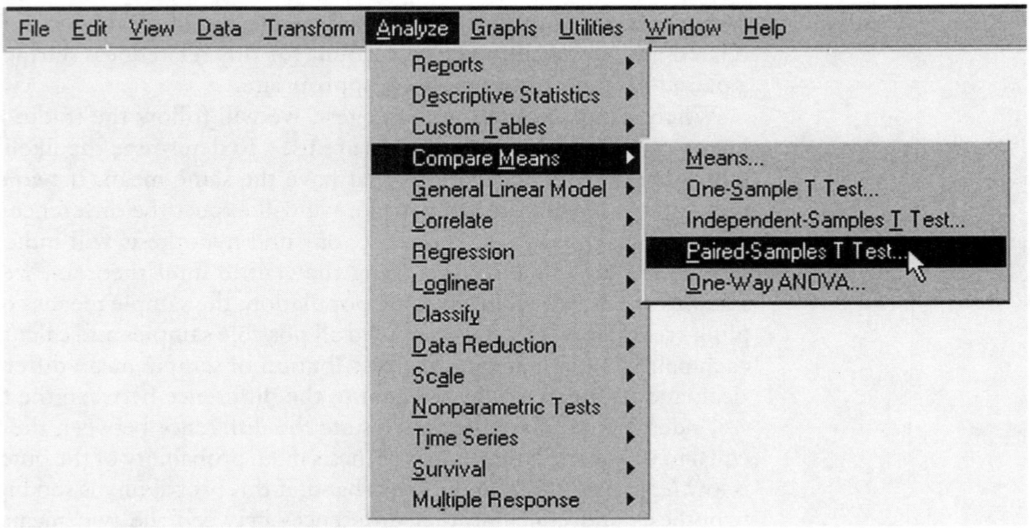

select the variables from the source variable list and place them in the **Paired Variables:** box for analysis. Below the source variable list is a box labeled **Current Selections.** As you select each variable to be paired, it will appear in this box. Finally, the five command push-buttons that you have used in all of the previous procedures appear at the far right.

Finally, there is an **Options...** button at the bottom right corner. Click on this button to view the Options dialog box. This dialog box is displayed in Figure 18.3.

There are only a few options available for the paired-samples t-test. You can specify a confidence interval and how missing values should be treated. By default, a 95% confidence interval will be computed, and missing values will be excluded on an analysis-by-analysis basis. These default settings are fine for most t-tests you will run. If you want a smaller or larger confidence interval, just type that number in place of the 95. In other words, if you wanted a 99% confidence interval, you would erase the 95 and type "99." Finally, if you wish to exclude missing values on a listwise basis, select that option.

Running a Paired-Samples T-Test

From the **Analyze** menu, select the **Compare Means** and **Paired-Samples T Test...** options. The next step is to select each pair of variables from the source variable list. The first pair will be COMPANX and STATANX. Scroll down the source variable list until you find COMPANX. Click your mouse once on this variable and it should appear in the Current Selections box next to the Variable 1 label. Continue to scroll down the list of variables until you locate the second variable, STATANX. Single-click your mouse and now this variable should appear in the Current Selections box next to the Variable 2 label. Transfer this first pair to the **Paired Variables:** box using the arrow button. The first pair selection is illustrated in Figure 18.4.

FIGURE 18.2
Paired-Samples T Test
dialog box

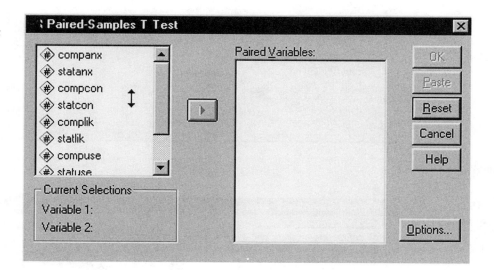

FIGURE 18.3
Paired-Samples T Test:
Options dialog box

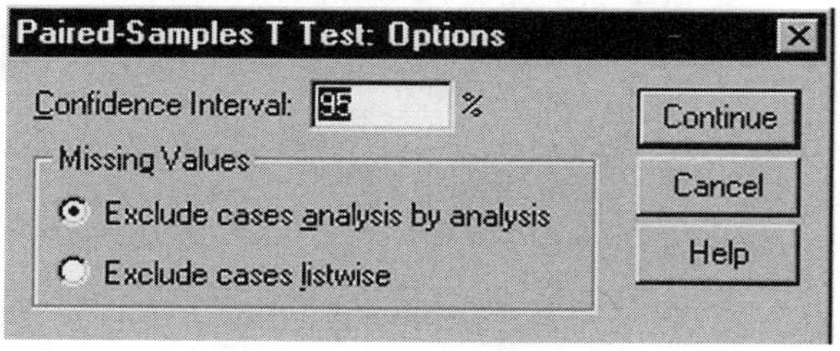

Continue this procedure for the next three pairs of variables. These pairs are listed below:

COMPCON — STATCON
COMPLIK — STATLIK
COMPUSE — STATUSE

Having identified all four pairs of variables, the Paired-Samples dialog box should look like that displayed in Figure 18.5.

We will leave the default options in place, so there's no need to specify anything else. Return to the Paired-Samples T Test dialog box using the **Continue** button, and use the **OK** command pushbutton to execute these t-tests.

The results from all the t-tests you produced in this session are stored in the output file. You should save this output file so that you will have a record of your efforts. We recommend using **chap18.spo** to identify this file as a listing of the results from Chapter 18. We will examine this output in the final section of this chapter.

FIGURE 18.4
Selection of a pair of variables for a Paired-Samples T Test

FIGURE 18.5
All pairs of variables selected for Paired-Samples T Test

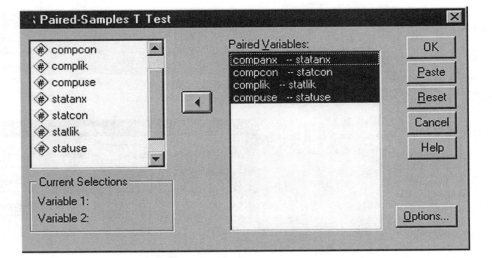

INTERPRETING SPSS PAIRED-SAMPLES T-TESTS RESULTS

You've generated results from four paired-samples t-tests in this SPSS session. Let's examine these results and try to make some sense of them. Each of these paired-samples t-tests examined attitudes toward computers and statistics. Specifically, each t-test will allow us to determine whether students' attitudes toward computers differ from their attitudes toward statistics. Under the null hypothesis, we assumed that these attitudes were not different. Therefore, we expected the difference between the means for each pair of these attitudes to be equal to 0. The results from our paired-samples t-tests will help us make a decision regarding this null hypothesis.

The results from the paired-samples t-tests are displayed in Figure 18.6. The first thing we'll examine from these results is the descriptive information. This descriptive information includes the mean, standard deviation, and standard error of the mean for each variable used in the analysis. In addition, the Pearson correlation coefficient for each pair of variables is presented. This information is presented in one table for all pairs of variables that we specified. In earlier versions of SPSS (Version 6.X), all of the information pertaining to one pair of variables was presented in the same section of the output.

You have already examined this descriptive information using other SPSS procedures. You used the Descriptives (see Chapter 6) and the Means (see Chapter 7) procedures to examine means and standard deviations and the Correlations procedure (see Chapter 14) to produce Pearson correlations.

Examine the mean, standard deviation, and standard error of the mean for each variable in our analysis. From this information, you can see that the mean is consistently higher for the computer scales. This indicates that students tend to have more positive attitudes toward computers than toward statistics. For each pair of variables, the standard deviations and standard errors are also reported. The greatest amount of variability appears to be associated with the anxiety scales, the smallest amount appears to be associated with the usefulness scales.

Next, examine the correlation coefficients. Pearson correlation coefficients describe the magnitude of the relationship between each pair of variables. The correlation is weakest (r = .502) between the two anxiety scales (i.e., COMPANX, STATANX) and strongest (r = .645) for the two liking scales (i.e., COMPLIK, STATLIK). All four correlations are statistically significant (p < .001).

The remaining information pertains to the paired-sample t-test procedure. The information reported in the output includes the mean and standard deviation of the difference between the pair of variables. The mean represents the average difference between the two variables being paired, while the standard deviation represents the variability of these differences. Finally, a standard error of the mean difference and a 95% confidence interval are reported. This information can be used to estimate the difference that might exist in the population. Using the reported confidence interval, you can estimate a range in which the population difference would occur 95 times out of 100. As with other confidence intervals, the smaller this interval, the better the estimate. Additionally, the confidence interval should not contain zero. If it does, then the true difference in the population could be 0. This would provide support for the null hypothesis. In our analysis, all four confidence intervals are positive, indicating that, were we to repeatedly sampled students their attitude toward computers would be higher (more positive) than their attitudes toward statistics 95 times out of 100. This information will be useful in making inferences about the population.

Finally, let's examine the results for the t-tests. For each t-test, a t value, degrees of freedom (df), and a 2-tailed significance is reported. The df for each of our four t-tests is 208 because each t-test was based on a sample of 209 students. The lowest t value (t = 4.935) is given for the confidence attitude scales; while the highest (t = 9.184) is reported for the comparison of the anxiety scales. You will also notice that the mean difference is lowest for the confidence scales and highest for the anxiety scales. In all four cases, the reported 2-tailed significance is .000. This means that we would expect these results less than 1 time in 1,000 (p < .001) if the null hypothesis were true.

Paired Samples Statistics

		Mean	N	Std. Deviation	Std. Error Mean
Pair 1	COMPANX	30.6029	209	6.3708	.4407
	STATANX	26.4211	209	6.8018	.4705
Pair 2	COMPCON	30.6077	209	5.2941	.3662
	STATCON	29.0478	209	5.2089	.3603
Pair 3	COMPLIK	29.6603	209	5.3155	.3677
	STATLIK	27.0813	209	4.2684	.2953
Pair 4	COMPUSE	34.9187	209	3.9000	.2698
	STATUSE	32.9139	209	4.6886	.3243

Paired Samples Correlations

		N	Correlation	Sig.
Pair 1	COMPANX & STATANX	209	.502	.000
Pair 2	COMPCON & STATCO	209	.622	.000
Pair 3	COMPLIK & STATLIK	209	.645	.000
Pair 4	COMPUSE & STATUSE	209	.608	.000

Paired Samples Test

		Paired Differences							
					95% Confidence Interval of the Difference				Sig. (2-tailed)
		Mean	Std. Deviation	Std. Error Mean	Lower	Upper	t	df	
Pair 1	COMPANX - STATANX	4.1818	6.5827	.4553	3.2842	5.0795	9.184	208	.000
Pair 2	COMPCON - STATCO	1.5598	4.5697	.3161	.9367	2.1830	4.935	208	.000
Pair 3	COMPLIK - STATLIK	2.5789	4.1504	.2871	2.0130	3.1449	8.983	208	.000
Pair 4	COMPUSE - STATUSE	2.0048	3.8674	.2675	1.4774	2.5322	7.494	208	.000

FIGURE 18.6
SPSS Paired-Samples T Test results

Because the probability of these results occurring, given the conditions of the null hypothesis, is so low, we reject the null hypothesis for each t-test. What do these results tell us about graduate students? Based on the information gathered from this sample, we would conclude that students have more positive attitudes toward computers than they do toward statistics. They are more comfortable, have more confidence, like computers more, and find computers more useful in their lives. We must keep in mind that most of these students are enrolled in their very first statistics course, or at least their first course in quite some time. It would be interesting to make these comparison again after the students had completed more statistics courses. We (the authors) believe that they would begin to have more positive attitudes toward statistics as they gain more experience and have more opportunities to apply statistical procedures.

CHAPTER SUMMARY

In this chapter, we used the Paired-Samples T Test procedure to perform t-tests on pairs of variables measuring attitudes toward computers and attitudes toward statistics. Under the null hypothesis, we assumed that there would be no difference in these attitudes. Because comparison of the pairs of attitude means revealed that observed differences were not likely due to chance, we rejected the null hypothesis. In the next chapter, we'll examine similar situations using a repeated measures ANOVA.

PRACTICE EXERCISES

Use the data set you created in Chapter 3 (i.e., student admission data).

1. Use the paired-samples t-test procedure to obtain the following information.
   a. Means and standard deviations for two pairs of variables
      (1) GRE-V and GRE-Q
      (2) RATING1 and RATING2
   b. Correlation between each pair of variables
   c. Difference between the means for each pair of variables
   d. T value for each paired-samples t-test

2. What can be concluded from the correlation between these two variables?
3. What can be concluded from the 95% confidence interval for the difference between the means?
4. Is there a difference between GRE-Q and GRE-V scores?
   Is there a difference between RATING1 and RATING2?
5. What conclusions can be drawn from the above comparisons for this pool of applicants?

19 | Within-Subjects ANOVA

In the previous chapter, you used a paired-samples t-test to make comparisons within the same group of subjects. Specifically, you compared students' attitudes toward computers with their attitudes toward statistics. Each comparison was made using a pair of attitude means, one for computers and one for statistics. However, the paired-samples t-test is limited to comparisons involving two related means. Therefore, if you need to compare more than two related means, more that one t-test would be required, and you know that error increases when multiple tests are performed.

You faced this situation when you needed to compare more than two independent groups in Chapter 16. One option would have been to perform multiple independent-samples t-tests. Instead, you used a one-way ANOVA to make comparisons among two or more independent group means. In Chapter 17, you used ANOVA to make comparisons among two or more related group means. Whereas comparisons between different groups are made using a between-subjects ANOVA procedure, comparisons within the same, or related groups, are made using within-subjects ANOVA.

A within-subjects ANOVA is appropriate for two types of comparisons. The first type is a comparison of repeated measures; wherein a subject repeats his or her performance under two or more conditions or time periods. For example, suppose a group of graduate students was measured regarding their attitudes toward statistics while they were enrolled in the first statistics course and again in the second and third statistics courses. In all, each student in the sample would have expressed his/her attitudes toward statistics three times. To make comparisons about attitudes toward statistics over three courses, a within-subjects ANOVA would be used.

The second type of comparison is a comparison of related or matched samples. As an example, suppose we wanted to make comparisons of student and instructor evaluations of the same course would be made using a paired-samples t-test. Suppose each course was also evaluated by a third source, the department chair. To make comparisons among these three sources of evaluation, a within-subjects ANOVA would be used since each of these three sources of information must be kept together during analysis.

The within-subjects ANOVA extends the applications of the paired-samples t-test, as a one-way ANOVA did for the independent-samples t-test. The assumptions and hypothesis testing procedure are similar to that for the paired-samples t-test. The assumptions are normality, independence, and homogeneity of variance. First, each sample was drawn from a normally distributed population. Second, each person's score is independent of all other scores, and each treatment level (i.e., group, sample) is independent of the others. Finally, the variances from each population are equal.

An additional assumption is made when using a within-subjects ANOVA. This is the condition of sphericity, or homogeneity of covariance. Under this condition, it is assumed that the levels of the within-subjects variables are equally related to each other. In other words, a person's performance under one condition influences that under other conditions about the same. For example, if a within-subjects ANOVA were used to examine the effects of a drug under three different conditions, we would assume that these effects equally influence each other, or have similar covariances, or correlations, between them.

When using a within-subjects ANOVA, you will follow a similar hypothesis testing process as you did with a paired-samples t-test. Using ANOVA, you make the assumption under the null hypothesis for as many groups, or variables, as we are comparing. Specifically the null hypothesis assumes that all population means are equal. For example, if you are comparing attitudes toward statistics over three courses or evaluations of a statistics courses based on three different sources, you assume that each of these three population means is equal. You will continue to assume that this null hypothesis is true until you gather sufficient evidence from your sample that makes this hypothesis improbable.

If the null hypothesis is rejected, it doesn't necessarily mean that all three groups have different population means. A rejection of the null hypothesis simply indicates that not all groups have the same population mean. In other words, you conclude that there is a significant amount of variation between at least two of the means, and therefore, a treatment effect exists. As you did when using one-way ANOVA in Chapter 16, you must make further comparisons among the different group means to determine which groups differ.

In the remaining sections of this chapter, we will explore the use of within-subjects ANOVA to make comparisons among students' attitudes toward computers and statistics. Before we begin, let's examine the variables we will use to illustrate these procedures.

VARIABLES USED IN THIS CHAPTER

In order to illustrate within-subjects ANOVA, we will make comparisons among the four attitudes toward computers (i.e., COMPANX, COMPCON, COMPLIK, COMPUSE). Each student responded to four different types of attitude scales regarding their anxiety, confidence, liking, and usefulness. We have stored these variables in a data file labeled **chap19 data** on the enclosed disk.

USING SPSS FOR WITHIN-SUBJECTS ANOVA DESIGNS

In this section, we will use SPSS for Windows to perform a within-subjects ANOVA. Specifically, we will use ANOVA to compare four types of attitudes toward computers. Activate SPSS and retrieve the file **chap19 data**.

GLM PROCEDURE

The GLM procedure is used in SPSS to process within-subjects ANOVA designs. You used the GLM procedure in earlier chapters when you explored factorial ANOVA. Earlier versions of SPSS used the ANOVA Models procedure. These procedures will yield the same results, no matter which software program you are using, but the specific process of each software will vary.

Beginning from the **Analyze** menu, select the **General Linear Model** and **Repeated Measures...** options, as illustrated in Figure 19.1.

These menu selections open the Repeated Measures Define Factor(s) dialog box (see Figure 19.2). This dialog box is used to define the within-subjects variable(s), or factor(s). By default, SPSS will label a repeated variable as "factor1." You can specify a different name in the **Within-Subject Factor Name:** box. For our repeated-measures ANOVA, the repeated

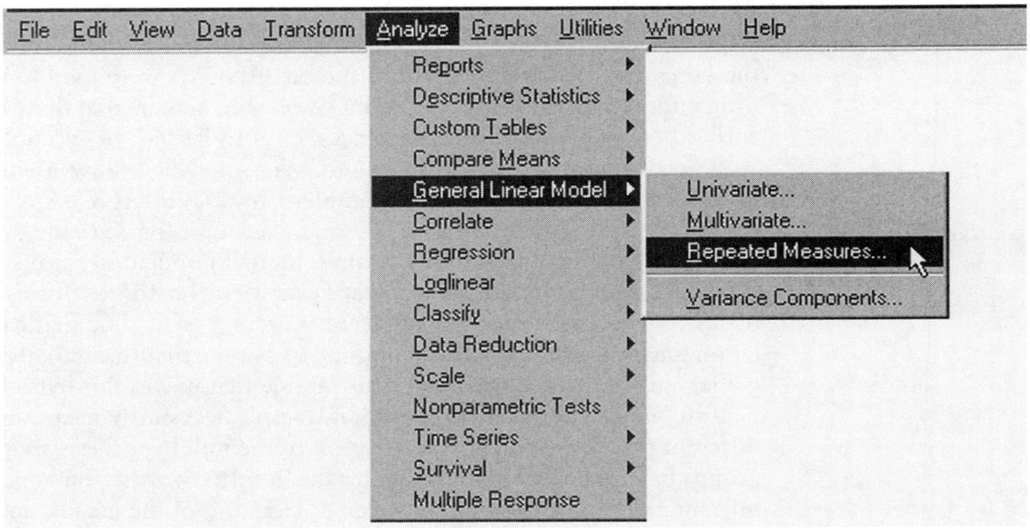

FIGURE 19.1
Analyze–GLM–
Repeated Measures
menu selections

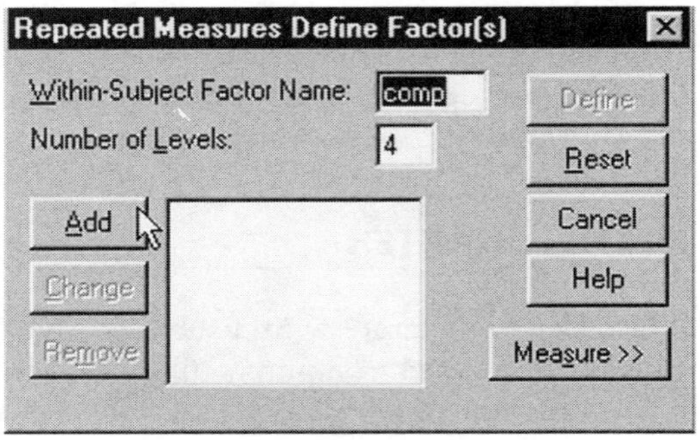

FIGURE 19.2
Repeated Measures
Define Factor(s) dialog
box

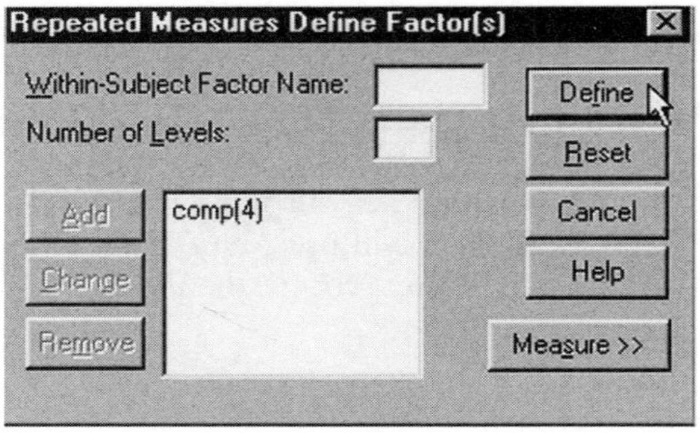

FIGURE 19.3
Repeated
Measures–COMP
factor identified

factor is computer attitudes, so label this within-subjects factor as "COMP." The next box prompts you for the **Number of Levels:** of this factor. There are four computer attitude scales, therefore our within-subjects factor has four levels. Type "4" in the Number of Levels box. Using your mouse, click on the **Add** button so that this within-subjects variable is added to our analysis. These selections are illustrated in Figure 19.3.

Next, you need to define the variables that correspond to each level of the within-subjects variables, so click your mouse on the **Define** button. This will open the Repeated Measures dialog box displayed in Figure 19.4.

Notice that the COMP label you gave the within-subject factor in the previous window now appears in this dialog box above the **Within-Subjects Variables** box. In this box, four

FIGURE 19.4
Repeated Measures
dialog box

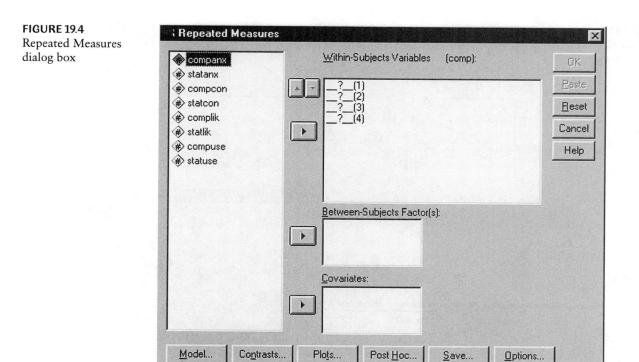

FIGURE 19.5
Within-Subject
Variable (COMP)

levels are listed and ready to be defined. We will use the four computer attitude scales as these levels. One at a time, select the four computer attitude scales from the source variable list (at left) and transfer them to the **Within-Subjects Variables**   (comp):, using the arrow button. These four variables are COMPANX, COMPCON, COMPLIK, and COMPUSE. After selecting each of these four variables, the **Within-Subjects Variables**   (comp): box should list them, as displayed in Figure 19.5.

Now that you have defined the four levels of the within-subjects factor, let's examine the options available with this procedure. First, you will see that there is a place to identify between-subjects factors and covariates. You will explore these options in the next chapter. At the bottom of this dialog box, there are six buttons that allow you to explore many statistical options for a within-subjects design. Let's explore these options as we continue with our example of a within-subjects ANOVA.

Specifying the Model

The first button, labeled **Model...**, is used to specify the model we want to use to examine the effects of the variables (factors) included in the design. Click on this button to open the Repeated Measures: Model dialog box (see Figure 19.6).

FIGURE 19.6
Repeated Measures:
Model dialog box

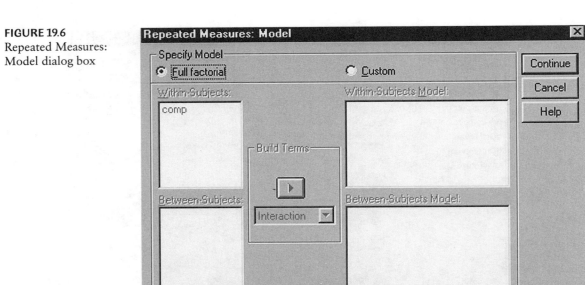

The default options are displayed in this dialog box. A full-factorial model is specified. This model will include all main effects, interactions, and covariate effects. For most situations, this default option will be appropriate. If you want to specify interaction effects involving a covariate, which would be useful in an analysis of covariance design, or just a partial listing of the interaction effects, you would specify a custom model. When specifying a custom model, you need to select the terms that define the model, including main and interaction effects. The final piece of information found in this dialog box pertains to the sums of squares. By default, Type III sums of squares are used. Other types of sums of squares can be specified for different situations. For example, you would specify Type I sums of squares to examine the effects in a hierarchical model. Type II sums of squares would be appropriate for a regression model, and Type IV would be used in situations where some of the comparison groups have no subjects. For most situations you encounter including the present example, Type III sums of squares will be appropriate.

Contrasts

Click on the **Contrasts...** button to open the Repeated Measures: Contrasts dialog box, displayed in Figure 19.7.

These are the same contrasts we discussed in Chapter 17. The default setting is Polynomial, which will examine trends. Our data are not suitable for such trends, so change the setting to None.

Profile Plots

You used plots earlier in this book to examine relationships between variables. Visual displays of effects are helpful in determining the nature of the effect. Click on the **Plots...** button to explore the available options. The Repeated Measures: Profile Plots dialog box appears in Figure 19.8.

Profile plots are especially useful in determining interaction effects, as you did in Chapter 17. Our current model includes only one variable, therefore an interaction is not

FIGURE 19.7
Repeated Measures:
Contrasts dialog box

FIGURE 19.8
Repeated Measures:
Profile Plots dialog box

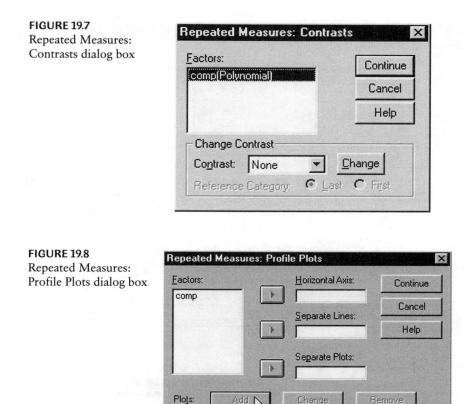

possible. However, a plot would be useful to display a profile of the overall group means across the four computer attitude scales, as you did in Chapter 16.

Select COMP from the source variable list at the left and place it in the **Horizontal Axis:** box. Next, click the **Add** button to specify this plot. This will result in a plot of the overall group means for each of the four computer attitude scales. In the next chapter, we will illustrate a situation with more than one group plotted to determine interaction effects. To return to the Repeated Measures dialog box, click on the **Continue** button.

Post-Hoc Multiple Comparisons

Click on **Post Hoc...** to open the Repeated Measures: Post Hoc Multiple Comparisons dialog box, displayed in Figure 19.9.

As you can see, there are several different post-hoc multiple-comparison tests displayed in this dialog box. You explored these in Chapter 16 when performing a one-way ANOVA. These tests are used to compare the observed means for levels of between-subjects variables. Since our current example includes only a within-subjects variable, these tests are not appropriate, and therefore, not available. We will examine some appropriate comparisons later in this chapter. You will explore the multiple comparisons found in this dialog box in the next chapter. To return to the Repeated Measures dialog box, click on the **Continue** button.

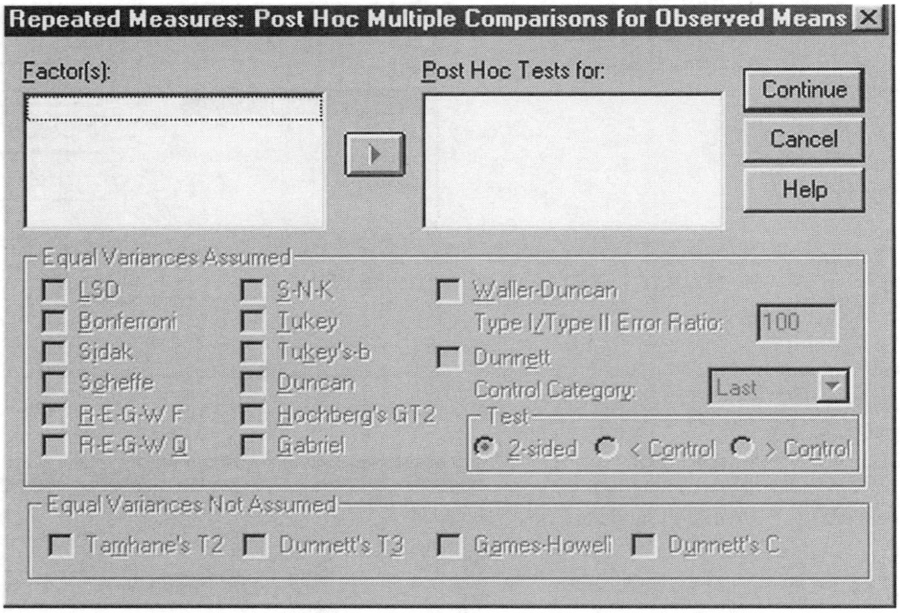

FIGURE 19.9
Repeated Measures:
Post Hoc Multiple
Comparisons dialog
box

FIGURE 19.9
Repeated Measures:
Post Hoc Multiple
Comparisons dialog
box

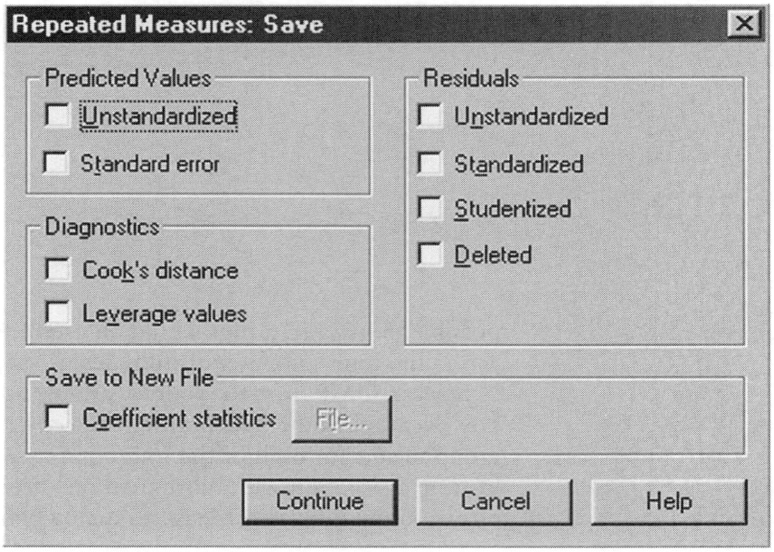

FIGURE 19.10
Repeated Measures:
Save dialog box

Saving New Variables

Using the GLM Repeated Measures procedure, predictions can be made about the performance of each subject in the sample. Specifically, predictions are made based on the relationship between the independent variable(s) and the dependent variable. The stronger the relationship, the better the prediction. These relationships (or effects) are evaluated using the analysis of variance procedure.

Predictions made using the GLM Repeated Measures procedure can be saved for each case. In addition, information regarding residuals (error) and diagnostics can also be saved. To explore these options, click on the **Save...** button to open the Repeated Measure: Save dialog box (see Figure 19.10). We will not be saving any new variables in the current analy-

FIGURE 19.11
Repeated Measures:
Options dialog box

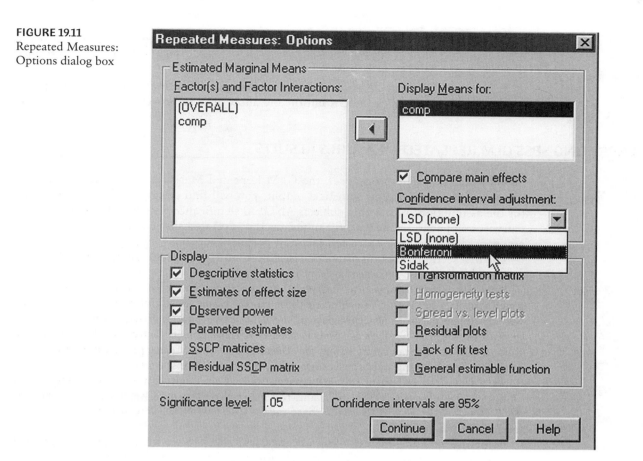

sis. We will examine these options in more detail when we discuss regression analysis. Return to the Repeated Measures dialog box using the **Continue** button.

Options

The final dialog box pertains to the various options available in the GLM Repeated Measures procedure. To examine these options, click on the **Options...** button. This will open the Repeated Measures: Options dialog box displayed in Figure 19.11. Once again, there are many options listed in this dialog box. These options include descriptive statistics, comparisons of main effects, effect size, and parameter estimates. You can also adjust the significance level used to identify statistically significant post-hoc tests and the width of the confidence interval.

Our current analysis includes only one within-subjects variable, COMP. Select this variable and place it in the box labeled **Display Means for:**. Also, select the option **Compare main effects**. This information will be useful in determining the extent to which the four different types of computer attitudes differ. To determine differences between pairs of computer attitude scales, specify post hoc pairwise comparisons.

These options are found in a menu under the **Confidence interval adjustment** heading. The three options include LSD, Bonferroni, and Sidak. You examined these options earlier when dealing with a one-way ANOVA. Remember, the LSD test is very liberal in that it does not control for the inflation of Type 1 error. The Bonferroni and Sidak do make such adjustments. Select the option of **Bonferroni.**

Under the Display heading, there are several options. Select the **Descriptive Statistics, Estimates of effect size,** and **Observed power** options. These options will produce means, standard deviations, effect size, and power estimates. We'll explore the other options regarding parameter estimates and matrices in the following chapters, and some of the other statistical options later when using regression analysis. Finally, leave the significance level set at the .05 default.

Return to the Repeated Measures dialog box using the **Continue** button. As with previous SPSS procedures, click the **OK** button and allow SPSS to process your data.

INTERPRETING SPSS GLM REPEATED MEASURES RESULTS

As with previous SPSS procedures, the GLM Repeated Measures component produces a great deal of output. In this statistical output, you will find descriptive information, tests for the assumptions of a within-subjects ANOVA, significance tests (i.e., F-tests), post-hoc pairwise comparisons, and a profile of means. If you printed all the output, it would be several pages long. We have extracted the most pertinent sections to interpret.

The first section of output provides descriptive information regarding the within-subject factor. This information is displayed in Figure 19.12.

First, the output displays the variables that correspond to each of the four levels of computer attitudes (COMP). You selected these earlier when specifying the four levels of the within-subject factor. The other part of the descriptive output provides means, standard deviations, and the number of subjects for the within-subjects factor. You have produced similar output several times using the Descriptives and Means procedures and in the process of performing hypothesis tests using the correlations, t-test, and ANOVA procedures. All we can tell from this information is that the highest mean was produced for computer usefulness (COMPUSE), and the other three attitude means are very similar. We'll examine the extent to which these means differ when we interpret the significance tests in the next sections.

Before we examine the tests of significance, let's check to see whether the assumption of sphericity can be maintained. This information is summarized in Figure 19.13.

FIGURE 19.12
Descriptive statistics output from GLM procedure

Within-Subjects Factors

Measure: MEASURE_1

COMP	Dependent Variable
1	COMPANX
2	COMPCON
3	COMPLIK
4	COMPUSE

Descriptive Statistics

	Mean	Std. Deviation	N
COMPANX	30.6029	6.3708	209
COMPCON	30.6077	5.2941	209
COMPLIK	29.6603	5.3155	209
COMPUSE	34.9187	3.9000	209

Mauchly's Test of Sphericity[b]

Measure: MEASURE_1

Within Subjects Effect	Mauchly's W	Approx. Chi-Square	df	Sig.	Epsilon[a]		
					Greenhouse-Geisser	Huynh-Feldt	Lower-bound
COMP	.467	157.333	5	.000	.674	.680	.333

Tests the null hypothesis that the error covariance matrix of the otrhonormalized transformed dependent variables is proportional to an identity matrix.

[a] May be used to adjust the degrees of freedom for the averaged tests of significance. Corrected tests are displayed in the layers (by default) of the Tests of Within Subjects Effects table.

[b] Design: Intercept
Within Subjects Design: COMP

FIGURE 19.13
Test for Sphericity

The test of significance is the Mauchly's test of sphericity. This test yields a W statistic which approximates a chi-square. You used chi-square in Chapter 12. Using the chi-square distribution, you (or SPSS) can determine the extent to which this result is likely to happen by chance when the null hypothesis is true. Before we examine more of this section, it is important to review the null hypothesis that is being tested.

Remember, the assumption of sphericity refers to the relationships (or covariances) between the levels of the within-subject factor(s). Specifically, it is assumed that these covariances are equal. Therefore, the null hypothesis specifies that these covariances are equal. Because we want to maintain the assumption of equal covariances, we do NOT want to reject the null hypothesis. This situation is similar to the one you encountered when you used Levene's test to assess homogeneity of variance prior to apply the t-test and ANOVA.

The Mauchly's W statistic is reported as .467, which has a chi-square value of 157.333 with 5 degrees of freedom. The significance is reported as .000. In other words, the probability of this result occurring by chance is less than 1 in a 1,000 ($p < .001$). This means that the observed differences between the covariances in our analysis are not likely due to chance. In other words, the relationships between levels of the repeated variable (i.e., computer attitude scales) are not equal; the assumption of sphericity can NOT be maintained, according to the results of the Mauchly's W statistic.

The information reported under the Epsilon heading will be helpful in further addressing the lack of sphericity. If we maintained the assumption of sphericity, these epsilon values would be 1. As you can see, these values are not 1. There are two primary epsilons reported, Greenhouse-Geisser (.674) and Huynh-Feldt (.680), with a lower-bound estimate of .333. To correct for the lack of sphericity, epsilon values can be used to adjust the degrees of freedom used in the tests of significance. The degrees of freedom are multiplied by the epsilon value. This results in smaller degrees of freedom and a more conservative test of significance. Using the Greenhouse-Geisser epsilon, we will multiply the degrees of freedom for our significance tests by .674 before evaluating the F ratio for statistical significance.

The results of the within-subjects tests of significance are summarized in Figure 19.14.

This table summarizes the results from the within-subjects ANOVA. Concentrate on the row for the COMP effect, as this is the effect we are examining. There are several lines of information in this row, each producing an F ratio of 127.979. However, note that the degrees of freedom are different for each of these F ratios. The first row reports the information based on the assumption of sphericity, while the remaining three rows offer adjustments for a lack of sphericity.

We know from examining the tests of sphericity in Figure 19.13 that the assumption can NOT be maintained. Notice that each of the three adjustments reported in Figure 19.14 were also reported as epsilon values in Figure 19.13. These epsilon values were used to adjust the degrees of freedom. For example, the Greenhouse-Geisser epsilon was reported as .674. Multiplying .674 by the unadjusted degrees of freedom (3 and 624) will result in 2.021 and 420.349. These adjusted degrees of freedom are reported in Figure 19.14. The adjustments made using the Huynh-Feldt epsilon (.680) are similar, while those made using the lower-bound epsilon (.333) are more severe. No matter which adjustment is used, the probability of this result occurring by chance is very small, less than 1 in a 1,000. Therefore, we conclude that the differences between the attitude scales did not happen by chance and we should explore these differences further.

Examine the profile plot in Figure 19.15. This profile displays the means for each of the four computer attitudes. You can see that the mean for the fourth attitude scale (i.e., computer usefulness) exceeds the other three. The first two attitude score means (anxiety and confidence) are very close, while the third (liking) is slightly lower. Let's examine the results of the statistical comparisons made between these attitude scales to determine what differences exist.

Tests of Within-Subjects Effects

Measure: MEASURE_1

Source		Type III Sum of Squares	df	Mean Square	F	Sig.	Eta Squared	Noncent. Parameter	Observed Power[a]
COMP	Sphericity Assumed	3482.321	3	1160.774	127.979	.000	.381	383.938	1.000
	Greenhouse-Geisser	3482.321	2.021	1723.147	127.979	.000	.381	258.635	1.000
	Huynh-Feldt	3482.321	2.041	1706.320	127.979	.000	.381	261.185	1.000
	Lower-bound	3482.321	1.000	3482.321	127.979	.000	.381	127.979	1.000
Error(COMP)	Sphericity Assumed	5659.679	624	9.070					
	Greenhouse-Geisser	5659.679	420.349	13.464					
	Huynh-Feldt	5659.679	424.494	13.333					
	Lower-bound	5659.679	208.000	27.210					

[a.] Computed using alpha = .05

FIGURE 19.14
Tests of within-subjects effects

FIGURE 19.15
Profile plot for computer attitude scales

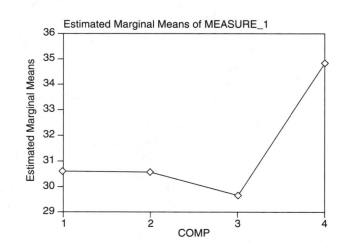

Comparative information was produced because you requested that main effects be compared. Locate the information regarding these effects in your output. If you use the outline pane, it will be listed under the Estimated Marginal Means heading. The first table is similar to the table of means that you have examined earlier. The second table, however, summarizes the results of making comparisons between each pair of means. These tables are displayed in Figure 19.16.

In all, there are six different comparisons. The results of each comparison are reported twice, so we've highlighted six unique comparisons for the purposes of discussion. Five of these six comparisons were found to be statistically significant. The only nonsignificant

Estimates

Measure: MEASURE_1

COMP	Mean	Std. Error	95% Confidence Interval	
			Lower Bound	Upper Bound
1	30.603	.441	29.734	31.472
2	30.608	.366	29.886	31.330
3	29.660	.368	28.935	30.385
4	34.919	.270	34.387	35.450

Pairwise Comparisons

Measure: MEASURE_1

(I) COMP	(J) COMP	Mean Difference (I-J)	Std. Error	Sig.[a]	95% Confidence Interval for Difference[a]	
					Lower Bound	Upper Bound
1	2	**−4.785E-03**	.207	**1.000**	−.555	.545
	3	**.943***	.281	**.006**	.193	1.692
	4	**−4.316***	.404	**.000**	−5.391	−3.241
2	1	4.785E-03	.207	1.000	−.545	.555
	3	**.947***	.214	**.000**	.377	1.518
	4	**−4.311***	.312	**.000**	−5.142	−3.480
3	1	−.943*	.281	.006	−1.692	−.193
	2	−.947*	.214	.000	−1.518	−.377
	4	**−5.258***	.305	**.000**	−6.071	−4.446
4	1	4.316*	.404	.000	3.241	5.391
	2	4.311*	.312	.000	3.480	5.142
	3	5.258*	.305	.000	4.446	6.071

Based on estimated marginal means

*. The mean difference is significant at the .05 level.

a. Adjustment for multiple comparisons: Bonferroni.

FIGURE 19.16

Pairwise comparison results

comparison was between the first two attitude scales (anxiety and confidence). This is the first result reported in Figure 19.16. The difference between these two scales is only −.00478, and the probability of this difference occurring is reported as 1.000. In other words, this difference is not statistically significant.

The other comparisons yielded larger differences, that are not likely due to chance. The greatest differences were found between the fourth scale (usefulness) and the other scales. Specifically, the mean for usefulness exceeded liking by 5.258 points. Usefulness also exceeded anxiety and confidence by 4.316 and 4.3110 points, respectively. All of these differences would occur by chance less than 5 times in 1,000 (p < .000). The other two comparisons indicate that the third scale (liking) has a significantly lower mean than anxiety and confidence.

CHAPTER SUMMARY

This chapter provided an illustration of a within-subjects ANOVA design. Each subject responded to four related computer attitude scales. Within-subjects designs are statistically powerful because a larger number of observations are gained from a small number of subjects. In this chapter, our design included 209 subjects, but each subject responded to four related computer scales, resulting in a total of 836 observations used in the statistical analysis.

Other common applications of this type of design are made when time is a factor. That is, the same subjects are asked to respond to conditions over a period of time. That is why these applications are typically referred to as repeated-measures designs. This would be the case if we asked subjects to respond to a computer attitude scale more than once. In the next chapter, we will examine a situation where different groups of subjects are asked to respond to a computer attitudes scales before and after a course using computers.

PRACTICE EXERCISES

Use the data pertaining to attitudes toward statistics to answer the following questions. The variables you need are found in the data you used in this chapter (chap19 data).

1. Use the GLM procedure to perform a within-subjects ANOVA.
   a. The within-subjects factor is defined by the four statistics attitude scales.
      (i.e., STATANX, STATCON, STATUSE, STATLIK).
      Name this factor STAT.
   b. Request a profile plot for these data.
   c. Request at least one post-hoc comparison for this analysis.

2. Examine the results from the test for sphericity.
   a. What statistic and probability are reported?
   b. Can the assumption of sphericity be maintained?
      If not, what adjustments will you make?

3. Examine the results of the F-test for the within-subjects effect.
   a. Summarize these results below.
                    df   MS   F   Probability
      STAT
      Error term
   b. Can the null hypothesis be rejected?

4. Examine the profile plot. Based on this plot, what would you conclude regarding students' attitudes toward statistics?

5. Examine the results from the post-hoc pairwise comparisons.
   a. Which post-hoc test(s) did you select? Why?
   b. What can be concluded about the differences between measures of attitudes toward statistics?

20 | Mixed-Model ANOVA

Until now, you have used a variety of statistical procedures to make comparisons both between and within groups of subjects. You used an independent-samples t-test, one-way ANOVA, and factorial ANOVA to make comparisons between independent groups, and a paired t-test and within-subjects ANOVA to make comparisons within groups. In this chapter, you will use a statistical procedure to make comparisons between groups *and* within groups. This procedure is referred to as a *mixed-model ANOVA* because it includes both between-group and within-group comparisons. That is, the analysis includes at least one between-subjects factor and at least one within-subjects factor.

Mixed-model ANOVAs are also referred to as split-plot designs. Imagine having a plot of land in your back yard on which you've planted tomatoes. Divide this area into two smaller plots. On each plot, you record the conditions of the tomato plants (dependent variable). Next, you treat one plot with some type of fertilizer. After a period of time, record the tomato plant conditions again. After you have gathered all the data, you will be able to make comparisons between each plot to examine the effectiveness of the fertilizer, and within each plot to determine if any changes have occurred over time.

The above example is also referred to as a pretest-posttest experimental design. In this design, a pretest and posttest are used before and after treatment to determine the extent to which the treatment had an influence on subjects' performance over time. In some cases, an additional follow-up may be used after a period of time to determine the extent to which the treatment has continued to have an impact. A mixed-model analysis also includes comparisons between different treatment groups. In the above example, there are only two groups, one receiving treatment and the other serving as a control group. This design can easily be expanded to more than two groups.

Determining that there is a difference between the pretest and the posttest is useful in that this difference demonstrates that a change has occurred over time. In addition, determining that there is some overall difference between treatment and control groups is helpful. However, the interaction between the within-subjects factor and the between-subjects factor is most useful in that it will allow you to determine whether subjects' change from pretest to posttest was dependent upon membership in a particular treatment group. In other words, did one treatment group change more than the other? In most cases, you would hope that at least one group changed more (or less) than others because of the different treatment(s) received.

In this chapter, we will use SPSS to illustrate a mixed model ANOVA design. Specifically, we will examine the extent to which four different groups of subjects responded to computer attitude scales before beginning and after completing a computer-based statistics course. Before we begin, let's examine the variables we will use in this chapter.

VARIABLES USED IN THIS CHAPTER

Since our original data did not provide appropriate opportunities for a mixed-model ANOVA, we created data to illustrate a mixed ANOVA design. These data are similar to those you used in previous chapters, in that they pertain to attitudes toward computers and statistics.

For this analysis, the dependent variable will be computer attitudes. However, computer anxiety was measured twice, once prior to the start of the course and once following the completion of the course. Therefore, the within-subjects factor is time (i.e., pretest and posttest).

In addition, this mixed design includes a between-subjects factor. Each subject belongs to one of four different groups. These four groups used different types of computer operating systems to run SPSS statistical procedures. In the first group, no computers were used by students. SPSS was demonstrated by the instructor and output was discussed in class. This group will act as the control group. The second group used the mainframe version of SPSS to perform all statistical procedures. In the third group, SPSS/PC+ was used. Finally, students in the fourth group used a Windows-based version of SPSS. The statistical procedures performed and discussed were the same for each group.

Using SPSS for Mixed-Model ANOVA Designs

Activate SPSS and retrieve the file **chap20 data**. As with the within-subjects ANOVA you performed in the previous chapter, you will be using the GLM procedure.

GLM Mixed-model ANOVA

The menu selections you will make to perform a mixed model ANOVA are similar to those you used in the previous chapter to perform a within-subjects ANOVA. The only difference is that we will specify more conditions for the mixed model design, as it also includes a between-subjects variable. Beginning from the **Analyze** menu, select the **General Linear Model** and **Repeated Measures...** options, as you did in the previous chapter (see Figure 20.1).

These menu selections open the Repeated Measures Define Factor(s) dialog box. Use this dialog box to define the within-subjects factor. By default, SPSS will label the repeated measures factor as "factor1." For our mixed model ANOVA, the within-subjects factor is time, so give the factor a name such as "TIME." The next box prompts you for the Number of Levels of this factor. Attitudes were measured twice, so type "2" in the Number of Levels box. Using your mouse, click on the **Add** button so that this within-subjects variable is added to the analysis. Your dialog box should specify the conditions illustrated in Figure 20.2.

Next, you need to define the variables that correspond to each level of the within-subjects variables, so click your mouse on the **Define** button. This will open the Repeated Measures dialog box. Notice that the TIME label you gave the within-subject factor in the previous window now appears in this dialog box above the **Within-Subjects Variables** box. In this box, two levels are listed and ready for you to define. We will use the pre and post computer attitude scales as these levels.

In this illustration, computer anxiety will serve as the dependent variable. Computer anxiety was measured before the course and after the course. These measures are recorded in the data set as COMPANX1 and COMPANX2. Select them from the source variable list and match them to the two levels of the within-subjects factor (TIME). It is important that COMPANX1 be matched to the first level and COMPANX2 matched to the second. These two variables represent the pre- and post-course anxiety scales, which define the within-subjects variable, TIME.

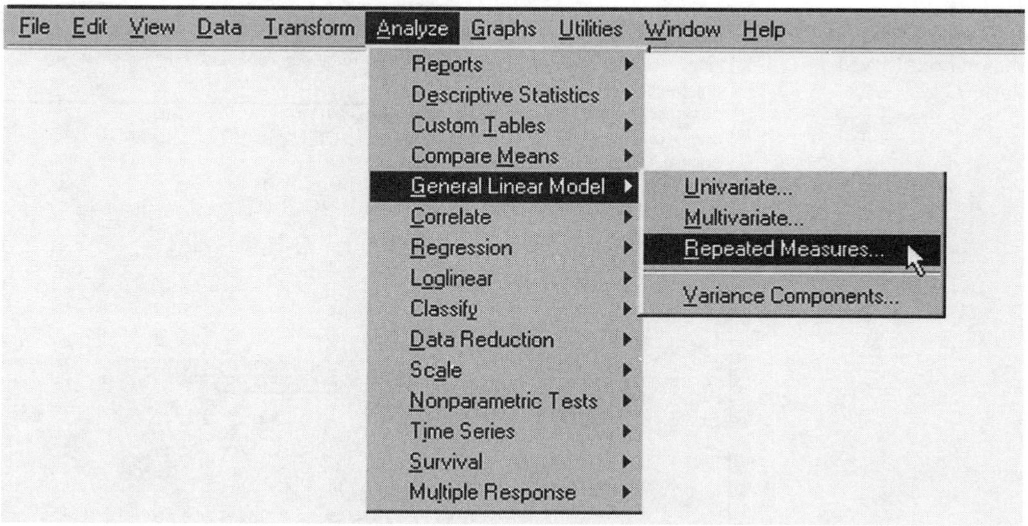

FIGURE 20.1
Analyze–GLM–Repeated
Measures menus

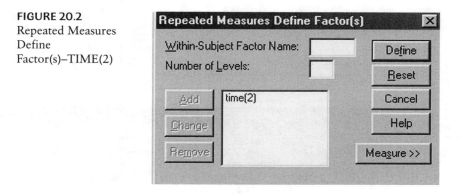

FIGURE 20.2
Repeated Measures
Define
Factor(s)–TIME(2)

The next thing to do is define the between-subjects variable. For this illustration, the between-subjects variable is identified as GROUP. This variable has four levels, each representing a different group of students that used a different version of SPSS. Select GROUP from the source variable list and place it in the box labeled Between-Subjects Factors. You have now defined the within- and between-subjects variables for the mixed design. The Repeated Measures dialog box should look like that displayed in Figure 20.3.

Specifying the Model

The first button, labeled **Model...**, is used to specify the method by which we want to model the effects of the variables (factors) included in our design. Click on this button to open the Repeated Measures: Model dialog box (see Figure 20.4).

The default options are displayed in this dialog box. A full-factorial model is specified and will include all main effects, interactions, and covariate effects. As in the previous chapter, this default option will be appropriate. Our model will yield two main effects (GROUP, TIME) and one interaction effect (GROUP X TIME). The final piece of information found in this dialog box pertains to the sums of squares. By default, Type III sums of squares are specified. This option is appropriate for this analysis.

Contrasts

Click on the **Contrasts...** button to open the Repeated Measures: Contrasts dialog box. By default, no contrasts are specified. We did not perform any contrasts in the previous

FIGURE 20.3
Repeated Measures
dialog box–Mixed
design

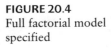

FIGURE 20.4
Full factorial model
specified

chapter when we were examining a within-subjects design. We will explore some contrasts in this chapter.

Contrasts can be used to test specific differences between levels of the within-subjects factor(s) or between-subjects factor(s). Because there are only two levels of the within-subjects variable, only one comparison is possible. Therefore, let's explore the use of contrasts with the between-subjects variable.

FIGURE 20.5
Simple contrasts (each group compared with control group)

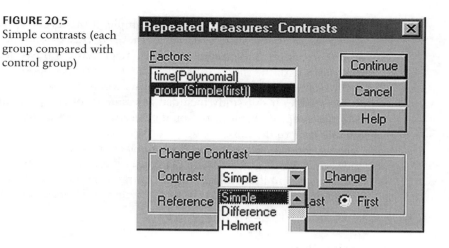

The between-subjects variable, GROUP, has four levels. The first level serves as a control group (i.e., the group did *NOT* get hands-on experience with SPSS). The remaining three groups all used a different version of SPSS to perform statistical procedures. One way to determine the extent to which using SPSS results in significantly different levels of computer anxiety would be to compare each of the three SPSS groups with the control group. This would require three simple comparisons.

To specify these comparisons, you should first highlight the GROUP variable in the Factors box. Next, you need to change the contrast type. Examine the options available using the **Co**ntrast: menu. Select the **Simple** option. Simple contrasts are used to make comparisons between one level and each of the remaining levels, and are particularly useful for models that have a control group. By default, the control group (or reference group) is identified as the last group. In our case, the control group is the first group, so change the Reference Category to First. Finally, click the **Change** button to implement these changes. Since there are only two levels of the within-subjects variable (TIME), change the contrast setting to None. Again, use the **Change** button to implement these changes.

The changes you have made will be recorded in the Repeated Measures: Contrasts dialog box, as displayed in Figure 20.5. The contrasts for GROUP are identified in parentheses as (Simple [First]), which instructs SPSS to perform simple contrasts using the first group as the reference category. Before you continue, let's examine the other contrast options.

Available Contrasts

The contrast options, found in the Contrasts menu, include None, Deviation, Simple, Difference, Helmert, Repeated, and Polynomial. As you would expect, the option None will result in no contrasts. You have specified that simple contrasts should be used to compare the first group (i.e., control group) with each of the remaining groups. There are, however, other types of contrasts that could be used.

Deviation contrasts are used to compare group means with the overall grand mean. Each group, except the reference group, is used to make these comparisons. Difference and Helmert contrasts are used to compare group means to all previous or subsequent groups. Specifically, difference contrasts compare the mean of each level to the mean of all previous levels. The first group mean is not included because there are no previous levels. On the other hand, Helmert contrasts are used to compare the mean of each group to the mean of all subsequent groups. The last group is not contrasted since there are no subsequent groups. Difference and Helmert contrasts are useful when there are increasing or decreasing levels to be compared. For example, if the levels represented increasing or decreasing levels of computer experience, these contrasts would be useful.

Another option is Repeated contrasts. Repeated contrasts are used to compare each group mean with the mean of its subsequent group (as opposed to *all* subsequent groups, as with Helmert contrasts). These contrasts would be useful in compairing levels of a repeated variable. If our study included assessments of computer anxiety over several periods of time, repeated contrasts would be useful to assess increases (or decreases in anxiety) from one time to the next.

Finally, there is an option for Polynomial contrasts. These contrasts are used to estimate trends across levels and are particularly useful for assessing trends in continuous variables.

For our current illustration, simple contrasts are most appropriate. Check to be sure the correct contrasts are specified. When everything is in order, use the **Continue** button to return to the main dialog box.

Profile Plots

Click on the **Plots...** button to explore the options that are available. In the previous chapter, you generated a plot of the four computer attitude means so that you could examine a profile of students' attitudes over the four scales. Profile plots are much more useful in examining interaction effects. In the current design, we are interested in the extent to which computer anxiety changed over time, and whether such changes depended upon the type of SPSS instruction the students received. A profile plot will help you determine if such a TIME × GROUP interaction exists.

Select TIME from the source variable list at the left and place it in the **Horizontal Axis:** box. Select GROUP and place it in the **Separate Lines:** box. Next, click the **Add** button. This will result in a plot of pre- and post-anxiety means for each group. If an interaction is present, the lines used to plot each group's means will not be parallel.

The options you have specified for your profile plots are displayed in Figure 20.6. Check to be sure these options are correct, then return to the Repeated Measures dialog box by clicking on the **Continue** button.

FIGURE 20.6
Profile plots
(TIME by GROUP
interaction)

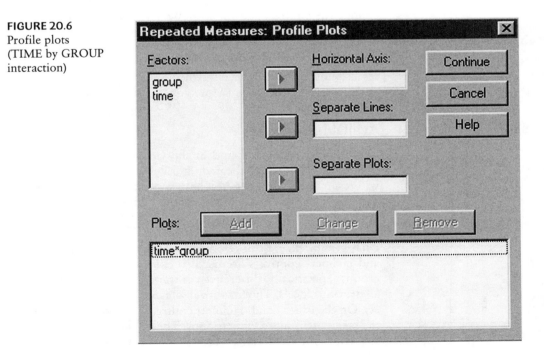

Post-Hoc Multiple Comparisons

Click on **Post Hoc...** to open the Repeated Measures: Post Hoc Multiple Comparisons dialog box. As you can see, there are several different post-hoc multiple comparison tests available. Because these tests are used to compare the observed means for levels of between-subjects variables, we were unable to use them in the previous chapter. These tests are divided into two groups. One group of tests is used when homogeneity of variance is assumed, while the others are used when this assumption is rejected. Since we created these data for this illustration, let's assume that the variances are equal.

Our current illustration involves four groups of equal-size. This is good, as equal cell sizes are recommended for most post-hoc tests. Two such tests that are commonly used are Bonferroni's and Tukey's tests. Both of these tests adjust the significance level in order to control for Type 1 error when multiple comparisons are being made. You used these tests previously when you performed one-way ANOVA. A third test, Sidak's t-test, also guards against the inflation of Type 1 error. Select these three post-hoc tests.

There are two tests that use a step-down approach in making multiple comparisons. These are the R-E-G-W-F (based on the F-test) and R-E-G-W-Q (based on the studentized range). These tests begin with a test of all group means. If all means are not equal, tests are performed to find differences among subsets of group means.

A special test, used to compare the means of treatment groups to the mean of a control group, is called Dunnett's test. This test will work well for our situation. You can identify the control group as the first or last group. You can also perform one- or two-tailed tests. Select Dunnett's test and use the control category menu to select the first group as the control group. Accept the setting for two-tail (2-sided) tests.

At this point, you have selected a few post-hoc tests, including Bonferroni's, Tukey's, Sidak's t-test, and Dunnett's test. Check your dialog box to be sure these tests are selected. Pay special attention to the settings for Dunnett's test. The control category should be set to First, and 2-sided test should be specified.

These selections are displayed in Figure 20.7. When these settings are correct, return to the Repeated Measures dialog box using the **Continue** button.

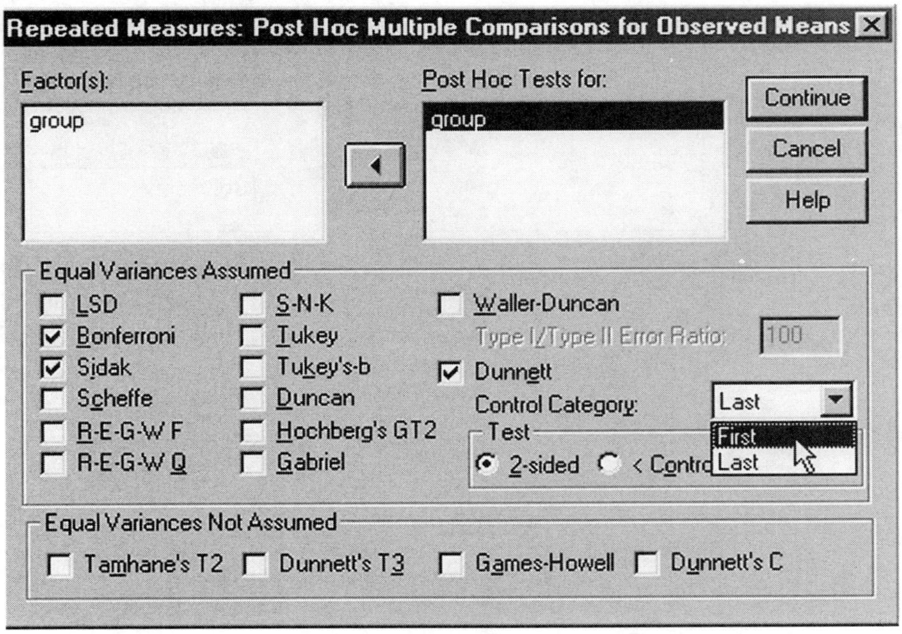

FIGURE 20.7
Post Hoc Multiple
Comparisons
(GROUP)

Saving New Variables

You explored these options in the previous chapter. We will not be saving any new variables in the current analysis. We will examine these options in more detail when we discuss regression analysis. Return to the Repeated Measures dialog box using the **Continue** button.

Options

To open the Repeated Measures: Options dialog box, click on the **Options...** button (see Figure 20.8). Our current analysis includes only one within-subjects variable, TIME and one between-subjects variable, GROUP. Select these variables and place them in the box labeled **Display Means for:,** and select the option to **Compare main effects.** This information will be useful in determining the extent to which the levels of these variables differ. To determine if differences exist between pairs of computer anxiety mean scores specify pairwise comparisons. We've selected the option for **Bonferroni's** test.

Under the Display heading, there are several options. You examined these options in the previous chapter. We've selected the first three options in order to produce means, standard deviations, effect size, and power statistics. Finally, leave the significance level set at the default value (p < .05).

Return to the Repeated Measures dialog box using the **Continue** button and you're ready to produce some more output. As with previous SPSS procedures, click the **OK** button and allow SPSS to process your data.

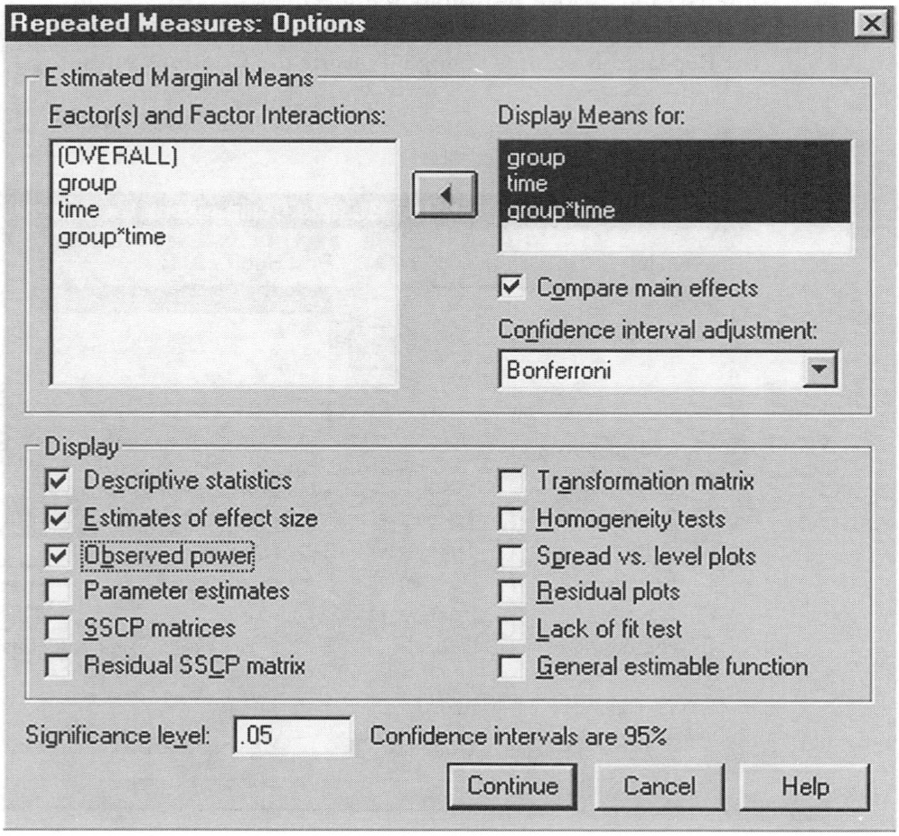

FIGURE 20.8
Repeated Measures:
Options

INTERPRETING SPSS GLM REPEATED MEASURES RESULTS

As in the previous chapter, there is a great deal of output to examine from the Repeated Measures procedure, including descriptive information tests of the assumptions significance tests (i.e., F-tests), post-hoc pairwise comparisons, and a profile of means. Again, we've extracted the most pertinent sections to interpret.

The first section of output provides descriptive information regarding the within- and between-subjects factors, as displayed in Figure 20.9.

First, this output defines the levels of the within- and between-subjects variables. COMPANX1 and COMPANX2 define the two levels of TIME, the within-subjects factor. The between-subjects factor, GROUP, has four levels with ten subjects in each level. The next table displays a descriptive summary (means and standard deviations) of

FIGURE 20.9
Descriptive output from GLM mixed model

Within-Subjects Factors

Measure: MEASURE_1

TIME	Dependent Variable
1	COMPANX1
2	COMPANX2

Between-Subjects Factors

		Value Label	N
GROUP	1.00		10
	2.00		10
	3.00		10
	4.00		10

Descriptive Statistics

	GROUP	Mean	Std. Deviation	N
COMPANX1	1.00	30.5000	2.0138	10
	2.00	31.7000	2.2632	10
	3.00	30.5000	2.1213	10
	4.00	31.3000	2.4060	10
	Total	31.0000	2.1839	40
COMPANX2	1.00	30.3000	1.9465	10
	2.00	30.0000	1.8257	10
	3.00	32.0000	1.8856	10
	4.00	33.4000	1.8379	10
	Total	31.4250	2.2746	40

Tests of Between-Subjects Effects

Measure: MEASURE_1
Transformed Variable: Average

Source	Type III Sum of Squares	df	Mean Square	F	Sig.	Eta Squared	Noncent. Parameter	Observed Power[a]
Intercept	7937.612	1	7937.612	1261.305	.000	.997	1261.305	1.000
GROUP	41.738	3	13.913	2.010	.130	.143	6.031	.473
Error	249.150	36	6.921					

a. Computed using alpha = .05

Tests of Within-Subjects Effects

Measure: MEASURE_1
Transformed Variable: Average

Source	Type III Sum of Squares	df	Mean Square	F	Sig.	Eta Squared	Noncent. Parameter	Observed Power[a]
TIME	3.613	1	3.613	2.475	.124	.064	2.475	.334
TIME* GROUP	44.337	3	14.779	10.125	.000	.458	30.374	.996
Error(TIME)	52.550	36	1.460					

a. Computed using alpha = .05

FIGURE 20.10
Between- and within-subjects effects

each group for each time. These means are similar for COMPANX1, ranging from 30.5 to 31.7. For COMPANX2, however, these means are more varied, ranging from 30.0 to 33.4. The standard deviations of COMPANX1 and COMPANX2 are similar for the four groups.

Figure 20.10 displays the results from the significance tests for the within- and between-subjects variables. Your output will also contain a test for sphericity. In this case, this test is not necessary, as there are only two levels of the within-subjects variable (two mean scores; one covariate). Let's examine the results of the analysis.

First, look at the results for between-subjects effects for the GROUP variable. These results fail to reveal a statistically significant difference (F = 2.010, p = .130). In other words, average anxiety does not vary significantly among these four groups. As the main effect for group is not significant, post-hoc tests are not necessary. Had there been a statistically significant difference among these four groups, you would have interpreted the post-hoc comparisons just as you have done previously.

Next, examine the within-subjects effects. The change in anxiety over time is not statistically significant. As is indicated by the results of the F-test for the TIME variable (F = 2.475, p = .124). Any changes over time for the overall sample are most likely due to chance. However, examine the results for the interaction effect (TIME by GROUP) in the within-subjects effects table. This effect is statistically significant (F = 10.125, p < .001). In other words, changes in computer anxiety depend on the group to which a student belongs. A good way to explore this interaction effect is with a profile plot.

FIGURE 20.11
Profile plot (TIME by GROUP interaction)

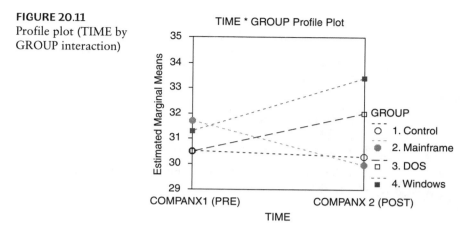

The profile plot for the TIME by GROUP interaction is displayed in Figure 20.11. Examining this plot, you will find that two group means decreased, while the other two increased. The lines for each group will appear on your screen in a different color (as long as you have a color monitor). However, unless you have a color printer, it will be difficult to tell which group is which. We have, therefore, changed the line and marker styles and labels for illustration purposes. You did this in Chapter 17 with the profile plots from factorial ANOVA.

Groups 1 and 2 (control, mainframe) experienced a decrease in their computer anxiety means, indicating greater anxiety, or less comfort with computers. If you examine the means summarized in Figure 20.9, you will see that the decrease was greater for the group receiving SPSS instruction using the mainframe version. The other two groups increased their mean anxiety score, indicating more comfort with computers. The greatest increase was for the fourth group, which used the Windows-based version of SPSS. Further analysis of the pre- and post-anxiety means within each group would be necessary to determine whether these differences are statistically significant.

CHAPTER SUMMARY

In this chapter, you explored a mixed model ANOVA design. These models are common in that there is often more than one group of subjects involved in a study, and they are often assessed on the dependent variables at more than one time. As with earlier within-subjects designs, mixed model designs are powerful because a larger number of observations are gained from a smaller number of subjects.

In the next section of this book, we will explore regression analysis. In the past few chapters, you have used the general linear model (GLM) to produce ANOVA results and have had options to create new variables based on how well the independent variables can be used to predict scores on the dependent variable. In the next few chapters, we will make these predictions using regression analysis.

PRACTICE EXERCISES

Use the data set you created in Chapter 3 (i.e., student admission data).

1. Using the GLM procedure in SPSS, perform a mixed ANOVA.
   a. The within-subjects factor is defined by the two faculty ratings (RATING1 and RATING2).
   b. The between-subjects variable is GENDER.
   c. Request a profile plot for these data (GENDER X RATING interaction).
      Use separate lines for GENDER and plot the RATING scores on the horizontal axis.

2. Examine the results of the F-test for the within-subjects effect.
   a. Summarize these results below.

	df	MS	F	Probability
GENDER				
Error term				
RATING				
GENDER X RATING				
Error term				

   b. What can you conclude based on these results?

3. Examine the profile plot. Based on this plot, what would you conclude regarding faculty ratings and gender of applicant?

SECTION VIII

Regression Analysis

21 | Bivariate Regression

In Chapters 12, 13, and 14, you have examined methods for describing relationships between variables. Recall that the Pearson product moment correlation coefficient was used to examine relationships between variables that were continuous, that is, measured on an interval or ratio level. In this chapter, you will once again use the Pearson coefficient to examine relationships. We will begin with something you have already examined, a bivariate correlation, and extends its use through regression analysis.

Regression analysis is used to explain and make predictions about a dependent variable using information provided by an independent variable or a set of independent variables. If you are using more than one independent variable, the process is referred to as multiple regression. In regression analysis, the dependent variable is called the criterion variable, while an independent variable is referred to as a predictor variable.

There are several types of regression analysis. The appropriateness of one type or another depends on the nature of the variables used and the relationship between them. The three common types of regression include linear, nonlinear, and logistic regression. We will focus on linear regression in the next three chapters.

As you might expect, linear regression is used to make predictions based on a linear relationship between the dependent and independent variables. These predictions are made using an equation to estimate a line that best fits the relationship between the dependent and independent variables. This line is called the regression line, or fit line, is determined by finding the linear equation that minimized the difference between the actual value of the dependent variable and the predicted value of the dependent variable as predicted by the independent variable. This is referred to as least-squares regression. If the independent and dependent variables correlate perfectly, then the independent variable will predict the dependent variable perfectly along a line, and there will be no error.

In linear regression, the regression line is determined using the mathematical equation for a straight line. This equation includes two important components: a slope and an intercept. The slope represents the change in the dependent variable for each one unit increase in the independent variable. The slope is represented in the equation as a coefficient or weight that is attached to the independent variable(s). This weight provides the equation with information about change in rise (or fall) in the value of the dependent variable for every unit of change in the independent variable. When standardized, larger values for the slope represent steeper slopes and therefore, a stronger relationship between the variables. The intercept represents the value of the dependent variable when the independent variable is equal to 0, or the point where the regression line crosses the Y-axis. We will examine the slope and intercept in greater detail later in the chapter.

Linear regression makes predictions about the dependent variable based on linear relationships, and nonlinear regression makes predictions based on nonlinear curvilinear relationships. A different type of equation is necessary for modeling nonlinear relationships. Using linear regression to model nonlinear relationships will often result in very poor predictions, because in such situations a curve is required to minimize the difference in actual and predicted scores.

Logistic regression is a special type of regression used when the dependent variable is categorical. For example, you might want to predict whether a student will or will not graduate from graduate school. In this case, the dependent variable is dichotomas; either a student will graduate or he/she will not. Using logistic regression, you can determine the probability that a student is a member of the graduating group based on other information you have about that student.

We will be focusing on simple linear regression in this chapter. That is, we will use only one predictor variable, and we will assume that the relationship between the dependent and independent variables is linear in the population. Other assumptions must be met in order to use linear regression. These include independence, normality, and homogeneity of variance. These assumptions should be familiar, since we made similar assumptions when using t-tests and ANOVA.

Independence refers to the condition that each observation be independent of all other observations in the sample. The second assumption, normality, refers to the requirement that the dependent variable be normally distributed in the population for all values of the independent variable. The third assumption homogeneity of variance also refers to the population distribution of the dependent variable and must be true of the dependent variable at all values of the independent variable.

Other assumptions must be made regarding error; the difference between a person's actual performance and his or her predicted performance. We realize that there will almost always be some error. That is, the value we predict for individuals will not always equal the value of their actual performance. However, the average of the errors across all subjects should be zero. We must also assume that errors in prediction from one subject to the next are not related, and that errors correlate with the independent variable. Finally, we assume that the variance of errors is homogeneous at all levels of the independent variable.

In the remaining sections of this chapter, we will explore the use of bivariate linear regression using SPSS. Before we begin, let's examine the variables we will use to illustrate these procedures.

VARIABLES USED IN THIS CHAPTER

In this chapter, you will explore the relationship between student employment hours (EMPHOURS) and the number of credits they are enrolled in during the quarter they are taking statistics (CREDNOW). Specifically, you will examine the extent to which employment hours can be used to predict the number of credits a student is enrolled in during the quarter. Therefore, EMPHOURS serves as the independent, or predictor variable, while CREDNOW is the dependent, or criterion variable.

USING SPSS TO PERFORM BIVARIATE REGRESSION

Activate SPSS and retrieve the file named **chap21 data.** As with most of the previous procedures in this book, you begin from the **Analyze** menu. From this menu, select the **Regression** and **Linear...** options, as illustrated in Figure 21.1.

These menu options will open the main Linear Regression dialog box. Figure 21.2 displays this dialog box.

The Linear Regression dialog box is similar to the boxes you navigated during previous procedures. You select variables for analysis from the source variable list at the far left of the dialog box. Selected variables are placed in either the **Dependent:** or **Independent(s):** boxes. There is room for only one dependent variable, but several independent, or predictor, variables can be used. You will use only one independent variable in this chapter, but you will have an opportunity to use several in the next chapter.

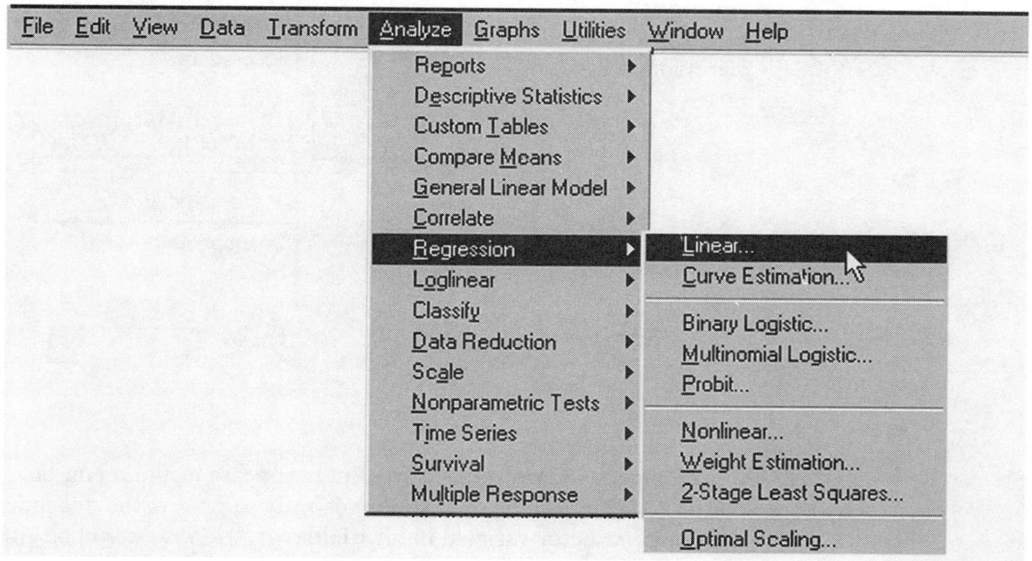

FIGURE 21.1
Analyze–Regression–
Linear menu selections

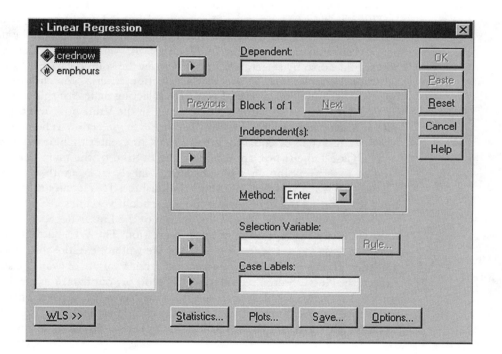

FIGURE 21.2
Linear Regression
dialog box

For our first bivariate regression, identify number of credits taken (CREDNOW) as the dependent variable and number of hours employed each week (EMPHOURS) as the independent variable. In other words, we will be predicting how many credits a students enrolls in using the number of hours he/she works as a predictor. The Linear Regression dialog box should look like that displayed in Figure 21.3.

Above the **Independent(s):** box, there is a rectangular box labeled Block 1 of 1 with a **Previous** button on the left and a **Next** button on the right. Using regression analysis, you can specify that predictor variables be entered in a specific order. Because we will be using only one predictor variable in this chapter, you will not use this feature. You will get a chance to use it in the next chapter.

Below the **Independent(s):** box is a menu used to specify the type of regression method you wish to use. This menu appears to the right of the **Method:** label. The default option is

FIGURE 21.3
Variables selected for
regression analysis

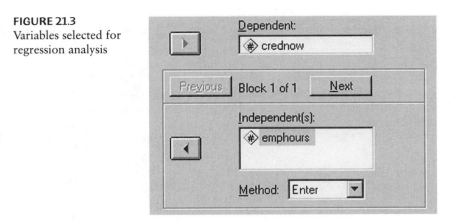

a simultaneous entry method, so Enter appears in the menu box. This means that all predictor variables will be used simultaneously to predict the dependent variable. There will be only one predictor variable in bivariate regression, so it will be entered in the first and only block. You can scroll down the menu to see what other methods are available. You will have a chance to use some of these other methods in the next chapter.

There is also an option to specify a **Selection Variable:**. For example, suppose you wanted to examine the extent to which employment hours could be used to predict number of credits taken for females. In this situation, you can use gender as a selection variable. You would do so by selecting GENDER from the source variable list and placing it in the **Selection Variable:** box. To specify the selection criteria, you click on the **Rule...** button to open the Set Rule dialog box. If you were selecting males for this analysis, you would specify GENDER as the selection variable and 1 in the Value box. You can use any type of variable as a selection variable and set the criteria for selection as being equal to, not equal to, less than, less than or equal to, greater than, or greater than or equal to a specified value.

The **Case Labels:** box appears near the bottom of the main dialog box. This option is used to identify points in a plot using the labels from another variable. You did this in Chapter 13 when you were plotting relationships. This feature is used along with other options for plotting the dependent and independent variables.

There are five pushbuttons at the bottom of the Linear Regression dialog box. These buttons will access many features of linear regression. The **WLS** button allows you to perform a weighted least-squares regression analysis. We will not explore this process in this book. The **Statistics...** button will allow you to choose from a variety of available statistics. As you might expect, the **Plots...** button is used to specify plots of your data. You use the **Save...** button if you want to save new variables that result from the regression analysis. Finally, the **Options...** button is used to specify options regarding the criteria for including predictors in the regression equation and the treatment of missing values. Let's examine these buttons in more detail.

Statistics

Click on the **Statistics...** button to open the Linear Regression: Statistics dialog box (see Figure 21.4). Readers using SPSS Version 9 will have more statistics to choose from than readers using older versions. Let's take a look at these options.

Regression Coefficients. There are three options pertaining to regression coefficients. The **Estimates** option is selected by default and provides a lot of useful information, including regression coefficients (both standardized and unstandardized), standard errors, t values, and two-tailed significance levels for each independent variable used in the regression equation. When there is more than one independent variable, additional information is provided for the independent variables not yet added to the equation. We'll discuss this information in the next chapter when we illustrate multiple regression.

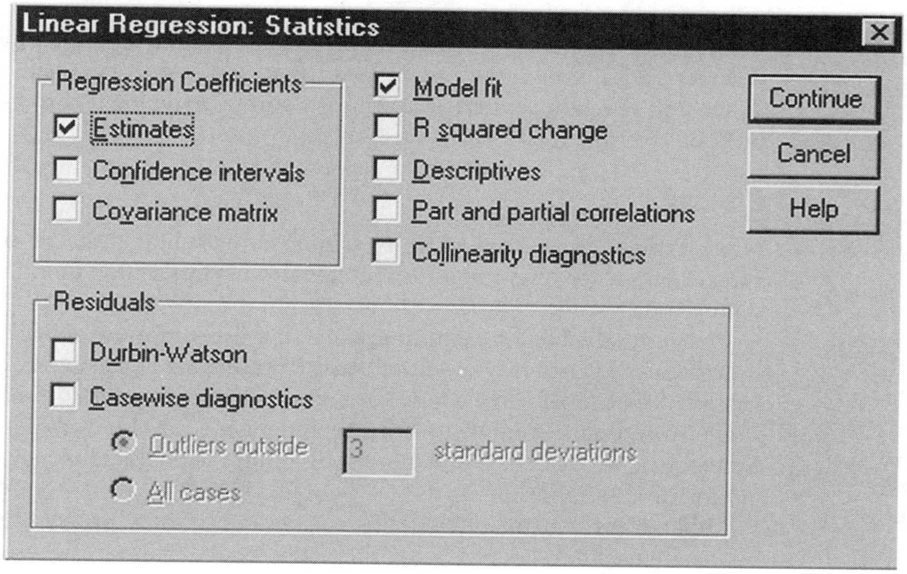

FIGURE 21.4
Linear Regression:
Statistics dialog box

The other two options available for regression coefficients are **Confidence intervals** and a **Covariance matrix.** Choosing the **Confidence intervals** option will result in a 95% confidence interval for each unstandardized regression coefficient. Select this option. The final option for regression coefficients is a **Covariance matrix.** If there is more than one independent variable, this matrix is useful in determining the extent to which the predictor variables are associated. We'll examine this option in the next chapter.

Residuals.   There are two available statistics under the Residuals heading. The **Durbin-Watson** option is useful for examining residuals, or error. This option produces a serial correlation among all the residuals, which we assumed to be zero. Select this option and we'll examine the output later.

The second option, **Casewise diagnostics,** produces information regarding the residuals (error) for each case in your sample. This can be useful for detecting outliers or those individuals with unusually high or low scores. Select this option. By default, casewise diagnostics will identify outliers that are outside 3 standard deviations from the mean of the predicted values of the dependent variable. Change this option to 2 standard deviations. You can also change this to list all cases, but the default setting suits our purposes.

Other Available Statistics.   There are five other statistics options available. The only default statistic is **Model fit.** The statistics generated from this option include the R value, R^2, adjusted R^2, standard error of estimate, and an ANOVA table. These statistics are essential to regression analysis, as we will find out when we examine the output later in the chapter. The **Descriptives** option will produce means, standard deviations, and a correlation matrix. You have generated this type of output in earlier chapters. Using this option will allow you to obtain basic descriptive statistics from within the regression procedure. Otherwise, it would be necessary to use the Descriptives and Correlations procedures in addition to Regression. Select this option as well.

The remaining three options will not be used in this illustration, but they will be useful later when we present multiple regression. These options are **R squared change**, **Part and partial correlations,** and **Collinearity diagnostics.** The R squared change option examines the increase (or decrease) in the prediction of the dependent variable when an additional independent variable is added to (or removed from) the regression equation. **Part and partial correlations** produces partial and semi-partial correlation coefficients for each independent variable. These coefficients are helpful in determining which independent variable relates most strongly with the dependent variable, when controlling for the influence of the other variables in the equation. Finally, the option for **Collinearity diagnostics** allows you to examine the extent to which the independent variables are related to each other.

Figure 21.5 shows the options box that you just completed. Check your selections. When you're ready, return to the Linear Regression dialog box by clicking on the **Continue** button.

Plots

Next, let's examine the options available regarding plots of our data. Click on the **Plots...** button to open the Linear Regression: Plots dialog box. Figure 21.6 displays this dialog box.

Plots are valuable for examining some of the assumptions of regression analysis. To specify variables for a plot, you select a pair from the list at the left of the dialog box. Let's select SRESID and ZPRED. These variables represent the studentized residual values and the standardized predicted values for the dependent variable for each person in the sample. Remember, we made a few assumptions about residuals. This plot will be useful as we examine these assumptions.

Other plots available include histograms and normal probability plots. These plots are especially useful for determining the extent to which the residuals follow a normal distribution. Check the options for **Histogram** and **Normal probability plot.**

Figure 21.7 displays our plot selections. After specifying these plots, return to the main dialog box using the **Continue** button.

Saving New Variables

To explore the options available in the Save dialog box, click on the **Save...** button at the bottom of the main dialog box. The Linear Regression: Save dialog box is displayed in Figure 21.8. As you can see, there are many variables that can be created as a result of regression analysis. These new variables pertain to predicted values, residuals, distances, influence statistics, and prediction intervals. All variables you choose will be added to your data file for each case.

Predicted Values.   Under the Predicted Values heading, there are four options. You can compute unstandardized or standardized predicted values for each case, adjusted predicted values, and a standard error of the mean prediction value. The unstandardized predicted

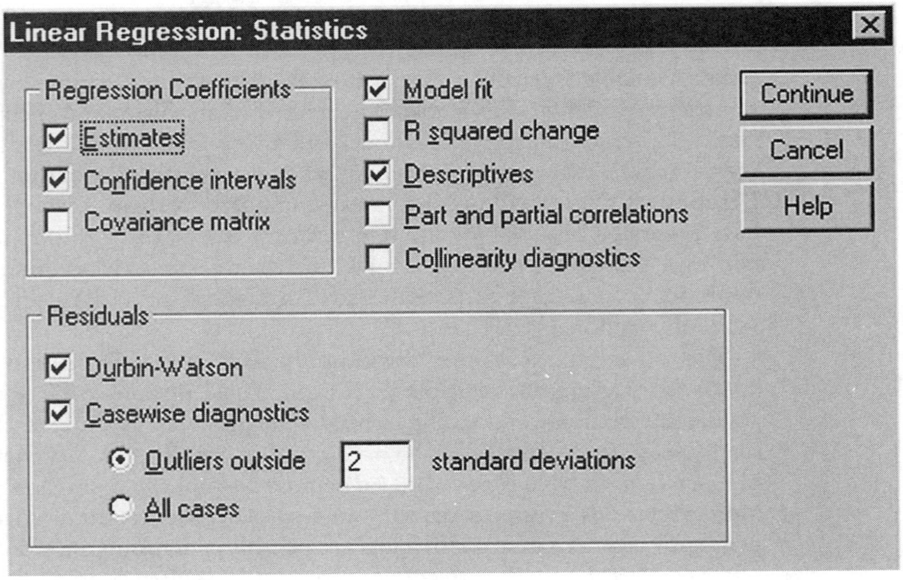

FIGURE 21.5
Statistics options
selected for bivariate
regression

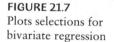

FIGURE 21.6
Linear Regression:
Plots dialog box

FIGURE 21.7
Plots selections for
bivariate regression

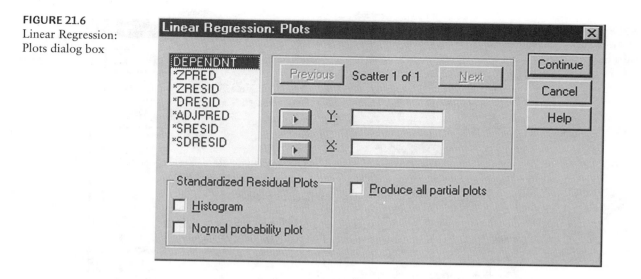

value is a direct result of regression analysis. This is the estimate of the dependent variable, given a specific score on the independent variable. Select this option. A standardized predicted value is simply a predicted values transformed into a z score.

The third option is an adjusted predicted value. This is the predicted value of a case if that case were excluded from the calculation of the regression coefficient(s). This must be done separately for each case in the sample. Can you imagine how long this would take without the assistance of the computer software. If a case is an outlier, this value will be farther from the actual predicted value. The final option allows you to compute a standard error for different values of the independent variable. Cases which are farther from the overall mean will have more error. Select both these options.

Residuals.   Next, examine the options under the Residuals heading. A residual is simply error in prediction. The bigger the residual, the greater the error. Again, you can compute both unstandardized and standardized residuals. A standardized residual is simply a z score created by dividing a residual by the overall standard error of all residuals. Select both these options. There is also an option for a studentized residual. A studentized residual is similar to a standardized residual with one exception. The standard error for each particular case is used as the divisor, rather than the standard error of all residuals. Select this option also. The final two options provide information about residuals for a case if that case were excluded

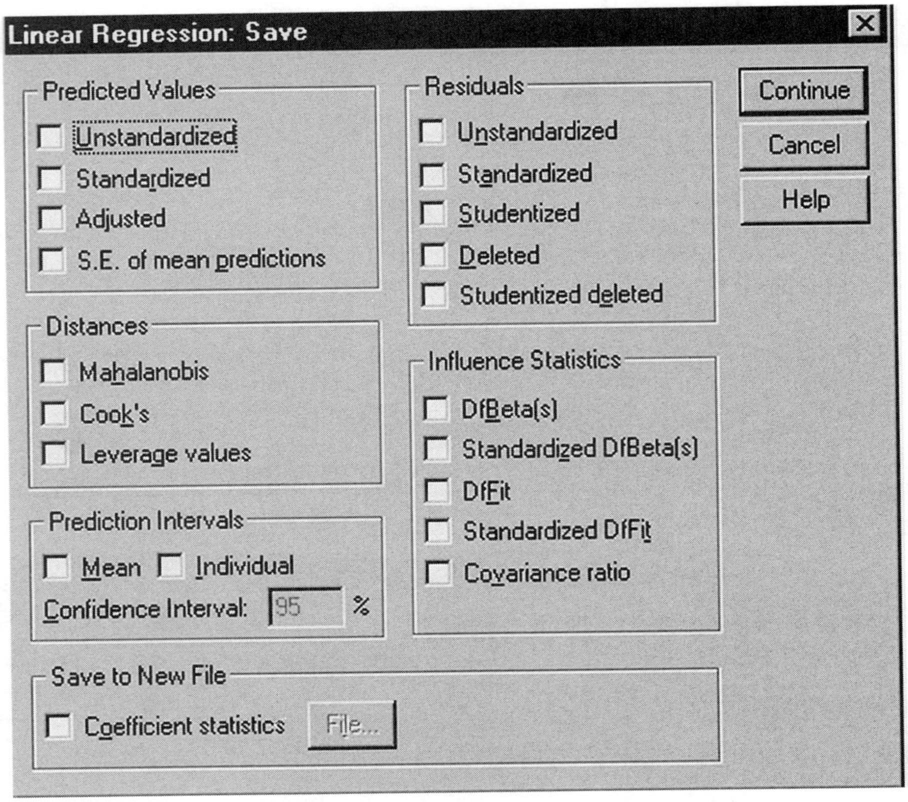

FIGURE 21.8
Linear Regression:
Save dialog box

Linear Regression: Save

Predicted Values
- ☐ Unstandardized
- ☐ Standardized
- ☐ Adjusted
- ☐ S.E. of mean predictions

Distances
- ☐ Mahalanobis
- ☐ Cook's
- ☐ Leverage values

Prediction Intervals
- ☐ Mean ☐ Individual
- Confidence Interval: [95] %

Save to New File
- ☐ Coefficient statistics [File...]

Residuals
- ☐ Unstandardized
- ☐ Standardized
- ☐ Studentized
- ☐ Deleted
- ☐ Studentized deleted

Influence Statistics
- ☐ DfBeta(s)
- ☐ Standardized DfBeta(s)
- ☐ DfFit
- ☐ Standardized DfFit
- ☐ Covariance ratio

[Continue] [Cancel] [Help]

from the regression analysis. Like the option for adjusted predicted value, this information is useful for examining the extent to which a case can be considered an outlier. The **Deleted** option produces the adjusted unstandardized residual, while the **Studentized deleted** option produces the adjusted studentized residual. Select the option for **Studentized deleted**.

Distances.   Next, let's examine the options under the Distances heading. There are three options. The first, **Mahalanobis,** is a measure of how far a case lies from the average of all cases on a particular independent variable. The second option computes **Cook's,** which indicates how much the residuals of all other cases would change if that case were excluded from the regression analysis. This is a measure of how much influence a case has on the overall regression results. The third option, **Leverage values,** is a somewhat weaker measure of the influence of a specific case, with values ranging from 0 to 1. Select the Cook's and **Leverage values** options for this analysis.

Influence Statistics.   More specific effects of a particular case can be determined using options listed under the Influence Statistics heading. The options listed in this category reveal the effects that the exclusion of a case would have on the slope and the intercept of the overall regression equation. This is done by computing new values for the slope and intercept of the regression equation based on a sample without a specific case included. Once the new parameters are computed, a new regression equation can be used to determine the extent to which predicted values have changed. The option for **DfBeta(s)** produces a new slope and intercept for the regression equation, while the **Standardized DfBeta(s)** option computes these values on a standardized scale. Select these options so we can examine these new values.

Three other options remain under the Influence Statistics heading. These include **DfFit, Standardized DfFit,** and **Covariance ratio. DfFit** provides you with the difference in the predicted value for a case were that case excluded from the regression analysis. The **Standardized**

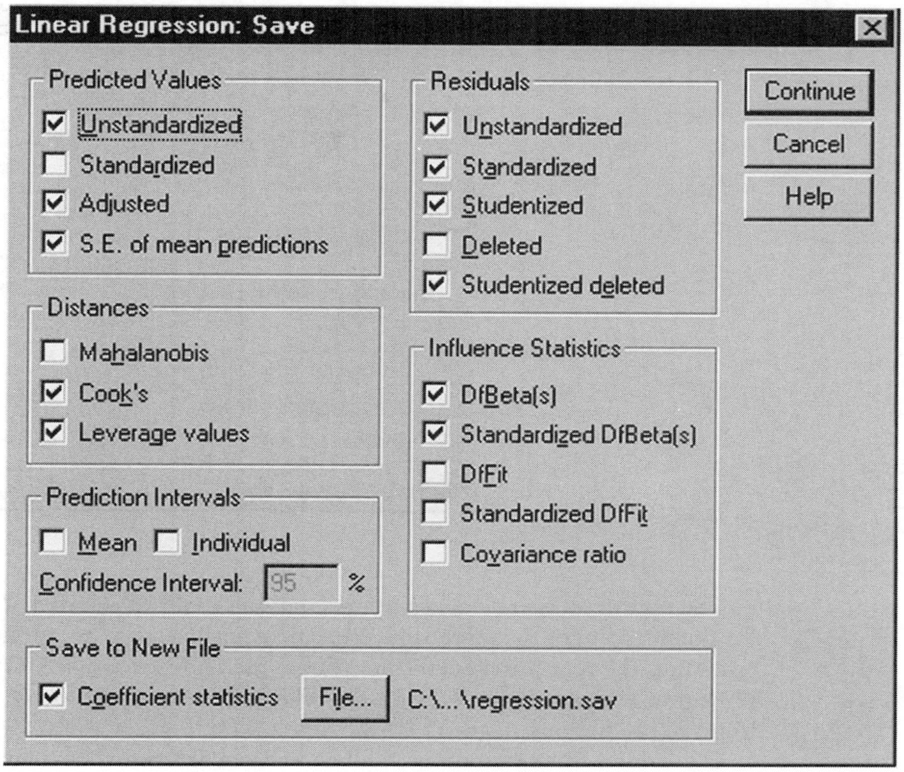

FIGURE 21.9
Options selected for
new variables

DfFit provides this same information in standardized form. Finally, the **Covariance ratio** provides information regarding the extent to which the relationships (covariances) among the variables included in the analysis would change if a particular case were excluded.

Prediction Intervals. Examine the two options under the Prediction Intervals heading. These options simply allow you to compute a confidence interval for either the mean of the actual value of the dependent variable or for all cases having a given value on the independent variable. You were able to specify the standard error of mean prediction earlier. These options will result in the lower and upper bounds of the confidence interval for each case, not just the standard error. The 95% confidence interval is the default, but you can specify any interval from 0 to 100.

Save to New File. Finally, there is an option to save regression coefficient statistics to a new file. If you wanted to examine these coefficients for each case, this would be the place to begin. We've specified that they be saved to a file identified as regression on the hard drive. If you would like to do the same, check this option and specify a name for the file.

The selections made in this session are summarized in Figure 21.9. When you're finished exploring these options, click on the **Continue** button to return to the main dialog box.

Options

Finally, let's explore the Options dialog box. Click on the **Options...** button at the bottom of the main dialog box. The Options dialog box appears in Figure 21.10. There aren't many options here that we will use in this chapter. The information labeled Stepping Method Criteria pertains to multiple regression situations. These criteria are used to guide the entry and removal of variables from the regression analysis. In the next chapter, we will have some use for these criteria.

FIGURE 21.10
Linear Regression:
Options dialog box

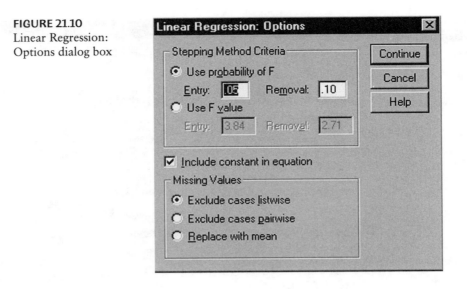

The option to Include constant in equation should be selected. This will estimate a value for the intercept of the regression line. There may be some occasions when all you are interested in is the regression coefficient (slope), perhaps for use in a structural equation model. However, you will typically want the intercept if you want to use the regression equation to make predictions.

Finally, as with previous procedures, you can determine how you want missing values to be treated. By default, cases are excluded listwise. That is, if a person has a missing value on any variable identified for the analysis, he/she will be excluded. You can change this setting to a pairwise deletion of missing cases, which was also available in most of the previous SPSS procedures. There is one more option for the treatment of missing values. This final option replaces a missing value with the mean of that variable. Using the variable mean will not impact the overall group performance and will prevent cases from being dropped from the analysis. We will use the default setting for our first illustration.

RUNNING THE REGRESSION ANALYSIS

For the first regression analysis, we will examine the extent to which the number of credits in which students are enrolled (CREDNOW) can be predicted from the number of hours of employment per week (EMPHOURS). Be sure that CREDNOW is identified as the dependent variable and EMPHOURS is selected as the independent variable (see Figure 21.3). You might also want to review the options you've selected in the Statistics, Plots, Save, and Options dialog boxes. After you're satisfied with these selections, click on the **OK** command pushbutton to perform the regression analysis.

INTERPRETING SPSS BIVARIATE REGRESSION RESULTS

Now that you have produced all this output, let's examine it in sections. The SPSS output from your regression analysis appears in several tables. We have broken the output down into different parts so that our interpretation will be easier to follow.

Descriptive Information

Figure 21.11 displays descriptive information relating to the variables in the regression analysis. This information includes means and standard deviations for each variable as well

FIGURE 21.11
SPSS linear
regression–Descriptive
information

Descriptive Statistics

	Mean	Std. Deviation	N
CREDNOW	10.47	3.63	150
EMPHOURS	25.41	14.28	150

Correlations

		CREDNOW	EMPHOURS
Pearson Correlation	CREDNOW	1.000	−.415
	EMPHOURS	−.415	1.000
Sig. (1-tailed)	CREDNOW	.	.000
	EMPHOURS	.000	.
N	CREDNOW	150	150
	EMPHOURS	150	150

as the correlation between the two variables. From this information, we can see that the average number of credits in which our sample of students is enrolled is 10.47, and the average number of hours worked each week is 25.41. The correlation between these two variables is −.415, which indicates that there is a tendency for students who work more hours to be enrolled in fewer credit hours. This is not surprising, since they would have less time to take classes.

Determining the Regression Equation

Figure 21.12 presents the information that typically results from regression analysis. This information includes the R value, R^2, standard error of estimate, ANOVA results, regression coefficients, and intercept. First, notice that the multiple R is .415. This value is reported as a positive number. The bivariate correlation value we obtained in Figure 21.11 was −.415, indicating a negative relationship. The relationship hasn't changed, as you will soon see. First, let's examine some other important information.

The R^2 value is .173. This means that the variables of CREDNOW and EMPHOURS share 17.3% of their variance in common. In other words, we can predict 17.3% of the variance in the number of credits taken by students by, knowing how many hours per week they are employed. However, the value of R^2 obtained from a sample is almost always an overestimation of what it would be in the population. Therefore, an adjusted R^2 is also reported. This value is .167. The extent to which R^2 is overestimated depends primarily on the ratio of the number of predictor variables to the size of the sample. Our ratio is 1:150, and the difference between the reported R^2 (.173) and the adjusted R^2 (.167) is very small. If we had fewer subjects, the difference would be greater.

Next, examine the information found in the ANOVA table. This table includes two sources of variation: Regression and Residual. The regression source identifies variation shared between the predictor (EMPHOURS) and the criterion (CREDNOW). The residual source represents the variation in CREDNOW that we were unable to explain with our predictor variable. The F-test is used to examine whether the amount of variance explained in the dependent variable is likely due to chance. Our reported F value is 30.877 with a significance level of .000. The amount of variance explained in CREDNOW using EMPHOURS is statistically significant.

Variables Entered/Removed[b]

Model	Variables Entered	Variables Removed	Method
1	EMPHOURS[a]	.	Enter

a. All requested variables entered.
b. Dependent Variable: CREDNOW

Model Summary[b]

Model	R	R Square	Adjusted R Square	Std. Error of the Estimate	Durbin-Watson
1	.415[a]	.173	.167	3.31	1.533

a. Predictors: (Constant), EMPHOURS
b. Dependent Variable: CREDNOW

ANOVA[b]

Model		Sum of Squares	df	Mean Square	F	Sig.
1	Regression	338.214	1	338.214	30.877	.000[a]
	Residual	1621.119	148	10.954		
	Total	1959.333	149			

a. Predictors: (Constant), EMPHOURS
b. Dependent Variable: CREDNOW

Coefficients[a]

Model		Unstandardized Coefficients		Standardized Coefficients	t	Sig.	95% Confidence Interval for B	
		B	Std. Error	Beta			Lower Bound	Upper Bound
1	(Constant)	13.147	.553		23.777	.000	12.055	14.240
	EMPHOURS	−.106	.019	−.415	−5.557	.000	−.143	−.068

a. Dependent Variable: CREDNOW

FIGURE 21.12
SPSS linear regression–Regression statistics

The next section pertaining to the regression equation is labeled Coefficients. This information is necessary to build the regression equation and make predictions. In this output, the unstandardized regression coefficient is labeled B and the standardized is labeled Beta. A standard error, 95% confidence interval, and a t-test are also reported for the unstandardized regression coefficients. Let's examine some of this information more closely.

The unstandardized regression coefficient for our predictor variable, EMPHOURS, is −.106. A negative coefficient indicates a negative relationship with the dependent variable, just as we discovered earlier. Specifically, this value represents the change in employment hours for every one credit hour increase in credits taken by students. Therefore, for every one credit increase, students are employed .106 fewer hours per week.

The 95% confidence interval is reported with a lower bound of −.143 and an upper bound of −.068. You examined confidence intervals in previous chapters when examining sample means and sample mean differences. This interval can be interpreted in the same manner. If you were to estimate the regression coefficient for EMPHOURS over and over, 95 times out of 100 it would range from −.143 to −.068. The values in this interval are all negative, which indicates a negative relationship. If this interval contained 0, you would have to conclude that the relationship in the population is not different from zero.

Next, examine the results for the t-test. This t-test is used as a test of the regression coefficient (B). Under a null hypothesis, the value of the regression coefficient is assumed to be zero. The t-test is performed to determine whether the obtained coefficient differs from zero. With a reported t value of −5.557 and a significance level of .000 (p < .001), we can safely conclude that our regression coefficient does differ from zero. Therefore, the contribution of EMPHOURS to the prediction of CREDNOW is statistically significant. This result agrees with that of the overall F-test reported earlier. Both the t test and the overall F address the question of whether EMPHOURS can be used to predict CREDNOW. In this case, squaring the result from the t-test here will result in the F ratio reported earlier. That is: $(-5.557)^2 = 30.877$.

The information reported for Constant pertains to the intercept of the regression line. A value of 13.147 is reported in the output. This is the point where the regression line crosses the Y-axis, or alternatively, the value predicted for the criterion (CREDNOW) when the predictor (EMPHOURS) is equal to 0. Using this value with the unstandardized regression coefficient (B), we can make predictions using the following equation:

$$CREDNOW = -.106(EMPHOURS) + 13.147$$

For example, if a student worked 10 hours per week, we would predict their credit hours using the following equation:

$$CREDNOW = -.106(10) + 13.147 = 12.087$$

In other words, a student who is employed 10 hours per week would be expected to be enrolled in approximately three courses, being that the typical graduate course is worth 4 credit hours. Similarly, a student who is employed 40 hours per week would be expected to be enrolled in about two graduate courses:

$$CREDNOW = -.106(40) + 13.147 = 8.907$$

These predictions, however, cannot be made without the consideration of error. If we could predict perfectly, the R value would be 1.0 and the standard error of estimate would be 0. This is rarely the case because we are rarely capable of measuring a variable without error. The standard error of estimate resulting from our analysis is 3.31 (see Model Summary table). This estimate can be used to create a confidence interval for predicted values.

You create confidence intervals using the normal distribution. The two most common confidence intervals are 68% and 95%. As long as you know the z values associated with these intervals in the normal distribution, you can construct a confidence interval. To construct the 68% confidence interval, the z values are -1 and $+1$. Remember that 68% of the cases in a normal distribution will appear between -1 and $+1$ z scores. The corresponding z values for the 95% confidence interval are -1.96 and $+1.96$. Between these two z values, 95% of the cases will be distributed.

Using a student who works 40 hours per week, we predicted an enrollment of 8.907 credits. The 68% and 95% confidence intervals for this predicted value are:

$$68\% \text{ CI} = 8.907 +/- 3.31 = 5.777 \text{ to } 12.2170$$
$$95\% \text{ CI} = 8.907 +/- (1.96)(3.31) = 2.4194 \text{ to } 15.3946$$

In other words, of all students working 40 hours per week, some could be enrolled in as few as 2.4 credit hours while others could be enrolled in as many as 15.4 credit hours. That's quite a range. As we have already noted, the smaller the standard error of estimate is, the better predictions we can make.

Examining Residuals

Next, let's examine some information regarding the residuals from this regression analysis. Information regarding individual cases appears in Figure 21.13. Remember, we asked for casewise diagnostics for those individuals with residuals that exceeded 2 standard deviations. Six cases met this criterion and are displayed in the output. Of these cases, the one with the largest residual was case number 95. This student was enrolled in just 4 credit hours, but based on our regression analysis, we predicted an enrollment of 12.73 credit hours. This residual differed from our prediction by 2.636 standard deviations. When you encounter potential outliers such as these six cases, you should examine them more closely and ask yourself if these data may be in error (i.e., miscoded, etc.).

More information regarding residuals for the entire sample of 150 students is summarized in Figure 21.14. We'll say just a few things about these statistics. The information pertaining to the predicted values and standardized predicted values simply indicates the ranges of predictions and the mean prediction. We selected the option to save unstandardized predicted values. These have been written into our data set and are available for analysis if we need them. The standard error of the predicted values can be used to provide a precise confidence interval for an individual's predicted credit hours. The adjusted predicted value is simply the predicted value for a case if that case were not included in the regression analysis. Let's examine these statistics for some individual cases. We've chosen two different cases from our sample to apply these statistics.

FIGURE 21.13
SPSS linear regression–Casewise diagnostics

Casewise Diagnostics[a]

Case Number	Std. Residual	CREDNOW	Predicted Value	Residual
7	-2.318	4	11.67	-7.67
61	-2.126	4	11.04	-7.04
95	-2.636	4	12.73	-8.73
128	2.423	18	9.98	8.02
140	-2.126	4	11.04	-7.04
180	2.473	15	6.82	8.18

[a.] Dependent Variable: CREDNOW

Return to the data editor and examine case numbers 57 and 181 (see Figure 21.15). Case number 57 was employed 25 hours per week, which is the average number of hours worked per week for our sample of students. This student had a predicted enrollment of 10.51, when he/she was actually enrolled in 14 credit hours. Note that the standard error of the mean predicted value for this case is .2703. The second student is case number 181. This student was employed 70 hours per week, which was far above the average. Based on this number of employed hours, we predicted a credit load of 5.76 hours, when the student was actually enrolled in 10 credit hours. The standard error of the mean predicted value is .8888; much higher than that reported for the student who was employed 25 hours per week. Based on these examples, we can see that the error is greater surrounding the mean credit hours for students who are employed 70 hours versus those who are employed 25 hours. Therefore, if we were to estimate population means, we would have a better estimate for those students employed 25 hours per week.

Residuals Statistics[a]

	Minimum	Maximum	Mean	Std. Deviation	N
Predicted Value	5.76	12.73	10.47	1.51	150
Std. Predicted Value	−3.123	1.499	.000	1.000	150
Standard Error of Predicted Value	.27	.89	.37	9.82E-02	150
Adjusted Predicted Value	5.43	12.92	10.47	1.52	150
Residual	−8.73	8.18	1.18E-17	3.30	150
Std. Residual	−2.636	2.473	.000	.997	150
Stud. Residual	−2.666	2.532	.000	1.004	150
Deleted Residual	−8.92	8.58	3.67E-04	3.35	150
Stud. Deleted Residual	−2.723	2.579	−.001	1.010	150
Mahal. Distance	.001	9.753	.993	1.306	150
Cook's Distance	.000	.155	.008	.016	150
Centered Leverage Value	.000	.065	.007	.009	150

[a] Dependent Variable: CREDNOW

FIGURE 21.14
SPSS linear regression–Residual statistics

FIGURE 21.15
Cases 57 and 181 from data

	crednow	emphours	pre_1	res_1	sep_1
57	14	25	10.50957	3.49043	.27034
181	10	70	5.76155	4.23845	.88882

Examining the Influence of Cases

Return to Figure 21.14 to examine a few more of the residual statistics. There are three statistics reported that describe the influence an individual case has on the fit of the regression line. Two commonly used statistics are leverage and Cook's D. Leverage values range from 0 to 1, with higher values indicating that the case has more influence on the fit of the regression line.

The average leverage value expected depends on the number of independent variables and the sample size. For our sample of 150, with one independent variable, the average leverage should be approximately .013. Our mean leverage is actually below that at .0067, which is good. A rule of thumb is to consider leverage values of twice the expected average (.026) or greater as high. We have some cases in our sample that exceed this value, as indicated by the maximum leverage of .0655. We may need to reexamine these cases. But, before we do this, let's examine the values for Cook's D.

The Cook's D statistic indicates what the change in the regression coefficients would be if a specific case was excluded from the analysis. The average Cook's D for our sample is .0077, which seems rather small. However, a maximum Cook's D of .1547 is also reported, so there may be some influential cases in the sample. You typically judge the Cook's D statistics against the remaining sample. Therefore, when examining the distribution of Cook's D statistics for entire sample, you look for gaps. To do so, you simply perform a frequency analysis of the values saved for Cook's D in your data file. The Cook's D statistic was saved as coo_1. Having done a frequency analysis, we found that three cases distanced themselves from the remainder of the sample. These three cases had values of .06869, .07899, and .15472. All other cases had values under .04. Before we discuss the leverage and Cook's D statistic further, let's discuss two other statistics we requested pertaining to the influence of a subject.

These two are the DfBeta and standardized DfBeta. Remember, the DfBeta is the amount of change which would result in the slope and intercept if a particular case were excluded from the analysis. Because the DfBeta is unstandardized, it is difficult to assess how much change is significant. Standardized DfBeta makes comparisons across different scales of measurement much easier. There is no consensus as to what constitutes a large standardized DfBeta. An absolute cutoff of 2 has been suggested, but because these values are impacted by sample size, less stringent cutoff criteria have also been suggested. One such cutoff criterion is calculated by dividing 3 by the square root of the sample size, $3/\sqrt{n}$. In our sample, this would be $3/\sqrt{150}$, or .2449. Using this criteria, we would conclude that some of the cases in our sample are influencing our results.

Let's see if we can identify the cases that have the greatest influence on our regression statistics. First, you will probably find several influential cases depending on which statistic you use. Therefore, we will use multiple influence statistics to examine our sample. These will include leverage, Cook's D and standardized DfBetas. All these statistics were saved as part of our data and can be used as variables in a variety of procedures.

Using the Select Cases procedure, we will select those cases that meet a minimum criteria according to at least one of these statistics. For leverage (lev_1), our criteria is established as .026. For Cook's D (coo_1), we will use .05. Finally, for the standardized DfBetas (sdb0_1 and sdb1_1), we will use .2449. Using the Select If procedure (see Chapter 10), select a subgroup of cases that meet the criteria on at least one of these influence statistics.

As a reminder, choose the option for **Select Cases...** from the **Data** menu. Select the second option, If condition is satisfied. Click on the **If...** button. The If statement should be written as follows: lev_1 >.026 or coo_1 > .05 or sdb0_1 > .2449 or sdb1_1 > .2449.

Using these criteria, eight cases are selected. A summary of these cases appears in Figure 21.16.

Using the information summarized in Figure 21.16, we can assess the extent to which specific cases are influencing our regression statistics. If you examine these cases individually, you will see that not all of these cases meet our criteria on all of the statistics. Only cases 180 and 181 exceed the criteria for leverage, Cook's D and standardized DfBetas. Case number 95 exceeds the influence criteria for all but the leverage statistic. Examining these cases in a scatter plot will help you visualize the influence of these cases. We have gen-

Case Summaries

	Case Number	ID	Cook's Distance	Leverage	Sdfbeta for Intercept	Sdfbeta for EMPHOURS
1	12	12	.02341	.03939	−.13434	.20009
2	90	90	.00762	.03939	.07650	−.11394
3	95	95	.07899	.01508	−.40480	.33808
4	143	143	.01833	.03939	.11878	−.17692
5	154	154	.04141	.02328	−.15591	.25520
6	158	158	.03775	.02883	−.15842	.24852
7	180	180	.15472	.03939	−.35193	.52417
8	181	181	.06869	.06546	−.25366	.35404
Total N		8	8	8	8	8

FIGURE 21.16
Case summaries of influential cases

FIGURE 21.17
Scatterplot with influential cases identified

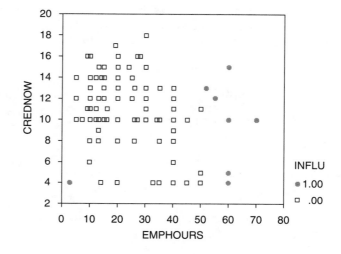

erated a scatterplot of the independent and dependent variables with these eight cases labeled. This plot appears in Figure 21.17

As you can see in this scatterplot, these cases may indeed be problematic. If we removed all of them, the scatterplot would appear profoundly different. It is possible that the relationship between employee hours and credit hours would also be quite different if we removed these cases. Cases 95, 180, and 181 may be particularly influential on the slope estimate. Case number 180 has the largest standardized DfBeta for the slope and the largest Cook's D statistic. You can see in the scatterplot that case number 180 also lies the furthest away from the remaining cases. It is almost as if this case pulls the line of best fit toward it, creating a weaker relationship. When examining cases to determine the extent to which they influence your regression statistics, it is always good practice to compute several measures of influence as well as a scatterplot.

Examining the Assumptions of Regression

Finally, let's examine some of the assumptions we made regarding regression analysis.

Linear Relationship. First, we assumed that the relationship was linear in the population. This assumption is best checked by examining a simple scatterplot between the two variables. You produced many such plots when examining relationships in Chapter 12. We've generated a simple scatterplot for the relationship between employments hours and credits taken. This plot is displayed in Figure 21.18.

Examining this plot, there does not appear to be any signs of a curvilinear relationship, so we should feel comfortable maintaining this assumption.

Residuals. Most of the assumptions we made pertained to error. For instance, we assumed that the residuals are normally distributed, they have a mean of zero and a constant variance across levels of the independent variables, they are independent across all subjects, and they are not systematically relate (correlated) to the independent variables. To check these assumptions, we can examine some of the remaining SPSS output.

Figure 21.14 summarizes the residual statistics you requested earlier in the chapter. Locate the information regarding the unstandardized residuals. This is labeled Residual in the SPSS Output. There is a range of residuals from −8.73 to +8.18. The mean of these residuals is reported as 1.18E-17 in the SPSS table. That's .0000000000000000118 (sixteen zeros). We can be satisfied that the mean of the residuals is pretty much equal to 0.

Next, locate the Durbin-Watson test statistic of 1.533. This value appeared in the Model Summary table in Figure 21.12 The Durbin-Watson test is a serial correlation among residuals. This test value will range from 0 to 4, with values close to 0 indicating a positive correlation among residuals and those close to 4 identifying a negative relationship. Values between 1.5 and 2.5 are expected. Our value of 1.533 falls in this range, so we shouldn't worry about the residuals being correlated.

FIGURE 21.18
Simple scatterplot of employment hours and credits taken

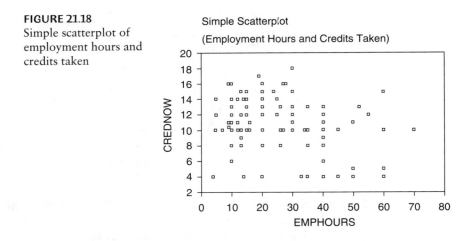

FIGURE 21.19
Histogram of standardized residuals

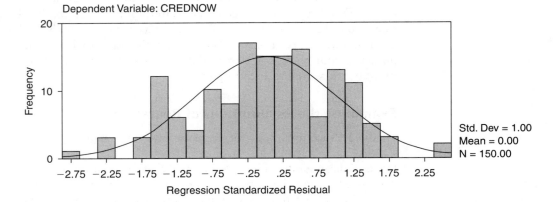

To examine the extent to which the residuals follow a normal distribution, we requested a histogram (see Figure 21.19) and a normal probability plot (Figure 21.20). These figures allow you to visually determine the extent to which the residuals are normally distributed. Figure 21.19 displays a histogram of the standardized residuals with a superimposed normal curve. Although our residuals do not adhere perfectly to a normal distribution, they do not appear to depart significantly. Figure 21.20 displays a normal probability plot for the standardized residuals. If our residuals followed a normal distribution perfectly, their cumulative probabilities would follow a straight line. Again, this is not perfect, but no significant departures appear. If you requested that the standardized residuals be saved, additional tests of normality can be computed. These include the Shapiro-Will's and K-S Lilliefors tests. These procedures are available using the Explore procedure.

To examine the distribution of residuals across levels of the independent variable, you selected a plot of the studentized residuals and the standardized predicted values (see Figure 21.21). If the variance of the residuals is constant, there will be no pattern of the points in the plot. In other words, the residuals will be randomly distributed throughout the scatterplot, as they are in Figure 21.21.

Finally, to check if the residuals are related to the independent variable, you can request a scatterplot of the residuals and the independent variable. Figure 21.22 displays the scatterplot of the residuals and the independent variable (EMPHOURS) and reports the correlation coefficient of 0. This supports the assumption that our residuals are not correlated with the independent variable (EMPHOURS).

FIGURE 21.20
Normal probability
plot

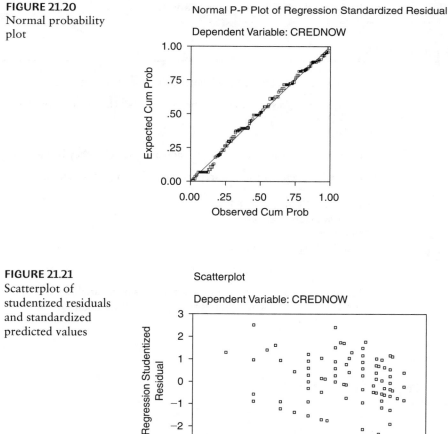

FIGURE 21.21
Scatterplot of
studentized residuals
and standardized
predicted values

FIGURE 21.22
Scatterplot of residuals
and independent
variable (r = 0)

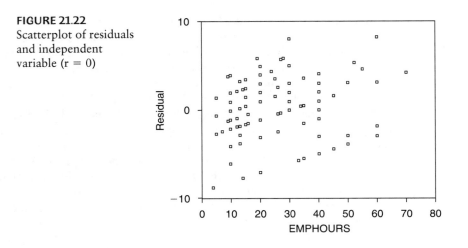

CHAPTER SUMMARY

In this chapter, you used linear regression to make predictions based on the relationship between two variables. Bivariate regression analysis is very useful in determining the extent to which an independent variable, or predictor, can be used to predict performance on a dependent, or criterion, variable. However, in most cases there will be several variables that can be used to predict scores on the dependent measure. We will explore regression with multiple predictors in the next chapter.

PRACTICE EXERCISES

Use the data set you created in Chapter 3 (i.e., student admission data).

1. Using linear regression, examine the extent to which a subject's pre-test score can be predicted using:
   a. GRE-V
   b. GRE-Q

2. Examine the assumptions of regression analysis. Can they be met for each regression?

3. For each regression analysis, report the following information:
   R^2
   F and significance of the F-test
   Regression coefficient for the independent variable
   Intercept
   Standard error of estimate

4. For each regression analysis, identify any outliers and influential cases.

5. Based on the information from question 2, which variable (GRE-V or GRE-Q) is a better predictor of the pre-test scores. Support your response using information from the regression analysis.

22 | Multiple Regression

In the previous chapter, you explored regression analysis using one independent variable. However, for most situations in education and the social sciences, there is more than one potential predictor. In this chapter, you will be working with more than one independent variable to make predictions about a dependent variable using a technique referred to as multiple regression analysis.

When making predictions with just one independent variable, it is easy to tell how much that variable contributes to the prediction of the dependent variable. You simply examine the correlation coefficient between the two variables. However, when examining more than one predictor, the influence of a specific predictor can not be determined solely by the correlation between the two variables. There are other variables to consider. It is likely that the predictor variables influence each other, and in doing so, influence the relationship between the predictor and the dependent variable. This is because when two predictor variables correlate strongly with each other, their ability to predict unique portions of the dependent variable decreases.

In this chapter, we will examine statistics that will help us to determine the influence of predictor variables in a multiple regression situation. Two such statistics are the partial and semi-partial correlation. A *partial correlation* is that portion of a bivariate correlation that remains after the influence of a third variable has been removed. It is also possible to remove the influence of more than one variable. When this is done, the resulting correlation is referred to as a higher-order partial correlation.

A *semi-partial correlation* is conceptually similar. A semi-partial correlation is that portion of the correlation between two variables that remains after the influence of a third variable has been removed from the predictor variable only. This process allows you to determine the unique influence of a predictor variable on the dependent variable, because you use only that part of the predictor variable that is not related to other predictors in assessing the predictor/criterion correlation The resulting correlation is likely to be much smaller than the original correlation because the influence of the other predictor variable(s) has been removed.

There are a variety of methods one can use to perform multiple regression. These methods pertain to the manner in which the predictor variables are entered in the analysis. In *simultaneous* analysis, you enter all of the independent variables at once into the prediction model. In *stepwise* analysis, you enter only those variables that contribute statistically to the prediction of the dependent variable. In *hierarchical* analysis, you determine the order of entry of the variables in steps determined by predictor variables supporting your decision with prior research or theory.

Before we begin working with SPSS to perform multiple regression, let's discuss sample size requirements. As you might expect, the more variables you have, the more subjects you need. With one independent variable, a single correlation is computed and used to estimate regression parameters (e.g., slope and intercept). However, when additional variables are included, more statistical calculations are required. First, correlations are computed between each independent variable and the dependent variable. Then, correlations are computed among all the independent variables. Finally, regression parameters are estimated and tests of significance (e.g., F, t) are applied. All these calculations can increase error and limit the extent to which your results will apply to the overall population. Therefore, a larger sample is recommended. As a rule of thumb, we recommend that the sample contain approximately ten subjects for each independent variable when using multiple regression. For example, when using five predictor variables, you should have a minimum sample size of 50 subjects.

VARIABLES USED IN THIS CHAPTER

In this chapter, we will continue our prediction of credit hours taken (CREDNOW) by introducing multiple predictor variables into the prediction model. These predictor variables will include age (AGE), employment hours (EMPHOURS), enrollment in night courses (NIGHT), and involvement in other activities (OTHACT).

USING SPSS FOR MULTIPLE REGRESSION

Activate SPSS and retrieve the file chap22 data. As with bivariate regression, you begin from the **Analyze** menu. From this menu, select **Regression** and **Linear...** (see Figure 22.1) to open the Linear Regression dialog box (see Figure 22.2), as you did in Chapter 21.

This is the same dialog box you used for bivariate regression. You select variables for a multiple regression analysis in the same manner as you did in the previous chapter. The dependent variable is placed in the Dependent box, while the predictor variables are placed in the Independents box. Before you select the variables for the multiple regression analysis, let's explore some features you didn't get a chance to use in the previous chapter. These features pertain to the selection of predictor variables for the analysis.

Selection of Variables for a Multiple Regression Model

If you examine Figure 22.3, you will notice that there is a rectangular box labeled Block 1 of 1, with a **Previous** button on the left and a **Next** button on the right, directly above the Independents box. Using multiple regression analysis, you often want to specify that predictor variables be entered in a specific order. To do so, you place the first predictor, or pre-

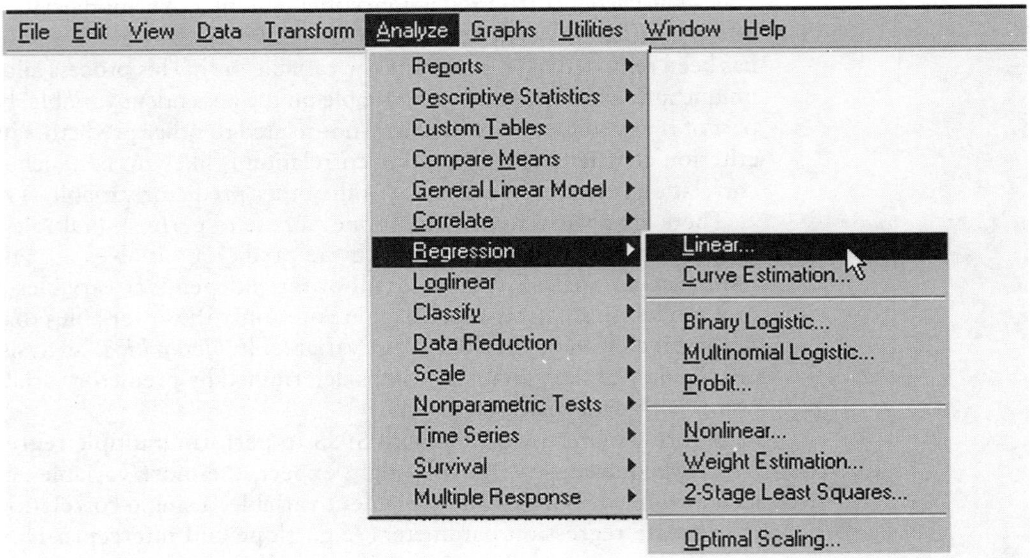

FIGURE 22.1
Analyze–Regression–
Linear menu selections

dictors, in the first block. Then select the **Next** button to identify the predictors for the second block. Continue until you've identified the predictors for each block.

Below the Independent(s) box is a menu used to specify the method used to select variables for the regression model. This menu appears to the right of the Method label. There are five options available. The default option is labeled **Enter.** Using the **Enter** method, predictor variables will be used in the manner you determine. If you place all the predictor variables in the Independents box in the first block, they will be used simultaneously to predict the dependent variable. If you place predictor variables in different blocks, they will be entered in the order you prescribed.

FIGURE 22.2
Linear Regression
dialog box

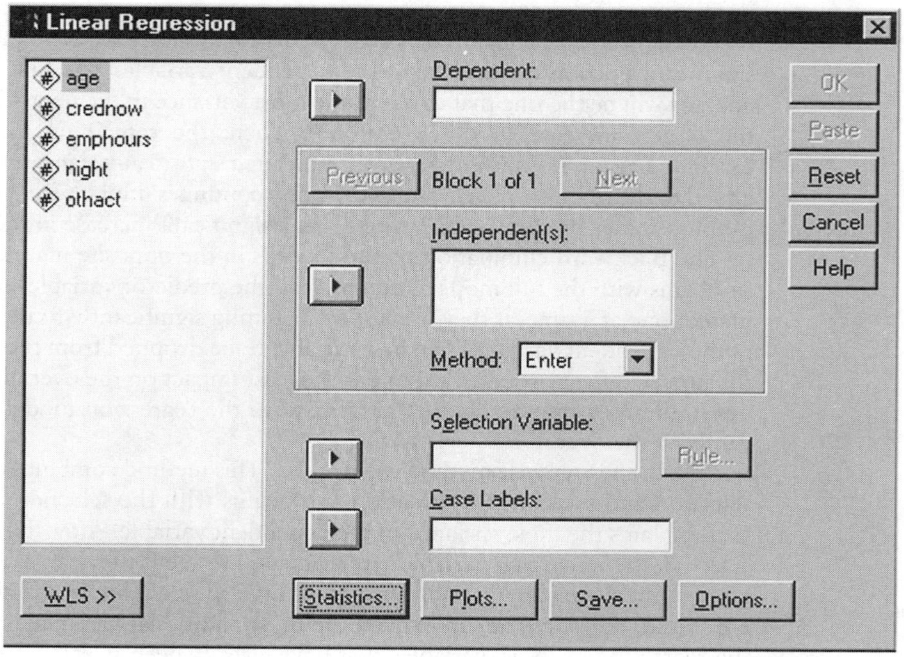

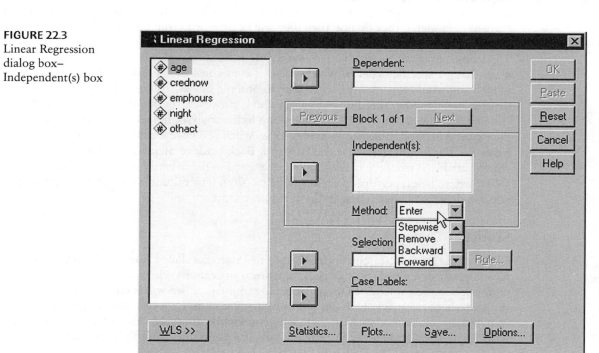

FIGURE 22.3
Linear Regression
dialog box–
Independent(s) box

The **Remove** option is used in the opposite manner as **Enter**. Using the **Remove** method, you specify that variables should be removed from the regression analysis at some point in the process. These two methods afford you a great deal of control in the selection of variables for the regression analysis.

The remaining three methods do not allow you as much control in the variable selection process. Using these methods, the selection or elimination of variables for the regression analysis is determined by the statistical qualities of the variables. Specifically, variables that explain statistically significant portions of variation in the dependent variables are selected for the regression.

The **Forward** selection method begins with a null model, for which it is assumed that the predictor variables do not explain any variance in the dependent variable. In other words, the R^2 is assumed to be equal to 0. All the predictor variables are examined to see if any explain a significant portion of variance in the dependent variable. The first variable selected for the analysis will be the one that explains the most variance in the dependent variable, resulting in the largest increase in the overall R^2. Then, the remaining independent variables are examined again. If a second variable results in a statistically significant increase in the R^2, it is added to the regression analysis. The process continues until it reaches a point at which the addition of other predictors fails to result in a significant increase in the overall R^2.

The **Backward** elimination method works in the opposite manner. The regression analysis begins with the full model containing all the predictor variables. Predictors are then eliminated, one at a time, if they are *not* contributing significantly to the explanation of variance in the dependent variable. The first variable to be dropped from the regression model will be the non significant predictor that has the least impact on the overall R^2. This process continues until all of the predictors that remain in the regression model are contributing significantly to the overall R^2.

Finally, the **Stepwise** method can be used. This method combines the properties of forward selection and backward elimination and begins with the selection of the predictor variable that explains the most variance in the dependent variable. After the first predictor variable is selected, the remaining variables are evaluated to see if they can explain any additional variation in the dependent variable, just as in forward selection. In addition significant predictors are found, the one that can explain the most additional variance is selected. At each step in the regression analysis, variables that have already been selected are also examined to see if they continue to contribute significantly to the overall R^2. If they do, they will remain in the regression model. If they do not, then they will be dropped, from the analysis as per the elimination method.

A combination of the five variable selection methods can also be used. For example, you might have a specific order in which you'd like to consider the predictors for a regression model. You would organize these variables in ordered blocks. To enter them sequentially into the regression model, you use the **Enter** method. However, you might also want to remove a variable, or a block of variables, at some point in the analysis. In this case, you would also use the **Remove** method. Another possibility exists when you have identified several variables in a particular block. You might use the **Forward, Backward,** or **Stepwise** methods to determine which variable(s) from the block should be retained in the overall regression model.

Before we begin performing multiple regression, let's examine a few other features that you didn't get a chance to use in the previous chapter.

Statistics Dialog Box

Click on the **Statistics...** button to explore the Statistics dialog box (see Figure 22.4). You have already examined most of these statistical operations when you performed bivariate regression in the previous chapter. To avoid redundancy, we will focus our efforts of those statistics that are especially useful in multiple regression. However, some options you used in bivariate regression, such as estimates, confidence intervals, descriptive statistics, casewise diagnostics, and model fit statistics will also be useful in multiple regression.

FIGURE 22.4
Linear Regression:
Statistics dialog box

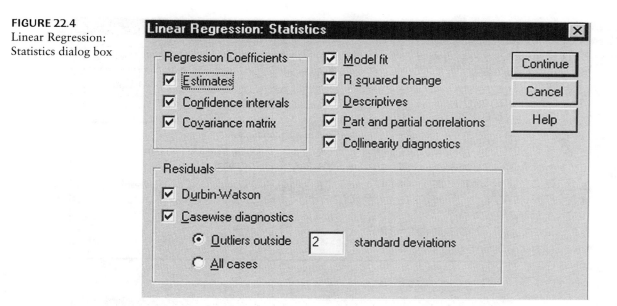

When examining multiple regression results, we will find several new statistical options useful. First, a **Covariance matrix** is appropriate because we now have more than one predictor variable, and these variables are likely to be related to each other. The correlation matrix displayed from the descriptives option will also be useful in examining the extent to which the predictor variables are related to each other. The option for **Collinearity diagnostics** examines the extent to which the predictor variables are correlated. Remember, the goal in regression is to explain variance in the dependent variable. If two or more predictors share too much in common, they will not be able to explain unique parts of the dependent variable.

When using multiple regression, several steps might be necessary as predictors are selected and/or eliminated from the regression model. Therefore, SPSS displays a summary of the variables that were added and/or deleted from the model at each step. Two additional options are extremely useful in multiple regression. These are **R squared change** and **Part and partial correlations**. At each step in the regression process, variables are examined in terms of their impact on the R^2. The **R squared change** computes the value of the change in R^2 as well as a significance test to determine whether the amount of the change is statistically significant. The **Part and partial correlations** option computes both partial and semipartial correlations for each predictor variable. Recall that these correlational procedures are used to examine the relationship of given predictor variables with the dependent variable, having controlled for the influence of other predictors. In prior versions of SPSS (Version 6.X), you had to specify options for **R squared change** and **Part and partial correlations** in the syntax. Recent versions automatically calculate it for you.

In this session, you should select all the options available in the Statistics dialog box. We will have a chance to examine the results from these selections at the end of the chapter.

Plots Dialog Box

Click on the **Plots...** button to open the Linear Regression: Plots dialog box. This dialog box appears in Figure 22.5. You examined plots options extensively in the previous chapter when working with a bivariate regression model. Specifically, you selected a histogram, normal probability plot, and a scatterplot. These same plots are useful in multiple regression to examine outliers and the assumptions made about residuals. Request the same options you did when performing bivariate regression. However, we will not be discussing this output.

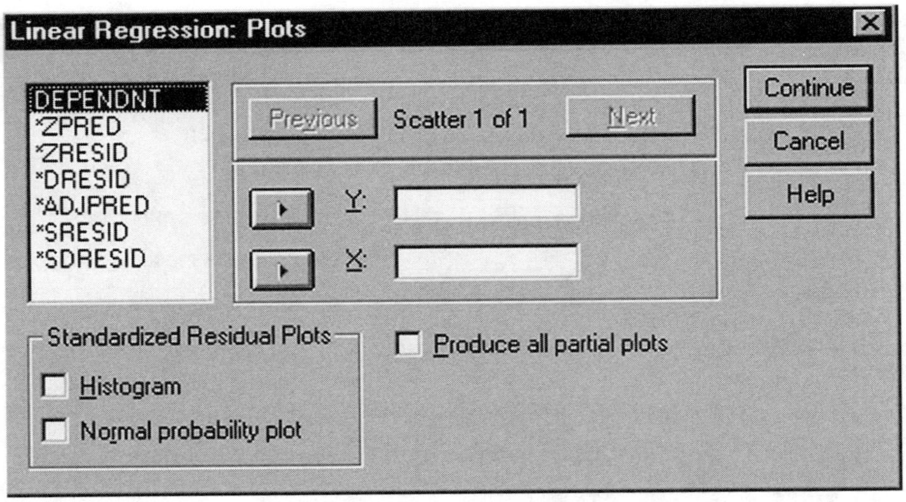

FIGURE 22.5
Linear Regression: Plots
dialog box

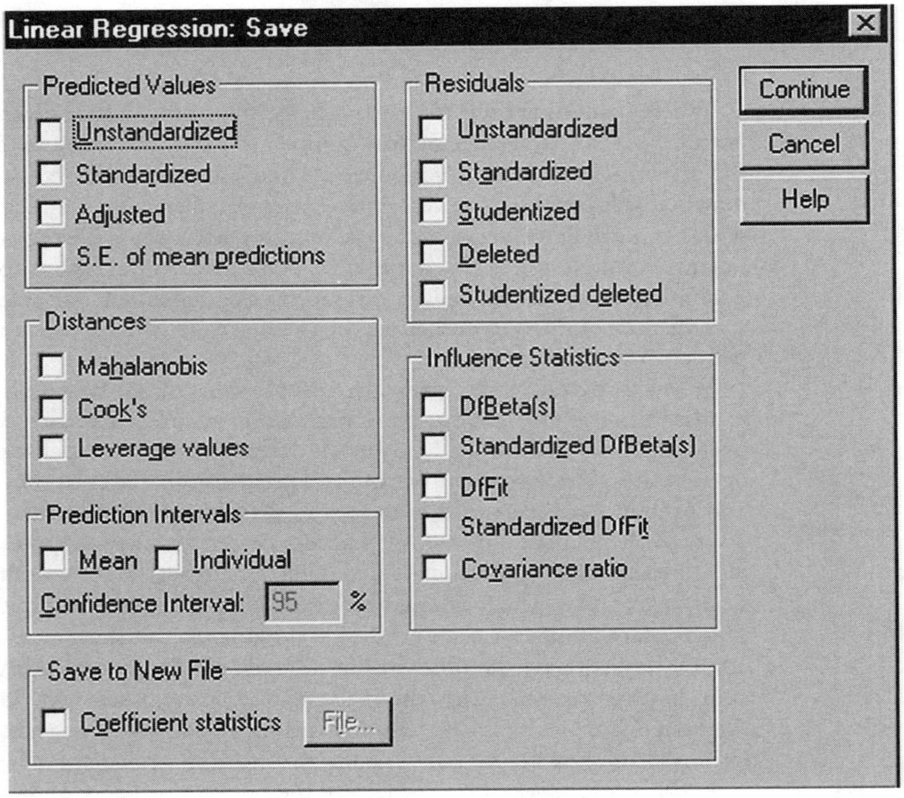

FIGURE 22.6
Linear Regression:
Save dialog box

Save Variables Dialog Box

Open the Linear Regression: Save dialog box by clicking on the **Save...** button (see Figure 22.6). Again, you examined these options extensively when using bivariate regression in the previous chapter. Whatever selections you make will result in the creation of new variables added to your data file.

The same variables you saved in bivariate regression will also be useful in multiple regression. We'll select a few options for residuals, such as **Standardized** and **Studentized** residuals. Also, select **Leverage values** and **Cook's.** Under the influence category, we'll se-

FIGURE 22.7
Linear Regression:
Options dialog box

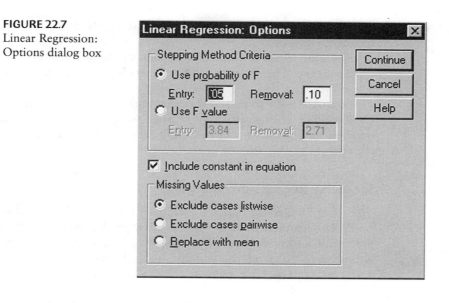

lect **Standardized DfBeta(s)** and **Covariance ratio**. You selected all but one of these options when using bivariate regression. The **Covariance ratio** was not useful in bivariate regression because there was only one predictor variable. However, we are now considering more than one predictor variable, so this is now useful.

Options Dialog Box

Finally, click on the **Options...** button to examine the Options dialog box. This dialog box appears in Figure 22.7. The options for Stepping Method Criteria pertain specifically to multiple regression situations. These criteria are used to guide the entry and removal of variables in the regression analysis.

By default, the process used to determine the selection or elimination of variables from the regression model will be based on the probability of the F statistic. Specifically, a probability of .05 is used as the criteria for selection of a variable and .10 for elimination. In other words, if the increase in the overall R^2 for the regression model is not likely due to chance ($p \leq .05$), the variable will be retained. On the other hand, if the decrease of the R^2 is more likely due to chance ($p \geq .10$), the variable will be eliminated from the regression model. To make the selection of predictors more conservative, you could lower the probability level for entry and raise the probability for removal. To make it easier to include a variable in the regression model, you would raise the probability for entry and lower the probability for removal. The criteria for selection and removal of variables can also be based of actual F values. The default settings for probability will suit our purposes.

The remaining options pertain to the inclusion of the constant, or intercept, and the treatment of missing values. We discussed these options in the previous chapter, and we will accept the default options.

RUNNING MULTIPLE REGRESSION ANALYSIS

For this illustration, we will perform several regression analyses, each using a different method of selecting the predictor variables for analysis. In each of these regressions, credits taken (CREDNOW) will serve as the dependent variable.

Simultaneous Regression

The first regression analysis will examine the influence of all predictor variables simultaneously. To select the variables for this analysis, move CREDNOW to the Dependent box.

Move the remaining four variables (AGE, EMPHOURS, NIGHT, OTHACT) to the Independent(s) box.

Check the Method menu. The default setting of Enter should be in effect. If not, specify this setting. This instructs SPSS to enter all of the predictor variables into the regression analysis at once.

You might want to review the selections you've made in the Statistics, Plots, Save, and Options dialog boxes. If you're satisfied with these selections, click on the **OK** button to perform the regression analysis. We'll examine the results from this regression analysis at the end of the chapter.

Stepwise Regression Analysis

The second regression analysis will examine the influence of the predictor variables in a stepwise manner. In other words, those predictors that contribute (statistically) to the prediction of the dependent variable will be added, while those that do not contribute will be excluded from the analysis. You selected the criteria for entering and removing variables from the regression analysis in the Options dialog box.

The selection of variables for stepwise regression is no different than it was for simultaneous regression. CREDNOW should be listed in the **Dependent:** box, while the remaining four variables (AGE, EMPHOURS, NIGHT, OTHACT) should be located in the **Independent(s):** box.

To specify a stepwise regression analysis, change the Method setting to **Stepwise**. After you've reviewed your selections, click on the **OK** button to perform this regression analysis. We will examine the results later.

Hierarchical Regression Analysis

Our third analysis will be a hierarchical regression model. We will specify the manner in which the predictor variables will be used to predict the dependent variable. Ideally, we would have a solid theory behind our selection of predictors. However, the best we are able to do is explain a rationale for the order in which we will enter our predictors.

We have four predictors: age, employment hours, enrollment in night courses, and involvement in other activities. All these things could potentially interfere with the number of credit hours a student enrolls in during the quarter. We know from the previous chapter that the more a student works, the less credit hours he/she generally takes. In addition, we could hypothesize about relationships of the other three predictors with credits taken (CREDNOW).

Older students might enroll in fewer credits because a larger percentage of older students are also part-time students. Student who enroll in night courses might also be enrolled in fewer courses because many of these students are also part-time. Finally, students who are involved in other activities might be enrolled in fewer credit hours because of the time given to these other activities.

Let's examine the influence of these variables in three steps. First, we'll examine the influence of a background variable (age). Next, we will examine the extent to which time-related variables (EMPHOURS and OTHACT) influence the number of credit hours taken. Finally, we will add enrollment status (NIGHT).

To make these variable selections, you use the **Pre_vious** and **Next** functions within the **Independent(s):** box. We will place different variables in different blocks. To indicate the first variable, select AGE and place it in the **Independent(s):** box. To specify the second block of variables, click on the **Next** button. Now, select EMPHOURS and OTHACT and place them in the Independents box. Finally, to specify the third block, use the **Next** button and place NIGHT in the **Independent(s):** box. These selections are illustrated in Figure 22.8.

Check these selections as well as those in other dialog boxes (Statistics, Plots, Save, Options). If everything looks good, use the **OK** button to perform this regression analysis.

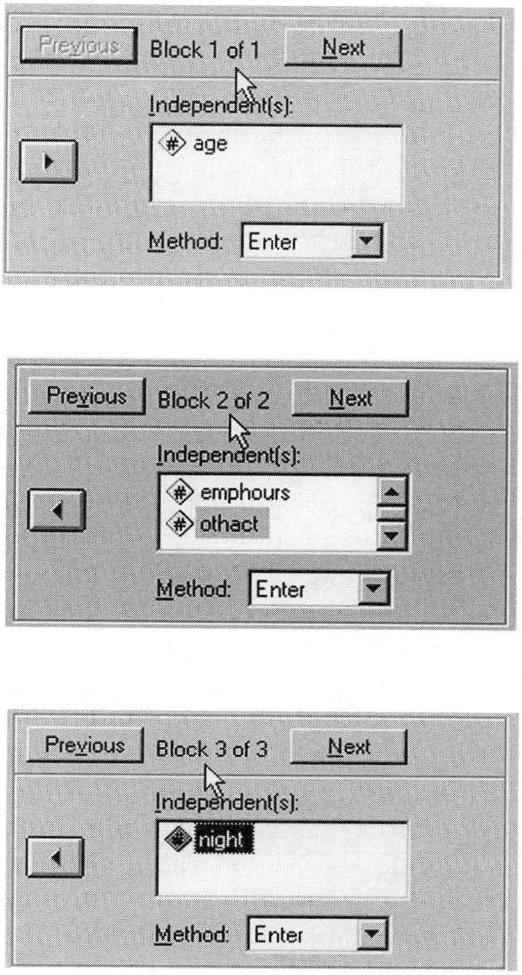

FIGURE 22.8
Selection of predictor variables for Blocks 1, 2, and 3

INTERPRETING MULTIPLE REGRESSION RESULTS

You've generated a lot of output in this SPSS session. Selected parts of the output are highlighted in this section, focusing on the types of information most useful in multiple regression. We will discuss this output within each of the three regressions you performed, beginning with the simultaneous regression analysis.

Simultaneous Regression

Descriptive Statistics and Correlations.   Descriptive information, including means, standard deviations, and correlations, is summarized in Figure 22.9. You have produced this type of information with other procedures such as Descriptives and Correlations.

Notice that our analysis included 150 students who had valid responses to each of the five variables we selected for the regression analysis. The average number of credit hours taken is 10.47, or about 2½ courses per quarter. The average age for this sample of students is just over 32 years old (32.69), while average numbers of hours employed per week is just over 25 (25.41). The means for night course enrollment (NIGHT) and involvement in other activities (OTHACT) are reported as .19 and .47. Since these variables are coded such that 1 represents Yes and 0 represents No, these averages indicate the percentage of

Descriptive Statistics

	Mean	Std. Deviation	N
CREDNOW	10.47	3.63	150
AGE	32.69	8.54	150
EMPHOURS	25.41	14.28	150
NIGHT	.19	.40	150
OTHACT	.47	.50	150

Correlations

		CREDNOW	AGE	EMPHOURS	NIGHT	OTHACT
Pearson Correlation	CREDNOW	1.000	−.397	−.415	−.526	−.241
	AGE	−.397	1.000	.331	.349	.237
	EMPHOURS	−.415	.331	1.000	.432	.116
	NIGHT	−.526	.349	.432	1.000	.178
	OTHACT	−.241	.237	.116	.178	1.000
Sig. (1-tailed)	CREDNOW	.	.000	.000	.000	.002
	AGE	.000	.	.000	.000	.002
	EMPHOURS	.000	.000	.	.000	.080
	NIGHT	.000	.000	.000	.	.015
	OTHACT	.002	.002	.080	.015	.
N	CREDNOW	150	150	150	150	150
	AGE	150	150	150	150	150
	EMPHOURS	150	150	150	150	150
	NIGHT	150	150	150	150	150
	OTHACT	150	150	150	150	150

FIGURE 22.9
Descriptive and correlations output from multiple regression

Yes responses. In other words, 19% of the students were enrolled in only night courses and 47% were involved in other activities during the quarter.

The table of correlations is useful in determining the relationship between the dependent variable (CREDNOW) and each of the predictor variables as well as the relationships among the predictor variables. All of the correlations between the predictors and CREDNOW are negative. The strongest of these is between night course enrollment (NIGHT) and CRED-NOW, reported as −.526. This correlation indicates that those students who are enrolled solely in night courses tend to take fewer credit hours, as you would expect. The second-strongest relationship is with employment hours (EMPHOURS) −.415. This correlation indicates that students who work more hours each week tend to enroll in fewer courses. Again, this is what we expected. The correlation between CREDNOW and AGE is reported as −.397, indicating that older students tend to be enrolled in fewer credit hours. Finally, the correlation between CREDNOW and involvement in other activities (OTHACT) is reported as −.241, indicating that those students who are involved in other activities tend to be enrolled in a fewer number of credit hours.

Next, examine the correlations among the four predictor variables. All these correlations are positive, ranging from .116 to .432. Of the six correlations, five are statistically signif-

Variables Entered/Removed[b]

Model	Variables Entered	Variables Removed	Method
1	OTHACT, EMPHOURS, AGE, NIGHT[a]	.	Enter

[a.] All requested variables entered.
[b.] Dependent Variable: CREDNOW

Model Summary[b]

Model	R	R Square	Adjusted R Square	Std. Error of the Estimate	Change Statistics R Square Change	F Change	df1	df2	Sig. F Change	Durbin-Watson
1	.606*	.367	.349	2.93	.367	20.993	4	145	.000	1.573

[a.] Predictors: (Constant), OTHACT, EMPHOURS, AGE, NIGHT
[b.] Dependent Variable: CREDNOW

ANOVA[b]

Model		Sum of Squares	df	Mean Square	F	Sig.
1	Regression	718.551	4	179.638	20.993	.000[a]
	Residual	1240.783	145	8.557		
	Total	1959.333	149			

[a.] Predictors: (Constant), OTHACT, EMPHOURS, AGE, NIGHT
[b.] Dependent Variable: CREDNOW

FIGURE 22.10
Model summary and ANOVA results–Simultaneous regression

icant ($p < .05$). Ideally, these predictors would not be related to each other, in order to maximize their contribution to the prediction of the dependent variable. We certainly do not want any high correlations ($r > +/-.80$) among the predictors. Using this criterion, we are safe in that the highest correlation is .432.

So what do these correlations tell us? Generally, older students tend to work more hours, are more likely to be enrolled as night students, and be involved in other outside activities. In addition, night students are more likely to be employed more hours and involved in other activities.

Model Summary and ANOVA Results. The next selection of output pertains to the simultaneous regression procedure. Figure 22.10 displays the first segment of this output. The first table in this figure indicates that all four predictors were used in the analysis and that CREDNOW was selected as the dependent variable. The second table provides a summary of the final regression model. This table summarizes information pertaining to the overall relationship (R) between the predictors and the dependent variable, the amount of variance explained by these predictors (R^2), and the results of the significance test used to test the regression model (F Change).

The overall relationship between the four predictors and CREDNOW is reported as .606. When this multiple correlation (R) is squared, we find that 36.7% of the variance in CREDNOW can be explained using these four predictors. The adjusted R^2 is .349, which is not that much different from our sample R^2 of .367. Recall from the previous chapter that the adjusted R^2 is an estimate that exists in the population. When the adjusted R^2 is close to the R^2 reported for the sample, the fit between the sample and population is good. When the adjusted R^2 differs substantially from the R^2 reported in the sample, the fit is worse. The adjustment is made primarily on the basis of the ratio of sample size to number of predictor variables. In our situation, we have 150 subjects and 4 predictors, or a ratio of 37.5 subjects per predictor. An acceptable rule of thumb is to have approximately 15 subjects per predictor.

Results from the test of significance appear in the Model Summary and the ANOVA table. The results of the F-test reveal a statistically significant F value of 20.933 (p < .001). The degrees of freedom for this F-test are 4 and 145. There are 4 df representing the number of predictor variable and 145 df representing error. Since there are 150 subjects, resulting in a total of 149 degrees of freedom, and we are using 4 df for the regression predictors, that leaves 145 degrees of freedom for the residual.

The reported standard error of estimate is 2.93. We will use this later when making predictions. One more piece of information appears in the Model Summary, the Durbin-Watson statistic. This value is reported as 1.573. This statistic describes the serial correlation among residuals. This test value will range from 0 to 4, with values close to 0 indicating a positive correlation among residuals and those close to 4 identifying a negative relationship. Values between 1.5 and 2.5 are expected. Our value of 1.573 falls in this range so we shouldn't worry about the residuals being correlated.

Regression Coefficients. Figure 22.11 summarizes the information pertaining to the regression coefficients. This information is necessary for making predictions about the dependent variable. The unstandardized regression coefficients (B) are reported in the first column and the standardized coefficients are reported in the third column. Whereas the unstandardized coefficients are dependent upon the scales used to measure each predictor and can rarely be compared directly, the standardized coefficients are based on the same scale. Comparisons can be made to assess the relative contribution of each predictor. We will make these comparisons later.

All the unstandardized coefficients are negative, indicating that these predictors are negatively related to the dependent variable, CREDNOW. Next, examine the informa-

Coefficients[a]

Model		Unstandardized Coefficients B	Std. Error	Standardized Coefficients Beta	t	Sig.	95% Confidence Interval for B Lower Bound	Upper Bound	Correlations Zero-order	Partial	Part	Collinearity Statistics Tolerance	VIF
1	(Constant)	15.227	.998		15.254	.000	13.254	17.200					
	AGE	−7.77E-02	.031	−.183	−2.491	.014	−.139	−.016	−.397	−.203	−.165	.810	1.235
	EMPHOURS	−4.72E-02	.019	−.186	−2.477	.014	−.085	−.010	−.415	−.202	−.164	.776	1.288
	NIGHT	−3.310	.694	−.362	−4.766	.000	−4.682	−1.937	−.526	−.368	−.315	.759	1.318
	OTHACT	−.806	.495	−.111	−1.629	.106	−1.785	.172	−.241	−.134	−.108	.934	1.071

a. Dependent Variable: CREDNOW

FIGURE 22.11
Coefficients for simultaneous regression

tion reported in the 95% Confidence Interval for B columns. You have examined confidence intervals before as they pertained to other sample statistics such as means. These intervals represent the range of values you would expect the unstandardized coefficients to have in the population 95 percent of the time. When examining these intervals, you should keep a few things in mind. First, narrow intervals indicate a better estimate than do wider intervals. Second, you want intervals that do not contain 0, because this would indicate a possibility of no relationship in the population. Examining these confidence intervals, we see that only the interval for OTHACT contains 0. The remaining three intervals are negative.

Next, examine the information pertaining to the t-tests. Three of the four t-tests are statistically significant ($p < .05$). Only the t-test for OTHACT failed to reach statistical significance. Remember that these t-tests are performed to determine whether the obtained unstandardized coefficients differ from zero, as a coefficient of zero would indicate the lack of relationship. Based on the results of these t-tests, we can say that the variables NIGHT, EMPHOURS, and AGE are contributing significantly to the prediction of CREDNOW, but the contribution of OTHACT is no more than we would expect by chance.

Let's examine a few more pieces of information that are helpful for determining the contribution of specific predictor variables. We mentioned earlier that the standardized coefficients offer some indication of a predictor's contribution. Examining standardized coefficients, we see that enrollment in night courses (NIGHT) has the value of −.362. This is followed by the predictors of employment hours (EMPHOURS) and age (AGE), with Beta coefficients of −.186 and −.183. Finally, the variable of OTHACT has a somewhat lower Beta coefficient of −.111.

Next, examine the three columns of information under the "Correlations" heading. There are three different types of correlations reported. The first column simply reports the zero-order correlation. You examined this earlier in the correlation matrix. From these coefficients, we know that NIGHT relates most strongly with the dependent variable ($r = −.526$). When squared, this tells us that NIGHT and CREDNOW share 27.7% common variance. This relationship is illustrated in the first row of Figure 22.12.

A zero-order correlation describes the relationship between two variables. This relationship, however, is typically influenced by other variables. We know that other variables (e.g., AGE, EMPHOURS, OTHACT) relate to both NIGHT and CREDNOW and, therefore influence this relationship. The next two correlation columns offer an indication of the relationship between each predictor and CREDNOW once the influence of the other predictors in controlled.

First, examine the partial correlations. The highest partial correlation is also reported for NIGHT. This relationship represents the correlation between NIGHT and CREDNOW, with the influence of the remaining predictors (AGE, EMPHOURS, OTHACT) removed from both NIGHT and CREDNOW. Removing the influence of these three variables results in the parts of NIGHT and CREDNOW that are not related to these three variables, or residual parts. This relationship is illustrated in the second row of Figure 22.12. Notice that only parts of each variable are used to form the partial correlation. The resulting partial correlation between NIGHT and CREDNOW is −.368. When squared, this coefficient represents the amount of variation shared between the residuals of NIGHT and CREDNOW. Specifically, the parts of NIGHT and CREDNOW, that are not related to AGE, EMPHOURS, and OTHACT share approximately fourteen (13.54%) percent in common.

The partial correlation coefficients for AGE and EMPHOURS are almost identical (−.203 and −.202) whereas that for OTHACT is lower at −.134. These values are lower than that reported for NIGHT, indicating less relationship with the dependent variable (CREDNOW) after controlling for the remaining predictor variables.

Next, examine the semi-partial correlations under the "Part" heading. As expected, the highest semi-partial correlation is also reported for NIGHT (−.315). This coefficient represents the extent to which NIGHT relates to CREDNOW, after the influence of the

FIGURE 22.12
Zero-order, partial,
and semi-partial
correlations

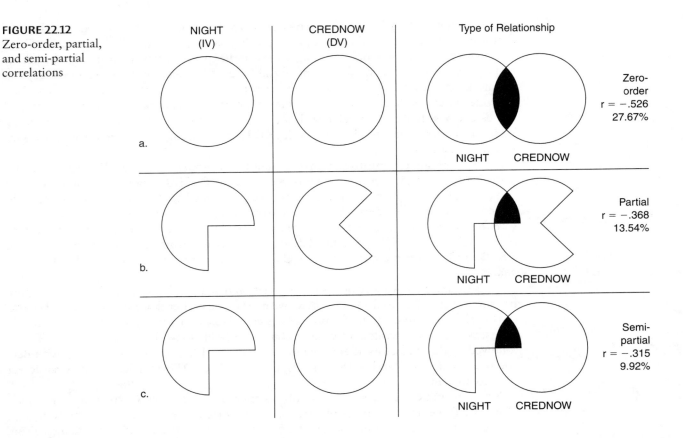

remaining predictors (AGE, EMPHOURS, OTHACT) has been removed from NIGHT. This represents the unique contribution of NIGHT. That is, only the part of NIGHT that is not influenced by the other three predictors is correlated with the in tact dependent variable, CREDNOW. When the semi-partial correlation is squared, it represents the unique portion of variance in the dependent variable explained by the predictor. Based on the semi-partial correlation between NIGHT and CREDNOW, we can say that 9.9 percent of the variance in CREDNOW can be explained by NIGHT and is not influenced by the other three predictors. In other words, of all the variance to be explained that could be explained in the dependent variable (100%), NIGHT explains approximately ten percent. This relationship is illustrated in the third row of Figure 22.12.

The unique contributions of AGE and EMPHOURS are similar, as the semi-partial correlations for each are −.165 and −.164. Squaring these coefficients, we find that each of these two predictors contribute about 3% to the prediction of variance in CREDNOW. Finally, the contribution of OTHACT is $(-.108)^2$, or just over 1%.

Next, examine the information presented under the Collinearity Statistics heading. We reviewed the correlation among the predictors earlier and determined that they were moderately related. There are also indicators from the multiple regression results that are helpful in determining the extent to which the predictors overlap. For example, examine the information regarding tolerance in Figure 22.11. This information shows the percentage of each variable that is not related to the other predictors. Lower tolerance values indicate that there is a great deal of overlap with other predictors, and therefore, little of that predictor's variance remains available to contribute to the dependent variable. On the other hand, higher tolerance values indicate little overlap with the other predictors, leaving a greater amount of the predictors variance available to share with the dependent variable. Of our four predictors, NIGHT has the lowest tolerance and OTHACT has the highest tolerance value. This agrees with the information you examined earlier in the correlation matrix, which indicated the strongest correlations involving NIGHT and the weakest involving OTHACT.

The second statistic reported for collinearity is VIF, or the variance inflation factor. This statistic is equal to 1 divided by the tolerance. Therefore, if the tolerance were a perfect 1, the VIF would also be a 1. Lower tolerances, which indicate overlap among the predictors, result in higher VIFs. Therefore, as the VIF becomes larger, greater overlap exists among the predictors. When there is a great deal of overlap among predictors, the variability of regression coefficients (B) becomes inflated. The reported VIF values for our four predictors are low, close to 1, so we have little to be concerned about.

Finally, let's return to the regression coefficients and use them to make predictions about the dependent variable, CREDNOW. These coefficients are found in the first column in Figure 22.11. Using these coefficients, we form the following regression equation:

Predicted CREDNOW =
15.227 − (.0777)(AGE) − (.0472)(EMPHOURS) − (3.310)(NIGHT) − (.806)(OTHACT)

Suppose a student is 50 years old, employed 40 hours per week, enrolled as a night student, and involved in other outside activities. A prediction of the number of credit hours taken by this student is made below:

Predicted CREDNOW =
15.227 − (.0777)(50) − (.0472)(40) − (3.310)(1) − (.806)(1)
15.227 − 3.885 − 1.888 − 3.310 − .806 = 5.338

This student is predicted to be enrolled in 5.338 credit hours, just over one course per quarter. Each of the four predictors is negatively correlated with CREDNOW, so this prediction should result in a low number of credit hours taken.

Try this example. What is the predicted course load of a student that is:

- 22 years old
- employed 10 hours per week
- not enrolled as a night student
- not involved in other outside activities

You should have predicted this student's CREDNOW value to be 13.046, or just over 3 courses per quarter. This student would have more time to take courses and is more likely a full-time student.

This concludes our examination of the first regression analysis. Let's examine some output from the second regression.

Stepwise Regression Results

The next three figures display selected output from the stepwise regression analysis. The types of output are similar to that which you examined in the first regression, so we will focus of the results that are different.

Figure 22.13 displays information from the Model Summary of this stepwise regression. Notice that the selection of predictor variables is different. Compare this information with the model summary information from first regression analysis. Whereas all four predictors were used simultaneously in the first regression, individual predictors were selected in steps for this regression. In fact, only three of the four predictors were used. The stepwise procedure did not include involvement in other activities (OTHACT) with the other predictors. We'll see why later.

Examine the model summary. Three models, or steps, are summarized. At each step, the multiple correlation (R), R^2, and significance tests are summarized. In the first step, the regression model contains only one predictor, NIGHT. Using this predictor, a multiple R of .526 is computed. This is really nothing more than a bivariate correlation, as there is only one predictor in the model. We already know that NIGHT explains a significant amount of variance in CREDNOW from examining previous results.

Variables Entered/Removed[a]

Model	Variables Entered	Variables Removed	Method
1	NIGHT	.	Stepwise (Criteria: Probability-of-F-to-enter <=.050, Probability-of-F-to-remove >=.100).
2	AGE	.	Stepwise (Criteria: Probability-of-F-to-enter <=.050, Probability-of-F-to-remove >=.100).
3	EMPHOURS	.	Stepwise (Criteria: Probability-of-F-to-enter <=.050, Probability-of-F-to-remove >=.100).

a. Dependent Variable: CREDNOW

Model Summary[d]

Model	R	R Square	Adjusted R Square	Std. Error of the Estimate	R Square Change	F Change	df1	df2	Sig. F Change	Durbin-Watson
1	.526[a]	.276	.271	3.10	.276	56.501	1	148	.000	
2	.573[b]	.328	.319	2.99	.052	11.366	1	147	.001	
3	.596[c]	.355	.342	2.94	.027	6.094	1	146	.015	1.597

a. Predictors: (Constant), NIGHT
b. Predictors: (Constant), NIGHT, AGE
c. Predictors: (Constant), NIGHT, AGE, EMPHOURS
d. Dependent Variable: CREDNOW

FIGURE 22.13
Stepwise regression–Model summary

An additional predictor, AGE, is added to the regression model in step 2. With both predictors, the multiple R becomes .573, with an R^2 of .328. In other words, the addition of AGE increased the R^2 by .052, or just over 5%. The results of the F-change-test (F = 11.366, p = .001) indicate that this additional explained variance is more than what we would expect by chance. When the third predictor, EMPHOURS, is added, the R^2 increases by 2.7 percent. To examine this increase for statistical significance, an F-change-test was performed. Again, these results (F = 6.094, p = .015) indicate that this increase in not likely due to chance.

The information summarized in the ANOVA table in Figure 22.14 is useful for addressing the question: Does the overall amount of variance explained by the predictors in the model differ from 0? The answer is 'yes' because in each case, the results of these F-tests are statistically significant. The final model includes three predictors (NIGHT, AGE, EMPHOURS). The results of the F-test (F = 26.802, p < .001) indicate that these predictor variables can be used to explain significant amounts of variance in CREDNOW.

Finally, examine the results displayed in Figure 22.15. These results include coefficients, t-tests, correlations, and collinearity statistics for variables selected and excluded from the regression analysis at each step. You have examined the information in the Coefficients table in the previous regression analysis. Therefore, we will focus on the new information pertaining the excluded variables.

Examine the information in the first row of the Excluded Variables table. This is the first step of the stepwise regression in which only one predictor, NIGHT, is being used to predict CREDNOW. The three variables excluded from this step are AGE, EMPHOURS and

ANOVA[d]

Model		Sum of Squares	df	Mean Square	F	Sig.
1	Regression	541.340	1	541.340	56.501	.000[a]
	Residual	1417.993	148	9.581		
	Total	1959.333	149			
2	Regression	643.109	2	321.555	35.912	.000[b]
	Residual	1316.224	147	8.954		
	Total	1959.333	149			
3	Regression	695.847	3	231.949	26.802	.000[c]
	Residual	1263.486	146	8.654		
	Total	1959.333	149			

a. Predictors: (Constant), NIGHT
b. Predictors: (Constant), NIGHT, AGE
c. Predictors: (Constant), NIGHT, AGE, EMPHOURS
d. Dependent Variable: CREDNOW

FIGURE 22.14
ANOVA results–Stepwise regression

OTHACT. There is a lot of information in this table that is useful for determining which, if any, of the excluded variables can be used to explain additional variance in CREDNOW.

First, examine the Beta In column. These are the standardized regression coefficients for each predictor, should they be added to the analysis. The largest beta value is reported for AGE, and indicates that AGE would make the greatest contribution of the three excluded predictors. If we look further, the results of the t-tests indicate the likelihood that the additional variance explained by each predictor is due to chance. In each case, this t-test is statistically significant ($p < .05$). In other words, if any of these variables were added to the regression analysis, the increase in explained variance would be greater than that expected by chance. So, which one should be added? Examine the partial correlations for each excluded predictor. When controlling for the influence of NIGHT, the strongest relationship is reported for AGE. Therefore, AGE was added to the regression analysis in the second step.

Next, examine the information in the second row. These two variables (EMPHOURS and OTHACT) are not included in the analysis at this point. Of these two excluded variables, EMPHOURS has the largest Beta, a statistically significant t-test, and the largest partial correlation. Therefore, EMPHOURS was added to the regression analysis in the third step.

Finally, examine the third row of excluded variables. Only OTHACT is listed. The Beta and partial correlation values are lower than those reported for variables in the earlier steps, and the t-test failed to reach statistical significance. When you were selecting options for this regression, you specified criteria for entry and removal of variables in the regression analysis. The criteria set for entering new variables specified a probability of .05 or less. In other words, the probability that the increase in R^2 due to the entry of the predictor is due to chance must be equal to or less than 5%. This information is generated from the t-test. In this case, $p = .106$, which exceeds .05, thus, OTHACT was not added to the regression model.

Finally, let's use the prediction equation from the stepwise regression. The final model includes three predictors. The regression coefficients used in the prediction of CREDNOW are found in the first column in Figure 22.15. This equation is written below.

Predicted CREDNOW =
15.175 − (3.420)(NIGHT) − (.087)(AGE) − (.0473)(EMPHOURS)

Coefficients[a]

Model		Unstandardized Coefficients		Standardized Coefficients			95% Confidence Interval for B		Correlations			Collinearity Statistics	
		B	Std. Error	Beta	t	Sig.	Lower Bound	Upper Bound	Zero-order	Partial	Part	Tolerance	VIF
1	(Constant)	11.397	.281		40.501	.000	10.841	11.953					
	NIGHT	−4.810	.640	−.526	−7.517	.000	−6.075	−3.546	−.526	−.526	−.526	1.000	1.000
2	(Constant)	14.623	.995		14.698	.000	12.657	16.589					
	NIGHT	−4.034	.660	−.441	−6.111	.000	−5.339	−2.729	−.526	−.450	−.413	.878	1.139
	AGE	−.103	.031	−.243	−3.371	.001	−.164	−.043	−.397	−.268	−.228	.878	1.139
3	(Constant)	15.175	1.003		15.125	.000	13.192	17.158					
	NIGHT	−3.420	.695	−.374	4.920	.000	−4.793	−2.046	−.526	−.377	−.327	.766	1.306
	AGE	−8.70E-02	.031	−.205	−2.824	.005	−.148	−.026	−.397	−.228	−.188	.838	1.193
	EMPHOURS	−4.73E-02	.019	−.186	−2.469	.015	−.085	−.009	−.415	−.200	−.164	.776	1.288

a. Dependent Variable: CREDNOW

Excluded Variables[d]

Model		Beta In	t	Sig.	Partial Correlation	Collinearity Statistics		
						Tolerance	VIF	Minimum Tolerance
1	AGE	−.243[a]	−3.371	.001	−.268	.878	1.139	.878
	EMPHOURS	−.232[a]	−3.071	.003	−.246	.813	1.229	.813
	OTHACT	−.152[a]	−2.161	.032	−.176	.968	1.033	.968
2	EMPHOURS	−.186[b]	−2.469	.015	−.200	.776	1.288	.766
	OTHACT	−.112[b]	−1.609	.110	−.132	.934	1.071	.847
3	OTHACT	−.111[c]	−1.629	.106	−.134	.934	1.071	.759

a. Predictors in the Model: (Constant), NIGHT
b. Predictors in the Model: (Constant), NIGHT, AGE
c. Predictors in the Model: (Constant), NIGHT, AGE, EMPHOURS
d. Dependent Variable: CREDNOW

FIGURE 22.15
Coefficients–Stepwise regression

Suppose a student is: (a) a night student, (b) 50 years old, and (c) employed 40 hours per week. The prediction equation would be applied to this student as follows:

$$\text{Predicted CREDNOW} = 15.175 - (3.420)(1) - (.087)(50) - (.0473)(40)$$
$$= 15.175 - 3.42 - 4.35 - 1.892 = 5.513$$

For this student, we predict that he/she is enrolled in 5.513 credits, or about one course per quarter. We worked a similar example for the simultaneous entry model. Compare the present result with that earlier example. The only difference between the two is that the stepwise model does not include the OTHACT variable. Note that, in this example, the exclusion of this variable made little difference in the prediction. Try another example. Suppose a student is: (a) not a night student, (b) employed only 8 hours per week, and (c) 25 years old. What is your prediction? You should have arrived at a predicted enrollment of 12.6216 credits, just over three courses per quarter.

Variables Entered/Removed[b]

Model	Variables Entered	Variables Removed	Method
1	AGE[a]	.	Enter
2	OTHACT, EMPHOURS[a]	.	Enter
3	NIGHT[a]	.	Enter

a. All requested variables entered.
b. Dependent Variable: CREDNOW

Model Summary[d]

Model	R	R Square	Adjusted R Square	Std. Error of the Estimate	R Square Change	F Change	df1	df2	Sig. F Change	Durbin-Watson
					Change Statistics					
1	.397[a]	.158	.152	3.34	.158	27.687	1	148	.000	
2	.517[b]	.268	.252	3.14	.110	10.955	2	146	.000	
3	.606[c]	.367	.349	2.93	.099	22.717	1	145	.000	1.573

a. Predictors: (Constant), AGE
b. Predictors: (Constant), AGE, OTHACT, EMPHOURS
c. Predictors: (Constant), AGE, OTHACT, EMPHOURS, NIGHT
d. Dependent Variable: CREDNOW

FIGURE 22.16
Model summary–Hierarchical regression

Hierarchical Regression Results

Finally, let's examine the results from our final regression analysis. In this analysis, we developed the model according to our logical, yet anecdotal theory about the variables that influence the number of credits taken by students. Figure 22.16 displays a summary of the results from this analysis.

AGE was used in the first step to predict CREDNOW. This resulted in a multiple R of .397 and an R^2 of .158. In the second step, we added two more predictors, OTHACT and EMPHOURS. This increased the R^2 by 11 percent, which was statistically significant (F Change = 10.955, p < .001). In the final step, we added NIGHT to the regression model. The R^2 increased by an additional 9.9 percent, which was also statistically significant (F Change = 22.717, p < .001).

Next, examine the ANOVA results in Figure 22.17. The results for each step in the model are statistically significant (p < .001). The final model, which includes all four predictors, resulted in an F ratio of 20.993 with a p < .001. This is the same result we found in our simultaneous model because the final models (see Figure 20.10), in these two analyses are identical.

Finally, let's examine the results displayed in Figure 22.18. This information summarizes the coefficients, correlations, t-tests, and collinearity statistics at each step in the regression model. Take a few minutes to look over this information. The final prediction equation is exactly the same as that obtained from the simultaneous regression analysis we completed earlier. Again this is because both analyses produced identical final models.

FIGURE 22.17
ANOVA
results–Hierarchical
regression

ANOVA[d]

Model		Sum of Squares	df	Mean Square	F	Sig.
1	Regression	308.776	1	308.776	27.687	.000[a]
	Residual	1650.557	148	11.152		
	Total	1959.333	149			
2	Regression	524.157	3	174.719	17.774	.000[b]
	Residual	1435.176	146	9.830		
	Total	1959.333	149			
3	Regression	718.551	4	179.638	20.993	.000[c]
	Residual	1240.783	145	8.557		
	Total	1959.333	149			

a. Predictors: (Constant), AGE
b. Predictors: (Constant), AGE, OTHACT, EMPHOURS
c. Predictors: (Constant), AGE, OTHACT, EMPHOURS, NIGHT
d. Dependent Variable: CREDNOW

Coefficients[a]

Model		Unstandardized Coefficients B	Std. Error	Standardized Coefficients Beta	t	Sig.	95% Confidence Interval for B Lower Bound	Upper Bound	Correlations Zero-order	Partial	Part	Collinearity Statistics Tolerance	VIF
1	(Constant)	15.978	1.082		14.762	.000	13.839	18.117					
	AGE	−.169	.032	−.397	−5.262	.000	−.232	−.105	−.397	−.397	−.397	1.000	1.000
2	(Constant)	16.580	1.026		16.164	.000	14.553	18.607					
	AGE	−.110	.033	−.260	−3.379	.001	−.175	−.046	−.397	−.269	−.239	.851	1.176
	EMPHOURS	−7.95E-02	.019	−.313	−4.167	.000	−.117	−.042	−.415	−.326	−.295	.889	1.125
	OTHACT	−1.036	.528	−.143	−1.961	.052	−2.079	.008	−.241	−.160	−.139	.942	1.061
3	(Constant)	15.227	.998		15.254	.000	13.254	17.200					
	AGE	−7.77E-02	.031	−.183	−2.491	.014	−.139	−.016	−.397	−.203	−.165	.810	1.235
	EMPHOURS	−4.72E-02	.019	−.186	−2.477	.014	−.085	−.010	−.415	−.202	−.164	.776	1.288
	OTHACT	−.806	.495	−.111	−1.629	.106	−1.785	.172	−.241	−.134	−.108	.934	1.071
	NIGHT	−3.310	.694	−.362	−4.766	.000	−4.682	−1.937	−.526	−.368	−.315	.759	1.318

a. Dependent Variable: CREDNOW

Excluded Variables[c]

Model		Beta In	t	Sig.	Partial Correlation	Collinearity Statistics Tolerance	VIF	Minimum Tolerance
1	EMPHOURS	−.319[a]	−4.210	.000	−.328	.890	1.123	.890
	OTHACT	−.155[a]	−2.022	.045	−.165	.944	1.059	.944
	NIGHT	−.441[a]	−6.111	.000	−.450	.878	1.139	.878
2	NIGHT	−.362[b]	−4.766	.000	−.368	.759	1.318	.759

a. Predictors in the Model: (Constant), AGE
b. Predictors in the Model: (Constant), AGE, OTHACT, EMPHOURS
c. Dependent Variable: CREDNOW

FIGURE 22.18
Coefficients–Hierarchical regression

CHAPTER SUMMARY

In this chapter, you used multiple regression analysis to examine the influence of several predictor variables on a dependent variable. Specifically, you explored three different approaches to building regression models. These regression models were similar in that they identified predictor variables that explained significant portions of the variance in a dependent variable. However, different methods of predictor variable selection may produce different prediction equations. In the following chapter, we will continue our examination of regression analysis. Specifically, we will explore the use of categorical predictor variables and coding techniques.

PRACTICE EXERCISES

Use the data set you created in Chapter 3 (i.e., student admission data).

1. Using multiple regression analysis, examine the extent to which a students' pre-test scores can be predicted using their GRE-V and GRE-Q Scores
   a. Perform a simultaneous regression.
   b. Perform a stepwise regression.

2. For each regression analysis, report the following information:
   R^2
   R^2change (if necessary)
   F and significance of the F-test
   F-change-test (if necessary)
   Regression coefficient for the independent variable, intercept, standard error of estimate

3. For each regression analysis, identify any outliers and influential cases.

4. Based on the information from question 2, which variable (GRE-V or GRE-Q) is a better predictor of the pre-test scores? Support your response using information from the regression analyses.

REFERENCE

Pedhazur, E. J. (1997). Multiple Regression in Behavioral Research (3rd Edition). Fort Worth, TX: Harcourt Brace College Publishers.

23 | Regression with Categorical Predictors

In Chapters 21 and 22, you explored bivariate and multiple regression using continuous variables as predictors. However, there will be situations when you want categorical predictors, or a combination of categorical and continuous predictors in your regression model. Before categorical predictors can be used with regression analysis, they must be coded properly. In this chapter, you will examine procedures for coding categorical predictor and using them to explain variance in a continuous dependent variable.

There are several methods that can be used to code categorical predictors. These include dummy coding, effect coding, orthogonal coding, and criterion coding. Each of these coding procedures will allow you to determine the overall influence of a particular categorical predictor. However, the information that pertains to the specific effects of that predictor will vary. Three of these coding procedures (dummy, effect, orthogonal) may require more than one set of codes to represent the overall variable; criterion coding requires only one.

Dummy coding is useful for determining the overall impact of a categorical predictor. The coding procedure uses 1 or 0 to indicate membership in a specific category. Once you've successfully dummy-coded a categorical predictor, you are able to examine its overall relationship with the dependent variable.

The coding procedures used for *effect coding* allow you to make specific comparisons between different categories within the predictor. Effect coding is, in fact, a form of contrast coding. You used contrasts when you performed a one-way ANOVA in Chapter 16. In one-way ANOVA example, you created a contrast that allowed you to compare the performance of one group with the performance of four other groups. You did this by assigning the following contrast coefficients: $-1, -1, -1, -1, 4$. This is just one of many contrasts that could be specified using effect coding.

Orthogonal coding also allows you to make specific group comparisons. However, the comparisons made using orthogonal contrasts are independent of each other. This condition of independence limits the variety of contrasts that can be specified, but eliminates overlap among such contrasts and their relationship with the dependent variable.

Finally, using *criterion coding*, each person is assigned a predicted score (i.e., the mean score of the group in which he/she is a member), as their code. The resulting correlation between a criterion-coded predictor and the dependent variable is nothing more than a correlation between predicted scores and observed scores. Stronger correlations indicate better predictions. If the predictions are perfect, the correlation would be $+1.0$.

In this chapter, we will illustrate dummy and criterion coding procedures. Dummy coding is straightforward, but usually requires several different coding vectors to fully represent a predictor variable. Specifically, the number of coding vectors required is equal to the degrees of freedom for the predictor variable. On the other hand, criterion coding will always be completed with one coding vector. For a more complete discussion of all of these coding procedures, see Pedhazur (1997). Before we begin to explore these coding procedures, let's briefly examine the variables that will be used in this chapter.

VARIABLES USED IN THIS CHAPTER

To illustrate coding procedures, we will use the computer experience (COMPEXP) as the categorical predictor. We will examine the extent to which computer experience can be used to predict computer anxiety (COMPANX). As a reminder, the five categories of computer experience are listed below.

Category	Label
1	week or less
2	between 1 week and 1 month
3	between 1 month and 6 months
4	between 6 months and 1 year
5	over 1 year

USING SPSS TO CODE CATEGORICAL INDEPENDENT VARIABLES

In this section, you will use SPSS to code a categorical variable for use as a predictor in regression analysis. Let's begin with dummy coding. The data you will need are stored in the file identified as **chap23 data** on the enclosed computer disk.

Dummy Coding

Dummy coding is a simple process in which people who belong to a given group are assigned the value of 1 and those who do not belong are assigned a 0. A set of codes is called a vector, and a variable may require more than one coding vector. The specific number of coding vectors required for a variable is equal to the degrees of freedom for that variable. By now, you should be familiar with degrees of freedom. There are five groups represented in the COMPEXP predictor variable. Therefore it has 5–1, or 4 degrees of freedom. It will require the same number of coding vectors to represent computer experience as a predictor in regression analysis. Let's see how this coding is done.

Remember, we assign a 1 if a person belongs to a particular group and a 0 if they do not belong to that group. To create the first vector, we assign everyone who has one week or less of experience a value of 1, while everyone else is assigned value of '0'. We will continue this coding scheme until all four coding vectors are computed. Altogether, there will be four dummy-coded vectors. For the lack of better names, we will identify these as DUM1, DUM2, DUM3, and DUM4.

To code this vector using SPSS, you can use the Compute or Recode procedures, which you used earlier in chapters 8 and 9. These procedures are found in the **Transform** menu. For illustrative purposes, we will use the Recode procedure. You used the Recode procedure earlier to reverse-code negatively-worded items. As you recall, the Recode procedure can be used to recode existing variables or create new ones. Earlier, you recoded existing variables. In this chapter, you will use the Recode procedure to create new variables (i.e. DUM1, DUM2, DUM3, DUM4).

Select the **Recode** and **Into Different Variables...** options from the **Transform** menu, as illustrated in Figure 23.1.

These menu selections will open the Recode into Different Variables dialog box. The variables from the data set are listed at the left in the source variable list. You select the variable from this list and place it in the box labeled **Input Variable -> Output Variable:**. Since we will

FIGURE 23.1
Transform–Recode–
Into Difference
Variables menu
selections

FIGURE 23.2
Recode into Different
Variables dialog box
(COMPEXP—DUM1)

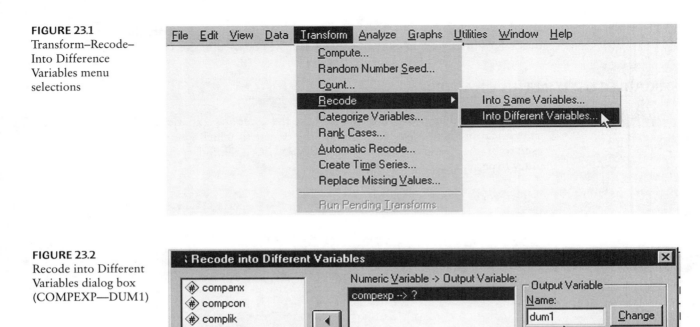

be recoding computer experience, select COMPEXP as the input variable. Identify the output variables as DUM1 in the box labeled Output Variable. These selections appear in Figure 23.2.

To create DUM1, you will recode the existing values associated with COMPEXP. Select the **Old and New Values...** button to get started (see Figure 23.3). The Old and New Values dialog box is divided into two halves, old values and new values. The old values refer to the existing variable, which is COMPEXP in this example. The new values pertain to the new variable, DUM1.

There are several ways to identify the values to be recoded. To specify a single value, you use the **Value:** option. You recode missing values using the **System-missing** or **System- or user-missing** options. There are three options you can use to specify a range of values. These options allow you to specify both the starting and ending values in the range, just the starting value, or just the ending value. Finally, there is an option labeled **All other values.** This option recodes all values that have not been previously specified.

Remember, DUM1 will be equal to 1 for those individuals in the first COMPEXP group and equal to 0 for those in the other four groups. To create the first category of DUM1, specify "1" for the old values and "1" for the new value. Use the **Add** button to complete this recode statement. Now, because all remaining values of COMPEXP should be coded to 0, use the option for **All other values** and specify "0" for the new value. Again, use the **Add** button to add this recode statement to the list. Both recode statements should appear in the **Old -> New:** window, displayed in Figure 23.4.

Once you have specified these options, use the **Continue** button to return to the Recode Into Different Variables dialog box. To create the new variable, DUM1, use the **Change** button to change the old values to new values, as illustrated in Figure 23.5.

FIGURE 23.3
Old and New Values
dialog box

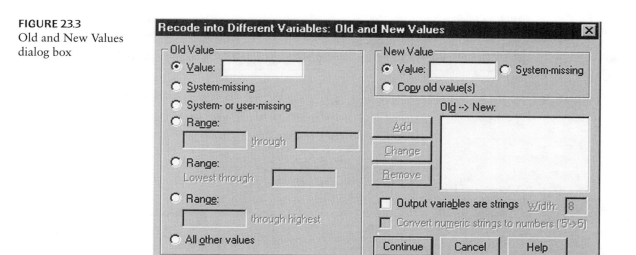

FIGURE 23.4
Old -> New values
displaying recode
statements for DUM1

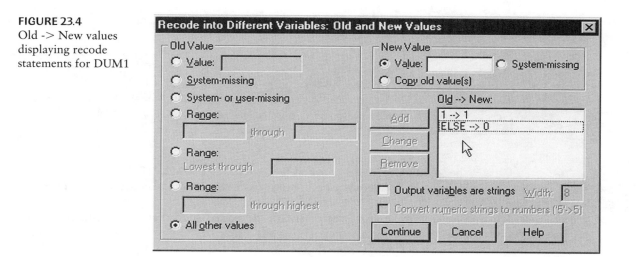

FIGURE 23.5
Recode into Different
Variables
(COMPEXP ->DUM1)

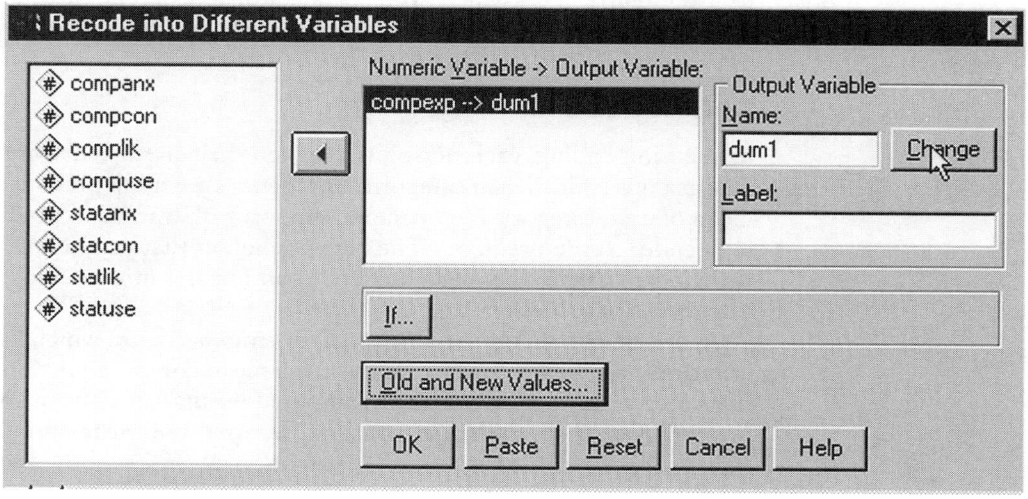

TABLE 23.1
Dummy Coding Vectors for Computer Experience

COMPEXP	DUM1	DUM2	DUM3	DUM4
1	1	0	0	0
2	0	1	0	0
3	0	0	1	0
4	0	0	0	1
5	0	0	0	0

Finally, use the **OK** button to execute the recode you just specified. DUM1 will be created and displayed in your data file. The steps you just completed to create DUM1 are summarized below:

Step 1	From the <u>T</u>ransform menu, select the <u>R</u>ecode and **Into <u>D</u>ifferent Variables...** options.
Step 2	Select the input variable from the source variable list.
Step 3	Name the output variable.
Step 4	Select the Old and New Values option.
Step 5	Specify the old and new values and use the **<u>A</u>dd** button after each recode statement. Use the **Continue** button when finished.
Step 6	Use the **<u>C</u>hange** button to change the old values into new values.
Step 7	Use **OK** to create the new variable.

Create the remaining dummy-coded vectors (i.e., DUM2, DUM3, DUM4) using the same procedures. Remember, each vector will consist of 1s and 0s, as indicated in Table 23.1.

The second dummy coding vector should be coded such that those students in the second computer experience category have a value of 1 and those in the remaining categories are assigned a 0. Therefore, an old value of 2 becomes a new value of 1, while all other old values become 0. Try to create the remainder of the dummy variables on your own.

When you are finished, four new variables (DUM1, DUM2, DUM3, DUM4) should appear in your data set. Check your data editor to examine these new variables. We will be using them later, but before we do, let's discuss criterion coding.

Criterion Coding

In criterion coding, each person is assigned their predicted score on the dependent variable as their code. When categorical predictors are used, predicted scores are equal to the mean of each category. For example, suppose you wanted to predict computer anxiety using gender as the predictor. The best prediction that can be made for any individual female in this case is the mean anxiety of all females in the sample. This holds true for all categorical variables.

Again, our predictor variable is computer experience, which has five categories. To use criterion coding, we need to compute the mean computer anxiety score for each of these five categories. You have already computed means using various SPSS procedures such as Frequencies, Descriptives, and Means. We used the Means procedure to generate mean

FIGURE 23.6
Old -> New values
(criterion coding–
CRITER1)

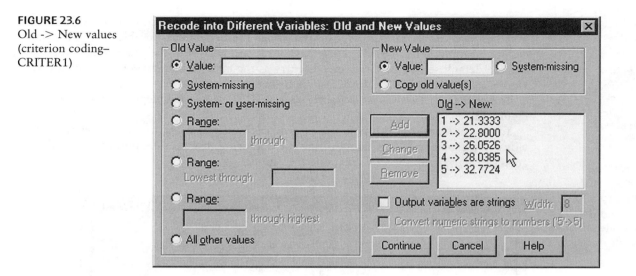

computer anxiety scores for each level (category) of computer experience. These means are displayed below.

Computer Experience Category	Computer Anxiety Mean
1	21.3333
2	22.8000
3	26.0526
4	28.0385
5	32.7724

As with dummy coding, you can use either the Recode or Compute procedures. We will use the Recode procedure in our illustration to create a new predictor (CRITER1), with values based on an existing variable (COMPEXP).

We will follow the steps used earlier when we created dummy-coded vectors. From the **Transform** menu, select the **Recode** and **Into Different Variables...** options. Select COMP-EXP as the input variable and name the output variable CRITER1. Select the Old and New Values option and specify the means for computer anxiety as the new values. Be sure to use the **Add** button after each recode statement. When completed, the Old and New Values window should look like that displayed in Figure 23.6.

Use the **Continue** button when finished and the **OK** button to create the new variable. The new variable, CRITER1, will now appear in your data file, and are ready for use.

USING CATEGORICAL VARIABLES AS PREDICTORS
IN REGRESSION ANALYSIS

Now that you have recoded computer experience using dummy coding and criterion coding, let's use it in regression analysis as a predictor of computer anxiety. The procedure you follow to perform this regression analysis is no different than what you have already done. Using the dummy-coded vectors, you will actually enter four predictors (i.e., DUM1, DUM2, DUM3, DUM4) into the model. However these 4 predictors contain the same information that the single predictor COMPEXP did. Using criterion coding, you will enter only one predictor CRITER1.

From the **Analyze** menu, select the **Regression** and **Linear...** options as you did in the previous two chapters. Identify COMPANX as the dependent variable. For the dummy coding example, select DUM1, DUM2, DUM3, and DUM4 as the independent variables. Use the default setting of simultaneous entry as the method of regression, as illustrated in Figure 23.7. Click on **OK** to process this regression analysis.

To use the criterion-coded variable, select CRITER1 as the independent variable, as in Figure 23.8.

You are welcome to explore the many available statistics and options you used in the previous two chapters. When you are finished exploring, use the **OK** button to run the regression analysis, and we will examine the output.

FIGURE 23.7
Dummy coded variables identified for regression analysis

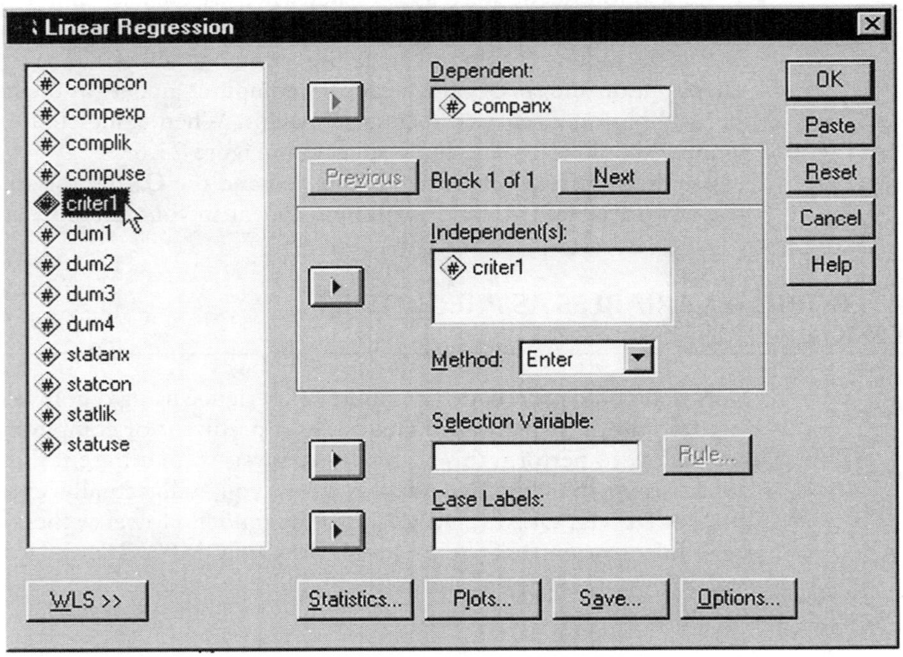

FIGURE 23.8
Criterion coded variable identified for regression analysis

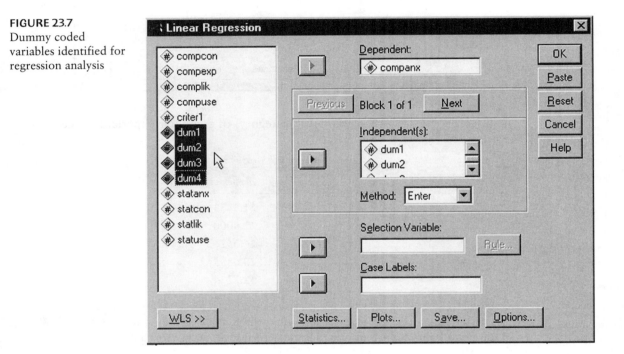

INTERPRETING SPSS REGRESSION WITH DUMMY- AND CRITERION-CODED VARIABLES RESULTS

The regression output produced using categorical predictors is similar to the output produced in the two previous chapters. The exact format and contents of the output will depend on the specific options you selected. Therefore, we will examine only a few general components of the regression analysis.

Using a Dummy-Coded Predictor

The results from our regression analysis using a dummy-coded predictor appear in Figure 23.9. The form of these results resembles that of a multiple regression, as four predictors are listed. Remember, however, that these four dummy-coded vectors are simply a transformation of predictor variable, computer experience. They contain the same information. Therefore, the multiple R reported in this output is nothing more than the correlation between two variables, computer experience and computer anxiety.

FIGURE 23.9
Regression analysis output with a dummy-coded predictor

Model Summary

Model	R	R Square	Adjusted R Square	Std. Error of the Estimate
1	.558[a]	.311	.298	5.3381

a. Predictors: (Constant), DUM4, DUM1, DUM2, DUM3

ANOVA[b]

Model		Sum of Squares	df	Mean Square	F	Sig.
1	Regression	2629.040	4	657.260	23.066	.000[a]
	Residual	5812.999	204	28.495		
	Total	8442.038	208			

a. Predictors: (Constant), DUM4, DUM1, DUM2, DUM3
b. Dependent Variable: COMPANX

Coefficients[a]

Model		Unstandardized Coefficients		Standardized Coefficients		
		B	Std. Error	Beta	t	Sig.
1	(Constant)	32.772	.443		73.928	.000
	DUM1	−11.439	1.834	−.365	−6.238	.000
	DUM2	−9.972	1.745	−.335	−5.714	.000
	DUM3	−6.720	1.302	−.304	−5.160	.000
	DUM4	−4.734	1.137	−.246	−4.164	.000

a. Dependent Variable: COMPANX

The reported correlation is .558, indicating a moderate positive relationship between computer experience and computer anxiety. In other words, the more experience a student has with computers, the more comfortable he/she will generally be working with computers. If this correlation is squared, an R^2 value of .311 is obtained. In other words, 31% of the variance in computer anxiety is explained by students' computer experience classification. This amount of variance is significantly higher than what we would expect by chance, evidenced by the F ratio of 23.066 ($p < .001$).

To make a prediction of computer anxiety based on computer experience, we follow the same process that we did earlier in multiple regression. Remember, there are four dummy-coded vectors that define 5 levels of computer experience. These vectors are treated as predictors in the regression equation. The unstandardized coefficients (B) are used as weights for each dummy-coded vector in the equation. This equation would be:

Computer Anxiety =
32.772 −11.439(DUM1) −9.972(DUM2) −6.720(DUM3) −4.734(DUM4)

Suppose you wanted to make a prediction for those students who have more than one year of computer experience (i.e., the fifth category of COMPEXP). A person with this amount of experience received a 0 on each of the four dummy-coded vectors, so the equation would be:

Predicted Computer Anxiety =
32.772 −11.439(0) −9.972(0) −6.720(0) −4.734(0) = 32.772

As expected, our prediction is equal to the mean of all students having one year or more of computer experience. The same holds true for the other levels of computer experience. Try the equation for yourself. To do so, you must use the appropriate dummy codes indicated in Table 23.1.

Using a Criterion-Coded Predictor

Figure 23.10 summarizes the results from your regression analysis using criterion coding. As we expected, the results indicate that computer experience and computer anxiety are related. The values for R and R^2 here are the same as those reported in the dummy coding analysis. This is expected because you have not changed the variable, just the coding method. What has changed is the F ratio. This is because of a change in the degrees of freedom. As you recall, we used four dummy vectors in the previous regression. Therefore, the regression analysis was performed using 4 degrees of freedom. For criterion coding, just one vector was required, so the regression analysis is based on 1 df. An F ratio of 93.620 ($p < .001$) is reported for this analysis indicating a relationship between computer experience and computer anxiety.

The regression equation derived from this analysis is also different from the equations you derived before because of the difference in coding method. This equation for the current model is: Predicted Computer Anxiety = 1.000(CRITER1) − .000007. In other words, you multiply the mean of a given COMPEXP category by 1 and subtract .000007, which is basically zero. Applying this prediction equation to those in the fifth category of COMPEXP, you have: 1.000(32.772) − .000007 = 32.772. Again, this prediction corresponds with the category mean.

Model Summary

Model	R	R Square	Adjusted R Square	Std.Error of the Estimate
1	.558[a]	.311	.308	5.2993

a. Predictors: (Constant), CRITER1

ANOVA[b]

Model		Sum of Squares	df	Mean Square	F	Sig.
1	Regression	2629.040	1	2629.040	93.620	.000[a]
	Residual	5812.999	207	28.082		
	Total	8442.038	208			

a. Predictors: (Constant), CRITER1
b. Dependent Variable: COMPANX

Coefficients[a]

Model		Unstandardized Coefficients		Standardized Coefficients	t	Sig.
		B	Std. Error	Beta		
1	(Constant)	−7.117E-06	3.184		.000	1.000
	CRITER1	1.000	.103	.558	9.676	.000

a. Dependent Variable: COMPANX

FIGURE 23.10
Regression analysis output with a criterion-coded predictor

CHAPTER SUMMARY

This chapter completes the section on regression analysis. We demonstrated dummy and criterion coding with categorical predictors. Either coding method will work with regression analysis. Dummy coding is perhaps the simplest method of coding categorical variables for use in regression analysis. However, if you were working with more than one categorical predictor, dummy coding may create some difficulty. Remember that all dummy-coded vectors must be entered into the regression equation to examine the influence of the categorical variable. It is likely that all coded vectors would not enter the equation if you were using a stepwise selection process. In such a case, criterion-coded variables are much easier to manage.

PRACTICE EXERCISES

Using the data on student applicants for the doctoral program (student admissions data), we are interested in predicting GRE-Q scores using SES.

1. Code SES using dummy and criterion coding.
   a. How many dummy vectors are needed?
   b. What values are used to code each dummy vector?

	SES level		
	1 (lower)	2 (middle)	3 (upper)
Dummy vectors:			

   c. What values are used to criterion code the levels of SES?

SES level	Criterion code value
1	
2	
3	

2. Use SPSS to predict GRE-Q using the dummy- and criterion-coded SES predictor variable.
   a. What evidence from your SPSS output is used to determine whether GRE-Q can be predicted from SES?
   b. Using the regression equation, determine the predicted GRE-Q score for middle SES students.

APPENDIX A

Student Admission Data

ID	Gender	SES	Ethnicity	GREQ	GREV	Pretest	Rating 1	Rating 2
01	1	2	1	667	449	87	9	8
02	2	1	2	356	480	55	7	5
03	2	2	2	445	666	75	8	7
04	1	3	1	750	679	94	10	9
05	1	2	2	589	550	80	8	9
06	2	2	1	490	450	74	8	6
07	2	2	3	705	405	97	7	7
08	1	1	2	380	360	55	5	4
09	1	1	4	450	385	69	7	6
10	2	3	2	666	765	85	10	9
11	1	2	3	675	499	88	8	6
12	1	1	1	422	435	72	6	6
13	1	2	1	555	666	81	8	7
14	2	3	1	600	755	74	6	5
15	1	2	4	533	485	68	7	8
16	2	2	1	500	535	79	8	7
17	1	1	1	375	490	65	6	6
18	2	3	1	725	750	95	8	10
19	2	2	2	575	650	78	10	9
20	1	2	1	475	550	63	7	6

Variables:

ID—Identification number

Gender—gender of applicant
    1 = male, 2 = female

SES—socioeconomic status of applicant
    1 = low, 2 = middle, 3 = upper

Ethnicity—ethnicity of applicant
    1 = White, 2 = African-American,
    3 = Asian, 4 = Hispanic

GREQ—score on Graduate Record
    Examination—Quantitative Section

GREV—score on Graduate Record
    Examination—Verbal Section

Pretest—score on pretest in area of specialty

Rating1—rating from an interview with a faculty
    member

Rating2—rating from another faculty member

APPENDIX B

Computer and Statistics Attitude Survey

FED Statistics Student Survey

Background Information

1. Undergraduate Major:

   _____

2. School awarding your undergraduate degree:

   _____

3. Please indicate college level completed.

   _____ Bachelors

   _____ Masters

   _____ Specialist

   _____ Doctorate

4. Please indicate your enrollment status at Auburn.

   _____ full-time

   _____ part-time

   _____ evening courses only

5. How many credits have you completed at Auburn? _____
   (*beyond your most recent degree*)

6. How many credits are you currently enrolled in? _____

Prior Coursework

7. Have you completed any of the following courses?
   Please use the following key:

   YES = Yes
   CE = Currently enrolled
   PLAN = No, but plan to take in the future
   NO = No, do not plan to take

   a. Intro. to Educational Research   YES   CE   PLAN   NO
      (e.g., FED 661)
      If YES,   Year completed _____)
              _____ Undergraduate, _____ Graduate

b. Tests and Measurements course   **YES   CE   PLAN   NO**
  (e.g., FED 400, 610)
  If YES,   Year completed _____)
           _____ Undergraduate, _____ Graduate

c. Beginning Statistics   **YES   CE   PLAN   NO**
  (e.g., FED 672)
  If YES,   Year completed _____)
           _____ Undergraduate, _____ Graduate

d. Analysis of Variance   **YES   CE   PLAN   NO**
  (e.g., FED 673)
  If YES,   Year completed _____)
           _____ Undergraduate, _____ Graduate

e. Multiple Regression   **YES   CE   PLAN   NO**
  (e.g., FED 775)
  If YES,   Year completed _____)
           _____ Undergraduate, _____ Graduate

f. Multivariate Statistics   **YES   CE   PLAN   NO**
  (e.g., FED 776)
  If YES,   Year completed _____)
           _____ Undergraduate, _____ Graduate

g. Other course(s) in statistics   **YES   CE   PLAN   NO**
  (please specify:_____)
  If YES,   Year completed _____)
           _____ Undergraduate, _____ Graduate

Teaching Experience

8. Do you have teaching experience?
  (* please include substitute teaching)
  _____ YES   _____ NO
  If YES,
  How many years? _____
  What grade levels? (please circle all that apply)

PK   K   1   2   3   4   5   6   7   8   9   10   11   12
  If secondary, what subject areas?

____ Math	____ Vocational Ed.
____ Science	____ Special Ed.
____ English/Language Arts	____ Reading
____ Social Sciences	____ Art/Music
____ Health/Physical Ed.	____ Other (please specify)

_____

Current Academic Information

9. What degree program are you currently enrolled in?
  (please circle specific degree at right)
      _____   Bachelors   (BA, BS, BS.Ed, Other)
      _____   Masters   (MA, MS, MS.Ed., MAT, Other)
      _____   Specialist   (Ed.S)
      _____   Doctorate   (Ed.D, Ph.D)

10. Area of specialization: _____

11. If not enrolled in a degree program, please indicate your reason for enrolling in this course.

_____

12. Do you have your graduate committee?

_____ YES   _____ NO

If YES,

Who is your committee chair? _____

13. Do you have a thesis/dissertation topic?

_____ YES   _____ NO

If YES, Briefly describe the topic.

_____

_____

_____

Outside Employment

14. Are you employed this quarter?

_____ YES   _____ NO

If YES, How many hours per week? _____

15. Are you involved in any other activities that consume a great amount of your free time?

_____ YES   _____ NO

If YES, How many hours per week? _____

Survey of Attitudes Toward Learning about and Working with Computers

The purpose of this survey is to gather information concerning people's attitudes toward and working with computers. It should take about five minutes to complete this survey. All responses will be kept confidential.

1. *Age:* _____

2. *Gender:*   ( ) Male   ( ) Female

3. *Experience with learning and working with computers:*

   (   )   1 week or less

   (   )   1 week to 1 month

   (   )   1 month to 6 months

   (   )   6 months to 1 year

   (   )   1 year or more

4. *Type of experience working with computers:*

   (check all that apply)

   a. *Microcomputer Software Packages*

   (   ) word processing (e.g., WordPerfect, Word Star, MacWord, etc.)

   (   ) database/spreadsheet (e.g., Lotus, Dbase, etc.)

   (   ) statistical analysis (e.g., SPSSPC, SAS, SYSSTAT, etc.)

   (   ) computer programming; please specify language(s):

   _____

   (   ) other (please specify)

   _____

b. *Mainframe Computers*

( ) statistical analysis

( ) electronic mail

( ) computer programming; please specify language(s):

_____

( ) other (please specify)

_____

Computer Attitudes Scale

Below are a series of statements. There are no correct answers to these statements. They are designed to permit you to indicate the extent to which you agree or disagree with the ideas expressed. Place a check mark in the parentheses under the label which is closest to your agreement or disagreement with the statement. Use the following key:

SA—Strongly Agree

 A—Agree

 D—Disagree

SD—Strongly Disagree

	SA	A	D	SD
1. Computers do not scare me at all.	( )	( )	( )	( )
2. I'm no good with computers.	( )	( )	( )	( )
3. I would like working with computers.	( )	( )	( )	( )
4. I will use computers many ways in the future.	( )	( )	( )	( )
5. Working with a computer would make me nervous.	( )	( )	( )	( )
6. Generally I would feel OK trying a new problem on the computer.	( )	( )	( )	( )
7. The challenge of solving problems with computers does not appeal to me	( )	( )	( )	( )
8. Learning about computers is a waste of time.	( )	( )	( )	( )
9. I do not feel threatened when others talk about computers.	( )	( )	( )	( )
10. I don't think I would do advanced computer work.	( )	( )	( )	( )
11. I think working with computers would be enjoyable and stimulating.	( )	( )	( )	( )
12. Learning about computers is worthwhile.	( )	( )	( )	( )
13. I feel aggressive and hostile toward computers.	( )	( )	( )	( )
14. I am sure I could do work with computers.	( )	( )	( )	( )
15. Figuring out computer problems does not appeal to me.	( )	( )	( )	( )
16. I'll need a firm mastery of computers for my future work.	( )	( )	( )	( )
17. It wouldn't bother me at all to take computer classes.	( )	( )	( )	( )
18. I'm not the type to do well with computers.	( )	( )	( )	( )
19. When there is a computer problem that I can't immediately solve, I would stick with it until I had the answer.	( )	( )	( )	( )
20. I expect to have little use for computers in my life.	( )	( )	( )	( )
21. Computers make me feel uncomfortable.	( )	( )	( )	( )
22. I am sure I could learn a computer language.	( )	( )	( )	( )
23. I don't understand how some people spend so much time working with computers and seem to enjoy it.	( )	( )	( )	( )
24. I can't think of any way that I will use computers in my career.	( )	( )	( )	( )
25. I would feel at ease in a computer class.	( )	( )	( )	( )
26. I think using a computer would be very hard for me.	( )	( )	( )	( )
27. Once I start to work with the computer, I would find it hard to stop.	( )	( )	( )	( )

	SA	A	D	SD
28. Knowing how to work with computers will increase my job possibilities.	( )	( )	( )	( )
29. I get a sinking feeling when I think of trying to use a computer.	( )	( )	( )	( )
30. I could get good grades in a computer class.	( )	( )	( )	( )
31. I will do as little work with computers as possible.	( )	( )	( )	( )
32. Anything that a computer can be used for, I can do just as well some other way.	( )	( )	( )	( )
33. I feel comfortable working with a computer.	( )	( )	( )	( )
34. I do not think I could handle a computer course.	( )	( )	( )	( )
35. If a problem is left unsolved in a computer class, I would continue to think about it afterwards.	( )	( )	( )	( )
36. It is important to me to do well in computer classes.	( )	( )	( )	( )
37. Computers make me feel uneasy and confused.	( )	( )	( )	( )
38. I have a lot of self-confidence when it comes to working with computers.	( )	( )	( )	( )
39. I do not enjoy talking with others about computers.	( )	( )	( )	( )
40. Working with computers will not be important to me in my life's work.	( )	( )	( )	( )

Statistics Attitudes Survey

Purpose:

The purpose of this survey is to gather information regarding students' attitudes toward math and statistics. It should take you about 5–10 minutes to complete this survey and all responses will remain confidential.

Directions:

Please read each of the following statements carefully. Indicate the extent to which you agree or disagree with each statement by placing a check between the parentheses under the most appropriate heading. Use the following key:

SA—Strongly Agree
A—Agree
D—Disagree
SD—Strongly Disagree

	SA	A	D	SD
1. I am not afraid of statistics.	( )	( )	( )	( )
2. I'm no good with numbers.	( )	( )	( )	( )
3. I would like working with statistics.	( )	( )	( )	( )
4. I will use statistics many ways in the future.	( )	( )	( )	( )
5. Working with statistics makes me nervous.	( )	( )	( )	( )
6. Generally I would feel OK trying a new problem in statistics.	( )	( )	( )	( )
7. The challenge of solving research problems with statistics does not appeal to me.	( )	( )	( )	( )
8. Learning about statistics is a waste of time.	( )	( )	( )	( )
9. I do not feel threatened when others talk about statistics.	( )	( )	( )	( )
10. I don't think I would do advanced statistics problems.	( )	( )	( )	( )
11. I think working with statistics would be enjoyable and rewarding.	( )	( )	( )	( )
12. Learning about statistics is worthwhile.	( )	( )	( )	( )
13. I feel aggressive and hostile toward statistics.	( )	( )	( )	( )

		SA	A	D	SD
14.	I am sure I could learn to use statistics.	( )	( )	( )	( )
15.	Figuring out statistical problems does not appeal to me.	( )	( )	( )	( )
16.	I'll need a firm mastery of statistics for my future work.	( )	( )	( )	( )
17.	It doesn't bother me at all to take statistics courses.	( )	( )	( )	( )
18.	I'm not the type to do well in statistics.	( )	( )	( )	( )
19.	When there is a statistical problem that I can't immediately solve, I would stick with it until I had the answer.	( )	( )	( )	( )
20.	I expect to have little use for statistics in my life.	( )	( )	( )	( )
21.	Statistics makes me feel uncomfortable.	( )	( )	( )	( )
22.	I am sure I could learn how to use statistics.	( )	( )	( )	( )
23.	I don't understand how some people spend so much time working with statistics and seem to enjoy it.	( )	( )	( )	( )
24.	I can't think of any way that I will use statistics in my career.	( )	( )	( )	( )
25.	I feel at ease in a statistics class.	( )	( )	( )	( )
26.	I think statistics will be very hard for me.	( )	( )	( )	( )
27.	Once I start to solve a statistics problem, I would find it hard to stop.	( )	( )	( )	( )
28.	Knowing how to use statistical techniques will increase my job possibilities.	( )	( )	( )	( )
29.	I get a sinking feeling when I think of trying to learn statistics.	( )	( )	( )	( )
30.	I could get good grades in a statistics class.	( )	( )	( )	( )
31.	I will do as little work with statistics as possible.	( )	( )	( )	( )
32.	Anything that statistics can be used for, I can do just as well some other way.	( )	( )	( )	( )
33.	I feel comfortable working with statistics.	( )	( )	( )	( )
34.	I do not think I could handle a statistics course.	( )	( )	( )	( )
35.	If a problem is left unsolved in a statistics class, I would continue to think about it afterwards.	( )	( )	( )	( )
36.	It is important to me to do well in statistics class(es).	( )	( )	( )	( )
37.	Statistics makes me feel uneasy and confused.	( )	( )	( )	( )
38.	I have a lot of self-confidence when it comes to working with statistics.	( )	( )	( )	( )
39.	I do not enjoy talking with others about statistics.	( )	( )	( )	( )
40.	Working with statistics will not be important to me in my life's work.	( )	( )	( )	( )

WHEW !

THANK YOU FOR COMPLETING THIS SURVEY

APPENDIX C

Syntax Commands Used to Run SPSS Procedures

This appendix contains the syntax commands used to generate statistical output throughout the text. In each chapter, you executed SPSS procedures by selecting options from menus and dialog boxes. As you made these selections, a record was being kept by SPSS in the form of syntax commands. You can view these syntax commands in a syntax editor simply by clicking on the Paste button.

You used this button to paste the syntax commands into the syntax editor several times throughout the text. Syntax commands are similar to those necessary to run earlier DOS-based and mainframe SPSS programs. It is a good practice to save these syntax commands as you perform SPSS procedures, just in case you need to perform the same operations again at a later time. Once you have saved a record of the syntax commands, all you need to do is retrieve the file to perform the same operations again. This saves you a great deal of time, eliminating the need to recreate all your menu and dialog box selections.

As a reminder, the steps necessary to create, save, and retrieve syntax commands are summarized below. After this summary, we present a listing of the syntax commands from each chapter.

To create syntax commands and view in the syntax editor:

1. Make all the necessary menu and dialog box selections.
2. Use the **Paste** button to view the syntax commands in the syntax editor.

To save the syntax commands to a file:

1. Select the **Save** option from the **File** menu.
    (These selections can also be made using the save file icon from the toolbar.)
2. Identify the location (e.g., floppy disk, drive C) to where you wish to save the syntax commands using the Save in menu.
3. Specify a name for the file in the File name box.
4. Identify the file as a syntax file using the .sps suffix.
5. Click the **Save** button.

To retrieve the syntax file:

1. Select the **Open** option from the **File** menu.
   (These selections can also be made using the open file icon from the toolbar.)
2. Specify the location of the file (e.g., floppy disk, drive C) using the Save in menu.
3. Identify the filename in the File name box.
   Be sure the Files of type menu box is set for Syntax (*.sps).
4. Click the **Open** button.

Chapter 4–Importing and Merging Data Files

** Fixed Width Format
```
data list file='A:\asciidat.txt' fixed records=1 /1 ID 1-2(F) GENDER 3-3(F) SES 4-4(F)
ETHNIC 5-5(F) GREQ 6-8(F) GREV 9-11(F) PRETEST 12-13(F) RATING1 14-15(F)
RATING2 16-17(F).
EXECUTE .
```

** Delimited Text Format
```
data list list(',') file='A:\asciidat2.txt' / ID(f8.2) GENDER(f8.2) SES(f8.2) ETHNIC(f8.2)
GREQ(f8.2) GREV(f8.2) PRETEST(f8.2) RATING1(f8.2) RATING2(f8.2).
EXECUTE .
```

**Adding new cases
```
ADD FILES /FILE=*
/FILE='A:\student1.add cases.sav'
/IN=source01.
VARIABLE LABELS source01
'Case source is A:\student1.add cases.sav'.
EXECUTE .
```

**Adding new variables
```
MATCH FILES /FILE=*
/FILE='A:\student2. add var.sav'
/RENAME (id = d0)
/DROP= d0.
EXECUTE .
```

Chapter 5–Frequency Analysis

```
FREQUENCIES
  VARIABLES=compexp gender degree group
  /STATISTICS=RANGE MEDIAN MODE
  /BARCHART FREQ
  /ORDER ANALYSIS .
```

Chapter 6–Central Tendency and Variability

** Default Statistics
```
DESCRIPTIVES
  VARIABLES=aucred teaexp age /SAVE
  /STATISTICS=MEAN STDDEV MIN MAX .
```

** Optional Statistics
```
DESCRIPTIVES
  VARIABLES=aucred teaexp age /SAVE
  /STATISTICS=MEAN STDDEV VARIANCE RANGE MIN MAX SEMEAN KURTOSIS
SKEWNESS .
```

Chapter 7–Describing Subgroups

```
**Select Cases (GENDER =1)
USE ALL.
COMPUTE filter_$=(gender = 1).
VARIABLE LABEL filter_$ 'gender = 1 (FILTER)'.
VALUE LABELS filter_$ 0 'Not Selected' 1 'Selected'.
FORMAT filter_$ (f1.0).
FILTER BY filter_$.
EXECUTE .
```

```
** SelectRandom Sample of Cases (25% of the sample)
USE ALL.
COMPUTE filter_$=(uniform(1)<=.25).
VARIABLE LABEL filter_$ 'Approximately 25 % of cases (SAMPLE)'.
FORMAT filter_$ (f1.0).
FILTER BY filter_$.
EXECUTE .
```

```
**Select Random Sample of Cases (n=50)
USE ALL.
do if $casenum = 1.
 compute #s_$_1=50.
 compute #s_$_2=209.
 end if.
 do if #s_$_2 > 0.
 compute filter_$ = uniform(1)* #s_$_2 < #s_$_1.
 compute #s_$_1 = #s_$_1 - filter_$.
 compute #s_$_2 = #s_$_2 - 1.
 else.
 compute filter_$ = 0.
 end if.
VARIABLE LABEL filter_$ '50 from the first 209 cases (SAMPLE)'.
FORMAT filter_$ (f1.0).
FILTER BY filter_$.
EXECUTE .
```

```
**Using a Filter Variable (Teaching Experience)
USE ALL.
FILTER BY teaexp .
EXECUTE .
```

```
**MEANS Procedure (One Independent Variable)
MEANS
 TABLES=age crednow BY status
 /CELLS MEAN COUNT STDDEV .
```

```
** MEANS Procedure (Two Independent Variables)
MEANS
 TABLES=age crednow BY status employed
 /CELLS MEAN COUNT STDDEV .
```

Chapter 8–Recoding Data

```
**Recode into SAME Variables
RECODE
 comp2 comp5 comp7 comp8 comp10 comp13 comp15 comp18 comp20 comp21
 comp23 comp24 comp26 comp29 comp31 comp32 comp34 comp37 comp39 comp40
 (4=1) (3=2) (2=3) (1=4) .
 EXECUTE .
```

```
**Recode into DIFFERENT Variables
RECODE
  age
  (Lowest thru 25=1) (26 thru 30=2) (31 thru 40=3) (41 thru 50=4) (51
  thru Highest=5) INTO agegroup .
EXECUTE .

**Categorize Procedure
RANK
  VARIABLES = age
  /NTILES(5)
  /PRINT = NO
  /TIES = MEAN .
```

Chapter 9–Computing New Variables

```
**Computing 4 Computer Attitude Scales
COMPUTE

companx = sum(comp1,comp5,comp9,comp13,comp17,comp21,comp25,comp29,comp33,comp37) .
compcon = sum(comp2,comp6,comp10,comp14,comp18,comp22,comp26,comp30,comp34,comp38) .
complik = sum(comp3,comp7,comp11,comp15,comp19,comp23,comp27,comp31,comp35,comp39) .
compuse = sum(comp4,comp8,comp12,comp16,comp20,comp24,comp28,comp32,comp36,comp40) .
EXECUTE .
```

Chapter 10–Reliability Analysis

```
**Coefficient Alpha
RELIABILITY
  /VARIABLES=comp1 comp5 comp9 comp13 comp17 comp21 comp25 comp29
  comp33 comp37
  /FORMAT=NOLABELS
  /SCALE(ALPHA)=ALL/MODEL=ALPHA
  /STATISTICS=DESCRIPTIVE SCALE CORR ANOVA
  /SUMMARY=TOTAL MEANS VARIANCE CORR .

** Split-half Reliability
RELIABILITY
  /VARIABLES=comp1 comp5 comp9 comp13 comp17 comp21 comp25 comp29
  comp33 comp37
  /FORMAT=NOLABELS
  /SCALE(SPLIT)=ALL/MODEL=SPLIT
  /STATISTICS=DESCRIPTIVE SCALE CORR ANOVA
  /SUMMARY=TOTAL MEANS VARIANCE CORR .
```

Chapter 12–Crosstabulation of Variables

```
**2-way Table (GENDER by COMPEXP)
CROSSTABS
  /TABLES=gender BY compexp
  /FORMAT= AVALUE TABLES
  /STATISTIC=CHISQ CC
  /CELLS= COUNT EXPECTED ROW COLUMN TOTAL RESID .

*3-way Table (STATUS by NIGHT by EMPLOYED)
CROSSTABS
  /TABLES=status BY night BY employed
  /FORMAT= AVALUE TABLES
  /STATISTIC=CHISQ CC PHI
  /CELLS= COUNT EXPECTED ROW COLUMN TOTAL RESID .
```

Chapter 13–Displaying Relationships

**Simple Scatterplot (Age and Employment Hours)
GRAPH
  /SCATTERPLOT(BIVAR)=age WITH emphours
  /MISSING=LISTWISE
  /TITLE= 'Simple Scatterplot' 'EMPHOURS with AGE'.

**Simple Scatterplot with a Third Variable (Age and Employment Hours by Gender)
GRAPH
  /SCATTERPLOT(BIVAR)=age WITH emphours BY gender
  /MISSING=LISTWISE
  /TITLE= 'Simple Scatterplot' 'EMPHOURS with AGE by GENDER'.

**Overlay Scatterplot ('Age and Credits with Employment Hours)
GRAPH
  /SCATTERPLOT(OVERLAY)=age crednow WITH emphours emphours (PAIR)
  /MISSING=LISTWISE
  /TITLE= 'Overlay Scatterplot' 'Age and Credits with Emplyment Hours'.

**Scatterplot Matrix (Computer Attitude Scales)
GRAPH
  /SCATTERPLOT(MATRIX)=companx compcon complik compuse
  /MISSING=LISTWISE
  /TITLE= 'Scatterplot Matrix' 'Computer Attitude Scales'.

**3-D Scatterplot ('Employment Hours by Age by Credits Taken)
GRAPH
  /SCATTERPLOT(XYZ)=age WITH emphours WITH crednow
  /MISSING=LISTWISE
  /TITLE= '3-D Scatterplot' 'Employment Hours by Age by Credits Taken'.

Chapter 14–Describing Relationships

**Student Background Variables
CORRELATIONS
  /VARIABLES=teayear emphours age
  /PRINT=TWOTAIL NOSIG
  /STATISTICS DESCRIPTIVES XPROD
  /MISSING=PAIRWISE .

**Computer Attitudes with Statistic Attitudes
CORRELATIONS
  /VARIABLES=companx compcon complik compuse with statanx statcon statlik statuse
  /PRINT=TWOTAIL NOSIG
  /STATISTICS DESCRIPTIVES XPROD
  /MISSING=PAIRWISE .

**Spearman rank-order Correlation
CORRELATIONS
  /VARIABLES=educ compexp companx compcon complik compuse
  /PRINT=TWOTAIL NOSIG
  /STATISTICS DESCRIPTIVES XPROD
  /MISSING=PAIRWISE .
NONPAR CORR
  /VARIABLES=educ compexp with companx compcon complik compuse
  /PRINT=SPEARMAN TWOTAIL NOSIG
  /MISSING=PAIRWISE .

Chapter 15–T-Test Procedures

```
**One-sample t-test
T-TEST
 /TESTVAL=4
 /MISSING=ANALYSIS
 /VARIABLES=crednow
 /CRITERIA=CIN (.95) .
```

**Independent-samples t-test (Comparing masters and doctoral students on computer and statistics attitudes)
```
T-TEST
 GROUPS=degree(2 4)
 /MISSING=ANALYSIS
 /VARIABLES=companx compcon complik compuse statanx statcon statlik statuse
 /CRITERIA=CIN(.95) .
```

**Independent-samples t-test (Comparing part- and full-time students on AGE, EMPHOURS, CREDNOW)
```
T-TEST
 GROUPS=status(1 2)
 /MISSING=ANALYSIS
 /VARIABLES=age emphours crednow
 /CRITERIA=CIN(.95) .
```

Chapter 16–ONE-WAY ANOVA

```
**Computer Attitudes by Computer Experience
ONEWAY
 companx compcon complik compuse BY compexp
 /CONTRAST= −1 −1 −1 −1 4
 /STATISTICS DESCRIPTIVES HOMOGENEITY
 /PLOT MEANS
 /MISSING ANALYSIS
 /POSTHOC = TUKEY SCHEFFE LSD ALPHA(.05).
```

Chapter 17–Factorial ANOVA

```
** DV=Computer Liking, IVs = MASTDOC and COMPEXP2
UNIANOVA
 complik BY mastdoc compexp2
 /METHOD = SSTYPE(3)
 /INTERCEPT = INCLUDE
 /PLOT = PROFILE(compexp2*mastdoc)
 /EMMEANS = TABLES(mastdoc) COMPARE ADJ(BONFERRONI)
 /EMMEANS = TABLES(compexp2) COMPARE ADJ(BONFERRONI)
 /EMMEANS = TABLES(mastdoc*compexp2)
 /PRINT = DESCRIPTIVE ETASQ OPOWER
 /CRITERIA = ALPHA(.05)
 /DESIGN = mastdoc compexp2 mastdoc*compexp2 .
```

**DV=Employment Hours, IVs=GENDER and MASTDOC
```
UNIANOVA
 emphours BY gender mastdoc
 /METHOD = SSTYPE(3)
 /INTERCEPT = INCLUDE
 /PLOT = PROFILE(mastdoc*gender)
 /EMMEANS = TABLES(gender) COMPARE ADJ(BONFERRONI)
```

```
/EMMEANS = TABLES(mastdoc) COMPARE ADJ(BONFERRONI)
/EMMEANS = TABLES(gender*mastdoc)
/PRINT = DESCRIPTIVE ETASQ OPOWER
/CRITERIA = ALPHA(.05)
/DESIGN = gender mastdoc gender*mastdoc .
```

Chapter 18–Paired-Samples T-Test

```
**Comparing computer and statistic attitude scales
T-TEST
  PAIRS= companx compcon complik compuse WITH statanx statcon statlik
  statuse (PAIRED)
  /CRITERIA=CIN(.95)
  /MISSING=ANALYSIS.
```

Chapter 19–Within-Subjects ANOVA

```
**Comparison Across Four Computer Attitude Scales
GLM
  companx compcon complik compuse
  /WSFACTOR = comp 4 Polynomial
  /METHOD = SSTYPE(3)
  /PLOT = PROFILE(comp)
  /EMMEANS = TABLES(comp) COMPARE ADJ(BONFERRONI)
  /PRINT = DESCRIPTIVE ETASQ OPOWER
  /CRITERIA = ALPHA(.05)
  /WSDESIGN = comp .
```

Chapter 20–Mixed Model ANOVA

```
**TIME (Pre- and Post- Computer Anxiety) by SPSS Group
GLM
  companx1 companx2 BY group
  /WSFACTOR = time 2 Polynomial
  /METHOD = SSTYPE(3)
  /POSTHOC = group (TUKEY SCHEFFE LSD)
  /PLOT = PROFILE(time*group)
  /EMMEANS = TABLES(group) COMPARE ADJ(BONFERRONI)
  /EMMEANS = TABLES(time) COMPARE ADJ(BONFERRONI)
  /EMMEANS = TABLES(group*time)
  /PRINT = DESCRIPTIVE ETASQ OPOWER
  /CRITERIA = ALPHA(.05)
  /WSDESIGN = time
  /DESIGN = group .
```

Chapter 21–Bivariate Regression

```
REGRESSION
  /DESCRIPTIVES MEAN STDDEV CORR SIG N
  /MISSING LISTWISE
  /STATISTICS COEFF OUTS CI BCOV R ANOVA
  /CRITERIA=PIN(.05) POUT(.10) CIN(95)
  /NOORIGIN
  /DEPENDENT crednow
  /METHOD=ENTER emphours
  /SCATTERPLOT=(*ZPRED ,*SRESID)
  /RESIDUALS DURBIN HIST(ZRESID) NORM(ZRESID)
```

```
/CASEWISE PLOT(ZRESID) OUTLIERS(2)
/SAVE PRED ADJPRED SEPRED COOK LEVER MCIN RESID ZRESID SRESID
SDRESID DFBETA SDBETA .
```

Chapter 22–Multiple Regression

```
** Simultaneous Regression
REGRESSION
  /DESCRIPTIVES MEAN STDDEV CORR SIG N
  /MISSING LISTWISE
  /STATISTICS COEFF OUTS R ANOVA COLLIN TOL CHANGE ZPP
  /CRITERIA=PIN(.05) POUT(.10)
  /NOORIGIN
  /DEPENDENT crednow
  /METHOD=ENTER night emphours othact age
  /RESIDUALS DURBIN
  /CASEWISE PLOT(ZRESID) OUTLIERS(2) .
```

```
** Stepwise Regression
REGRESSION
  /DESCRIPTIVES MEAN STDDEV CORR SIG N
  /MISSING LISTWISE
  /STATISTICS COEFF OUTS R ANOVA COLLIN TOL CHANGE ZPP
  /CRITERIA=PIN(.05) POUT(.10)
  /NOORIGIN
  /DEPENDENT crednow
  /METHOD=STEPWISE night emphours othact age
  /RESIDUALS DURBIN
  /CASEWISE PLOT(ZRESID) OUTLIERS(2) .
```

```
**Hierarchical Regression
REGRESSION
  /DESCRIPTIVES MEAN STDDEV CORR SIG N
  /MISSING LISTWISE
  /STATISTICS COEFF OUTS R ANOVA COLLIN TOL CHANGE ZPP
  /CRITERIA=PIN(.05) POUT(.10)
  /NOORIGIN
  /DEPENDENT crednow
  /METHOD=STEPWISE age /METHOD=ENTER emphours othact /METHOD=
    ENTER night
  /RESIDUALS DURBIN
  /CASEWISE PLOT(ZRESID) OUTLIERS(2) .
```

Chapter 23–Regression with Categorical Predictors

```
**Creating 4 DUMMY Code Vectors for the Five Categories of Computer Experience
RECODE
  compexp
  (1=1) (ELSE=0) INTO DUM1 .
  (2=1) (ELSE=0) INTO DUM2 .
  (3=1) (ELSE=0) INTO DUM3 .
  (4=1) (ELSE=0) INTO DUM4 .
EXECUTE .
```

```
** Using DUM1, DUM2, DUM3, DUM4 in Regression Analysis
REGRESSION
  /MISSING LISTWISE
  /STATISTICS COEFF OUTS R ANOVA
```

```
/CRITERIA=PIN(.05) POUT(.10)
/NOORIGIN
/DEPENDENT companx
/METHOD=ENTER dum1 dum2 dum3 dum4 .
```

**Recoding Computer Experience using Criterion Coding
```
RECODE
  compexp
  (2=22.8) (1=21.3333) (3=26.0526) (4=28.0385) (5=32.7724) INTO
  CRITER1 .
EXECUTE .
```

**Using Criterion-coded Variable in Regression Analysis
```
REGRESSION
  /MISSING LISTWISE
  /STATISTICS COEFF OUTS R ANOVA
  /CRITERIA=PIN(.05) POUT(.10)
  /NOORIGIN
  /DEPENDENT companx
  /METHOD=ENTER criter1 .
```

APPENDIX D

Answers to Chapter Practice Exercises

Chapter 3–Data Entry and Definition

For each of these variables, identify the level of measurement and how the variable will be coded for SPSS.

Variable	Level of Measurement	Coding Information
College	nominal	1 = Agriculture 2 = Business 3 = Education 4 = Engineering 5 = Liberal Arts 6 = Science and Math
Tenure Status	nominal	1 = tenure-track 2 = tenured
Academic Rank	ordinal	1 = Instructor 2 = Assistant Professor 3 = Associate Professor 4 = Full Professor
Years of Experience	ratio	# of years of experience

Chapter 5–Frequency Analysis

1–using student admission data

1a1. There are 9 females in the sample.
1a2. There are 5 students from low SES backgrounds.
1a3. Thirty (30) percent of the sample is African-American.

1a4. Eighty (80) percent of the student received a rating of 8 or lower from the first faculty member (RATING1), while 75% received an 8 or lower from the second faculty member (RATING2).

2–using chap5 data

2a1. In this sample, 134 (64.1%) of the students have teaching experience.

2a2. Eighty-four (40.2%) have a Bachelors degree.

2a3. Over fifty percent (51.7%) have earned a Masters degree.

Chapter 6–Measures of Central Tendency and Variability

Descriptive Statistics

	N	Minimum	Maximum	Mean	Std. Deviation	Skewness		Kurtosis	
	Statistic	Statistic	Statistic	Statistic	Statistic	Statistic	Std. Error	Statistic	Std. Error
GREQ	20	356.00	750.00	546.6500	123.2137	.084	.512	−1.194	.992
GREV	20	360.00	765.00	550.2000	128.7857	.375	.512	−1.134	.992
PRETEST	20	55.00	97.00	76.7000	12.1962	−.096	.512	−.563	.992
RATING1	20	5.00	10.00	7.6500	1.3870	.180	.512	−.272	.992
RATING2	20	4.00	10.00	7.0000	1.6222	.164	.512	−.764	.992
Valid N (listwise)	20								

1a. Descriptive information is reported in the above table.

1b. When examining GRE scores, our sample is slightly more varied in terms of verbal ability, as GREV has standard deviation of 128.7857 compared to 123.2137 for GREQ.

1c. Of the above variables, GREV is most skewed, having the largest absolute value for the skewness statistic (.375). This statistic is positive, which indicates that the tail of the GREV distribution is slightly flatter toward the positive (or right) side and higher on the left side. The frequency distribution below illustrates this skewness.

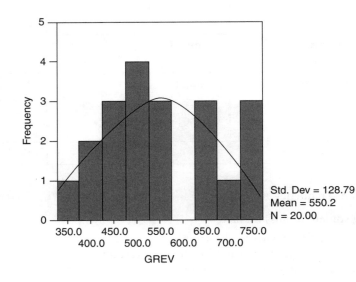

Std. Dev = 128.79
Mean = 550.2
N = 20.00

1d. Z scores were created when performing the descriptive analysis by checking the box labeled "Save standardized values as variables." These z scores have been added to your data file.

1e. The selection of the top three applicants will vary depending on the criteria you use to make this selection. For example, you might think that GRE scores are most important or you might think that each of the five variables is equally important. If you used a weighted criteria, we recommend that you use the z scores, not the original variables.

Chapter 7—Selecting and Describing Subgroups

1a. The average GREQ score for students from a low SES background is 396.6.

1b. The average ratings for female students are 8 for RATING1 and 7.2 for RATING2.

1c. The average GREV score for students who received a rating of 8 or above on RATING1 is 605.4.

2. The selection of random samples is made by selecting the Random sample of cases option from the Select Cases dialog box.

3. Using the Means procedure, we obtained the following descriptive information.

3a. Summary of GREV and GREQ by GENDER

Report

GENDER		GREV	GREQ
1.00	Mean	504.3636	533.7273
	N	11	11
	Std. Deviation	102.1590	126.4002
2.00	Mean	606.2222	562.4444
	N	9	9
	Std. Deviation	141.1593	124.7989
Total	Mean	550.2000	546.6500
	N	20	20
	Std. Deviation	128.7857	123.2137

3b. Summary of GREV and GREQ by SES

Report

SES		GREV	GREQ
1.00	Mean	430.0000	396.6000
	N	5	5
	Std. Deviation	57.1183	38.3640
2.00	Mean	536.8182	564.4545
	N	11	11
	Std. Deviation	91.2566	87.3217
3.00	Mean	737.2500	685.2500
	N	4	4
	Std. Deviation	39.3309	66.8599
Total	Mean	550.2000	546.6500
	N	20	20
	Std. Deviation	128.7857	123.2137

3c. Summary of GREV and GREQ by GENDER and SES

GENDER	SES			GREV	GREQ
1.00	1.00	Mean		417.5000	406.7500
		N		4	4
		Std. Deviation		57.5181	35.7153
	2.00	Mean		533.1667	582.3333
		N		6	6
		Std. Deviation		75.8720	78.1042
	3.00	Mean		679.0000	750.0000
		N		1	1
		Std. Deviation		.	.
	Total	Mean		504.3636	533.7273
		N		11	11
		Std. Deviation		102.1590	126.4002
2.00	1.00	Mean		480.0000	356.0000
		N		1	1
		Std. Deviation		.	.
	2.00	Mean		541.2000	543.0000
		N		5	5
		Std. Deviation		116.5320	101.8946
	3.00	Mean		756.6667	663.6667
		N		3	3
		Std. Deviation		7.6376	62.5327
	Total	Mean		606.2222	562.4444
		N		9	9
		Std. Deviation		141.1593	124.7989
Total	1.00	Mean		430.0000	396.6000
		N		5	5
		Std. Deviation		57.1183	38.3640
	2.00	Mean		536.8182	564.4545
		N		11	11
		Std. Deviation		91.2566	87.3217
	3.00	Mean		737.2500	685.2500
		N		4	4
		Std. Deviation		39.3309	66.8599
	Total	Mean		550.2000	546.6500
		N		20	20
		Std. Deviation		128.7857	123.2137

Chapter 8–Recoding Variables

1. Retrieving a data file.

To retrieve an SPSS Data file:

Step 1   From the menubar, click on the **File** menu.
Step 2   **Open.**
Step 3   **Data.**
Step 4   Select the drive which contains your file.

> **Step 5** **Identify the type of file you wish to retrieve. The setting is *.sav for SPSS data files.**
>
> **Step 6** **Highlight the file and click twice with your mouse to retrieve it into the data editor.**

(Double-clicking on the open file icon on the toolbar will lead directly to the window containing the names of files found on specific disks.)

2. Use the Recode in Different Variables procedure to recode GREV and GREQ scores into new variables with five categories.

2a. There are three (3) applicants having GREQ scores in the 701 to 800 category.

2b. There are two (2) applicants with GREV scores in the 0 to 400 category.

Chapter 9–Computing New Variables

1. Compute the new variable, GRETOT, using the COMPUTE procedure. Either of the following expressions could be used to compute this new variable:

   COMPUTE gretot = greq + grev .

   COMPUTE gretot = sum(greq,grev).

2. The average GRE score is computed by dividing the total, GRETOT, by 2.

   COMPUTE greavg = gretot/2.

3. Descriptive information regarding these new variables is summarized below.

Descriptive Statistics

	N	Minimum	Maximum	Mean	Std. Deviation
GRETOT	20	740.00	1475.00	1096.8500	216.0607
GREAVG	20	370.00	737.50	548.4250	108.0304
Valid N (listwise)	20				

Chapter 10–Reliability Analysis

1. Reliability estimates (Cronbach's alpha) are summarized for each of the four statistics attitude scales below.

Scale	Reliability Estimate
Anxiety	.9500
Confidence	.9095
Liking	.9063
Usefulness	.8902

2. Examining the inter-item correlations for each scale, we have noted some of our observations.

   Scale 1–Anxiety–Item 37 generally has higher correlations with the remaining items. The inter-item correlations for item 37 range from .55 to .84, indicating consistency with the other items in the scale. On the other hand, item 13 has three inter-item correlations below .5 with items 1, 5, and 9.

Scale 2–Confidence–Item 18 correlates strongly with the other items in the scale with these correlations ranging from .48 to .74, whereas item 10 relates in a weaker manner with correlations ranging from .26 to .50.

Scale 3–Liking–Item 11 correlates most strongly with inter-item correlations ranging from .42 to .72, while item 35 relates somewhat weaker as correlations range from .34 to .64.

Scale 4–Usefulness–Item 16 has the highest inter-item correlation with item 4 (.73), while the lowest overall inter-item correlation exists between items 36 and 20 (.19).

3. The average inter-item correlations for each scale are reported below.

Scale	Average Inter-Item Correlation
Anxiety	.6532
Confidence	.5229
Liking	.4928
Usefulness	.4464

The above information indicates that items in the anxiety scale correlate most strongly with each other, while those in the usefulness scale correlate the least. This agrees with the reliability information presented in response to the first question.

4. Scale 1–Anxiety–Item 13 correlates least strongly with the overall scale evidenced by a .5890 item-total correlation. All other items correlate at or beyond .65. If item 13 were deleted from the overall scale, the reliability would increase slightly from .9500 to .9523.

Scale 2–Confidence–All items except item 10 have item-total correlation above .60. Item 10 correlates .5500 with the overall scale. The deletion of this item would increase the reliability slightly from .9095 to .9116.

Scale 3–Liking–Items 31, 35, and 39 had item-total correlations slightly below .60. The deletion of any of these items will not increase the overall scale reliability estimate.

Scale 4–Usefulness–Item 36 has the lowest item-total correlation (.3946). All other items have item-total correlation in excess of .60 except item 32 (.46). The deletion of item 36 would increase the reliability from .8904 to .8934.

In summary, no items correlate negatively with their respective scale and impact the overall reliability in a severe manner.

5. These reliability estimates are comparable to those obtained for the four computer attitude scales. A summary of these estimates appears below.

	Computer	Statistics
Anxiety	.9432	.9500
Confidence	.9143	.9095
Liking	.9095	.9063
Usefulness	.8370	.8902

Chapter 11–Hypothesis Testing

1a. If the mean number of days is 5 days and the standard deviation is 1 day, then 7 days is 2 standard deviations above the mean. In a normal distribution, about 2% of the scores lie above (or below) a standard deviation of 2. Thus, about 2% of the students will spend 7 or more days in the hospital.

1b. We know that, on a normal curve, the 84th percentile lies at a point very close to the 1st standard deviation above the mean. Since the mean is 5 days and moving one standard deviation to the right is one additional day, there are about 6 days on the distribution of length of hospital stay (in days) that lie to the left of this point; the 84th percentile.

1c. Since the mean length of stay is 5 days and the standard deviation is 1 day, 4 and 6 represent points on the distribution that are 1 standard deviation below and 1 standard deviation above the mean. We know that length of stay for approximately 68% of the students can be found between these two points. Sixty-eight percent of 50 students is 34 students.

1d. Using the same logic as we used for Question 3, we add 14% (the proportion of the distribution that lies between the 1st and 2nd standard deviation) to our figure of 68% and get 82%. Eighty-two percent of the students will spend between 3 and 6 days in the hospital.

Chapter 12–Crosstabulation of Variables

1a. The smallest subgroups, identified in the Count box, are low SES females (SES=1, GENDER=2) and high SES males (SES=3, GENDER=1). Each group has only 1 member. The largest group is the middle SES male group (SES=2, GENDER=1) with 6 members. Due to the fact that some of the cells have counts of less than 5, we should use the chi-square statistic cautiously. Its value will likely be inflated.

1b. Pearson's chi-square and related statistics are found in the Chi-Square Tests box. The value for the chi-square statistic is 2.72 with 2 degrees of freedom with a probability of .257.

1c. The chi-square reported in this analysis is not statistically significant as the p value for the statistic (.257) exceeds our chosen level of significance, .05. Thus, we would conclude that there is no significant relationship between GENDER and SES.

1d. The appropriate measure of association for this analysis is the contingency coefficient since one of our variables (SES) is not dichotomous. The value of this statistic, .35, is not statistically significant since its associated p value (.26) is above .05.

Chapter 13–Displaying Relationships

1. Three scatterplots are displayed here.

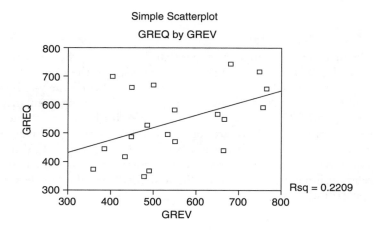

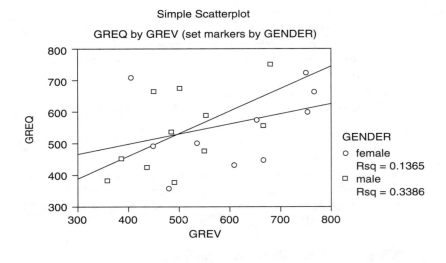

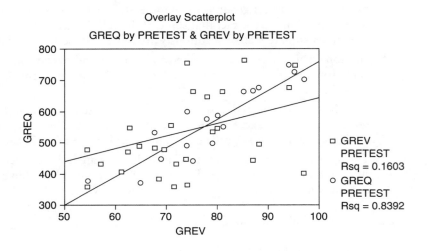

2. The first thing one might notice is that, for all plots, the low scores tend to be grouped at the left of the chart and the high scores are to the right. This represents a positive relationship in which a high value for the variable on the y-axis is generally related to a high value for the variable on the x-axis. The strongest relationship exists between GREQ and PRETEST scores. Examine the third scatterplot and notice that the solid squares are very tightly grouped and follow a clear positive pattern. On the other hand, examine the relationship between GREQ and GREV in the first scatterplot. This relationship is weaker as the data points are more widely scattered. The weakest relationship exists between GREQ and GREV for the female subjects (see the second scatterplot).

3. A scatterplot matrix of the statistics attitude scales appears here.

Scatterplot Matrix
Statistics Attitudes Scales

Chapter 14–Describing Relationships

1a. We would use Pearson's r, since both variables are interval data.

1b. As above, we would use Pearson's r, for the same reason.

1c. Since SES is an ordinal variable, we would use Spearman's r.

2a. The Pearson correlation between GREQ and GREV is .470 (p = .037)

2b. The Pearson correlation between PRETEST and GREQ is stronger at .916 (p < .001).

2c. The Spearman correlation between RATING1 and SES is .590 (p = .006).

3a, 3b, 3c.–Reject the null hypothesis for each relationship and conclude that these relationships are not likely due to chance.

Chapter 15–T-Tests

1. H_o: The doctoral applicants do not differ from the typical student in terms of the GREQ and therefore come from a population having a mean of 500.

   H_o: The doctoral applicants do not differ from the typical student in terms of the GREV and therefore come from a population having a mean of 500.

The results of each one-sample t-test are summarized.

	GREQ	GREV
Sample Mean	546.65	550.20
Test Value	500	500
Mean Difference	46.65	50.20
95% CI	−11.02 to 104.32	−10.07 to 110.47
t	1.693	1.743
df	19	19
2-tail Sig.	.107	.097
Decision about null hypothesis	Fail to reject	Fail to reject

What conclusions can be made based on these t-test results?

The differences between our sample of 20 applicants and a population having a mean GREQ and GREV of 500 are most likely due to chance.

2. H$_o$: Male doctoral applicants do not differ from female doctoral applicants in terms of the GREQ.

   H$_o$: Male doctoral applicants do not differ from female doctoral applicants in terms of the GREV.

The results from each independent-samples t-test are reported.

	GREQ	GREV
Means		
Males	533.73	504.36
Females	562.44	606.22
Standard Deviations		
Males	126.40	102.16
Females	124.80	141.16
Levene's test for Equality of Variances		
F	.002	3.061
Sig.	.967	.099
Can homogeneity of variance be assumed?	Yes	Yes
t	−.508	−1.872
df	18	18
2-tail Sig.	.617	.078
Mean Difference	−28.72	−101.41
95% CI	−147.41 to 89.97	−216.17 to 12.45
Decision about null hypothesis (Reject/Fail to Reject)	Fail to reject	Fail to reject

What conclusions can be made based on these t-test results?

The differences between males and females in terms of GREQ and GREV scores are most likely due to chance.

3. You should have used an independent-samples t-test to compare your selected applicants with the remaining applicant pool on GREQ, GREV, and PRETEST.

Chapter 16–One-Way ANOVA

1. The independent variable is SES, having 3 levels. Three one-way ANOVAs were performed using GREQ, GREV, and RATING average as the dependent variables.

2. A summary of these ANOVAs appears here. Group means are reported in each cell.

	SES			
	Low	Middle	High	F ratio (Probability)
GREQ	396.6	564.45	685.25	17.161 (< .001)
GREV	430.0	536.82	737.25	18.029 (< .001)
RATING	5.8	7.64	8.38	6.912 (.006)

Homogeneity of variance was maintained in each analysis as the probability of the Levene's statistic exceeded .05

3. Three different post-hoc tests were performed for comparison purposes. These were Tukey, Scheffe, and LSD. The results from these tests are summarized.

	Tukey	Scheffe	LSD
GREQ	High > Middle, Low Middle > Low	High > Middle, Low Middle > Low	High > Middle, Low Middle > Low
GREV	High > Middle, Low Middle > Low	High > Middle, Low	High > Middle, Low Middle > Low
RATING	High > Middle, Low	High > Middle, Low	High > Middle, Low

The only inconsistency among these three tests regards GREV scores. Whereas the Tukey and LSD tests detected a difference between middle and low SES, the more conservative Scheffe did not.

4. Using pre-planned contrasts, high SES students were compared to the average of middle and low SES students. The results of this contrast was statistically significant for each dependent variable. High SES students scored higher on the GREQ and GREV and were rated higher in faculty interviews.

Chapter 17—Factorial ANOVA

1. The independent variables are COMPEXP2 and MASTDOC, each having two levels. The dependent variable is STATLIK, statistics liking scale.

2. Profile Plot (MASTDOC by COMPEXP2)

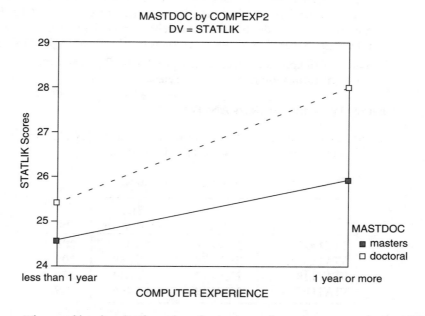

The profile plot displays that the impact of computer experience (COMPEXP2) is similar for both masters and doctoral students, indicating the lack of an interaction effect.

3. The results (F ratios) from the factorial ANOVA are summarized here.

Effect	F (Probability)
Computer Experience (COMPEXP2)	6.719 (< .001)
Degree Program (MASTDOC)	2.446 (.121)
Interaction (COMPEXP2 × MASTDOC)	.335 (.564)

There is a significant main effect (p < .05) for computer experience. Specifically, those with more than one year of experience like statistics more than those with less than one year experience. There is no significant main effect for degree program (p = .121) and no significant interaction effect (p = .564).

Chapter 18—PAIRED-SAMPLES T-TEST

1. The results from the paired-samples t-tests are summarized.

Paired Variables	Means	Correlation	t	Probability
GREV	550.2	.470	−.122	.904
GREQ	546.65			
RATING1	7.65	.722	2.795	.012
RATING2	7.00			

2. The correlations between the pairs of variables indicate that these variables are positively related to each other. That is, there is a tendency for applicants who score low on the GREV to score low on the GREQ, and those who score high on the GREV to also score high on the GREQ. The relationship between faculty ratings is higher, indicating a stronger relationship.

3. The 95% CI for the pair of GRE scores ranges from −64.31 to 57.21. This is a very wide range that contains zero. Therefore, the true difference in the population could be negative, positive or zero. The CI for the pair of ratings communicates a different message. This range is from .16 to 1.14. The interval contains all positive values. Therefore, we can say that 95 times out of 100, the difference between the two ratings will be positive.

4. We fail to reject the null hypothesis for GRE scores. The likelihood of this difference occurring by chance is high (.904). We can reject the null hypothesis for faculty ratings, as the probability of this difference occurring by chance is .012. Examining the rating means, we conclude that ratings received from the first interview (RATING1) are significantly higher than those from the second interview (RATING2).

5. The pool of applicants scored similarly on the GRE tests, but they received significantly different ratings on their first interview.

Chapter 19–Within-Subjects ANOVA

1. The descriptive results from the within-subjects ANOVA are summarized here along with a profile plot of statistics attitudes means.

Descriptive Statistics

	Mean	Std. Deviation	N
STATANX	26.4211	6.8018	209
STATCON	29.0478	5.2089	209
STATLIK	27.0813	4.2684	209
STATUSE	32.9139	4.6886	209

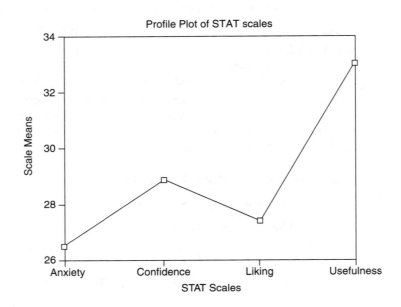

2. The assumption of sphericity is not met according to the results of the chi-square test and the epsilon values. The reported chi-square is 243.293, $p < .001$, indicating a bad fit with the condition of equal covariances. The epsilon values are also very low (.576 and .580).

3. The reported F statistic is 146.458 ($p < .001$). The null hypothesis is rejected and a difference among the four statistics attitudes scales can be concluded.

4. Based on the profile plot of means, the most positive attitudes regard the usefulness of statistics, whereas the attitude scores pertaining to anxiety and liking are somewhat lower.

5. The adjusted Bonferroni post-hoc comparison was used to detect specific differences among statistics attitude scale means. The results of these comparisons revealed responses to the scales of Usefulness were significantly more positive than each of the other three scales. In addition, responses to the Confidence scale were more positive when compared with the Liking and Anxiety scales.

Chapter 20–Mixed-Model ANOVA

1. A mixed-model ANOVA was used to examine the between-subjects effect of GENDER and the within-subjects effect of RATING. In addition, an interaction between these two variables was explored. A profile plot of GENDER by RATING appears here.

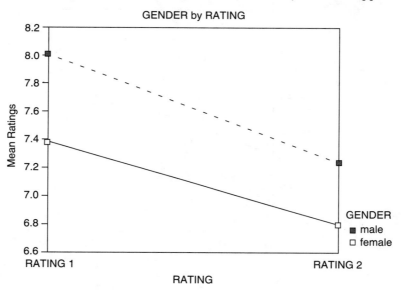

2a. The results from the mixed-model ANOVA are summarized.

Between-Subjects Effects	df	MS	F	Probability
GENDER	1	2.679	.655	.429
Error	18	4.089		
Within-Subjects Effects				
RATING	1	4.34	7.692	.013
GENDER by RATING	1	.134	.237	.632
Error	18	.563		

2b. There is a significant main effect for RATING. Specifically, the first interview (RATING1) resulted in higher faculty ratings than the second interview (RATING2).

3. Examining the profile plot, you can see that the ratings for females are consistently higher than males. Also, RATING1 is higher than RATING2 for both males and females. The effects of each independent variable are consistent for each level of the other independent variable, indicating no interaction effect.

Chapter 21–Bivariate Regression

1. Two bivariate regressions were performed. The DV, or criterion measure, was PRETEST for each regression while the IV's, or predictors, were GREV and GREQ.

2. The assumptions have been met for these regression analyses: The residuals are normally distributed with a mean of zero. A linear relationship exists between the each IV and the DV. There is no correlation between error and the IV. The Durbin-Watson statistics fall within an acceptable range (2.023, 2.329)

3. The results of each regression are summarized.

	Predictor	
	GREQ	GREV
R Square	.839	.160
F (Probability)	93.94 (< .001)	3.44 (.080)
B (slope)	.09068	.03792
A (intercept)	27.131	55.836
Standard Error of Estimate	5.0247	11.4819

4. When using GREV as a predictor, case #7 was identified as a potential outlier. This case has a standardized residual of over two standard deviations (2.248). See plot.

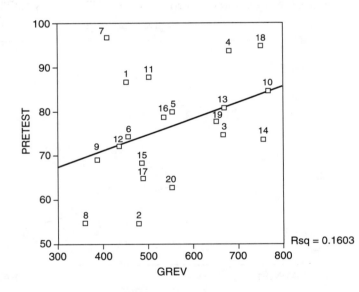

5. Based on the results of these regressions, GREQ is the better predictor. It resulted in a higher, and statistically significant, R Square (.839 vs. .160). It also resulted in a much lower standard error of estimate (5.02 vs. 11.48).

Chapter 22–Multiple Regression

1. Two regression analyses were performed. The first regression used a simultaneous approach, while the second was a stepwise regression.

2. The results from each regression analysis are summarized.

	Regression	
	Simultaneous	Stepwise
R Square	.840	.839
F (Probability)	44.745 (< .001)	93.94 (< .001)
Regression coefficients	.092 (GREQ)	.091 (GREQ)
	− .004 (GREV)	
Intercept	28.161	27.131
Standard Error of Estimate	5.1516	5.0247

3. No outliers or influential cases were identified.

4. Based on the regressions, we would recommend a regression model using only GREQ as the predictor. The addition of GREV to the model does not significantly impact the prediction of PRETEST scores. An examination of the information regarding GREV reveals extremely low partial (−.085) and semi-partial (−.034) correlations. In addition, the significance test on GREV's slope (B) was not statistically significant (p=.729), and the confidence interval surrounding this slope contained 0.

Chapter 23–Regression with Categorical Predictors

1. The dummy coding and criterion coding used for SES is summarized here.

Dummy Coding	SES		
	Low	Middle	High
SESDUM1	1	0	0
SESDUM2	0	1	0
Criterion Coding			
SESCRIT	396.6	564.45	685.25

2a. Using the coded SES variable, an R Square of .669 (p < .001) resulted with a standard error of estimate of 72.86.

2b. The predicted GREQ for an applicant from a middle SES background is 564.4545.

INDEX